EMPLOYMENT, LABOUR AND INDUSTRIAL LAW IN AUSTRALIA

Employment, Labour and Industrial Law in Australia provides a comprehensive, current and accessible resource for the undergraduate and Juris Doctor student.

With a social and political background to the law, this text provides insightful legal analysis underscored by practical business experience, while exploring key principles through a close evaluation of laws and lively discussion of prominent cases.

Recognising the multi-faceted nature of the subject, the authors have included content on employment, labour and industrial law in the one text, while also presenting critical topics not often dealt with, namely:

- current and in-depth analysis of trade union regulation
- public work including the public sector, the judiciary and academics
- workplace health and safety including worker's compensation, bullying, anti-discrimination and taxation
- emerging issues including topics such as transnational and international employment law, migration and employment, as well as volunteers and work experience.

To maintain currency within this rapidly changing area of law, the text has a website which will include updates for any major developments in the field as well as responses to end-of-chapter questions.

Written by respected academics and practising lawyers in the field, *Employment, Labour and Industrial Law in Australia* is a relevant and contemporary guide to this fascinating area of law.

Louise Floyd (PhD) is Associate Professor of Law at James Cook University and a Barrister to the Supreme Court of Queensland.

William Steenson is a Sydney-based government lawyer and accredited mediator.

Amanda Coulthard is Associate Professor of Law at Bond University and has a part-time practice at the Brisbane Bar.

Daniel Williams is a Partner at Minter Ellison Lawyers, Brisbane.

Anne C Pickering is undertaking a PhD at the University of Queensland TC Beirne School of Law, where she is also a tutor.

EMPLOYMENT, LABOUR AND INDUSTRIAL LAW IN AUSTRALIA

Louise Floyd, William Steenson, Amanda Coulthard,
Daniel Williams and Anne C Pickering
with Jim Jackson and Annaliese Jackson

CAMBRIDGE
UNIVERSITY PRESS

CAMBRIDGE
UNIVERSITY PRESS

University Printing House, Cambridge CB2 8BS, United Kingdom

One Liberty Plaza, 20th Floor, New York, NY 10006, USA

477 Williamstown Road, Port Melbourne, VIC 3207, Australia

4843/24, 2nd Floor, Ansari Road, Daryaganj, Delhi – 110002, India

79 Anson Road, #06–04/06, Singapore 079906

Cambridge University Press is part of the University of Cambridge.

It furthers the University's mission by disseminating knowledge in the pursuit of
education, learning and research at the highest international levels of excellence.

www.cambridge.org
Information on this title: www.cambridge.org/9781316622995

© Cambridge University Press 2018

First published 2018

Cover designed by Adrian Saunders
Typeset by SPi Global
Printed in Singapore by Markono Print Media Pte Ltd, September 2017

A catalogue record for this publication is available from the British Library

A Cataloguing-in-Publication entry is available from the catalogue of the National Library of Australia at www.nla.gov.au

ISBN 978-1-316-62299-5 Paperback

Additional resources for this publication at www.cambridge.edu.au/academic/employmentlaw

Reproduction and communication for educational purposes
The Australian *Copyright Act 1968* (the Act) allows a maximum of
one chapter or 10% of the pages of this work, whichever is the greater,
to be reproduced and/or communicated by any educational institution
for its educational purposes provided that the educational institution
(or the body that administers it) has given a remuneration notice to
Copyright Agency Limited (CAL) under the Act.

For details of the CAL licence for educational institutions contact:

Copyright Agency Limited
Level 15, 233 Castlereagh Street
Sydney NSW 2000
Telephone: (02) 9394 7600
Facsimile: (02) 9394 7601
E-mail: info@copyright.com.au

For God, my mother Jessica and my dog Mack, who are my best friends.
And for Justices Margaret McMurdo and David Octavius Joseph North,
who have been inspirations, mentors and supports in my career.

Louise Floyd, Brisbane, May 2017

FOREWORD

Until the Industrial Revolution, the regulation of employment was not a subject which engaged the minds of legislators to any great extent. Even so, attempts to control employment had been made as early as 1351 when, in the reign of Edward III, the Statute of Labourers sought to reduce wages to the levels which applied before the Black Death. The labour shortage caused by that awful plague had seen wages rise and labourers move in search of improved conditions. As has often been the case, the statute failed to realise its goal.

In this country, colonial governments made sporadic attempts to control the labour market, and often with the same lack of success as had been experienced half a millennium earlier in England. It was not until the great strikes of the 1890s that a concentrated effort was made to create a system which might prevent or settle disputes. Legislation to establish systems of conciliation and arbitration emerged, first in Western Australia (1900) and then New South Wales (1901), the Commonwealth (1904), South Australia (1915) and Queensland (1916). Tasmania and Victoria retained a curious attachment to wages boards until 1984 and 1992 respectively.

The slow march in legislation was mirrored in the common law of employment, where principles established in the 19th century and earlier were applied with varying degrees of precision well into the late 20th century. But the market for labour does not wait for parliaments or courts. While changes in the types and styles of employment have been recognised to a limited extent by the various industrial commissions through awards and agreements, the pace of change continues to quicken.

This book recognises that the acceleration in change means that decades of labour law jurisprudence are being relegated on a continuing basis to the file marked 'of historical interest'. Knowledge of the interstices of interstate industrial disputes or the effect of ambit claims was once an essential part of an industrial lawyer's armoury. After the *WorkChoices* case, the thousands of pages devoted to those matters are now consigned to the dusty shelves of unvisited libraries.

The factors which give rise to the inevitable mutation of the law come from both within and without this country. Australia long ago ceased to be immune from the influence of world trade and international corporate employers. To that end, this book contains a very welcome consideration of transnational and international employment law and the special problems it engenders.

The authors provide, to both the student and the professional, a clear description of the law and rigorous analyses of both the challenges which exist and the changes which are in prospect.

The Hon Justice Glenn Martin AM
President, Industrial Court of Queensland and
Queensland Industrial Relations Commission
Judge of the Supreme Court of Queensland

CONTENTS

TABLE OF CASES

Australia

Fair Work Ombudsman v Quest South Perth Holdings Pty Ltd (2015) 228 FCR 346, 28, 30, 33–4
Fair Work Ombudsman v Quest South Perth Holdings Pty Ltd (2015) 256 CLR 137, 26, 29, 34
Fair Work Ombudsman v Quest South Perth Holdings Pty Ltd (No. 2) [2013] FCA 582, 25–6, 28, 32
Fair Work Ombudsman v Ramsey Food Processing Pty Ltd (2011) 198 FCR 174, 20–1, 23, 27
Federal Commissioner of Taxation v Barrett (1973) 129 CLR 395, 12
Federal Commissioner of Taxation v J Walter Thompson (Australia) Pty Ltd (1944) 69 CLR 227, 12
Finance Sector Union of Australia v Police and Nurses Credit Society Ltd (Unreported, Australian Industrial Relations Commission, Commissioner O'Connor, 29 November 2003), 191
Fingleton v The Queen (2005) 227 CLR 166, 292–3
Fisher v Edith Cowan University (No. 2) (1997) 72 IR 464, 216
Fitzgerald v Smith [2010] FWA 7358, 61
Flinders Operating Services Pty Ltd v Australian Municipal, Administrative, Clerical and Services Union (2010) 204 IR 1, 128
Forstaff Pty Ltd v Chief Commissioner of State Revenue (2004) 144 IR 1, 5, 23
Frijters v University of Queensland [2016] FWC 2746, 311
Gallagher v Pioneer Concrete (NSW) Pty Ltd (1993) 113 ALR 159, 2
Gaylene May McDonald [2016] FWC 300, 365
General Manager of the Fair Work Commission v Health Services Union [2013] FCA 1306, 171
General Manager of the Fair Work Commission v McGiveron [2017] FCA 405, 171, 187
General Manager of the Fair Work Commission v Thomson (No. 3) [2015] FCA 1001, 167
General Manager of the Fair Work Commission v Thomson (No. 4) [2015] FCA 1433, 167
General Manager of the Fair Work Commission v Transport Workers' Union (Unreported, Federal Court of Australia NSD2041/2016), 171
General Manger of the Fair Work Commission v Musicians Union of Australia [2016] FCA 302, 170
Giannerelli v The Queen (1983) 154 CLR 212, 177
Golden Plains Fodder Australia Pty Ltd v Millard (2007) SASR 461, 20–1
Goldman Sachs JB Were Services Pty Ltd v Nikolich (2007) 163 FCR 62, 357, 400
Gordon v Carroll, Catoni and Hospital Employees Federation of Australia (1975) 27 FLR 129, 161
Gothard, Re AFG Pty Ltd (recs and mgrs apptd) (in liq) v Davey (2010) 80 ACSR 56, 20–1
Gramotnev v Queensland University of Technology (2015) 251 IR 448, 59, 110, 232, 301
Gramotnev v Queensland University of Technology (No. 2) [2015] QCA 178, 301
Grant v BHP Coal Pty Ltd [2014] FWCFB 3027, 60, 62
Grant v BHP Coal Pty Ltd (No. 2) [2015] FCA 1374, 62
Gregory v Philip Morris (1988) 80 ALR 455, 235
Griffith University v Tang (2005) 221 CLR 99, 320
Grocon Pty Ltd Enterprise Agreement (Victoria) (2003) 127 IR 13, 141
Grove v Cameron (1972) 21 FLR 59, 159
H v Centre [2014] FWC 6128, 361
Hall v A & A Sheiban Pty Ltd (1989) 20 FCR 217, 373–4
Hammon v Metricon Homes Pty Ltd [2016] FWCFB 1914, 365
Hansen v Calvary Health Care Adelaide Ltd [2016] FWCFB 5223, 366
Harpreet Singh [2015] FWC 5850, 357
Harry M Miller Attractions Pty Ltd v Actors and Announcers Equity Association of Australia [1970] 1 NSWR 614, 207

European Court of Human Rights

New Zealand

United Kingdom

Australia

TABLE OF INTERNATIONAL INSTRUMENTS

ABOUT THE AUTHORS

Louise Floyd (PhD) is Associate Professor of Law, James Cook University Law School and a Barrister to the Supreme Court of Queensland. Louise was awarded the MacCormick Fellowship to the University of Edinburgh Law School, Scotland, and is International Visiting Fellow at Cornell University in New York State. Louise has been awarded numerous teaching prizes. She is former Sub Dean of the University of Queensland Law School and was awarded that institution's Promoting Women Fellowship. Louise's career began when she was Judge's Associate to Hon MA McMurdo AC.

William ('Bill') Steenson is a government lawyer and a lecturer in industrial and labour law at the University of Technology Sydney. He was General Counsel and Director Legal and Policy for the Royal Commission into Trade Union Governance and Corruption. Previously, Bill worked as a Principal Lawyer for WorkCover NSW, and has also worked as an Industrial Officer and as a part-time member of the Government and Related Employees Appeals Tribunal (GREAT), dealing with employment-related appeals and grievances. Bill is an accredited mediator and a member of the Professional Conduct Committee of the Law Society of NSW.

Dan Williams is a Partner at Minter Ellison Lawyers, Brisbane. He has a particular interest and expertise in industrial relations strategy and has for many years provided advice and support in these matters for some of the largest employers in Australia in both the private and public sectors. His practice has spanned the entire period of enterprise bargaining in Australia from the early 1990s, and this historical perspective allows him to bring valuable insight to an analysis of this complex topic.

Anne C Pickering is undertaking a PhD at the University of Queensland TC Beirne School of Law, where she is also a tutor. She completed her LLM (Research) at the Queensland University of Technology. Anne has practised as a solicitor, and most recently worked for both the Queensland Law Society and the Legal Practitioners Admissions Board.

Amanda Coulthard is Associate Professor of Law at Bond University and has a part-time practice at the Brisbane Bar. She has previously worked at a variety of Brisbane law firms.

Jim Jackson (PhD) is Emeritus Professor and the former Chair of the Academic Board at Southern Cross University where he was the Foundation Dean of the Law School. He is an academic lawyer specialising in higher education law, including academic employment law. He has also worked for Wollongong and Bond Universities and internationally for Kaplan in Singapore.

Annaliese Jackson is a solicitor at Queensland University of Technology. She has previously been a Senior Lawyer at the Fair Work Ombudsman, specialising in employment law, and an Associate at Minter Ellison Lawyers in the Human Resources and Industrial Relations Team.

PREFACE

The photograph on the front cover of this book was taken by me whilst flying in a Qantas charter flight over the South Pole. To many, there might not be any immediate connection between that photo and labour and employment law. The South Pole is vast and beautiful, but it is largely uninhabited; it is not a thriving hub of either businesses or trade unions.

But the photograph is a metaphor. The South Pole is, at once, something that has been with us forever, and something that is undergoing great change. There are settlements that have been in existence since Mawson's hut, yet there are vast expanses comprising a new frontier. Terrain that is majestic yet challenging (even threatening) on the ground can be enjoyed for all its magnificence comparatively easily from the sky. There is wildlife and nature so spectacular that it must not be destroyed as the world changes and develops.

In what some would call a crowded market of good employment or labour texts, this book offers its own perspective and contribution. The book:

- analyses the **key elements and new developments of both employment and labour law** – issues relating to the employment of workers as well as trade union-related issues and new developments such as **the responses to the Trade Union Royal Commission** and **anti-bullying laws**;
- analyses the **crucial emerging issues and new frontiers, such as transnational labour law** (including a discussion of Chinese labour standards and Brexit, and their relevance to Australia); immigration and employment; volunteering; as well as **the impact of robots and automation**;
- **analyses areas of work that either have not previously been considered in texts or that are important, yet do not regularly appear in labour and employment texts**, such as public sector work and 'The Big Society'; judicial work; and taxation;
- provides **teaching materials**, such as tutorial and group work questions and chapter summaries at the end of chapters; and
- has **accompanying web materials** – so developing areas (such as workplace policy) have a flexible medium with which materials can be presented in a useful and timely way.

The book is useful for law and business students and also for the profession. It is written in an accessible way.

Broadly, the book begins, in Chapters 1 and 2, by studying the contract of employment, the differences between contractors and employees (and sham contracting), outsourcing and supply chains; as well as the duties implied into the employment relationship (including the remaining questions after the High Court of Australia decision in *Barker*). Chapter 3 then considers theories of labour and employment law and why Australia has the unique legislative system that it has and why the contract of employment is not like any other contract. Adverse action forms part of that discussion as it relates in part to that other feature of the Australian system, the prominence of group representation. Chapter 4 deals with the terms of employment and connects with that enterprise bargaining, Modern Awards and the National Employment Standards, as well as the statutory provisions and case law that govern the processes of bargaining (such as bargaining in good faith). In Chapter 5, the machinery provisions covering trade unions are analysed (as unions typically bargain for enterprise agreements); so too is the law on industrial action. In this context, there is a useful discussion of the recent Trade Union Royal Commission and the subsequent legislative developments relating to trade union governance. Chapter 6 deals with the end of the employment relationship. It traverses statutory unfair dismissal laws (which cover vast swathes of the Australian workforce); wrongful dismissal (which is often relevant for high-income earners); and further issues arising at the end of the employment relationship, such as: restraint of trade,[1] transfer of business (what happens to employment conditions when workers transfer with a business) and the fair entitlements guarantee (which applies in the event of job loss through employer insolvency). Chapter 7 deals with public work – public sector employment, judicial work (something not often considered in texts) and academic employment. Chapter 8 deals with specialist employment law issues: workplace health and safety (including bullying), anti-discrimination law and taxation. (Areas such as tax are so complex that they are specialties unto themselves, yet it is important for all employment lawyers to understand the connection between labour and tax, and to be able to flag issues that might require specialist tax expertise.) Finally, Chapter 9 deals with those emerging issues and new frontiers – transnational labour law (dealing with transnational corporations, conflicts of laws, and with China, Brexit and key issues in trading blocs) as well as labour and immigration, volunteer work and robots/automation. At the end of each chapter, there are summaries and work questions, and there are accompanying web materials for the entire book.

In writing this book, there are many people to be thanked. First, my co-authors. Bill Steenson of the Fair Work Commission and University of Technology, Sydney, wrote Chapter 5 on trade union law as well as the health, safety and bullying section in Chapter 8. He was a delight to work with and extremely diligent and punctual. Chapter 4, on enterprise bargaining, was written by Dan Williams (Partner, Minter Ellison – Brisbane) along with some of his work group. Another tremendous colleague, Dan's practical perspectives as a top lawyer, negotiator and litigator are invaluable for such a practical topic as bargaining. Professor Jim Jackson and his wonderful daughter Annaliese wrote the academic employment section of Chapter 7 – which is a significant contribution, as Jim is Australia's leading academic employment lawyer and Annaliese was a Judge's Associate to both the late President David Hall, of the Queensland Industrial Court, and Justice Philip McMurdo, of the Queensland Court of Appeal and she has worked for both the Fair Work Commission and Griffith University as an employment lawyer. I am grateful to call the Jacksons colleagues and friends. I am happy to introduce Anne Pickering of the Queensland Law Society, in her first foray into writing a major work. (She is also undertaking her PhD through the University of Queensland TC Beirne School of Law,

---

1   While these are in employment contracts from their inception, the clause is usually litigated at the end of the relationship.

where she is also a tutor.) Anne wrote Chapter 2 on very short notice after the original person assigned that task proved unable to do it and withdrew shortly before the deadline. Anne showed her typical good nature and efficiency in writing. Amanda Coulthard wrote Chapter 1. For my part, I thoroughly enjoyed writing Chapter 3, Chapter 6 and Chapter 9, as well as all the material on judicial work, public sector employment and the big society theory in Chapter 7 and the material on discrimination and taxation in Chapter 8.

Secondly, I thank the many brilliant people who provided invaluable support other than writing. Lucy Russell of Cambridge University Press has been a strong support to the vision I have had in planning, designing and writing this work. She is truly first class in her commitment and organisational skills. Thanks to her whole team for their editing (Emily Thomas and Sarah Shrubb). Thanks to the anonymous referees for their comments, especially one whose table on the choice of remedy for job loss now forms a part of this book. My family, to whom this book is dedicated (my mother, Jessica, and my dog, Mackie), have been ever-present supports, as have the judges to whom this book is also dedicated. Hon President Margaret McMurdo AC of the Queensland Court of Appeal (to whom I was Judge's Associate in 1993) and Hon Justice David Octavius Joseph North of the Queensland Supreme Court (whom I first met as my lecturer in civil procedure in the 1990s) show a dedication to the profession that demonstrates their talent, professionalism and intellect. They have been particularly decent in their dealings with me. Justice Glenn Martin AM, also of Queensland's Supreme Court, who wrote the foreword, is similarly committed and respected by all. Thanks to Professor Michael Gold and his colleagues (especially the librarians) at the Industrial and Labor Relations School at Cornell University in New York State (where I was International Visiting Fellow while I was finalising this work) – I am grateful. Thanks also to Professors Tom Mayo and Fred Moss at Southern Methodist University Dedman School of Law, Dallas, Texas, which I was also visiting (for the fourth time) as this book was in its final stages. Tom and Fred are wonderful friends and colleagues, and they have been for years. Finally, thanks to Professor Neil Walker at Edinburgh Law School for his time in discussing some aspects of Brexit with me while I was visiting there in February 2017.[2]

Enjoy reading this work. May it provide useful insights for the established and not-so-established frontiers of Australian labour and employment law and the transnational employment law developing around it.

Dr Louise Floyd (Lead Author and Associate Professor of Law, JCU)
Barrister, Supreme Court of Queensland, and International Visiting Fellow,
Industrial and Labor Relations School, Cornell University, New York

---

[2]   But obviously any discussion of Brexit in this book is my own work and I take responsibility for any opinions or flaws.

ACKNOWLEDGEMENTS

Dan Williams would like to thank Toby Walthall, Leyla Sandeman, Jessica Mansell, Lauren Crome, Lachlan Jolly, Mia Williams and Harriet Crouch for their assistance in drafting and researching Chapter 4.

ABBREVIATIONS

AAS	Australian Accounting Standards
ABCC	Australian Building and Construction Commission
ACCC	Australian Competition and Consumer Commission
ACLEI	Australian Commission on Law Enforcement Integrity
ACNC	Australian Charities and Non-Profits Commission
ACTU	Australian Council of Trade Unions
AEC	Australian Electoral Commission
AFP	Australian Federal Police
AHEIA	Australian Higher Education Industrial Association
AIRC	Australian Industrial Relations Commission
AMIEU	Australasian Meat Industry Employees Union
APRA	Australian Prudential Regulatory Authority
APS	Australian Public Service
ASIC	Australian Securities and Investments Commission
ATO	Australian Taxation Office
AWA	Australian Workplace Agreement
BCA	Business Council of Australia
BCII Act	*Building and Construction Industry Improvement Act 2005* (Cth)
BCOM	Branch Committee of Management
BOOT	better off overall test
CEACR	Committee of Experts on the Application of Conventions and Recommendations (ILO)
CLSs	Core Labour Standards (ILO)
EA	enterprise agreement
FBT	fringe benefits tax
FWA	Fair Work Act
FWBC	Fair Work Building and Construction
FW(BI) Act	*Fair Work (Building Industry) Act 2012* (Cth)
FWBII	Fair Work Building Industry Inspectorate
FWC	Fair Work Commission
FWO	Fair Work Ombudsman
GEER	General Employee Entitlements on Redundancy Scheme
GPFR	General Purpose Financial Report
HEPs	higher education providers
HESF	Higher Education Standards Framework
HEWRR	Higher Education Workplace Relations Requirements
GRC	Human Rights Commission
HREOC	Human Rights and Equal Opportunity Commission
HSRs	health and safety representatives

HSU	Health Services Union
HWCA	Heads of Workers Compensation Authorities
ICCPR	International Covenant on Civil and Political Rights
IFA	individual flexibility arrangement
ILO	International Labour Organization
IR	industrial relations
IR Act	*Industrial Relations Act 1993* (Cth)
IR Act 1988	*Industrial Relations Act 1988* (Cth)
IR Act (NSW)	*Industrial Relations Act 1996* (NSW)
ITWF	International Transport Workers Federation
MSD	majority support determination
MUA	Maritime Union of Australia
NERR	notice of employee representational rights
NES	National Employment Standards
NTEU	National Tertiary Education Union
OAIC	Office of the Australian Information Commissioner
PABO	protected action ballot order
PCBU	person conducting a business or undertaking
PID	public interest disclosure
PID Act	*Public Interest Disclosure Act 2013* (Cth)
PINs	Provisional Improvement Notices
RD Act	*Racial Discrimination Act 1975* (Cth)
RICO	Racketeer Influenced and Corrupt Organisations Act (US)
RO Act	*Fair Work (Registered Organisations) Act 2009* (Cth)
ROC	Registered Organisations Commission
SD Act	*Sex Discrimination Act 1984* (Cth)
SDA	Shop, Distributive and Allied Employees Association
TCF	textile, clothing and footwear industry
TUC	Trade Union Council (UK)
TURC	Royal Commission into Trade Union Governance and Corruption
TWU	Transport Workers' Union
WHS	workplace health and safety
WHS Act	*Work Health and Safety Act 2011* (Cth)
WR Act	*Workplace Relations Act 1996* (Cth)
WTO	World Trade Organization

1 SETTLING THE CONTRACT: ESSENTIALS OF FORMATION AND CHARACTERISATION

1.05 Introduction

This book commences with a discussion about the relationship between employer and employee. Whether a contractual relationship pursuant to which a person works for remuneration for the benefit of another is one of employment is of fundamental importance in Australian employment law. This is because many rights and obligations, principally rights under legislation, depend on the work relationship being one of employer and employee as opposed to some other relationship, such as that of principal and independent contractor. This chapter explains how the courts go about determining whether an individual is an employee. It then goes on to examine the difficulties that can arise in identifying an employee's employer where there are complex corporate arrangements, labour hire arrangements and labour supply chains. Consideration is then given to how the law deals with arrangements in which an employer seeks to disguise an employment relationship as an independent contractor relationship; in particular, by examining the sham contracting provisions in the *Fair Work Act*. The chapter then concludes with a summary of the federal legislation on independent contractors.

1.10 The significance of the employment relationship

There are a number of relationships within which work might be performed by one person for the benefit of another for remuneration.[1] Whether the relationship is one of employer and employee is important in determining what rights and obligations, both at common law and pursuant to legislation, are conferred upon the parties. Indeed, many (although, not all) of the rights and obligations that are the focus of this book depend upon determining whether or not the relationship is one of employment.

1.10.05 Vicarious liability

At common law, perhaps the most significant remaining reason for determining whether or not the relationship is one of employer and employee is vicarious liability.[2] At common law, an employer will be vicariously liable for the negligent acts of its employee carried out in the course of the

---

1   The employment relationship is contractual: this is discussed further below. The requirement for remuneration is necessary, because without remuneration there would be no consideration and therefore no contract of employment, or of any other kind: *Ready Mixed Concrete (South East) Ltd v Minister of Pensions and National Insurance* [1968] 2 QB 497 at 515.

2   *Sweeney v Boylan Nominees Pty Ltd* (2006) 226 CLR 161 (*Sweeney*) at [27]. See *ACE Insurance Ltd v Trifunovski* (2011) 200 FCR 532 (*ACE Insurance (decision at first instance)*) at [25] for a discussion of other reasons at common law for which the distinction was once important. This point was not disturbed on appeal: *ACE Insurance Ltd v Trifunovski* (2013) 209 FCR 146 (*ACE Insurance (decision on appeal)*). Although vicarious liability is the most fundamental issue at common law concerning the distinction between independent contractor and employee, it should be noted that a number of duties implied into the contract of employment (discussed in Chapter 2) are also now implied into contracts between principal and independent contractor: see, for example, *Gallagher v Pioneer Concrete (NSW) Pty Ltd* (1993) 113 ALR 159, where the court implied a duty to give reasonable notice to terminate a contract between principal and independent contractor.

employment. By contrast, a principal will generally not be vicariously liable for the negligent acts of an independent contractor that it has engaged to perform work.[3] The distinction between employees and independent contractors remains critical to the ambit of vicarious liability. [4]

1.10.10 Statutory rights and obligations

Determining whether or not a work relationship is one of employer and employee is of particular significance with respect to a number of legislative rights and obligations in respect of which the right or obligation attaches only to the relationship of employer and employee.

In the context of industrial relations legislation, for example:

- the *Fair Work Act 2009* (Cth) (*Fair Work Act*) predominantly confers rights and obligations on (national system) employers and employees.[5] Such rights and obligations include minimum employment standards in respect of, for example, minimum hours of work, leave, minimum wages and the right to bring an unfair dismissal claim;[6]
- awards made by industrial tribunals such as the Fair Work Commission generally regulate only the terms and conditions of employment;[7]
- enterprise agreements that can be approved by the Fair Work Commission are made between employer and employees about matters pertaining to the employment relationship.[8]

There are many other legislative rights and obligations dealing with matters such as workers' compensation, taxation, superannuation and intellectual property in respect of which the employment relationship is an important distinguishing feature.[9]

There are also legislative rights and obligations which arise irrespective of whether or not the relationship is one of employer and employee. This is so, for example, in the areas of workplace health and safety, discrimination and victimisation at work.[10]

1.15 Identifying an employee
1.15.05 The employment relationship is contractual

Before turning to the common law's approach to determining whether or not a relationship is one of employment, that is, one of employer and employee, it must be understood that the

---

3   *Hollis v Vabu Pty Ltd* (2001) 207 CLR 21 (*Hollis v Vabu*) at [32]. Although a principal might be vicariously liable for the negligent acts of an independent contractor where the duty is non-delegable duty: see, for example, *Leichhardt Municipal Council v Montgomery* (2007) 230 CLR 22.
4   *Sweeney* at [27].
5   'National system employee' and 'national system employer' are defined in ss 13 and 14 respectively of the *Fair Work Act*.
6   These rights and obligations and the concept of 'national system' employers and employees (and the types of employment to which various rights and obligations extend under the *Fair Work Act*) is discussed in Chapter 3.
7   The making of modern awards under the *Fair Work Act* is discussed in Chapter 3.
8   The making of enterprise agreements under the *Fair Work Act* is discussed in Chapter 4.
9   Aspects of these legislative rights and obligations are discussed in Chapter 4.
10   Workplace health and safety is covered in Chapter 5, discrimination is covered in Chapter 8, and victimisation at work is covered in Chapter 8.

employment relationship is contractual. Without a contract between the putative employer and the putative employee there can be no employment relationship.[11]

This chapter proceeds on the assumption that there is a valid and enforceable contract between the parties. Nevertheless, it is useful to summarise very briefly the key requirements for the formation of a valid and enforceable contract (of employment).

The formation of a contract of employment is governed by the same well-settled common law principles that govern the formation of any valid contract: agreement between the parties; an intention to create legal relations; consideration; and certainty and completeness of terms.[12] Of course, the parties must also have the capacity to contract. At common law the question of capacity – in the employment context – usually arose where the employee was a minor.[13] The employment of minors is now the subject of specific legislative provisions.[14] It is also possible for issues to arise around the capacity of corporations, unincorporated associations and the crown and its instrumentalities.[15]

It is important to note that the law does not require a contract of employment to be in writing. Indeed, it is often the case that there is no formal or detailed written contract. Given the informal way in which parties often enter into an employment relationship, it is not always possible to identify with precision a formal offer and acceptance as might be the case in commercial negotiations. Nevertheless, the parties must have reached an agreement. Where there is no formal offer and acceptance and a dispute arises as to whether the parties have reached a concluded agreement, the court will determine whether an agreement can be inferred from considering all the facts and circumstances objectively.[16]

The parties may have reached an agreement but they must also have intended their agreement to be legally binding. Without this intention the agreement will be unenforceable as a contract. The issue does not usually arise where the person is paid a wage for the work they do, although payment in some form does not of itself necessarily establish an intention to create legal relations.[17] In the employment context, the issue of intention to create legal

---

11   *R v Brown; Ex parte Amalgamated Metal Workers and Shipwrights' Union* (1980) 144 CLR 462, 475; see also *Advanced Workplace Solutions Pty Ltd v Fox and Kangan Batman TAFE* [1999] AIRC 731, where the relationship had all of the characteristics of an employment relationship but the absence of any contract between the putative employer and employee meant that there was no employment relationship.

12   These principles are dealt with exhaustively in textbooks on contract law. See, for example, JW Carter *Contract Law in Australia* (LexisNexis Butterworths, 3rd ed, 2105) Chs 3–8. For a discussion of the principles in the context of employment contracts see M Irving *The Contract of Employment* (LexisNexis Butterworths, 2012) Ch. 3, and I Neil and D Chin *The Modern Contract of Employment* (Thomson Reuters, 2012) Ch. 3.

13   To be valid, the contract had to meet the test of necessity and be for the benefit of the minor: see Carter *Contract Law in Australia* (2105) 325.

14   This legislation is discussed in Chapter 2.

15   See Carter *Contract Law in Australia* (2105) 328–34. In the context of employment contracts see Irving *The Contract of Employment* (2012) 139–41.

16   *Brambles Holdings Ltd v Bathurst City Council* (2001) 53 NSWLR 153 at [75]; *Damevski v Giudice* (2003) 133 FCR 438 at [84]–[85]. For a discussion of the objective approach to determining offer and acceptance in the employment context, see Irving *The Contract of Employment* (2012) 84–105.

17   See, for example, *Redeemer Baptist School Ltd v Glossop* [2006] NSWSC 1201. In that case the school paid the teachers but the payment was discretionary and also dependent upon the needs of the teacher and the school's capacity to pay. It was significant that both the school and the teachers said that they did not intend to make a binding contract.

relations has usually arisen in arrangements involving trainees, voluntary workers, ministers of religion and family members. The courts' approach was generally to presume that in those sorts of relationships the parties did not intend to create legal relations. After the High Court's decision in *Ermogenous v Greek Orthodox Community of SA Inc* (2002) 209 CLR 95,[18] the better approach is not to presume the absence of an intention to create legal relations but to objectively examine all the facts and circumstances of the relationship between the parties.

To be enforceable, a contract of employment (like any contract) must be supported by consideration.[19] This issue does not often arise in the context of employment as the requirement for consideration will usually be satisfied by the payment of wages (or the provision of other benefits) for the work performed.[20] There must generally, however, be what is called a mutuality of obligation.[21] This means that there must be an obligation to perform work or provide services and an obligation on the other side to pay the agreed remuneration for those services.[22]

The essential terms of a contract must be complete and certain. A contract will be incomplete if it does not contain all of the essential terms.[23] As will be seen in Chapter 2, however, incompleteness might be remedied through the implication of a term. Generally, a term will only be uncertain if it is so unclear or ambiguous that a court is unable to give meaning to it.[24]

There are other matters that can affect the enforceability of a contract. For example, a contract or a term of a contract might not be enforceable because it contravenes a statute or public policy. This is a complex area and a proper treatment of it is beyond the scope of this book.[25] Finally, there must be no vitiating factors which could affect the enforceability of the contract, such as duress, unconscionability, undue influence or misleading conduct.[26]

---

18   (2002) 209 CLR 95 at [24]–[27]. The High Court held that the relationship between the incorporated association that held property for use by the church and the archbishop was intended to have legal consequences.

19   An exception arises if a contract is made under seal: Carter *Contract Law in Australia* (2105) 116–17. It is rare for an employment contract to be made under seal.

20   The payment must, however, be in exchange for the work performed: see *Teen Ranch Pty Ltd v Brown* (1995) 87 IR 308, where the board and lodging provided to a worker at a Christian camp was not provided in exchange for the work he performed at the camp as a helping hand and group leader. The question of consideration in the context of the variation to an employment contract can be complex: see Irving *The Contract of Employment* (2012) 311–22 and Neil and Chin *The Modern Contract of Employment* (2012) 77–8.

21   The requirement for this obligation in the engagement of piece workers and casual employees is more complex: see Irving *The Contract of Employment* (2012) 106–09.

22   *Forstaff Pty Ltd v Chief Commissioner of State Revenue* (2004) 144 IR 1 at [90]. In *Dietrich v Dare* (1980) 30 ALR 407, the High Court held that there was no contract of service because there was no mutuality of obligation: the person, who was engaged on a trial basis and who was to be paid for any work done during that trial, was under no obligation to perform any work.

23   For a discussion about whether a term is essential in the employment context, see Irving *The Contract of Employment* (2012) 121–2.

24   For a discussion about whether a term is uncertain in the employment context, see Irving *The Contract of Employment* (2012) 124–5.

25   Ibid 177–86.

26   Ibid Ch. 4. Misleading and deceptive conduct is discussed in the context of termination of employment in Chapter 6.

1.15.10 A contract for the provision of personal services

A contract of employment is a contract for the provision of personal services. This means that a contract which permits the work to be done in another manner or by another person is generally not a contract of employment. So the capacity of a putative employee to delegate their services is a factor which tells against the relationship being one of employment. So, too, it follows that employment is something which cannot be unilaterally assigned.[27] These matters are taken up later in this chapter in discussing the common law tests for determining whether or not a person is an employee.

It is also important to appreciate that the requirement that the contract be one for the provision of personal services means that an employee must be a natural person.[28] As a consequence, a company cannot be an employee.[29] This will be so even where the company that has entered into the contract is the personal company of the worker and it is the worker who provides the services under the contract and ultimately benefits from the remuneration paid to the company.[30] This does not mean that the court might not look behind the contract and find that in fact the individual is truly the employee and the company has been interposed simply for the purpose of receiving payment under the contract.[31] Such an arrangement might also come under scrutiny under the sham contracting provisions in the *Fair Work Act*, which are discussed later in this chapter.

1.15.15 The employee/independent contractor distinction

As noted, there are a number of other (contractual) relationships pursuant to which work might be performed for reward.[32] However, the distinction between the relationship of employer and employee and that of principal and independent contractor is that which is most often made. It is the one that is most encountered in practice for the purposes of determining the conferral of the rights and obligations outlined above in respect of which the status of the person as an employee is necessary.

1.15.20 The express intention of the parties

The parties are free to choose the legal relationship which best suits their circumstances.[33] However, care needs to be taken as parties must conduct themselves, in their relations with

---

27   The personal nature of contracts of employment was discussed by Buchanan J in *ACE Insurance (decision on appeal)*, [25]. This is also discussed in Chapter 6.

28   *Humberstone v Northern Timber Mills* (1949) 79 CLR 389 at 404–05.

29   *ACE Insurance (decision on appeal)* at [25].

30   See, for example, *Zoltaszek v Downer EDI Engineering Pty Ltd (No. 2)* [2010] FMCA 938.

31   *Roy Morgan Research Pty Ltd v Commissioner of Taxation* (2010) 184 FCR 448 (*Roy Morgan*) at [43]; *ACE Insurance (decision on appeal)* at [152]–[153]. Note also that under the Part 3 of *Independent Contractors Act 2006* (Cth) the court's power to review a 'services contract' on the basis that it is harsh and/or unfair does not apply to a contract in which the independent contractor is a body corporate unless the work to which the contract relates is wholly or mainly performed by a director of the body corporate or a member of the family of a director of the body corporate: s 11(1)(b).

32   This includes the relationship of bailor and bailee, directors and officers of a corporation, partnerships and holders of public office. That is not to say that an individual might not have dual status as an employee and, for example, a director of the employer company. Officers within the public service are often also employees: public sector employment is dealt with in Chapter 7.

33   Some of the reasons for it suiting an individual worker to be treated as a contractor rather than an employee were noted by Buchanan J in *ACE Insurance (decision on appeal)* at [32].

regulatory agencies such as the Australian Taxation Office, in accordance with the legally correct interpretation of their relationship.[34]

The parties might expressly set out their choice in a term in the written contract by which they declare the nature of their relationship. The parties' expressed intention will not, however, be conclusive.[35] It may be conclusive where an examination of the relationship points clearly to the relationship being that which accords with the parties' expressed intention. Where, however, the relationship is capable of being one or the other, the court will often resolve the ambiguity in favour of the parties' expressed intention.[36] However, the courts will go behind the parties' expressed intention when it does not accord with the 'true' character of the relationship. In short, the parties cannot change the true character of the relationship by calling it something it is not.[37] The courts will be the ultimate arbiter of whether the relationship is, at law, one of employer and employee or (for example) principal and independent contractor.[38] In the end, the parties' expressed intention is simply one factor to be considered.

The question has arisen as to whether the putative employee might be estopped from asserting that they are not an independent contractor in circumstances where they have proceeded with the relationship on the basis of that understanding. This question arose in *ACE Insurance Ltd v Trifunovski*, a case concerning whether insurance salespersons were employees and so entitled to paid leave under industrial legislation and awards. The insurance company that engaged them raised the defence of estoppel by convention on the basis that the parties had for many years proceeded upon the understanding that the agents were independent contractors. The insurance agents gave evidence that they had always believed, until more recent legal advice was obtained, that they were independent contractors. The estoppel argument was rejected.[39] In another case, although no argument based on estoppel was raised, the result was also that an employee's insistent statement to their putative employer to the effect that he was not an employee, had been self-employed by the organisation for a number

---

34   This point was emphasised by Buchanan J in *ACE Insurance (decision on appeal)* at [32].

35   *ACE Insurance (decision on appeal)* per Buchanan J at [32] and [36]. The parties' expressed intention is not the same as their subjective understanding of the legal nature of their relationship. That understanding is not relevant to the question. Nevertheless, how the parties regarded their relationship, in the sense of how they conducted themselves, will be relevant: see *Stevens v Brodribb Sawmilling Co. Pty Ltd* (1986) 160 CLR 16 (*Stevens v Brodribb Sawmilling*) per Mason J at 26.

36   *Massey v Crown Life Insurance Co.* [1978] 1 WLR 676 at 679, applied in *Australian Mutual Provident Society v Chaplin* (1978) 18 ALR 385 at 389–90; see also *Building Workers' Industrial Union of Australia v Odco Pty Ltd* (1991) 29 FCR 104 (*Odco*); *ACE Insurance (decision at first instance)* at [114], a point which was not disturbed on appeal.

37   See, for example, *Re Porter; Re Transport Workers Union of Australia* (1989) 34 IR 179 at 184, where Gray J said that 'the parties cannot create something which has every feature of a rooster, but call it a duck and insist that everybody else recognise it as a duck'; see also *Hollis v Vabu* at [58]; *Roy Morgan* at [39]. And, in *On Call Interpreters & Translators Agency Pty Ltd v Commissioner of Taxation (No. 3)* (2011) 214 FCR 82 (*On Call Interpreters*) Bromberg J summarised the approach in saying, at [193], that 'The trend of Australian courts is to look beyond contractual descriptions and at the substance and truth of the relationship'.

38   For a discussion of the nature of the inquiry as one involving fact and law, see Neil and Chin *The Modern Contract of Employment* (2012) 36–8. As to the assessment being objective, see *On Call Interpreters* at [188].

39   Per Perram J at [145]. The estoppel argument was not pursued on appeal.

of years and would 'not be told what to do', was not a bar to his arguing that he was an employee when seeking an unfair dismissal remedy.[40]

1.15.25 The true nature of the relationship: a practical and realistic approach

The courts will also look beyond other terms of the contract which might be relied upon as determinative of the character of the relationship and look to the 'real substance' or 'reality' of the relationship in question.[41] This requires going 'beyond and beneath the contractual terms'[42] and examining the contract and the work practices to establish the totality of the relationship.[43] The court's approach is one that is 'practical' and 'realistic'.[44] The practical approach requires the analysis to commence with a proper identification of the parties to the relationship, their role and function and the nature of the interactions constituting their relations.[45]

The importance of the court's focus on the reality of the relationship, and not merely its form, is particularly important given the diversity of modern-day work arrangements. It is also important in the context of what has been described as an increasing trend towards 'disguised employment relationships'.[46] Further, the *Fair Work Act* prohibits sham arrangements including where an employer misrepresents that a relationship as one of employer and employee when it is in truth that of principal and independent contractor.[47] Sham arrangements under the *Fair Work Act* are discussed in s 1.20.

1.15.30 The lack of a unifying definition and the search for an ultimate question

The question then is how to distinguish between the relationship of employer and employee and that of principal and independent contractor given that the employment relationship remains largely undefined as a legal concept.[48] Most of the statutes (and by derivation, industrial instruments[49]) conferring rights and liabilities in respect of employment do not define or

---

40   *Meena v Biripi Aboriginal Corporation Medical Centre (t/as Werin Aboriginal Medical Centre)* [2013] FWC 4502.

41   *Damevski v Giudice* (2003) 133 FCR 438 per Marshall J at [144] and [172].

42   Ibid [77] and [78].

43   *Hollis v Vabu* at [24] citing *Stevens v Brodribb Sawmilling* at 29 per Mason J with approval.

44   *Hollis v Vabu* at [47] and [57]. For a discussion of these principles and authorities see *On Call Interpreters* at [188]–[199].

45   *On Call Interpreters* at [201].

46   *On Call Interpreters* at [204], and [196], where Bromberg J referred to the use of the expression 'disguised work relationships'.

47   *Fair Work Act* s 357.

48   *Stevens v Brodribb Sawmilling* at 35 per Wilson and Mason JJ.

49   Industrial instruments such as awards and enterprise agreements will usually define types of employment – for example, whether the employment is full-time, part-time or casual – and provide for various classifications by reference to an employee's experience and duties. However, whether a person is an employee remains to be determined by reference to the common law.

set out any test for determining who is an employee.[50] For example, a number of sections in the *Fair Work Act* provide that 'employer' and 'employee' have their 'ordinary meanings'.[51] It has been held that this phrase imports into the *Fair Work Act* the common law meaning of employee.[52] This is perhaps paradoxical, given that, as already discussed, the only significant reason at common law for determining whether an individual is an employee or independent contractor relates to the imposition of vicarious liability.[53]

The lack of a definition can be problematic given the number of statutes (and industrial instruments) conferring rights and imposing obligations in respect of employment and where legal consequences follow for failure to comply with those obligations.[54] For example, a contravention of the National Employment Standards in the *Fair Work Act* attracts a civil penalty.[55] Indeed, as Justice Bromberg noted in *On Call Interpreters and Translators Agency Pty Ltd v Commissioner of Taxation (No. 3)* (*On Call Interpreters*), the *Fair Work Act* – whilst avoiding any definition of 'employee' – provides for the imposition of a civil penalty on an employer who misrepresents a contract to be one of employment in circumstances where it is not.[56]

As a starting point, the contract of employment is often described as a contract *of* service and the contract between principal and independent contractor as a contract *for* services.[57] Describing the employment relationship as one *of* service suggests that the relationship is one of dependency and control. Yet, where a relationship might lie on the spectrum from dependency to independence, or on which side of the 'binary divide' it may lie, will not always be readily apparent. It will fall to be determined on a case-by-case basis, and no two cases will be the same given the multitude of ways in which the parties might organise and conduct their relationship and work arrangements.

The courts, whilst not seeking to provide a unifying definition, have, at times, approached the task by framing an 'ultimate question' in a way that seeks to provide a focal point around which the relationship can be examined.[58] So, for example, in *Marshall v Whittakers' Building Supply Co*[59] the 'ultimate question' was posed by Windeyer J when he said that the distinction

---

50 Sometimes a statute will broaden the reach of a particular right by deeming workers who might not otherwise be employees at common law to have the benefit of that right. The issue of deemed employees is discussed below.
51 See, for example, *Fair Work Act* s 335 (in respect of Part 3-1), and ss 15, 30E, 30P and 770.
52 *C v Commonwealth* (2015) 234 FCR 81 at [34]. By way of contrast, see *Konrad v Victoria Police* (1999) 91 FCR 95 at 127, where a meaning of 'employee' wider than that used at common law was accepted on the basis that the provisions of the then *Industrial Relations Act 1988* (Cth) provided that the terms 'employer' and 'employee' (in respect of unfair dismissal) imported the meaning ascribed to those terms in the International Labour Organization Termination of Employment Convention in which the words 'worker' and 'employer' did not bear common law meanings because the Convention applied to many countries in which the common law did not apply.
53 *ACE Insurance (decision at first instance)* at [25]–[26]. The point was not disturbed on appeal.
54 *On Call Interpreters* at [206].
55 The National Employment Standards (NES) are contained in Part 2-2 of Chapter 2 of the *Fair Work Act* and provide a number of minimum terms and conditions of employment for employees in relation to such matters as hours of work and leave. The *Fair Work Act* s 44(1) provides that a breach of the NES attracts a civil penalty. The same is true with respect to the contravention of awards or enterprise agreements: ss 45 and 50 respectively of the *Fair Work Act*.
56 *On Call Interpreters* at [206].
57 See, for example, *Stevens v Brodribb Sawmilling* per Wilson and Dawson JJ at 36.
58 *On Call Interpreters* at [207]–[209].
59 (1963) 109 CLR 210 at 217.

between a servant[60] and an independent contractor 'is rooted fundamentally between a person who serves his employer in his, the employer's business, and a person who carries on a trade or business of his own'.[61] This statement was cited with approval by the plurality of the High Court in *Hollis v Vabu Pty Ltd*, in what is widely regarded as a landmark case on the modern approach to differentiating between an employee and an independent contractor.[62]

The question has been similarly framed in industrial relations tribunals. For example, in *Abdalla v Viewdaze Pty Ltd* a full bench of the (then) Australian Industrial Relations Commission, in deciding whether a travel agent was an employee for the purposes of the unfair dismissal laws, approached the question by asking whether the person was a servant of another in that other's business or was conducting a business of their own.[63]

1.15.35 Restating the ultimate question

A more recent judicial restatement of the 'ultimate question' is to be found in the decision of Bromberg J in *On Call Interpreters*. This case was concerned with whether On Call was liable to pay a superannuation guarantee charge in relation to a number of translators and interpreters it engaged to perform translating and interpreting services for its clients on an assignment basis. On Call had treated them as independent contractors and so had not made any superannuation contributions on their behalf.[64] The Commissioner of Taxation views the translators and interpreters as employees and, accordingly, levied a superannuation guarantee charge. On Call challenged the assessment. In discussing how to distinguish an employee from an independent contractor, his Honour said:[65]

---

60   The use of the word 'servant' here harks back to the relationship of master and servant, from which the contractual relationship of employer and employee has evolved.

61   Interestingly, Wilson and Dawson JJ in this passage in *Stevens v Brodribb Sawmilling* say that Windeyer J was really posing the ultimate question in a different way, or restating the problem, rather than offering a definition which could be applied for the purpose of providing an answer: 35. Their Honours said they would be doing no more themselves if they were to 'suggest that the question is whether the degree of independence overall is sufficient to establish that a person is working on his own behalf rather than acting as the servant of another': 35.

62   *Hollis v Vabu* at [40]. Taking the same approach, in relation to the question of whether a person performing personal services for the benefit of another was an employee or an independent contractor, in the context of vicarious liability, the majority of the High Court in *Sweeney* [33] described the worker (a mechanic) who had performed the work as doing so 'not as an employee of the respondent but as a principal pursuing his own business or as an employee of his own company pursuing its business'. See also *Roy Morgan* at [45] and *ACE Insurance (decision at first instance)* at [29] (not disturbed on appeal).

63   (2003) 122 IR 215 at 227–8. See also *ACT Visiting Medical Officers Association v Australian Industrial Relations Commission* (2006) 153 IR 228 where, in the context of an application to the (then) Australian Industrial Relations Commission by an association of visiting medical officers for registration as an association of employees, it was held that visiting medical officers who had their own private practices and had entered into contracts for the provision of their professional services (as visiting medical officers) with the hospital did so as an integral part of their private practices and so were held not to be employees; see also *Jiang Shen Cai (t/as French Accent) v Do Rozario* [2011] FWAFB 8307 at [30].

64   The effect of the *Superannuation Guarantee (Administration) Act 1992* (Cth) (which is read together with the *Superannuation Guarantee Charge Act 1992* (Cth)) is to impose a superannuation guarantee charge upon employers (as defined) who fail to pay prescribed contributions for the benefit of their employees. 'Employee' is given its ordinary common law meaning but also an extended meaning to include, relevantly, a person who works under a contract that is wholly or principally for the labour of the person: *Superannuation Guarantee (Administration) Act 1992* (Cth) ss 12(1) and 12(3).

65   *On Call Interpreters* at [208].

Simply expressed, the question of whether a person is an independent contractor in relation to the performance of particular work, may be posed and answered as follows:

Viewed as a "practical matter":

(i) is the person performing the work [of] an entrepreneur who owns and operates a business; and

(ii) in performing the work, is that person working in and for that person's business as a representative of that business and not of the business receiving the work?

If the answer to that question is yes, in the performance of that particular work, the person is likely to be an independent contractor. If no, then the person is likely to be an employee.

Bromberg J used the two elements of this question as the focal point around which to organise and examine the indicia 'thrown up' by the totality test.[66] Of the first element, his Honour said that to carry on a business was to 'conduct a commercial enterprise as a going concern'.[67] As to the second element – whose business is the economic activity being performed in and for – his Honour said a range of indicia fell to be considered, depending upon the nature of the economic activity and the circumstances in which it is being carried out.[68] Whilst an affirmative answer to the first element of the question is likely to mean that the individual is an independent contractor, this will not always or necessarily be the case when the second element of the question is considered. Indeed, Bromberg J found that whilst two of the translators were conducting their own businesses, they were nevertheless employees having regard to the totality of the indicia including control, so that the economic activity in which the interpreters were engaged was being performed 'in and for' On Call.[69] Accordingly, they were employees at common law.[70]

In the end, however, the framing of the question does not alter the test. Indeed, the Full Federal Court has recently held that to view the matter through the prism of a dichotomy between a situation in which the putative employee works in the business of another and a situation in which he or she conducts his own business as an entrepreneur deflects the central question of whether or not the person is an employee. The question is not whether or not the person is an entrepreneur. It is whether or not he or she is an employee.[71] This question continues to involve – as we will see – an assessment of all the indicia of the relationship, in the context and setting in question.

1.15.40 The totality test: control and its continuing relevance

For many years, the distinction between employee and independent contractor lay in examining the 'degree of control' the putative employer had over the work to be done and the manner in which the

66   Ibid [209]–[220].
67   Ibid [210]–[217].
68   Ibid [218]–[220].
69   Ibid [296]. His Honour also found that the panel interpreters were not operating their own businesses and so they too were employees.
70   His Honour found that they were also employees, applying the extended meaning in s 12(3) of the *Superannuation Guarantee (Administration) Act 1992* (Cth).
71   *Tattsbet Ltd v Morrow* (2015) 233 FCR 46 at [61]; approved in *Fair Work Ombudsman v Ecosway Pty Ltd* [2016] FCA 296.

work was to be done.[72] The more control was exercised the more likely it was that the relationship was that of employer and employee. Conversely, a lack of control pointed to the relationship being one of principal and independent contractor. This is described as the 'classic test'.[73]

It was a test developed when social conditions were different and reflected a time when work was largely unskilled and was more closely and directly supervised.[74] However, things changed. The master–servant relationship evolved into the modern contract of employment. Society industrialised and workers became more skilled and specialised and were thus able to work independently and largely without supervision. Work arrangements changed with, for example, the advent of practices such as working from home or tele-working. Industrial legislation too has become more complex.[75] The common law responded to these changing social and regulatory conditions by shifting the emphasis on control from the actual exercise of control to the right to exercise it, even if only in relation to 'incidental or collateral matters'.[76] Despite this adaptation of the control test, it was becoming a less relevant determinant of the nature of the work relationship.[77]

Ultimately, in *Stevens v Brodribb Sawmilling*, a case concerning vicarious liability, the High Court clearly stated that the existence of control, whilst significant, is not the sole criterion by which to gauge whether or not a relationship is one of employment.[78] Control is but one of a number of indicia to be considered in determining the nature of the relationship. Before turning to consider those other indicia, it is important to emphasise that the right to control the manner in which work is performed remains an important factor. In some cases it might be the predominant factor, yet in others it might be a mistake to treat it as decisive.[79] This approach was endorsed by the High Court in *Hollis v Vabu*.[80]

In assessing control, the court will consider the way in which and the extent to which control, or the right to control, is exercised. Control might be exercised over a number of matters. For example:

- the arrangements by which work is performed, such as place and hours of work;[81]
- the nature of the work and the manner in which it is to be performed,[82] taking into account, as already noted, that skilled or specialised work might not leave much room for actual control;[83]

---

72   For an early statement of the control test, see *Federal Commissioner of Taxation v J Walter Thompson (Australia) Pty Ltd* (1944) 69 CLR 227 at 231 per Latham J.

73   See, for example, *Stevens v Brodribb Sawmilling* per Wilson and Dawson JJ at 35.

74   Ibid per Mason J at 28.

75   See, for example, the observations of Dixon J in *Humberstone v Northern Timber Mills* (1949) 79 CLR 389 at 404.

76   *Zuijs v Wirth Brothers Pty Ltd* (1955) 93 CLR 561 at 571; *Stevens v Brodribb Sawmilling* per Mason J at 29.

77   See, for example, *Marshall v Whittaker's Building Supply Co.* (1963) 109 CLR 210 at 218; *Federal Commissioner of Taxation v Barrett* (1973) 129 CLR 395 at 401–02.

78   *Stevens v Brodribb Sawmilling* per Mason J at 24, Wilson and Dawson JJ at 36.

79   Ibid 36 per Wilson and Dawson JJ, citing the observations of Dixon J in *Queensland Stations Pty Ltd v Federal Commissioner of Taxation* (1945) 70 CLR 539 at 571, where his Honour observed that the reservation of a right to direct or superintend the performance of work could not transform into a contract of service what in essence is an independent contract.

80   *Hollis v Vabu* at [44]. See also *On Call Interpreters* at [204] and [269].

81   *Stevens v Brodribb Sawmilling* at 24 and 36.

82   *On Call Interpreters* at [262]–[263]. *Hollis v Vabu* at 43–45, 49 and 57; *Stevens v Brodribb Sawmilling* at 35–6; *Roy Morgan Research* at [36] and [49].

83   *Zuijs v Wirth Brothers Pty Ltd* (1955) 93 CLR 561 at 571–2.

- attendance at training courses and compliance with training manuals;[84]
- compliance with workplace rules, a code of conduct or ethics;[85]
- a requirement to wear a uniform or otherwise be attired in a particular way;[86]
- the existence of performance, compliance and disciplinary processes and the right to dismiss;[87]
- the right to direct that work be performed and an obligation to work;[88]
- a requirement that the putative employee work particular hours at particular times, although the absence of that requirement is not necessarily demonstrative of a lack of control.[89]

1.15.45 The totality test: control and the other relevant indicia

Having discussed control and its continuing relevance, we now turn to examine the other indicia that are examined in determining whether a relationship is one of employer and employee.

THE MULTIPLE INDICIA TEST

The approach in modern Australian employment law[90] to determining whether or not a person performs work as an employee involves examining the 'totality of the relationship'[91] by reference to a list of criteria or indicia. This approach is often described as the multi-factor or multi-indicia test.

These indicia are regarded as characteristics of an employment relationship of which the employer's right to control the work done by the employee is often the most significant indicium.[92] Whilst not exhaustive, aside from control, the following is a list of the key indicia to which the courts and tribunals have regard in examining the totality of the relationship:

- the right to perform work for others or reject work that is offered;
- the right to delegate work or provide another person to perform the work;

---

84   *ACE Insurance (decision at first instance)* at [65], a point not disturbed on appeal.
85   *On Call Interpreters* at [262]–[263]; *Hollis v* Vabu at 42 and 44–5.
86   *Hollis v* Vabu at 42.
87   *On Call Interpreters* at [264]–[265]; *Hollis v Vabu* at [68].
88   This is also considered as an indicium separate from the question of control.
89   *Hollis v Vabu* at [49]. This point was made by Bromberg J in *On Call Interpreters* at [268]. His Honour further noted that this would be no different from the case of employees who are engaged as casuals.
90   In Britain, the courts have developed the 'organisation or integration' test as an alternative test: see, for example, *Ready Mixed Concrete (South East) Ltd v Minister for Pensions and National Insurance* [1968] 2 QB 497. This test involves assessing whether the putative employee was employed as part of the business and did his work as an integral part of the business. In Australia, this is not a separate test but is one of the factors to be considered in the multi-indicia approach: *Stevens v Brodribb Sawmilling* at 26–7; *On Call Interpreters* at [285]–[289].
91   *Stevens v Brodribb* Sawmilling at 29. The approach has been endorsed in numerous cases since, such as *Hollis v Vabu* at [24]; *On Call Interpreters* at [209]; *ACE Insurance (decision at first instance)* at [29], and which approach was not disturbed on appeal.
92   *Stevens v Brodribb* Sawmilling, at 24 and 36; *Hollis v Vabu* at [45].

- the ability to engage other staff;
- economic dependence on the business of the putative employer;
- the extent to which the putative employee is represented as part of the business;
- the provision and maintenance of own tools and equipment;
- responsibility for other significant business expenses or the provision of a place of work;
- whether remuneration is based on hours worked rather than based on result;
- whether there is provision for paid leave;
- how taxation and superannuation obligations are accounted for.

The list of relevant indicia is not closed. It has expanded over time to reflect the multiplicity and diversity of arrangements by which work is performed.

Leaving aside control and the expressed intention of the parties (if any), what follows is a discussion of a number of the indicia that are frequently considered by the courts. It is not an exhaustive list. Nor is the intention here to provide a review of the vast number of cases in which these indicia have been considered and applied in different contexts, on different facts, and producing different outcomes. It is also important to bear in mind that the indicia might overlap with each other in the particular factual context. Further, it is also the case that some of the factors, whilst considered separately from the question of control, might themselves be regarded as aspects of control.

It is also important to emphasise that the task of examining the indicia is not a mechanistic one to be performed by checking off against a list of indicia without recognising that different significance may attach to the same indicia in different cases[93] or that one spotlight might not necessarily adequately illuminate the totality of the relationship.[94] It is necessary to evaluate, weigh and balance the indicia to come to a conclusion as to the true nature of the relationship. Some indicia will be more useful or relevant than others, depending on the nature of the work arrangement.[95] Further, no one indicium is necessarily afforded more weight than another. They are – along with control – considered in combination to produce an overall picture of the relationship. This means that in many cases the outcome is necessarily impressionistic and the same or similar facts might produce different results. The approach of the courts must necessarily be – at least to some extent – 'impressionistic' and 'intuitive'. [96]

A CONSIDERATION OF THE MULTIPLE INDICIA

- *the right to perform work for others or reject work*: such a right suggests a relationship of principal and independent contractor, whilst on the other hand exclusivity is said to be indicative of an

---

93   *On Call Interpreters* at [220], citing *Lopez v Deputy Commissioner of Taxation* (2005) 143 FCR 574.
94   Ibid [204].
95   Ibid.
96   Ibid.

employment relationship.[97] This factor might, however, not be of particular utility in the context of casual and part-time employment, where it is likely that the putative employee will be working for others.[98] In that event, the real question will be whether the person is not to pursue other activities when they are actually performing work for the putative employer.[99] Further, economic considerations might mean that the right to work for others, or to refuse work, might be a notional freedom with the consequence that less weight is placed on this factor.[100] And it has been said that the right to reject work or not be available to accept it from time to time does not change the relationship when the person did choose to accept the work;[101]

- *the right to delegate or substitute*: a contract of employment is a contract for the provision of personal services. Accordingly, if the putative employee is entitled to delegate the performance of the work to others this will be indicative of a relationship of principal and independent contractor.[102] This is particularly so where the right to delegate is unlimited, although even then it may not be determinative;[103]

- *the ability to engage other staff*: being permitted to engage other staff to assist in the performance of the work is a factor tending against the existence of an employment relationship;[104]

- *economic dependency*: being financially self-reliant suggests that the person is not an employee, whereas economic dependency on the business of the putative employer suggests that the person is an employee;[105]

- *integration into the business*: where the person is integrated into the putative employer's business this will be an indicator that the person is an employee. This might occur through, for example, regular contact and communication, attending social functions organised by the putative employer, attending training courses and seminars and so demonstrating a concern on the putative employer's part in the professional development of the person;[106]

- *representation as part of the business*: being represented and portrayed to the public as part of or an emanation of the putative employer's business is a strong indicator that the person is an employee.[107] This might be done, for example, by requiring the person to wear a uniform or an identification badge or to display the livery of the business;[108]

---

97   Ibid [218]; *Commissioner of Taxation v Barrett* (1973) 129 CLR 395 at 407.
98   *Stevens v Brodribb Sawmilling* at 526–7 per Wilson and Dawson JJ; *On Call Interpreters* at [286]; *Roy Morgan Research* at [50]–[51].
99   *Roy Morgan Research* at [51].
100   *Re Porter; Re Transport Workers Union of Australia* (1989) 34 IR 179 at 184–5. *Roy Morgan Research* at [49].
101   *Roy Morgan Research* at [48].
102   *Stevens v Brodribb Sawmilling* at 26 per Mason J: the power to delegate is an 'important factor' in determining whether the worker is a servant or independent contractor; see *On Call Interpreters* at [281]. See also *Abdalla v Viewdaze Pty Ltd* (2003) 122 IR 215 at 230.
103   *Stevens v Brodribb Sawmilling* at 38, citing *Australian Mutual Provident Society v Chaplin* (1978) 18 ALR 385 at 391 (Privy Council).
104   *ACE Insurance Ltd v Trifunovski* (2011) 200 FCR 532 at [96].
105   *On Call Interpreters* at [218].
106   Ibid [287]–[288].
107   *Hollis v Vabu* at [50]; *On Call Interpreters* at [270]. *ACE Insurance (at first instance)* at [82], a point not disturbed on appeal.
108   This was the case for the bicycle couriers in *Hollis v Vabu*.

- *provision and maintenance of tools and equipment*: provision and maintenance by the individual of their own tools and equipment is a factor indicative of the relationship of principal and independent contractor.[109] Much depends, however, on the extent of the capital outlay. So, in *Hollis v Vabu* the fact that bicycle couriers were required to bear the cost of providing and maintaining their own bicycles was not contrary to the existence of an employment relationship. The capital outlay was relatively small. Further, it was relevant to the court's consideration of this indicium that the bicycles were not inherently capable of use only for courier work but were also a means of personal transport and recreation out of work time.[110] The question of whether the mode of transport could be used for personal use or only in the course of earning the remuneration has since been seen as significant in other cases.[111] By contrast, in *Stevens v Brodribb Sawmilling*, the provision and maintenance by the worker of his own truck for undertaking the work of hauling timber was significant. The item not only involved a significant capital outlay but it was also specialised equipment for carrying timber;
- *payment of other significant business expenses*: the incurring of other significant expenses such the rental of premises, accommodation and travel expenses, and office expenses in an ordinary case will be a good pointer to the absence of an employment relationship;[112]
- *provision of own place of work*: where the person has their own separate premises from which they carry out or coordinate the work, this is indicative that they are carrying on their own business as an independent contractor;[113]
- *goodwill*: where the goodwill created by the performance of the work benefits the putative employer and is not a marketable part of any business that might be carried out by the putative employee, this will be a strong indicator that the relationship is one of employer and employee;[114]
- *opportunity for profit and the risk of loss*: such an opportunity is indicative of a finding that the person is in business for themselves; the ability to earn profit and the taking of economic risk in the earning of that profit is also indicative of the person being in business on their own account;[115]
- *method of remuneration*: the distinction is sometimes made that employees are paid a wage or salary by reference to the hours worked whereas an independent contractor is paid for a result or on commission. This is not, however, always the case and so care must be taken with the application of this indicium.[116] Employees might be paid by result and independent contractors might be paid on a

---

109   *Stevens v Brodribb* at 24 and 37.
110   *Hollis v Vabu* at [56].
111   See, for example, *ACE Insurance Ltd (decision at first instance)* at [88]. In that case, although not a contractual requirement, the work of insurance salespersons necessitated that they had a motor vehicle. The vehicles could, however, be used for personal use; and in *Roy Morgan Research* at [41] a requirement that interviewers have their own transport in which to keep the interview documentation secure when they were in the field was not significant and the vehicles were also used as a means of personal transport.
112   *ACE Insurance Ltd (decision at first instance)* at [94] (although, when balanced against the other factors this factor was accorded less weight).
113   *On Call Interpreters* at [290].
114   This was the case in *On Call Interpreters* at [274]; *Roy Morgan Research* at [46]; *Hollis v Vabu* at [48]; *ACE Insurance Ltd (decision at first instance)*, at [83]–[84].
115   *Roy Morgan Research* at [47]. Bromberg J in *On Call Interpreters* at [217] regarded the taking of risks in the pursuit of profits as an indicium that a person is operating their own business.
116   *On Call Interpreters* at [277]; *Roy Morgan Research* at [42].

time basis. For example, in *Hollis v Vabu* the plurality of the High Court held that the fact the bicycle couriers were paid per delivery was not determinative. The method of payment – per delivery and not per time engaged in making the delivery – was described as 'a natural means to remunerate employees whose sole duty is to perform deliveries, not least for ease of calculation and to provide an incentive more efficiently to make deliveries';[117]

- *the capacity to bargain for remuneration:* the absence of any scope to bargain for remuneration and the overall control exercised by Vabu over the couriers' finances was a factor considered by the plurality of the High Court in *Hollis v Vabu* as an indicator of the relationship of employer and employee;[118]

- *the provision of skilled labour or labour requiring specialist qualifications:* where the work involves a profession, trade or distinct calling this may point to the relationship of independent contractor. So in *Hollis v Vabu*, the fact that the bicycle couriers were not providing skilled labour or labour requiring specialist qualifications was a factor pointing against a finding that they were independent contractors;[119]

- *payment for leave:* a similar approach can be taken to this indicium. A failure to pay leave may be no more than a reflection of the parties' understanding of their relationship. And in this regard it should be noted that the absence of paid leave is a feature of casual employment;[120]

- *taxation and superannuation:* regard to these indicia involves some circularity in reasoning.[121] In short, these obligations flow as a matter of law from a correct analysis of the character of the relationship. The parties' treatment of their taxation obligations might do little more than serve to confirm their intention and understanding of the nature of their relationship and so fall into the same category as declarations in the contract itself.[122] The absence of PAYG deductions might make it more difficult to characterise the relationship as one of employment. On the other hand, the presence of GST collections by the putative contractor point strongly against the relationship being characterised in that way.[123]

- *incorporation:* as already noted, a contract of employment is a contract for personal services. The contract between the parties might provide that the person being engaged to provide the services can incorporate. Where such a contractual opportunity is in fact illusive, the court will place little weight on it.[124] Where the person does provide their services through a corporation, this will not necessarily lead to the conclusion that the relationship is one of principal and independent contractor: there may be circumstances where, for example, it is still the individual who is being selected to do the work and the company's role is only as the recipient of the remuneration.[125]

---

117   *Hollis v Vabu* at [54].
118   Ibid. See also *On Call Interpreters* at [292] and *ACE Insurance Ltd (decision at first instance)* at [97].
119   *Hollis v Vabu* at [48].
120   *On Call Interpreters* at [295].
121   Ibid.
122   *ACE Insurance Ltd (decision at first instance)*, 90 and on appeal, [37].
123   *Tattsbet Ltd v Morrow* (2015) 233 FCR 46; 321 ALR 305 at 322 per Jessup J, with whom Allsop CJ and White JJ agreed.
124   *ACE Insurance Ltd (decision at first instance)* at [95].
125   *Roy Morgan Research* at [43], cited with approval in *ACE Insurance Ltd (decision at first instance)* at [94].

1.15.50 A flexible application of the totality test

It can be seen from the above discussion that the cases in which the issue is the characterisation of the relationship as one of employee or independent contractor are diverse. However, it is possible to say that the three main areas in which the need to make the characterisation arises are where the issue is concerned with:[126]

(i)   duties and obligations that one of the contracting parties might owe to third parties;

(ii)   the obligations owed by contracting parties to each other; and

(iii) where a regulatory agency asserts that there is a liability to pay a tax or other charge.

The first category is principally, if not entirely, concerned with the question of vicarious liability for injuries caused by the negligence of the putative employer for the negligent conduct of the putative employee. The focus in such cases is on the interests of the third party, and on where the loss should lie. Of the cases already cited, *Stevens v Brodribb Sawmilling*, *Sweeney* and *Hollis v Vabu* are examples.

The second category of cases involve a claim by the putative employee that the putative employer owes him or her an obligation (usually, arising under statute). These disputes involve a characterisation of the relationship for the purposes of determining the obligations that the parties owe directly to each other. Examples of such obligations include entitlements under an award or enterprise agreement, a right to entitlements under the *Fair Work Act*, such as minimum entitlements under the NES or a right to bring an unfair dismissal application. Of the cases referred to so far, *ACE Insurance Ltd v Trifunovski* is an example where the issue was the worker's entitlement to annual and long service leave arising under award and statute; *Abdalla v Viewdaze Pty Ltd* concerned an unfair dismissal application.

The third category of cases concern obligations, for example, to make pay as you go taxation payments, make superannuation contributions or remit payroll tax. As we have seen, *On Call Interpreters* was a case concerned with the liability to make superannuation contributions.

It has been suggested that where the outcome has an impact on third parties the focus of the examination may sometimes subtly influence the answer to the question.[127] A court or tribunal's weighing up of the various indicia of the relationship might be influenced the differing policy bases for the legislative obligation that is the subject of the inquiry. If that is so, then a similar set of facts might produce a different decision depending on whether the issue is one, for example, of vicarious liability, taxation obligations, award entitlements, access to an unfair dismissal remedy or an entitlement to workers' compensation.[128]

1.15.55 Deemed employees

There are a number of statutes which deem workers who might not otherwise be employees at common law to have the benefit of a particular right under the statute. The rationale is that in

---

126   See the discussion about this in *ACE Insurance Ltd (decision on appeal)* at [26]–[28].

127   *ACE Insurance Ltd (decision on appeal)* per Buchanan at [28], citing Lord Denning in *Denham v Midland Employers Mutual Assurance Ltd* [1955] 2 QB 437 at 443–4.

128   Neil and Chin *The Modern Contract of Employment* (2012) 5 and the discussion at [1.70].

respect of the particular right it is considered that workers should have the same benefit regardless of whether they are employees or independent contractors at common law. So, for example, the obligation to make superannuation contributions for employees is extended beyond an employee at common law to a person who works under a contract that is wholly or principally for the labour of the person.[129] There are similar sorts of provisions in payroll tax legislation and workers' compensation legislation.

In the context of industrial relations legislation, there is a variety of legislative approaches used to ensure that entitlements and protections extend to particular categories of workers who might not be employees at common law. For example, some State industrial relations legislation deems workers in certain industries to be employees,[130] or gives a power to the industrial tribunal to deem a class of persons who perform work in an industry as contractors to be employees for the purposes of rights under that legislation.[131] The impact of the *Independent Contractors Act 2006* (Cth) on some of these deeming provisions is considered later.

Another example has arisen as a response to the growth in the use of outworkers in certain industries – notably the clothing industry. These are workers who work away from their (putative) employer's business premises – often in their own homes. Outworkers can certainly be employees on the application of the multiple indicia test. There is nothing in the mere fact of working away from what would be traditionally regarded as a workplace that would necessarily lead to the conclusion that an outworker is an independent contractor. However, the *Fair Work Act* deems a person who performs work as an outworker in the textile, clothing and footwear industry as a contractor to be an employee for most of the purposes of the Act.[132]

1.20 Identifying the employer

Usually the identity of the employer will be clear. However, circumstances can arise in which it becomes necessary to identify the 'true' employer. The issue typically arises in two situations. First, where the employer is one or other of a corporation in a group of related or associated corporations and second, in what are generally called labour hire arrangements. Determining who the employer is in each of these circumstances is the subject of this section.

It is important to note at the outset that Australian law has not to date accepted the concept of joint employment.[133] So the starting premise for the discussion that follows is that at any one time an employee can only have one employer in respect of the same position.

---

129   *Superannuation Guarantee (Administration) Act 1992* (Cth) ss 12(1) and 12(3). This provision was considered in *On Call Interpreters*.
130   *Industrial Relations Act 1996* (NSW) Schedule 1.
131   *Industrial Relations Act 1999* (Qld).
132   Outworker is defined in the *Fair Work Act* s 12. Part 6-4A contains special provisions dealing with contract outworkers in the textile, clothing and footwear industry (TCF). Section 789BB deems TCF contract outworkers to be employees where they perform work directly or indirectly for a Commonwealth outworker entity (defined in s 12) or for a constitutional corporation where the work is performed for the purposes of a business undertaking of the corporation. The result is that the TCF contract outworkers will be taken to be employees for the purposes of most of the provisions of the Act.
133   *Fair Work Ombudsman v Eastern Colour Pty Ltd* (2011) 209 IR 263.

1.20.05 Employment by related or associated corporations

The way in which a business has arranged its affairs may give rise to uncertainty as to the identity of the 'true' employer. There may have been a series of engagements involving a number of related or associated corporations and it is unclear whether there has been a secondment (with no change in the identity of the employer) or a change in the identity of the employer. Also, it is not unusual amongst a group of related or associated corporations for one of them to be selected as the entity that engages the employees whose services are rendered for the benefit of another corporation or corporations in the group that operates the business. This form of 'labour hire' might be described as an intra-group labour hire arrangement. Such arrangements are common and not unlawful.[134] In such circumstances, the identity of the 'true' employer becomes of particular practical relevance when the entity that the corporate group contends is the true employer has no assets of substance from which to pay employee entitlements.[135] As will be seen, the question is not answered by simply determining which entity remunerated the employee. That will be but one factor to be considered in assessing the totality of the circumstances.[136]

Before exploring the approach that the court takes in determining the identity of the employer in these types of circumstances, it is important to note that employment is not something which can be transferred without the consent of the employee.[137] The consent of the employee, whether express or implied, must be real.[138] Transfer of employment is to be contrasted with the secondment or 'loan' of an employee. In that instance, there is no change in the employment relationship: the original employer remains as the employer even where practical control over the work being done is exercised by the hirer.[139]

Otherwise, in circumstances where there are multiple possible employers of a person, Finn J in *Re C & T Grinter Transport Services Pty Ltd (in liq)* [2004] FCA 1148 (*C & T Grinter*) held that the principles to be applied in the identification of the employer are as follows (citations omitted):[140]

- a contract of service cannot be transferred by one employer to another or novated as between them without the employee's consent;

---

134   *Fair Work Ombudsman v Ramsey Food Processing Pty Ltd* (*Ramsey Food Processing*) (2011) 198 FCR 174 at [77]; *Golden Plains Fodder Australia Pty Ltd v Millard* (2007) SASR 461 at [91].

135   This is of course not the only circumstance in which the question is important. The issue might be, to give further examples, one of identifying the employer for the purposes of vicarious liability or determining payroll tax obligations.

136   *Australian Insurance Employees Union v WP Insurance Services Pty Ltd* (1982) 42 ALR 598 at 606, cited with approval by Edmonds J in *Gothard, Re AFG Pty Ltd (recs and mgrs apptd) (in liq) v Davey* (2010) 80 *ACSR* 56 (*Gothard*) at [61].

137   *Noakes v Doncaster Amalgamated Collieries Ltd* [1940] AC 1014 at 1026, cited with approval in *McCluskey v Karagiozia* [2002] FCA 1137 at [11].

138   *Denham v Midland Employers Mutual Assurance Ltd* [1955] 2 QB 437 at 433, cited with approval by Finn J in *Re C & T Grinter Transport Services Pty Ltd (in liq)* [2004] FCA 1148 at [20]; *Romero v Auty* (2001) 19 ACLC 206 at [43].

139   *Ramsey Food Processing* at [47]. There is a limited exception to this rule where an employment relationship might be found to exist between the hirer and the employee for the purposes of a tortious act by the employee: see the discussion in Neil and Chin *The Modern Contract of Employment* (2012) [2.40].

140   [2004] FCA 1148 at [20], cited with approval by Edmonds J in *Gothard* at [54] and by Collier J in *Fair Work Ombudsman v Eastern Colour Pty Ltd* (2011) 209 *IR* 263 at [75].

- the totality of the circumstances surrounding the relationships of the various parties including conduct subsequent to the creation of an alleged employment relationship is relevant to the assessment to be made;
- documentation created by one or more of the parties describing or evidencing an apparent employment relationship will be relevant to, but not necessarily determinative of, the true character of that relationship and in determining the identity of the disputed employer;
- the court is entitled to consider the reality of the purported contractual arrangements;
- conversations and conduct at the time of the alleged engagement of the employee is of considerable significance;
- the beliefs of the employees as to the identity of their employer is admissible and entitled to weight;
- in cases of the engagement of new employees to work in a business in which a number of separate corporate entities participate otherwise than as partners it was open to those controlling the business to select the employer provided that the selection was consistent with the financial and administrative organisation of the business and was not otherwise a sham.

As can be seen, the court takes a wide view of the putative relationship, having regard to how the parties conducted themselves in practice. Where there is documentation the court will look beyond the documents to the reality of the situation.[141] The practical matters which might be considered in identifying the employer include a consideration of which entity:

- had practical and legal control and direction of the employees;
- made decisions about hiring;
- made decisions about disciplinary issues;
- made decisions about the level of remuneration;
- actually paid remuneration;
- communicated with employees about leave; and
- made decisions about termination of employment.[142]

The last point on the list of principles identified by Finn J in *C & T Grinter* is worth further comment: the necessity to identify a rational explanation for the arrangement, which explanation must be satisfactorily related to a tangible business objective.[143] This requirement makes clear that it is possible for the court to find on the evidence that an administrative arrangement whereby one corporation is selected to employ the labour is not legally effective to alter the identity of the employer where the separate employing company is completely reliant on the company to whom it supplies the labour, has no assets or management structure and exists only as shell to protect another company in the group (which does have assets) from liability to the employees.

---

141   *Gothard* at [52]; see also *Golden Plains Fodder Australia Pty Ltd v Millard* (2007) SASR 461 per Gray J (David J agreeing) at [32]–[33].
142   *Gothard* at [59].
143   *Ramsey Food Processing* at [78].

So, for example, in *Romero v Auty*, an arrangement was put in place between two related companies whereby one of them (the 'new employer') would be the corporate vehicle which received funds from another company (the previous employer) on a weekly basis sufficient to meet the weekly payroll and would receive a transfer of funds as required to meet other obligations such as bonus payments, superannuation contributions and other entitlements. The 'new employer' paid the labour and associated costs of this administrative arrangement. It had no significant assets and made no provision in its accounts for the accrued employee entitlements. The 'new employer' issued group certificates and was the insured party for workers' compensation purposes. Warren J found that these arrangements were ineffective to change the true identity of the employer and were done for the administrative convenience of the 'real' employer.[144] Such an arrangement may be regarded not only as legally ineffective but also as a sham if it has been set up to disguise which entity is the true employer so as to avoid or minimise employment obligations.[145]

1.20.10 Labour hire arrangements

Now we turn to arrangements in which an unrelated business provides the labour of a worker to another business. This practice is called a labour hire arrangement. We are principally concerned here with what has been called the 'pure' labour hire industry: where the supplier of the labour is genuinely conducting a business of its own as such and the workers are hired out at the outset of the relationship. As we will see later, this can be contrasted with a situation in which there is a restructure of an existing employment relationship through the interposition of a labour hire company.

1.20.15 What is a labour hire arrangement?

Labour hire arrangements typically involve a tripartite arrangement in which a labour hire business (the supplier) supplies the labour of a worker (the worker) to a third party business (the client) who pays the supplier a fee. The worker usually renders an invoice to the supplier, who remunerates the worker for the work done. The commercial reward for the supplier is in the difference between the fee paid by the client and the remuneration paid to the worker. There are a number of reasons why the client may choose to obtain labour through a labour hire arrangement. For example:[146]

- filling short-term vacancies;
- filling regular seasonal requirements;
- filling specific functions within a business with workers with specific skills;

---

144   19 ACLC 206 at [23]–[26]; see also *Textile Footwear & Clothing Union of Australia v Bellechic Pty Ltd* [1998] FCA 1465, another example of a case in which such a rearrangement was ineffective. Compare, however, *Golden Plains Fodder Australia Pty Ltd v Millard* (2007) SASR 461.

145   This was the case in *Fair Work Ombudsman v Ramsey Food Processing Pty Ltd* (2011) 198 FCR 174, where the court regarded as a contrivance the interposition of another entity as the employer in a business rearrangement. Although not concerning an intra-group arrangement but instead the interposition of an unrelated purportedly independent company to provide labour, Buchanan J held that even if the situation were to be evaluated as an intra-group arrangement, the arrangements were ineffective to isolate employment and employment obligations from the true employer: at [91]. His Honour went on to find that the arrangement was a sham: at [115].

146   For an explanation of the nature of labour hire arrangements see, for example, *Victorian Inquiry into the Labour Hire Industry and Insecure Work, Background Paper*, October 2015 (Victorian Inquiry).

- using labour as a longer-term supplement to an ongoing workforce; and
- using labour hire to entirely replace an ongoing workforce.

Labour hire arrangements are a 'longstanding and unremarkable' feature of the labour market in Australia.[147] Their utilisation has increased in Australia in past decades. It is recognised in Australia that there is no assumption of illegality or illegitimate purpose from the mere fact that a labour hire arrangement is in place as long as certain objective criteria are met. A desire to avoid liability for employment-related obligations through using a labour hire arrangement is not in itself illegal as an objective.[148] Nevertheless, allegations that labour hire arrangements are being used to avoid workplace laws and other statutory obligations and the disadvantages and risks of such arrangements for workers are the subject of inquiry.[149] Further, some targeted regulation of the labour hire industry has been introduced.[150]

As noted earlier, Australia has not accepted the doctrine of joint employment. Accordingly, it is not possible for both the supplier and the client to be the employer of the worker. The question then is whether it is the supplier or the client that is the employer. Of course, whether or not the worker is an employee falls to be determined first by the application of the 'totality test' discussed above. It is only where the worker is an employee that the identity of the employer needs to be considered in the inquiry, which is concerned with obligations imposed on an employer and not on a principal in a principal–independent contractor relationship.[151]

1.20.20 Identifying the employer in a labour hire arrangement

Labour hire arrangements are diverse and the identity of the employer in each case will be determined according to the facts. There are cases where the court has held that neither the supplier nor the host is the employer; where the supplier was held to be the employer; and where the host was held to be the employer.[152]

BUILDING WORKERS' INDUSTRIAL UNION OF AUSTRALIA v ODCO PTY LTD (1991) 29 FCR 104 (ODCO)

Odco Pty Ltd ran a business called Troubleshooters Available, which supplied labour to clients who were builders, construction managers and contractors in the building industry in Victoria. In conducting its business, Odco encountered hostility from officials in the trade union movement

---

147   Ibid 7, for a reference to temping in the 1950s. See also *Ramsey Food Processing* at [60].
148   *Ramsey Food Processing* at [60].
149   See Victorian Inquiry; disadvantages and risks for workers are identified on 9. A South Australian parliamentary inquiry was announced in May 2015. There has also been a Fair Work Ombudsman (FWO) inquiry.
150   See Victorian Inquiry.
151   See *Personnel Contracting Pty Ltd (t/as Tricord Personnel) v Construction, Forestry, Mining and Energy Union of Workers* (2001) 141 IR 31, in which the worker was an independent contractor engaged by the hirer.
152   See *Forstaff Pty Ltd v Chief Commissioner of State Revenue* (2004) 144 IR 1; *Wilton v Coal & Allied Operations Pty Ltd* (2007) 161 FCR 300; and the authorities referred to by Merkel J in *Damevski v Giudice* (2003) 133 FCR 438, [173].

who were concerned that the provision of labour for an 'all-in' daily rate would undermine adherence to award conditions in the building industry. This hostility led to various incidents at building sites where the workers supplied by Troubleshooters were working. It was those incidents which led Troubleshooters to seek remedies in the Federal Court in relation to claims that (inter alia) the union was engaging in conduct that hindered or prevented its clients from acquiring labour services provided by it. One of the main issues in the proceedings was whether the workers were employees of the client or Troubleshooters. This issue was relevant to whether or not the award applied to the workers. The essential features of the tripartite arrangement were:

- the workers were screened at interviews conducted by Troubleshooters at which inquiry was made as to whether or not they were self-employed and why they wanted to be self-employed;
- they then entered into a contract with Troubleshooters which expressly provided that they were not employees but were self-employed; there was no guarantee of work and the worker was not obliged to accept work; no claim would be made for leave of any type; the worker was responsible for work-related injury insurance; the worker would provide their own plant and equipment; and, no deductions would be made in respect of PAYE taxation;
- the contract further provided that the worker would be paid a specified rate per hour for actual on-site hours worked and that Troubleshooters would have no liability to the worker except in respect of the agreed rate of pay for work done;
- the worker agreed to carry out the work in a workmanlike manner and to guarantee Troubleshooter against faulty workmanship;
- after signing the contract, the worker would be placed on Troubleshooters' 'books' and offered work at a particular site with a particular client site when that work became available;
- Troubleshooters' contract with its clients required them to pay Troubleshooters in accordance with an invoice rendered per week for all the workers on site provided by Troubleshooters. The amount invoiced was for the hourly rate agreed between Troubleshooters and the worker together with on-costs.

On appeal, the full court of the Federal Court found that there was no contract between the client and the worker. Accordingly, the client could not be the employee of the worker, irrespective of the direction or control the client exercised over the work done by the worker and the client's ability to send the worker off-site if it were unhappy with the worker for whatever reason. The court concluded that there was no contract because there was no promise of payment of periodic sums by the client to the worker and no agreement between the client and the worker as to what that sum should be. The client's only obligation was to pay Troubleshooters and the worker's only entitlement was against Troubleshooters (and that in accordance with a different calculation). At the time the worker reported to the foreman on a site he had already entered into a contract with Troubleshooters to perform the work and Troubleshooters had assumed an obligation to pay him.[153] The question then

---

153   *Odco* at 742–52. See also *Advanced Workplace Solutions Pty Ltd v Fox and Kangan Batman TAFE* [1999] AIRC 731 (*AWS*), in which the absence of a contractual relationship between the client and the worker meant that there could be no contract of employment irrespective of the control and direction exercised by the client over the worker.

was whether the contract between the worker and Troubleshooters – and there was undoubtedly a contract – was one of employment. The court focused on the control test and concluded that the worker was not subject to Troubleshooters' control or directions. Troubleshooters had no power to direct or require workers to, for example, rectify defective work. Its role was that of mediator between the client and the worker. The court regarded the other indicia of an employment relationship as inconclusive and so emphasised the express intention of the parties to conclude that the relationship was not one of employment.

The decision in *Odco* is often credited as being responsible for the dramatic growth of the labour hire industry in the late 1980s and throughout the 1990s, and for spawning the use of what became called the 'Odco-style arrangement' by which subsequent labour hire companies sought to implement the same type of arrangement.[154]

1.20.25 The interposition of a labour hire agency

The above discussion was concerned with labour hire arrangements in which the supplier was not only in the business of labour hire but the hiring occurred at the outset of the work relationship. But what of cases in which there has been an attempt to restructure an existing employment relationship by interposing a labour hire company?

Typically in such cases, what happens is that the employee is told by their employer that the arrangement by which they are offered work is to change. Instead of being employed directly by their employer they are to be engaged by a labour hire company who will provide their services back to the employer. They will be required to submit time sheets or similar documentation to the labour hire company. The labour hire company will be responsible for remunerating them. Otherwise, 'nothing will change': the 'worker' will do the same work, for the same (ex) employer and under the control and supervision of the (ex) employer. In these circumstances, the cases demonstrate that the courts are prepared to go behind the purported arrangement and the documents used to set it up to examine the true nature of the relationship as it operates between the parties. The search is for the 'substance' and 'reality' of the relationship.

That is what happened in the case of *Damevski v Giudice*. Mr Damevski was employed for 3 years by Endoxos as a cleaner on a full-time basis. Endoxos then gave him the 'choice' to resign his employment and be engaged by a labour hire company called MLC Workplace Solutions (MLC) as an independent contractor, or not be provided with further work by Endoxos. He was given a letter setting out this choice. At a meeting with Endoxos to discuss the 'transition' to MLC, it was explained to Mr Damevski (and other Endoxos employees) that 'nothing would change'. Mr Damevski signed a letter of resignation prepared by Endoxos. Some time later, his services as a cleaner were terminated. He brought an unfair dismissal

---

154 *Damevski v Giudice* (2003) 133 FCR 438; *Fair Work Ombudsman v Quest South Perth Holdings Pty Ltd (No. 2)* [2013] FCA 582, where reliance on 'Odco-style documents' was unsuccessful in creating a contract between the employee and the labour hire company. See also *AWS*, in which 'Odco-style documents' were used but in which the full bench of the AIRC said that the decision in *Odco* was not determinative of the case before it.

application against Endoxos. Not surprisingly, Endoxos defended the application on the basis that it was no longer Mr Damevski's employer. On an application for judicial review of the decision of the (then) Australian Industrial Relations Commission, which had agreed with Endoxos, the full court of the Federal Court concluded that on the facts there was no 'clear and unambiguous' contract between Mr Damevski and MLC. There was no evidence of any signed agreement or of any negotiations between him and MLC concerning such an agreement. Further, even if his purported agreement with Endoxos to accept an offer of engagement by MLC could be sufficient to create a contract with MLC, there was no evidence that the contract was ever fulfilled or exercised. Mr Damevski continued to perform the same work for Endoxos and continued to be subject to the control and direction of Endoxos. MLC remunerated Mr Damevski as an agent of Endoxos.[155] The ambiguity of the arrangement between Mr Damevski and MLC required the court to consider the entire 'factual matrix' to establish what legal relationship, if any, existed. The court concluded that whilst there was no evidence of an express contractual relationship between Endoxos and Mr Damevski, one could be implied from the conduct of the parties. To imply such a contract, it was not necessary that there be a formal offer to re-employ by Endoxos and an acceptance by Mr Damevski. When Mr Damevski began working again for Endoxos after his resignation, viewed objectively, a contract of service on the same terms and conditions could be implied, as nothing had changed.[156]

Another attempt to 'convert' existing employees to independent contractors to be engaged by an interposed labour hire agency was considered by the full court of the Federal Court in *Fair Work Ombudsman v Quest South Perth Holdings Pty Ltd* [2015] FCAFC 37. The facts of the case are discussed in s 1.25.20 below, as the case principally concerned allegations of contravention of the sham contracting provisions in the *Fair Work Act*. The labour hire agency, Contracting Solutions, also used 'Odco-style documents'. The employees resigned and accepted the proposal by Contracting Solutions. They continued to work for their original employer (Quest) and 'nothing changed' other than that they were now remunerated by Contracting Solutions. The full court of the Federal Court found that the 'conversion' was ineffective and that the employees continued to be employees of Quest by reason of an implied contract of services between them.[157] On appeal (although not on this point) the High Court held this conclusion to be an uncontroversial conclusion of law.[158]

1.20.30 Labour supply chains

In addition to the typical tripartite labour hire arrangement, the procurement of labour through complex labour supply chains is an increasingly common practice. This typically involves a company that is the ultimate beneficiary of the work performed entering into a commercial contract with another entity, which in turn enters into contracts with subcontractors, who in turn enter into employment contracts with individuals. This type of arrangement presents a challenge when trying to determine the nature of the various contractual relationships. The entity at the top of the chain will have no direct contractual relationship with the worker and is

155   *Damevski v Giudice* at [48]–[51], Wilcox and Merkel JJ concurring.
156   Ibid [81], [84], [89] per Marshall J.
157   *Fair Work Ombudsman v Quest South Perth Holdings Pty Ltd* [2015] FCA 37 at [129]–[234].
158   *Fair Work Ombudsman v Quest South Perth Holdings Pty Ltd* (2015) 256 CLR 137.

unlikely to know the structure of the relationships in the chain or know whether or not there is compliance with workplace laws.[159]

A recent example of this type of arrangement involving trolley collection at Coles supermarkets was the subject of an inquiry and proceedings by the Fair Work Ombudsman. Coles had entered into a contract with an unrelated entity for the provision of trolley collection services at its supermarkets across Australia. That entity entered into a series of subcontracts with other entities and individuals who in turn employed the trolley collectors. The trolley collectors were underpaid. In proceedings for contraventions of the *Fair Work Act*, the Fair Work Ombudsman alleged that Coles was involved in the contraventions and liable as an accessory to the contraventions by the employer of the trolley collectors.[160] As a consequence, Coles entered into an Enforceable Undertaking with the Fair Work Ombudsman, implemented changes to its trolley contracting process, and commenced a process of bringing trolley collection services 'in-house' so that the trolley collection would be performed by its direct employees.[161] It also made ex-gratia payments to the underpaid trolley collectors.

1.25 Sham contracting

The identification of the 'true' employer may involve not only an inquiry as to whether a particular arrangement was 'legally effective' in establishing or changing the identity of the employer but also whether the arrangement was a 'sham'.

1.25.05 Common law sham and pretence

At common law a 'sham' arises where the parties have a common intention to disguise the true nature of their transaction.[162] Making out a common law case of sham is to be distinguished from the popular use of the word as a means of emphatically expressing disapproval of conduct.[163]

For example, in *Sharrment Pty Ltd v Official Trustee in Bankruptcy*,[164] Lockhart J described a sham as:

> ... something that is intended to be mistaken for something else or that is not really what it purports to be. It is a spurious imitation, a counterfeit, a disguise or a false front. It is not

159   For another example of the issues that arise in labour supply chains, see *A Report on the Fair Work Ombudsman's Inquiry into the labour procurement arrangements of the Baiada Group in New South Wales*, available at http://www.fwo.gov.au.
160   *Fair Work Ombudsman v Al Hilfi* [2016] FCA 193.
161   *Enforceable Undertaking Between the Commonwealth of Australia (as represented by the Fair Work Ombudsman) and Coles Supermarkets Australia Pty Ltd (ABN 45 004 189 708)* 6 October 2014, available at https://www.fairwork.gov.au (About Us/Our Role/Enforcing the Legislation).
162   *Fair Work Ombudsman v Contracting Solutions Australia Pty Ltd* [2013] FCA 7, [18], citing *Equuscorp Pty Ltd v Glengallan Investments Pty Ltd* (2004) 218 CLR 471 at [46].
163   Buchanan J noted these limitations in *Ramsey Food Processing* at [112]–[113].
164   (1988) 18 FCR 449 at 454; approved in *Raftland Pty Ltd v Commissioner of Taxation* (2008) 238 CLR 516 at [111]–[112].

genuine or true, but something made in imitation of something else or made to appear to be something which it is not. It is something which is false or deceptive.

In *Fair Work Ombudsman v Quest South Perth Holdings Pty Ltd*, a case concerning a purported labour hire arrangement, North and Bromberg JJ described a sham at common law as an agreement not intended by the parties 'to have substantive, as opposed to apparent, legal effect; and which is the product of the common intention of the parties to deliberately deceive third parties'.[165] Their Honours noted that this requirement of a common intention between the parties to deceive third parties will be of little utility in exposing a disguised employment in which the employee is 'usually either ignorant of the deceit or a victim of it'.[166] The common law doctrine of sham – and the obvious limitation imposed by the requirement of common intention – has been supplemented by the broader doctrine of pretence, in which a common intention to deceive is not required and the issue is whether or not the agreement in truth represents what was agreed.[167]

1.25.10 Statutory provisions on sham arrangements

There has also been a statutory response to disguised employment arrangements. Division 6 of Part 3-1 of Chapter 3 of the *Fair Work Act* is headed 'Sham arrangements'.[168]

Broadly speaking, sham contracting is said to occur where an employer disguises an employment relationship as an independent contracting relationship. It is regarded as conduct that 'unfairly deprives workers of the benefits of employment and undermines the effective operation of the system established by the *Fair Work Act 2009* (Cth) and other industrial legislation'.[169]

Specifically, Division 6 contains three provisions dealing with conduct that involves sham contracting arrangements by an employer:

(i)   representing to an individual that the contract of employment under which they are employed or are to be employed is a contract for services under which they perform the work as an independent contractor: s 357;

(ii) dismissing an employee in order to engage the employee as an independent contractor to perform the same or substantially the same work: s 358;

(iii) making a statement known to be false to an employee to persuade or influence them to enter into a contract for services under which they will perform the same or substantially the same work as an independent contractor: s 359.

Each of the three sections is a 'civil remedy provision' under Part 4-1 of the *Fair Work Act*. This means that a finding of contravention may result in the imposition of a penalty and/or the

---

165   *Fair Work Ombudsman v Quest South Perth Holdings Pty Ltd* (2015) 228 FCR 346 at [144], citing *Raftland Pty Ltd v Commissioner of Taxation* (2008) 238 CLR 516 at [33]–[35], [58] (Gleeson CJ, Gummow and Crennan JJ) and [85], [112] and [148] (Kirby J).

166   *Fair Work Ombudsman v Quest South Perth Holdings Pty Ltd* (2015) 228 FCR 346 at [145].

167   Ibid [145]–[146].

168   Provisions in similar terms to ss 357 and 358 were also to be found in the *Workplace Relations Act 1996* (Cth): ss 900, 901 and 902.

169   *Fair Work Ombudsman v Quest South Perth Holdings Pty Ltd (No. 2)* [2013] FCA 582 at [2].

ordering of compensation to a party (most obviously, the employee) that suffers loss as a result of the contravention.[170] The standard of proof is the civil standard: that is, the balance of probabilities.[171] Further, where the contravention involves an allegation that the person took action for a particular reason or with a particular intent – such as is the case with respect to s 358 – it is presumed that the action was taken for that reason unless the respondent proves otherwise. Additionally, a person will be taken to have taken action for a particular reason if the reasons for the action included that reason. It is not necessary that the contravening reason be the substantial or dominant reason for which the action was taken.[172]

Whilst the heading to Division 6 uses the word 'sham', none of the three sections contains the word 'sham'. So an alleged contravention does not require a finding that an arrangement is a sham in the common law sense although, indeed, it might be.[173] Conduct contravening these sections depends upon a proper construction of each of the elements that comprise the prohibited conduct. The heading, however, forms part of the Act. Accordingly, regard is to be had to the concept of 'sham arrangements' in construing the sections, having regard to the mischief to which the prohibitions are directed: that is, an arrangement through which an employer seeks to cloak a work relationship so that it falsely appears to be an independent contracting arrangement.[174]

There have been numerous decisions on these sham contracting provisions. A selection of these decisions is discussed below.[175]

1.25.15 Misrepresenting employment as an independent contracting arrangement

Section 357(1) provides:

> A person (the employer) that employs, or proposes to employ, an individual must not represent to the individual that the contract of employment under which the individual is, or would be, employed by the employer is a contract for services under which the individual performs, or would perform, work as an independent contractor.

It can be seen that there are two elements that make up a contravention of s 357:

(i) the proposed or existing contractual relationship is, or will be, one of employment; and

(ii) a representation is made by the employer to the employee or prospective employee that the contract, is or will be, a contract for services.

---

170   See *Fair Work Act* Part 4-1.
171   *Evidence Act 1995* (Cth) s 140; see *Fair Work Ombudsman v Maclean Bay Pty Ltd* (2012) 200 FCR 57 per Marshall J at [7]–[8] (*Maclean Bay*) for an explanation of the court's approach to the standard of proof. See also, for example, *Fair Work Ombudsman v Metro Northern Enterprises Pty Ltd* [2013] FCCA 216 at [376] (*Metro Northern*); *Director, Fair Work Building Industry Inspectorate v Linkhill Pty Ltd (No. 7)* [2013] FCCA 1097 at [318] (*Linkhill*).
172   The operation of this reverse onus is taken up in Chapter 3 on adverse action.
173   *Fair Work Ombudsman v Contracting Solutions Australia Pty Ltd* [2013] FCA 7 at [18]–[20] (a decision in relation to the similar provisions in Part 22 of the *Workplace Relations Act 1996 (Cth)* where the heading to the provisions was also sham arrangements).
174   *Fair Work Ombudsman v Quest South Perth Holdings Pty Ltd* (2015) 256 CLR 137.
175   To date there have been no decisions on s 359.

Whether the contractual relationship or proposed contractual relationship is or will be one of employment (as opposed to a relationship of principal and independent contractor) is determined by the application of the totality test already discussed. The application of that test is undertaken no differently when the case is concerned with an alleged contravention of s 357.[176]

As to the making of a representation which mischaracterises the relationship, this might be established by evidence of:

(i)   a direct statement made by the employer that the relationship is or will be one of principal and independent contractor in, for example, job advertisements or interviews;[177]

(ii)   the provision of a contract or other document in which statements are made as to the relationship being one of principal and independent contractor;[178]

(iii)   statements or descriptions characterising the relationship that are made in documents provided to the putative employee by the putative employer;[179]

(iv)   requiring the workers to provide an ABN to the employer;[180]

(v)   requiring the workers to produce invoices in order to receive payment for work performed;[181]

(vi)   not withholding income tax or making superannuation contributions in relation to the workers;[182]

(vii)   not providing any workers' compensation insurance coverage.[183]

Where the representation is made in relation to prospective employment, whether or not there was a contravention of s 357 is answered by reference to what was proposed at the time the representation was made. The question is whether the nature of the agreement proposed was misrepresented at the time of the proposal, not whether the representation turned out to be false by reference to the agreement actually made.[184] This means that the focus is not upon what actually eventuated or evolved over time but on whether when the workers were being engaged they were in fact and law being engaged as employees whilst it was being represented to them that they were being engaged as independent contractors. That is not to say,

---

176   See *Metro Northern Enterprises* at [20]; *Director, Fair Work Building Industry Inspectorate v Bavco Pty Ltd* (2014) 291 FLR 380 at [39] (*Bavco*); *Linkhill* at [228]–[288].

177   See *Fair Work Ombudsman v Centennial Financial Services Pty Ltd* (2010) 245 FLR 242 at [267].

178   Ibid [268].

179   *Fair Work Ombudsman v Maclean Bay Pty Ltd* (2012) 200 FCR 57 at [93]; *Fair Work Ombudsman v Metro Northern Enterprises Pty Ltd* [2013] FCCA 216 at [372].

180   *Fair Work Ombudsman v Happy Cabby Pty Ltd* [2013] FCCA 397 at [10] (*Happy Cabby*), relying upon the Agreed Statement of Facts made by the parties as to the relevant representations; *Fair Work Ombudsman v Joonie (Investment) Pty Ltd* [2013] FCCA 2144 at [5] (*Joonie*), relying upon the Agreed Statement of Facts made by the parties as to the relevant representations; *Linkhill* at [315] (not disturbed on appeal: [2014] FCFCA 1124).

181   *Happy Cabby* at [10]; *Joonie* at [5]; *Linkhill* at [315]–[316].

182   Ibid.

183   Ibid.

184   *Fair Work Ombudsman v Quest South Perth Holdings Pty Ltd* (2015) 228 FCR 346 at [72] and [245].

however, that the agreement as it eventuated is not important; it may be relevant in determining whether or not the contravening representation was made.[185]

A contravening representation might be made at the time at which the person is being engaged and may continue to have effect during the period of time following the date upon which the representation was made.[186] In that event, the representation will also be a representation that an existing contract is a contract for services.

To establish a contravention of s 357 there is no need to establish that the putative employee relied upon the representation in entering into the arrangement.[187]

If a finding is made that the employer made a representation misrepresenting the relationship, it may be able to make out the defence provided for in subsection 357(2), which provides:

> Subsection (1) does not apply if the employer proves that, when the representation was made, the employer:
>
> (a)   did not know; and
>
> (b)   was not reckless as to whether;
>
> the contract was a contract of employment rather than a contract for services.

It is the employer's subjective actual knowledge, not suspicion, that is in issue under s 357(2)(a) and this must be seen in light of the fact that there is no single indicator or test for determining the existence of an employment relationship.[188] So, for example, the fact that the documents provided by the employer are found not to be indicative of the nature of the relationship in its totality does not mean that the employer is unable to prove a lack of actual knowledge that the contract was one of employment.[189] The question of knowledge will thus obviously be a matter of evidence, including, for example, such matters as whether the employer obtained relevant legal advice and the substance of that advice.[190]

As to the concept of 'recklessness' under s 357(2)(b), the term is not defined in the Act. It is accepted that 'reckless' has its common law meaning in civil law, but not in criminal law.[191] However, different views have been expressed as to the approach to be taken to the concept in the context of the *Fair Work Act* and the mischief to which s 357 is directed. Most recently, in *Fair Work Ombudsman v Ecosway Pty Ltd* (*Ecosway*), White J held that the concept of recklessness involves an element of objectivity. Accordingly, the employer must, in addition to proving that they did not know that the contract was one of employment rather than a contract for services, prove that in the circumstances known to them at the time they made the misrepresentation, they could not reasonably have been expected to have known that the

---

185   Ibid [72].
186   *Maclean Bay* at [138], cited with approval and applied in *Linkhill* at [314]–[316].
187   *Metro Northern* at [374].
188   Ibid [378]–[379]; *Bavco* at [52], where Manousaridis J held (despite the wording of s 357(2)) that the requisite knowledge is not as to a 'contract of employment' but as to whether the person is or will be 'an employee', which his Honour described as a word of 'common currency'.
189   *Metro Northern* at [395].
190   *Linkhill* at [326], and [322], where O'Sullivan J had regard to a submission that the employer had the requisite knowledge because of previous proceedings in which the question of whether workers were engaged as employees or independent contractors was determined in relation to engagement of workers by a related entity. As to the potentially relevant classes of evidence from which knowledge might be inferred, see *Bavco* at [71].
191   It is accepted that the *Criminal Code Act 1995* (Cth) does not apply: *Construction, Forestry, Mining and Energy Union v Nubrick Pty Ltd* (2009) 190 IR 175 at [18] and *Metro Northern* at [381].

contract may be a contract of employment.[192] In applying that approach, evidence about advice the employer received, any relevant investigations into the employer's engagement practices by, for example, the Fair Work Ombudsman or other regulatory bodies, will be relevant in terms of what the employer knew or might reasonably be expected to have known.[193]

1.25.20 Dismissing an employee to engage them as an independent contractor

Section 358 provides:

> An employer must not dismiss, or threaten to dismiss, an individual who:
>
>   (a)   is an employee of the employer; and
>   (b)   performs particular work for the employer;
>
> in order to engage the individual as an independent contractor to perform the same, or substantially the same, work under a contract for services.

Whether a dismissal or threat of dismissal has occurred is a matter of fact to be determined on all the evidence.[194]

As noted above, the unlawful reason need only be one of the reasons for the termination of employment. Neither does it need be the dominant reason. Further, it is not necessary that the unlawful purpose – that the dismissed employee is engaged as an independent contractor – ultimately be achieved.[195]

FAIR WORK OMBUDSMAN v QUEST SOUTH PERTH HOLDINGS PTY LTD (2015) 256 CLR 137

Proceedings for a contravention of the sham contracting provisions in the *Fair Work Act* have also arisen in the context of an arrangement involving an attempt to convert existing employees to independent contractors by interposing an unrelated labour hire supplier to engage the employees as independent contractors using the Odco Contracting System. The application of the provisions in that context gave rise to sufficiently novel or complicated issues that the matter ultimately had to be resolved by the High Court.

---

192   *Ecosway* at [196]–[199].
193   In *Ecosway*, White J considered the origins of a template agreement used by the company and advice that had been obtained about it: [200]–[217]; see also *Metro Northern* at [403]; *Bavco* at [90], where an audit by the ABCC did not negate the defence as the employer had not been informed at the relevant time that the outcome of the audit was that its practices did not comply with the Act. See also Fair Work Ombudsman, 'Sham contracting and the misclassification of workers in the cleaning services, hair and beauty and call centre industries: Report on the preliminary outcomes of the Fair Work Ombudsman Sham Contracting Operational Intervention', November 2011, where at p. 19 the Fair Work Ombudsman stated that in certain circumstances a Letter of Caution to an employer about the practice of engaging independent contractors might negate the defence.
194   See *Fair Work Ombudsman v Quest South Perth Holdings Pty Ltd (No. 2)* [2013] FCA 582 at [232]–[239]. These findings were not challenged on appeal.
195   *Director, Fair Work Building Industry Inspectorate v Robko Construction Pty Ltd* [2014] FCCA 2257 at [81].

Quest South Perth Holdings Pty Ltd (Quest) operated a business of providing serviced apartment accommodation. Quest employed housekeepers (including, for some years, a Ms Best and a Ms Roden) to clean its serviced apartments. Quest wanted to change the basis upon which it engaged the housekeepers by putting in place 'the ODCO system'. To that end, it entered into a hiring agreement with a company called Contracting Solutions Pty Ltd (Contracting Solutions), which operated a labour hire business. Contracting Solutions held a licence with Odco Contracting Systems Australia Pty Ltd which permitted it to utilise the Odco business procedures and systems in its labour hire business. Pursuant to the hiring agreement, Contracting Solutions would provide labour to Quest and be responsible for the 'administrational management' of the workers, whom it would engage as independent contractors. Contracting Solutions would pay the contractors a rate equivalent to the ordinary time award rate as a flat rate for all hours worked and on-charge that to Quest plus a percentage. Contracting Solutions told Quest that its existing employees would be 'converted' to contractors and it (Contracting Solutions) would sign up all new staff at Quest's request. Amongst the advantages of this arrangement was the assurance by Contracting Solutions that Quest would not have to pay penalty rates. Quest was assured that it would have peace of mind as to the 'legitimacy of its workers' because the Odco system had been tested, as a result of which the workers would be classified as independent contractors operating outside the industrial relations system. Quest explained the new arrangement to Ms Best and Ms Roden and represented to them that they would carry out their work for Quest as independent contractors of Contracting Solutions. They were given a 'sign up pack' including a contractor guide and a contractor application form. The documents described them as independent contractors. Ms Best and Ms Roden were encouraged to take up the arrangement offered to them and various statements were made as to the benefits of the arrangement. Ms Best and Ms Roden accepted the offered arrangement. They each believed that they had no option but to accept. Thereafter, they continued to work as housekeepers. Nothing changed in any practical sense. They continued to clean Quest's apartments according to the same roster and under the supervision of the same manager. They continued to wear a uniform supplied by Quest and used equipment supplied by Quest. They continued to complete the same time sheets, although these were no longer headed Quest. Contracting Solutions, however, now paid them. They had no contact with Contracting Solutions except in the case of Ms Best, when as a result of an injury she was unable to work for Quest. She was required by Quest to contact Contracting Solutions, who told her (when she was able to work) that it would contact its clients to see if they required any cleaning services.

The Fair Work Ombudsman brought a proceeding in the Federal Court claiming, amongst other things, pecuniary penalty orders against Quest for contraventions of s 357 of the *Fair Work Act* in respect of the 'conversion' of Ms Best and Ms Roden. At first instance, McKerracher J dismissed the claim.[196] The Fair Work Ombudsman appealed to the Full Federal Court.

The Full Federal Court construed s 357(1) as having a confined operation. It held that a 'representation made by an employer to its employee that he or she is providing work as an

---

196 As noted, the Fair Work Ombudsman also claimed that Quest had contravened s 358 in respect of the dismissal of a receptionist engaged by Quest.

independent contractor under a contract for services made with a third party is not actionable under s 357'.[197] This, the court said, was because the representation must be directed to the contract between the employer (in this case named as Quest) and the employee and not simply to the status of the employee. The contract being referred to is the contract between the employer and the employee, and it is the character of that contract and not another contract (in this case, the contract between the workers and the labour hire supplier) about which the representation must be made.[198] In that circumstance, the representation by Quest, previously the employer, that the worker has a contract with a labour hire company as an independent contractor is not a mischaracterisation of a contract with the employer but a denial of the existence of a contract between the employer (again, Quest) and the employee.[199] As discussed in s 1.15.10, the Full Federal Court went on to find that the contract between the employees and Contracting Solutions was legally ineffective and that there was an implied contract of employment between the employees and Quest.

The Fair Work Ombudsman was granted special leave to appeal to the High Court. The question for the High Court was whether s 357(1) of the *Fair Work Act* 'prohibits an employer from misrepresenting to an employee that the employee performs work as an independent contractor under a contract for services with a third party'. The High Court unanimously answered this question in the affirmative.[200]

The High Court rejected the confined interpretation of s 357(1) arrived at by the Full Federal Court and said that there was nothing in the language of the section that confines the representation to a representation that the contract under which the employee performs or would perform work as an independent contractor is a contract for services with the employer. The section, the High Court said, is silent as to the counterparty to the represented contract for services. To otherwise confine the statutory prohibition would not achieve the evident statutory purpose, which is to protect an individual who is in truth an employee from being misled by his or her employer about his or her employment status, and would give the provision a capricious operation. Accordingly, the court concluded that the representation by Quest fell squarely within the scope of s 357(1).

1.30 Independent contractors legislation

To conclude this chapter, we touch upon the provisions of the *Independent Contractors Act 2006* (Cth).

The principal objects of the Act, set out in s 3, are:

(i)   to protect the freedom of contractors to enter into contracts to supply their services;

(ii)   to recognise independent contracting as a legitimate form of work arrangement; and

(iii) to prevent interference with genuine contracting arrangements.

---

197   *Fair Work Ombudsman v Quest South Perth Holdings Pty Ltd* (2015) 256 CLR 137 [77].
198   Ibid [80].
199   Ibid [77].
200   *Fair Work Ombudsman v Quest South Perth Holdings Pty Ltd* (2015) 256 CLR 137.

The Act applies to a contract for services to which an independent contractor is a party and which relates to the performance of work.[201] The contract must have a requisite 'constitutional connection'.[202] 'Independent contractor' is not defined, although the independent contractor need not be a natural person.[203] The meaning of 'independent contractor' is otherwise left to the common law and the application of the tests already discussed.[204]

The objects of the Act are, principally, achieved by providing that the contract for services is to be governed by the terms of the contract.[205] More particularly, the objects of the Act are achieved by excluding any State or Territory legislation which does any of the following:

(i) deems contractors to be employees for the purpose a law relating to a workplace relations matter;[206]

(ii) confers rights or imposes obligations on a party to a services contract that in an employment relationship would be about workplace relations matters;[207]

(iii) enables a contractor to bring proceedings to have their contract varied or set aside on the basis that it is unfair.[208]

The freedom to enter into a legitimate and genuine contract for services is balanced by the jurisdiction of the Federal Court or Federal Circuit Court in Part 3 of the Act to review a contract on the ground that it is a unfair or harsh. This jurisdiction is dealt with in Chapter 2.

SUMMARY

We have seen that in any study of Australian employment law it is important to understand how the courts determine whether a person performing work is an employee. This is because the employment

---

201   *Independent Contractors Act 2006* (Cth) s 5(1).
202   Either party must be a trading, financial or foreign corporation or a Commonwealth authority, or the contract must have some connection with a Territory: s 5(2).
203   *Independent Contractors Act 2006* (Cth) s 4.
204   In *ATS (Asia Pacific) v Dun Oir Investments Pty Ltd* (2012) 212 FCR 566 Cowdroy J (in dealing with a strike out application) held that the contract was not a contract for services because the services to be provided did not relate to the workplace or the provision of labour: at [40]. However, in *Kerrisk v DC Holdings Western Australia Ltd* [2013] FCA 1217 it was suggested that 'independent contractor' might have a broader meaning than a meaning in contradistinction to that of employee: at [85].
205   *Independent Contractors Act 2006* (Cth) s 2.
206   *Independent Contractors Act 2006* (Cth) s 7(1)(a). This would be exclude, for example, s 275 of the *Industrial Relations Act 1999* (Qld).
207   Section 7(1)(b). 'Workplace relations matters' is defined in s 8 to include matters such as remuneration, leave and hours of work. There are a number of matters that are expressly stated not to be workplace relations matters, including discrimination, workplace health and safety, superannuation and workers' compensation: s 8(2). Further, State laws on outworkers are exempt, as are some specific pieces of legislation: for example, those dealing with contracts in the road transport industry: s 7(2).
208   *Independent Contractors Act 2006* (Cth) s 7(1)(c). Section 106 of the *Industrial Relations Act 1996* (NSW) gives the NSW Industrial Relations Commission power to review contracts and arrangements – including those involving independent contractors – and which involve the performance of work and to set aside or vary those contracts and/or award the payment of money on the basis of unfairness. As result of the *Independent Contractors Act* this jurisdiction no longer applies to contracts for services that are covered by the Act. A similar but narrower provision in s 276 of the *Industrial Relations Act 1999* (Qld) is also precluded from operating.

relationship is a determinant for many important rights and obligations. There is no unifying definition. Rather, the court approaches the question by examining the totality of the relationship. We have seen that the court is concerned to identify the true nature of the relationship between the parties, having regard to a range of indicia and all the circumstances of the relationship. The variety and complexity of modern-day work arrangements can make the court's task difficult, and it will not always be easy to predict whether a court will find the worker is an employee or, for example, an independent contractor. Nevertheless, the court's task is to determine the true nature of the relationship and the true identity of the employer and in doing so look behind any contrivance or sham.

REVIEW QUESTIONS

1. Whether a worker is an employee (and not an independent contractor) is significant for a number of reasons. What are those reasons?
2. What is the test in modern Australian employment law for determining whether or not a worker is an employee?
3. Discuss how you think an Australian court would approach determining whether or not Uber drivers are employees or independent contractors.
4. Explain why Mr Damevski in *Damevski v Giudice* (2003) 133 FCR 438 was found not to have entered into a contract with the labour hire agency and was still an employee of his original employer. Why was this finding significant for Mr Damevski?
5. Explain why Quest (*FWO v Quest South Perth Holdings Pty Ltd*) was found to be in breach of s 357(1) of the *Fair Work Act*.

FURTHER READING

Fair Work Ombudsman, 'Sham contracting an the misclassification of workers in the cleaning services, hair and beauty call centre industries: Report on the preliminary outcomes of the Fair Work Ombudsman Sham Contracting Operational Intervention', November 2011 (available at https://fairwork.gov.au).

M Irving, *The Contract of Employment* (LexisNexis Butterworths, 2012), Ch. 2.

I Neil and D Chin, *The Modern Contract of Employment* (Thomson Reuters, 2012), Ch. 1.

C Roles and A Stewart 'The Reach of Labour Regulation: Tackling Sham Contracting' (2012) 25 *Australian Journal of Labour Law* 258.

A Stewart, 'Redefining Employment? Meeting the Challenge of Contract and Agency Labour' (2002) 15 *Australian Journal of Labour Law* 234.

2 THE EMPLOYMENT CONTRACT: IMPLIED TERMS

2.05 Introduction

In Chapter 1 we established the nature of a contract and how to distinguish between a contract of employment and an independent contract. The terms of an employment contract set out the various rights and duties of the employer and the employee.

In addition to the express terms in an employment contract, there are implied terms. These are duties and obligations imposed on the employer and employee under the common law.[1] They are based on public policy or originate from the nature of the contract of employment (for example, between master and servant).[2] Duties implied by common law can be imposed on the employee or the employer or they can be mutual obligations. In Australia at present, there is much debate about that latter group.

In the 2014 High Court of Australia decision in *Commonwealth Bank of Australia v Barker* (2014) 253 CLR 169 (*Barker* (2014)) the court did not imply a mutual duty of trust and confidence into the employment relationship flowing from the employer to the employee. As will be seen throughout this chapter, debate as to whether there is a reciprocal duty of good faith continues. Further, issues arise as to the interconnection between work, remuneration and strikes. So it is with those reciprocal duties that this discussion begins.

2.10 No work, no pay[3] – work earns remuneration

That workers are entitled to earn remuneration, whether it is by way of wages or salary, for work they perform was confirmed by the decision in *Automatic Fire Sprinklers Pty Ltd v Watson*.[4] The employee's duty to render services and the employer's duty to pay wages may seem straightforward, in that if services are not rendered then wages may not be paid. However, there are several issues arising from this seemingly simple interdependent duty.

For example, there is a question as to whether it is justified for employees to extract wages, based on the employer's duty to pay wages, during lawful industrial action such as a go-slow or a work-to-rule. Chapter 5 of this book deals with industrial action and limits on payment of salary to workers who strike under the *Fair Work Act 2009* (Cth). But there are difficulties in practice.

In a go-slow, work is performed, but at a very slow rate. In a work-to-rule, work is performed, but only to the letter of the contract of employment. Both of these industrial

---

1   In Australia, the common law implied terms in employment contracts are settled after the decision in *Byrne v Australian Airlines Ltd* (1995) 185 CLR 410 (*Byrne*), where features of common law contracts of employment were revisited. For an in-depth analysis of this High Court decision in the context of implied terms in employment contract read R Naughton 'Revisiting the contract of employment – *Byrne and Frew v Australian Airlines Limited*' (1995) 17 *Sydney Law Review* 88.
2   C Sappideen et al. *Macken's Law of Employment* (Law Book Co., 7th ed, 2011) 146. In the well-known English case of *BP Refinery (Westernport) Pty Ltd v Shire of Hastings* (1977) 180 CLR 266 (*BP Refinery*) the Privy Council set down a set of requirements for implying a term into a contract.
3   Also referred to as 'wages-work bargain'.
4   *Automatic Fire Sprinklers Pty Ltd v Watson* (1946) 72 CLR 435. See further the exposition in Chapter 6 in the context of termination of employment. This chapter includes other relevant cases such as *Ulan Coal Mines Ltd v Honeysett* (2010) 199 IR 363; *Dawnay Day & Co. Ltd v de Braconier d'Alphen* [1997] IRLR 442, [45]–[46]; *Aussie Home Loans v X Inc Services Pty Ltd* (2005) ATPR 42-060, [24]–[26]; and *Kearney Pty Ltd v Crepaldi* [2006] NSWSC 23 at [58].

strategies can have a negative impact on a business's productivity, but it is hard to prove their effect before a court. So if this conduct is alleged, it may be some time before it can be proved legally, and hence before payment for the defective work may occur.

2.10.05 Does the employer have a duty to provide work?

There is no obligation on an employer to provide work to an employee unless the contract of employment requires the employer to provide work. The exception to this was examined in *Blackadder v Ramsey Butchering Services Pty Ltd* (*Blackadder* (2005).

BLACKADDER *v* RAMSEY BUTCHERING SERVICES PTY LTD (2005) 221 CLR 539

Blackadder (2005) confirmed that this exception is 'where it was necessary for the employee, an actor' to continue to be employed in order to maintain a profile, or where the employee's career and future prospects depended on the employee working in a particular way, or where the employee's remuneration depended upon the amount of actual work performed by the employee'.[5] Their Honours also noted that in modern times, job satisfaction also contributes to 'determining whether work in fact should be provided'.[6]

Despite these observations, the decision in *Blackadder* (2005) was in part due to the unusual facts of the case. The High Court decision in Mr Blackadder's unfair dismissal case was in favour of Mr Blackadder and ordered the employer to reinstate him to the position he had immediately prior to the termination of employment.[7] In deciding so, the High Court noted that the 'the employer must provide work to be done by the employee of the same kind and volume as was being done before termination'.[8]

Mr Blackadder had been employed as a boner at Ramsey Butchering Services since 1998.[9] The day after his appearance as a witness in a case brought by another employee against the employer, concerning an unlawful termination of employment, Mr Blackadder was transferred from the boning room, where he had worked since commencing work, to the slaughterfloor.[10] Additionally, the work Mr Blackadder was required to perform in the slaughterhouse involved tasks not performed by him before.[11] Mr Blackadder refused to carry out the duties, which he considered beyond his current skills and capacity.[12] On Mr Blackadder's refusal, his employment was terminated by the employer. The Industrial Commission found the termination to be unfair and unlawful and ordered reinstatement of his employment (*Blackadder v Ramsey Butchering Services Pty Ltd* (29 March 2000), Redmond C).[13]

---

5   *Blackadder v Ramsey Butchering Services Pty Ltd* (2005) 221 CLR 539 at [80].
6   Ibid.
7   Ibid [44].
8   Ibid.
9   Ibid [23].
10   Ibid [22].
11   Ibid [23].
12   Ibid [24].
13   Ibid [26].

Subsequently, the employer reinstated Mr Blackadder in the position of boner with full pay, but required that he undergo a medical assessment by a doctor nominated by the employer.[14] Although he was reinstated to his position as a boner, Mr Blackadder was not given work. He then applied to the Federal Court of Australia for an order to impose penalties on the employer, to make a declaration to reinstate him as a boner, and to recover lost wages. He succeeded in this.[15]

However, Ramsey Butchering appealed to the Full Court of the Federal Court of Australia.[16] The primary issue was whether these orders affirmed the contract of employment and thereby the common law rule that an employee does not have a right or entitlement to work.[17] The Full Court of the Federal Court of Australia relied on the common law position that there is no obligation on the employer under the employment contract to provide work to the employee unless it is specifically stated in that contract.[18]

In deciding whether the employer was obliged to give work to Mr Blackadder, the High Court concluded that the employer 'must recommence paying or providing the financial or other benefits attached to the position' and 'also must put the employee back to the performance of those duties which the employee was fulfilling before termination'.[19] In other words, he must be given work to make his reinstatement meaningful.

2.10.10 Duty to provide work distinguished from a direction to not perform work

An employer's direction to the employee not to perform work depends on 'the circumstances of the direction, the work that is not to be performed and the terms of the contract of employment'.[20] There is a difference between a direction to not perform a certain task due to faulty equipment and a direction not to perform work as a result of a contentious work issue or breakdown of the employer–employee relationship.

DOWNE v SYDNEY WEST AREA HEALTH SERVICE (NO. 2) (2008) 71 NSWLR 633

This case is an example of a 'significant and crucial distinction between a duty to provide work and a direction not to perform work'.[21] The facts of the case relate to the terms of the contract

---

14   Ibid [57]–[58].
15   *Blackadder v Ramsey Butchering Services Pty Ltd* (2002) 118 FCR 395 (*Blackadder* (2002)).
16   *Ramsey Butchering Services Pty Ltd v Blackadder* (2003) 127 FCAFC 20 (*Blackadder* (2003)).
17   Ibid [15].
18   Ibid [65].
19   *Blackadder* (2005) at [43].
20   *Downe v Sydney West Area Health Service (No. 2)* (2008) 71 NSWLR 633 (*Downe*) at [421].
21   Ibid [420]. Rothman J referred to the UK decision of *Collier v Sunday Referee Publishing Company* [1940] 2 KB 647 in making this observation.

entered into between the employer and Dr Downe. She had arrived in Australia from Canada in 1990 with the intention of establishing and running (as Director) a Neonatal Intensive Care Unit.[22] Sometime in 2004, while she was on long service leave, Dr Downe was suspended from her duties as a result of a number of complaints made against her. An investigation commenced.[23] The investigation was completed in 2005 but did not find evidence to prove the complaints against Dr Downe.[24] Despite this, the Health Service continued its indefinite suspension of Dr Downe.[25] In 2006, Dr Downe was directed to work at a different hospital, Westmead Hospital, as a staff specialist, under a State award.[26] Dr Downe's case was against the indefinite suspension from work and the employer's direction to work at Westmead Hospital.[27]

While the Health Service had given a specific direction to Dr Downe during the period of investigation – not to perform work – it had not informed her when she could return to her job.[28] The court decided that the suspension of Dr Downe indefinitely and the direction to work as a specialist in Westmead Hospital were a breach of the terms her employment contract and therefore unlawful.[29] It decided that in these circumstances the employer could not direct Dr Downe to work at a different location, as that contravened the location specified in the employment contract.[30]

2.15 Duty to cooperate

An essential aspect of an employer–employee relationship is the expectation that the parties will cooperate towards the mutual goals and business objectives.[31] This reflects the 'participatory and consultative'[32] approach adopted in the modern (and changing) employee–employer relationship – the master–servant relationship is obsolete. Stewart et al. observe that the duty to cooperate owed by each party to a contract 'is imposed by a term implied by law and also operates as a rule of construction'.[33]

There is a reciprocal nature to the duty to cooperate. For example, in an 1881 case, *Mackay v Dick*,[34] Lord Blackburn noted that although an express obligation to cooperate is not specified in a contract, the nature of general cooperation is such that when two parties have agreed to something by a written contract, 'the construction of the contract is that each agrees

---

22   *Downe* [8]–[9].
23   Ibid [32].
24   Ibid [101].
25   Ibid [215]–[221].
26   Ibid [3]; [376].
27   Ibid [1]–[5].
28   Ibid [5]; [424].
29   Ibid [408].
30   Ibid [429].
31   J Riley 'Siblings but not twins: making sense of "mutual trust" and "good faith" in employment contracts' (2012) 36(2) *Melbourne University Law Review* 536.
32   Sappideen et al, *Macken's Law of Employment* (2011) 209, with reference to *Barker* (2014) at [25], [30], [37] and [61]. See also *Byrne* at 436 (McHugh and Gummow JJ).
33   A Stewart et al. *Creighton and Stewart's Labour Law* (Federation Press, 6th ed, 2016) 527.
34   (1881) 6 App Cas 251 (*Mackay*).

to do all that is necessary to be done'[35] to carry out his part of the obligation.[36] Most importantly, Lord Blackburn observed that the question regarding what part each party is to assert should be decided by the circumstances.[37]

The reciprocal nature of a contract was observed in another early decision – *Butt v McDonald*, in 1896[38] – by Griffith CJ, when His Honour stated: 'It is a general rule applicable to every contract that each party agrees, by implication, to do all such things as are necessary on his part to enable the other party to have the benefit of the contract.'[39]

The duty to cooperate is considered to be based 'upon the need for one party to take a positive step without which the other party is unable to enjoy a right or benefit conferred upon it by the contract.'[40]

Because of its mutual nature, there was an attempt in *Commonwealth Bank of Australia v Barker* (*Barker* (2013)) to argue that the duty of cooperation should be seen as providing an alternative approach to, or an extension of, the recognition of an implied duty of mutual trust and confidence in Australia.[41] However, the High Court rejected that suggestion.[42] While it was the main subject of discussion in *Barker* (2014), our discussion of trust and confidence can be found in the next section of the chapter. For now it is instructive to consider the High Court's reasoning on cooperation and trust and confidence.

In the High Court decision in *Barker* (2014), French CJ, Bell and Keane JJ examined the obligation of cooperation and the proposition that terms 'implied in law are in fact rules of construction and that all implied "terms" of universal application fall into this category', as against being part of the contractual duty to cooperate.[43] Their Honours observed that discussion on this topic generally does not address 'whether, and when, implication of a term is to be regarded as an exercise in the construction of a contract or a class of contract'.[44]

To this end their Honours referred to the observations of Mason J in *Secured Income Real Estate (Australia) Ltd v St Martins Investments Pty Ltd*,[45] which endorsed the principles applied in both *Mackay* and *Butt* regarding the rule of construction.[46] In that case, Mason J specifically

35   Ibid 263. Their Honours in *Barker* (2014) noted that Lord Blackburn's observation indicates a rule of construction as opposed to the necessity for implication. See also *South Australia v McDonald* (2009) 104 SASR 334 at [271].

36   As referred to and quoted by French CJ, Bell and Keane JJ in *Barker* (2014), [25]. Also, see G Kuehne 'Implied obligations of good faith and reasonableness in performance of contracts: old wine in new bottles?' (2006) 33 *University of Western Australia Law Review* 68.

37   *Mackay*, 263. *Barker* (2014) at [25].

38   (1896) 7 QLJ 68 (70–71) (*Butt*).

39   Ibid.

40   *Barker* (2014) at [88].

41   *Barker* (2013) at [121]–[122]; [126]–[128].

42   *Barker* (2014) at [26].

43   Ibid [24]. Their Honours referred to some important texts and written work on this topic, including J Carter *Contract Law in Australia* (LexisNexis, 6th ed, 2013) 32–33 [2–19]; NC Seddon and RA Bigwood *Cheshire and Fifoot Law of Contract* (LexisNexis Butterworths, 10th Aust. ed, 2012) 461 [10.41]; and GJ Tolhurst 'Contractual confusion and industrial illusion: a contract law perspective on awards, collective agreements and the contract of employment' (1992) 66 *Australian Law Journal* 716. In relation to good faith, see J Allsop 'Good faith and Australian contract law: a practical issue and a question of theory and principle' (2011) 85 *Australian Law Journal* 361.

44   *Barker* (2014) at [24].

45   (1979) 144 CLR 596.

46   *Barker* (2014) at [25].

referred to the implied 'duty to co-operate', which His Honour stated is necessary to fulfil the obligations under a contract for all the parties to the contract. However, he also noted that it is not easy to ascertain when this is necessary: it depends on the intentions of the parties and the circumstances of the matter.[47] Mason J further stated that:

> the question arises whether the contract imposes a duty to co-operate on the first party or whether it leaves him at liberty to decide for himself whether the acts shall be done, even if the consequence of his decision is to disentitle the other party to a benefit. In such a case, the correct interpretation of the contract depends, . . . it seems to me, not so much on the application of the general rule of construction as on the intention of the parties as manifested by the contract itself.[48]

Jessup J's dissenting judgement in *Barker* (2013) in the Full Federal Court is also important in this respect. His Honour stated that the implied term of mutual trust and confidence and good faith cannot be justified as a 'mutualisation of the employee's duty of fidelity to the employer' or as a 'development of the implied duty of cooperation between parties to the contract'.[49] Furthermore, His Honour observed that an implied term of mutual trust and confidence and good faith is prescriptive and lacks description. He then went further, saying that it has the 'potential to act as a Trojan horse' because it can reveal 'only after the event the specific prohibitions which it imports into the contract'.[50]

This exposition highlights how necessary it is to consider the circumstances of each case when trying to ascertain the parties' intentions regarding the duty to cooperate.[51]

2.20 The duty of trust and confidence

As alluded to above, *Barker* (2014) is the first High Court of Australia decision to consider whether or not there is a duty of mutual trust and confidence, as well as the legal position on good faith. In Australia, the question of an implied duty of mutual trust and confidence was settled in the negative in *Barker* (2014), although there are residual issues, such as the reciprocal duty of good faith from employer to employee, that still require attention.[52] For the first time, the High Court had the opportunity to examine the question of whether the

---

47 Ibid [27]. Mason J in *Secured Income Real Estate (Australia) Ltd v St Martins Investments Pty Ltd* (1979) 144 CLR 607 at 607–609.
48 Ibid.
49 *Barker* (2013) at [340]. See also *Barker* (2014) at [13].
50 Ibid.
51 Also pointed out in *Barker* (2014), which both Lord Blackburn in *Mackay* and Mason J in *Secured Income Real Estate (Australia) Ltd v St Martins Investments Pty Ltd* (1979) 144 CLR 596 emphasised. See *Barker* (2014) at [25]–[26].
52 Although this decision appears to indicate that the Australian position is settled, there is divided opinion as to whether *Barker* (2014) settled the position regarding whether Australian employment law recognises the English law doctrine of the implied term of mutual trust and confidence between employers and employees. Some scholarly material includes R Naughton 'Termination of employment and workplace investigations' (2016) *Employment Law Bulletin* 186; J Riley 'Developments in contract of employment jurisprudence in other common-law jurisdictions' in Alan Bogg et al. (eds) *The Contract of Employment* (Oxford University Press, 2016) 273–94; J Carter et al. 'Terms implied in law: 'trust and confidence' in the High Court of Australia' (2015) 32(3) *Journal of Contract Law* 203–30.

English principle recognised in *Malik v Bank of Credit and Commerce International SA (in liq)* (*Malik*) [1998] AC 20 should be implied into employment contracts in Australia. However, in *Barker* (2014), Gageler J strongly opined, that the statutory circumstances in the UK have no similarity to the Australian circumstances,[53] and therefore cautioned against the direct application of the UK's position in Australia.

Although the High Court refused to apply the English development in this area, in *Barker* (2014) much of the debate on the central question on the duty of trust and confidence in Australia was based on English law, and some of the cases considered were English cases. Therefore it is necessary to discuss the development of trust and confidence in English law in order to understand the High Court decision in *Barker* (2014) and its impact on Australian employment law.

2.20.05 Development of mutual trust and confidence in English law

The common law doctrine of mutual trust and confidence in employment contracts is a well-established principle in the UK. Its origins can be traced to cases which emerged as a result of the introduction of unfair dismissal laws in the UK in the 1970s.[54] The *Industrial Relations Act 1971* (UK), which was replaced in 1975 and amended in 1996, provided statutory remedy for an employee who may have been unfairly dismissed by an employer, but not for an employee who may have resigned due to unacceptable behaviour by an employer.[55] This gap, or lack of clarity, is considered to have prompted the development of the common law principle of mutual trust and confidence to enable those employees who are not dismissed per se but wish to claim against an employer on the basis that they had been constructively dismissed to do so.[56] Employees can now make a common law claim based on this implied term.[57]

The criteria to ascertain the duty of trust and confidence was articulated by Arnold J in *Courtaulds Northern Textiles Ltd v Andrew* (*Courtaulds*) [1979] IRLR 85. There needs to be 'an implied term of the contract that the employers would not, without reasonable and proper

---

53   *Barker* (2014) at [116].
54   There is a raft of academic work which examines this obligation. See D Cabrelli 'The implied duty of mutual trust and confidence: an emerging overarching principle?' (2005) 34 *Industrial Law Journal* 305; Riley 'Siblings but not twins' (2012) 522–52; and Riley 'Developments in contract of employment jurisprudence in other common-law jurisdictions' (2016) 273–94. For a commentary on English law, see D Cabrelli *Employment Law in Context: Text and Materials* (Oxford University Press, 2014); D Brodie 'Mutual trust and the value of employment contract' (2001) 30 *Industrial Law Journal* 84; and D Brodie 'Mutual trust and confidence: catalysts, constraints and commonality' (2008) 37 *Industrial Law Review* 329.
55   The development of trust and confidence as an implied term in contracts is explained by Lord Nicholls of Birkenhead in *Eastwood v Magnox Electric plc* [2004] UKHL 35, [4]. Brodie provides a comprehensive analysis in D Brodie 'Beyond exchange: the new contract of employment' (1998) 27 *Industrial Law Journal* 79.
56   *Eastwood v Magnox Electric plc* [2004] UKHL; Brodie 'Beyond exchange: the new contract of employment' (1998).
57   Ibid.

cause, conduct themselves ... in a manner calculated or likely to destroy or seriously damage the relationship of confidence and trust between the parties'.[58]

What constitutes relevant 'conduct' of an employer – Arnold J made observations about this in *Courtaulds* – was elaborated by Lord Steyn in the appeal before the House of Lords in *Malik*.[59] It encompasses 'any conduct' that may affect the relationship of trust and confidence between the employer and the employee.[60] In *Courtaulds*, when determining whether or not the employer's conduct contributed to the repudiation of the contract and so led to constructive dismissal, Arnold J observed that it is important to ascertain whether the conduct of the employer was (a) 'a fundamental breach of the contract' or (b) 'a breach of a fundamental term of the contract'.[61]

In *Mahmud v Bank of Credit and Commerce International SA* [1996] ICR 406 at 411–12, it was held that the obligation for mutual trust and confidence may be affected by an act or conduct that is 'directed at a particular employee' which 'is likely seriously to damage the relationship of employer and employee'.[62] Although the employees were held to have no remedy available in cases of constructive dismissal, Morritt J observed that:

> it is inherent in conduct of the kind which we are required to assume in this case that, if it is to be successful, it is secret and hidden from most of the employees as well as the rest of the world. So long as it remains secret it can have no effect on the trust and confidence of the employee from whom it is concealed. Moreover, not only could there be no breach without knowledge, there could be no stigma damage either until the fraud was revealed. Once the employee has left his employment the subsequent revelation of the fraud can have no effect on the trust and confidence for, by definition, it has ceased anyway.[63]

MALIK v BANK OF CREDIT AND COMMERCE INTERNATIONAL SA (IN LIQ) [1998] AC 20

In the landmark English decision *Malik*,[64] for the first time the duty of mutual trust and confidence articulated in *Courtaulds* was explained clearly with regard to the purpose of and the obligations placed on the employment relationship.[65]

In *Malik*, the duty of mutual trust and confidence was explained by their Lordships with reference to *Woods v WM Car Services (Peterborough) Ltd* [1981] ICR 666 at 670. According to Browne-Wilkinson VC in *Woods*, there is an implied term of trust and confidence imposed on the

58 *Courtaulds* at [11].
59 This Court of Appeal decision was contested in a joint application by Raihan Nasir Mahmud and Qaiser Mansoor Malik in *Malik*.
60 Lord Steyn in *Malik* at [47].
61 *Courtaulds* at [11].
62 Morritt J in *Mahmud v Bank of Credit and Commerce International SA* [1996] ICR 406 at 411–412 (*Mahmud*), as quoted by Lord Steyn in *Malik* at [47].
63 Morritt J in *Mahmud* as quoted by Lord Steyn in *Malik* at [48].
64 This case is further explored in Chapter 6 in terms of its relevance to termination of employment.
65 Sappideen et al. *Macken's Law of Employment* (2011) 213.

employer: 'the employer will not, without reasonable and proper cause, conduct itself in a manner calculated or likely to destroy or seriously damage the relationship of confidence and trust between employer and employee'.[66]

In *Malik*, Lord Steyn affirmed that the trust and confidence term was implied in all contracts of employment in the UK and opined that it was a good development.[67] The basis for the House of Lords' decision in *Malik* was that that the employer was liable for engaging in corrupt business without the knowledge of the employees and that damages may be available for a breach of mutual trust and confidence as long as the breach is found on the part of the employer and it impacts the prospects of employment of the employees.[68] In this case, the House of Lords decided that the employer's dishonest business practices did amount to a breach of mutual trust and confidence.[69]

It is important to compare *Malik* with the earlier case of *Addis v Gramophone Co. Ltd.*[70]

ADDIS v GRAMOPHONE CO. LTD [1909] AC 488

The key issues in *Addis* were whether in a wrongful dismissal case damages were available for the manner of dismissal, for distress suffered as a result of the dismissal or for the loss due to the employee being unable to gain other employment.[71] The House of Lords confirmed that the employee cannot recover damages for injuries suffered due to the manner of dismissal.[72] Their Lordships also noted that damages are not recoverable for mental distress or inability to secure employment as a result of wrongful dismissal, although they awarded damages for 'pecuniary loss, such as loss of salary and commission'.[73]

In *Malik*, Lord Steyn addressed the question of the extent to which *Addis* could be applied.[74] His Lordship affirmed that *Addis* articulated the principle that 'an employee cannot recover exemplary or aggravated damages for wrongful dismissal',[75] emphasising

---

66   *Woods v WM Car Services (Peterborough) Ltd* [1981] ICR 666 at 670 as referred to in *Malik*, [23]. See also Sappideen et al. *Macken's Law of Employment* (2011) 156; J Riley 'Mutual trust and confidence on trial: at last' (2014) 36 *Sydney Law Review* 151; Brodie 'Mutual trust and confidence: catalysts, constraints and commonality' (2008) 329.
67   *Malik* at [46].
68   Ibid [36]–[38]; [44].
69   As per Lord Nicholls of Birkenhead in *Malik* at [34]–[35].
70   [1909] AC 488 (*Addis*).
71   *Addis* at [493] and Lord Nicholls of Birkenhead's observations in *Malik* at [34]–[42], with reference to *Addis*.
72   *Addis*, as referred to by Lord Nicholls of Birkenhead in *Malik* at [41].
73   Lord Steyn's observations in *Malik* at [50] with reference to *Addis*. See also *Addis* explained further in Chapter 6, especially with reference to I Neil and D Chin *The Modern Contract of Employment* (Thomson Reuters, 2012) 293 and in relation to damages for the manner in which employment was terminated. Neil and Chin reiterate that damages for disappointment and distress are unlikely in the event of a contract termination. Neil and Chin, 309–10.
74   Lord Steyn in *Malik* at [50]–[51].
75   Lord Steyn in *Malik* at [51] with reference to *Addis*.

the fact that the proposition in *Addis* was specifically concerned with 'wrongful dismissal'.[76] His Lordship's proposition was that this assertion in *Addis* did not mean that:

> [the] employee may not recover financial loss for damage to his employment prospects caused by a breach of contract. And no Law Lord said that in breach of contract cases compensation for loss of reputation can never be awarded, or that it can only be awarded in cases falling in certain defined categories.[77]

This interpretation of *Addis* by Lord Steyn leaves room to recover damages for financial loss based on loss of employment opportunities as a result of a breach of the contract of employment in the UK.

In the context of its application to employment contracts in the UK, scholars such as Brodie and Cabrelli have explored the distinct nature, origin and development of the implied duty of trust and confidence.[78] Although the concept of an implied duty of mutual trust and confidence has developed significantly in the UK in the space of the last four decades, the decision in *Johnson v Unisys Ltd* [2003] 1 AC 518 places limitations on that development.[79]

JOHNSON v UNISYS LTD [2003] 1 AC 518

In *Johnson,* the House of Lords identified some constraints on the application of the obligations of trust and confidence in wrongful dismissal cases.[80] Brodie aptly observes that 'this is somewhat ironic given that the very same piece of legislation (that is, the law of unfair dismissal) was the catalyst leading to the creation of the obligation'.[81]

In their decision to dismiss the application for damages in *Johnson*, Lord Nicholls of Birkenhead made the observation that 'a common law right embracing the manner in which an employee is dismissed cannot satisfactorily co-exist with the statutory right not to be unfairly dismissed'.[82] His Lordship further explained that the Parliament had already

---

76   Ibid.
77   Ibid.
78   Cabrelli 'The implied duty of mutual trust and confidence' (2005) 305. For a commentary on English law, see D Cabrelli *Employment Law in Context: Text and Materials* (Oxford University Press, 2014); Brodie 'Mutual trust and the value of employment contract' (2001) 84; Brodie 'Mutual trust and confidence: catalysts, constraints and commonality' (2008) 329; Riley 'Developments in contract of employment jurisprudence' (2016) 273–94.
79   This case has been examined in a large number of academic works, including Sappideen et al. *Macken's Law of Employment* (2011) 171; Brodie 'Mutual trust and confidence: catalysts, constraints and commonality' (2008) 329; H Collins 'Compensation for dismissal: In search of principle' (2012) 41 *Industrial Law Journal* 208–27; Riley 'Developments in contract of employment jurisprudence' (2016) 273–94.
80   *Johnson* at [541].
81   Brodie 'Mutual trust and confidence: catalysts, constraints and commonality' (2008) 329; Riley 'Developments in contract of employment jurisprudence' (2016) 273–94.
82   *Johnson* at [526].

specified categories of employees who can have recourse to a statutory right, the limitation period for claims, and the amount of compensation payable.[83]

Similarly, Lord Hoffman observed that these criteria were based on policy which attempted 'to balance fairness to employees against the general economic interests of the community'.[84] In making this observation, Lord Hoffman was expressing views similar to those of Lord Steyn, who noted that only the Parliament has the power to override policies and that 'judges, in developing the law, must have regard to the policies expressed by Parliament in legislation'.[85] His Lordship observed that there were express contractual terms that entitled Unisys to terminate the employee's employment with four weeks' notice without an adequate reason.[86]

On the question of damages, the rationale for the decision in *Johnson*, known and referred to as the 'Johnson exclusion zone',[87] is that if damages arose as a result of the termination of employment and the relevant statutes – whether unfair dismissal statutes or others – provide remedies, then damages under a breach of common law duty of mutual trust and confidence for the manner in which termination occurred are not available.[88] In other words, it attempts to prevent employees double dipping, by making a clear statement that if statutory damages are available, replicating damages in common law is not possible.[89]

The decision in *Johnson* has been adopted in a number of later cases, including *Eastwood v Magnox Electric plc* [2004] 1 AC 503 (*Eastwood*) and in *Edwards v Chesterfield Royal Hospital NHS Foundation Trust* ; [2012] ICR 201 (*Edwards*).[90] *Eastwood* was one of two adjoined appeal cases; the second was *McCabe v Cornwall County Council* [2004] UKHL 35. The decision in *Eastwood* affirmed *Johnson* on the one hand, but also found a way around the exclusion area specified in *Johnson* to allow for damages. The House of Lords held that although common law obligation to act in a fair manner in a decision to dismiss an employee and statutory provisions on unfair dismissal cannot co-exist, conduct prior to a dismissal did not fall within this. In reversing the decision of the Court of Appeal, the House of Lords noted that the cause of action in *Eastwood* had ensued prior to the dismissals and therefore allowed the matter to proceed to trial.

The decision in the appeal of *Edwards* examined whether damages were available for reputational loss as a result of a breach of contract and whether the claim in *Edwards* fell within Johnson exclusion zone.

The decision in *Edwards* extends the English law principle advocated in *Johnson* regarding the unavailability of common law damages for unfair dismissal if statutory damages are

---

83   Ibid.
84   Ibid [54].
85   Ibid [37]
86   Ibid [42].
87   For an explanation of the 'Johnson exclusion zone' see Sappideen et al. *Macken's Law of Employment* (2011) 167–70; Riley 'Siblings but not twins' (2012) 528; Riley, 'Developments in contract of employment jurisprudence in other common-law jurisdictions' (2016) 273–94; Lord Hoffman and Lord Millett's observations in *Johnson* at [47] and [80]; and more recently Lord Dyson (for the majority) in *Edwards v Chesterfield Royal Hospital NHS Foundation Trust* [2012] ICR 201 (*Edwards*) at [1]–[2].
88   Lord Hoffman and Lord Millett in *Johnson* at [47] and [80].
89   Ibid.
90   *Edwards* was a combined appeal, with the other case being *Botham v Ministry of Defence* [2012] ICR 201 (*Botham*).

available. In Australia, although the implied term of trust and confidence did not develop with the same intensity as in the UK, the principles in *Johnson* and *Eastwood* have been considered in later cases (see below).

In *Edwards*, the majority (Lord Dyson, Lord Phillip and Lord Mance) held that the Johnson exclusion zone extended to the breach of an express as well as an implied term in an employment contract and that the losses claimed by Mr Edwards fell within the Johnson exclusion area.[91]

2.20.10 Australia and the 'duty' of mutual trust and confidence

Duty does NOT flow from the employer, but questions remain concerning good faith. See (*Barker* (2014))[92] and its impact.

COMMONWEALTH BANK OF AUSTRALIA v BARKER (2014) 253 CLR 169 (BARKER (2014))

The High Court decision in *Barker* (2014) is considered as firmly addressing Australia's position regarding trust and confidence.[93] For the first time, the High Court of Australia had the opportunity to examine whether or not the English principle recognised in *Malik* should be implied into employment contracts in Australia.

The dissenting judgement of Jessup J in the Full Court of the Federal Court decision of *Barker* (2013) is important for understanding the High Court decision in *Barker* (2014). In the Full Court of the Federal Court decision, Jessup J examined relevant authorities and the judicial decisions in the UK[94] and Australia[95] and concluded that the implied term of trust and confidence does not form a part of the common law in Australia.[96] The extensive examination of the juridical basis presented by Jessup J is important, as the High Court unanimously affirmed His Honour's observations in concluding that the implied term of

91   *Edwards v Chesterfield Royal Hospital NHS Foundation Trust* and *Botham v Ministry of Defence* [2012] ICR 201 at [55]–[57].

92   The Full Federal Court decision is *Commonwealth Bank of Australia v Barker* (2013) 214 FCR 450 and *Barker v Commonwealth Bank of Australia* (2012) 296 ALR 706.

93   A number of decisions in Australia prior to *Barker* (2014) have suggested that the implied term of mutual trust and confidence in English law is part of Australian employment contracts. For example, *Shaw v New South Wales* (2012) 219 IR 87; *Concut Pty Ltd v Worrell* (2000) 176 ALR 693; *Codefa Construction Pty Ltd v State Rail Authority of New South Wales* (1982) 149 CLR 345. A few other decisions have noted the term's existence but refused to grant damages (*Russell v Trustees of the Roman Catholic Church for the Archdiocese of Sydney* (2008) 72 NSWLR 559), noted the term's existence but held that it was subject to statute, regulation and industrial award (*South Australia v McDonald* (2009) 104 SASR 344) or precluded damages for breach of implied terms of mutual trust and confidence in unfair dismissal cases (*Burazin v Blacktown City Guardian Pty Ltd* (1996) 142 ALR 144). In *Byrne* the question of the co-existence of common law and statutory rights arose. Professor Riley alludes to a potential co-existence of the two when she said that these may 'co-exist without necessarily intermingling' with reference to *Byrne*. See Riley 'Mutual trust and confidence on trial: at Last' (2014) 164.

94   *Barker* (2013) at [211]–[235].

95   Ibid [236]–[279].

96   Ibid [340].

mutual trust and confidence does not form a part of the Australian common law.[97] In *Barker* (2013) Jessup J concluded that failing to comply with the redeployment policy in the event of a CBA restructure did not breach an implied term.[98] His Honour agreed with the primary judge that damages for loss of reputation was not available.[99]

So it is important to examine the Full Court of the Federal Court's decision before considering the impact of the High Court's decision in *Barker* (2014).

The road to the High Court

COMMONWEALTH BANK OF AUSTRALIA *v* BARKER (2013) 214 FCR 450 (BARKER (2013))

Barker (2013) was the Commonwealth Bank's appeal against the decision of the primary court judge on the basis that there was no implied term of mutual trust and confidence. The key questions before the Full Court of the Federal Court of Australia were whether the redeployment policy formed part of the contract and whether the bank was in breach of its redeployment policy.[100] In the appeal case, the majority of the Full Court of the Federal Court (Jacobson and Lander JJ, Jessup J dissenting) agreed with Besanko J in the Federal Court that a term of mutual trust and confidence was implied into the employment agreement.[101] However, their Honours did not endorse Besanko J's finding that the non-compliance with the redeployment policy of the bank came within the scope of a breach of the implied terms.[102] Their Honours' reasoning was that the terms of the redeployment policy did not form a part of the employment contract and did not constitute a benefit because they were not contractually binding.[103] The majority of the Full Court of the Federal Court decided that an implied term did exist, based on the fact that the bank had failed to take appropriate steps to liaise with Mr Barker and explore alternative employment opportunities.[104]

Jacobson and Lander JJ relied on the test of necessity applied in two cases, *Byrne v Australian Airlines Ltd* (*Byrne*)[105] and *Breen v Williams* (*Breen*).[106] Their Honours noted with approval that necessity is a crucial aspect of the justification for the implication of a term into

---

97   *Barker* (2014) at [13], [40], [82] and [115]–[120].
98   *Barker* (2013) at [351].
99   Ibid [371].
100 This was examined by Besanko J in *Barker v Commonwealth Bank of Australia* (2012) 296 ALR 706 [334]. See *Barker* (2013) at [44], [51], [53]–[55] and [112]–[116].
101 *Barker* (2013) at [13].
102 Ibid [113]–[114].
103 Ibid [114] and [116].
104 Ibid [117].
105 *Byrne* at [450] per McHugh and Gummow JJ.
106 *Breen* at [103] per Gaudron and McHugh JJ; *Barker* (2013) at [88]–[91].

law, but that it is an 'elusive concept' which involves a range of factors, including the integral aspects of a contract, the relationship the contract establishes and the policy considerations relevant to a certain class of contract.[107]

In terms of damages for past economic loss, the Full Court of the Federal Court of Australia increased slightly the sum the primary court judge had awarded.[108] Besanko J's observations regarding general damages for hurt, distress and lost reputation were upheld by the majority in the Full Court of the Federal Court.[109] Their Honours conceded that damages for hurt and distress were not available for a breach of contract 'because the object of the contract was not to provide peace of mind'.[110]

Jessup J (dissenting), in the Full Court of the Federal Court, was of the view that the implied term of mutual trust and confidence does not form a part of the common law of Australia and that in this case the bank only owed 'duties which are already conventionally associated with contracts of that class'.[111] His Honour concluded that even if there had been a breach of an implied term, the bank's non-compliance with its redeployment policy was not a breach of this term.[112]

In His Honour's dissenting judgement, he provided a summary of reasons for not supporting the development of the common law principle of an implied term of trust and confidence:

(a) Despite the passage of 25 years since the first articulation of the implied term in England, there has, on my reading of the authorities, been no wholly satisfying defence of the term, locating it within the norms, obligations and entitlements which arise under the contract of employment.

(b) I can find no solid basis for the premise, implicit in the implied term, that, under the contract of employment, the employer owes a duty of trust and confidence to the employee beyond those duties which are already conventionally associated with contracts of that class.

(c) The proposition that the introduction of the implied term is justified as the mutualisation of the employee's duty of fidelity to the employer does not withstand examination.

(d) Neither can the implied term be justified as a principled development of the implied duty of co-operation as between the parties to the contract.

(e) Of its nature, the implied term is a mechanism for the regulation of the conduct of employers. It is prescriptive, and speaks prospectively, but, as expressed, the term is content-free and has the potential to act as a Trojan horse in the sense of revealing only after the event the specific prohibitions which it imports into the contract.

(f) The term would enable defined limits in the existing fabric of common law and equitable remedies to be sidestepped.

---

107   *Barker* (2013) at [93].
108   Ibid [151].
109   Ibid [152]–[158].
110   Ibid [154]. The Majority of the Full Court of the Federal Court, with reference to *Baltic Shipping Co. v Dillon* (1993) 176 CLR 344 at [365], [371]–[372], [382], [387] and [394].
111   *Barker* (2013) at [12] and [340].
112   Ibid.

(g)   The term would overlap a number of legislated prohibitions and requirements in particular dimensions of the employment relationship, thus tending to compromise the democratically-drawn architecture of the relevant obligations.[113]

2.20.15 Did the High Court settle the common law position in Australia?

Although Stewart et al. observe that the debate regarding whether the implied term of mutual trust and confidence forms part of common law of Australia was settled in *Barker* (2014) (that is, that there is no duty), they also express disappointment at the decision, for several reasons.[114]

Stewart et al. note that the High Court failed to distinguish between or give reason as to why there was a difference between Australian employees and those in other common law countries. According to Professor Stewart, the court did not 'engage in any meaningful way with the reasons referred to in earlier judgements justifying the implication of the term, including the notion that a person's work is not only a source of livelihood but of identity, self-worth, dignity, and self-confidence'. Nor did the court consider the implying of the term in relation to the statutory regime applicable to Australian employment law.[115]

Regardless of Stewart's complaint on that point (see discussion below), whether or not the High Court left its position as to mutual good faith and the employment contract open remains a valid question.

Barker and the High Court: settled and residual questions

COMMONWEALTH BANK OF AUSTRALIA *v* BARKER (2014) 253 CLR 169 (BARKER (2014))

The key question before the High Court was whether under the common law of Australia contracts of employment contain an implied term of mutual trust and confidence.[116] In following Jessup J's line of reasoning in the Full Court of the Federal Court's decision, the High Court in *Barker* (2014) rejected the proposal that mutual trust and confidence can be a part of the Australian employment law by referring to it as a development of the implied duty of cooperation.[117]

---

113   Ibid.
114   Stewart et al. *Creighton and Stewart's Labour Law* (2016) 526.
115   Ibid 167.
116   *Barker* (2014) at [15].
117   Ibid [26]. This decision by the High Court rejects the decision by Jacobson and Lander JJ in the decision of the Full Court of the Federal Court in *Barker* (2013) that the implication of the implied term was necessary by law.

A significant observation of the High Court was that although courts are familiar with framing some broad standards to apply to matters of common law and statutory matters, when it comes to a new standard contained in a new implied contractual term, the grounds for the 'implication in law of contractual terms' must be the starting point. [118] The High Court also noted the implication of terms by law and the test of necessity.[119] To this end French CJ, Bell and Keane JJ noted a number of ways courts have implied terms into contracts in order to give business efficiency to a contract, by custom or in law, and relating to particular classes of contract or to all classes of contracts.[120] The term 'business efficiency' in itself is broad. There may be space to infer implied trust and confidence in future cases, but the High Court decided that this duty does not exist in Australian employment law.

Although the High Court accepted that the duty to cooperate conforms to the test of necessity explained in *Byrne*,[121] their view was that an implied term of mutual trust and confidence would create a mutual obligation beyond what is 'necessary'.[122] Their Honours were particularly concerned that to imply a term of mutual trust and confidence could appear to reflect a view that employment contracts are 'relational', which, they observed, is 'a characteristic of uncertain application' and so would have a significant impact on employment relationships and the law of contracts of employment in Australia.[123]

Their Honours also formed the opinion that implications in law should be constrained within judicial function[124] but that the policy considerations encompassed in such implications were a matter to be determined by the legislature.[125] In expressing this reasoning, the High Court left it to the legislature to give implied terms statutory relevance and emphasised that the courts' role is to apply the statutory form to cases.[126] Of particular significance are Gageler J's views (which echo Jessup J's observations) regarding the relevance of the implied term to Australian employment law: his Honour is of the opinion that the statutory environment in the UK which led to the recognition of the implied term is not similar to that in Australia.[127]

The High Court in *Barker* (2014) specifically noted that it did not consider the 'related question of whether contractual powers and discretions may be limited by good faith and rationality requirements analogous to those applicable in the sphere of public law'.[128]

To this end, Kiefel J noted several questions that are not conclusively resolved in Australia. These include '[t]he question whether a standard of good faith should be applied generally to contracts' and 'whether such a standard could apply to particular categories of contract (such as employment contracts)'.[129] Her Honour's assertion that good faith need not be considered

118   *Barker* [2014] at [20].
119   Ibid [56]–[62] and [20]; see also [88]–[90].
120   Ibid [21].
121   Ibid [116].
122   Ibid [37].
123   Ibid.
124   Ibid [29].
125   Ibid [40].
126   Ibid.
127   Ibid [116].
128   Ibid [42].
129   Ibid [107].

further due to its wider importance leads to the possibility that the application of an implied term of the duty of good faith has scope for development. At some point in the future the court may still be required to consider these matters.

2.25 The duty of good faith

It is important to understand the nature of good faith.[130] Primarily, good faith is considered 'a principle of construction in certain kinds of contracts'.[131] Peden, who examines whether good faith is implied into a contract or merely forms a part of the construction of the contract by the operation of principles of contract law,[132] states that since good faith is inherent in contract rules and construction principles, if a court then asserts an implied term of good faith there is the likelihood that the court may be implying an unnecessary term or a term which contains a far more burdensome obligation.[133]

Stewart et al. refer to three views of good faith in Australia:[134]

(a) 'a term requiring good faith and fair dealing is implied by law' in all commercial contracts, but there is no clarity regarding whether an employment contract is a commercial contract;

(b) the duty of faith may exist as an implied term in a contract in some cases, but it does not exist generally due to its lack of clarity around its content, application and implication; and

(c) good faith is a principle which explains scope of the express terms in a contract.[135]

Kiefel J found that 'fairness in dealings' between parties to a contract is an aspect of the duty of good faith, but also observed that some legal systems consider it an essential element of 'modern general law of contract'.[136]

Although some cases before *Barker* may have suggested otherwise, the duty of mutual trust and confidence and the duty of good faith are two separate principles originating from one source: the employment relationship. The distinction between the two duties should be examined.

While both duties are traced to the employment relationship, mutual trust and confidence relates to the interaction between the parties in the actual relationship and good faith relates to the construction of the employment contract and the obligations it imposes on the parties.[137] If the mutual trust and confidence in the employment relationship is breached in some manner, this may affect the employment contract, leading to a breach of contract.[138] In this case, the distinction between mutual trust and confidence and good faith is that good faith dictates the interpretation of the obligations specified in the employment contract.

Amidst all the debate, there are settled aspects of good faith, especially as it is owed from employee to employer.

---

130   Stewart et al. *Creighton and Stewart's Labour Law* (2016) 528 also point out that Australian courts have failed to arrive at appropriate conclusions regarding some matters relating to good faith.
131   J Riley 'Siblings but not twins' (2012) 536.
132   E Peden '"Implicit good faith" – Or do we still need an implied term of good faith?' (2009) 25 *Journal of Contract Law* 50.
133   Ibid 60.
134   Stewart et al. *Creighton and Stewart's Labour Law* (2016) 528.
135   Ibid 528–9.
136   *Barker* (2014) at [104].
137   See Peden '"Implicit good faith"' (2009); Riley 'Siblings but not twins' (2012).
138   Riley 'Siblings but not twins' (2012) 535–7.

ROBB v GREEN [1895] 2 QB 315 CA

The duty of good faith in terms of an employee–employer relationship is considered well settled after the decision in the English case of *Robb*, which involved an employee who left his employment to set up a similar business to that of the employer. Prior to leaving his employment the employee had obtained copies of the names and addresses of customers from the employer's order book.[139] Evidence indicated that the employee had obtained this information without authorisation and without the knowledge of the employer – thus, in a calculated manner.[140]

In *Robb*, Lord Esher observed that the employee had breached the trust of the employer. His Lordship further added that that the 'question arises whether such conduct is a breach of contract', because with any employment contract there is 'a stipulation that the servant will act with good faith towards the master' and 'such must necessarily have been in the view of both parties when they entered the contract'.[141] The question in this early case was whether a breach of the employer's trust amounted to a breach in law. In Lord Fisher's opinion, it was a breach of an implied term of the contract that there is a duty to be honest.[142]

In a later English case, *Sanders v Parry* [1967] 1 WLR 753 (*Sanders*), the question of the implied term of a duty of good faith was revisited. Justice Havers affirmed that the defendant had an obligation at all times to protect the interests of the master, which included doing his best to retain the master's clients. Therefore, by accepting an offer from the plaintiff's number one client to do business independently, the defendant was not furthering the master's interests.

In both *Robb* and *Sanders*, the employees were found to have acted against the interest of the employer during the subsistence of their employment. Both *Robb* and *Sanders* indicate the well-settled nature of the employees' 'duty to act with fidelity and good faith'[143] and that it forms part of the law of implied terms of contracts in the UK.

2.25.05 Trade secrets, confidential information and the use of confidential information

One of the lingering questions, and a residual issue from the decision in *Barker* (2014), is whether good faith is different from confidentiality. To this extent, the English case of *Faccenda Chicken Ltd v Fowler* (*Faccenda*) is important, as it examined the scope of good faith.

The principle of good faith from an employee towards the employer and his business, especially regarding the use of confidential information that comes into the hands of an employee, and the obligations placed on employees was addressed in *Faccenda*. In *Faccenda*,

---

139   *Robb.*
140   Ibid.
141   Ibid.
142   Ibid 317.
143   The Full Bench in the matter of *Kim Michelle Hollingsworth v Commissioner of Police* [1999] NSWIRC 240 noted cases where a duty of faith is imposed on the employees, including *Courtaulds Northern Textiles Ltd v Andrew* [1979] IRLR 84; *Woods v WM Car Services (Peterborough) Ltd* [1981] ICR 666 at 670–2; and *Robinson v Crompton Parkinson Ltd* [1978] IRLR 61 at 62. This was recently referred to by Jessup J in his dissenting judgement in *Barker* (2013) at [245].

the English court also distinguished between trade secrets, which the employee has an obligation not to disclose, and other information, regardless of whether or not it is classified as 'confidential' and acquired by the employee in course of his employment.[144] However, in *Faccenda* the judge was of the opinion that disclosing 'confidential' information without authorisation during the subsistence of the employment contract would be a breach of the duty of good faith.[145] But when considered in the context of the facts in *Faccenda*, the court decided that the prices and sales information, when taken 'as a whole had the degree of confidentiality necessary',[146] but did not amount to a trade secret.

FACCENDA CHICKEN LTD v FOWLER [1986] ICR 297

In this case, the employee (Fowler), who had established a fresh chicken delivery business for the employer (Faccenda Chicken Ltd), resigned and formed his own business, which was a similar business, even using the same routes as his previous employer.[147] A number of other employees from the employer's business joined Fowler's business as his employees, leading to the plaintiff's action against Fowler and eight former employees.[148] The basis of the claim was that Fowler and the group of employees who had left Faccenda Chicken had used their knowledge and access to sales and other information to assist Fowler in his new business.[149] The plaintiff alleged that Fowler and the other former employees had breached an implied term in their employment contracts regarding the use of confidential information gathered during the course of their employment.[150]

Neill LJ noted that in the absence of an express term in the contract of employment, the employees' obligation regarding the use of information is subject to implied terms.[151] He added that during the employment of the employee in the business of the employer, this obligation is an implied term which imposes a duty of good faith or fidelity on the employee.[152] However, as to the scope of this duty, Neill LJ observed that the exact limits of it 'will vary according to the nature of the contract'[153] and that the duty will be breached if the employee engages in a deliberate act to obtain, memorise or retain information about employer's customers.[154]

Neill LJ applied three legal concepts as follows:

(1) The duty of an employee during the period of his employment to act with good faith towards his employer: this duty is sometimes called the duty of fidelity.

---

144   *Faccenda* at 298 and 309. Neill LJ with reference to *Amber Size & Chemical Co. Ltd v Menzel* [1913] 2 Ch. 239 and *Reid & Sigrist Ltd v Moss and Mechanism Ltd* (1932) 49 RPC 461.
145   *Faccenda* at 309. (Specific reference was made to the judgement of Cross J in *Printers & Finishers Ltd v Holloway* [1965] RPC 239.)
146   *Faccenda* at [310] and [312].
147   Ibid Headnote.
148   *Faccenda*.
149   Ibid.
150   Ibid 298.
151   Ibid 308.
152   Ibid.
153   Ibid 309: Neill LJ, with reference to *Vokes Ltd v Heather* [1945] 62 RPC 35.
154   Ibid: Neill LJ, with reference to *Robb*.

(2) The duty of an employee not to use or disclose after his employment has ceased any confidential information which he has obtained during his employment about his employer's affairs.

(3) The prima facie right of any person to use and to exploit for the purpose of earning his living all the skill, experience and knowledge which he has at his disposal, including skill, experience and knowledge which he has acquired in the course of previous periods of employment.

Although Neill LJ affirmed the three legal concepts as above, *Faccenda* emphasises the necessity to consider all circumstances of a case when deciding whether a piece of information collected in the course of employment is subject to the implied terms, thereby preventing its use by an employee.[155] In considering the circumstances, the court decided that some of the important matters are the nature of the employment and the information, whether the employer considered the information confidential and indicated this to the employees, and whether such information can be easily identified from other information which can be considered free for use by employees.[156]

It was held that in the absence of express terms, although the employee was subject to an implied duty of good faith to his employer not to use – for the duration of his employment and thereafter – confidential information gathered during the course of his employment, in *Faccenda* the information in question was not a trade secret.[158] Therefore, the employees were free to use the information once they left the employment.[158] *Faccenda* further cements the English law position on the duty of good faith, which was first developed in *Robb* and further developed in *Sanders*.

Stewart et al. note that good faith is implied in all commercial contracts but there is no clear guidance as to whether employment contracts should be considered commercial contracts.[159] In this context, it may be practical to provide for those rules and provisions that apply in respect of commercial contracts to be applied to employment contracts. Lord Millet's observation in *Johnson* regarding the fact that in *Addis* the House of Lords considered the contract of employment a commercial contract certainly supports this proposition.[160] In *Johnson*, rejecting the appellant's claim for damages and dismissing the appeal, Lord Millett strongly concluded that 'the coexistence of two systems, overlapping but varying in matters of detail and heard by different tribunals, would be a recipe for chaos. All coherence in our employment laws would be lost.'[161]

---

155   Ibid 310.

156   Ibid 311.

157   Ibid 313 and 298.

158   Ibid.

159   Stewart et al. *Creighton and Stewart's Labour Law* (2016) 528.

160   Lord Millett, in *Johnson*, noted that the Parliament intends that matters such as the one before His Lordship are considered and decided by special tribunals set up for that purpose and not courts of law, and that there is no necessity to replicate a right in common law which a person already has as a statutory right: at [80].

161   Ibid.

On the other hand, using Jessup J's description of the implied term of trust and confidence, if the 'Trojan horse'[162] is to be conquered, the prudent approach may be to introduce a statutory framework rather than determining the existence or non-existence of an obligation of good faith by an implied term. This might be effective in providing some clarity, especially in the case of employment contracts, and may also address the fact that terms implied by common law into contracts, including the duty of good faith, are susceptible to being replaced by the express terms of a contract or a statute.[163] To this end, their Honours provide some clarity in *Barker* (2014), to the effect that statutory form would allow the legislature to consider and apply its policy choices and the courts to interpret and apply the law.[164]

Although Australian cases have not conclusively stated the nature of the duty of good faith, there are several cases where the obligation was considered. For example, in *Blackadder* (2005), which was considered earlier in this chapter, the primary judge, Madgwick J, found that 'the contract has an implied term of mutual good faith and . . ., concretely, upon reinstatement, no alteration of consequence in the ordinary incidents of the reinstated employee's employment could be made, except in good faith'.[165] However, Madgwick J did not perceive the right of an employee to be treated in good faith by the employer as a right separate from the terms of the employment contract. He noted that 'any such other term, as, for example, to be actually given work to do, must be either expressly found or otherwise implied in the circumstances or as a matter of law'.[166]

The question of good faith left unanswered by the High Court in *Barker* (2014) was considered by the Court of Appeal of New South Wales in *New South Wales v Shaw* (*Shaw* (2015)).

NEW SOUTH WALES v SHAW (2015) 248 IR 206

In this case,[167] brought by the State of New South Wales to set aside the primary court judge's order for a judgement in favour of the respondents: probationary teachers who had been dismissed from their employment,[168] the respondents cross-appealed on the ground that there was an implied duty of good faith in their employment contract.[169] In rejecting this claim, their Honours held that as a statutory regime exists in respect of unfair dismissal, an implied duty of good faith in the employment contract was not necessary and therefore there could be no breach of good faith.[170]

---

162   *Barker* (2014) at [13] and [27]; *Barker* (2013) at [93] and [340].
163   *Barker* (2014) and *Barker* (2013))
164   *Barker* (2014) [29] and [40].
165   *Blackadder* (2002) at [41].
166   Ibid [42].
167   This is an appeal by the State of New South Wales against the decision in *Shaw v New South Wales* (2012) 219 IR 87. The 2012 decision was subsequently challenged in an action brought by the State of New South Wales in *New South Wales v Shaw* (2015) 248 IR 206 where the orders made by Sorby DCJ in 2013 awarding judgement for two plaintiff teachers and ordering the defendant (State of NSW) to pay costs (but no damages) was reversed.
168   *Shaw* (2012) at [86].
169   Ibid [88].
170   See *Shaw* (2015) at [111] and [130]–[155].

This decision indicated that the contract was considered to include neither an implied term of mutual trust and confidence nor a duty of good faith.[171] Their Honours note that even if a duty of good faith was implied as a matter of law into the respondents' employment contracts, relying on Kiefel J's observation in *Barker* (2014), 'such a question has been recognised as still being an unresolved issue',[172] and in any case there was no breach of such an obligation.

The question of good faith was considered again recently by the Supreme Court of Queensland (by Jackson J, with whom Margaret McMurdo P and Holmes JA agreed) in *Gramotnev v Queensland University of Technology* (*Gramotnev*). Of particular interest is Jackson J's observation that the decision in *Barker* (2014) does not give a conclusive answer regarding the existence of the implied term of good faith,[173] and that on the last occasion when the Queensland Court of Appeal had to decide the existence or otherwise of an implied term of good faith in an employment contract, the court rejected its existence.[174] Jackson J rejected Mr Gramotnev's allegation of the existence of an implied duty of good faith and noted that the language used in Mr Gramotnev's employment contract was the 'language of a duty of care'.[175] His Honour stated that it was not language 'to describe the obligations of an employer in exercising contractual rights or performing contractual obligations' and noted that there is no other case which supports 'a formulation of an implied term of good faith in those particular terms'.[176]

The observations by Ward JA in *Shaw* (2015) and the decision in *Gramotnev* regarding the question of the existence of the implied duty of good faith, in the light of the decision in *Barker* (2014), indicate that it is now generally accepted that *Barker* (2014) did not authoritatively conclude whether or not there is an implied duty of good faith in employment contracts in Australia.

2.30 Interplay between duty of trust and confidence and good faith

The interplay between duty of trust and confidence[177] and duty of good faith in an employer–employee relationship is such that in some cases the two obligations are considered as being related, even one, while other cases draw a distinction between them.[178] Professor Riley quite

---

171   Ibid.
172   Ibid [129].
173   *Gramotnev v Queensland University of Technology* (2015) 251 IR 449 (*Gramotnev*) at [160]–[161].
174   Ibid [163]. See Jackson J with reference to the *Laurelmont Pty Ltd v Stockdale & Leggo (Qld) Pty Ltd* [2001] QCA 212.
175   *Gramotnev* at [169] and [172].
176   Ibid [169].
177   In describing the duty of trust and confidence, the words 'trust' and 'mutual trust' are used interchangeably.
178   Australian examples include *Russell v Trustees of the Roman Catholic Church for the Archdiocese of Sydney* (2008) 72 NSWLR 559, where both terms were considered, *Shaw* (2012), which focused on mutual trust and confidence, and *Downe v Sydney West Area Health Service (No. 2)* (2008) 71 NSWLR 633, where both terms were considered. Writing by Australian academics on this topic includes Stewart et al. *Creighton and Stewart's Labour Law* (2016); Sappideen et al. *Macken's Law of Employment* (2011) 156; Riley 'Siblings but not twins' (2012); and Peden '"Implicit good faith"' (2009).

aptly likens this relationship to that of siblings, because they are founded on an employment relationship yet better understood as two separate principles.[179] The duty of mutual trust and confidence between an employer and employee is an inherent aspect of the contract of employment where both parties cooperate to achieve a common business goal.[180] Any act by either party that is detrimental to this relationship may be construed as a breach of the employment contract.[181] Good faith is best described as a principle that relates to the construction of some contracts, which infers the intention of the parties to perform their contractual obligations leading to the shared benefits of the contract.[182]

The High Court in *Barker* (2014) appears to consider mutual trust and confidence and good faith as two distinct terms, regardless of whether or not they are implied into Australian contracts.

2.35 Further duties: employee obeying reasonable directions

It is an established principle that an employee has a common law obligation to obey the lawful and reasonable directions of the employer.[183] There are several questions in this regard.

First, what does 'lawful and reasonable direction' refer to? For a start, an employer cannot give a direction to an employee which involves breaching a law[184] or that may place the employee's life in danger.[185] The duty to obey an employer's orders does not extend to unlawful and illegal acts. The authors of *Macken's Law of Employment* observe that unlawful acts are those which employees are not required to obey because they 'transgress some positive law'.[186] For example, a direction by an employer to an employee to drive a defective vehicle to make a delivery in the course of employment would transgress a positive law which requires vehicles to meet certain roadworthy standards.[187]

Activities not specified in the employment contract are considered unlawful directions. For example, in *Downe v Sydney West Area Health Service (No. 2)* (2008) 71 NSWLR 633, a direction to work at a hospital not specified in the contract of employment in a lesser capacity was considered an unlawful direction. However, an employee is expected to follow directions related to their job although not specifically stated in the contract of employment,[188] such as a workplace policy against bullying. The interaction between common law, contractual terms

---

179   Riley 'Siblings but not twins' (2012) 536.
180   Ibid 536–7.
181   Ibid 532.
182   Peden '"Implicit good faith"' (2009) 50–51, 53–54.
183   *McManus v Scott-Charlton* (1996) 70 FCR 16 at 21. *Australian Telecommunications Commission v Hart* (1982) 43 ALR 165.
184   Sappideen et al. *Macken's Law of Employment* (2011) 208.
185   Stewart et al. *Creighton and Stewart's Labour Law* (2016) 496.
186   Sappideen et al. *Macken's Law of Employment* (2011) 208.
187   *Grant v BHP Coal Pty Ltd* [2014] FWCFB 3027 [118].
188   Stewart et al. *Creighton and Stewart's Labour Law* (2016) 496.

and statutory provisions is important when trying to understand whether an employer's direction is lawful direction.[189]

The reasonableness of an employer's direction to an employee is determined in common law by ascertaining whether the direction (a) 'relates to the subject matter of the employment'[190] and (b) 'involves no illegality'.[191] The common law position on the duty of an employee to obey reasonable direction depends on the facts of each case.[192]

Employment does not necessitate 'total subordination'[193] of the employee's independence to the direction of the employer unless it affects the performance of the employee's work. This further clarifies what is lawful and reasonable, as was confirmed by Goldberg J in *Thompson v IGT (Australia) Pty Ltd* (2008) 173 IR 395 (*Thompson*).[194] In *Thompson*, Goldberg J observed that requiring an employee to attend a specific religious place of worship or dictating what they may wear outside of work was unlawful (see *Australian Tramways Employees' Association v Brisbane Tramways Co. Ltd* (1912) 6 CAR 35 at [42] (*Tramways*)).[195] In that case, both Goldberg and Finn JJ noted that the obligation to obey lawful and reasonable direction does not impede the employee's right to wear clothes at their discretion when clothing is not a matter that affects the performance of his work.[196]

The second question is whether lawful and reasonable direction are two different requirements. And if they are separate, does one override the other? The analysis presented in this section shows that they are interconnected requirements. The criteria applied by courts to determine the scope of lawful and reasonable direction can be found in an array of cases. The following cases examine employers' capacity to issue a direction to employees in various

---

189   Ibid 496 and 497. Stewart et al. note that a court may consider all circumstances, including 'the terms of any written contract or applicable industrial instrument or statute, custom and practice, and any work rules which have contractual effect – in short, all the sources which may supply contractual terms' to ascertain whether or not a direction is within the scope of the employment, and is therefore a lawful direction.

190   Dixon J in *R v Darling Island Stevedoring & Lighterage Co. Ltd; Ex parte Halliday; Ex parte Sullivan* (1938) 60 CLR 601 at 621–22. The 'standard or test' in this case has been considered in other Australian cases, including *Thompson v IGT (Australia) Pty Ltd* (2008) 173 IR 395; *Australian Telecommunications Commission v Hart* (1982) 43 ALR 165; and *Anderson v Sullivan* (1997) 78 FCR 380.

191   *R v Darling Island Stevedore & Lighterage Co. Ltd; Ex parte Halliday and Sullivan* (1938) 60 CLR 601 at 621.

192   Stewart et al. *Creighton and Stewart's Labour Law* (2016) 497.

193   Goldberg J made these observations with reference to Finn J (in *McManus v Scott-Charlton* (1996) 70 FCR 16 at [21] (*McManus*)), who referred to several cases in *McManus*, including *Australian Telecommunications Commission v Hart* (1982) 43 ALR 165; *Bayley v Osborne* (1984) 4 FCR 141 regarding the common law obligation of an employee to obey lawful and reasonable directions of the employer; *R v Darling Island Stevedoring and Lighterage Co. Lt.; Ex parte Halliday* (1938) 60 CLR 601 at 621–622 regarding the standard of this obligation; and *Australian Tramways Employees' Association v Brisbane Tramways Co. Ltd* (1912) 6 CAR 35 at [42] regarding the scope of this obligation. See also *Thompson v IGT (Australia) Pty Ltd* (2008) 173 IR 395 at [48].

194   Thompson at [48]–[52]. Finn J in *McManus*, as referred to by Goldberg J in *Thompson*. Despite this decision, employees may still be held responsible for out-of-work, conduct especially in the social media space, where the conduct affects the employment relationship. See, generally, *Dover-Ray v Real Insurance Pty Ltd* (2010) 204 IR 399; *Fitzgerald v Smith* [2010] FWA 7358; and *Stutsel v Linfox Australia Pty Ltd* (2011) 217 IR 28.

195   *Thompson.*

196   Ibid [48]–[52]. Goldberg J made these observations with reference to Finn J (in *McManus v Scott-Charlton* (1996) 70 FCR 16 [21] (*McManus*)).

circumstances and what criteria the court has used to decide the lawfulness and reasonableness of such direction.

2.35.05 An employer's direction to attend a medical examination at a nominated medical practitioner

The lawfulness and the reasonableness of an employer's direction to attend a medical examination at a nominated medical practitioner depends on the facts of each case, the terms of the contract of employment and the relevant legislation.

According to case law, an employer's obligation under the *Coal Mining Safety and Health Act 1999* (Qld) (CMSH Act) overrides its obligations under the relevant Enterprise Agreement (Agreement).[197]

GRANT v BHP COAL PTY LTD (NO. 2) [2015] FCA 1374[198]

In *Grant* (2015), it was decided that the direction to Mr Grant to attend the medical examination was lawful under 39(1)(c) of the CMSH Act.[199] The primary reason for deciding that the employer's request was lawful and reasonable was because the employer had a statutory obligation as a coal mine operator under the CMSH Act to ensure the health and safety of Mr Grant and others working around him in the mine.[200] Although under this Agreement only a medical certificate was required from an employee's medical practitioner, in cases where the employee was returning to work from a non-work-related injury, the Fair Work Commission (FWC) was of the view that the employer also had an 'obligation to ensure a safe system of work, and a duty of care is owed to all those on their worksites, in particular employees'.[201] The judges noted that:

> In the circumstances it is entirely reasonable that the first respondent would have at least sought further advice and information on the applicant's fitness to ensure that it was not exposing the applicant, or others, to unacceptable risks from a limitation arising from the applicant's injury or by virtue of his lengthy absence.[202]

Similarly, an employer can request an employee to provide a medical report from the treating doctor to find out the employee's likelihood of returning to work, in order to assist the efficiency of the business and the rostering arrangements.[203] An example is *Australian and International Pilots Association v Qantas Airways Ltd* (*AIPA v Qantas*).

---

197   *Grant v BHP Coal Pty Ltd (No. 2)* [2015] FCA 1374 at [29] and [41].
198   This case is an appeal against a decision by the Fair Work Commission (*Grant v BHP Coal Pty Ltd* [2014] FWCFB 3027 (*Grant* (2014)).
199   *Grant v BHP Coal Pty Ltd (No. 2)* [2015] FCA 1374 at [22].
200   Ibid [31].
201   Ibid.
202   Ibid.
203   Ibid [61].

AUSTRALIAN AND INTERNATIONAL PILOTS ASSOCIATION v QANTAS AIRWAYS LTD (2014) 240 IR 342

In *AIPA v Qantas*, the court held that although the information requested by Qantas was not covered by the provisions in the enterprise agreement, the purpose for which additional information was being sought was appropriate and lawful, and that it was not intended to impose on the employee's right to take his sick leave.[204] In this case the employee had provided a medical certificate from the treating doctor stating that he was unfit to work during a period of time, and had used personal leave available for him, but had refused to provide a report from his treating doctor.[205]

In contrast to the previous two cases considered, the decision in *Transport Workers' Union of Australia v Cement Australia Pty Ltd* [2015] FWC 158 (*Cement Australia*) was different.

TRANSPORT WORKERS' UNION OF AUSTRALIA v CEMENT AUSTRALIA PTY LTD [2015] FWC 158

In *Cement Australia,* an employer's order for employees to attend a health assessment program was ruled not lawful or reasonable, on two grounds: the health assessment results were not directly related to the requirements of performing the employees' job, and there was no connection between the employer's direction and a reduction in the injury rate.[206] The FWC considered the distinction between a reasonable and lawful direction to an employee based on 'specific circumstances' relevant to an individual, as distinct from 'a direction to a sector of the workforce, based on a general concern regarding' the trend of a particular injury for such a group.[207]

It is important to note the observations by Madgwick J in *Blackadder* (2002), that the employer can require an employee to attend a medical assessment 'on reasonable terms' to confirm fitness 'where there is a genuine indication of a need for it'.[208] In *Blackadder* (2002) Madgwick J observed that:

[t]he question whether it is reasonable for an employer to request an employee to attend a medical examination will always be a question of fact as will the question of what are

204   Ibid [71] and [72]–[76].
205   *Australian and International Pilots Association v Qantas Airways Ltd* (2014) 240 IR 342 at [44]. There is a difference between a medical certificate which was provided by the employer in this case and the medical report requested by the employer. According to the *Workplace Relations Act 1996* s 254(4), a medical certificate includes a general statement from a medical practitioner that in his or her opinion the employee would be unfit to work during a specified period due to a personal injury or illness. However, the medical report requested by the employer in this case required additional and specific information such as the employee's actual medical condition, prognosis and his likelihood of returning to work.
206   *Transport Workers' Union of Australia v Cement Australia Pty Ltd* [2015] FWC 158 at [126].
207   Ibid.
208   *Blackadder v Ramsey Butchering Services Pty Ltd* (2002) 118 FCR 395 at [68].

reasonable terms for the undertaking of the medical examination. The matters will generally require a sensitive approach, including, as far as possible, respect for privacy.[209]

It is clear yet again that whether an order is lawful and reasonable depends on the specific factual circumstances of each case.

2.35.10 An employer's direction regarding outside of work activities

When considering whether a direction regarding outside work activities is lawful and reasonable, courts will consider the extent of the connection between the after-hour activity and the nature of job of the employee.[210] For example, this was addressed in the case of *King v Catholic Education Office Diocese of Parramatta*.

KING v CATHOLIC EDUCATION OFFICE DIOCESE OF PARRAMATTA (2014) 242 IR 249

Mr King had been a long-serving teacher at a Catholic high school in Blacktown and sometimes transported students of the school in his car outside school hours to participate in surf lifesaving training.[211] The school issued a specific direction to Mr King not to transport school students to and from outside school activities and also directed that he no longer be involved in surf lifesaving training.[212] During this time, several teachers of the school had been charged for previous child sexual abuse and two students had made allegations of inappropriate conduct by Mr King towards them.[213]

One of the questions before the FWC was whether the employer could direct the employee regarding his activities outside of his work hours.[214] The FWC confirmed that although the activity was outside of normal school hours, the direction by the employer was lawful and reasonable.[215] The reason was that the school owed a duty of care to its students and the after school hour activities were directly connected to student and teacher relationships.[216] In addition, the FWC agreed that the employer had a duty to protect students from potential harm and its employees and itself from potential liability.[217] This duty was not confined to school hours.[218]

209   Ibid [69].
210   Whether the failure to comply with lawful and reasonable instructions of an employer is a reason for the termination of employment of an employee is examined in Chapter 3.
211   *King v Catholic Education Office Diocese of Parramatta* (2014) 242 IR 249 at [11]–[12].
212   Ibid [12].
213   Ibid [97]: see paragraph 95 of the witness statement of Mr Passarello mentioned by the Commissioner.
214   Ibid [30].
215   Ibid [33]. (The FWC considered the High Court decision of *New South Wales v Lepore* (2003) 212 CLR 511 in asserting this proposition.)
216   Ibid [53], [51], [54] and [60].
217   Ibid [54].
218   Ibid [33]. The FWC noted Gleeson CJ's observations in *New South Wales v Lepore* (2003) 212 CLR 511 [142].

2.35.15 Lawful and reasonable direction to employees in the public service

The scope of lawful and reasonable direction required to be complied with by employees in the public service has been considered in several cases. One of the main issues on this topic is that a public service employee's common law duty to obey lawful and reasonable direction should not impinge on the employee's constitutional right of freedom of communication about government and political matters.[219]

This issue was considered in *Bennett v President Human Rights and Equal Opportunity Commission* (*Bennett*).

BENNETT v PRESIDENT HUMAN RIGHTS AND EQUAL OPPORTUNITY COMMISSION (2003) 134 FCR 334

In this case, the applicant, Peter Phillip Bennett, a public servant employed in the Australian Customs Service, was also the Federal President of an industrial organisation, the Customs Officers Association.[220] He lodged a complaint to the Human Rights and Equal Opportunity Commission (HREOC) claiming, among other matters, that his employer had discriminated against him on the basis of his political opinions and his trade union activity.[221] After considering the complaint, HREOC exercised its statutory right to refuse to continue inquiries on the basis that it was satisfied that such discrimination did not exist.[222] The High Court application challenged the decision by HREOC not to continue its inquiry.[223] Mr Bennett challenged the validity of reg 7(13) of the *Public Service Regulations 1999*.[224] He further contended that this provision infringes the implied constitutional freedom of political communication that was confirmed in the High Court decision *Lange v Australian Broadcasting Corporation* (*Lange*).[225]

Finn J found that reg 7(13) of the *Public Service Regulations 1999* did infringe the implied constitutional freedom of political communication, and that even if that right were not infringed, the employer's direction infringed the employee's right to freedom of expression under Art 19(2) of the International Covenant on Civil and Political Rights (ICCPR),[226] since

---

219   *Bennett v President Human Rights and Equal Opportunity Commission* (2003) 134 FCR 334 at [123]–[124]. In his observation, Finn J referred to the test formulated in *Lange v Australian Broadcasting Corporation* (1997) 189 CLR 520 (*Lange*) at [578], which confirmed an implied constitutional freedom of political communication.

220   *Bennett v President Human Rights and Equal Opportunity Commission* (2003) 134 FCR 334 (*Bennett*) at [1].

221   Ibid.

222   Ibid [2].

223   Ibid [3].

224   Ibid. (The provision states: 'An APS employee must not, except in the course of his or her duties as an APS employee or with the Agency Head's express authority, give or disclose, directly or indirectly, any information about public business or anything of which the employee has official knowledge.')

225   Ibid.

226   Art 19(2): Everyone shall have the right to freedom of expression; this right shall include freedom to seek, receive and impart information and ideas of all kinds, regardless of frontiers, either orally, in writing or in print, in the form of art, or through any other media of his choice.

such direction was not specifically to protect public disorder (Art 19(3) of the ICCPR).[227] His Honour allowed the application and referred the matter for further consideration by HREOC because Art 19 was not considered by HREOC in view of the employee's duty of loyalty and fidelity as an Australian public servant.[228]

2.40 Duty to use care and skill

There is a general duty imposed on an employee to use reasonable care and skill in discharging their duties. It is reasonable that employees are expected to perform duties using the skills required to perform those duties. For example, if an employee is engaged in a clerical capacity in a medical practice it is unreasonable to expect the employee to perform some of the duties required of a nurse. The use of relevant skills in performing their duties to the expected skill level may have performance implications, but regardless of their skill level, all employees are required to show a certain level of care in carrying out their duties.[229]

The area requiring clarity in the duty to use care and skill is the question of liability in tort in relation to the employee's and the employer's liability for a negligent act of the employee in the course of his employment.[230] For example, in *McClymont v Egerton* [2015] QCATA 161 it was decided that a bus driver who had gone home in the bus after dropping off passengers – when he had been required to drop them off and then wait to pick them up – and had had an accident while returning, was not acting in the course of his employment.[231] It was further decided that the employee was liable to pay for the damage to the bus even though the employer had insurance.[232]

However, both the employer and the employee may be liable for an employee's negligent acts committed in the course of his employment. For example, an employed truck driver who accidentally kills a pedestrian while delivering goods in the course of his employment may be liable, along with the employer, to pay damages; alternatively, if the employer is held liable, the employer may have an action in common law (to recover the damages paid out) against the employee for failure to exercise due care.[233] For example, in *Lister v Romford Ice and Cold Storage Co. Ltd* [1957] AC 55 an employer who paid compensation to an injured person

227   See *Bennett* at [47]–[48]. Art 19(3): The exercise of the rights provided for in paragraph 2 of this article carries with it special duties and responsibilities. It may therefore be subject to certain restrictions, but these shall only be such as are provided by law and are necessary: (a) For respect of the rights or reputations of others; (b) For the protection of national security or of public order (*ordre public*), or of public health or morals.
228   Ibid [52]–[53].
229   Stewart et al. *Creighton and Stewart's Labour Law* (2016) 503.
230   This is further considered in both Stewart et al. *Creighton and Stewart's Labour Law* (2016) 503–04 and Sappideen et al. *Macken's Law of Employment* (2011) 210. See also Brodie 'Mutual trust and the value of employment contract' (2001) 97.
231   *McClymont v Egerton* [2015] QCATA 161 [46].
232   Ibid.
233   This example is loosely based on the actual facts in *Lister v Romford Ice and Cold Storage Co. Ltd* [1957] AC 55. Also see Stewart et al. *Creighton and Stewart's Labour Law* (2016) 503–04.

successfully recovered the damages from the employee based on the employee's failure to exercise a duty of care.[234]

2.45 Duty of fidelity

The authors of *Macken's Law of Employment* identify the development of the duty of good faith and fidelity as predating but forming a part of the more modern concept of the duty of trust and confidence.[235] This duty is closely linked to the English law principle of mutual trust and confidence. It is difficult to extrapolate the duty of fidelity, but on a general level it encompasses a range of duties imposed on the employee towards the employer.[236]

Although not limited to these areas, for the purpose of this chapter the duty of fidelity is considered in relation to the use of information, intellectual property, obligations regarding inventions, post-employment restraints, the duty to account for property, and bribes and secret commissions.

The practical difficulty of ascertaining the extent of 'that rather vague duty of fidelity' was noted by Finn J in *Bennett*[237] with reference to Lord Greene MR in *Hivac Ltd v Park Royal Scientific Instruments Ltd* [1946] Ch. 174.[238] In relation to duty of loyalty and fidelity Finn J further observed:

(a) The common-law duty must only be developed in a way that does not unnecessarily obstruct the constitutional freedom of communication about government and political matters.[239]

(b) When considering whether Phillip Bennett was disloyal, his status as a public servant and his obligations to the Commonwealth, and his status as the Federal President of the Customs Officers Association, should be considered.[240]

(c) The duty of loyalty 'overlaps with the equitable duty of confidence as it applies in employment settings to protect confidential information'.[241]

Some of the areas considered within the duty of fidelity are briefly examined below.

2.45.05 Use of information

Employees are required to refrain from disclosing information acquired during the course of employment. The contract of employment might also contain specific clauses which would expressly prevent employees from sharing any information with those specified.

The equitable duty of confidence[242] also ensures that information is protected.[243]

---

234   Stewart et al. *Creighton and Stewart's Labour Law* (2016) 503–04.
235   Sappideen et al. *Macken's Law of Employment* (2011) 156.
236   Ibid 215.
237   *Bennett* at [124].
238   Ibid.
239   Ibid [123].
240   Ibid [126].
241   Ibid [127].
242   This equitable duty can exist even after the employment finishes: Sappideen et al. *Macken's Law of Employment* (2011) 220.
243   Ibid 231, for a list of requirements to prove that the information is confidential information capable of being wrongfully used.

2.45.10 Intellectual property and obligations regarding inventions

Closely aligned with obligations related to the use of information are those related to intellectual property and inventions. Unless the contract of employment specifically states otherwise, the intellectual property rights for all inventions and material produced generally belong to the employer.

2.45.15 The duty to account for property

The duty to account for property covers all property which the employee acquires in the course of and during employment. For example, a police officer who raids the premises of an illegal drug syndicate is required to account for all property collected from the offender's premises. In addition, there may be official protocols, processes and checklists that police officers may be required to comply with to account for all property seized as a result of an investigation. However, if a police officer has a win on a lottery ticket purchased while off duty or at his lunch break, it does not fall within the duty to account for property.

2.50 Employer's duty to use care and to indemnify

As there is an implied duty imposed on an employee to use care and skill, so there is a duty on the employer to use care and to indemnify their employees in certain circumstances. This implied duty to use care requires the employer to take adequate measures to ensure that an employee is not exposed to risks at the workplace. For example, the employer has an obligation to ensure that a person employed as a crane worker has undertaken workplace safety and health training and is provided with mechanically sound equipment. A breach of the duty of care by an employer is likely to lead to a breach of contract and an action for damages in tort.[244] The duty of care and skill has been decided as being implied by tort, and this duty extends to all tasks, whether they are specialised or not.[245]

The duty of an employer to take reasonable care may include – but is not limited to – ensuring a safe workplace, mechanically sound and safe plant, equipment and appliances, safe systems of work and staff competent to perform the jobs they are assigned to do.[246]

The employer is responsible for reimbursing the employee for expenses approved by the employer and incurred by the employee during the course of his employment. For example, awards made under s 139(1)(g) of the *Fair Work Act 2009* (Cth) specifically allow for 'expenses incurred in the course of employment'.

---

244   *Strategic Management Australia AFL Pty Ltd v Entertainment Group Pty Ltd* (2016) 114 ACSR 1 at [59]; and *Wylie v ANI Corporation Ltd* [2002] 1 Qd R 320.

245   *Strategic Management Australia AFL Pty Ltd v Entertainment Group Pty Ltd* (2016) 114 ACSR 1 at [59]; and *Wylie v ANI Corporation Ltd* [2002] 1 Qd R 320. See also *Lister v Romford Ice and Cold Storage Co. Ltd* [1957] AC 55; and *Owners – Units Plan No. 1917 v Koundouris* (2016) 307 FLR 372.

246   Sappideen et al. *Macken's Law of Employment* (2011) 182–3.

SUMMARY

A contract of employment includes implied duties and obligations imposed on both the employee and the employer. The employee must obey reasonable direction and use care and skill, and has duties of fidelity and loyalty, cooperation and trust to the employer. The employee's duty of fidelity and loyalty also encompasses various duties and obligations relating to intellectual property, use of information, inventions, confidentiality, trade secrets, post-employment restraints, accounting for employer's property, and bribes and secret commissions. The employer must remunerate employees, use care and indemnify employees, and has a duty of cooperation and good faith towards the employee.

The duties of the employee to the employer are relatively settled in Australia. However, although the employer–employee relationship has evolved from that of master and servant, there are residual issues still emerging and developing. For example, the duty of good faith from employee to employer is well settled, but whether or not it is reciprocal remains unclear. The High Court decision in *Barker* (2014) authoritatively addressed Australia's position regarding the application of the principle of the mutual duty of trust and confidence recognised in the English decision of *Malik* (that is, it does not exist in Australia) but did not conclusively resolve questions around the obligation of good faith. There are other Australian cases that have considered the duty of good faith, also without making binding decisions. *Barker* (2014) rejected the proposition that the duty of trust and confidence is applicable to contracts of employment in Australia and specifically dismissed the application of English law to Australian employment law in this area.

REVIEW QUESTIONS

1. (a) What is the significance of the decision in *Commonwealth Bank of Australia v Barker* (2014) 253 CLR 169 in Australian employment law? What are the residual issues?

    (b) In the wake of *Barker* (2014), do English principles of mutual trust and confidence apply to contracts of employment in Australia?

    (c) What is the rationale for the decision regarding the question of damages in *Johnson v Unisys* [2003] 1 AC 518? What is the relevance, if any, of that case to Australian law?

2. What is the current position regarding the duty of good faith in Australia? What is the relevance of the decision in *Robb v Green* [1895] 2 QB 315 CA? What is the rationale for the decision in *Faccenda Chicken Ltd v Fowler* [1986] ICR 297 regarding the implied duty of good faith and trade secrets?

3. Although the duty of good faith in Australian employment law was affirmed in *Russell v Trustees of the Roman Catholic Church for the Archdiocese of Sydney* (2008) 72 NSWLR 559, as Riley describes, it is a 'failed' case for several reasons. In the light of Basten JA's observations, what is one basis for why it might be regarded as failed, especially from the point of view of *Russell*? Is there enduring significance in *Russell's* case? If so, what is that significance?

4. Research question: Quite apart from the duties implied by the common law into employment contracts, an employee's employment may be subject to workplace policies. That too is an area of law which is complex and changing. Research, analyse and present the current Australian legal position on workplace policy – what is the legal status of workplace policy?

5.   Group work: Find a number of practical examples of workplace policies and analyse them. When is policy used? What sorts of issues are included in policies? Create a model business then write a policy for that business.

FURTHER READING

D Cabrelli 'The implied duty of mutual trust and confidence: an emerging overarching principle?' (2005) 34 *Industrial Law Journal* 305.

MM Cope, *Equitable Obligations: Duties, Defences and Remedies* (Law Book Co., 2007).

G Kuehne 'Implied obligations of good faith and reasonableness in performance of contracts: old wine in new bottles?' (2006) 33 *University of Western Australia Law Review* 68.

MJ Pittard and R Naughton *Australian Labour and Employment Law* (LexisNexis, 2015).

J Riley 'Developments in contract of employment jurisprudence in other common-law jurisdictions' in Alan Bogg et al. (eds) *The Contract of Employment* (Oxford University Press, 2016) 273–94.

3 INTRODUCTION TO THE *FAIR WORK ACT*

3.05 Introduction

The opening chapters of this book outlined the basics of the contract of employment – offer and acceptance are required, as are consideration and certainty of terms. Characterising a contract as being one of either employment (contract of service) or a contract for services (independent contractor) is important. The law has 'special protections' aimed at preventing the misuse of the independent contractor relationship (in other words, stopping one party engaging others in such a way as to avoid paying the entitlements that the law stipulates for employees). Further, the common law implies various duties into the employment contract – to some extent there is still debate in Australia on the nature and scope of those duties and the protections they deliver.

Some authors, such as US law professor Stewart Schwab, would argue that the contract of employment is no different from most other contracts and it is not necessary for there to be a sophisticated body of law tailored to governing an employment contract or workplace relationship.[1] However, although the extent of regulation varies from country to country (and the US is at the less interventionist end of the regulatory spectrum), many acknowledge the special nature of the contract of employment: for many, a job is crucial to their identity and is their means of buying food and shelter; being exploited at work can have negative impacts on their health, and depending on the worker's skill set and the economic circumstances of the day, a different job may be difficult to find. And finally, the productivity of the workplace affects society as a whole.[2]

Debates on legal theory, together with the historical and social settings of Australia, have produced the labour and employment law that we have today. That law draws from both common law and statute; it finds a central place for organised labour and a strong national regulator, yet also aspires to promote flexibility and productivity. It is complex and extensive in nature, and in the last twenty or thirty years has seen enormous change. Our system is unique, though it draws on international concepts. It is largely nationally driven, yet has a history of innovation at the State government level.

The purpose of this chapter is to:

- outline the main theories of labour law as well as the major shifts in the Australian system and why the law is as it is;
- explain the background to the relationship between employment and labour laws, statute and case laws, State and Federal laws, international and local law, the main organs of the system – as well as laying the groundwork for the analysis in Chapter 4 of enterprise bargaining and awards; and
- critically analyse one of the key developing features of the system – adverse action (another 'special protection' like that aimed at contractors).

---

1   S Schwab *Employment Law: Cases and Materials* (Lexis Law Publishing, 2002) 7–8. See also
     S Schwab 'Predicting the future of employment law: reflecting or refracting market forces?' (2001) 76
     Indiana Law Journal 29–48. See also the theories of Hayek discussed further below.
2   See below for the theories of Kahn-Freund and Lord Wedderburn, for example.

3.10 Legal theories – a justification for labour law?

The provision for fair and reasonable remuneration (as required under the legislation) is obviously designed for the benefit of the employees in the industry; and it must be meant to secure to them something which they cannot get by the ordinary system of individual bargaining with employers. If Parliament meant that the conditions shall be such as they can get by individual bargaining – if it meant that those conditions are to be fair and reasonable, which employees will accept and employers will give, in contracts of service – there would have been no need for this provision. The remuneration could safely have been left to the usual, but unequal, contest, the 'higgling of the market' for labour with the pressure for bread on one side, and the pressure for profits on the other. The standard of 'fair and reasonable' must, therefore, be something else: and I cannot think of any other standard appropriate than the normal needs of the average employee, regarded as a human being living in a civilised community.[3]

These were the findings of Justice HB Higgins in 1907 in the judgement for which he became famous – the Harvester Judgement. His Honour had been assigned a task under the relevant legislation, the *Excise Tariff Act 1906* (Cth), of determining what was the amount of a 'fair and reasonable' wage, for it was only if such were paid that the employing business concerned would be exempted from duty.[4] So he looked at it simply: 'If A lets B have the use of his horses, on terms that he give them fair and reasonable treatment, . . . it is B's duty to give them proper food and water, and such shelter and rest as they need.'[5] Applying that logic to the treatment of men, His Honour relied on extensive evidence about the cost of living of the day to ensure a comfortable life – and that was the fair and reasonable (living) wage.[6]

Over and above this actual statement of the law, Justice Higgins' judgement is famous for his acknowledgement that there is a power imbalance between worker and employer that meant that some kind of intervention to protect workers from exploitation was required.[7] Indeed, throughout his judgement, His Honour acknowledges the difficulties working people face. For one thing, there are slightly substandard labourers who will undercut the costs of a skilled workman and thus lower all wage rates.[8] And, no matter how good-hearted an employer may be, there is always the temptation to treat the acquisition of labour like the acquisition of any other commodity (such as wood or iron) and pay no more than is necessary.[9] Redressing those problems required intervention. One might also consider the need for workers to combine against their employer in a bargaining role.[10]

---

3   *Ex parte H v McKay* (1907) 2 *CAR* 1–33 *(The Harvester Judgement)* at 3 per Higgins J. Much of this discussion is drawn from L Floyd 'Glass houses and rock solid guarantees: a legal analysis of the Commonwealth "no disadvantage" test', unpublished PhD thesis, University of Sydney, 2004.
4   Ibid 2 per Higgins J.
5   Ibid 3 per Higgins J.
6   Ibid.
7   Ibid.
8   Ibid.
9   Ibid.
10   Ibid.

Over the last hundred years much has altered – and the bargaining chapter of this book (Chapter 4) is testament to the influence that flexibility and productivity (rather than simply living wages) now play in our laws. And yet for all that, the sentiments in the above quotation remain highly relevant to some of the core issues in labour and employment laws, namely:

- Is there an imbalance between worker and employer such that legal intervention is necessary in the contract of employment?
- If so, what is the best method of intervention – allowing workers to combine as a countervailing force against their stronger employers or legislating for a floor of rights, beneath which no contract can be struck?

The labour scholars who have championed and debated these points are renowned. British scholar Otto Kahn-Freund, in *Labour and the Law*,[11] viewed the contract of employment as a legal fiction – although the law perceived a bargain as having been struck, in truth all but the most skilled and sought-after worker often had no choice but to accept the terms determined by the employer.[12] To Kahn-Freund, the situation was akin to a passenger on a train who was viewed by the law as assenting to conditions on the back of the ticket even if they are blind or illiterate.[13] In Kahn-Freund's view, the way to address the situation was to allow workers to combine – the employer had collective resources and staff, so why not workers?[14]

Taking the contrary view was Friedrich Hayek, especially in *The Road to Serfdom*,[15] *The Constitution of Liberty*[16] and *Law, Legislation and Liberty*.[17] To Hayek, the individual, not the collective, will enrich society. Employers create job opportunities, and take the risks and accumulate the capital that enable workers to gain a job and earn a living.[18] While some workers may be disadvantaged and have to take a pay cut or change jobs they do not like,[19] government intervention and trade unions are not the answer. Such intervention is too arbitrary, and may rely on the popularity of a cause, rather than analysing its value to the economy, to drive decision-making. Unions in particular may drive up prices.[20] Unions should exist simply as friendly societies to help employees choose between jobs – all offered on the employer's terms.[21]

Views such as those of Hayek have numerous advocates, from Professor Richard Epstein, who wrote 'In Defense of the Contract at Will',[22] through to Professor Schwab,

---

11   O Kahn-Freund *Labour and the Law* (Stevens & Maxwell, 2nd ed, 1977).
12   K Renner *The Institutions of Private Law and their Social Function* (Routledge & Kegan Paul Limited, 1949) 39. In fact, Kahn-Freund described the contract of employment as the 'indispensable figment of the legal mind': *Labour and the Law* (1977) 6.
13   Renner *The Institutions of Private Law and their Social Function* (1949) 39.
14   Kahn-Freund *Labour and the Law* (1977) 6.
15   F Hayek *The Road to Serfdom* (Routledge & Kegan Paul, 1944).
16   F Hayek *The Constitution of Liberty* (The University of Chicago Press, 1960).
17   F Hayek *Law, Legislation and Liberty* (The University of Chicago Press, 1973) (Vols 1–3).
18   Hayek *Law, Legislation and Liberty* (1973) Vol 3 151; Hayek *The Constitution of Liberty* (1960) 119.
19   Hayek *Law, Legislation and Liberty* (1973) Vol 3 93–96.
20   Ibid 93 et seq; Hayek *The Constitution of Liberty* (1960) 119–21, 124, 275–7 and 300–03; Hayek *Law, Legislation and Liberty* (1973) Vol 1 119–21.
21   Hayek *Law, Legislation and Liberty* (1973) Vol 1 95–6; and Hayek *The Constitution of Liberty* (1960) 275–6.
22   R Epstein 'In defense of the contract at will' (1984) 51 *University of Chicago Law Review* 955.

who rather condescendingly regards the power imbalance theory as something that 'appeals to students'.[23] To Schwab the contract of employment is like any other and an unhappy worker can simply change jobs in much the same way people change supermarkets.[24]

A scathingly brilliant rebuttal of that viewpoint was written by Lord Wedderburn, whose works include the fabled *The Worker and the Law*.[25] Lord Wedderburn was highly critical of Hayek's opposition to any form of trade union organisation. 'It is not a question of balance,' objected Wedderburn, 'of organisations being too strong or too weak, or of the vulnerability of the individual employees. Such group organisation is in itself a threat to law and society.'[26] The critique continued: Hayek placed too much faith in corporations playing a proper and responsible role in a productive society, and that view seemed 'antique' in a world of pyramid corporations and white collar crime.[27] Lord Wedderburn doubted how workers could stand up against transnational corporations, which made even some national governments look like 'parish councils'.[28] To Lord Wedderburn the answer lay not in a floor of rights (laid out in government legislation), as this was not part of the contract of employment and still required the worker to stand alone.[29] Power for labour was collective.[30] Lord Wedderburn also regarded Hayek's faith in freedom of contract as 'an astonishingly naif belief in the neutrality of the principles of common law'.[31] To Wedderburn, the crux of the common law is the protection of property.[32]

These sorts of views have been eloquently and persuasively advocated by many Australian labour law academics. The relationship of the common law to the promotion of the managerial prerogative was discussed by Professor Andrew Stewart in his article 'Procedural flexibility, enterprise bargaining and the future of arbitral regulation'.[33] In a similar vein, Professor Ron

---

23   S Schwab *Employment Law: Cases and Materials* (Lexis Law Publishing, 2002) 7–8. See also S Schwab 'Predicting the future of employment law: reflecting or refracting market forces? (2001) 76 *Indiana Law Journal* 29–48.

24   Schwab *Employment Law: Cases and Materials* (2002) 7–8

25   Lord Wedderburn, *The Worker and the Law* (Pelican Books, 3rd ed, 1986) 10 et seq. See also Lord Wedderburn 'Collective bargaining or legal enactment: the 1999 Act and union recognition' (2000) 29 *Industrial Law Journal* 28 and 29. There, Lord Wedderburn applauds the Webbs for their 'embryonic thought' that the growth of corporate entities placed the position of workers at greater risk. Wedderburn also cites Kahn-Freund as noting the advent of the transnational company as something that threatened the very institution of labour law.

26   Lord Wedderburn 'Freedom of association and philosophies of labour law' (1989) 18 *Industrial law Journal* 9. It is interesting to note that Kahn-Freund, in *Labour and the Law* (1977), specifically notes that regulation of power relationships is a matter of degree (7).

27   Wedderburn 'Freedom of association and philosophies of labour law' (1989) 12.

28   Wedderburn 'Collective bargaining or legal enactment' (2000): Lord Wedderburn notes that some corporations have become so global and large that even national governments resemble 'parish councils' in comparison. He also notes that there seems to be no corresponding globalisation of labour (29 et seq).

29   Lord Wedderburn *The Worker and the Law* (Pelican Books, 3rd ed, 1986) 5–6. As to the many methods of dealing with power imbalance, Lord Wedderburn offers diagrams at 14 and 15.

30   Wedderburn 'Collective bargaining or legal enactment' (2000) 25.

31   Wedderburn 'Freedom of association and philosophies of labour law' (1989) 11.

32   Ibid 11–12, 28. In Wedderburn 'Collective bargaining or legal enactment' (2000) 41 Lord Wedderburn observed that some earlier judges may have viewed unions as a restraint on trade.

33   A Stewart 'Procedural flexibility, enterprise bargaining and the future of arbitral regulation' (1992) 5 *Australian Journal of Labour Law* 101–33.

McCallum has intimated that there may be a power imbalance even for well-qualified employees;[34] and, in one speech, Professor Breen Creighton referred to power imbalances as almost a fact of life.[35]

Perhaps the most influential writings in recent times are those of Professor Hugh Collins, who wrote the ground-breaking 1989 article, 'Labour law as a vocation'.[36] Importantly, the article is not diametrically opposed to Kahn-Freund or Lord Wedderburn. It does accept that there can be a power imbalance but argues that it must not be overstated – depending on prevailing market circumstances, workers may be in a strong position at the point of engagement. Further, once employed, it may be the hierarchy within an organisation which causes the worker to become subordinate. If these factors are not taken into account, it may be possible for union power to bring the economy into disequilibrium, with possibly high levels of unemployment.[37] According to this 'third way', fertile areas for study therefore range from minimum conditions of work through to industrial democracy and the regulation of corporations.[38]

Such thinking has shaped much of New Labour in Great Britain[39] and, according to Phillip Blond,[40] also the governments of Hawke and Keating in Australia and Clinton in the US.

The emerging labour theories of writers such as Blond are discussed in Chapter 7. The final chapter, Chapter 9, includes discussion of other theories and issues such as the law of unemployment. But in this early chapter, it is worth observing that it is Collins' theory that has been influential on the present laws of the Australian system. Having said that, as academics such as the late Professor Weeks have observed, unions still play a highly significant role in this country:

> Workers' interests are pursued both collectively and individually and, while it is evident that unions have been losing the allegiance of workers to the point where they recognise the need to become more responsive to their actual and potential members, collective strategies remain indispensable. Bennett's warning that the allocation of rights to individuals against unions leaves employers' 'unacknowledged and overwhelming' rights and powers 'untouched while stripping unions of rights and impeding the individual employee's ability to engage in collective action' ought to be heeded.[41]

---

34   R McCallum 'Australian workplaces, the rise of contractualism and industrial citizenship' in *Employment Contracts: Their Role in Industrial Relations?* (Fourth Annual Labour Law Conference, University of Sydney, 1996) 2.

35   B Creighton 'Reforming the contract of employment' in *Employment Contracts: Their Role in Industrial Relations?* (Fourth Annual Labour Law Conference, University of Sydney, 1996) 16–18.

36   H Collins 'Labour law as a vocation' (1989) 105 *Law Quarterly Review* 468–84.

37   Ibid 479.

38   Ibid 481.

39   A Giddens *The Third Way* (Polity Press, 1998); and A Giddens *The Third Way and its Critics* (Polity Press, 2000). See also T Blair *New Britain: My Vision of a Young Country* (Fourth Estate, 1996). Blair discusses partnerships at, for example, 31–32.

40   P Blond *Red Tory: How Left and Right Have Broken Britain and How We Can Fix It* (Faber & Faber, 2010).

41   P Weeks *Trade Union Security Law – A Study of Preference and Compulsory Unionism* (Federation Press, 1996) 263.

3.15 Practical, historical and constitutional development of the Australian system – how we got here[42]

The original key industrial legislation in Australia was the *Conciliation and Arbitration Act 1904* (Cth). It passed the Parliament with support from both sides of politics relying on s 51(xxxv) of the Constitution – the industrial relations power, which empowered the newly created Commonwealth to pass laws for the 'prevention and settlement of industrial disputes extending beyond the limits of any one State'.

The enactment ultimately saw the creation of a central 'umpire' – then known as the Conciliation and Arbitration Commission (later Industrial Relations and now Fair Work Commission) – which would, in the first place, try to conciliate disputes (today's alternative dispute resolution). If that were not possible, it would arbitrate, and so create an award of terms and conditions of employment to be followed in the future. The parties to appear before the Commission were typically representative organisations – unions or employer bodies – and the jurisdiction would be triggered by the serving of a so-called log of claims.

The Australian system was a deliberate alternative to unbridled collective bargaining. As Sir Alfred Deakin observed in his second reading of the legislation:[43]

> This Bill marks, in my opinion, the beginning of a new phase of civilization. It begins the establishment of the People's Peace, under which the conduct of industrial affairs . . . may be guided . . . Hitherto, there has been but one method of dealing with strikes and lockouts, and one inevitable result. The strongest party has always prevailed. The cause was not in question; the matter of dispute was not weighed. Give to one side numbers and means now, and it wins. The cause counts for nothing; power counts for everything; might makes right. Under the new system – and here is the revolution – a different aim will operate. Might is not to make right. But, as soon as it can be discerned and determined, right is to make right.

Such a system for the peaceful and sensible resolution of disputes would avoid exploitation of working people – that in turn would enrich the fabric of the new country of Australia and give it the enduring stability it needed to move ahead.[44] This became known as the Deakin Settlement.[45]

As Macintyre and Mitchell were to observe later, that need for peace and stability was spawned by the bruising strikes of the late 1800s.[46] Walker also saw national character as part

---

42   Much of this discussion on the historical development of the Australian system is based on L Floyd 'Enron and One.tel: Employee entitlements after employer insolvency in the United States and Australia – Australian renegades championing the Australian dream' (2003) 56 *Southern Methodist University Law Review* 975–1004.

43   Sir Alfred Deakin, House of Representatives, Commonwealth of Australia Parliamentary debates, 2868 (30 July 1903).

44   Ibid 2868.

45   Ibid.

46   S Macintyre and R Mitchell *The Foundations of Arbitration* (Oxford University Press, 1989).

of the equation – the working men who had come to Australia had often been very harshly treated in England, so a system of this nature had immediate appeal.[47]

Sidney and Beatrice Webb referred to the system as 'the remarkable experiment in the Britains beyond the seas'.[48] Politicians of the day remarked that the Commission had the elasticity of an 'elephant's trunk'[49] because it could deal with the complexities of each matter that came before it. In explaining the system to the world, Justice Higgins wrote, in the *Harvard Law Review*, that the system was 'The new province for law and order'.[50]

For many years there was a political consensus behind the system. Labor politicians such as Prime Minister Chifley spoke lyrically of the 'Light on the Hill' as being a fair return for one's labour, so that 'our less fortunate fellow citizens are protected from those shafts of fate which leave them helpless and without hope'.[51] Although Prime Minister Menzies was known for standing up to unions, he was no zealot. In his 'Forgotten People' speech, he insisted:

> *The functions of the State will be much more than merely keeping the ring within which the competitors will fight. Our social and industrial obligations will be increased. There will be more law, not less; more control, not less.* But what really happens to us will depend on how many people we have who are of the great and sober and dynamic middle-class – the strivers, the planners, the ambitious ones. We shall destroy them at our peril.[52]

But of course, times change.

3.15.05 Changing economic, structural and policy considerations[53]

In considering the development of the constitutional industrial relations power and, for example, how it was interpreted by the High Court of Australia, Gunningham[54] correctly observed that, with the passage of time, various elements of the power were given an increasingly broad interpretation. So, for example, 'industrial disputes' went from being disputes within heavy industry to including disputes within clerical disciplines.[55] The effect of this

47   KF Walker 'Conciliation and arbitration in Australia' in J Loewenberg (ed) *Compulsory Arbitration: An International Comparison* (Lexington Books, 1976) 2–3.

48   S and B Webb *Industrial Democracy* (Longmans, Green & Co., 1902) li and xxii.

49   Sir Alfred Deakin, Commonwealth of Australia Parliamentary Debates, 2868 (30 July 1903). See also 2865: it could 'pick up a pin or lift an enormous load' – it was not rigid legislation.

50   Higgins 'A new province for law and order' (1915–16) 29 *Harvard Law Review* 1, 39. In that paper, Higgins reflected on the position of the Australian worker: 'give them reasonable certainty that their essential material needs will be met by honest work, and you release infinite stores of human energy for higher efforts, for nobler ideas'. As Walker noted, Australia's labour laws were 'an antipodean curiosity as exotic as the kangaroo or the boomerang' (1).

51   Prime Minister JB Chifley (14 November 1949), Australian Labor Party Campaign Launch. The author is indebted to Roslyn Russell, who provided this extract from this speech.

52   Sir Robert Menzies (radio broadcast, 22 May 1942), reprinted in *The Forgotten People* (Angus & Robertson, 1943) (emphasis added).

53   Much of the following paragraphs on changes to the system are based on L Floyd's PhD thesis, 'Glass houses and rock solid guarantees: a legal analysis of the Commonwealth "no disadvantage" test' (2004) and on her article 'For everything there is a season' (2007) 14 *James Cook University Law Review* 25–50.

54   N Gunningham *Industrial Law and the Constitution* (Federation Press, 1988).

55   See *Re State Public Service Federation; Ex parte Attorney-General (Western Australia)* (1993) 178 CLR 249 (*SPSF*).

was significant. When the Australian system was first created, the prime movers in government were the States; the Commonwealth was the new government with carefully delineated powers. Over time, the reach of Commonwealth power expanded, and that of the States declined.[56] Parallel to this, the Commonwealth's Conciliation and Arbitration Commission began to include similar terms in awards within an industry, so industry standards emerged. Further, the Commission decided test cases, such as the *Termination Change and Redundancy Case*,[57] which set up benchmarks for how certain issues that were common to numerous industries, such as redundancy, would be handled. Although there was clearly merit in some of these developments, the net effect was an ever-strengthening Commonwealth jurisdiction and a centralisation of power federally and throughout various industries.[58] When the Commonwealth Parliament began to use heads of power additional to the industrial relations power – for example, the foreign affairs power – to ground further federal laws (such as unfair dismissal based on international treaties and conventions), the trend became even more pronounced.[59]

Colliding head-on with these Australian developments were the changes going on throughout the world, after the 1970s particularly. Globalisation, the development of IT and instantaneous communication (and a general resurgence of neoliberal theory) all caused many to question the Australian system's capacity to handle the modern world. In other words, was a system based on large representative unions, third-party intervention and industry or national standards flexible enough to facilitate business and employment when the circumstances in which business operated could change so quickly and when competition could come from far afield?[60]

In a highly influential paper, 'Enterprise-based bargaining units – a better way of working',[61] the Business Council of Australia (BCA) urged parliamentarians to place a greater emphasis on the employing enterprise – the actual unit that employed workers and had to respond to business pressures (be they pressures as to price, international competition or changing tastes). That basic unit was viewed as being small, responsive and flexible enough to adapt to the demands of the changing economy, whereas industry, in the larger sense, was more cumbersome.

The law did begin to change, and enterprise bargaining became a significant part of the industrial law equation.[62] Using enterprise bargaining (discussed in detail in Chapter 4), unions and employers would negotiate terms and conditions of employment for the workers at a particular workplace or enterprise, so terms and conditions of employment moved away from the detailed, prescriptive industry-style awards of the past. Importantly, the support structures

---

56   Some other examples of the interpretation of this constitutional head of power are raised in Chapter 4.
57   *Termination Change and Redundancy Case* (1984) 8 IR 34.
58   See, for example, Floyd 'For everything there is a season' (2007).
59   *Victoria v Commonwealth* (1996) 187 CLR 416. Indeed, the argument was that if the Federal government had agreed to international obligations (on dismissal, for example), then it was the correct level of government to enact those obligations, and it could do so under the foreign affairs power.
60   See Chapter 4.
61   Business Council of Australia, 'Enterprise-based bargaining units – a better way of working' (1989) *Business Council of Australia* 3–4.
62   The author has a detailed history in, for example, 'Glass houses and rock solid guarantees' (2004).

of the old system were not abandoned. The Commission would still vet agreements, by comparing the proposed ones with the current ones, to ensure that there was no disadvantage to workers in moving from the award to an agreement.

The original incremental moves towards enterprise bargaining (outlined above) took place under the Hawke-Keating Labor Government. When the Howard Coalition Government won office, further decentralisation took place. For the purposes of this chapter, one of the major changes was the introduction of Australian Workplace Agreements (AWAs), which were essentially individual statutory agreements. From a practical perspective, these agreements ushered individuals out of the collective (union) system for the setting of terms and conditions of employment.[63] Further, there were fewer legislative supports for unions and the no disadvantage test was further relaxed. Despite all these changes, it seemed that as long as the Coalition held a majority only in the House of Representatives, and not in the Senate, the more left-leaning parties in the Senate would always nullify what some would say were the more extreme and individualistic aspects of Coalition labour policy. In other words, despite the advent of AWAs and the relaxation of the no disadvantage test, the traditional safeguards (that is, a role for unions and the Australian Industrial Relations Commission [AIRC]) were still clearly present.

3.15.10 WorkChoices

In 2004, the Coalition gained a majority in both houses of parliament; free from opposition, the government ushered in the infamous and ill-fated WorkChoices regime.[64]

Before outlining some key features of WorkChoices, two observations should be made. First, this is the most Hayekite that Australian industrial relations has ever got – it was a celebration of the individual. Second, WorkChoices did not simply appear like the proverbial bolt from the blue. In 1993, the Liberals had lost the so-called unlosable election by launching a very detailed policy called Fightback, which spelled out the extremely individualistic policies a Liberal Government would bring in, should it win the next election, under then leader John Hewson.[65] It scared workers. In 1996, Mr Howard – an extremely astute politician – gave a 'rock solid guarantee' that Liberal policies would not cause a cut in take-home pay.[66] But as the present writer observed,[67] that guarantee was limited. If one reads the speech in its entirety, it is clear that Mr Howard's intention had always been to individualise the system and effect broad structural change – he regarded the AIRC and unions as 'arthritic, old fashioned . . . [and] the biggest single impediment . . . to removing the speed limits on economic growth . . . [The] Australian Industrial Relations system . . . [owed] its origins to the mores of pre-World War One Australia.'[68]

---

63   Technically, one could be a unionist and have an AWA, but as a practical reality, if the union was not negotiating for a worker's conditions of employment, many workers questioned the need to be in a union.

64   This discussion of WorkChoices is based on the author's previous work: Floyd 'Glass houses and rock solid guarantees' (2004) and 'For everything there is a season' (2007).

65   Liberal Party of Australia, 'Fightback! It's your Australia' (Online Offset Printers, 1992) 1–67.

66   John Howard MP, 'Address to 28th Young Liberal Movement Convention' (delivered at the Australian National University, 8 January 1996) (supplied to the author by the then Prime Minister's Office). See also L Taylor, 'Bullets removed from IR gun', *The Australian*, 9 January 1996, 1.

67   Floyd 'Glass houses and rock solid guarantees' (2004) Chs 1 and 2.

68   Howard, 'Address to 28th Young Liberal Movement Convention' (1996).

Professor Mitchell was correct when he said that the only thing that had held former Prime Minster Howard back from such reforms was the Senate – when Mr Howard had the numbers to pass WorkChoices, he was in effect fulfilling his political dream.[69]

For present purposes, the key features of WorkChoices were:[70]

- The abolition of the no disadvantage test – agreements were now to be binding on lodgement. The effect of this is obvious: the safety net of the AIRC to vet agreements for fairness was removed.

- The emphasis was now on AWAs, individual statutory agreements, so unions had a marginalised place in the system.

- Philosophically, the system was less collective and more individualistic, so it was less connected to its past and more akin to Hayek.

- Further worker protections were circumscribed: for instance, unfair dismissal laws still existed on the statute books, but for 60 per cent of the workforce employed by businesses employing up to 100 people, there was limited access to that relief.

- Bizarre concepts were created, such as greenfields agreements, in which an employer could agree with itself as to what terms of employment would apply to a new workplace.

- The heads of power in the Constitution on which the legislation relied were largely the corporations power (s 51(xx)) and the foreign affairs power (s 51(xxix)) rather than the industrial relations power, with all its rich history about egalitarianism.

- The State jurisdictions were also gutted and the system became largely Federal in operation.

It is a part of Australian political folklore now how unpopular WorkChoices was. Within a year of its becoming law, cases emerged[71] that clearly demonstrated that workers could be worse off under the new system. Despite the government's attempts to reintroduce a form of no disadvantage test, called the Fairness Test, it was too little too late. The government was defeated by Kevin Rudd's Labor Party in November 2007, Mr Howard became one of the few Prime Ministers to lose his seat in the election,[72] and the law was repealed and replaced by what is the current statute, the *Fair Work Act*.

---

69   R Mitchell, 'Juridification and labour law: a legal response to the flexibility debate in Australia' (1998) 14 *International Journal of Comparative Labour Law and Industrial Relations* 122.

70   See L Floyd 'Workplace relations: employment and industrial law' in C Turner *Australian Commercial Law* (Thomson Legal and Regulatory, 26th ed, 2006–07) 783–806; See also Floyd 'For everything there is a season' (2007).

71   M David 'Spotlight abandons confusing AWAS', *Sydney Morning Herald (SMH)* online, 19 September 2007, http://www.smh.com.au/news/national/spotlight-abandons-confusing-awas/2007/09/18/1189881513631.html (accessed 12 March 2017).

72   See 'John Howard concedes defeat', *SMH* online, 24 November 2007, http://www.smh.com.au/news/federal-election-2007-news/howard-phones-rudd/2007/11/24/1195753366680.html (accessed 12 March 2017).

3.20 The *Fair Work Act 2009* (Cth): an overview

The *Fair Work Act*, which proclaimed a third way mantra of flexibility for business and fairness for workers,[73] is both a stunning departure from WorkChoices and something which actually extends what that legislation started.

The stunning departure involves the place of unions within the Australian system. AWAs (those statutory individual agreements which, practically, marginalised unions) were abolished. In this connection, the objects of the legislation were amended to include: 'ensuring that the guaranteed safety net of fair, relevant and enforceable minimum wages and conditions can no longer be undermined by the making of statutory individual employment agreements of any kind given that such agreements can never be part of a fair workplace relations system'. One interpretation of this might be that *to be fair means to be collective*! To this was added the relatively new concept of good faith bargaining, which effectively reversed decisions such as *Australian Workers' Union v BHP Iron-Ore Pty Ltd* (2001) 106 FCR 482, and meant that employers could no longer simply ignore unions in a bargaining process.[74] And there are the special protections of adverse action (outlined further at the end of this chapter). A watered down 'relative' of the old no disadvantage test (called the better off overall test or BOOT) was also enacted[75] – and the renamed Fair Work Commission had a more important role than any umpire had played under WorkChoices. So third-party safety nets were given legislative support.

Continuing trends that WorkChoices developed, the *Fair Work Act* still relies on heads of constitutional power other than the original industrial relations power (such as the corporations power); and it embedded the march towards a federal system (and, therefore, national employment standards or legislative floors of rights – see Chapter 4).

3.20.05 State and Federal laws and revisiting constitutional issues

It was mentioned earlier that the States had originally been the prime movers in legislation in Australia. However, the power balance between Federal and State parliaments began to shift over the decades.[76] Despite that, when WorkChoices was introduced, in States such as Queensland, 60 per cent of the workforce were still covered by State industrial law. WorkChoices effectively pushed the majority of that 60 per cent into the federal system; government servants and those

---

73   *Fair Work Act 2009* (Cth) s 3.
74   Essentially BHPIO was offering pay rises to those who would enter into an AWA with the company. Although unions could still represent their members in some matters, the links between pay increases and AWAs raised questions about the utility of belonging to a union. Would workers still seek union membership if their pay rise was underpinned by an individual document? The bargaining position of BHPIO was held to be legal, so one interpretation of the judgement was that unions could be ignored on key terms in the bargaining process.
75   *Fair Work Act 2009* (Cth) s 228, discussed in Chapter 4.
76   For a further discussion of this see Floyd 'The *Fair Work Act*'s forgotten issues: why Richard Tracey's study of trade union regulation and the issues in the High Court's McJannet decision are worth a second thought' (2010) 33(3) *Australian Bar Review* 276–92.

employed other than by corporations made up the majority of those still under the Queensland Act. Not surprisingly, Queensland, along with most other State governments and some unions, embarked on a High Court constitutional challenge to the new national system.

NEW SOUTH WALES *v* COMMONWEALTH (2006) 229 CLR 1

The applicants raised questions as to the constitutional validity of the WorkChoices legislation and its reliance on the corporations power to ground a new national industrial relations system. Their arguments included:

- That the new system used the corporations power for a purpose that was beyond contemplation when it was introduced into the Constitution. Unlike s 51(xxxv), which had been the subject of lively and vigorous debate about the position of workers in Australian society, there had been little debate about s 51(xx) and the British position had simply been adopted in Australia.
- The new legislation sought to use the corporations power to create a system to govern workers, and that was not naturally connected to a corporation's power.
- There was already a specialist industrial relations power and it should not be ignored.

In rejecting virtually every argument, the High Court (with Kirby and Callinan JJ dissenting) upheld the WorkChoices legislation. In the court's view, the Constitution was a living document, not something cast in the cement of history. The fact that there was an exclusive industrial relations (IR) power did not preclude the use of other powers in an IR forum (indeed government had been incrementally doing this for some time).[77] Further, there was not necessarily a disconnect between the operation of corporations and the conditions of those who worked for them. This broad interpretation of the corporations power dramatically expanded the ability of the Commonwealth to legislate on most matters pertaining to constitutional corporations.[78]

In the wake of *WorkChoices* there was some very technical litigation on whether particular entities were in fact constitutional corporations.[79] However, when Labor returned to power federally, in 2007, most of the States entered into negotiations to hand over their powers to the Commonwealth to form a 'national system'. At that time there was much talk of a new age of 'co-operative federalism'.[80]

These days the lion's share of the IR and employment law jurisdiction is Federal, apart from the various State public servants (for example). While some, such as Professor Stewart, appear to be ardent supporters of this move (it cuts down red tape, for example),[81] it is well worth spending some time on considering the place of the States.

---

77   See observation above about *Victoria v Commonwealth* (1996) 187 CLR 416.
78   See, for example, A Stewart and G Williams, *The WorkChoices Case: What the High Court said* (Federation Press, 2007).
79   See, for example, *Educang Ltd v QIRC & QIEU* (2006) QIC 43; 182 QGIG 491.
80   Floyd 'The *Fair Work Act*'s forgotten issues' 276–92.
81   A Stewart 'Testing the boundaries: towards a national system of labour regulation' in A Stewart and A Forsyth *Fair Work, The New Workplace Laws and the Work Choices Legacy* (Federation Press, 2009).

Systems such as that in Queensland had been real innovators in IR. At the height of the WorkChoices regime, its State-funded body, Wageline, provided invaluable free assistance to workers in terms of understanding their rights and investigating their problems. There have also been child labour protection laws in Queensland. Most importantly, the State systems were very well equipped to deal with workers in regional areas.

In States such as Queensland, the State-based Australian Workers' Union was richer than the Federal Australian Workers' Union and covered workers who were not even included in the Federal rules! So when the two bodies merge – as they are to do so under the national system – what are the guarantees that State employees (especially in regional and rural areas) will be effectively represented? How can regional workers be assured that their voices will be heard if senior management of a union is based in a capital city in a separate State? And given that the money of State unionists may end up in the Federal union's coffers (even though it may well have been contributed to advance State concerns), how can there be a reassurance funds will be used effectively?

The position as regards the changing laws on trade union governance is examined by Bill Steenson in Chapter 5 of this book. The present writer has also discussed these State-related issues in both the *Australian Bar Review* and *The International Lawyer*. One further idea was contemplated by Hon Justice Christine Wheeler: one day a State might raise the actual Federal compact – the State–Federal relations balance and the characterisation of Commonwealth power – in litigation.[82]

There were alternatives to the national system. We could have developed a harmonised system whereby the States would have legislation similar to that of the Commonwealth but not hand over power.

As highlighted in the final chapter of this book, perhaps the arguments associated with Brexit may cause people to reconsider the issues around State–Federal relations and regionalism in a globalised world.

3.25 The matrix of workplace law and tribunals

The discussion so far has centred on how we got to where we are and the important lingering questions around Federal–State relations and the position of regional workers. While the rest of this book deals with the details of the system, there are still some introductory concepts that need clarification. As acknowledged at the opening of this chapter, this area of the law involves rather technical, sometimes seemingly contradictory relationships – between industrial and employment law; case and statute law; and international and domestic law.

3.25.05 Employment and industrial or labour law

As a rule of thumb, 'employment' law is the law pertaining to the ongoing employment relationship, while 'labour' or 'industrial' law is the term used to discuss trade union-related

---

82   Hon Justice C Wheeler 'Shifting sands: implications and the Constitution' (2007) 81 *Australian Law Journal* 548–49 as cited in Floyd 'The *Fair Work Act*'s forgotten issues' 290 et seq.

laws. In recent times, both areas are sometimes referred to as 'workplace' law; some use the expression 'the law of work'.[83] That phraseology is interesting. It is similar to that used in occupational or workplace health and safety statutes, which speak of 'the worker' – it is a means of covering those who perform an act of work, be they employees or independent contractors (for example).

3.25.10 Case and statute law or common law and legislation

The obvious preliminary point is that cases can *exemplify* a statutory term (see Chapter 6, which examines cases which exemplify what is an unfair dismissal under the relevant statutory provisions). Further, cases can *explain* a term of a statute. For example, what constitutes causation in adverse action is considered at the end of this chapter. The distinction between the employment relationship and an employment contract, elaborated on in Chapter 2 and Chapter 6, is rather tricky – wrongful dismissal can end an employment relationship even though the contract of employment continues. Also, the common law (or case law) can *imply* certain duties into a contract of employment, as discussed in Chapter 2 – and these duties may not appear in any statute. But statute law may still prevent the contract from containing certain terms: discriminatory terms, and conditions of work that fall beneath the level of the statutory safety net (the National Employment Standards – see Chapter 4).

One might ask how this web of statute and case law can impact the terms and conditions under which one works. Below are some starting points when endeavouring to answer the question: What are my terms and conditions of employment? The question is easy to ask but tricky to answer. It is worth reprising here the major points from the author's *Employment Law in a Nutshell*:

- Start with the written words of the contract. Ensure that what is offered is not below the statutory safety net (National Employment Standards) or in breach of other relevant statutes (such as anti-discrimination laws). It may be hard to argue that spoken words (if someone promised a one-year contract would be renewed, for example) are contractually binding. It is always best to get those things in writing.
- The common law may imply into the contract the sorts of duties discussed in Chapter 2, but the scope of some of those implied duties and their utility is still unclear.
- Especially if you are working in an industry that was traditionally unionised, there may be a modern award (a type of industry standard) or enterprise bargain (a detailed agreement governing a specific workplace) which forms part of the terms of employment, but is not usually part of the contract. (The legal status of these agreements influences which remedies are available in the event of a breach. See Chapter 4.)
- As well as the contract of employment, there may be workplace policies. Their status, too, is often contested: it may not be clear whether or not they bind both employer and employee.

---

83   For example, R Owens and J Riley *The Law of Work* (Oxford University Press, 2007).

- If you are employed in specialist employment – as a public servant, for example – there will be specialist law that is relevant, such as the *Public Service Act* (see Chapter 7).
- Specialist legislation on specific topics will often apply as well: anti-discrimination legislation, and superannuation and related tax laws, as well as workplace health and safety laws (see Chapter 8).
- Check unfair dismissal and other termination of employment legislation, and restraint of trade law, and see if any terms of the original contract were specifically directed at those areas.[84]

If you are not an employee but a contractor, some of the above may still be relevant. Superannuation is relevant to contractors, as is a lot of workplace health and safety law, and anti-discrimination law. Whether or not you are an employee, if you have worked in different jurisdictions or for a multinational, you may need to see whether or not there are conflicts of laws issues (see Chapter 9).

The laws pertaining to unions and bargaining exist alongside this framework as they regulate the process by which the bargains (that lay down terms of employment) are made, the rights the employee has within the union and, importantly, the obligations of unionists themselves.

3.25.15 Tribunals

When a problem arises in relation to terms and conditions of employment, a question to be resolved is which is the appropriate forum in which to raise a complaint. Some agreements will have an internal employer-specific complaints mechanism. As part of that process, or allied to it, there may be recourse to a union or employer group. If the matter cannot be resolved internally or if the employee has no confidence in the system, there might be an external avenue – someone in the public sector challenging an employment decision, for example, might have recourse to judicial review (Chapter 7); or an employee suffering harassment may take a matter to a discrimination tribunal (Chapter 8). An employee may take an unfair dismissal matter to the Fair Work Commission (FWC) (Chapter 6). It is often wise to seek professional advice in relation to complaints, as formal complaints are likely to affect the employment relationship, and if the relationship is fatally damaged, an employee might be awarded damages but still be out of a job. Further, where multiple issues arise in one dispute, there could be multiple tribunals and causes of action an employee may access, so advice as to choice of action and tribunal would be beneficial (see Chapter 6)

The FWC[85] is the modern equivalent of the Australian Industrial Relations Commission and, before that, the Conciliation and Arbitration Commission. These tribunals have an extremely rich history. Their decisions have shaped the terms and conditions of generations of Australian workers and put in place safety nets – in relation to redundancy, for example – that have benefited many workers. In addition, these tribunals have traditionally regulated the bargaining process and unions. Very significantly, the Federal government has recently passed

---

84   L Floyd *Employment Law in a Nutshell* (Thomson Reuters, 2010).
85   Further details of its role and legislation can be found at https://www.fwc.gov.au.

legislation to establish separate regulation for unions and the building and construction industry (see Chapter 5).

3.25.20 The International Labour Organization (ILO)[86]

The final chapter of this book (Chapter 9) deals with the ILO and its contribution in the changing world of the 21st century. It is therefore important to establish what the body actually is, and what Australia's relationship to it is. We shall begin with its creation and aims.

As Valticos explains, the ILO was established by the Treaty of Versailles at the end of World War I.[87] The ILO would draw up conventions and recommendations in the area of labour law and these would form part of the member states' local laws once their Parliament had ratified the conventions and legislated them into domestic law.[88] The advent of the ILO was the product of a century of debate on international and national labour standards. From the beginning of the 19th century, British and French industrialists had argued that some type of international labour benchmark was supportive of trade, so that nations with lower labour standards could not gain an unfair advantage.[89] By the time of the signing of the Treaty of Versailles (1919), there was much more than trade at the heart of the ILO. It began to be recognised that labour costs were only part of the trade equation – competence and resources were also significant factors. Labour standards had additional benefits: they brought peace and social and economic stability, which was seen as particularly important after the war.[90] These ideals were recognised in the ILO Constitution – and fifty years later, in 1969, the ILO won a Nobel Peace Prize.[91]

As the organisation grew, it evolved.[92] In 1944, the ILO's Declaration of Philadelphia proclaimed:

> All human beings, irrespective of race, creed or sex, have a right to pursue both their material well-being and their spiritual development in conditions of freedom and dignity, of economic security and equal opportunity. [93]

The ILO saw unions and workplace democracy as facilitating peace and dignity, which led to its adoption of the Freedom of Association and Protection of the Right to Organise Convention 1948 (No. 87) and the Right to Organise and Collective Bargaining Convention 1949 (No. 98). These instruments together created international standards which provide workers with rights (enforceable at international law) to form and join trade unions, which can act as an effective body to represent and further the concerns of working people.[94]

---

86   Some of the material in this section and the discussion of adverse action is taken from Floyd 'Castles in the sand: a legal analysis of s 45D secondary boycotts – prohibitions and trade union power', unpublished LLM thesis, University of Queensland (1998); L Floyd, 'Weipa and the wharves: Australian strike law and its effects on trade union power' (1999) 18 *University of Tasmania Law Review* 65–125; and L Floyd 'Freedom of association (introduction to Pt XA)' (2000) *Federal Industrial Law* 3809–3810.3.
87   N Valticos and G Von Potobsky *International Labour Law* (Kluwer Law and Taxation, 2nd ed, 1995) 18.
88   Ibid.
89   Ibid 20–21.
90   Ibid 21 et seq; 24 et seq.
91   Ibid 25.
92   Ibid 25 et seq.
93   Declaration of Philadelphia. Annex, II(a), as cited in Valticos and Von Potobsky 19.
94   Valticos and Von Potobsky *International Labour Law* (1995) 93–94 et seq.

The other aspects of the ILO that are significant at this stage are its enforcement and review mechanisms. The ILO collects from and produces reports on the compliance of member states with its labour standards.[95] It works with developing nations such as China to give effect to its standards.[96] It can also hear complaints brought to it by parties.[97] The ILO performs valuable work which has improved the lives of workers. However, there are questions as to how effectively its recommendations can be enforced – this is an issue with many international law bodies. That problem is further considered in Chapter 9.[98]

3.30 A role for unions: freedom of association and adverse action

So far in the chapter, it has been observed that for all the structural reform of the Australian system, unions still have a significant place in the legislative scheme. Two aspects of that are freedom of association and adverse action.

Prior to the *Fair Work Act*, there were provisions addressing freedom of association in the *Workplace Relations Act 1996* (Cth) (*WR Act*): ss 298J, 298K, 298L and 298M.[99] Essentially, the provisions aimed to prevent one party altering the other's position to their detriment for a prohibited reason – these included union membership or refusal to join a union. There was some debate about the desirability of that situation. For much of the 20th century, Australian law had actually contained a statutory preference towards union membership,[100] and some argued that international law, too, aimed to foster unionism as a worker protection.[101] However, the British case *Young, James and Webster v United Kingdom* (1982) 4 EHRR 38 made the excellent point:

> To construe [the freedom of association article] as permitting every kind of compulsion in the field of trade union membership would strike at the very substance of the freedom it is designed to guarantee.

That UK decision involved workers who did not want to be compelled to join a union which was using membership money to support British Labour.

That debate aside, the importance of the law came to the fore in the infamous waterfront dispute in Australia.

95   Ibid 277 and 284, and V-Y Ghebali *The International Labour Organisation: A Case Study on the Evolution of UN Specialised Agencies* (Nijhoff Publishers, 1988).
96   Ghebali *The International Labour Organisation* (1988) 116–25.
97   Valticos and Von Potobsky *International Labour Law* (1995) 290 et seq. See also KP McEvoy and R Owen 'On a wing and a prayer: the pilots' dispute in the international context' (1993) 6 *Australian Journal of Labour Law* 1–3.
98   See also Valticos and Von Potobsky *International Labour Law* (1995) 290 et seq; 315.
99   See L Floyd 'Freedom of association (introduction to Pt XA)' (2000) *Federal Industrial Law* 3809–10.3. That original commentary dealt with ss 298K etc. It was updated when the provisions were renumbered: see L Floyd 'Freedom of association: introduction to Part 16' (2006) *Federal Industrial Law* 19 17063–68.
100   P Weeks *Trade Union Security Law: A Study of Preference and Compulsory Unionism* (Federation Press, 1995).
101   R Ben-Israel *International Labour Standards: The Case of Freedom to Strike* (Kluwer Law and Taxation, 1987) 8–10.

PATRICK STEVEDORES OPERATIONS NO. 2 PTY LTD v MARITIME UNION OF AUSTRALIA (1998) 195 CLR 1

Patrick Stevedoring reorganised its companies so that union stevedores (formerly employed wharfies) became labour for hire, through a company, the only real asset of which was a supply contract which effectively stated that the contract could be revoked without significant penalty if there was a disruption in the supply of labour.

On learning that Patricks was training an alternative, non-union workforce in Dubai, the Australian wharfies went on strike. That triggered the revocation term of the labour supply contract: termination of the agreement with limited compensation. The wharfies were laid off and the Dubai-trained non-union labour started work as replacements. The company that laid off the wharfies avoided claims of unfair dismissal due to its use of labour supply contracts. The company the Voluntary Administrators were trying to salvage (the one that had engaged the union labour) was worth next to nothing. Winding up the company so that there were no places left for union workers on the waterfront seemed highly likely.

The union, the Maritime Union of Australia (MUA), relied on the freedom of association provisions of the *WR Act* to argue that the corporate reorganisation stemmed from the employer's desire to remove the MUA and its members from the waterfront. To that end, the union relied on a minute of discussions between the Commonwealth Workplace Relations Minister's office and the stevedoring companies which spoke of 'what would be needed for the MUA's influence on the waterfront to be significantly weakened' and of carrying out 'well-prepared strategies to dismiss their workforce, and replace them with another'.[102] The union argument also claimed that the corporate restructure left the Voluntary Administrators as innocent agents who would have no choice but to shut down the corporation through which the unionists gained work. That closure would damage the MUA and its employee-members as there would be no employed MUA members on the wharves.

Before the Federal Court (North J at first instance, then the Full Court) the union had some success gaining an injunction.

Before the High Court the obvious was raised: how could an applicant win an action to guarantee work for union members when the company they gained work from was insolvent? After all, s 588G of the *Corporations Act 2001* (Cth) prevented a company trading while insolvent. There was one promising finding for the union in the High Court judgement: there was a serious question to be tried – whether or not the actions of the company (which were clearly altering the unionists' position to their detriment) were motivated by the workers' membership of the MUA.

In the event, the matter settled out of court and the unionists relied on the evidence described above to regain work for the union workforce in return for productivity increases and some redundancies. The unionists regained their jobs, the non-unionists left, and the waterfront increased its productivity for many years thereafter.

---

102 *Maritime Union of Australia v Patrick Stevedores (No. 3)* (1998) 153 ALR 602 at 610 ff per North J. See also Floyd 'Weipa and the wharves: Australian strike law' (1999) 113 et seq.

3.30.05 *Fair Work Act* provisions (elements of adverse action)

Adverse action is part of the general protections of the *Fair Work Act*, Part 3-1. Those general protections are broader than protecting freedom of association: Chapter 1 discussed the general protections against sham contracting, for instance.[103] Here we will concentrate on adverse action, especially in the context of exercising workplace rights or having some connection to membership or non-membership of a union. In other words, those matters broadly encompassing freedom of association or the exercise of rights flowing from an industrial instrument.[104]

Essentially, adverse action has three 'elements':

1. a workplace right, which is exercised (s 340), or the complainant was or was not a union member, or was taking industrial action (s 346);

2. action taken against the person which is adverse – such as dismissing the person or injuring them in their employment (see the table in s 342); and, crucially

3. the cause of that adverse action is the workplace right or union membership or non-membership (see ss 340 and 346).

So a worker (who was or was not a union member) experiencing negative treatment in the workplace will not automatically succeed in an adverse action claim – the exercise of the right or the status of union membership or non-membership must be the *driver* behind the adverse treatment.

Before discussing the case law on adverse action and causation, some further complexities in the legislation should be acknowledged. First, adverse action may be alleged by contractors who are not engaged; and employers technically may be able to access the provisions (see, for example, s 342).[105] Second, while those applying s 340 and following can treat the old ss 298K, L and M of the *WR Act* as a predecessor for purposes of statutory interpretation, Rinaldi et al.[106] argue that the newer *Fair Work Act* provisions cover a broader range of conduct – for example, including the giving of evidence against someone in proceedings – and that there are many uncertainties in the interpretation of the new Act. This is discussed below.

3.30.10 Causation – the crucial element

The central element of adverse action is causation – which was defined by the High Court of Australia in *Board of Bendigo Regional Institute of Technical and Further Education v Barclay* [2012] HCA 32 (*Barclay*).

---

103   The breadth of the series of provisions is also borne out by the objects of the Part, which include protection from discrimination (see s 336, which is given effect by s 351 et seq).

104   But even then, the legislation is sweeping in its operation, and covers other matters (broadly akin to freedom of association measures). See the review questions, and see s 342, s 355 (coercion) and s 353 (bargaining services fee).

105   For academic discussion of the ability of contractors to unionise see, for example, S McCrystal *The Right to Strike in Australia* (Federation Press, 2010); 'Collective bargaining beyond the boundaries of employment: a comparative analysis' (2014) 37(3) *Melbourne University Law Review* 662. As to employers and adverse action, the case law is testament to the fact that many of the adverse action, claims are brought by employees (see cases discussed below).

106   M Rinaldi et al. *Fair Work Legislation 2015* (Thomson Reuters, 2015).

BOARD OF BENDIGO REGIONAL INSTITUTE OF TECHNICAL AND FURTHER EDUCATION *v* BARCLAY (2012) 248 CLR 500

This case was the High Court of Australia's first consideration of the adverse action provisions and the authoritative judgement on the meaning of causation. The case found that 'the central question on causation was whether the exercise of a workplace right was a substantial and operative reason for the adverse action and, in determining what was a substantial and operative reason, the evidence of the person executing the action was relevant (and could be tested through cross examination)'.[107]

The case involved the actions of Mr Greg Barclay. Significantly, Mr Barclay was both a union representative at the Bendigo TAFE and a member of the team responsible for ensuring that the courses at Bendigo TAFE were accredited. In the former capacity, Mr Barclay sent an email to union members employed at Bendigo TAFE in these terms:[108]

> Hi all
>
> The flurry of activity across the Institution to prepare for the upcoming reaccreditation audit is getting to the pointy end with the material having been sent off for the auditors to look through prior to the visit in February.
>
> It has been reported by several members that they have witnessed or been asked to be part of producing false and fraudulent documents for the audit.
>
> It is stating the obvious but, DO NOT AGREE TO BE PART OF ANY ATTEMPT TO CREATE FALSE/FAUDULENT [sic] DOCUMENTATION OR PARTICIPATE IN THESE TYPES OF ACTIVITIES. If you have felt pressured to participate in this kind of activity please (as have several members to date) contact the AEU and seek their support and advice.
>
> Greg Barclay,
> President,
> BRIT AEU Sub Branch.

The Bendigo TAFE treated Mr Barclay's actions in sending this email as potential serious misconduct – why had he not informed them of the alleged problem, given the significance of the accreditation process and his role (as a TAFE employee) in that process? Why had he only circulated the email to union members?[109]

Confronted with suspension and possible further disciplinary action, Mr Barclay alleged adverse action (s 346) – the actions he was confronted with were clearly adverse and were, he alleged, brought about by his actions: it was as a union member and representative that he sent the email.[110]

The High Court found in favour of the TAFE College, relying on the evidence of Dr Louise Harvey, who also worked for the TAFE, who underscored:[111] the importance of the

---

107   Floyd and Spry 'Four burgeoning IR issues' 156 referring to *Barclay* at 59–65 per French CJ and Crennan J, at 104 and 121–9 per Gummow and Hayne JJ, and at 144–6 per Haydon J. This is not the same as a sole, dominant reason (see Gummow and Hayne JJ at 103–05).

108   Ibid [11] per French CJ and Crennan J.

109   *Barclay* at [12]–[14].

110   Ibid [23].

111   Ibid [12]–[30].

accreditation to the TAFE; Mr Barclay's direct role in that process; the requirement for possible issues (such as the ones raised by Mr Barclay) to be formally reported and investigated; and the fact this email may cast aspersions on the character of employees of the TAFE. Those were the substantial and operative reasons for the treatment of Mr Barclay and not his actions as a union representative. As Floyd and Spry note:[112]

> The High Court, especially Chief Justice French and Justice Crennan, held that it was 'erroneous to treat the onus imposed on an employer by s 361 as being heavier (or rendered impossible to discharge) because an employee affected by adverse action happens to be an officer of an industrial association'.[113] Instead, their Honours insisted, there should not be an advantage for a unionist which is not enjoyed by other workers.[114] Indeed, an employee's union position should not be regarded as 'something which can never be dissociated from adverse action'.[115] On the evidence, Dr Harvey's account of why she took the action she took should be accepted by the High Court (as it was at first instance) and it was a mistake to regard Mr Barclay's union position as something inherently intertwined with the matter.[116] For future cases, 'it is appropriate for a decision-maker to give positive evidence comparing the position of the employee affected by the adverse action with that of an employee who has no union involvement'.[117]

The case was quite a departure from the reasoning of the Full Federal Court, from which the matter was appealed.[118] After the High Court judgement the test became less liberal and more objective.[119] That is significant, not the least because under s 361, in adverse action claims, there is a reverse onus of proof as to causation: in other words, there is a presumption that the action was taken with intent. At a practical level, the case clearly demonstrates the importance of barristers drawing sufficient evidence if defending a claim on behalf of an accused employer. Further, the case makes it clear that the mere fact that a complainant is a union member undertaking union business will not always found a claim of adverse action.[120]

3.30.15 Workplace right

Essentially, under s 341 a workplace right includes a benefit or role stemming from a workplace law, instrument or ruling, as well as a process or proceeding, complaint or inquiry that

---

112   L Floyd and M Spry 'Four burgeoning IR issues' (2013) 160.
113   *Barclay* at [60] per French CJ and Crennan J.
114   Ibid.
115   Ibid [62].
116   Ibid [61] and [65].
117   Ibid [65].
118   See Floyd and Spry 'Four burgeoning IR issues for 2013 and beyond' (2013).
119   The case is especially important given s 360, which notes that the fact that a person has multiple reasons for doing something does not prevent an adverse action claim being made.
120   The later High Court decision in *Construction, Forestry, Mining and Energy Union v BHP Coal Pty Ltd (No. 3)* [2012] FCA 1218 is considered in the review questions at the end of this chapter.

may stem from such law or instrument. The section provides a list of examples, including cashing out leave, but protects some employers in the event of transfer of business.

There is a considerable body of case law on the meaning of s 341, and while those cases settle some matters, there are many boundaries which remain to be settled.[121] Rinaldi et al., in *Fair Work Legislation 2016–2017*, highlight some of the key questions about the meaning and scope of s 341:[122]

- Federal Court Judge Hon Justice Logan in *Australian Licenced Aircraft Engineers Association v Sunstate Airlines (Qld) Pty Ltd* (2012) 208 FCR 386 suggested that 'workplace instrument' does not include a law in relation to which employment is simply incidental. Interestingly, the *Superannuation Guarantee Charge Act 1992* (Cth) was found not to be a 'workplace law' in *Tattsbet Ltd v Morrow* (2015) 233 FCR 46. However, the *Equal Opportunity Act 1995* (Vic) was found to be a workplace law even though it regulates relationships in addition to employment (compare *Bayford v Maxxia Pty Ltd* (2011) 207 IR 50).

- There is also a split in the authorities as to whether a complaint must arise from a statutory or a contractual provision: *Murrihy v Betezy.com.au Pty Ltd* (2013) 238 IR 307 per Jessop J compared to *Shea v TRUenergy Services Pty Ltd (No. 6)* (2014) 242 IR 1 per Dodds-Streeton J.

- Further, some cases have found that a worker's complaint about management competency (rather than about the manner in which the worker has been treated by management) could not ground an action, while others have distinguished that reasoning (compare *Rowland v Alfred Health* [2014] FCA 2 with *Construction, Forestry, Mining and Energy Union v Pilbara Iron Company (Services) Pty Ltd (No. 3)* (2012) 64 AILR 101-659).

3.30.20 Adverse action

The meaning of adverse action is contained in s 342 and includes dismissal; injuring an employee in their employment; altering their position to their detriment; or discrimination against the employee. Clearly, the sort of treatment captured by the provision is broad.

The case of *Qantas Airways Ltd v Australian Licensed Aircraft Engineers Association* (2012) 202 FCR 244 outlines the importance of a 'real and substantial' detriment to the employee (even if no legal right was actually violated, for example suspending overseas postings for a group of staff). The case further notes that there may be detriment even when an act is directed at a group of employees, of whom the complainant is one.[123]

In contrast, there might not be a finding of adverse action where the act of investigation is taken on reasonable grounds or where an employer advertises externally for staff where there is no suitable internal applicant – when such an argument was raised in *Wolfe v Australia and*

---

121   An excellent discussion of this body of case law may be found in M Rinaldi et al. *Fair Work Legislation 2016–2017* (Thomson Reuters, 2016) 388 et seq.
122   Ibid Commentary on s 341.
123   This case is considered in detail in the review questions at the end of this chapter.

New Zealand Banking Group Ltd [2013] FMCA 65 the observation was made that the decision not to internally advertise did not decrease the terms the employee already had.

3.30.25 Procedure and remedies

In the event of dismissal, parties may take the matter to the Fair Work Commission, which in the first instance will try to settle matters. It is important to note the Chapter 6 table of actions available in the event of dismissal and the need for complainants to avoid double-dipping in terms of remedies.

SUMMARY

A central question for labour regulation is whether the contract of employment requires its own body of regulation beyond the common law of contract. Parallel to that question is the debate as to whether there should be collective power (unions) or the more individualist statutory floor of rights as a means of ensuring the conditions of workers. Theorists from Kahn-Freund to Wedderburn, and many Australian commentators, argue that the employment contract is special because there is a power imbalance between employers and employees, and employees cannot always easily switch jobs. In contrast, Hayek and others reject the power imbalance argument and instead argue that business-oriented laws lead to job creation, which is good for workers. The 'third way' of Professor Collins is the theory embraced by Australian law: that fairness and flexibility are mutually reinforcing, not mutually exclusive goals. To that end, the governing *Fair Work Act* includes both a statutory floor of rights (National Employment Standards) and a role for a statutory commission and unions (in, for example, enterprise bargaining), and the aims of the legislation acknowledge the importance of productivity, for business and the national economy as well as fairness. A fourth theory, favoured by Britain's (former) Cameron Government – the Big Society – argues for a reduced role for government and greater use of social enterprise. That theory in particular overtly supports the use of contractors and small business owners as alternatives to large businesses. It does not oppose unions *per se*, but favours smaller unions closely connected to their worker-members.

Those are the theories that drive labour law debate (which is a very policy-driven area of law), and that then find their expression in legislation. Over the years, legislation has evolved in terms of both the substance of industrial law and the constitutional powers used by the Federal government to pass industrial laws.

The Australian Constitution has a specialised industrial relations power, but that power did not directly create an industrial commission – it is a machinery provision, which facilitated the establishment by the Federal government of a commission which took submissions from representative unions and employer groups and then conciliated or arbitrated. That was part of the Deakin Settlement by which young Australia would emphasise the 'merits' of a dispute, rather than industrial strength (pure collective bargaining). This aimed to lay the foundation for a peaceful, egalitarian society. It had bipartisan support for much of the 20th century.

From the 1980s, however, Australian governments have used other heads of power (foreign affairs and corporations) in addition to or as an alternative to the original IR power. Those heads of power have been used to support laws covering areas ranging from unfair dismissal to enterprise bargaining.

The adoption of those laws has reflected Australia's commitment to international conventions (in the case of dismissal law) and to 'structural reform' in the economy (in the case of enterprise-based bargaining); it has also reflected ideological shifts of government. The high-water mark of this turning towards the corporations power as the constitutional basis of the Australian labour and employment law system was WorkChoices. The constitutional challenge to its reliance on the corporations power failed. The current system still shows significant reliance on the corporations power, so the Federal government has broad power in the field, and although traditional safeguards (such as unions and the FWC) still clearly have a strong legislative role, the importance of actual businesses (that is, enterprise bargaining) is also significant.

As mentioned above, until the 1980s there was a consensus on the Australian system of centralised unions, employer groups and a commission to conciliate and arbitrate claims. Despite its obvious fairness in that period, the system became cumbersome and based on industry standards, whereas the economy faced new challenges – technology, globalisation – which required flexible enterprise-based solutions. A new consensus emerged, supporting enterprise bargaining underpinned by the safety nets of the commission and unions. There were some other individualistic developments, such as AWAs – individual statutory contracts. The most radical change was WorkChoices, which essentially sought to remove the old safeguards and have only an extremely individualistic system. WorkChoices was rejected by the electorate. The present system aims to work for both business and unions, though it does include some measures aimed clearly at protecting unions (adverse action and the abolition of AWAs). There are statutory minimum standards, as well as the FWC to facilitate bargaining at the level of the workplace or enterprise.

The operation of the law obviously requires that there be tribunals. The FWC is a key industrial relations body in Australia, with newer legislation ushering in specialist governance of unions. There is also recourse to the common law court system in Australian industrial law, however: sometimes by way of appeal from the FWC and sometimes because of common law contractual issues (and in a few cases, by way of judicial review). The ILO sets standards which underpin some of Australia's labour laws. Recourse to the ILO is available, but like all international law measures, its enforcement capacity is lacking.

Despite the moves towards a 'third way' system, there is still a significant amount of statutory support for unions in Australia. In addition to the abolition of AWAs, and other matters discussed later in this book (such as the requirement for parties to bargain in good faith for an enterprise agreement), adverse action is one of the general protections of the *Fair Work Act*. Its predecessor was the freedom of association laws – it is an offence to inflict a detriment on a party due to union membership or non-membership – but it is broader. Its precise scope is still to be determined.

REVIEW QUESTIONS

1. Consider the reasoning of the High Court of Australia in *Construction, Forestry, Mining and Energy Union v BHP Coal Pty Ltd* (2014) 253 CLR 243. Critically analyse the relationship of that reasoning to the decision of the High Court in *Board of Bendigo Regional Institute of Technical and Further Education v Barclay* (2012) 248 CLR 500 and the effect of the case on claims made by unionists under s 346 of the *Fair Work Act*.

2. This chapter discusses the freedom of association laws, especially in connection with adverse action. There are further provisions of the *Fair Work Act* that deal with coercion, undue influence and misrepresentation. What are those provisions and what is their legal effect?

3. In light of the above questions, critically analyse the Full Federal Court of Australia decision in *Qantas Airways Ltd v Australian Licensed Aircraft Engineers Association* (2012) 202 FCR 244.

4. Practical exercise and discovery research:

    (a) This chapter provides a foundation for considering the history, role and functions of the FWC. At a practical level, what are the functions of the Commission? What sorts of cases does it have jurisdiction to hear? How do matters proceed? What is its relationship to other tribunals and government bodies?

    (b) If you are employed, work out your terms and conditions of employment, including the agreements, policies and awards applicable to your work.

5. Group debate or discussion. The above commentary on the theories of labour and the means of regulating labour and employment law raises questions as to the flexibility of the FWC as opposed to a reliance on statutory standards. Discuss that debate in light of the development of Australian law.

FURTHER READING

R Blanpain and E Engels *Comparative Labour Law and Industrial Law in Industrialized Market Economies* (Kluwer, 5th ed, 1993).

A Chapman 'Judicial method and the interpretation of industrial discrimination' (2015) 28 *Australian Journal of Labour Law (AJLL)* 1.

D Hall 'Deregulating the labour market in the pioneer state' (Legislative Comment)' (1988) 1 *AJLL* 59–69.

R Mitchell and M Rimmer 'Labour law, deregulation and flexibility in Australian industrial relations' (1990) 12 *Comparative Law Journal* 1–34.

A Orifici '*CFMEU v Endeavour Coal*: severing workplace rights from their organisational impact?' (2016) 29 *AJLL* 327.

A Stewart 'A question of balance: Labor's new vision for workplace regulation' (2009) 22 *AJLL* 3.

4 BARGAINING, AWARDS AND THE NATIONAL EMPLOYMENT STANDARDS

4.05 Overview: some basic concepts
4.05.05 What is enterprise bargaining?

Enterprise bargaining is the primary process by which employers and groups of employees collectively negotiate and agree terms and conditions of employment which will apply to their employment relationship.

There are many forms of enterprise bargaining. An informal discussion between a work team and their supervisor, if it leads to an agreement which is then followed in respect of that work team, can be categorised as enterprise bargaining. However, the term is mostly used to describe a formal process which takes place under either State or Federal industrial relations legislation. For the private sector, the legislation is the *Fair Work Act 2009* (Cth).[1]

The key characteristics of enterprise bargaining, which have changed incrementally over time as legislation has changed but which have remained relatively constant in practical application, are:

- Enterprise bargaining occurs between an employer, or in some cases a group of employers, and employees who are within a defined scope. In some cases, the scope can be as broad as the employees in a particular industry. In other cases, the scope can include all of an employer's employees. In other cases, the scope will be limited to particular employees, and in many cases, employees in one particular work location.

- There are formal rules which govern how enterprise bargaining can commence (and who has the capacity to commence it).

- Once commenced, there are rules which govern the obligations of all parties involved, including formal requirements in respect of administrative processes.

- Both the employer and employees, or different sub-groups of the relevant employees, are entitled to be represented by bargaining representatives. Trade unions are generally permitted to be bargaining representatives for employees who are their members or for employees within their eligibility rules who have not joined the union but who have appointed them as bargaining representatives. Under the *Fair Work Act* unions are in fact the default bargaining representative for their members and will have that role unless the employee appoints a different bargaining representative.

- Under the *Fair Work Act* and some of the State regimes, there are rules which govern the way in which parties to enterprise negotiations and their bargaining representatives must bargain. Under the *Fair Work Act* these are called the 'good faith bargaining' obligations.

- An enterprise agreement can generally only contain terms which are relevant to or which 'pertain' to the employment relationship between the employer and the relevant employees. Areas which have been contentious in this regard over the years include attempts to

---

1   Most States retain their powers over State and local government employees: *Industrial Relations Act 1996* (NSW); *Industrial Relations Act 1999* (Qld); *Fair Work Act 1994* (SA); *Industrial Relations Act 1984* (Tas); *Industrial Relations Act 1979* (WA). Victoria, the Northern Territory and the Australian Capital Territory (ACT) operate wholly within the Federal jurisdiction for employment law.

restrict the use of contractors, matters which deal with the relationship between the employer and a trade union, and clauses which attempt to set remuneration levels for employees of other entities.

- An agreement will be reached when a majority of employees have accepted an employer's proposal. It is not necessary for each individual employee to have agreed to the terms and conditions, and employees who disagree with the terms, and may have voted against them, will nonetheless be bound. New employees within the scope of the enterprise agreement will also be bound by it.

- Once agreed, an enterprise agreement must be formally approved by the relevant industrial tribunal; under the *Fair Work Act* this is the Fair Work Commission (FWC).

- When approving an enterprise agreement, the tribunal will have to be satisfied that employees are at least not disadvantaged in the terms and conditions as against the terms which would apply under an award. Under the current *Fair Work Act* regime they must be better off as against those terms. This has variously been called the 'no disadvantage test' or the 'better off overall test'.

- Once approved, enterprise agreements will override any applicable modern award and also, to the extent of inconsistency, an employment contract.

- Enterprise agreements take effect as a form of statutory instrument, and breach of an enterprise agreement will usually also constitute a breach of the legislation, which can result in civil penalties being ordered against the responsible party.

4.05.10 The historical context

As acknowledged in Chapter 3 of this book, enterprise agreements are a relatively new addition to the Australian industrial relations landscape. Until 1991, terms and conditions for employees were more commonly fixed on an industry basis through a system of centralised wage fixing, administered by the relevant State or Federal industrial tribunal. Individual employers were rarely directly represented in the public hearings by which terms and conditions were set in industry awards, and to the extent that they were represented it was through their industry bodies – for example, the Chambers of Commerce and Industry. Employees were similarly rarely ever represented directly; their interests were represented by trade unions.

One of the implications of the centralised wage fixing system was that common terms and conditions applied across industries, and employees working in the same industry in any part of the country could expect to receive the same terms and conditions. As a consequence, competition between businesses based on the terms and conditions they were able to offer employees was muted. Conversely, there was little capacity for a business which could not afford to pay the prevailing award conditions to compete based on its capacity to attract and maintain employees who were prepared to work for lesser terms.

The first cracks in this system occurred in 1991, when the Minister in the Hawke Labor Government, with support from the then President of the Australian Council of Trade Unions (ACTU), Bill Kelty, urged the Australian Industrial Relations Commission (AIRC) to allow a limited system of bargaining on an enterprise-by-enterprise basis. On this occasion, the AIRC refused the request, preferring to maintain the existing 'one size fits all' system.[2] However, the pursuit of a broader agenda to deregulate the economy at all levels (tariffs, trade barriers, competition policy and the labour market) continued, and the AIRC relented later in 1991, although with the following caveat:

> The submissions again revealed a diversity of opinions and a failure to confront practical problems. Despite this, the parties and interveners once more press us to move toward a more devolved system. Collectively, they have left to us the task of translating a general concept into workable arrangements. There is little prospect, it would seem, that further postponement will lead to more fully developed proposals or to the resolution of points of disagreement. Although the concerns expressed in our April decision have not been allayed, we are satisfied that a further and concerted effort should be made to improve the efficiency of enterprises. In all the circumstances confronting us, we are prepared, on balance, to determine an enterprise bargaining principle. In deciding the best way to proceed, we have taken account of the views of the parties and interveners and the need to limit the risks inherent in the approach chosen.[3]

The first machinery for a system of enterprise bargaining appeared in the *Industrial Relations Act 1988* (Cth) in 1992.[4] Ever since, enterprise bargaining has been the preferred mechanism for setting the terms and conditions which employees actually receive, and the award system has played the role of setting a minimum set of terms and conditions below which no employer may go (except in exceptional circumstances), whether or not they engage in enterprise bargaining.

The objective of enterprise bargaining – which remains embodied in the objects of the *Fair Work Act* and in specific objects of the enterprise bargaining provisions[5] – is to allow employers, cooperatively with their employees, to negotiate terms and conditions which are appropriate for the particular enterprise, and which allow productivity and efficiency improvements to be made in a cooperative and consensual way.

Not all stakeholders believe the system is effective in this regard; the enterprise bargaining framework has been criticised for its inflexibility and its administrative complexity and some employers have drawn the conclusion from their own experience with it that it provides an opportunity for employees to negotiate a pay rise without any genuine productivity benefits to the employer. Nevertheless, enterprise bargaining is a regular process for many employers, and for many is the primary way that they refresh and update the terms and conditions of employment in their workplace.

4.05.15 Why do employers and employees bargain for enterprise agreements?

The usual reasons why employers and employees (and the unions which represent them) will enter into enterprise bargaining negotiations may be summarised as follows:

---

2   *National Wage Case April 1991* (1991) 36 IR 120 at 156.
3   *National Wage Case October 1991* (1991) 39 IR 127 at 130.
4   Via the *Industrial Relations Legislation Amendment Act 1992* (Cth).
5   *Fair Work Act 2009* (Cth) ss 3 and 171.

- There may be inflexibility or inappropriate terms in the underlying modern award (which are necessarily a 'one size fits all' solution in the relevant industry), and the employer may wish to negotiate to eliminate those inflexibilities, usually in exchange for higher wages or other terms seen by employees as beneficial to them.

- Employers may see enterprise bargaining as a defensive process, because when an enterprise agreement is in force (which can be for up to 4 years[6]) employees are essentially prevented from taking industrial action in support of improved terms and conditions of employment.

- Employees, often represented by unions, may wish to negotiate terms and conditions more favourable than those contained in the relevant modern award. Wages are the most obvious example, but employees and unions also commonly seek improvements in relation to dispute resolution (for example, a guaranteed right to have disputes arbitrated by the industrial tribunal), restrictions on the employer's right to make employees redundant or to make changes to working arrangements (such as to rosters) without agreement, or, in some industries (for example, construction and mining), to restrict the employer's right to use contractors instead of directly employed workers to carry out particular tasks.

4.05.20 The minimum standards which underpin enterprise bargaining

Under the *Fair Work Act*, enterprise bargaining is underpinned by two sources of minimum standards: the National Employment Standards (NES) and the system of modern awards.

4.05.25 The National Employment Standards (NES)

The NES[7] are a set of statutory minimum employment terms which apply to all national system employees in Australia. The NES cover 10 basic employment terms:

- maximum weekly hours;
- flexible working hours;
- parental leave and related entitlements;
- annual leave entitlements;
- personal/carer's leave and compassionate leave;
- community service leave;
- long service leave;
- public holidays;
- notice of termination and redundancy entitlements; and
- the provision of the Fair Work Information Statement.

---

6   *Fair Work Act 2009* (Cth) s 186(5).
7   Ibid Ch. 2 Part 2-2.

Table 4.1 summarises the NES terms as at the time of publishing:

Table 4.1:   NES terms

Maximum weekly hours	The maximum hours an employee can be required to work are 38 hours per week, plus reasonable additional hours.
Requests for flexible working arrangements	An employee with more than 12 months' service may request a change in their working arrangements from their employer if they require flexibility because they:
	• are the parent, or have responsibility for the care, of a child who is of school age or younger;
	• are a carer (within the meaning of the *Carer Recognition Act 2010* (Cth));
	• have a disability;
	• are 55 or older;
	• are experiencing violence from a member of their family; or
	• provide care or support to a member of their immediate family or household, who requires care or support because they are experiencing violence from their family.
	If an employee is the parent of a child or has responsibility for the care of a child and is returning to work after taking parental or adoption leave, the employee may request to return to work on a part-time basis to help them care for the child.
	Employer must respond to request in writing within 21 days, stating whether employer grants or refuses the request.
	Employer may only refuse request on reasonable business grounds.
Parental leave (including pay)	Employee with more than 12 months' service is entitled to 12 months unpaid parental leave (maternity, paternity, adoption). Parents may only take 3 weeks of consecutive parental leave.
	Although not part of the NES, means-tested government-paid parental leave of up to 18 weeks based on federal minimum wage was introduced in January 2011 (in lieu of employee receiving baby bonus).
	Employees may request a further period of unpaid leave (up to 12 months). Employer must respond to the request in writing within 21 days, stating whether employer grants or refuses the request.
	Employer may only refuse request on reasonable business grounds.
	Employer has an obligation to consult with employee on parental leave if employer makes a decision that will have a significant effect on the status, pay or location of the employee's pre-parental leave position.
	Employee is entitled to return to pre-parental leave position – or, if it no longer exists, an available position for which they are qualified and suited.
Annual leave	Employee is entitled to take 4 weeks' annual leave per annum, or 5 weeks for shift workers.

Table 4.1   (cont.)

Maximum weekly hours	The maximum hours an employee can be required to work are 38 hours per week, plus reasonable additional hours.
	Employer must not unreasonably refuse a request by the employee to take annual leave and must pay the employee at the employee's base rate of pay for the employee's ordinary hours of work in the period. Employer and an award/agreement-free employee may agree on when and how annual leave may be taken by the employee. Employer may require an award/agreement-free employee to take a period of annual leave, but only if the requirement is reasonable. A requirement may be reasonable if, for example: • the employee has accrued an excessive amount of paid leave; or • the employee's enterprise is being shut down for a period. A modern award or enterprise agreement may include terms requiring an employee, or allowing for an employee to be required, to take paid annual leave in particular circumstances, but only if the requirement is reasonable. Employee covered by a modern award or enterprise agreement can only cash out annual leave if the award or agreement provides for this. If awards or agreements include cashing out terms, they must require: • that the employee's remaining accrued annual leave is not less than 4 weeks; • each period of cashed out leave needs to be covered by a separate agreement; and • employee to be paid full amount they would have been entitled to if they had taken the leave. Award/agreement-free employees may enter into an agreement with their employer regarding cashing out their annual leave. The employer cannot agree to cash out the employee's annual leave if it would result in the employee's remaining annual leave being less than 4 weeks. If the period during which an employee takes paid annual leave includes a period of other leave, for example personal leave or community service leave, the employee is taken not to be on annual leave for the period of that other leave or absence.
Personal/Carer's leave and compassionate leave	Employee is entitled to: • 10 days paid personal/carer's leave per annum; • up to 2 days unpaid carer's leave per occasion (if paid personal/carer's leave is exhausted); and • up to 2 days paid compassionate leave per occasion.

Table 4.1   (cont.)

Maximum weekly hours	The maximum hours an employee can be required to work are 38 hours per week, plus reasonable additional hours.
	Casual employees are entitled to unpaid carer's leave and compassionate leave.
	There is no cap on the amount of personal/carer's leave that an employee can take in a 12-month period.
	Modern awards or enterprise agreements may provide for cashing out of personal/carer's leave. The employer cannot agree to cash out the leave if it would result in their remaining personal/carer's leave balance being less than 15 days.
	Award/agreement-free employees cannot cash out personal/carer's leave.
Community service leave	Employee who engages in an eligible community service activity is entitled to be absent from his or her employment.
	If employee is absent because of jury service, employer is required to 'top up' the employee's base rate of pay for the first 10 days.
Long service leave	Employee's entitlement to long service leave is derived from an award, industrial instrument or State legislation depending on employee's circumstances.
Public holidays	Employee is entitled to be absent from employment on a public holiday and to be paid for that day.
	Employer may request an employee to work on a holiday if the request is reasonable. An employee can refuse a request to work in certain circumstances.
Notice of termination and redundancy pay	Employer must give the following minimum notice of termination (or payment in lieu of notice):

Notice of termination and redundancy pay:

- not more than 1 year of service – 1 week
- more than 1 year but not more than 3 years – 2 weeks
- more than 3 years but not more than 5 years – 3 weeks
- more than 5 years – 4 weeks.

The notice period is increased by 1 week if the employee is over 45 years of age and has completed at least 2 years of service with the employer.
Notice must be in writing and must specify the termination date.
An employee is entitled to redundancy pay if employment is terminated because:

- the employer no longer requires the job done by the employee to be done by anyone; or
- the employer is insolvent or bankrupt.

Employees who are made redundant are eligible to receive redundancy pay in accordance with the following:

Table 4.1 (cont.)

Maximum weekly hours	The maximum hours an employee can be required to work are 38 hours per week, plus reasonable additional hours.
	• at least 1 year but less than 2 years' service – 4 weeks • at least 2 years but less than 3 years – 6 weeks • at least 3 years but less than 4 years – 7 weeks • at least 4 years but less than 5 years – 8 weeks • at least 5 years but less than 6 years – 10 weeks • at least 6 years but less than 7 years – 11 weeks • at least 7 years but less than 8 years – 13 weeks • at least 8 years but less than 9 years – 14 weeks • at least 9 years but less than 10 years – 16 weeks • at least 10 years – 12 weeks Service before 1 January 2010 does not count for the above scale if the employee did not have redundancy pay entitlements before that date (for example, if they were award-free with no contractual entitlement). Employers are not obliged to pay redundancy pay if: • the employee's period of continuous service with the employer is less than 12 months; or • the employer is a small business employer.[8] Applications can be made to the Fair Work Commission to vary amount of redundancy pay (where other acceptable employment has been secured for the employee, for instance). 'Transfer of employment' situations may affect the obligation to pay redundancy pay.
Fair Work Information Statement	An employer must give each employee the Fair Work Information Statement before, or as soon as practicable after, the employee starts employment.

An enterprise agreement cannot exclude a term of the NES.[9] If an enterprise agreement contains a term which excludes a term of the NES it will not be approved. A term of an enterprise agreement has no effect to the extent that it excludes a term of the NES.

However, an enterprise agreement can include terms that the NES expressly permits it to include.[10] For example, an enterprise agreement may include terms providing for the cashing out of paid personal/carer's leave by an employee.[11]

---

8   Ibid s 23, which states that an employer is a *small business employer* at a particular time if the employer employs fewer than 15 employees at that time.
9   Ibid s 55(1).
10   Ibid s 55(2).
11   Ibid s 101.

To the extent that an enterprise agreement includes a term that the NES expressly permits it to include, then the NES operates subject to that term in the enterprise agreement.[12]

Enterprise agreements may also contain terms which are ancillary or incidental to the operation of the NES, or terms that supplement the NES, so long as the effect of those terms is not detrimental to an employee in comparison with their entitlement under the NES.[13] An example of a term of an enterprise agreement which is ancillary or incidental to the operation of the NES is a term which provides that, instead of taking paid annual leave at the rate of pay required under the NES, an employee may take twice as much leave at half that rate of pay. An example of a term which is supplementary to the NES is a term which provides that employees are to be paid for annual leave at a rate that is higher than the employee's base rate of pay (that is, higher than the NES requirement).

4.05.30 Modern awards

Modern awards are industry or occupation-based minimum employment standards which apply in addition to the NES. From 1 January 2010, Federal and State-based awards (pre-modern awards) were replaced by modern awards.

Section 134(1) of the *Fair Work Act* sets out the modern awards objective: namely that they, together with the NES, provide a fair and relevant minimum safety net of terms and conditions, taking into account:

(a)   relative living standards and the needs of the low paid; and

(b)   the need to encourage collective bargaining; and

(c)   the need to promote social inclusion through increased workforce participation;

(d)   the need to promote flexible modern work practices and the efficient and productive performance of work;

(da)   the need to provide additional remuneration for:

- employees working overtime;
- employees working unsocial, irregular or unpredictable hours;
- employees working on weekends or public holidays;
- employees working shifts;

(e)   the principle of equal remuneration for work of equal or comparable value;

(f)   the likely impact of any exercise of modern award powers on business, including on productivity, employment costs and the regulatory burden;

(g)   the need to ensure a simple, easy to understand, stable and sustainable modern award system for Australia that avoids unnecessary overlap of modern awards; and

(h)   the likely impact of any exercise of modern award powers on employment growth, inflation and the sustainability, performance and competitiveness of the national economy.

12   Ibid s 55(3).
13   Ibid s 55(4).

Each modern award establishes a single set of minimum conditions of employment for employers and employees who work in the same industries and occupations. In some respects these conditions mirror or supplement the NES terms, and in other respects they build on those terms.

4.05.35 Modern award reviews by the Fair Work Commission

Modern awards are intended to be subject to regular, systematic review by the FWC. Section 156 of the *Fair Work Act* obliges the FWC to conduct a review of all modern awards on a 4-yearly basis, and enables it to make determinations varying, creating or revoking modern awards in the process.

The 4-yearly review process has tended to be lengthy and cumbersome – the most recent review process commenced in 2014 and at the time of writing had not yet come to an end. Consequently, it has been the cause of a significant drain on not only the FWC's resources, but also those of employers, employer groups and unions involved in challenging or defending the terms of modern awards.[14]

Employer groups and unions have advocated for the abolition of the 4-yearly review process, on the basis that the present scheme is unsustainable because of the burden it places on all parties involved. Their position follows the Productivity Commission's recommendation (that the review process ought to cease due to the burden placed on parties and their resources). At the time of writing there is a bipartisan agreement to abolish the mandatory requirement for a four-year review.[15]

Modern award coverage

Modern awards cover employees performing work that has historically been regulated by awards. Employees in senior or management roles were traditionally not covered by awards, a situation which continues under the modern award regime.[16]

Apart from these exceptions, most Australian employees below managerial and executive level are covered by a modern award. All modern awards must contain terms setting out the employers, employees and organisations (unions, for example) who are to be covered by the award.[17] References to the employees to be covered by the award should be set out according to particular classes or categories of workers,[18] usually described with regard to the occupation or activities generally performed by those employees. Employers may similarly be listed by class, or can be individually named.[19]

High-income employees[20] who are covered by a modern award can elect to enter into a written guarantee of annual earnings. The effect of that guarantee will be that the relevant modern award will not apply to them (though they will continue to be covered by it for some

---

14   *Workplace Relations Framework – Productivity Commission Inquiry Report*, No. 76, 30 November 2015, 346.

15   Ibid.

16   *Fair Work Act 2009* (Cth) s 143(7).

17   Ibid s 143(1).

18   Ibid s 143(5)(b).

19   Ibid s 143(5)(a).

20   The high-income threshold changes each year as a result of the FWC's annual wage reviews. From 1 July 2016, it is $138,900.

purposes, notably the unfair dismissal jurisdiction). These employees continue to be covered by the NES.

Required content in modern awards

Modern awards usually include the following additional minimum conditions of employment, tailored to the needs of the particular industry or occupation:[21]

- minimum wages, classification structures and incentives;
- types of employment (full-time, part-time or casual);
- arrangements for when work is performed (hours of work, rostering and breaks);
- overtime and penalty rates;
- provision for annualised wage or salary arrangements;
- allowances;
- leave-related matters (including loading and when leave is to be taken);
- superannuation; and
- procedures for consultation and dispute settlement.

Modern awards must also contain a 'flexibility term',[22] allowing the award to be varied under an individual flexibility arrangement to meet the genuine needs of an individual employee and their employer – for example, starting and finishing work earlier to allow an employee to pick their children up from school.

However, employers will be required to ensure that such arrangements result in the employee being 'better off overall' than they would have been if no arrangement had been agreed. If an individual flexibility arrangement (IFA) is entered into, the relevant modern award will have effect as varied by the IFA. Originally, IFAs could be unilaterally terminated by either the employer or employee on 28 days' written notice.[23] The model flexibility term contained in awards was amended in 2013 to increase the notice period to 13 weeks to enhance the operational effectiveness of the model term in line with the modern awards objective.[24]

All modern awards must include a consultation clause that requires employers to notify all affected employees, and their representatives, if an employer has decided to introduce major changes within or around the workplace. Such changes could be in relation to the production, program, organisation, structure or technology, and must be likely to have significant effects on the company's employees. Significant effects include termination of employment, major changes in composition or operation of the business, changes to the size of the employer's workforce or skills required, the transfer of employees to other work locations and the restructuring of jobs.[25] Finally, modern awards must include a procedure for settling disputes about matters covered by the award or the NES.[26]

---

21 *Fair Work Act 2009* (Cth) s 139.
22 Ibid s 144.
23 Ibid s 145(4), noting that s 145 only applies in circumstances where the purported IFA does not meet the requirements of *Fair Work Act* s 144.
24 *Modern Awards Review 2012 Award Flexibility* (2013) 232 IR 159.
25 The requirement for a consultation clause is set by *Fair Work Act* ss 139(1)(j) and 145A. An example is clause 8 of the Black Coal Mining Industry Award 2010.
26 *Fair Work Act 2009* (Cth) s 146.

4.05.40 Relationship between enterprise agreements and other sources of employment terms

For those employees to whom an enterprise agreement applies, the enterprise agreement, in conjunction with the NES, will apply to the exclusion of the otherwise applicable award (except for minimum rates of pay).

Modern awards

Once approved (which requires the FWC to ensure that employees will be better off overall than if the applicable modern award applied), the modern award will be excluded from operation. However, the enterprise agreement can never provide for base rates of pay which are lower than the rates in the underlying award, and to this limited extent the award remains relevant.

Other enterprise agreements

Only one enterprise agreement can apply to an employee at any particular time.[27] An earlier enterprise agreement that applies to an employee in relation to particular employment will continue to apply, even if another enterprise agreement that covers the employee in relation to the same employment comes into operation, until the earlier agreement has passed its nominal expiry date. Once the earlier agreement has passed its nominal expiry date, it ceases to apply to the employee and can never again apply.[28]

Contracts and policies

For an employee covered by an enterprise agreement, their employment contract can contain terms and conditions which supplement the terms of the enterprise agreement (where the enterprise agreement is silent as to a particular matter, for example), or provide for terms and conditions which are move favourable than the enterprise agreement, but cannot undercut terms and conditions which are provided for in the enterprise agreement.

Unless an employment contract expressly states that terms of an enterprise agreement are incorporated into the contract, then the terms are unlikely to be so incorporated and will not take effect as contractual terms between the employer and the employee. A reference in an employment contract to an employee's employment being 'governed by', 'subject to' or 'as prescribed by' an enterprise agreement will normally be interpreted as providing a 'sign post' which identifies the separate application of the enterprise agreement, rather than as incorporating the terms of the enterprise agreement into the employment contract.[29]

An employer's policies may contain terms and conditions which are supplementary, ancillary or incidental to the terms of an enterprise agreement, but to the extent that they provide for terms and conditions which are less favourable than those contained in the enterprise agreement, the enterprise agreement terms will still prevail.

---

27   Ibid s 58(1).
28   Ibid s 58(2).
29   *Australian Workers' Union v BHP Iron-Ore Pty Ltd* (2001) 106 FCR 482; *ACTEW Corporation Ltd v Pangallo* (2002) 127 FCR 1; *Soliman v University of Technology, Sydney* (2008) 176 IR 183; *Gramotnev v Queensland University of Technology* (2015) 251 IR 448.

The general rule with respect to the incorporation of policies into enterprise agreements is that a simple reference in an enterprise agreement to a policy will not normally mean the policy is incorporated into the enterprise agreement unless that is plainly specified by the terms of the enterprise agreement.[30]

4.05.45 Who can bargain?

There are no restrictions on who can be covered by an enterprise agreement, and the *Fair Work Act* regime provides considerable flexibility in relation to both the employees who can be covered and the employers. Most enterprise agreements are between a single employer and a section of the employer's workforce;[31] usually (but not always) excluding managerial and executive staff. However, there is no reason why employees at any level cannot be included, and in some industries (notably the public sector and higher education) the enterprise agreements often cover quite senior employees.

More than one employer can be covered by one enterprise agreement.[32] Employers who are related (for example, in a group company situation) can negotiate an enterprise agreement which covers them and their respective workforces. So can distinct employers who are engaged in a common enterprise (a joint venture, for example). There is also the capacity for the Minister for Employment to grant any number of employers who have a so-called single interest (for example, employers who may not be related or associated but have a common focus, such as Catholic school employers or all the hospital employees in a particular State) authorisation to negotiate collectively.[33]

Other than within one of the circumstances where collective bargaining by multiple employers is permitted, neither employers nor their employees (or unions who represent them) are permitted to bargain on a 'pattern' basis,[34] namely where claims are made either by unions or by employers across multiple enterprises on an inflexibly 'pattern' basis.

Except in the case of so-called greenfields agreements[35] (agreements which are made between an employer and a union before any of the employees for a particular project have been employed) all enterprise agreements under the Federal system are made between an employer and the employees who are within the scope of the proposed enterprise agreement. The role of unions in these negotiations is to be a bargaining representative on behalf of their members. Previously in the Federal system, and still in most State systems, enterprise agreements could be made between an employer and a union or an employer directly with its employees. In practice, even where both models are available, there are very few real differences between an enterprise agreement made directly with a union and an enterprise agreement made with employees. In both cases the rights and obligations of the employer and employees are substantially the same.

---

30   *Australian Rail, Tram and Bus Industry Union v KDR Victoria Pty Ltd (t/as Yarra Trams)* [2013] FCA 330.
31   *Fair Work Act 2009* (Cth) s 172(2).
32   Ibid ss 172(2), 172(3) and 172(5).
33   Ibid ss 172(5)(c) and 247–52. See also *Stuartholme School v Independent Education Union of Australia* (2010) 192 IR 29. See also *Victorian Hospitals' Industrial Association* [2011] FWA 8376.
34   *Fair Work Act 2009* (Cth) s 412.
35   Ibid ss 172(2) and 172(4).

4.05.50 Who is covered by an enterprise agreement?

A crucial feature of enterprise bargaining is that although an enterprise agreement is made between an employer and the employees who are employed at the time the agreement is made,[36] the enterprise agreement will then cover all employees who are within the scope of the enterprise agreement at any time during the life of the enterprise agreement, including if they are recruited after the agreement is made.[37] One implication of this is that employees who join an organisation where there is an applicable enterprise agreement covering the work which the employee is recruited to do will not have a free choice in relation to his or her terms of employment.

This has not always been the case. From 1996 until the Rudd Government came to power in 2007 there was an option for employers and employees to enter into individual work agreements (called Australian Workplace Agreements or AWAs). These had features similar to those of an enterprise agreement but were not negotiated collectively. During that period, even if there was an enterprise agreement in place in the workplace, both current or prospective employees were entitled to make agreements in relation to terms of employment which would then apply only between the employer and that single employee.

Individual agreements of this kind have always been inconsistent with Labor Party industrial relations policy, and they were abolished shortly after the Rudd Government came to power.[38] At the time of writing, although there is business support for this option (and thousands of employees accepted the option when it was available), there has been no move to reintroduce it.

The scope of an enterprise agreement (or the employees who will be covered by it) is often a controversial matter during enterprise bargaining. It is not uncommon for employees and unions and the relevant employers to disagree in relation to scope. In some cases unions and employees want a broader scope. In the coal mining industry, for example, a point of contention is often whether or not supervisors and subordinate managers should be within the scope of the enterprise agreement which covers production and maintenance employees. In other cases, it will be the employer who wants a single enterprise agreement covering all classifications of employees (production, maintenance, administrative, clerical etc), whereas the unions which represent the different classification groups may want to have an enterprise agreement which just covers the group of employees they represent, without having their negotiation or their industrial terms linked to those applying to other sections of the workforce.

Issues of scope can be negotiated, like any other term.[39] However, the FWC (upon application by one party or another) also has the capacity to intervene by determining the scope of a particular enterprise agreement negotiation.[40]

---

36   Except in the case of greenfields agreements.
37   *Fair Work Act 2009* (Cth) ss 51–53.
38   Further, enterprise agreements cannot contain a term that provides a method by which an employee or employer may elect (unilaterally or otherwise) not to be covered by the agreement. A term of this sort is unlawful pursuant to *Fair Work Act* s 194(ba).
39   *Stuartholme School v Independent Education Union of Australia* (2010) 192 IR 29 at [16].
40   *Fair Work Act 2009* (Cth) ss 238–39. See also *United Firefighters' Union of Australia v Metropolitan Fire & Emergency Services Board* (2010) 193 IR 293.

The issue of scope within an enterprise agreement can be legally and industrially controversial in other ways. The only restriction on how many employees must be employed before an enterprise agreement can be made is that an enterprise agreement cannot be made with a single employee.[41] So, for example, there is nothing to prevent an employer making an enterprise agreement with a workforce of two individuals. Given that one implication of an enterprise agreement is that all future employees will be covered, this is often a concern for unions if they believe an employer is adopting a strategy of employing a few employees and making an enterprise agreement with them, on the basis that it may then cover a much larger workforce, none of whom will have the capacity to influence the terms and conditions under which they will be employed while the agreement operates.

The only qualification on an employer's right to select a group of employees as it chooses is that the group must be 'fairly chosen'.[42] To be 'fairly chosen', there must be a rational basis for the selection of the cohort, and no exclusion of employees on a basis which is capricious or not aligned with the operational structure of the organisation. This means, for example, that it would ordinarily not be available to an employer to pick a subset of employees doing similar work (perhaps on the basis that they wanted an enterprise agreement but others did not) and then negotiate directly with them to the exclusion of other employees who are in similar roles. In some circumstances it might equally not be fair to choose all the employees of an employer as a group covered by an agreement, because a minority group which had distinct industrial issues would be 'swamped' by superior numbers in a different work group.[43]

If an enterprise agreement does not cover all the employees of the employer or employers covered by the agreement, the Commission has to take into account whether the group chosen is 'geographically, operationally or organisationally distinct' in deciding whether it has been 'fairly' chosen.[44] The *Fair Work Act* does not specify how these matters are to be taken into account (in s 186(3A)), and the weight given to these considerations will differ according to the matter at hand. Consideration can also be given to the interests of employees who are excluded from the coverage of an agreement.

CIMECO PTY LTD v CONSTRUCTION, FORESTRY, MINING AND ENERGY UNION (2012) 219 IR 139 (CIMECO)

In *Cimeco*, a Full Bench of Fair Work Australia quashed a decision of Deputy President McCarthy to not approve an enterprise agreement on the basis that the group of employees covered by the particular agreement was not 'fairly chosen' within the meaning of s 186(3) of the *Fair Work Act*. The Full Bench held that the requirement that an enterprise agreement be made with the employees who 'will' be covered by the enterprise agreement meant there had to be legal certainty that they would be covered; that is, they would be employed by the relevant employer within the scope of the enterprise agreement at the time it was made. At

---

41   *Fair Work Act 2009* (Cth) s 172(6).
42   Ibid ss 186(3) and 186(3A).
43   *Re ANZ Stadium Casual Employees Enterprise Agreement 2009* [2010] FWAA 3758.
44   *Fair Work Act 2009* (Cth) s 186(3A).

first instance, McCarthy DP had held that 'for Cimeco to make an agreement of a geograph-ical nature, it should include a much more representative group of existing employees for that group to be regarded as fairly chosen'.[45] The Full Bench held that this statement was erroneous because an agreement can only be made by a vote of the employees who will be covered by it. They on to say that '[a] "much more representative group of existing employ-ees" cannot vote to make a geographically distinct agreement unless at the time of the vote they will be covered by that agreement'.[46]

The *Cimeco* decision is notable because of the literal interpretation of the term 'will be covered'. The phrase is used in several parts of the bargaining framework in contexts which suggests that such a literal meeting was not intended by Parliament; see the Full Federal Court decision in *Shop, Distributive and Allied Employees Association v ALDI Foods Pty Ltd* (2016) 245 FCR 155.

Bargaining with small groups of employees during a start-up phase has also led to controversy. The Full Court of the Federal Court in *Construction, Forestry, Mining and Energy Union v John Holland Pty Ltd* (2015) 228 FCR 297 (*John Holland*) and the Full Bench of the FWC in *Communications, Electrical, Electronic, Energy, Information, Postal, Plumbing and Allied Services Union of Australia and Australian Manufacturing Workers' Union Queensland Divisional Branch v Main People Pty Ltd* [2014] FWCFB 8429 (*Main People*)[47] accepted that there is nothing inherently problematic about an employer making an enterprise agreement with a limited number of employees, even when the intention is that the workforce will subsequently be significantly expanded. The union argument has consistently been that this is inconsistent with the aims of the bargaining framework because it disenfranchises employ-ees who are contemplated but not employed, but this has not been accepted. The FWC and the Federal Court have both firmly rejected the notion that it is inconsistent with the concept of 'fairly chosen' for an employer to make an agreement with a small cohort of employees who are the first employed, even when it is clear that the intention is to employ many more employees in similar classifications. An employer is, generally, at liberty to make an agreement with its employees at any time, irrespective of its future intentions in relation to the size of its workforce. However, caution must still be exercised, as Buchanan J noted in *John Holland*:[48]

There is no requirement that employees who vote to make an agreement must have been in employment for any length of time, and there is no requirement that they remain in employment after the agreement is made. Presumably, the presently employed members of such a group will act from self-interest, rather than from any particular concern for the interests of future employees. The potential for manipulation of the agreement-making procedures is, accordingly, a real one. However, no suggestion of that kind is made in the

---

45   *Cimeco Pty Ltd v Construction, Forestry, Mining and Energy Union* (2012) 219 IR 139 at [39].
46   Ibid [38].
47   *Communications, Electrical, Electronic, Energy, Information, Postal, Plumbing and Allied Services Union and Australian Manufacturing Workers' Union Queensland Division v Main People Pty Ltd* [2014] FWCFB 8429.
48   (2015) 228 FCR 297 at [33].

present case and the possibility may therefore be put to one side for the purpose of the discussion. That is an important consideration because it suggests, as the primary judge thought, that determination of whether the group of employees was fairly chosen in the present case needed to bring to account the business rationale for the choice, as well as deal with any possibility of unfair exploitation. It was not irrelevant in that assessment to bear in mind, as the primary judge said, that the agreement provided benefits, not detriments, for those to whom it would apply.

It is vitally important for employers and employees to take care in how they define the scope of the agreement – who will be covered. If there is ambiguity or uncertainty in relation to the way the scope is drafted, arguments may arise as to whether the right group of employees voted. One example can be seen in a series of related FWC and Federal Court decisions involving the Teys Australia Group. Consistent with industrial arrangements over many years, Teys had allowed a group of employees described as 'trainee supervisors' to vote in an enterprise agreement which was approved by a very narrow majority of the employees concerned. Upon challenge by the union (the AMIEU) the Full Bench eventually accepted that trainee supervisors were not within the scope of the enterprise agreement (as defined by the terms of the enterprise agreement itself) and therefore they should not have voted.[49]

Bargaining representatives (usually unions) can apply to be 'covered' by an enterprise agreement if it otherwise covers employees within the scope of their eligibility.[50] They must do so after an application for approval of the enterprise agreement is made to the FWC, but before the agreement is approved.[51]

4.05.55 What matters can be included in an enterprise agreement?

The *Fair Work Act* has specific rules in relation to what terms and what subject matter can be dealt with in an enterprise agreement.[52] The basic rule is that an enterprise agreement can only contain terms which relate to or 'pertain' to the employment relationship between the employees and their employer.[53]

Under the 1996 changes introduced by the Howard Government the content of enterprise agreements was restricted to matters which pertained strictly to the relationship between employers and unions. This continued until the fall of the Howard Government in 2007, and in the *Fair Work Act* as it was introduced by the Rudd Labor Government, the matters which could be included in an enterprise agreement were extended to include matters pertaining to the relationship between the employer and unions covered by the agreement. This, for example, allowed enterprise agreements to contain terms about the rights which union officials and organisers would have within a particular workplace. However, other matters, such as

---

49   *Australasian Meat Industry Employees Union v Teys Australia Beenleigh Pty Ltd* (2014) 245 IR 170, upheld by the Full Court in *Teys Australia Beenleigh Pty Ltd v Australasian Meat Industry Employees Union* (2015) 234 FCR 405.
50   *Fair Work Act 2009* (Cth) s 53.
51   Ibid ss 183 and 201.
52   Ibid s 172.
53   Ibid s 172(1)(a).

right of entry, still may not be included in an enterprise agreement, and the statutory regime in respect of right of entry must prevail.[54]

The limits of what subject matter can be characterised as having a sufficient connection with the employment relationship to be allowable content in an enterprise agreement has been both legally and politically controversial. The aim of the general restriction to content directly relevant to the employment relationship is to ensure that negotiating parties cannot bargain for, and use their industrial weapons in support of, claims which, if agreed, would travel beyond the limits of the employment relationship. So a term which purported to fix the prices which an employer could charge for its product would not be permissible. Nor would a term which restricted employees' personal activities in ways which did not have any proper connection with employment. The essential principle emerging from a number of judgements is that a matter pertains to the employer–employee relationship if it affects employers and employees in their capacity as such.[55] However, as outlined by (then) French J in *Wesfarmers Premier Coal Ltd v Automotive, Food, Metals Engineering, Printing and Kindred Industries Union (No. 2)*:[56]

> The question whether a matter affects the relations of employer and employee in their 'capacity' as such has the potential to generate arcane debates about characterisation particularly where a person may be affected in more than one capacity. The Court should not … propose elaborate sub-principles to guide that characterisation. The process should be kept as simple and as straightforward as its language and judicial exegesis permits having regard to the practical consequences that may attend error.

It is now clear from the Explanatory Memorandum to the *Fair Work Act* that, despite earlier controversy, the following subject matter is 'permitted':[57]

- terms relating to particular staffing levels (subject to any other applicable legislative requirements or limitations), particularly if those terms are aimed at ensuring the health, safety and well-being of employees; and
- terms relating to conditions or requirements about employing casual employees or engaging labour hire or contractors if those terms sufficiently relate to employees' job security – for example, a term which provided that contractors must not be engaged on terms and conditions that would undercut the enterprise agreement (also known as a 'jump-up' or 'contractor' clause).

The determination as to whether a particular term is a matter pertaining to the employment relationship depends on the wording of the term in the context of the particular employment relationship.

One particular legal and political controversy relates to the extent to which content in an enterprise agreement can or should qualify or restrict an employer's capacity to engage contractors to perform work which might otherwise be carried out by employees (which is commonly sought as either a political or industrial objective by employees and unions on their behalf). The High Court in *Re Cram; Ex parte NSW Colliery Proprietors Association Ltd* (1987) 163 CLR 117 held that a dispute about manning and recruitment, in particular about the mode of recruitment, was a dispute

---

54   Terms or conditions in relation to right of entry are prohibited content: *Fair Work Act* s 152.
55   See, in particular, *Electrolux Home Products Pty Ltd v Australian Workers' Union* (2004) 221 CLR 309; *R v Portus; Ex parte ANZ Banking Group Ltd* (1972) 127 CLR 353 at 359 and 362; *R v Kelly; Ex parte Victoria* (1950) 81 CLR 64 at 84.
56   (2004) 138 IR 362 at [79].
57   See Fair Work Bill 2009 (Cth), Explanatory Memorandum [666]–[674].

as to 'industrial matters', since it impacted on and therefore pertained to the employer–employee relationship. This can be contrasted with the earlier High Court decision in *R v Commonwealth Industrial Court; Ex parte Cocks* (1968) 121 CLR 313, which held that a general prohibition on the engagement of independent contractors was not an 'industrial matter'.

WESFARMERS PREMIER COAL LIMITED *v* AUTOMOTIVE, FOOD, METALS ENGINEERING, PRINTING AND KINDRED INDUSTRIES UNION (NO. 2) (2004) 138 IR 362 (WESFARMERS)

One example where the line was crossed was in *Wesfarmers*, where French J found that a clause that restricts or qualifies the employer's right to use individual contractors imports into the proposed agreement a discrete matter which does not pertain to the employer–employee relationship. French J went on to say that a proposed agreement containing such a clause, and where the clause is not merely ancillary, but substantive and distinct, is not an agreement of the kind required by the legislation.[58]

CONSTRUCTION, FORESTRY, MINING AND ENERGY UNION *v* BROOKFIELD MULTIPLEX AUSTRALASIA PTY LTD (2012) 221 IR 15

Another more recent example is *CFMEU v Brookfield Multiplex Australasia Pty Ltd*. In that case, the 'contractor' clause proposed by the CFMEU extended to the regulation of the terms and conditions of subcontractors who performed work of a kind that would not be performed by any employee of Brookfield Multiplex who would be covered by the proposed agreement. In circumstances where Brookfield Multiplex did not intend to expand its workforce beyond the current classifications, the 'contractor' clause was found to travel beyond any ascertainable nexus with the relationship between Brookfield Multiplex and its employees who would be covered by the agreement.

Another area of controversy is the capacity for employees to negotiate for a term that employees must pay a so-called bargaining fee, which is a payment made by employees who choose not to join a union to compensate unions for the role that they commonly play in negotiating terms and conditions for all employees in the workplace, whether union members or not. Clauses of this kind were disavowed by the High Court in *Electrolux Home Products Pty Ltd v Australian Workers' Union* (2004) 221 CLR 309, following the High Court's earlier decision in *Re Alcan Australia Ltd; Ex parte Federation of Industrial, Manufacturing and Engineering Employees* (1994) 181 CLR 96. 'Bargaining fees' terms remain outlawed under the *Fair Work Act*,[59] but terms which permit deductions of union membership fees are permitted by s 172(c)

---

58   (2004) 138 IR 362 (*Wesfarmers*) at [109].
59   *Fair Work Act 2009* (Cth) s 353.

of the *Fair Work Act* (along with deductions authorised by employees who will be covered by the agreement for other purposes, called 'salary sacrificing').

Finally, s 172(1)(d) of the *Fair Work Act* permits an agreement to contain terms about how the agreement operates. As per the Fair Work Bill's Explanatory Memorandum, this could include terms setting out how and when the negotiations for a replacement agreement will be conducted, about the nominal expiry date or terms specifying who the agreement will cover (subject to s 186(3)).[60]

4.05.60 Mandatory content in enterprise agreements

The *Fair Work Act* prescribes that all enterprise agreements must contain some particular prescribed content, called 'mandatory' content.[61]

Currently, mandatory content includes a consultation clause which meets the requirements of the *Fair Work Act*,[62] including that shift changes must specifically be the subject of consultation before being introduced, and a dispute resolution procedure which provides for industrial disputes arising out of the terms or operation of the enterprise agreement or the NES to be resolved.[63]

RE WOOLWORTHS (T/AS PRODUCE AND RECYCLING DISTRIBUTION CENTRE) (2010) 194 IR 386

In *Re Woolworths* an issue arose concerning whether a dispute resolution clause needed to provide for compulsory arbitration if the dispute could not be resolved by discussions and conciliation. At first instance, the Commissioner rejected a Woolworths/SDA deal covering employees at a Melbourne distribution centre because it only empowered Fair Work Australia (as it then was) to arbitrate a dispute with the parties' agreement, on the basis that disputes might be left unresolved if there was no requirement for compulsory arbitration. However, a Full Bench found otherwise.[64] Having tracked through the history of industrial dispute resolution[65] and other parts of the *Fair Work Act*,[66] the Full Bench concluded that there was no reason to prescribe how a dispute must be 'resolved', and that, historically, dispute resolution processes had emphasised conciliation as a means of achieving an outcome, as well as arbitration. Accordingly, following this decision, a dispute resolution clause need not provide for compulsory arbitration if conciliation processes do not succeed. However, the dispute resolution clause must still provide for a mechanism pursuant to which disputes can be resolved.

It is common for the FWC to be identified as the independent body which will help parties resolve industrial disputes under their enterprise agreements, whether through conciliation or compulsory arbitration. Historically, the State and Federal industrial tribunals have had wide

---

60   Fair Work Bill 2009 (Cth), Explanatory Memorandum at [681].
61   *Fair Work Act 2009* (Cth) ss 202–205.
62   Ibid s 205.
63   Ibid s 186(6).
64   (2010) 194 IR 386.
65   Particularly *Appeals by Ampol Refineries (NSW) Pty Ltd and Australian Institute of Marine and Power Engineers* (1998) 43 AILR 3-724.
66   *Fair Work Act 2009* (Cth) ss 595 and 739.

powers to identify and resolve industrial disputes, limited only in the case of the Federal tribunal by a requirement that the dispute had an interstate aspect to it. When the Howard Government passed the *Workplace Relations Amendment (Work Choices) Act 2005* (Cth) it did not rely on the constitutional head of power which allows the Commonwealth Parliament to pass laws in relation to interstate industrial disputes,[67] and instead relied on the corporations power for most of the legislation,[68] including the enterprise bargaining provisions. The broad-based industrial disputes settlement powers were removed from the Commission, and were replaced with a regime whereby the Commission was only given a function to resolve industrial disputes if the parties themselves gave it that authority.

The extent to which the FWC could resolve disputes between industrial parties arising out of their enterprise agreements was also challenged on the basis that it was an impermissible exercise of judicial power by a tribunal which is not a Federal Court.[69] This controversy was laid to rest by the High Court in *Construction, Forestry, Mining and Energy Union v Australian Industrial Relations Commission* (2001) 203 CLR 645 (the private arbitration case) on the basis that the resolution of an industrial dispute pursuant to an authority given to the Commission by industrial parties was not an exercise of judicial power but rather a function given to the tribunal by the parties, and therefore the outcome of an arbitration was in effect an extension of the enterprise agreement itself. The critical finding made by the High Court in relation to the role of the Commission was that when exercising its powers under the dispute settlement clause in the Gordonstone coal certified agreement (certified agreements were the precursors to enterprise agreements under the *Fair Work Act*), the Commission exercises a power of *private arbitration*, being neither a judicial power nor an arbitral power under the relevant piece of industrial relations legislation. This was because the parties have agreed to submit disputes as to their legal rights and liabilities for resolution by a particular person or body and to accept the decision of that person as binding on them, in contrast to exercises of judicial power which are exercised independently of the consent of the person against whom the proceedings were brought and result in a judgement or order that is binding of its own force.

Although a dispute resolution clause in an enterprise agreement must provide for the resolution of disputes arising out of the enterprise agreement itself and the NES, the parties are free to expand the scope of the dispute resolution clause to all matters arising out of the employment relationship. Provisions of this kind give the FWC extraordinarily broad power to resolve disputes which arise in the workplace, as it is limited only by the particular clause itself.

Perhaps unsurprisingly, the limits of the Commission's power to intervene in a dispute between an employee and an employer have been legally controversial. A clause which allows the Commission to resolve disputes (including by arbitration) which arise broadly under the employment relationship can be, and has been, used to resolve disputes about performance management processes, promotion decisions, redundancy processes and many other circumstances.[70] An employer who has agreed in an enterprise agreement that the dispute resolution procedure will be as broad as this can expect that employees, or unions on their behalf, will

---

67   Constitution s 51(xxxv).
68   Ibid s 51(xx).
69   Chapter III of the Constitution commits power to make judicial determinations exclusively to the courts.
70   Some further examples include disputes about the payment of allowances under an enterprise
       agreement and back-pay issues.

utilise the machinery of the FWC to dispute any decision within the employment relationship to which they object.

There are two limitations on the FWC's authority to deal with disputes. First, the FWC has no jurisdiction to intervene until preceding steps in the dispute resolution process have been followed (for example, formal discussions at escalating levels of authority)[71] and a dispute which arises under one enterprise agreement cannot be pursued under a successor enterprise agreement unless the later enterprise agreement specifically reserves the employee's capacity to do so.[72]

4.05.65 Prohibited content in enterprise agreements

The *Fair Work Act* and all its predecessors have also identified content which may *not* be included in an enterprise agreement. Over the various iterations of the legislation, this has been described as 'objectionable', 'unlawful' or 'prohibited' content.

Under the *Fair Work Act*, the broad categories of content which are unlawful, and which may not be included in an enterprise agreement are set out in s 194. They include:

- discriminatory terms, which are defined by s 195 to mean terms which discriminate against an employee covered by the agreement because of, or for reasons which relate to, a protected attribute such as race, colour and age;
- objectionable terms, which is defined in s 12 to mean terms that:
  - require, have the effect of requiring, or purport to require or have the effect of requiring; or
  - permit, have the effect of permitting, or purport to permit or have the effect of permitting;
  either of the following:
    - a contravention of Part 3-1 (which deals with general protections);
    - the payment of a bargaining services fee.

CENTENNIAL NORTHERN MINING SERVICES PTY LTD v CONSTRUCTION, FORESTRY, MINING AND ENERGY UNION (NO 2) (2015) 247 IR 350 (CENTENNIAL)

In *Centennial*, Justice Buchanan held that a clause which capped an employee's redundancy payment by reference to their age was discriminatory (on the basis of age) and therefore unlawful. The effect of the retrenchment clause was that an employee over the age of 60 was not entitled to any payment. Buchanan J held that there had never been a

71   *Transport Workers' Union of Australia v Torrens Transit Services Pty Ltd* (2013) 236 IR 263 and *United Firefighters' Union of Australia v Country Fire Authority* [2013] FWC 7013.
72   *Construction, Forestry, Mining and Energy Union Mining and Energy Division Queensland District Branch v North Goonyella Coal Mines Pty Ltd* [2015] FWCFB 5619; *ING Administration Pty Ltd v Jajoo* (2006) 158 IR 239; *Telstra Corporation Ltd v Communications, Electrical, Electronic, Energy, Information, Postal, Plumbing and Allied Services Union of Australia* (2007) 163 IR 134; and *Deakin University v Rametta* (2010) 196 IR 42.

generally accepted industrial principle that employees approaching or passing some 'average' general age of retirement thereby became disentitled to payment for the generally accepted hardship of compulsory retrenchment. Because an employee was permitted to continue working after 60 years of age, a provision in an enterprise agreement which subjected them to disadvantage by reference to attaining that age was directly discriminatory against them on the ground of their age, and therefore unlawful.

An additional consequence of a particular term being prohibited under one of the above headings is that employees are not entitled to take protected industrial action in support of claims for an enterprise agreement which includes unlawful or non-permitted terms. Examples include:

- *Construction, Forestry, Mining and Energy Union v Brookfield Multiplex Australasia Pty Ltd*,[73] where the FWC refused to grant orders allowing a protected action ballot to take place (a precursor to the taking of protected industrial action) because of a finding that one of the union's claims on behalf of its members was not a term which sufficiently pertained to the employment relationship.
- *Construction, Forestry, Mining and Energy Union v AGL Loy Yang Pty Ltd (t/as AGL Loy Yang)* [2016] FWC 4364, where a Deputy President came to the same conclusion in relation to other clauses which were found not to be permissible content.
- *National Union of Workers v Phillip Leong Stores Pty Ltd* [2014] FWC 6459, where, amongst other things, a clause which limited casuals or contractors to 30 per cent of the permanent workforce was held to be outside the employment relationship and a non-permitted matter.

It is allowable for industrial parties to include content in an enterprise agreement by incorporating it from another document. The terms of the underlying modern award are often incorporated in this way, though this drafting style can lead to confusion and ambiguity as to what terms actually apply. A better course is to be very specific about what terms are incorporated.

Other types of documents which are commonly incorporated into enterprise agreements include workplace policies.

TEYS AUSTRALIA BEENLEIGH PTY LTD v AUSTRALASIAN MEAT INDUSTRY EMPLOYEES' UNION [2016] FCAFC 122

As is made clear in this case, although it is permissible under s 257 of the *Fair Work Act* for an incorporated document to be incorporated as it exists from time to time, the incorporated content cannot later effect a variation of the enterprise agreement itself. In *Teys*, the parties agreed to a term which allowed the union and the employer to subsequently reach an agreement which replaced the remuneration system in the enterprise agreement (for some employees) with a 'piece-rates' system. There was no such agreement in existence at the time the employees were asked to vote on the enterprise agreement, and it was only after the agreement was approved that the union and the employer reached agreement on a piece-rates system. The Full Court of the Federal Court (overturning a first instance decision which concluded that the incorporation was valid and did vary the enterprise agreement) made declarations to the effect that the piece-rates agreement was not incorporated and did not vary the enterprise agreement.

In some industries there have been policy decisions which have restricted the content in enterprise agreement in other ways. For example, in 2003 the Howard Government introduced the so-called Higher Education Workplace Relations Requirements (HEWRRs),[74] which made a condition of university funding that they eliminate from their enterprise agreements content which was viewed by the then government as unduly restrictive. These restrictions were unwound when the Rudd Government came to power in 2008, and most universities have subsequently agreed to reintroduce content which had to be stripped out during the HEWRR regime.

Similarly, in the building and construction industry, the Federal government has sought to regulate the content of enterprise agreements reached within the industry by making it a condition of tender for Commonwealth-funded projects that building industry participants do not have particular content in their enterprise agreements, content which would otherwise be lawful content under the *Fair Work Act*.

As is not uncommon, this policy has also waxed and waned over the years; during the Howard Government period the policy was highly prescriptive in relation to content, outlawing, for example, clauses which were viewed as interfering unduly with productivity and efficiency in construction workplaces, and requiring strict compliance with right of entry provisions.

In 2013, the then Employment Minister, Bill Shorten, promulgated the Building Code 2013 as a statutory instrument under the *Fair Work (Building Industry) Act 2012* (Cth). This Code[75] replaced the previous Guidelines (which had existed as policy only) but was far less prescriptive in relation to enterprise agreement content. The Turnbull Government subsequently passed legislation which meant that a new Code, containing significant restrictions on content, came into effect.[76]

4.05.70 The better off overall test (BOOT)

With the brief exception discussed in Chapter 3 (under WorkChoices), a consistent feature of enterprise agreements under all governments has been a requirement that employees be protected from having their terms and conditions reduced below the minimum standard, including the underlying award if one exists for the relevant employees.

---

74   Via the *Higher Education Support Act 2003* (Cth).

75   Which could be issued by the relevant Minister pursuant to the *Fair Work (Building Industry) Act 2012* (Cth) s 27.

76   The new code came into effect when the *Building and Construction Industry (Improving Productivity) Act 2016* (Cth) commenced operation on 2 December 2016.

For most of the history of enterprise bargaining, the test has been a 'no disadvantage test', which meant that employees could not be worse off, but did not have to be better off. Since 2010, the relevant test has been the 'better off overall test',[77] which contains the crucial difference that employees have to in fact be better off than they would have been under the award; it is not enough that they will be no worse off. Although the distinction seems minor, in some situations the application of the test can produce markedly different outcomes.

The application of the BOOT (as it has become known) is often a matter of considerable controversy. Although the test is expressed as a 'global' test (meaning that some terms can be traded off against others, as well as that the deal overall is better than the underlying award), in practice the FWC has been careful to ensure that terms in enterprise agreements do not sit below the relevant award in any respect unless the overall advantage to employees is very carefully explained.

Whether each and every employee has to be better off in all circumstances has also been controversial.

HART v COLES SUPERMARKETS AUSTRALIA PTY LTD AND BI-LO PTY LTD (T/AS COLES AND BI-LO) [2016] FWCFB 2887

This controversy was exposed in the Coles enterprise agreement approval process, when it was demonstrated that as a consequence of a negotiated reduction in penalty rates on weekends, some employees (who work predominantly on weekends) would be worse off even though the base rates in the enterprise agreement were higher than the modern award. Accordingly, even though the enterprise agreement was supported by the relevant union (the SDA) and was approved by a significant majority of employees, the FWC found that it could not be approved because, upon objection by one employee who could demonstrate that he would be worse off, it did not pass the BOOT for all employees in all circumstances.

The issue continues to be a controversial one, with many contractors and some members of the FWC maintaining that it was never intended for the test to be applied in such a technical and inflexible way, and that it should not be necessary to descend to an analysis of the import of the agreement in every conceivable work situation.[78] However, the wording of the test does suggest that all possible circumstances must be considered.

4.10 Bargaining for an enterprise agreement

In the Federal system, the *Fair Work Act* carefully prescribes the way bargaining must take place. There are administrative requirements, time prescriptions for particular steps and carefully defined processes which must be followed for the negotiation process to be valid.

---

77   *Fair Work Act 2009* (Cth) ss 186(2)(d) and 193.
78   *Beechworth Bakery Employee Co. Pty Ltd (t/as Beechworth Bakery)* [2016] FWCA 8862 at [6], reversed by *Shop, Distributive and Allied Employees Association v Beechworth Bakery Employee Co. Pty Ltd (t/as Beechworth Bakery)* [2017] FWCFB 1664.

4.10.05 How does bargaining commence?

There are several mandatory steps that must be taken when starting to bargain for a proposed enterprise agreement. Some of these steps have specific timeframes set by the *Fair Work Act*. If they are not met, the parties will be required to start again.[79]

The point at which the parties start the bargaining and agreement-making process, whether by agreement or by order of the Commission, is the 'notification time'. The notification time is the time when:[80]

(a) the employer agrees to bargain, or initiates bargaining, for the agreement; or

(b) a majority support determination in relation to the agreement comes into operation; or

(c) a scope order in relation to the agreement comes into operation; or

(d) a low-paid authorisation in relation to the agreement that specifies the employer comes into operation.

4.10.10 Majority support determination

If a majority of employees want to bargain with their employer to make an enterprise agreement but the employer has not yet agreed to bargain or initiated bargaining, a bargaining representative of the employees may apply to the Commission for a majority support determination (MSD).[81] As the name suggests, for an MSD to be made, the Commission must be satisfied that a majority of the employees who are employed by the employer at a time determined by the Commission who will be covered by a proposed agreement want to bargain.[82] The Commission can use any method it considers appropriate to work this out, including:

- a comparison of a petition signed by employees with a list of employees provided by an employer;[83] and

- ordering the Australian Electoral Commission to conduct a ballot of the relevant employees.[84]

There are a number of other factors which the Commission must take into account before it will issue an MSD:

- the employer or employers must not have agreed to bargain or initiated bargaining.[85] If an employer agrees to bargain after an application is made for an MSD, no MSD can be issued.[86]

---

79   For example, see *Fair Work Act* ss 173(3) and 180, discussed further below.
80   Ibid s 173(2).
81   Ibid ss 236–237, noting this only applies to a proposed single-enterprise agreement.
82   Ibid s 237(2)(a).
83   *Australasian Meat Industry Employees Union v Somerville Retail Services* [2012] FWA 7484; c.f. the outcome in *Australian Workers' Union v F Laucke Pty Ltd (t/as Laucke Mills)* [2013] FWC 4632.
84   *Australian Manufacturing Workers' Union v Cochlear Ltd* (2009) 186 IR 120, with the result of the ballot discussed in *Australian Manufacturing Workers' Union v Cochlear Ltd* (2009) 186 IR 122.
85   *Fair Work Act 2009* (Cth) s 237(2)(b).
86   *Australian Municipal, Administrative, Clerical and Services Union v Salvation Army (Peninsula Youth and Family Services)* [2013] FWC 6287.

Further, an MSD cannot be issued where an employer has agreed to bargain but does not agree with the scope or coverage of the agreement proposed:[87]

- whether the group of employees who will be covered by the agreement has been fairly chosen;[88] and
- it is reasonable in all the circumstances to make the MSD.[89]

If an MSD is made, the employer is required to bargain and triggers the notification time under s 173(2)(b) of the *Fair Work Act*. Once an MSD is issued, a bargaining representative is able to make an application for a protected action ballot order.[90] If the employer refuses to bargain, the employee bargaining representative may also seek a bargaining order to require the employer to meet the good faith bargaining requirements.[91]

4.10.15 Notice of employee representational rights

An employer that will be covered by a proposed enterprise agreement that is not a greenfields agreement[92] must take all reasonable steps to give notice of the right to be represented by a bargaining representative to each employee who:

- will be covered by the agreement; and
- is employed at the notification time for the proposed agreement.[93]

The notice of employee representational rights (NERR) must be given to each employee who will be covered by the proposed enterprise agreement as soon as practicable, and no later than 14 days, after the notification time.[94] If the NERR is issued after the 14-day period it is invalid, with the effect that no agreement can be approved by the Commission.[95]

NERRs must comply strictly with s 174 of the *Fair Work Act*. A failure to comply will, again, mean that no agreement can be approved by the Commission. The key case in this regard is *Peabody Moorvale Pty Ltd v Construction, Forestry, Mining and Energy Union* (*Peabody*).

PEABODY MOORVALE PTY LTD v CONSTRUCTION, FORESTRY, MINING AND ENERGY UNION (2014) 242 IR 210

In *Peabody*, the employer stapled two additional pages (containing forms for nominating a bargaining representative for the proposed enterprise agreement) to the NERR which was provided to employees.

---

87   *Liquor, Hospitality and Miscellaneous Union v Coca-Cola Amatil (Australia) Pty Ltd* (2009) 191 IR 124.
88   *Fair Work Act 2009* (Cth) ss 237(2)(c) and 237(3A).
89   Ibid s 237(2)(d).
90   Ibid s 437(2A), discussed further below.
91   Ibid s 230.
92   This is because there are no employees employed to give the notice to. No notice is required to be given to union(s) when negotiating a greenfields agreement.
93   *Fair Work Act 2009* (Cth) s 173(1).
94   Ibid s 173(3).
95   For example, *Transport Workers' Union of Australia v Hunter Operations Pty Ltd* [2014] FWC 7469.

A central issue in the case was the (then) relatively new s 174(1A) of the *Fair Work Act*, which came in force on 1 January 2013 under the Gillard Labor Government. The provision was in response to a recommendation from the Fair Work review panel that notice modifications should not be permitted and it was not sufficient for the notice to be substantially the same as the notice template. The amendment said the notice must contain the content and be in the form prescribed by the regulation and must not contain 'any other content'.

The five-member Full Bench held that under s 174(1), the notice template could not be changed. 'In our view [the *Fair Work Act*'s] s 174(1A) is clear and unambiguous,' it said. 'There is simply no capacity to depart from the form and content of the notice template provided in the regulations.' Any NERR that modifies the content or form of the notice template would be invalid. With respect to the additional pages stapled to the NERR by Peabody, the Full Bench said the question was whether those documents formed part of the NERR. In this case, the Full Bench held that they did form part of the NERR. As a result, the Full Bench found Peabody's NERR contained 'other content' and so did not comply with s 174(1A) of the *Fair Work Act* and was invalid.

The Full Bench did, however, state that s 174(1A) of the *Fair Work Act* did not preclude providing additional material or require the notice to be given in isolation. '[T]o construe the provision in that way would produce some absurd results. For example, it would prevent an employer from providing employees with a simple covering letter or an offer of interpreter services,' it said.

Following on from the decision in *Peabody*, the Full Bench in *Australian Maritime Officers' Union v Harbour City Ferries Pty Ltd* discussed (in obiter) whether an NERR deficient in a minor or trifling way would be a barrier to the agreement being approved, despite the operation of s 174(1A) of the *Fair Work Act*. The Full Bench stated that even minor and insignificant departures from the prescribed notice would not be in compliance applying a strict reading of s 174(1A). However, the Full Bench did go on to say, 'We accept that when [an NERR] contains a minor typographical error there may remain some room for judgement by a Commission member as to whether it renders the notice invalid.'[96]

Despite this optimistic statement, the FWC has found itself precluded from approving an enterprise agreement in circumstances where the NERR provided by the employer makes reference to the website of the FWC, rather than the website of the Fair Work Ombudsman (which is included in the prescribed form), on the basis that the reference to the incorrect website could not be described as being insignificant, minor or inconsequential.[97] The position has perhaps yet to be determined by the Federal Court, with Jessup J (with whom White J agreed) and Katzmann J making contrasting remarks in obiter in *Shop, Distributive and Allied Employees Association v ALDI Foods Pty Ltd*.[98]

---

96   (2015) 250 IR 1 at [38].
97   *Re Transit (NSW) Services Pty Ltd* [2016] FWC 2742.
98   (2016) 245 FCR 155.

4.10.20 Bargaining and the good faith bargaining requirements

Bargaining representatives are required to comply with the good faith bargaining obligations in the *Fair Work Act* during negotiations for enterprise agreements. These obligations establish what can described as the 'rules of engagement' and, if breached, can result in good faith bargaining orders being made by the FWC. If such an order is not complied with, the Commission can make a 'serious breach declaration', which can ultimately lead to the FWC arbitrating any outstanding matters, as well as parties potentially becoming liable for penalties in enforcement proceedings.

The obligations regulate parties' conduct during negotiations, but they do not require employers or employees to make concessions or reach agreement on any proposed terms. In fact, the Federal Court has overturned good faith bargaining orders made by the FWC which required an employer to accept certain bargaining proposals.

The good faith bargaining obligations are set out in s 228 of the *Fair Work Act* as follows:

- attend and participate in meetings at reasonable times;
- disclose relevant information (other than confidential or commercially sensitive information) in a timely manner;
- respond to bargaining proposals in a timely manner;
- genuinely consider proposals and give reasons for responses;
- refrain from capricious/unfair conduct that undermines freedom of association or collective bargaining; and
- recognise and bargain with other bargaining representatives.

These are administrative requirements which govern the process of negotiating the agreement – not the terms of the agreement itself.

Importantly, a bargaining representative is not required to:[99]

- make concessions during bargaining for an agreement; or
- reach agreement on terms to be included in an agreement.

A breach of the requirements is not a breach of the *Fair Work Act*. It means only that the FWC may make a good faith bargaining order.

Attendance

Bargaining representatives (including the employer) are required to attend and participate in meetings at reasonable times with other bargaining representatives until either bargaining has concluded or the employer has indicated an intention to put a proposal to a vote.

Denying a particular bargaining representative access to a bargaining meeting is likely to be a breach of good faith bargaining. This can be problematic if a small number of employees are members of a union but have not advised the employer of this membership. In these

---

99   *Fair Work Act 2009* (Cth) s 228(2).

circumstances the union will be the default bargaining representative for these employees, but that may not be known to the employer, and so the union may not be invited. An employer is required to recognise a bargaining representative as soon as they are identified and ask to be involved.

This obligation may require an employer to grant union delegates leave to attend bargaining meetings if reasonable to do so. What is 'reasonable' will depend on the circumstances, the number of delegates who seek to attend, the issues to be discussed and operational requirements.[100] However, there does not appear to be any requirement to pay employee bargaining representatives to attend bargaining meetings.[101]

The rationale is that the role of an employee bargaining representative is, essentially, a voluntary job. In some cases the existing enterprise agreement will provide for paid time for employee delegates to attend such meetings and there is no reason why this will not be enforceable.

Refusing to consent to a union holding meetings during work time to discuss industrial action has been held not to be a breach of good faith bargaining requirements.[102]

Disclosing relevant information in a timely manner

The key to complying with the obligation is determining whether the information sought is:

- 'relevant' to the negotiations – only relevant information is required to be disclosed; and
- 'confidential' or 'commercially sensitive' – which is not required to be disclosed even if it is relevant.

The FWC has determined that:

- Information that does not exist or is not in possession of the bargaining representative is not required to be disclosed or created.
- Information about the arrangement of hours of employees to be covered by the proposed agreement, and a comparison of payments to be made under the proposed agreement with the relevant modern award, was required to be disclosed.[103]
- If the employer does not assert an incapacity to pay a wage increase sought, it is not (absent other factors) required to disclose information about the financial affairs of the employer.[104]
- Failing to inform bargaining representatives that the employer is putting an agreement to a vote of employees can be a failure to provide relevant information to bargaining representatives.[105]

---

100   *Flinders Operating Services Pty Ltd v Australian Municipal, Administrative, Clerical and Services Union* (2010) 204 IR 1.

101   *Bowers v Victoria Police* [2011] FWA 2862.

102   *Liquor, Hospitality and Miscellaneous Union v Foster's Australia Ltd* [2009] FWA 750.

103   *Australian Municipal, Administrative, Clerical and Services Union v Aero-Care Flight Support Pty Ltd* [2012] FWA 7214.

104   *Queensland Nurses' Union of Employees v TriCare Ltd* [2010] FWA 7416.

105   *Alphington Aged Care and Sisters of St Joseph Health Care Services (Vic) (t/as Mary Mackillop Aged Care)* [2009] FWA 301.

Responding to proposals in a timely manner

Providing prompt responses to a bargaining representative's claims during bargaining is a relatively simple and important way to avoid breaching this obligation.

AUTOMOTIVE, FOOD, METALS, ENGINEERING, PRINTING AND KINDRED INDUSTRIES UNION v COCHLEAR LTD (2012) 231 IR 1

In *Automotive, Food, Metals, Engineering, Printing and Kindred Industries Union v Cochlear Ltd*, the FWC found that the company had not bargained in good faith because it failed to respond to the AMWU's proposal for an enterprise agreement in a timely manner and refused the union access to the lunch room for meetings with members. However, Cargill C said, 'a bargaining party cannot be required to bargain in any particular way or to put any particular type of response'.[106] Cargill C found that Cochlear was entitled to ask questions of the union in order to understand its claim, and its response to the union's claim – although a very minimal position – was not a breach. The problem was that the response took 6 or 7 months. The Commission found that there was nothing in Cochlear's response that could not have been put earlier, and that it had dragged out its response by refusing to respond until bargaining representatives had formally filled out the bargaining issues table. At least some positive engagement with the process is required.[107]

Genuinely consider proposals and give reasons for responses

The FWC and the Federal Court will not prescribe a set course for bargaining to follow, as the way that a bargaining process should be conducted varies from case to case. However, one party 'sitting mute' throughout the entire bargaining process or failing to put forward a counter-proposal may have failed to satisfy the good faith bargaining requirements.

ENDEAVOUR COAL PTY LTD v ASSOCIATION OF PROFESSIONAL ENGINEERS, SCIENTISTS AND MANAGERS, AUSTRALIA (2012) 217 IR 131 (ENDEAVOUR COAL)

In *Endeavour Coal*, a Full Bench of the FWC found that Endeavour had breached the good faith bargaining requirements by failing to genuinely bargain. While Endeavour had superficially complied with the formal requirements by participating in meetings and responding to the proposals put by the union, it did not show a genuine effort to bargain. Over a period of 12 months it did not present any proposals of its own. It took the view that APESMA needed to convince the company

---

106   (2012) 231 IR 1 at [545].
107   Ibid [545]–[546].

that it should make an agreement in the first place. In this case the employer did not want to bargain with the union at all. Bargaining commenced because the union successfully applied for a majority support determination. The company had never had an enterprise agreement for this group of employees. However, once bargaining commences, the employer is bound by the good faith bargaining obligations irrespective of its preference that bargaining not occur.

While there is no obligation to make substantive concessions during negotiations, employers are required to give genuine consideration to proposals and giving genuine reasons for rejecting a proposal. Otherwise, there is a risk that the employer will have engaged in 'surface bargaining'. Surface bargaining is a strategy in collective bargaining where one party merely 'goes through the motions' with no real intention of reaching an agreement. It can amount to a breach of good faith bargaining.

Refrain from capricious or unfair conduct

The Explanatory Memorandum of the *Fair Work Act* makes it clear that this obligation was intended to cover a broad range of conduct. It is the most widely used basis for criticising the behaviour of employers during bargaining.

The circumstances will be critical in determining whether particular conduct breaches this obligation. As a guide, the FWC has found the following conduct is not unfair or capricious:

- communicating directly with employees if the purpose is to influence employees rather than to negotiate directly with them;[108]

- putting a proposed enterprise agreement to a vote of employees without the agreement of the bargaining representatives when bargaining is at an impasse.[109] In contrast, it has been found to be 'capricious and unfair' to put an offer to bargaining representatives, and when the offer is not accepted treat negotiations as at an end, and then put a different offer to a vote of employees;[110]

- protected industrial action by the employer during negotiations (such as locking out employees);[111]

- restructuring during bargaining, subject to consultation requirements under an enterprise agreement or modern award;[112] and

- changing rosters for sound operational reasons.[113]

---

108   *Construction, Forestry, Mining and Energy Union v Tahmoor Coal Pty Ltd* (2010) 195 IR 58.

109   Ibid.

110   *Community and Public Sector Union v Victoria Legal Aid* [2013] FWC 1441; see also *Automotive, Food, Metals, Engineering, Printing and Kindred Industries Union v Coates Hire Operations Pty Ltd (t/as Coates Hire Ltd)* [2012] FWA 3357.

111   *United Voice v MSS Security Pty Ltd* [2013] FWC 4557.

112   *Liquor, Hospitality and Miscellaneous Union v Coca-Cola Amatil (Australia) Pty Ltd* [2009] FWA 153 and Transcript of Proceedings, *Construction, Forestry, Mining and Energy Union v Anglo Coal (Capcoal Management) Pty Ltd* (Fair Work Commission, Deputy President Abury, 17 November 2016). The decision was upheld on appeal: *Construction, Forestry, Mining and Energy Union v Anglo Coal (Capcoal Management) Pty Ltd (t/as Capcoal)* (2017) 262 IR 370.

113   *Australian Workers' Union v Woodside Energy Ltd* [2012] FWA 4332.

Withdrawing from previously expressed bargaining positions can amount to capricious behaviour in breach of the good faith bargaining obligations. However, a bargaining representative will not breach the obligations by withdrawing from previously agreed terms, clauses or conditions if:

- there are changed economic circumstances;[114] and/or
- some terms of an offer are removed in later bargaining after an offer has been put to employees and voted down.

An employer will usually be able to 'reset' its bargaining position in those circumstances.

In some circumstances changing positions on previously agreed terms will be a breach of the requirements. For example:

- Seeking scope orders late in bargaining (even where it had earlier disputed scope) has been found to be 'capricious' and inconsistent with good faith bargaining.[115]
- A union's action in suddenly increasing a wage claim from 5 per cent to 10 per cent following lengthy negotiation and two unsuccessful ballots was found to be a breach of good faith bargaining requirements. The Commission ordered the union to give genuine consideration to the proposals of other bargaining representatives and construct any of its proposals without increasing previously stated wage claims.[116]

An employer needs to be careful about altering terms and conditions of employment – particularly pay – during bargaining. The FWC has made several orders against employers who have unilaterally changed the terms and conditions of employees during the bargaining process.

There is no rule that an employer is prevented from providing a pay increase outside the enterprise agreement negotiation process, but employers should consult with bargaining representatives about any intention to do so, and should ensure that their wage position is consistent with their position in the negotiation (for example, they should not propose wage increases to employees which are higher than their negotiating position in the formal negotiation).

An employer might not be able to unilaterally offer pay increases (or alter employees' terms and conditions of employment) during bargaining in circumstances where it had said it was not in a position to discuss pay at the time of the negotiations. However, unilaterally granting pay increases may be acceptable where it is customary for the employer to do so at a particular time and the employer consults with bargaining representative about the proposed increases. In *Re Finance Sector Union of Australia* [2010] FWA 2690, for example, the FWC ordered the bank to give 24 hours' notice to the union of any information which changed its position on wage increases.

However in *Endeavour Coal*, a Full Bench of the FWC (supported on appeal to the Federal Court)[117] upheld an order preventing the employer from taking any further action to

---

114   *Construction, Forestry, Mining and Energy Union v Shingawa Refractories Australasia Pty Ltd* [2011] FWA 8304.

115   *Capral Ltd v Australian Manufacturing Workers' Union (Qld Branch)* [2010] FWA 3818.

116   *Australian Municipal, Administrative, Clerical and Services Union v NCR Australia Pty Ltd* [2010] FWA 6257.

117   *Endeavour Coal Pty Ltd v Association of Professional Engineers, Scientists and Managers, Australia* (2012) 206 FCR 576.

unilaterally alter terms and conditions of new staff, or terms in existing staff's contracts of employment, outside the enterprise bargaining process.

In *Australian Workers' Union v Woodside Energy Pty Ltd*,[118] the FWC found that Woodside had not breached the good faith bargaining requirements even though it introduced new rosters during the negotiations, as this did not affect bargaining. The Commission said that Woodside did not act unfairly or capriciously because it had discussions with some employees about new rosters.

Recognise and bargain with other bargaining representatives

Most cases in relation to this obligation concern an employer negotiating directly with employees, or resolving issues arising out of the challenges of juggling numerous bargaining representatives.

Some principles have emerged from case authorities:

• Where a bargaining representative indicates that they do not wish to participate in negotiations, it is not a breach of this obligation to proceed with negotiations without that representative.[119]

• Bargaining directly with employees without giving a bargaining representative an opportunity to be involved can be a breach of this obligation.[120]

• Conducting bargaining through a company's Joint Consultative Committee, which includes employees who are not bargaining representatives, is not a breach of this obligation provided that bargaining representatives are also advised of meetings and invited to participate.[121]

• Conducting separate bargaining meetings where there are multiple bargaining representatives is not, of itself, a breach of this obligation (although breaches could arise in some other circumstances, such as if the employer had different negotiating positions with each 'group').[122]

Breaches of the good faith bargaining obligations – what can happen?

The FWC has the power to make 'bargaining orders' enforcing the good faith bargaining obligations and has a broad discretion as to the types of orders it can make.[123] They include restraining a termination of employment, or making an order for reinstatement, with compensation, where an employee (for example, one who was a bargaining representative for other employees and who was a 'thorn in the employee's side' in the bargaining process) was dismissed.

The breach of a bargaining order attracts a penalty.[124] Where a bargaining representative has continually flouted bargaining orders, another bargaining representative can apply to the

118   [2012] FWA 4332.
119   *Construction, Forestry, Mining and Energy Union v Ostwald Brothers Pty Ltd* (2012) 64 AILR 101-565.
120   *Communications, Electrical, Electronic, Energy, Information, Postal and Allied Services Union v Pro-Built Control Pty Ltd* (2013) 230 IR 424.
121   *Australasian Meat Industry Employees Union v T & R (Murray Bridge) Pty Ltd* [2010] FWA 1320.
122   *Australasian Meat Industry Employees Union v Woolworths Ltd* (2009) 195 IR 5.
123   *Fair Work Act 2009* (Cth) ss 229–233.
124   Ibid s 233 (a civil penalty provision) and s 539.

FWC for a serious breach declaration[125] which, if made, leads to an arbitrated workplace determination.

4.15 Protected industrial action in support of claims

Industrial action is lawful (or 'protected') if it is taken by employees in support of the claims in an enterprise agreement negotiation process. An employer is also entitled to take protected industrial action (by 'locking out' employees in response to protected action by some or all of the employees who are proposed to be covered by the enterprise agreement).

Australian Bureau of Statistics data shows that even though industrial action can now be lawful, it is much rarer than it was 20 years ago, when many more employees were members of unions. In 1992, nearly 1 million days were lost to industrial action. For much of the 20th century levels of industrial action in Australia were relatively high.

Somewhat paradoxically, the pattern of disputation has changed dramatically since 1993, when workers and their unions were first given the capacity to lawfully engage in industrial action in the context of negotiation for enterprise agreements. Previously, almost any form of industrial action was unlawful, and could be the subject of injunction proceedings and actions for damages. The 'legitimising' of industrial action during the course of bargaining has in fact been associated with a decline in the overall incidence of industrial action.

There has been a similar fall in disputes in virtually all developed countries. That may be linked to the decline in the proportion of the workforce that is unionised, resulting in a reduced capacity for unions to mount effective campaigns to organise industrial action.

4.15.05 The definition of industrial action

Industrial action is defined broadly to cover any situation whereby employees work in a manner different from the customary manner. 'Industrial action' is defined in s 19 of the *Fair Work Act* to mean:

- the performance of work by an employee in a manner different from that in which it is customarily performed, or the adoption of a practice in relation to work by an employee;
- a ban, limitation or restriction on the performance of work by an employee or on the acceptance of or offering for work by an employee (for example, a formal ban on accepting overtime even if the working of overtime is strictly voluntary);
- a failure or refusal by employees to attend for work or a failure or refusal to perform any work at all by employees who attend for work;
- a lockout of employees from their employment by the employer of the employees.

All of these actions can also constitute protected industrial action provided certain administrative prerequisites are met, as set out in ss 413 and 414 of the *Fair Work Act*.

125   Ibid ss 234 and 235.

4.15.10 What is the significance of industrial action being protected?

The significance of industrial action being protected is that no action lies under any law (whether written or unwritten) in force in a State or Territory in relation to any industrial action unless the industrial action has involved or is likely to involve:

- personal injury; or
- wilful or reckless destruction of, or damage to, property; or
- the unlawful taking, keeping or use of property.[126]

However, a workforce which has taken protected industrial action is not 'protected' from the employee's legitimate responses to the harm caused by the industrial action, even where that response includes a restructuring which makes the roles of some of the employees redundant.[127]

4.15.15 Procedural requirements for protected industrial action

There are a number of procedural steps which must be taken before bargaining parties can lawfully take protected industrial action.

The FWC must first order that a secret ballot of employees take place. The process starts with an application by an employee bargaining representative, usually the union, for a protected action ballot order (PABO).[128]

Where an enterprise agreement is already in place, an application for a ballot can be made no earlier than 30 days before the nominal expiry date of the existing enterprise agreement.[129]

The bargaining representative(s) making the application for a PABO need to show that they have genuinely been trying to reach agreement with the employer.[130]

This is not a high threshold, but merely demonstrating that some meetings have taken place between the bargaining parties will not necessarily meet that threshold.[131] On the other hand, an impasse between the negotiating parties does not need to have been reached. As a Full Bench of the FWC said in *Total Marine Services v Maritime Union of Australia* (2009) 189 IR 407:

> [31] In our view the concept of genuinely trying to reach an agreement involves a finding of fact applied by reference to the circumstances of the particular negotiations. It is not useful to formulate any alternative test or criteria for applying the statutory test because it is the words of s 443 which must be applied ...

---

126   Ibid s 415, noting the exclusion relating to actions for defamation in s 415(2).
127   *Construction, Forestry, Mining and Energy Union v Anglo Coal (Capcoal Management) Pty Ltd (t/as Capcoal)* (2017) 262 IR 370.
128   *Fair Work Act 2009* (Cth) s 437, noting that there may be joint applicants pursuant to s 439.
129   Ibid s 438.
130   Ibid s 443(1).
131   Ibid s 443(1). See also *Construction, Forestry, Mining and Energy Union v Brookfield Multiplex Australasia Pty Ltd* [2012] FWA 3374.

[32] We agree that it is not appropriate or possible to establish rigid rules for the required point of negotiations that must be reached. All the relevant circumstances must be assessed to establish whether the applicant has met the test or not. This will frequently involve considering the extent of progress in negotiations and the steps taken in order to try and *reach* an agreement. At the very least one would normally expect the applicant to be able to demonstrate that it has clearly articulated the major items it is seeking for inclusion in the agreement, and to have provided a considered response to any demands made by the other side. Premature applications, where sufficient steps have not been taken to satisfy the test that the applicant has genuinely tried to reach an agreement, cannot be granted.

Until recently, a PABO could be made where an employer chose not to enter into any negotiations for an enterprise agreement. In *JJ Richards & Sons Pty Ltd v Fair Work Australia* (2012) 201 FCR 297, the Transport Workers' Union (TWU) requested that JJ Richards start negotiations for an enterprise agreement. JJ Richards did not agree to negotiate. In turn, the TWU made an application for a PABO. Ultimately, the Full Court of the Federal Court held that the FWC was mandated to make the order for a protected action ballot if the two conditions prescribed by s 443(1) of the *Fair Work Act* were satisfied, 'even if bargaining between an employer and employees has not commenced'.

After the *JJ Richards* decision, the Abbott/Turnbull Government inserted a new s 437(2A) into the *Fair Work Act*, which requires that there has been a notification time in relation to the proposed enterprise agreement. This now means that a PABO cannot be issued unless an employer:

- has initiated or agreed to bargain; or
- has been required to bargain through the making of an MSD or a scope order.

Applications for a PABO will not usually be granted if the applicant bargaining representative is seeking the inclusion of a term in the enterprise agreement outside the scope of those matters permitted under the *Fair Work Act*. If an applicant is or has been pursuing a substantive claim for a non-permitted matter, that is *relevant* to whether or not a party is genuinely trying to reach agreement. However, it is *not determinative* of the issue. In considering this issue, a Full Bench has explained that the diversity of factual circumstances and nuances in cases means that it is not possible that one factor or consideration will be determinative of the result.[132]

In *Esso*, the Full Bench determined that three unions who were seeking a clause restricting the employer's right to engage independent contractors were nevertheless genuinely trying to reach agreement. Such a term is clearly not permitted under s 172(1) of the *Fair Work Act* in new enterprise agreements. However, in the particular context, the unions were genuinely trying to reach agreement because:

- the non-permitted clause was merely a draft proposal;
- the unions had not adopted a rigid position in relation to the draft clause;
- the draft clause did not feature prominently in discussions between the parties;

---

132   *Esso Australia Pty Ltd v Automotive, Food, Metals, Engineering, Printing and Kindred Industries Union* (2015) 247 IR 5 (*Esso*). Cf. *Airport Fuel Services Pty Ltd v Transport Workers' Union* (2010) 195 IR 384.

- the employer never expressed a view in negotiations that the draft clause was a non-permitted term; and
- the draft clause was withdrawn before the end of the proceedings before the FWC.

The secret ballot process involves several more steps after an order is made by the FWC.[133] At least 50 per cent of the voters on the ballot roll (usually compiled by the Australian Electoral Commission) must vote, and more than 50 per cent of those voters must approve the action.[134] The voters can approve stoppages of varying lengths, including of an unlimited duration.[135]

Protected industrial action must also commence within 30 days of the result of the ballot being declared (although there is provision for one extension of a further 30 days).[136] Once a form of industrial action is taken once, and as long as the ballot authorises multiple instances of a particular form of industrial action, it can continue to be taken. Prior to taking protected action, the relevant bargaining representative must give the employer written notice of the 'employee claim action'.[137] This must be done at least 3 clear working days prior to the action occurring, and the notice must specify the nature of the action and the day on which it will start.[138] There is scope to increase the notification period up to 7 working days where there are exceptional circumstances, generally in relation to essential services important to the public interest, such as health services,[139] public transport services,[140] correctional services,[141] fire services,[142] the provision of power,[143] airport security,[144] power stations[145] and customs and border protection services.[146]

4.15.20 Suspending or terminating protected industrial action

In very limited circumstances the FWC can suspend or terminate protected industrial action.

One such circumstance (which is rarely satisfied) is the industrial action causing (or having the capacity to cause) significant economic harm to the bargaining participants and the dispute being unlikely to be resolved in the reasonably foreseeable future.[147]

---

133   *Fair Work Act 2009* (Cth) ss 449–458.
134   Ibid s 459.
135   The question or questions to be put to employees who are to balloted must be included in an application for a PABO – see *Fair Work Act* s 437(3).
136   *Fair Work Act* s 459.
137   Ibid ss 413–414.
138   Ibid s 414(2).
139   *Health Services Union v Victorian Institute of Forensic Mental Health* (2012) 222 IR 8; *Australian Nursing Federation v Victorian Hospitals Industrial Association* (2011) 214 IR 131.
140   *Transport Workers' Union of Australia v Chief Executive, ACT Internal Omnibus Network* [2010] FWA 3355; *Australian Rail, Tram and Bus Industry Union v Queensland Rail Ltd* [2011] FWA 6073.
141   *Community and Public Sector Union v G4S* [2011] FWA 2115.
142   *United Firefighters' Union of Australia v Country Fire Authority* [2013] FWC 5360.
143   *Re Construction, Forestry, Mining and Energy Union* [2013] FWC 2748; *Automotive, Food, Metals, Engineering, Printing and Kindred Industries Union v Clyde Babcock-Hitachi (Australia) Pty Ltd* [2011] FWA 2291.
144   *Transport Workers' Union of Australia v ISS Security Pty Ltd* [2012] FWA 7141.
145   *Re AGL Loy Yang Pty Ltd (t/as AGL Loy Yang)* (2017) 69 AILR 102-740.
146   *Community and Public Sector Union v Commonwealth Government – Australian Customs and Border Protection Service* [2011] FWA 3919.
147   *Fair Work Act 2009* (Cth) s 423.

The FWC must also make an order to suspend or terminate protected action that is being engaged in or is threatened, impending or probable if it is satisfied that the protected action has threatened, is threatening or would threaten:

- to endanger the life, personal safety or health, or the welfare of the population or of part of it; or
- to cause significant damage to the Australian economy or an important part of it.[148]

This latter ground led to the termination of the industrial action which had culminated in the worldwide grounding of the Qantas fleet in 2011.[149] There, the Minister for Workplace Relations made the application to terminate the lockout on the basis that it threatened to cause significant economic damage to the tourism and air transport industries and indirectly to industry generally because of the effect on consumers of air passenger and cargo services. The Qantas evidence was that the cost to it alone was $20 million per day.[150] The overall cost to the business community and dislocation to the flying public was incalculable.

This decision was eventually considered by the Full Federal Court,[151] which found the Full Bench decision to be within jurisdiction. The Full Federal Court found that there was no requirement for 'proportionality' in employer response action; the requirement was simply that the lockout was genuinely in 'response' to the employee action.

More recently, the FWC proceeded to terminate protected industrial action being taken by employees of the Department of Immigration and Border Protection on the basis that the protected industrial action was creating an 'unacceptable risk to the life, personal safety, health and welfare of the Australian community'.[152] Commissioner Wilson terminated protected action (rather than suspending it, as was sought by the employer) because suspension would have provided a 'non-permanent conclusion' to the bargaining dispute, which had been long-standing. More recently, the FWC terminated threatened industrial action at the Loy Yang A Power Station which, according to evidence, threatened to cause severe economic disruption and potential risk to safety in Victoria and South Australia.[153]

There is also scope for the FWC to make orders suspending protected action to give the bargaining representatives a chance to resolve the matters at issue without protected action,[154] and the Commission can also make an order to suspend protected action if it is causing significant harm to a third party.[155]

These powers are intended to only be used in exceptional circumstances, and usually where significant harm is being caused (or is likely to be caused) by the action. It is not intended that these mechanisms be capable of being triggered where the industrial action is merely causing an

---

148   Ibid s 424.
149   *Minister for Tertiary Education, Skills, Jobs and Workplace Relations* (2011) 214 IR 367. This decision was upheld on appeal to the Full Court of the Federal Court: *Australian and International Pilots Association v Fair Work Australia* (2012) 202 FCR 200.
150   *Re Minister for Tertiary Education, Skills, Jobs and Workplace Relations* [2011] FWAFB 7444 at [10].
151   *Australian and International Pilots Association v Fair Work Australia* (2012) 202 FCR 200.
152   *Commonwealth of Australia (represented by the Department of Immigration and Border Protection) v Community and Public Sector Union* [2016] FWC 7184 per Commissioner Wilson at [40].
153   *Minister for Industrial Relations for the State of Victoria v AGL Loy Yang Pty Ltd and others* [2017] FWC 2533.
154   *Fair Work Act 2009* (Cth) s 425.
155   Ibid s 426.

inconvenience. With respect to what amounts to 'significant economic harm', this is harm above and beyond the sort of loss, inconvenience or delay that is commonly a consequence of industrial action.[156]

The Minister has a power to make a 'declaration' terminating protected industrial action on the same grounds as the tribunal can under s 424 of the *Fair Work Act*, including to avoid significant damage to the economy.[157] This power has never been exercised as at the time of writing.

Once protected industrial action is terminated, the FWC must arbitrate the bargaining dispute and issue an order settling the applicable terms and conditions (called a 'determination') if the parties are unable to reach agreement during a compulsory 21-day post-termination bargaining period.

4.15.25 Prohibition on payments for periods of industrial action

Sections 470 to 473 of the *Fair Work Act* provide rules on payments relating to periods of protected and industrial action. Generally, employers are prohibited from paying employees who have failed or refused to attend for work for the total duration of any protected industrial action.

The general prohibition on strike pay does not apply in an unqualified way to partial work bans, other than overtime bans, that are protected industrial action. A more complex regime prevails. In that case employers can:

- choose to accept partial performance and pay in full;
- issue a partial work notice and reduce payments accordingly; or
- issue a notice rejecting partial performance and withhold payments altogether for the industrial action period, subject to notice requirements.

Accepting or seeking strike pay is unlawful, and is subject to civil penalty provisions under the *Fair Work Act*.[158]

4.20 The approval process
4.20.05 Pre-approval steps

When an employer believes a suitable proposed enterprise agreement has been negoti-ated (with or without the agreement of the other bargaining representatives), the employer may put the proposed enterprise agreement to a vote of the employees to

---

156   *Construction, Forestry, Mining and Energy Union v Woodside Burrup Pty Ltd* (2010) 198 IR 360, notwithstanding that Woodside was concerned with s 426 of the *Fair Work Act*; *Prysmian Power Cables and Systems Australia Pty Ltd v National Union of Workers* [2010] FWA 9402.
157   *Fair Work Act 2009* (Cth) s 431.
158   Ibid s 473.

be covered by the agreement.[159] The vote cannot be held until at least 21 days after the last NERR is provided to employees.[160] Before a vote can take place, the employer must comply with the procedural and administrative requirements of s 180 of the *Fair Work Act*.

The period commencing 7 clear days before the vote is called the 'access period'.[161] Before the access period commences, the employer must take all reasonable steps to inform the employees of the time and place where the vote will occur and the voting method that will be used.[162]

Employees must also be given, or have access to, a written version of the agreement and everything that is incorporated into the agreement by reference, such as the terms from a relevant award, during the 7-day access period.[163] Section 180 of the *Fair Work Act* also requires the employer to take 'all reasonable steps' to ensure that the terms of the agreement, and the effect of those terms, are explained to the relevant employees during the access period. In doing so, an employer is required to consider the particular needs of its workforce, giving consideration to such issues as the age of employees and whether employees are non-English speaking.[164]

A single-enterprise agreement will be made if a majority of employees who will be covered by a proposed agreement who vote cast a valid vote approve the agreement.[165] If a majority of employees vote against the agreement, it cannot come into operation. There is no prescribed format for a ballot (a 'show of hands' may suffice), but increasingly employees are utilising different forms of secret ballot, including postal votes, 'locked box' attendance ballots and electronic means, including email and text message formats.

4.20.10 Approval of an agreement by the FWC

If an enterprise agreement is made, the bargaining representatives for the agreement must apply to the FWC for approval of the agreement.[166] The application is usually made by the employer, although there is scope for the application to be made by any bargaining representative. If an employee organisation wants to be covered by the agreement, it is required to give written notice to the FWC and the employer before the agreement is approved.[167] Unions who are bargaining representatives are also able to advise the FWC whether or not they support the approval of a particular agreement. Where they indicate that they do not support the approval, there may be a contested hearing. Further, a union may seek to be heard in a matter where

---

159   Ibid s 181, noting the method for voting can be by any means such as a ballot, electronic or even a show of hands.
160   Ibid s 181(2).
161   Ibid s 180(4), though as is clear from *Re McKechnie Iron Foundry Pty Ltd Single Enterprise Agreement 2010* [2010] FWA 3171, the 7-day period is exclusive of the day the Notice is given and exclusive of the day the vote starts.
162   Ibid s 180(3).
163   Ibid s 180(2).
164   Ibid ss 180(5) and 180(6).
165   Ibid s 182(1). See s 182(2) for the requirements for a multi-enterprise agreement to be made, and s 182 (3) for when a greenfields agreement is made.
166   Ibid s 185.
167   Ibid s 183.

they have industrial coverage of the workers who would be covered by the enterprise agreement but the union was not a bargaining representative during the negotiation stage (usually in circumstances where all employees have appointed themselves or another person as bargaining agents rather than the union as a default bargaining agent).[168]

Subject to s 192 of the *Fair Work Act*, the FWC is bound to approve an enterprise agreement if it is satisfied that certain conditions are met, as set out in ss 186[169] and 187 of the *Fair Work Act*.

4.20.15 'Genuinely agreed'

One of the prerequisites in s 186 of the *Fair Work Act* is that 'the agreement has been genuinely agreed to by the employees covered by the agreement'.[170] The requirement that an agreement be 'genuinely agreed' is expressed in terms of satisfaction that particular bargaining provisions within the Act have been complied with (ss 188(a) and 188(b)) and satisfaction of a more general criterion in s 188(c) of the Act.[171] There is usually no scope for inquiry into the subjective beliefs of individual employees, although the Commission will consider and take into account any evidence that employees were misled about any aspect of the process or the effect of the terms of the agreement.

The approach to considering whether or not employees have genuinely agreed has been discussed in a number of cases, and similar provisions in earlier versions of the legislation, and was summarised by Deputy President Asbury in the decision of *Re Central Queensland Services Pty Ltd*[172] as follows:

- The circumstances to be considered are those that existed when the agreement was voted on.[173]

- A consideration of all relevant circumstances revealed by the material before the FWC, at the time it considers the application for approval, is required, in order to ascertain whether there are reasonable grounds for rejecting the genuineness of the agreement.[174]

- Circumstances including the provision of material or information to employees which has the character of being misleading or intimidating,[175] or where approval is affected by a material non-disclosure, or there is a scheme underpinning the agreement about which

168   See *Re Main People Pty Ltd Agreement 2014* [2015] FWC 2560, noting the power under s 590 of the *Fair Work Act* is discretionary.
169   Noting the discussion earlier in the chapter about whether the group of employees covered by the agreement is fairly chosen for the purpose of *Fair Work Act* ss 186(3) and 186(3A).
170   *Fair Work Act 2009* (Cth) ss 186(2)(a) and 188.
171   *Ostwald Brothers Pty Ltd v Construction, Forestry, Mining and Energy Union* (2012) 227 IR 134.
172   [2015] FWC 1554 at [65].
173   *CJ Manfield Pty Ltd v Communications, Electrical, Electronic, Energy, Information, Postal, Plumbing and Allied Services Union* [2012] FCA 253.
174   *Manfield Coalair and CEPU Electrical Division Northern Territory Enterprise Agreement Gove Alumina Refinery and Mine Site – 2010/2012* [2011] FWAA 9129.
175   *Peabody Moorvale Pty Ltd v Construction, Forestry, Mining and Energy Union* (2014) 242 IR 210 at [70] (Although this observation was made in the context of additional written material distributed at the same time as the Notice of Employee Representational Rights it is equally relevant in circumstances where oral presentations are made to employees); *Re MSS Security Pty Ltd* [2010] FWA 3687.

employees are not informed,[176] will be relevant to the FWC's assessment of whether or not the agreement has been genuinely agreed by the employees;

- Genuine agreement requires that the consent of employees was informed and that there was an absence of coercion.[177]

4.20.20 The BOOT

One of the key prerequisites for approval under s 186(2) of the *Fair Work Act* is the requirement that a proposed enterprise agreement pass the BOOT. As noted earlier in the chapter, the FWC needs to be satisfied that, weighing the agreement provisions as a whole with those in the relevant modern award or awards, an employee is better off overall.[178]

When the approval of an enterprise agreement by the FWC is contested on the basis that the elements in the enterprise agreement are inferior to the entitlements under a relevant modern award, the FWC will usually make an assessment of whether or not the alleged detriment does exist and, if it does, its nature and extent. Once that assessment has been made, the Commission may consider any counterbalancing features which may warrant a conclusion that despite the identified detriments, the employee is nevertheless better off overall.

Some employers have attempted to overcome issues with the BOOT by including 'make-good' clauses in enterprise agreements: clauses which create a mechanism by which an employee can request comparisons of the benefits they have received under the relevant agreement and what they would have received under a modern award. However, for the reasons outlined by White J (with whom Katzmann J agreed) in *Shop, Distributive and Allied Employees Association v ALDI Foods*, a clause of this sort could only be classified as a term being more beneficial to employees if the make-good clause entitles employees to a payment which is *more* than the award entitlement.[179]

4.20.25 Undertakings

Where the FWC has a concern that the agreement does not meet the requirements set out in ss 186 and 187 of the *Fair Work Act*, s 190 provides that the Commission may still approve an agreement if it is satisfied that a written undertaking from the employer covered by the agreement meets its concern. Generally, the concerns are limited to issues as to whether the agreement passes the BOOT or where a term might contravene the NES, though it may be possible for other concerns of the FWC to be cured by accepting undertakings.

---

176   *Grocon Pty Ltd Enterprise Agreement (Victoria)* (2003) 127 IR 13 at 48; *Manfield Coalair and CEPU Electrical Division Northern Territory enterprise agreement Gove Alumina Refinery and Mine Site – 2010–2012* [2011] FWAA 9129.

177   *Re Toys R Us (Australia) Pty Ltd Enterprise Flexibility Agreement 1994* Print L9066; *Grocon Pty Ltd Enterprise Agreement (Victoria)* (2003) 127 IR 13.

178   *National Tertiary Education Industry Union v University of New South Wales* (2011) 210 IR 244.

179   (2016) 245 FCR 155 at [151]–[174].

However, an undertaking can only be accepted if the Commission is satisfied that the effect of doing so is not likely to cause financial detriment to any employee covered by the agreement, or result in substantial changes to the agreement.[180]

4.20.30 Effect of approval of an enterprise agreement

Once an enterprise agreement has been approved by the FWC, it begins to operate on the date which is 7 days after the approval unless the agreement fixes a later date of commencement.[181] The agreement can itself set a later date of commencement of operation. Although an enterprise agreement cannot commence before the 7-day period has passed, the benefits of the agreement may be expressed to be payable from an earlier date (wage increases may be back-dated, for example).

Only one enterprise agreement can apply to an employee at a particular time as it relates to their particular employment.[182] If an earlier enterprise agreement applies to an employee in relation to particular employment, and a later enterprise agreement comes into operation, the coverage rules are as follows:

- if the earlier agreement has not passed its nominal expiry date – the later agreement cannot apply to the employee in relation to that employment until the earlier agreement passes its nominal expiry date;[183] or
- if the earlier agreement has passed its nominal expiry date – the earlier agreement ceases to apply to the employee when the later agreement comes into operation,[184] and
- once an agreement ceases to apply, it can never apply again.[185]

4.25 Enforcing rights and obligations under enterprise agreements

Enterprise agreements create obligations and entitlements for both employers and employees.[186] These obligations and entitlements can be enforced in various ways, including through a dispute resolution process[187] (which may result in the FWC arbitrating the dispute) or an

---

180   *Australasian Meat Industry Employees Union v Teys Australia Beenleigh Pty Ltd* (2014) 245 IR 170.
181   *Fair Work Act 2009* (Cth) s 54(1), noting that a later date can be included in an agreement per s 54(1)(b).
182   Ibid s 58(1).
183   Ibid s 58(2).
184   Ibid s 58(2).
185   Ibid s 54(3), noting that a subsequent quashing of the approval of an enterprise agreement has the effect that the 'new' enterprise agreement never existed and the 'old' enterprise agreement is taken to have always applied: *Teys Australia Beenleigh Pty Ltd v Australasian Meat Industry Employees Union* (2015) 230 FCR 565.
186   Ibid s 51, noting when enterprise agreements 'applies' to particular persons or organisations (ss 52 and 53 of the *Fair Work Act*).
187   Ibid ss 738–740.

enforcement application to either the Federal Circuit Court of Australia or the Federal Court of Australia.[188]

4.25.05 Dispute resolution

As noted earlier in the chapter, every enterprise agreement must contain clauses which provide for the resolution of disputes about matters arising under that agreement. Examples of the sort of disputes which have been dealt with this way are:

- *Communications, Electrical, Electronic, Energy, Information, Postal, Plumbing and Allied Services Union v Thiess Degremont Joint Venture* [2011] FWA 6698, in which the FWC dealt with a dispute concerning a roster change and the proposed redundancy of 160 electrical employees.
- *United Voice v Wilson Security* [2014] FWC 4550, where the Commission heard a dispute regarding arrangements that were to apply to employees (that is, the payment of accommodation expenses and overtime) when attendance at training was required by the employer.
- *Appo and Amos v Broadspectrum (Australia) Pty Ltd* [2016] FWC 7561, where the Commission dealt with a dispute regarding whether shift workers should be paid double time for all overtime worked.

4.25.10 Enforcing obligations via the courts

In some circumstances, parties to enterprise agreements will apply to the court when terms of enterprise agreements are alleged to have been breached.[189] The courts have wide powers under ss 545 and 546 of the *Fair Work Act* to make any order they consider appropriate, including orders for reinstatement, compensation, penalties and injunctions. Some examples are set out below:

- *CEPU v QR Ltd and Ors* (2010) 198 IR 382, where Logan J held that Queensland Rail employers had failed to fulfil the obligation contained in the relevant enterprise agreements to consult with employees about a proposal which affected the employees' terms and conditions of employment as a result of implementing a direction of the Queensland Government to privatise part of the QR business. As a consequence of the breaches, each employer was ordered to pay the maximum penalty[190] (although this was reduced on appeal).[191]
- *Construction, Forestry, Mining and Energy Union v North Goonyella Coal Mine Pty Ltd* [2013] FCA 1444, where the employer admitted (amongst other things) that it had breached a term of its enterprise agreement during a redundancy selection process when it selected certain employees for redundancy.

---

188   Ibid ss 50 and 539.
189   Noting that inspector can also bring proceedings pursuant to *Fair Work Act* s 539(2).
190   [2010] FCA 652.
191   (2010) 204 IR 142.

- *National Tertiary Education Union v Royal Melbourne Institute of Technology* (2013) 234 IR 139, where the employer was held to have failed to offer an employee the option of participating in a voluntary redeployment process during a redundancy process as required by its enterprise agreement.

- *Director, Fair Work Building Industry Inspectorate v Foxville Projects Group Pty Ltd* [2015] FCA 492, where the employer admitted (amongst other breaches) that it had breached various terms of its enterprise agreement by failing to confer certain entitlements onto specified employees.

- *Construction, Forestry, Mining and Energy Union v Hail Creek Coal Pty Ltd (No. 2)* [2016] FCA 727, where the employer was penalised for contravening a term of its enterprise agreement by denying six employees access to sick leave.

4.30 Varying and terminating enterprise agreements

4.30.05 Varying enterprise agreements

It is possible to vary an enterprise agreement once it has been approved by the FWC. First, employers and employees may agree to vary an enterprise agreement, but the variation has no effect unless it is approved by the FWC.[192] This process is similar to that which applies during the approval process. The varied enterprise agreement still has to pass the BOOT, but can be approved with undertakings.[193]

Although this process has similarities to the approval of a new enterprise agreement, there is no scope for protected industrial action to take place, the good faith bargaining obligations do not apply and there is no scope for bargaining orders to be sought or issued.[194] Of course, the FWC may consider whether or not the 'bargaining' for a variation has been altogether fair, as it needs to consider whether there has been 'genuine agreement' to the variation.[195]

One peculiar case involving a proposed variation of an enterprise agreement involved the Toyota Motor Corporation. Toyota's enterprise agreement contained a 'no further claims' clause which stated that the parties would not 'make any further claims in relation to wages or any other terms and conditions of employment' prior to the end of the agreement. At first instance, Justice Bromberg ruled that Toyota contravened that clause when it asked its employees to vote on 27 variations to the agreement.[196] However, on appeal, the Full Court accepted Toyota's argument that a no further claims clause was inconsistent with or repugnant to the *Fair Work Act* because it imposed restrictions on (but did not wholly exclude) on Toyota and its employees having access to the provisions of the Act which allowed variations of enterprise agreements to occur.[197]

---

192   *Fair Work Act 2009* (Cth) ss 207 and 211, noting a vote must take place in accordance with ss 208–209.
193   Ibid ss 212–213.
194   There is scope for the FWC to deal with a dispute about a proposed variation under s 217A of the *Fair Work Act*, but the Commission cannot arbitrate the dispute.
195   *Application by LCR Group Pty Ltd* [2015] FWC 7311.
196   *Marmara v Toyota Motor Corporation Australia Ltd* [2013] FCA 1351.
197   *Toyota Motor Corporation Australia Ltd v Marmara* (2014) 222 FCR 152.

An enterprise agreement may also be varied by the FWC to remove an ambiguity or uncertainty in the agreement.[198] An enterprise agreement can also be varied by the FWC if there is a referral by the Australian Human Rights Commission under s 218 of the *Fair Work Act*, where an enterprise agreement has the effect of requiring a person to do an act which is unlawful under certain pieces of anti-discrimination legislation.

4.30.10 Terminating enterprise agreements

There are two methods of terminating enterprise agreements. First, it can be done by agreement (which requires a majority of employees to support termination). This can take place at any time during the life of an agreement.[199] More controversial, however, are applications to terminate without agreement, where the FWC can only terminate an agreement if it is in the public interest and appropriate to do so, taking into account the views of the parties covered by the enterprise agreement and the likely effect of termination on them.[200]

Until recently, applications of this type (usually made by employers) have been repeatedly rejected by the industrial tribunal for the reasons summarised in *Re Tahmoor Coal Pty Ltd* (*Tahmoor Coal*).[201] In that case, Vice President Lawler held that although it was not intended by the legislation that agreements should remain in place indefinitely, and it is unreasonable to lock an expired agreement in place indefinitely, this does not mean that a party to an agreement has a prima facie right to have the agreement terminated merely because the agreement has passed its nominal expiry date.[202] Vice President Lawler went on to say:

> It seems to me that under the scheme of the FW Act, generally speaking, it will not be appropriate to terminate an agreement that has passed its nominal expiry date if bargaining for a replacement agreement is ongoing such that there remains a reasonable prospect that bargaining (in conjunction with protected industrial action and or employer response action) will result in a new agreement. This will be so even where the bargaining has become protracted because a party is advancing claims for changes that are particularly unpalatable to the other party. While every case will turn on its own circumstances, the precedence assigned to achieving productivity benefits through bargaining, evident in the objects of the FW Act, suggests that it will generally be inappropriate for FWA to interfere in the bargaining process so as to substantially alter the status quo in relation to the balance of bargaining between the parties so as to deliver to one of the bargaining parties effectively all that it seeks from the bargaining.[203]

---

198 *Fair Work Act 2009* (Cth) s 217; *Automotive, Food, Metals, Engineering, Printing and Kindred Industries Union v Toyota Motor Corporation Australia* [2011] FWAFB 2132.
199 *Fair Work Act 2009* (Cth) ss 219–224.
200 Ibid ss 225–227, noting applications of this sort can only be made after an enterprise agreement has passed its nominal expiry date.
201 (2010) 204 IR 243 (*Tahmoor Coal*).
202 Ibid [54].
203 Ibid [55].

However, the landscape changed in 2015 following the decision in *Aurizon Operations Ltd*.[204] The Full Bench disagreed with the reasoning in *Tahmoor Coal*, finding that it will not always be inappropriate to terminate an expired enterprise agreement where the bargaining process for its replacement is afoot. It found that there is nothing in s 226 of the *Fair Work Act* that indicates a 'predisposition' against termination. The Full Bench accepted that termination would disturb the current bargaining position in this case, but strongly disagreed with the earlier interpretation of the *Fair Work Act*'s objectives, holding that although the termination of agreements may disturb the bargaining position in some negotiations, this is not contrary to the objects of the Act. In this case, nothing suggested that bargaining for new agreements would cease, and the Full Bench noted that employees and unions still had access to other bargaining tools under the *Fair Work Act*.

Since then termination decisions have been more readily granted.[205]

4.35 The future of enterprise bargaining and possible reform

On 21 December 2015, the Productivity Commission's report into the Australian workplace relations framework was publicly released; it had been commissioned in December 2014.[206] The report contained a number of recommendations regarding enterprise bargaining, including the following:

- amending the *Fair Work Act* to allow the FWC wider discretion to overlook minor procedural or technical errors when determining an application to approve an enterprise agreement so long as the Commission was satisfied that the employees were not likely to have been placed at a disadvantage because of an unmet procedural requirement. That amendment should include the potential for discretion to be used when there are minor errors or defects relating to the issuing or content of an NERR;[207]

- amending s 186(5) of the *Fair Work Act* to allow an enterprise agreement to have a nominal expiry date that is up to 5 years after the day on which the enterprise agreement is approved or matches the life of a greenfields project (which could exceed 5 years);[208]

- replacing the BOOT with a no disadvantage test, requiring each class of employee, and each prospective class of employee, to not be placed at a net disadvantage on

---

204   *Aurizon Operations Ltd* (2015) 249 IR 55 upheld by the Full Court of the Federal Court of Australia in *Communications, Electrical, Electronic, Energy, Information, Postal, Plumbing and Allied Services Union v Aurizon Operations Ltd* (2015) 233 FCR 301.

205   For example, *Construction, Forestry, Mining and Energy Union v Peabody Energy Australia PCI Mine Management Pty Ltd* [2016] FWCFB 3591, upholding the earlier decision in [2016] FWCA 1595; *Australian Manufacturing Workers' Union v Griffin Coal Mining Co. Pty Ltd* [2016] FWCFB 4620, upholding the earlier decision in [2016] FWCA 2312; *Re AGL Loy Yang Pty Ltd (t/as AGL Loy Yang)* (2017) 69 AILR 102-740, upheld on appeal, but reversed by *CFMEU v Loy Yang* [2017] FWCH 1019.

206   Productivity Commission Report.

207   Ibid Recommendation 20.1.

208   Ibid Recommendation 20.4.

an overall basis by the enterprise agreement compared with the relevant modern award(s);[209]

- limiting who is able to be an employee bargaining representative;[210]

- amending the *Fair Work Act* so that if an employer and union(s) have not reached a negotiated outcome for a greenfields agreement after 3 months, the employer may:

  - continue negotiating with the union;

  - request that the FWC undertake 'last offer' arbitration by choosing between the last offers made by the employer and the union

  - submit the employer's proposed greenfields arrangement for approval with a 12-month nominal expiry date;[211]

- allowing for the establishment of project proponent greenfields agreements under the *Fair Work Act*. This would involve a project proponent (such as a head contractor) seeking to have its agreement recognised as a project proponent greenfields agreement which subcontractors (who do not have a current enterprise agreement covering their employees on the projects) could then seek to have cover the work by their employees on the project;[212]

- amending Part 3-3 of the *Fair Work Act* regarding protected action ballot orders and the timeframes for taking protected industrial action;[213]

- amending the *Fair Work Act* to clarify that when determining whether to suspend or terminate industrial action under ss 423 or 426, the FWC should interpret the word 'significant' as 'important or of consequence', along with other amendments to ss 423(2) and 424(1)(c);[214] and

- providing other avenues of industrial action to be taken by employers rather than limiting this to lockouts.[215]

As noted in the Productivity Commission's report, applications to suspend or terminate protected industrial action under ss 423 and 426 of the *Fair Work Act* are very rarely successful given the very high bar set by the FWC in its interpretation of the word 'significant'. That interpretation is derived from a Full Bench decision from 2010 in the *Woodside Burrup* case,[216] where it was said that 'significant' meant 'exceptional in its character or magnitude when viewed against the sort of harm that might ordinarily be expected to flow from industrial action in a similar context'. Although there are good reasons for having a high threshold before applications of this sort are granted,[217] it may be that lowering the threshold slightly will enable disputes to be brought to a conclusion without both sides 'going to the wall'.

---

209   Ibid Recommendation 20.5.
210   Ibid Recommendation 20.6.
211   Ibid Recommendation 21.1.
212   Ibid Recommendation 21.2.
213   Ibid Recommendation 27.1.
214   Ibid Recommendations 27.2–27.4.
215   Ibid Recommendation 27.7.
216   *Construction, Forestry, Mining and Energy Union v Woodside Burrup Pty Ltd* (2010) 198 IR 360.
217   The withdrawal of labour being employees' primary mode of applying bargaining pressure on an employer.

At the time of publication, the Federal government has shown no appetite to implement these (and many other) recommendations of the Productivity Commission. However, changes of this sort would assist in meeting the objectives of the enterprise bargaining regime as set out in the *Fair Work Act*. In particular, providing the FWC with discretion to overlook some trivial indiscretions made during the pre-approval and approval stages would ensure that only issues of substance, not issues of form, are in dispute.

SUMMARY

Enterprise agreements are collective agreements that cover the conditions of employment of all employees within the scope of the agreement at any time during the life of the agreement, including those employees who join the workplace after the agreement is made. Thus there are debates between employers and employees about the scope and coverage of enterprise agreements. Although there is legislative capacity to make individual flexibility agreements, which vary the main agreement in relation to an individual employee, there are few of these in existence.

Enterprise agreements stand in a relationship to the floor of rights contained in the NES (such as minimum leave and other entitlements that apply to Australian national employees) and modern awards (largely industry-related standards). Enterprise agreements may subsume those standards or those standards may stand parallel to the enterprise agreement.

There are laws governing what may and must be included within an enterprise agreement. As a general rule, enterprise agreements can only contain terms which relate to or pertain to the employment relationship between the employer and employee. Significantly, that might include the relationship between the employer and the employee association. There is controversy about the extent to which an enterprise agreement might include the use of contractors by the employer.

Further laws govern mandatory content within an enterprise agreement (such as terms relating to consultation or the settlement of disputes).

There is also prohibited content – terms that must not be included in agreements: for example, terms must not discriminate, and must not breach the general protections.

Enterprise agreements are reviewed by the FWC before being approved and coming into effect. One significant test is the BOOT, by which the enterprise agreement is compared to the award. There is legal debate as to the operation of this test – for example, whether it means that all employees must be better off. There is also legal debate about the limits of the FWC's power to intervene in disputes between employee and employer.

The above summary defines what is an enterprise agreement and the relationship between agreements and awards and the NES; also, what must and must not be included in agreements. It also highlights that a core feature of agreements (apart from their collective nature) is the fact that they must be approved by the FWC. This involves a comparison between agreements and awards. There is also clearly a procedure that must be followed for agreements to reach this stage.

The procedure to be followed in making agreements includes formally starting bargaining. In the course of bargaining, parties must negotiate in good faith. That obligation requires them to meet and consider proposals, but it does not compel the making of concessions leading to a bargain. Case law deals with the difference between hard bargaining and bargaining in breach of the good faith bargaining laws, as well as with how to deal with confidential commercial information.

Strikes may be used as a bargaining chip once there is a formal bargaining period. Those strikes generally take the form of protected industrial action – if the industrial action is genuinely in support of bargaining, unions cannot be sued other than in specific situations: if the industrial action threatens human life, for example. Where industrial action overreaches what is protected, the bargaining period may be terminated.

There are procedures for approval of enterprise agreements as well as laws governing the variation or the termination of an enterprise agreement.

A 2015 Productivity Commission report has raised issues for potential law reform.

There are various State bargaining laws which apply to State and local government employees. Those State laws are not exactly the same as the Federal ones. There are also different legislative approaches amongst the States.

REVIEW QUESTIONS

1. Good faith bargaining is often said to have its origins in North American law. Is that correct? If so, to what extent has it been adopted here? Why has Australia adopted good faith bargaining laws? What was the position in Australia before the laws were introduced? Can the laws ever be used against unions or are they only something that can be adopted against employers?

2. As a practical exercise, conduct a search for individual flexibility agreements (IFAs). They exist on the statute books, but how many exist in practice? Is it possible to find out? How?

3. The Qantas dispute broke new ground in Australia. It was a significant industry which was of national importance but (being aviation) was also international; it saw the shutdown of an entire airline; and involved issues ranging from the use of contractors through to offshoring. Research (individually or in groups) the actual bargains being negotiated in the Qantas dispute. How did the matter reach the stage of an international lockout or shutdown? What is the enduring legal significance of the dispute as well as the relevant case law on bargaining?

4. (a) Union X was determined to retain its basic terms and conditions of employment from its last agreement even though circumstances in the industry had changed considerably (there had been privatisation and increased competition, say). The union kept insisting on the retention of those terms despite the fact that the employer proffered much evidence of the new and less favourable market conditions in which it was operating.

    (b) Employer Y started the negotiating process by saying it would gut the agreement of many key terms considered standard in the sector (such as academic freedom within an academic institution). Once negotiating began, the employer then stated that it wished to hold a vote for a non-union agreement.

    What is the legal position for Union X and Employer Y? What further evidence might you need? If Union X or Employer Y would encounter legal problems on the above facts, is there any way they could modify their position to achieve most of their goals while complying with the law?

5. Sally is employed as a lawyer for a Commonwealth government department. She has been asked to be on standby for the last three Christmases in case a legal issue arises. Sally is not married and does not have children and is told it is only fair for her to be on standby as she has the fewest people depending on her in her personal circumstances. Advise Sally on her position under the NES. Are there further legal provisions (perhaps covered in later chapters of this text) that might govern Sally's situation?

6. Read and consider the decisions of *Peabody Moorvale Pty Ltd v Construction, Forestry, Mining and Energy Union* (2014) 242 IR 210, appeal by Re *Uniline Australia Ltd* (2016) 263 IR 255 and *AMIEU*

v Teys Australia Beenleigh Pty Ltd (2014) 241 IR 119 and (2014) 245 IR 170. Do you agree with the concerns raised in the Productivity Commission report that the current *Fair Work Act* scheme is too focused on issues of form over substance?

FURTHER READING

K Blake and A Watkins 'Participation of casual and "sessional" employees in enterprise agreement ballots: Full Federal Court says only those employed at the time can vote' (2015) 21 *Employment Law Bulletin (ELB)* 119–21.

J Daraus 'Dispute resolution terms in enterprise agreements: is Fair Work Commission private arbiter?'' (2016) *ELB* 144–8.

L Floyd 'Unions overplaying their hand? Bargaining in the mining sector: an analysis of Aurizon' (2015) 43 *Australian Business Law Review (ABLR)*.

A Forsyth 'Could Canadian-style interest arbitration work in Australia?' (2015) 43 *ABLR* 121.

'Full Federal Court upholds a government's capacity to regulate enterprise bargaining through procurement policy' (2014) 20 *ELB*.

'Good faith bargaining requires that bargaining representatives endeavour to reach agreement: a review of *Endeavour Coal v APESMA*' (2012) 18(3) *ELB* 41.

K Gulle 'A critical look at some issues in collective bargaining under the *Fair Work Act 2009*' (2013) 19 *ELB* 125–6.

K Gulle 'The Fair Work Act four years on: true collective bargaining?' (2013) *ELB* 12732.

R Hamilton 'The changing interpretation of agreements' (2016) 7 *Workplace Review* 11–16.

L Howard 'Industrial action as a means to compel employers to commence bargaining' (2013) 26 *Australian Journal of Labour Law (AJLL)* 214–23.

J Howe and A Newman 'Collective bargaining and the ownership of employee creations' (2013) 26 *AJLL* 273–99.

S McCrystal 'Collective bargaining beyond the boundaries of employment: a comparative analysis' (2014) *Melbourne University Law Review (MULR)* 662–98.

R Naughton 'Public interest in Australian labour law – reshaping an old concept in the enterprise bargaining era' (2014) 27 *AJLL* 112.

C Sutherland 'Streamlining enterprise agreements to reduce complexity: an empirical assessment' (2016) *AJLL* 25–57.

C Sutherland 'The problem of uncertainty: an empirical analysis of indeterminate language and ambiguous provisions in enterprise agreements' (2016) 44 *Federal Law Review* 111–42.

J Vincent 'Forcing employers to bargain and the industrial relations playing field after *JJ Richards*: implications for employers, employees and unions' (2014) 20 *ELB* 38–46.

5 TRADE UNION LAW AND REGULATION – UNIONS AND INDUSTRIAL ACTION

Yet what force on earth is weaker than the feeble strength of one, But the union makes us strong.

(from *Solidarity Forever*, R Chaplin (1915))

5.05 Introduction

This chapter deals with the separate but closely related topics of industrial action, unions, and the Royal Commission into Trade Union Governance and Corruption (also referred to as TURC for Trade Union Royal Commission) conducted by the Hon. JD Heydon AC QC throughout 2014 and 2015.

It considers the forms that industrial action takes, its consequences, and the law as it relates to industrial action, including restrictions and sanctions. It compares Australian law to international law as it relates to principles such as freedom of association.

Industrial action is a very public manifestation of collective union action and therefore the treatment of these topics in the chapter is closely related.

The legal status of unions and their regulation at both Federal and State level is also considered, using specific examples – such as the series of problems that beset the Health Services Union in recent times – to illustrate the regulatory regime's powers and challenges.

Other constraints on union action, including the right of entry regime imposed by legislation, are also considered because, in both legal and practical terms, they impact on union operations.

In considering TURC, the focus will be on the two major aspects of the Commission's work: (i) the matters dealt with by the Commission in its hearings; and (ii) the law reform recommendations arising from the Commission's work.

Before dealing with unions and the regulation of their activities, it is important to have a clear notion of what unions are and what they do. In essence, a union is:

> an organisation of workers or employees who have joined together to achieve common goals. These goals can include seeking higher pay and better working conditions, fighting for job security and protecting the integrity of a trade.[1]

As the quotation at the beginning of the chapter suggests, the effectiveness of unions, and indeed their fundamental purpose, stems from the notion of collective action – that the actions of the many in support of particular objectives provide greater bargaining power in negotiations and in disputes.

While their coverage of the workforce has declined,[2] there remain approximately 2 million members of federally registered employee organisations (that is, unions)[3], in addition to those that remain registered under State jurisdictions.

---

1   Australian Workers Union *What is a Union?*, http://www.awu.net.au/what-union.
2   Australian Bureau of Statistics (ABS) Survey 6310.0 *Employee Earnings, Benefits and Trade Union Membership*, August 2013 (released 4 June 2014).
3   Fair Work Commission (FWC) *Annual Report 2016*. There are also approximately 100,000 members of employer organisations.

5.10 The origins of trade union regulation

The Universal Declaration of Human Rights includes 'the right to work; to equal pay for equal work; to just remuneration; and the right to join trade unions'.[4] These freedoms are also confirmed in the United Nations' core Covenants on civil and political rights, and on economic, social and cultural rights.[5]

However, since the earliest legal recognition of trade unions, long before the Universal Declaration, legislatures have sought to prescribe the rights, obligations and constraints placed on unions. This first part of the chapter deals with the evolution of trade union regulation in Australia.

In more recent years, the concept of freedom of association in Australia has been extended to include freedom not to join a union[6] – sometimes referred to as freedom *from* association – with accompanying sanctions to prevent 'closed shop' union-only workplaces.[7] In both cases, the *Fair Work Act 2009* (Cth) (*Fair Work Act*) offers 'general protections', in Part 3-1, for a range of industrial activity, as defined in s 347 of the Act.[8]

5.10.05 The system inherited and the colonial experience

With the transmission of British laws to the Australian colonies, the colonies were subject to the primacy of legislation enacted by the British Parliament – its reception into particular colonies was confirmed in the *Australian Courts Act 1828* (Imp).[9] Not only did British laws apply in the colonies, but also, until the enactment of the *Colonial Laws Validity Act 1865* (Imp),[10] laws enacted in the colonies, if they conflicted with British domestic law, could be declared invalid.

This meant that the colonies were subject to the often repressive laws governing masters and servants as well as combinations of workers (unions and their precursors). These included, for example, the *Combinations Acts* of 1799 and 1800, which restricted the ability of groups of people to meet and which made gatherings or combinations of workers for any purposes related to their employment unlawful.[11]

It was in this environment that in 1834 a group of Dorset agricultural workers, who had formed the 'Friendly Society of Agricultural Labourers', were arrested for unlawful assembly

---

4   United Nations Universal Declaration of Human Rights (1946), Art 23.
5   United Nations International Covenant on Civil and Political Rights 1966 (ICCPR), Art 22, and International Covenant on Economic, Social and Cultural Rights (ICESCR), Art 8.
6   Since the enactment of the *Workplace Relations Act 1996* (Cth); now contained in s 349, *Fair Work Act 2009* (Cth).
7   See, for example, *Director, Fair Work Building Industry Inspectorate v Construction, Forestry, Mining and Energy Union* [2016] FCA 1262.
8   By way of example, in *Director, Fair Work Building Industry Inspectorate v Construction, Forestry, Mining and Energy Union* [2016] FCA 413, insistence that union flags be flown from cranes was held to be 'industrial activity' and action taken to coerce the employer to comply was held to be a breach of the Act. In *Alcoa of Australia Ltd v Australian Workers' Union* [2016] FWC 3582, insistence on work uniforms without union logos on them was held to be a valid exercise of management functions and workplace policy.
9   9 George IV, Ch. 83, in particular s 24.
10   28 & 29 Vict. 63.
11   39 Geo III c.81 and 39 & 40 Geo III c.106, discussed in JV Orth *Combination and Conspiracy: A Legal History of Trade Unionism 1721–1906* (Clarendon Press, 1991) 43–67.

and convicted of swearing (unlawful) oaths of loyalty.[12] These early trade unionists (heralded as the 'Tolpuddle Martyrs', from the name of the village in Dorset from which they came) also had an Australian connection: they were sentenced to transportation for 7 years. As a post-script, following a major petition and protest, they were allowed to return to Britain after serving barely 2 years of their sentence.[13]

The adoption of British laws also meant, however, that when the legislative shackles on assemblies and combinations of workers were loosened (as in 1824) and tightened (as in 1825), these too applied in Australia.[14]

By the mid 19th century, the restrictions on colonial laws were significantly reduced, enabling the colonies to enact their own laws on domestic matters, including regulating the master and servant relationship and, in due course, unions and their activities.[15] However, many activities engaged in by unions and their members remained subject to the criminal law for the remainder of that century.[16]

While the great maritime and shearers' strikes of the early 1890s are often considered to be the genesis of sophisticated industrial relations (IR) systems in the Australian colonies (and later federally), and with them the regulation of trade unions, they were not the only contributors.[17] Prior to the strikes, the *Trade Union Act 1881* (NSW) had implemented a system of registration of unions[18] and an 1890 Bill introduced in the South Australian Parliament proposed the registration of organisations of employers and employees.[19] Ultimately, registration of organisations was enacted in South Australia in 1894.[20] However, these Acts relied upon employer bodies and trade unions to register as 'organisations' under the Act,[21] and this largely did not occur.[22] The *Industrial Arbitration Act 1900* (NSW), as well as introducing compulsory arbitration, also enshrined the system of registration of unions, providing significant benefits associated with registration.[23]

5.10.10 Development: *Conciliation & Arbitration Act 1904* (Cth) and its successors

One of the central notions in workplace relations in Australia is the industrial dispute. This can be traced to the 'industrial relations power' in s 51(xxxv) of the Australian Constitution,

---

12   *R v Lovelass* (1834) 172 ER 1380 – contraventions of the *Unlawful Oaths Act 1797* (37 Geo III, c.123).
13   See works such as HV Evatt *The Tolpuddle Martyrs: Injustice within the Law* ([1937] 2009) for a more detailed discussion of the case and associated issues.
14   *Combination of Workmen Act 1824* and *Combination of Workmen Act 1825* respectively.
15   For detailed discussion of the historical development of trade unions in Australia, see JH Portus *The Development of Australian Trade Union Law* (Melbourne University Press, 1958).
16   S Svenson *The Shearers' War* (University of Queensland Press, 1989) 302.
17   R Naughton 'The contribution of Charles Kingston to the cause of compulsory arbitration', paper presented to the Australian Labour Law Association Conference, November 2014.
18   *Trade Union Act 1881* (NSW) ss 2, 3, 6–13 and Schedule 2 – although compulsory arbitration was not a feature of this Act.
19   The *Industrial Disputes Settlement Bill*, South Australian Parliamentary Debates, House of Assembly, 17 December 1890.
20   *Conciliation Act 1894* (SA).
21   Naughton 'The contribution of Charles Kingston to the cause of compulsory arbitration', 19.
22   DW Smith and DW Rawson *Trade Union Law in Australia* (Butterworths, 2nd ed, 1985).
23   *Industrial Arbitration Act 1901* (NSW) ss 4–12.

enabling the Commonwealth Parliament to legislate in relation to 'conciliation and arbitration for the prevention and settlement of industrial disputes extending beyond the limits of any one State'.

The first Federal IR legislation, the *Conciliation and Arbitration Act 1904* (Cth) (*C&A Act*) was the manifestation of this power. It included not just the making of Federal IR jurisdiction and the tribunal to go with it – the Court of Conciliation and Arbitration – but also the first effort to regulate trade unions in that jurisdiction. Under the *C&A Act* unions were required to be registered in order to gain access to the system as parties and to be afforded the protections that registration afforded. Similar provisions existed in State legislation.

The Act enshrined the right to join a trade union, by prohibiting dismissal of an employee by reason of their union membership. It also protected an employee from being dismissed for accessing an entitlement that they had in an agreement or award.[24] The Act provided for the registration of trade unions, their rules and their legal personality,[25] with these functions administered by the court's registry.[26] There was a nexus between registration and the exercise of particular rights under the legislation: for example, having standing to submit industrial disputes to the court for determination.[27]

Apart from changes to administrative arrangements required as a result of judgements such as *R v Kirby; Ex parte Boilermakers' Society of Australia* (*Boilermakers*),[28] parallel systems of Federal and State registration of unions (and indeed of IR generally) continued throughout the 20th century, with additional measures being introduced to address particular issues.[29] The result was a more detailed and prescriptive system of union regulation.[30]

A feature of the union movement and its regulation in the 1980s and early 1990s was the push for amalgamation of small unions into larger and more broadly based unions, sometimes referred to as 'super unions'. In 1988, the Australian Bureau of Statistics recorded that there were 308 unions, of which 143 had fewer than 1000 members.[31] Within 8 years, there were 133 unions remaining (46 of them federally registered), several with more than 100,000 members.[32]

Indeed, the *Industrial Relations Act 1988* (Cth) (*IR Act 1988*) specified that unions were *required* to have 1000 members in order to be federally registered. In 1990, the minimum membership requirement was increased to 10,000 members. These requirements on the number of members that a union was required to have were found by the ILO's Committee

24   A protection which has remained in subsequent versions of Federal industrial legislation (see K Harvey and C Ozich 'Justice @ work: free to associate?' (Australian Institute of Employment Rights, 2016) 5 et seq.
25   *C&A Act* ss 55, 56, 58 and 66.
26   Ibid ss 51, 59 and 60.
27   Ibid s 65.
28   [1956] HCA 10; (1956) 94 CLR 254.
29   For example, the 1984 amendments to the *Conciliation and Arbitration Act* inserting s 133AB to deal with the issue of casual vacancies and ensure that appointment to vacant union positions (rather than election) did not occur for lengthy periods.
30   The *C&A Act* was 22 pages long, and only four of its pages regulated registered organisations. By comparison, the *Fair Work (Registered Organisations) Act 2009* (Cth) (*RO Act*) alone by 2016 had 203 pages, with an accompanying Regulation of 104 pages.
31   ABS 1988, cited in B Creighton and A Stewart *Labour Law* (Federation Press, 2010) 685.
32   ABS 1996, cited in Creighton and Stewart *Labour Law* (2010) 686.

on Freedom of Association to be a violation of the principles of freedom of association.[33] The *Industrial Relations Act 1993* (Cth) (*IR Act*), consistent with its expressed desire to comply with international obligations, removed this requirement – albeit at a point at which the amalgamation push had largely achieved its objective of bigger, more broadly based unions. However, smaller unions are certainly not unknown, even now: for example, the niche Union of Christmas Island Workers had 312 members in a recent annual return published on the Fair Work Commission's (FWC) website.[34]

The regulation of unions remained within the primary IR legislation – first the *Conciliation and Arbitration Act*, then the *IR Act* (in its 1988 and 1993 iterations) and later the *Workplace Relations Act 1996* (Cth) (and its schedule) (*WR Act*) until the enactment of the *Fair Work (Registered Organisations) Act 2009* (Cth) (*RO Act*).

The *RO Act* (as the current registered organisations legislation is known) and its provisions are discussed in further detail below. Many of the requirements in relation to registration and associated matters have featured in the legislation for many years – some since the days of the 1904 Act – with some of the 'newer' provisions (in relation to union elections, for example) themselves several decades old.[35]

Under the previous legislation, it was apparent that the Commission's functions in relation to unions were linked to its mainstream IR functions.[36] As indicated below, this is a matter that required clarification when the *Fair Work Act* and the *RO Act* became separate pieces of legislation.

5.15 Corporate status of a union

Conceptually, and without another form of legal recognition, a union is essentially an unincorporated association comprised of its members and not otherwise having legal personality.[37] However, from the earliest requirements for union registration at both Federal and State levels in Australia, legislation has given unions status to participate as a party in proceedings arising from that legislation.[38]

Such legislation also provided that the purposes of a trade union were legitimate in circumstances where they might otherwise be considered unlawful for being in restraint of trade and liable to prosecution for conspiracy.[39] These protections remain today in the IR legislation of most jurisdictions.

The *RO Act* provides the current framework for registration of unions and their regulation at the Federal level. While not identical, the requirements in most States are similar.

With the move to a national system for private sector employees of corporations as a consequence of the *Fair Work Act* and the referral of remaining private sector employees from

33 Ibid 682, referring to ILO 1992 *Case no. 1559 (Australia)*.
34 UCIW *Annual Return 2015*, https://www.fwc.gov.au/documents/documents/organisations/registered-orgs/290V/290V-AR2015-117.pdf.
35 *RO Act* s 146, virtually replicating s 133AB of the *C&A Act* (s 133AB having been inserted in 1984).
36 *Australian Federation of Air Pilots v Hamilton Island Enterprises Pty Ltd (No 2)* (1989) 32 IR 46.
37 *Re McJannet; Ex parte Minister for Employment, Training and Industrial Relations (Qld)* (1995) 184 CLR 620 at 639–640; Creighton and Stewart *Labour Law* (2010) 672.
38 See, for example, *Trade Union Act 1881* (NSW) ss 6 and 7, now reflected in *RO Act* s 27.
39 *Trade Union Act 1881* (NSW) ss 2 and 3.

the State systems to the Federal system (other than in Western Australia), many employees who had previously been covered by State IR systems moved into the Federal sphere. These employees would previously have been covered by State-registered unions in the State system.

Consequently, transitional registration arrangements for State-registered unions were inserted into the *RO Act*. In particular, Schedule 1 of that Act – in essence a continuation of Schedule 10 of the former *WR Act*, enabled State-registered unions and employer associations to apply for Federal registration on the basis of having at least one member who was previously covered by a State award or agreement and is now covered by an instrument in the national system. However, as transitional provisions, these arrangements will expire and a more lasting arrangement will be required.

There remains, however, the problem of dual personality of unions: having a State union and a Federal union, each with separate legal personality.[40]

These issues are discussed in the Heydon Royal Commission's *Final Report* and its Recommendations,[41] and the complementary issue of rationalising State registration is discussed later in this chapter at 5.40.

5.20 The *Fair Work (Registered Organisations) Act 2009* (Cth) (*RO Act*)

5.20.05 Overview

The General Manager of the FWC is responsible for the registration of 'organisations' (unions and employer associations). There are 110 registered organisations – 63 employer organisations and 47 unions.[42] However, from May 2017 it is the Registered Organisations Commission that is responsible for regulating the activities of these organisations.[43]

The *Fair Work Act* provides certain rights, responsibilities and protections for unions – such as the right to be a bargaining representative in negotiations for enterprise agreements, the right of entry to workplaces (discussed in more detail below) and certain protections if industrial action is taken in compliance with the provisions of the Act (protected action rather than unprotected industrial action, also discussed below).

In earlier versions of the legislation governing registered organisations, the relevant provisions were contained within the primary IR legislation (such as the *C&A Act* and the *IR Act*) or as a schedule to that legislation.[44]

However, the *RO Act* is entirely concerned with regulating the operations of organisations that have registered for recognition in accordance with the legislation and its predecessors.

---

40   *Moore v Doyle* (1969) 15 FLR 59.
41   JD Heydon Royal Commission into Trade Union Governance and Corruption (TURC), *Final Report*, Vol. 5.
42   FWC: http://www.fwc.gov.au/registered-organisations/find-registered-organisations.
43   http://www.roc.gov.au.
44   For example, the 'RAO Schedule' of the *WR Act*.

Even though the provisions are contained in their own Act, a Full Bench of the FWC concluded that the powers exercised under the *RO Act* could be used for the purpose of administering both that Act and the *Fair Work Act*, but not for other purposes.[45]

The *RO Act* deals with a range of matters fundamental to the operation of registered organisations, including:

* Registration (Ch. 2)
* Amalgamation (Ch. 3)[46]
* Rules of the organisation (Ch. 5)
* Eligibility for membership (Ch. 6)
* Democratic Control, including elections and disqualification (Ch. 7)
* Records and Accounts, including reporting requirements (Ch. 8)
* Conduct of Officers and Employees (Ch. 9).

While the objects of the Act, including 'democratic control of unions'[47] mean that many matters are left to registered organisations to determine themselves, there are some essential parameters within which these activities must fall.[48] This topic, considering some of the above matters as examples, provides an insight into the relationship between the *RO Act* and a registered organisation's rules.

5.20.10 Eligibility and rules

In relation to eligibility for membership, s 166 of the *RO Act* deals with who is eligible to join a union and associated matters, such as being occupationally (or otherwise) qualified to do so in accordance with the union's eligibility rules. Section 133 of the *RO Act* empowers the FWC to make determinations as to the right of a particular organisation to represent a particular group of employees and for the rules of an organisation to reflect those membership eligibility determinations.

The courts have found, in considering eligibility clauses of a trade union's registered rules, that the wording 'in such a context, [is] no doubt intended to have a wide meaning and it should be interpreted and applied in accordance with its ordinary and popular denotation rather than with some narrow or formal construction'.[49] They have also acknowledged that

---

45 *Construction, Forestry, Mining and Energy Union v Director, Fair Work Building Industry Inspectorate* (2016) 261 IR 1, affirming the position in *Australian Federation of Air Pilots v Hamilton Island Enterprises Pty Ltd (No. 2)* (1989) 32 IR 46 (the decision in *AFAP* having been handed down when the *RO Act* provisions were contained within the primary *IR Act*).

46 Though note the intention of the Coalition (in its 'Commitment to Fairness and Transparency in Workplaces' 17 June 2016) to introduce a 'public interest' test for union mergers: 'Coalition targets MUA-CFMEU nuptials', *Workplace Express*, 21 June 2016.

47 *RO Act* s 5(3)(d) and Ch. 7; consistent with cases such as *Grove v Cameron* (1972) 21 FLR 59. See also RRS Tracey 'The legal approach to democratic control of trade unions' (1985) 14 *Melbourne University Law Review* 177–210.

48 See, for example, *Allen v Townsend* (1977) 16 ALR 301, where the court struck down a rule that gave the union executive a power of veto over a decision by members.

49 *R v Cohen; Ex parte Motor Accidents Insurance Board* (1979) 141 CLR 577; also *Electrical Trades Union of Australia v Waterside Workers Federation of Australia* (1982) 56 FLR 430.

eligibility rules must be objectively construed and have regard for the understanding of those working in the industry:[50]

> an employee's classification can be described in a number of ways and the fact that it falls within one description does not mean it does not fall within another. The determining factor of whether the eligibility provisions of a union's registered rules apply in the case of 'occupational rules', is not their job title but the duties which they undertake.[51]

The need for eligibility rules to be read so as to be adaptable to changes in technology,[52] company structures and the location of operations[53] has also been recognised.

The entitlement of an organisation to represent the industrial interests of an employee in relation to the work performed under an industrial agreement is particularly relevant in relation to when the organisation seeks to be covered by that agreement or to exercise the right to participate in proceedings – and may be discerned by considering the membership eligibility rules of the registered organisation, whether or not a particular person is currently a member.[54]

While the case law confirms that the content of an organisation's rules is primarily a matter for its members,[55] in more recent times, and consistent with progress in fields such as anti-discrimination, a registered organisation's eligibility rules are not permitted to exclude members on certain specified grounds. Where such rules may have been popular in earlier times, such as the push to exclude communists from particular unions during the 1950s,[56] they would likely fall foul of the requirements of s 142(1)(d) of the *RO Act*, which are to not discriminate between applicants for membership on prescribed grounds (including political opinion). A recent example was the decision of the General Manager's Delegate to decline certification of a rule seeking to exclude members who expressed certain political views, with the decision also noting that some other provisions of existing rules might also contravene that section of the *RO Act*.[57]

5.20.15 Elections

In relation to union elections, the default position in the legislation is that elections are to be conducted by the Australian Electoral Commission (AEC) as the independent returning officer and that direct elections for union office-bearers be conducted by secret postal ballot.[58] On application, the regulator may grant exemptions from these requirements if satisfied that it is

---

50   *R v Williams; Ex parte Australian Building Construction Employees' and Builders Labourers' Federation* (1982) 153 CLR 402 at 408.
51   *Transport Workers' Union of Australia v Coles Supermarkets Australia Pty Ltd* (2014) 284 FLR 238 at [133], citing *R v Isaac; Ex parte Transport Workers' Union of Australia* (1985) 159 CLR 323.
52   *Electrical Trades Union of Australia v Waterside Workers' Federation of Australia* (1982) 56 FLR 430.
53   *Australian Manufacturing Workers' Union v ResMed Ltd* [2016] FWCFB 2714.
54   *Australian Rail, Tram and Bus Industry Union v Railtrain Pty Ltd* [2016] FWCFB 3153; *Regional Express Holdings Ltd v Australian Federation of Air Pilots* (2016) 244 FCR 344.
55   *Doyle v Australian Workers' Union* (1986) 12 FCR 197; *Municipal Officers Association of Australia v Lancaster* (1981) FLR 129, per Deane J at 165.
56   By the so-called 'Industrial Groups'.
57   *Shop Distributive and Allied Employees Association* [2016] FWCD 1939.
58   *RO Act* ss 182 and 144(1) respectively.

appropriate to do.[59] However, such exemptions may also be revoked if it is no longer appropriate to continue the exemption.[60]

In order for an election to be held, the organisation must lodge prescribed information (PI) with the ROC at least 2 months before the election is due to be held.[61] The PI is then assessed and a decision is issued specifying to the applicant and the AEC the positions for which elections are to be conducted.

The positions comprising the office-bearers of a registered organisation, and the terms of office of those positions, may be set by the organisation, subject to an upper term limit imposed by s 145 of the *RO Act*.[62]

While registered organisations may make rules for filling casual vacancies that arise between scheduled elections (either by appointment or election),[63] there are limitations on the proportion of the term for which an appointment may be made.[64] Where a casual vacancy election is held, the term of office is the balance of the term to which the original office-holder was elected.[65]

In addition to declaring the poll, at the conclusion of each election the AEC is required to provide a report in relation to any rules of the organisation that made the election difficult to conduct, as well as any irregularities in the election process. The organisation is obliged to consider these matters.[66]

5.20.20 Disqualification

Sections 210–220 of the *RO Act* deal with the circumstances in which a union official is disqualified or excluded from holding office. Section 212 details which offences are prescribed offences. They include:

- an offence involving fraud or dishonesty which carries a maximum term of imprisonment of 3 months or more (s 212(a));
- a range of (listed) offences against the *RO Act* in relation to elections (s 212(b));
- offences in relation to the formation and registration of organisations (s 212(c));[67]

---

59   Ibid ss 144(2) and 183 respectively. In respect of s 144(3), in *Local Government and Shires Association NSW* [2013] FWCG 1322 the applicant demonstrated much higher rates of participation in voting via attendance ballots when compared to postal voting.

60   *Construction, Forestry, Mining and Energy Union, Mining and Energy Division, Queensland District Branch* [2016] FWCFB 197 affirming the decision of the Delegate in *Queensland District Branch of the Mining and Energy Division of the Construction, Forestry, Mining and Energy Union* [2015] FWCD 7109.

61   *RO Act* s 189 and *Fair Work (Registered Organisations) Regulations 2009* Reg 138(3).

62   A 4-year maximum term, except where a longer term is required to synchronise with other elections, in which case the term may extend to a maximum of 5 years in that circumstance only.

63   *RO Act* s 146.

64   Ibid s 146(2) and its predecessors in response to cases such as *Gordon v Carroll, Catoni and Hospital Employees Federation of Australia* (1975) 27 FLR 129 at 177.

65   *RO Act* ss 146(2) and 146(5).

66   Ibid s 141.

67   Ibid s 213(b) if the relevant offence is an indictable offence.

- offences in relation to intentional injury or violence or intentional damaging or destruction of property – but only if they result in a term of imprisonment or a suspended sentence (s 212(d) and s 213(c)).

By virtue of these sections, former union officials such as the HSU's Michael Williamson and Craig Thomson[68] would be ineligible to hold office or to stand as a candidate for union office during the exclusion period prescribed by the legislation.

The exclusion period applies for a period of 5 years *starting from* the latest of the following events: conviction for the prescribed offence; the end of a suspended sentence; the day on which the period of imprisonment for the offence ends.[69] However, pursuant to ss 216 and 217, the Federal Court has a discretion to reduce the exclusion period if, on application, the court is satisfied having regard to the matters set out in s 218 in relation to the nature of the offence, the circumstances of the offence and the fitness and character of the person to be involved in the management of organisations.

The Heydon Royal Commission also recommended the introduction of disqualification periods for union officials who seriously and/or repeatedly breach industrial or other laws.[70] While this would be a step away from the 'democratic control' principle enshrined in the *RO Act*, it would certainly be in keeping with similar provisions in the corporations legislation and those already existing in the *RO Act*.

5.20.25 Financial and other records

The *RO Act* requires registered organisations (both employer organisations and unions) to submit annual returns and financial returns.[71] The annual return includes details of current office-bearers; the office of the organisation and each of its branches; any new branches that commenced operation; each election that must be held during the year; and a record of the number of members as at 31 December of the previous year. This information must be lodged with the ROC by 31 March each year.[72]

In relation to financial reporting, unions may have their entire organisation as a 'reporting unit' or, in the case of unions with Branches or Divisions, each Branch or Division may be a reporting unit.[73] The regulator also has the power to determine reporting units on an alternative basis, either upon application or on its own initiative.[74] In some cases, particularly in very large unions, Branches and Divisions are reporting units: the NSW Branch of the Construction Division of the Construction, Forestry, Mining and Energy Union (CFMEU) – one of approximately 30 reporting units that comprise the CFMEU – is a reporting unit, for instance.[75]

---

68   Both convicted of dishonesty offences.
69   *RO Act* s 213A.
70   TURC *Final Report*, Vol. 5, 230–6 and Recommendation 38.
71   *RO Act* Ch. 8, Parts 2 and 3.
72   Ibid s 230, and *Fair Work (Registered Organisations) Regulations 2009* Regs 147 and 149.
73   *RO Act* s 245.
74   Ibid ss 246 and 247 respectively.
75   See CFMEU registered organisations page on the FWC website at http://www.e-airc.gov.au/105N.

The financial reports submitted must include an operating report and a General Purpose Financial Report (GPFR). The latter must be produced in accordance with the Australian Accounting Standards (AAS) and the guidelines issued by the ROC,[76] and the auditor must be given full and free access to relevant documents and records and is entitled to report to the organisation's Committee of Management.[77] The financial reports are required to include matters such as legal costs and amounts paid to employers in return for employers making payroll deductions of membership fees.[78] The financial reports are also obliged to disclose related party transactions, affiliation fees paid to other bodies, grants and donations made, and details of officers and employees who are directors of a company or members of a board.[79] The full financial report must ordinarily be presented to a general meeting of members within 6 months of the end of the financial year, and then filed with the regulator.[80]

In addition, there is a requirement for the union to declare the remuneration paid to the top five officers of the organisation, ranked by remuneration, along with the top two officers of each branch (also ranked by remuneration), along with the identity of those officials.[81]

As well as their reporting obligations, registered organisations are required to keep specified records and to make these available to the Commissioner or his/her authorised representative[82] for the purpose of administering the legislation.[83] These records include a register of members, showing the names and addresses of each, as well as other prescribed information detailed in s 230 of the *RO Act*. In addition to the financial reporting obligations, the organisation must also keep proper financial records capable of being audited.[84] It is an offence to fail to keep such records, and civil penalty proceedings may be pursued.

Interestingly, all of these provisions pre-date the establishment of the Heydon Royal Commission into Trade Union Governance and Corruption, though they do not necessarily pre-date some of the earlier *conduct* investigated by it.

The Commissioner of the Registered Organisations Commission (ROC) has the power to conduct inquiries and investigations in relation to compliance of registered organisations,[85] in particular where they are reasonably suspected of contravening the guidelines, Part 3 of Ch. 8 of the *RO Act* (in relation to financial management only), suspected contravention of any civil penalty provision[86] and irregularities and deficiencies in auditors' reports submitted.[87] This power was held by the General Manager of the FWC until the establishment of the ROC.

76   *RO Act* ss 253, 254 and 255 (a function previously carried out by the General Manager, FWC).
77   *Fair Work Act 2009* (Cth) ss 257 and 260.
78   *RO Act* s 255.
79   FWC General Manager 'Reporting guidelines for the purposes of s 253', 26 June 2013.
80   *RO Act* ss 266 and 268.
81   Ibid ss 293B–293H.
82   Ibid s 235.
83   *Construction, Forestry, Mining and Energy Union v Director, Fair Work Building Industry Inspectorate* (2016) 261 IR 1.
84   *RO Act* s 252.
85   Ibid ss 330 and 331.
86   Ibid s 305 (civil penalty provisions).
87   Ibid s 332.

5.25 Union officials
5.25.05 Who is regarded as a union official?

As the conduct of union officials is the focus of both relevant sections of the *RO Act* and the proceedings of the Heydon Royal Commission, first principles require a determination of who is regarded as a union official.

On any view, elected office-bearers paid to undertake full-time union work come within the scope of union official. But does it include unpaid members of a Branch Committee of Management (BCOM)? And what about employees of the union not elected to their positions?

Section 12 of the *Fair Work Act* defines an official as a person who holds office in or is an employee of an association. In addition, s 9 of the *RO Act* defines 'office' as including any positions that are part of the decision-making body of a registered organisation, which means that its scope includes Committee of Management members.

Section 141 of the *RO Act* allows a registered organisation to determine its structure and office-bearers, provided that these do not offend other provisions of the Act.[88]

Sections 293B to 293J of the *RO Act* require disclosure of remuneration paid to officers and disclosure of material personal interests and payments to related parties. The Act also requires that persons elected to a Committee of Management must also complete financial management training.[89]

5.25.10 Duties of union officials

Union officials are said to owe a fiduciary duty to their members. A requirement for a person to be a fiduciary is that the person 'must first and foremost have bound themselves in some way to protect or to advance the interests of another'.[90] It is readily apparent that in unions this extends beyond simply taking care of the funds contributed by members. It goes to issues as fundamental as the trust that members repose in their officials to act in their best interests in negotiating on their behalf for their pay and working conditions, and the judgement as to whether or not to commence legal action to advance or defend members' interests.

In their 1989 report, Heydon, Meagher and Reynolds recommended that trade union officials should have the same fiduciary duties and responsibilities as company directors.[91] This approach was also recommended in an earlier paper analysing the duties of union officials and the nature of their obligations.[92]

The *RO Act* (particularly following amendments in 2012) places obligations on registered organisations, their officers and employees similar to those that ss 180 to 183 of the

---

88   Consistent with cases such as *Doyle v Australian Workers' Union* (1986) 12 FCR 197; *Municipal Officers Association of Australia v Lancaster* (1981) FLR 129, per Northrop and Evatt JJ at 150.
89   *RO Act* s 293K.
90   S Fridman 'An analysis of the proper purpose rule' [1998] *Bond Law Review* 11; 10(2) *Bond Law Review* 164, referring to P Finn *Fiduciary Obligations* (LBC, 1977).
91   JD Heydon, R Meagher and G Reynolds 'Report on the Duties and Fiduciary Obligations of Officials of Industrial Unions of Employers and Employees' (1989).
92   M Christie 'Legal duties and liabilities of federal union officials' (1986) 15 *Melbourne University Law Review* 591–617.

Corporations Act 2001 (Cth) place on directors and other relevant personnel,[93] albeit that the nature of the obligations is not identical.

Amendments to the *RO Act* in 2012 introduced particular duties of disclosure in relation to union officials. These include disclosure of remuneration paid to officers who are members of boards to which they were appointed by the registered organisation or by virtue of their union position; material personal interests of officers and their relatives as they relate to the affairs of the registered organisation; and payments made to a related party or to a body in which an officer or their relative has a personal interest.[94] Importantly, these officer obligations apply to persons exercising decision-making powers as part of a governing body of the organisation and therefore apply to those holding positions on the Committee of Management and similar bodies (many of those persons hold those positions in a part-time and or honorary capacity).

The duties owed under the *RO Act*, particularly as they relate to matters for which the regulator may seek penalties, are largely limited to matters with a link to 'financial management'.[95]

While union members can seek declarations that an official has breached particular rules and the members may then seek recourse in relation to that official, the civil penalty proceedings that the regulator may take against individual officials are essentially in relation to those financial management matters which would be a breach of ss 285, 286, 287 and/or 288 of the *RO Act*.

While there is limited case law on those particular sections of the current *RO Act*, the courts may draw upon a body of case law that has developed, particularly in the Federal Court, under the previous legislation.[96] While the provisions were not necessarily identical (especially in relation to specific financial reporting obligations), the themes of protecting the rights of members and of officers holding positions of trust are certainly shared.

Noting the parallels with company directors, in *Allen v Townsend* the Federal Court held that 'subject to necessary adaptations, similar principles of law should apply' to the duties of directors of corporations and in relation to members of committees of management of registered organisations.[97]

One of the matters that would appear to be at the heart of a union office-bearer's obligations is compliance with the organisation's own rules. This is something with direct parallels in the corporate sphere, with Ford's *Principles of Corporations Law* noting that 'an aspect of directors' duties which is often overlooked is the duty to act in accordance with the corporate constitution'.[98]

Indeed, this is reflected in the provisions in the *RO Act* enabling a union member to seek declarations in relation to an officer's compliance with the union's own rules.[99]

---

93   R Read and Z Smith 'The next phase of regulation of Registered Organisations in Australia: is there any need for corporate style regulation?', paper presented to the Australian Labour Law Association Conference, November 2014, 6–8. The duties in those sections of the *Corporations Act 2001* (Cth) are: s 180 (acting with care, skill and diligence, in the best interests of the organisation), s 181 (good faith and proper purpose), s 182 (not to act for the purpose of gaining a financial advantage for oneself) and s 183 (refraining from using information for the advantage of themselves or another person).

94   Now *RO Act* ss 293B–293G (previously ss 148A–148C).

95   Ibid s 283.

96   For example, *Allen v Townsend* (1977) 16 ALR 301; *Scott v Jess* (1984) 3 FCR 263; *Morris v O'Grady; Re Application of Raffa* (1991) 37 IR 196.

97   *Allen v Townsend* (1977) 16 ALR 301 at [66].

98   RP Austin and IM Ramsay *Ford's Principles of Corporations Law* (LexisNexis,14th ed, 2010) 400.

99   *RO Act* s 162.

Forsyth has noted distinctions between registered organisations and corporations, in particular their different natures and objectives, as part of the consideration of the applicability of corporate-style regulation to unions.[100] One particular distinction, long recognised, is the inherent dissension in an organisation concerned with political and social objectives and with different groups (often referred to as factions) seeking to influence the control and policy of the organisation. As described by Cameron, in some unions, 'union officialdom ... is in constant conflict with its own membership'.[101]

(DON'T) FOLLOW THE LEADER(S): THE HEALTH SERVICES UNION AND ITS ERRANT OFFICIALS

Michael Williamson was the Secretary of the HSU's NSW Branch (later HSU East) from 1995 to 2012, as well as National President from 2003 to 2011.

Mr Williamson set up an arrangement with a printing company to produce the union's newsletter at greatly inflated prices (up to 10 times what it would otherwise cost) and to split the proceeds between the publisher, himself and another union employee. He was also provided with a credit card paid for by the company. A Williamson family company, Canme, received payments of more than $600,000 from the union but did not provide any services. In addition, a company of which he was a director provided IT services to the union, without a competitive tender and without his involvement being adequately declared.

Following Williamson's suspension as Secretary, an independent report was commissioned by the HSU into its financial affairs. The report found that approximately $20 million had been paid by the union without any form of tendering or contract, including $5 million to Williamson family companies.[102]

Williamson was charged with more than 50 criminal offences, which were ultimately rolled into four major charges, to which he pleaded guilty. The charges were in relation to cheating and defrauding the HSU of approximately $1 million, creating false documents in order to deceive, and recruiting others to hinder police investigations. In March 2014, he was sentenced to 7½ years' imprisonment with a non-parole period of 5 years.[103]

The union instituted civil proceedings against Williamson, resulting in an agreed settlement whereby judgement was entered against Williamson for $5 million. The court also set aside Williamson's claimed (higher) pay rates from 2003 onwards, thereby reducing what would have been a substantial superannuation and leave liability for the union. The HSU also received a letter of apology from Williamson, which was published to members.[104]

100   A Forsyth 'Trade union regulation and accountability of office holders: examining the corporate model' (2000) 13 *Australian Journal of Labour Law* 1.
101   C Cameron *Unions in Crisis* (Hill of Content, 1982) 18.
102   Ian Temby QC and Dennis Robertson 'Final Report on HSUeast', 3 July 2012, http://progressivepsa.org/pdf/hsueast_temby_report_final_full_july2012.pdf.
103   *R v Williamson* (Unreported, District Court of NSW, 28 March 2014).
104   HSU NSW Branch 'Message from Secretary Gerard Hayes in relation to Michael Williamson', 21 October 2013, available at http://www.hsu.asn.au/message-from-secretary-gerard-hayes-in-relation-to-michael-williamson.

Williamson's Assistant Secretary, Peter Mylan, was subsequently the subject of a referral by the Royal Commission in relation to his actions while Acting Secretary in Williamson's absence, in particular for payments made for the benefit of Williamson's companies.

Craig Thomson, the National Secretary of the HSU from 2002 to 2007, was also the subject of both criminal and civil proceedings. An investigation of financial irregularities following Thomson's departure as National Secretary (to enter Parliament) identified apparent misuse of union funds, including Thomson's union-issued credit card and an apparent use of union funds to pay for an election campaign worker. Many of the transactions were never authorised (other than by Thomson himself) and were not disclosed to the National Executive. Thomson denied any wrongdoing.

The FWC conducted an investigation into the use of union funds by Thomson and commenced civil proceedings against him in October 2012. Later that month, police conducted searches of Thomson's home and office, seizing computers and boxes of documents. He was arrested on 31 January 2013 and charged with 173 offences arising from his time as an HSU official. Thomson denied the allegations.

In February 2014, he was found guilty of defrauding the union and was sentenced to 1 year of imprisonment (with 9 months of that suspended). The court found that his actions were a 'breach of trust of the highest order',[105] and noted that Thomson showed no remorse.

Thomson appealed both the conviction and the sentence. On appeal, Thomson's convictions on 13 of the charges were sustained; however, he was acquitted of another 49 charges (arising from an error by the prosecution). A fine of $25,000 was imposed, with the court observing that Thomson's actions were 'self-indulgent' and 'at their heart involved the use of other people's money'.[106]

Once the criminal charges had been finalised, the FWC proceedings against Thomson were able to proceed. In September 2015, the Federal Court found that Thomson's conduct on multiple occasions had breached his duties as a union official.[107] In December 2015, the court ordered that Thomson pay $231,243.42 in compensation as well as interest of $146,937.16.[108]

Kathy Jackson, the former National Secretary of the HSU and former State Secretary of its Victoria No. 1 Branch, was the subject of civil proceedings by the union to recover funds allegedly misused by her in relation to the purchase of personal items, travel and other expenditure. Jackson also set up a slush fund, the National Health Development Account (NHDA), for personal purposes, and directed payments from the HSU into the NHDA, as well as inducing an employer, the Peter McCallum Cancer Centre, to pay a grossly inflated amount misleadingly referred to as a reimbursement of legal expenses.

105 *R v Thomson* (Unreported, Melbourne Magistrates Court, 25 March 2014). Comments of Magistrate Rozencwajg reported at http://www.abc.net.au/news/2014-03-25/craig-thomson-fraud-hsu-sentencing/5342428.
106 *Thomson v R* (Unreported, County Court of Victoria, Douglas J, 15 December 2014).
107 *General Manager of the Fair Work Commission v Thomson (No. 3)* [2015] FCA 1001.
108 *General Manager of the Fair Work Commission v Thomson (No. 4)* [2015] FCA 1433.

In August 2015, the Federal Court determined that Ms Jackson owed the HSU the amount of $1,406,538,[109] which included $1,338,626 as compensation to the union as a result of her contraventions as an officer, and a further $67,912 of overpaid salary to which she was not entitled. (During a period of personal overseas travel she had remained 'at work' rather than taking leave.) In December 2015, the court ordered that she pay a further $356,500 in costs.[110]

Matters involving Ms Jackson were also referred to Victoria Police by the HSU directly and by the Royal Commission.[111] Ms Jackson was subsequently charged by Victoria Police with numerous criminal offences relating to these matters.

5.25.15 What constitutes a breach of a union official's duties?

Sections 285 to 288 of the *RO Act* set out clear obligations in relation to the way that officers (and in some cases, their employees) conduct themselves, albeit these are limited to matters with a financial aspect to them.[112]

Section 285 requires officers to discharge their duties with the degree of care and diligence that a reasonable person would exercise in such a position. Section 286 requires officers of registered organisations to exercise their powers in good faith in what they (reasonably)[113] believe to be in the best interests of the organisation and for a proper purpose.

Section 287 requires that an officer or employee not use their position to gain an advantage for themselves or others, or to cause a detriment to the organisation or another person.

Section 288 requires a person who obtains information by virtue of being an officer or employee to not use that information improperly.

In considering how these obligations apply in practice, findings made in the Federal Court proceedings involving Craig Thomson and Kathy Jackson (respectively) are of assistance. In *Thomson*,[114] the use of union funds to pay for personal expenses that had nothing to do with the business of the union 'amounted to an improper use of his position to gain an advantage for himself, and to cause detriment to the HSU, within the meaning of s 287(1) of the schedule'.[115] Causing the HSU to pay the sums concerned gave rise to the breach.[116]

In relation to the issue of acting for a proper purpose, the court found that:

> by causing the HSU to pay for these personal expenses, the respondent failed to discharge his duties in good faith in what he believed to be the best interests of the HSU ... Had there been any such belief, I can think of no reason why the respondent would not have informed the National Executive, even before the event, and had it give the necessary

---

109   *Health Services Union v Jackson (No. 4)* (2015) 108 ACSR 156.
110   *Health Services Union v Jackson (No. 5)* [2015] FCA 1467.
111   TURC *Final Report*, Vol. 2, Ch. 5.1 – for alleged breaches of ss 81 and 82 of the *Crimes Act 1958* (Vic) (fraud offences) as well as false evidence to the Royal Commission.
112   *RO Act* s 283.
113   *General Manager of the Fair Work Commission v Thomson (No. 3)* [2015] FCA 1001, in which Thomson had argued (unsuccessfully) that he believed his actions were not contrary to the union's interests – the court found that that belief was not reasonable.
114   Ibid.
115   *WR Act* s 287(1) of the RAO Schedule – now replicated in *RO Act* s 287.
116   [2015] FCA 1001 at [46].

authorisation ... in passing on the responsibility for this expenditure to the HSU, the respondent was not acting for a proper purpose: his purpose was to avoid having to pay for the excursion himself.[117]

And in relation to the exercise of the appropriate level of diligence as an officer, the extent to which Thomson crossed, blurred or erased the line between personal and union matters was a significant factor. The court found that:

> by failing to maintain a scrupulous separation between the matters and transactions for which he might properly use the funds and resources of the HSU and the matters and transactions which he ought to have funded otherwise, he exercised his powers and discharged his duties without the degree of diligence that a reasonable person would have exercised in like circumstances, in contravention of s 285(1) of the schedule.[118]

As to the argument that the union had the power to choose to spend its funds in that way, the observations of Jessup J in *Thomson (No. 3)* are instructive:

> It may well have been legitimate for the HSU to invest its funds and staff resources in ways that assisted community groups and promoted their aims. However, not being 'the business of the union' within the meaning of rule 32(n), and not being 'the general administration of the union' or 'reasonably incidental' thereto under r 36(b) of the Rules, no such investment could have been undertaken by the National Secretary on his own initiative. The authorisation of the National Council or the National Executive would have been necessary ... In circumstances where such authorisation had not been sought or granted, the respondent took it upon himself to select, of all the places in Australia where valid claims for assistance of this kind might have been advanced, the specific location where assistance would be provided. When it is realised that the respondent himself had only recently moved into the relevant area with the general project of increasing his own profile in the community to further his own political career, the potential for a conflict of interest to have arisen is all too obvious. Indeed, I would go further. In the absence of evidence from the respondent justifying how he proceeded in relevant respects, I would infer that his decision to commit the funds and staff resources of the HSU to Coastal Voice, a group which he himself established, was substantially influenced, if not wholly driven, by the advancement of that general project. In short, the respondent used his fiduciary position to benefit himself, at the expense of the organisation which he served. That was a conspicuous impropriety.[119]

In *Jackson*,[120] Tracey J (comparing the obligations under the *RO Act* and the *Corporations Act*) noted that the constraints on officers and employees are applied using an objective standard and cited the High Court's judgement in *Byrnes*, a case involving a companies provision indistinguishable from s 287, which held that for the conduct in question to be improper, it was not necessary that the offender be conscious of the impropriety:

> Impropriety consists in a breach of the standards of conduct that would be expected of a person in the position of the alleged offender by reasonable persons with knowledge of the duties, powers and authority of the position and the circumstances of the case. When

---

117   Ibid [47].
118   Ibid [99], [106] and [109].
119   Ibid 97.
120   *Health Services Union v Jackson (No. 4)* (2015) 108 ACSR 156 at [113].

impropriety is said to consist in an abuse of power, the state of mind of the alleged offender is important ... But impropriety is not restricted to abuse of power. It may consist in the doing of an act which a director or officer knows or ought to know that he has no authority to do.[121]

Thus the court found (amongst other contraventions) that Jackson's creation of a separate account and the payment of union funds into it was improper within the meaning of the legislation.[122]

It is clear from these matters that the court will always look to the nature of the expenditure, the relevant authorisation requirements and the role played by the office-bearer, particularly where the decision is likely to benefit them or where a conflict of interest otherwise arises.

5.25.20 Accountability to the regulator

As indicated above, s 330 and s 331 of the *RO Act* give the ROC Commissioner power to conduct inquiries and investigations into particular matters. These include suspected contraventions of ss 285 to 288 – obligations imposed variously on officers and employees of registered organisations.

Previously such investigations were uncommon. As at February 2012, the investigations into the HSU were reportedly the only two such investigations undertaken under the *RO Act* and apparently only one other had occurred under the previous legislation.[123] While this appears disconcerting, given the FWC's previous role as the regulator, it is perhaps unsurprising considering that these compliance functions were traditionally just a part of the overall FWC registry functions, which were to support the tribunal; the investigations function 'wasn't considered to be the main work we did'.[124] It should therefore come as little surprise that the KPMG Review of the HSU investigation identified flaws in relation to investigation management systems and the resources dedicated to investigations.[125]

The frequency of inquiries and investigations has increased, with a total of 18 completed by the FWC between December 2011 and 30 June 2016.[126] The FWC's website details all its inquiries and investigations, both current and completed.[127]

These inquiries and investigations have been in respect of both registered organisations and their officials. Amongst the investigations completed have been:

* The Musicians Union of Australia and its former Secretary, who (following investigation and civil penalty proceedings) each had fines imposed in relation to failure to submit financial reports over a period of several years;[128]

121 Ibid [114] (citing *R v Byrnes* (1995) 183 CLR 501 at 514–15 per Brennan, Deane, Toohey and Gaudron JJ).
122 Ibid [121].
123 Evidence of the FWC to the Education, Employment and Workplace Relations Legislation Committee, Parliament of Australia, Canberra, 16 February 2012.
124 KPMG *Process review of Fair Work Australia's investigations into the Health Services Union*, 17 August 2012, 3.
125 Ibid 4.
126 FWC *Annual Report 2013* 70; FWC *Annual Report 2016* 92–5.
127 Details of FWC investigations and inquiries are available at https://www.fwc.gov.au/registered-organisations/inquiries-investigations.
128 *General Manger of the Fair Work Commission v Musicians Union of Australia* [2016] FCA 302.

- The Health Services Union of Australia for failing to prepare or provide operating and financial reports to its Committee of Management for particular periods;[129]

- The Transport Workers' Union (TWU) for failing to maintain registers of its members as at specific dates and not removing unfinancial members more than 2 years after they had ceased membership (which inflated membership figures by more than 20,000);[130] and

- James McGiveron and Rick Burton, former Secretaries of the TWU's WA Branch, in relation to unauthorised use of union funds and using funds for personal benefit in respect of the purchase of vehicles, the implementation of a particularly generous redundancy policy that benefited one of them and payments for personal entertainment and hire expenses, resulting in fines being imposed on both individuals. [131]

5.25.25 Consequences for union officials

The consequences for union officials of improper conduct (at least in relation to 'financial management') include the civil penalty proceedings that may arise from breaches of the *RO Act*.

Currently the sanctions on individual union officials in the *RO Act* are civil penalty provisions for breach of their duties under ss 285, 286 and 287. These sections, however, only relate to financial management obligations. Therefore, any breaches by an official must have a financial aspect to them before the regulator is able to proceed for breaches of the Act.

In relation to 'non-financial' matters, such as breaches of the union's rules by an official, the regulator could seek a declaration that the official has breached his/her union's rules. However, that of itself will not result in a sanction. Indeed, individual union members could seek such a declaration themselves – either as the precursor to the members taking civil action or for the sake of the declaration itself (for its embarrassment value, perhaps). In contrast, expending time, effort and funds seeking declaratory relief without an accompanying penalty is unlikely to be routinely viewed as an effective use of the regulator's finite regulatory resources.

Sections 201 to 220 of the *RO Act* also deal with the circumstances in which an official's action can result in disqualification from office (such as certain criminal offences).

Ultimately, if a union official's conduct contravenes not only the expected standards of behaviour set out in the union's rules and the *RO Act* but also the criminal law, the fact that the conduct occurred in the IR sphere will not save them from the consequences of their actions.[132]

---

129   *General Manager of the Fair Work Commission v Health Services Union* [2013] FCA 1306.
130   *General Manager of the Fair Work Commission v Transport Workers' Union* (Federal Court of Australia matter number NSD2041/2016).
131   *General Manager of the Fair Work Commission v McGiveron* [2017] FCA 405 and FWC Media Release 'Penalties imposed on two former Secretaries of the TWU WA Branch', 21 April 2017, https://www.fwc.gov.au/documents/documents/media/releases/21-april-2017.pdf
132   B Norington 'Parasitic ex-union boss Michael Williamson jailed for fraud', *The Australian*, 28 March 2014; S Deery 'Former MP Craig Thomson sentenced to 3 months jail', *Herald Sun*, 25 March 2014 (on appeal, Thomson's sentence was reduced to a series of fines).

5.30 The regulator

5.30.05 The Fair Work Commission – dual role

While best known for its work in adjudicating workplace relations disputes and making awards and agreements, the FWC also performs the role of overseeing particular aspects of registered organisations[133] – this mix of roles has been the subject of attention and legislative amendment. The mix is discussed in detail in the section of this chapter dealing with the Registered Organisations Commission (ROC), suffice to say in summary that the *RO Act* as it existed in mid 2017 vested some of these powers in the new ROC, with others remaining with the FWC.

5.30.10 Powers available to the regulator

As the *Fair Work Act* and the *RO Act* dealt extensively with matters that affect unions and the work with which they are involved – enterprise bargaining, industrial action, registration and deregistration of unions – it is apparent that many of the actions of a union and its officers and employees could bring it to the (adverse) attention of the FWC (and/or the ROC).

While not every action by a union will find favour with the regulator, this does not always translate into sanctions against the union or its officials. However, as indicated in the sections on industrial action and right of entry elsewhere in this chapter, there are certainly sanctions available to deal with behaviour that contravenes legislation.

The powers of the regulator in relation to unions are vested with the General Manager of the FWC and the ROC Commissioner. It is the Commissioner (previously the General Manager) who determines whether to initiate an inquiry or investigation into a registered organisation or an official pursuant to s 330 and s 331 of the *RO Act*, and it is in their name that litigation is commenced.

The General Manager and ROC Commissioner may delegate some of their powers and functions to other officers, subject to those officers meeting particular criteria in terms of their rank or professional expertise.[134] Other functions, however, may not be delegated.[135] These include, for example, the power to exempt registered organisations from election requirements such as the conduct of ballots by the AEC.[136]

The regulator has available to it, in relation to many of the provisions of the *RO Act*, the option of commencing civil penalty proceedings. Section 305 of the *RO Act* defines the matters for which a civil penalty may be sought.

The regulator may also, in appropriate cases, issue a 'rectification notice' and can apply to the Federal Court for enforcement of that notice.[137] Such an order may be appropriate where remedial action is required by a union and the instituting of court proceedings may be an ineffective use of resources and/or may not itself achieve the rectification. An example of this

133   Department of Employment & Workplace Relations (DEWR) 'Towards more productive and equitable workplaces: an evaluation of the Fair Work legislation' (2012) 250.
134   *RO Act* s 343A(2) and s 343A(3).
135   Ibid s 343A(1).
136   Ibid s 183.
137   Ibid s 336(5).

may be where previous financial reports by a union have not included certain transactions as 'related party transactions' as required by the *RO Act*.

Where this omission has occurred as a result of relying on advice from an auditor and is subsequently identified to the union, the union is entitled to rely upon the professional advice of the auditor by way of a defence to proceedings,[138] but still needs to amend the financial reports to ensure that a true picture is provided to its members and to the regulator.

5.30.15 Industry-specific regulator: construction

The question of a building industry-specific regulator, which had long been prominent in the debate about workplace regulation, came to the fore again in 2016 with the double dissolution election trigger and the ultimate passage of legislation to reinstate the Australian Building and Construction Commission (ABCC) in November 2016.[139]

The creation of a body with specific oversight of the building and construction industry was a key recommendation from the Cole Royal Commission.[140] This recommendation was implemented in 2005 with the passage of the *Building and Construction Industry Improvement Act 2005* (Cth) (*BCII Act*). The Act established the ABCC, whose task was to regulate 'building work'.[141]

The industry-specific nature of the regulator, coupled with its coercive powers,[142] and the perception of an anti-union approach, led the Gillard Government to replace it in 2012 with the Fair Work Building Industry Inspectorate (FWBII), also known as Fair Work Building and Construction (FWBC).[143]

While the FWBC retained many of the former ABCC's powers, a number of the ABCC's coercive powers (such as the issuing of examination notices) were the subject of sunset clauses. These required the passage of additional legislation to extend the period in which such powers could be used by the FWBC.[144]

The FWBC had the right to make submissions in a matter before the FWC if the matter arose under the *Fair Work Act* and involved a building industry participant or building work.[145] This was a broad right and necessarily included matters such as right of entry permits (discussed later in this chapter). This right has been retained by the reinstated ABCC.[146]

It has often been mistakenly assumed that the ABCC (and the FWBC, its replacement between 2012 and 2016) only had responsibility for policing the activities of the construction union, the CFMEU. However, as the definition of 'building industry participants' and 'building work' in the *Fair Work (Building Industry) Act 2012* (Cth) (*FW(BI) Act*) made clear,[147] it

---

138   Ibid s 292.
139   *Building and Construction Industry (Improving Productivity) Act 2016* (Cth) (*BCII Act*).
140   *Royal Commission into the Building & Construction Industry* 2001–2003 (Cole Royal Commission).
141   *BCII Act* s 5.
142   These are discussed in detail in G Williams and N McGarrity 'The investigatory powers of the Australian Building and Construction Commission' (2008) 21 *Australian Journal of Labour Law* 244.
143   *Fair Work (Building Industry) Act 2012* (Cth) (*FW(BI) Act*).
144   *Construction Industry Amendment (Protecting Witnesses) Act 2015* (Cth), which extended the period from June 2015 to June 2017.
145   *FW(BI) Act* s 72.
146   *Building and Construction Industry (Improving Productivity) Act 2016* (Cth) s 112.
147   *FW(BI) Act* ss 4 and 5 respectively.

extended to other unions (such as the CEPU, which covers electrical and plumbing workers) as well as to employers,[148] provided that they fall within these criteria. It was also empowered to deal with sham contracting in the industry, as evidenced in matters such as *Linkhill v FWBC*.[149]

The legislation that reinstated the ABCC[150] also substantially extended the meaning of 'building work' in s 6 of that Act, to the extent that it now also encompasses:

> (b)   the construction, alteration, extension, restoration, repair, demolition or dismantling of railways (not including rolling stock) or docks;
>
> (c)   the installation in any building, structure or works of fittings forming, or to form, part of land, including heating, lighting, air-conditioning, ventilation, power supply, drainage, sanitation, water supply, fire protection, security and communications systems;
>
> . . .
>
> (e)   transporting or supplying goods, to be used in work covered by paragraph (a), (b), (c) or (d), directly to building sites (including any resources platform) where that work is being or may be performed.

Even a cursory glance at the nature of the above work makes it apparent that the ABCC's jurisdiction will now extend to many activities that may otherwise be considered either preparatory or ancillary to building work. A significant aspect of this is that many of these activities are not carried out by construction workers, but by members of other unions, such as the Maritime Union of Australia (MUA) and the Transport Workers' Union (TWU), bringing them under the spotlight of the ABCC's attention.

There were constraints on the extent to which the FWBC could intervene in building industry matters. For example, where parties took civil action against a union, its officials and/or individual employees for taking unprotected industrial action (or 'unlawful action' to use the term in the *FW(BI) Act*) the FWBC had the right to intervene in the proceedings or take action against persons contravening those provisions.[151] However, where the parties to those civil proceedings resolved their proceedings (through settlement and/or discontinuation, for example) the FWBC was unable to intervene[152] or could only do so in respect of building industry participants not the subject of those finalised proceedings.[153]

Notably, these restrictions do not appear in the legislation that reconstituted the ABCC.[154]

---

148   See, for example, discussion of *FWBC v Devine Constructions* in FWBC Industry Update, 27 November 2015, https://www.fwbc.gov.au/news-and-media/industry-update/latest-industry-update/industry-update-27-november-2015.

149   *Linkhill Pty Ltd v Director, Fair Work Building Industry Inspectorate* [2015] FCAFC 99, in which the FWBC successfully resisted an appeal by the company against a finding that it had engaged in sham contracting. The company's application to the High Court for special leave to appeal from the Full Bench of the Federal Court was refused on 11 December 2015, *Linkhill Pty Ltd v Director, Fair Work Building Industry Inspectorate* [2015] HCATrans 340.

150   *Building and Construction Industry (Improving Productivity) Act 2016* (Cth).

151   *FW(BI) Act* s 71.

152   Ibid ss 73 and 73A.

153   *Director, Fair Work Building Industry Inspectorate v Ingham* [2016] FCA 328.

154   *Building and Construction Industry (Improving Productivity) Act 2016* (Cth).

It is also significant (for reasons distinguished in the 'Picketing' section of this chapter) that the ABCC is empowered to take action against both 'unlawful industrial action'[155] and 'unlawful picketing'.[156] This appears to confirm the distinction drawn between industrial action and picketing as two separate types of activity, consistent with cases such as *Davids Distribution Pty Ltd v National Union of Workers* (1999) 91 FCR 463, yet for practical purposes the Act effectively treats them the same way.

5.30.20 State regulators

Those registered organisations that remain involved in the State jurisdiction, for example by virtue of the fact that some or all of their members work in State or local government (or in WA are employed by sole traders or members of partnerships), are subject to the requirements of the various States' IR laws.[157] This is the result of the historical coverage of State jurisdictions by virtue of s 51(xxxv) of the Constitution, under which matters that did not extend beyond the borders of a single State remained in the State IR jurisdiction. This led to the development of well-established (and in many cases well-resourced) State unions.[158]

Where registration, for the purposes of the participating in the State system, is concerned, these functions invariably sit with the Registry of each State's Industrial Relations Commission or equivalent.[159] However, the enforcement of breaches of State IR laws often sits with another agency. For example, in NSW the authority to prosecute for breaches of s 268 of the *Industrial Relations Act 1996* (NSW) – 'use of a position for profit' – rests with the Minister, an authorised inspector or other prescribed person,[160] not with the Registrar of the NSW Industrial Relations Commission (NSWIRC).

The Heydon Royal Commission considered the position of State regulation in its *Final Report*, noting that the requirements of each system varied. While recognising the very likely continuation of separate State systems, the Royal Commission urged the adoption of uniform measures in relation to the regulation of registered organisations at the State and Federal level.[161]

5.30.25 Registered Organisations Commission

After multiple attempts,[162] and becoming (with the ABCC Bill) a trigger for the July 2016 double dissolution election, the Coalition government was ultimately successful in legislating for a

155 Ibid s 46.
156 Ibid s 47.
157 *Industrial Relations Act 1996* (NSW); *Industrial Relations Act 2016* (Qld); *Fair Work Act 1994* (SA); *Trades Unions Act 1889* (Tas); *Industrial Relations Act 1979* (WA). Victoria, while retaining the *Trade Unions Act 1958*, in effect does not have a separate industrial relations regime.
158 See, for example, *Re McJannet: Ex parte Minister for Employment, Training and Industrial Relations (Qld)* (1995) 184 CLR 620.
159 The Industrial Relations Commission of NSW (NSWIRC), Tasmanian Industrial Commission (TIC), South Australian Industrial Relations Commission (SAIRC), Western Australian Industrial Relations Commission (WAIRC) and Queensland Industrial Relations Commission (QIRC).
160 *Industrial Relations Act 1996* (NSW) s 399.
161 TURC *Final Report*, Vol. 5, Ch. 2 (in particular Recommendation 2).
162 Fair Work (Registered Organisations) Amendment Bill 2013 (Cth), Fair Work (Registered Organisations) Amendment Bill 2014 (Cth) and Fair Work (Registered Organisations) Amendment Bill (No. 2) 2014 (Cth).

separate regulator of registered organisations. The *Fair Work (Registered Organisations) Amendment Act 2016* (Cth) amended the *RO Act* to remove some of (but not all) the registered organisations functions of the FWC and to move them to a separate Registered Organisations Commission (ROC), headed by a Commissioner but located within the structure of the Fair Work Ombudsman.

The rationale for a separate ROC was that the registered organisations functions of the FWC were essentially regulatory and administrative, whereas the other functions of the FWC were said to be essentially those of a tribunal.

The FWC's dual role of regulator and tribunal was criticised by the Heydon Royal Commission, which asserted that it was 'apt to confuse the public about the role of the Fair Work Commission, which is essentially adjudicative',[163] and argued that the range of responsibilities given to the General Manager could result in insufficient resources being dedicated to the regulation of organisations.[164]

Read and Smith[165] observed that trade unions are already subject to a high level of regulation that, they note, in some cases exceeds that which applies to corporations and their directors. They argue that a change in the compliance and enforcement practices of the regulator is to be preferred to a separate Commission or further changes to the legislation governing registered organisations.[166]

Much of the criticism of the FWC as a regulator of registered organisations stems from the FWC's response to matters involving the Health Services Union and its officers. However, as the above details of the FWC's investigations into registered organisations indicate, the FWC's spotlight on registered organisations and their compliance certainly increased substantially in the period 2012 to 2016.

The Heydon Royal Commission supported the establishment of the Registered Organisations Commission as a stand-alone regulator,[167] and explicitly rejected options to place responsibility for registered organisations with the corporate regulator, ASIC, or the with the regulator of other not-for-profit organisations, the Australian Charities and Non-Profits Commission (ACNC).

While the Coalition government supported the work of the Heydon Royal Commission, the *Fair Work (Registered Organisations) Amendment Act* did not incorporate the Royal Commission's recommendations, but was instead substantially the same as the previously rejected Bill.

The government confirmed that while it was supportive of most of the recommendations of the Trade Union Royal Commission, these would be put to Parliament no earlier than 2017.[168]

---

163   TURC *Final Report*, Vol. 5, 58.
164   Ibid, citing KPMG *Process Review* (2012) 3 and 27.
165   R Read and Z Smith 'The next phase of Regulation of Registered Organisations in Australia: is there any need for corporate-style regulation?', paper presented to the Australian Labour Law Association Conference, November 2014, 2–3.
166   Ibid 3–5, citing I Ayers and J Braithwaite *Responsive Regulation – Transcending the Deregulation Debate* (Oxford University Press, 1992) and J Braithwaite 'The essence of responsive regulation' (2011) *UBC Law Review* 475 et seq.
167   TURC *Final Report*, Vol. 5, 54–64, Recommendations 3 and 4, consistent with the submissions from various parties, http://www.tradeunionroyalcommission.gov.au/submissions/pages/2015-submissions-pages/submissions-in-response-to-discussion.paper-options-for-law-reform.aspx.
168   Senate Education & Employment Legislation Committee, Estimates Hearing, 19 October 2016, 74–5.

Ironically, with the government delaying legislation to implement these recommenda-tions,[169] the FWC retained many of its functions relating to registered organisations, including registration and rules,[170] as well as the *Fair Work Act* function of issuing right of entry permits.

5.35 The Trade Union Royal Commission (TURC)

5.35.05 Previous union-related Royal Commissions and inquiries

In Australia, Royal Commissions have come to be regarded as the highest form of public inquiry,[171] possessing significant powers to obtain documents and compel evidence, even in circumstances where it would otherwise be self-incriminating,[172] and to impose criminal sanctions for non-compliance.[173]

At the Federal level, the Governor-General appoints Commissioners via an instrument of appointment known as Letters Patent, which also contains the Inquiry's terms of reference. However, in practice the decision to hold a Royal Commission and the formulation of its terms of reference are matters that the government of the day determines – consistent with the convention of the Governor-General acting on ministerial advice in relation to the day-to-day government administration. The terms of reference of a Commonwealth-appointed Royal Commission can be as broad as the ambit of Commonwealth powers.

In addition, each State has its own legislation governing the operation of Royal Commis-sions and other types of inquiry in its jurisdiction.[174] There is also provision for States to provide a Federal Royal Commission with an appointment to conduct an inquiry under the relevant State legislation.[175]

This issuing of 'State Letters Patent' provides the advantage of: (a) investigating matters that would otherwise not be in the scope of a Commonwealth-appointed Royal Commission (that is, matters other than those which the Commonwealth has constitutional control over); and (b) allowing the Commission to exercise powers available under the relevant State Act, where appropriate.[176] Where the activities under investigation span both Federal and State

---

169   P Coorey 'Turnbull to mount fresh IR push in 2017', *Australian Financial Review*, 2 December 2016, 1.

170   *RO Act*, as amended by the *Fair Work (Registered Organisations) Amendment Act 2016*.

171   Australian Law Reform Commission *ALRC Report 111 – Making inquiries*, paragraph 1.16, http://www.alrc.gov.au/report-111.

172   *Royal Commissions Act 1902* (Cth) ss 2, 2(3A) and 6 (respectively). The High Court in *Giannerelli v The Queen* (1983) 154 CLR 212 confirmed that the protection against self-incrimination in the Act overrides contrary State provisions when the Commission holds a dual (Federal and State) appointment but only conducts one set of hearings.

173   *Royal Commissions Act 1902* (Cth) ss 2, 3 and 6H–6O inclusive.

174   In relation to Royal Commissions, these are: *Royal Commissions Act 1923* (NSW); *Inquiries Act 2014* (Vic); *Commissions of Inquiry Act 1950* (Qld); *Royal Commissions Act 1917* (SA); *Royal Commissions Act 1968* (WA); and *Commissions of Inquiry Act 1995* (Tas).

175   *Royal Commissions Act 1902* (Cth) s 7AA.

176   For discussion of this aspect see S Prasser 'When should Royal Commissions be appointed?' (2005) *Public Administration Today* and E Campbell *Contempt of Royal Commissions*, Faculty of Law, Monash University, Melbourne, 1984.

jurisdictions, the availability of State powers and jurisdiction is a useful addition to an inquiry's repertoire.

The Heydon Royal Commission (also referred to as TURC, for Trade Union Royal Commission) is far from being the first Royal Commission or other inquiry to have considered issues associated with unions. In recent decades there have been, at the Federal level:

- Royal Commission into Alleged Payments to Maritime Unions (1974–76) headed by JB Sweeney;
- Royal Commission into the Activities of the Australian Building Construction Employees' and Builders Labourers' Federation (1981–82) headed by JS Winneke;
- Royal Commission on the Activities of the Federated Ship Painters and Dockers Union (1980–84) headed by FX Costigan; and
- Royal Commission into the Building and Construction Industry (2001–03) headed by TRH Cole.[177]

Indeed, the apparently regular occurrence of such inquiries was summarised in the comment that 'every Liberal Prime Minister since Billy McMahon has had at least one Royal Commission into trade unions' and that it was perhaps only the shortness of McMahon's term of office that prevented him doing so.[178]

The Commissioner's own opening address on the first day that his Commission sat gave an indication of the long history of the topic.[179] The most recent predecessor of the TURC was the Royal Commission into the Building and Construction Industry conducted by retired judge Hon. Terence Cole. That inquiry, as its name suggests, was primarily focused on the construction industry and union issues associated with it. Amongst the reforms to come out of that Royal Commission was the establishment of a construction industry-specific IR regulator, the ABCC (discussed above).

5.35.10 Terms of reference

In the lead-up to the 2013 Federal election, the Coalition promised to establish a judicial inquiry into matters related to union governance and corruption. In February 2014 (now in government), the Coalition announced the establishment of a Royal Commission headed by former High Court Justice John Dyson Heydon AC QC.

The terms of reference given to Heydon when commissioned by Letters Patent dated 13 March 2014 were broad, and dealt with:

---

177   At the State level, examples span from the Royal Commission into Strikes (NSW) in 1891 through to the Royal Commission into Productivity in the Building Industry in New South Wales by R Gyles QC (NSW) in 1992. Indeed, Heydon, in conjunction with R Meagher and G Reynolds, in 1989 delivered the Report on the Duties and Fiduciary Obligations of Officials of Industrial Unions of Employers and Employees to the NSW government.

178   T Lyons 'Crippling unions: Abbott's anti-worker agenda', address to Chifley Research Centre, Melbourne, 29 October 2014. Winneke and Costigan were commissioned under the Fraser Government; Cole under the Howard Government. (However, Sweeney was commissioned under a Federal Labor government.)

179   TURC public hearing, Sydney, 9 April 2014 – referring, for example, to the Erle Royal Commission (UK) 1867–69, and the Cockburn Royal Commission (UK) 1874–75.

- Governance arrangements of separate entities established by unions or their officers, including their financial management, whether used for any unlawful purpose, the accountability of union officials to their members in respect of funds and assets in these bodies, the use of these funds, and the adequacy of laws as they relate to such bodies;[180]
- Activities relating to separate entities established or operated by five named unions: the Australian Workers Union (AWU); Construction Forestry Mining and Energy Union (CFMEU); Communications Electrical and Plumbing Union (CEPU); Health Services Union (HSU); and Transport Workers' Union (TWU); as well as any other person or body about whom credible allegations of involvement are made;[181]
- The circumstances in which funds are sought;[182]
- The extent to which union members are informed of the existence of related entities, are able to have any influence in relation to them, are protected from adverse effects and have the opportunity to hold officers accountable;[183]
- Conduct that may amount to breach of a law, regulation or professional standard by a union officer, in order to procure an advantage for themselves or another, or cause detriment to a person;[184]
- Conduct in relation separate entities that may amount to a breach of a law, regulation or professional standard by union officials who hold a position in a separate entity by virtue of their union position;[185]
- Bribes, secret commissions or unlawful payments arising from contracts or other arrangements between unions, their officers and others;[186]
- Participation of persons other than unions and their officers in the above types of conduct;[187]
- The adequacy and effectiveness of existing systems of regulation and law enforcement to deal with these matters, and the remedies available to unions and their members who have suffered a detriment as a result of such conduct;[188] and
- Matters reasonably incidental to the above terms of reference.[189]

In October 2014, the terms of reference were amended to include an additional matter '(ia)' in relation to acts undertaken to facilitate or conceal conduct that may be investigated by the Commission and extending the reporting date to 31 December 2015.[190]

---

180   Commonwealth Letters Patent issued by Governor-General, the Hon. Quentin Bryce, 13 March 2014, Term of Reference (TOR) 1.
181   Ibid TOR 2.
182   Ibid TOR 3.
183   Ibid TOR 4.
184   Ibid TOR 5.
185   Ibid TOR 6.
186   Ibid TOR 7.
187   Ibid TOR 8.
188   Ibid TOR 9.
189   Ibid TOR 10.
190   Amended Letters Patent issued 30 October 2014 by Hon. Sir Peter Cosgrove, https://www.tradeunionroyalcommission.gov.au/About/Pages/Letterspatent, 21 May 2016.

Throughout the course of 2014 each State appointed Heydon to a Commission of Inquiry under their respective legislation, with each also later providing amended terms of reference and an extended reporting date consistent with the amended Commonwealth Letters Patent.[191]

5.35.15 Hearings

The TURC conducted hearings in relation to each of the 'named' unions in the terms of reference – the AWU, CEPU, CFMEU, HSU and TWU – as well as in relation to the Maritime Union of Australia (MUA) WA Branch, the Shop Distributive and Allied Employees Association (SDA) Qld Branch, and the National Union of Workers (NUW) NSW Branch.

Royal Commissions may make their own arrangements in relation to the conduct of hearings and other aspects of their work, often doing so through the use of Practice Directions (PDs). The TURC's 'Practice Direction 1' – which postponed cross-examination of some witnesses until a date some weeks after their initial examination by Counsel Assisting, and then only with the leave of the Commissioner and the potential requirement to put on contrary evidence before getting that leave[192] – was the subject of some criticism by parties, as well as in the media.[193] However, that Practice Direction was similar to one used in the Cole Royal Commission, which successfully resisted a challenge contending that it did not provide procedural fairness to parties,[194] with the Federal Court finding that the postponement of cross-examination and the requirement for contrary evidence were not a denial of procedural fairness. Ultimately, the TURC Practice Directions were not subject to legal challenge.

The TURC adopted a case study approach, seeking to deal with matters that appeared to demonstrate conduct of a particular nature by reference to specific cases.[195] Its terms of reference meant that the scope of hearings necessarily went beyond just that of unions themselves. The hearing topics or case studies, of which there were some 75, encompassed the following subjects (with examples of the applicable case studies in brackets):

- superannuation funds (Cbus; TWU Super);
- income protection funds (Protect, CIPL; Incolink);
- redundancy funds and their alleged misuse (BERT);
- welfare funds and charitable foundations (Construction Charitable Works, Building Trades Group Drug & Alcohol Foundation);

---

191   The TURC website 'State Letters Patent' page outlines the State instruments, http://www.tradeunionroyalcommission.gov.au/About/Pages/Stateletterspatent, 21 May 2016.
192   TURC *Practice Direction 1*, paras 43–50, outlines the requirements for examination and cross-examination in hearings conducted under that Practice Direction (reproduced at TURC *Final Report*, Vol. 1, 249–51). Also available at http://www.tradeunionroyalcommission.gov.au/Pages/PracticeDirections.aspx.
193   See, for example, TURC public hearing, 7 July 2014 transcript; P Karp 'Smears left unanswered at the Royal Commission on trade unions will stick', *The Guardian*, 8 September 2014, http://www.theguardian.com/commentisfree/2014/sep/08/smears-left-unanswered-at-the-trade-union-royal-commission-will-stick.
194   *Kingham v Cole* (2002) 118 FCR 289.
195   TURC *Interim Report* (2014), Vol. 1, 3–4; TURC *Final Report*, Vol. 1, 21–3. The case study approach has been used in a number of other inquiries, including the *Royal Commission into Institutional Responses to Child Sexual Abuse*.

- registered clubs (Canberra 'Tradies' clubs);
- privacy (Cbus; SDA Qld Branch);
- alleged cartel conduct (CFMEU ACT);
- payments to unions in return for sympathetic treatment by unions (various AWU case studies including Chiquita Mushrooms, Thiess John Holland, UniBilt);
- misleading membership figures (TWU NSW re: inflated membership figures; AWU re: members apparently being signed up without their knowledge as part of a deal between the union and their employer);
- campaign funds for union elections (HSU Officers' fund, the McLean Forum);
- 'slush funds' for a mix of personal and campaign purposes (National Health Development Account, Industry 2020, AWU Workplace Reform Association); and
- examples of office-bearers allegedly using union funds for personal expenses (Jackson (HSU), Belan (NUW), Burton (TWU WA)).

The TURC held 189 days of public hearings between April 2014 and October 2015, receiving the evidence of 505 witnesses at those hearings. It also issued in excess of 2000 Notices to Produce requiring the production of documents or other material to the Commission.[196]

The findings in relation to the various case study hearings are detailed in the TURC *Final Report* and *Interim Report*, available at http://www.tradeunionroyalcommission.gov.au. A number of aspects of the Royal Commission's findings and recommendations are discussed below.

5.35.20 Policy issues and consultation

In addition to its program of hearings, the TURC engaged in consultations in each State and Territory. These included conferring with regulators, tribunals, employer associations, unions and others in the IR sphere.

During 2014, the TURC also released four Issues Papers for the purpose of policy consultation – one on each of the following topics:

- Duties of union officials;
- Funding of union elections;
- Relevant entities; and
- Protections for whistleblowers.

These documents attracted a total of 27 submissions (with some contributors making submissions in response to more than one topic).[197] Some of these submissions were from unions.

The TURC also convened an Academic Dialogue in July 2014 to inform itself of relevant issues in relation to unions and their regulation, and other significant topics, such as whistleblowers. The information from this session and from the submissions to issues papers fed into the TURC's policy considerations.

---

196   TURC *Final Report*, Vol. 1, 14–15.
197   The 2014 Issues Papers and Submissions in response are available on the TURC webpage at http://www.tradeunionroyalcommission.gov.au/submissions/pages/issues-papers.aspx.

During 2015, the TURC released its major policy and law reform paper, *Discussion Paper: Options for Law Reform*. It contained 80 questions on a range of law reform and policy topics ranging from superannuation to questions of the adequacy of current legal sanctions. A total of 20 submissions were received in response to the *Discussion Paper*.[198]

Following a determination by the ACTU not to participate in the Royal Commission,[199] the TURC used other approaches in order to consider their views as part of the assessment of information in the lead-up to policy and law reform recommendations. For example, the Commission sought out and considered submissions made by the ACTU to a range of other relevant inquiries, such as its submission to the committee considering the Fair Work (Registered Organisations) Amendment Bill 2014.[200]

The next section will consider the recommendations arising from these TURC processes.

5.35.25 Law reform recommendations

In addition to the recommendations concerning the Registered Organisations Commission and the associated State regulation of registered organisations (see earlier in this chapter), the Royal Commission also considered a number of other areas for law reform.

Indeed, an entire volume of the TURC *Final Report* – Volume 5 – dealt with law reform.[201] This section seeks to provide an overview of the areas considered and the reforms proposed. When the *Final Report* was tabled by the Federal government in December 2015, the Prime Minister challenged the Opposition to support the Commissioner's recommendations.[202] However, any adoption of Royal Commission recommendations into legislation was delayed until 2017. This has been a consequence of matters such as the ABCC and Registered Organisations Bills being rejected by the Senate on multiple occasions (though ultimately passed in late 2016), combined with the government's intention to introduce the legislation regarding the TURC recommendations after the other matters had been dealt with.[203]

The law reform recommendations made by Royal Commission dealt with the following areas (with the corresponding Chapter of the TURC *Final Report* Volume 5 in brackets):

- Regulation of Unions (Chapter 2);
- Regulation of Union Officials (Chapter 3);
- Corrupting Benefits (Chapter 4);
- Regulation of Relevant Entities (Chapter 5);
- Enterprise Agreements (Chapter 6);
- Competition Issues (Chapter 7);

---

198   The Discussion Paper and published submissions in response to it are available at http://www.tradeunionroyalcommission.gov.au/submissions/Pages/default.aspx.

199   A Patty 'ACTU boycotts Royal Commission', *Sydney Morning Herald (SMH)*, 24 June 2014, http://www.smh.com.au/national/actu-boycotts-royal-commission-20140624-zsjwn.html.

200   TURC *Final Report*, Vol. 5, 4 and 56–7.

201   Ibid Vol. 5.

202   ABC News Online 'Trade union royal commission findings: Malcolm Turnbull says report shows widespread malpractice in unions', 31 December 2015, http://www.abc.net.au/news/2015-12-30/trade-union-royal-commission-turnbull-report/7060250.

203   Refer to discussion of the ABCC and Registered Organisations Commission legislation elsewhere in this chapter.

- Building & Construction Industry (Chapter 8);
- Rights of Entry (Chapter 9).

The *Final Report* also made recommendations in relation to the operation of the *Royal Commissions Act 1902*. These are not discussed in this section.

In relation to the Regulation of Unions, the TURC made numerous recommendations, including:

- calling on the Commonwealth and States to consider adopting a national approach to registration, deregistration and regulation of registered organisations, with a single regulator overseeing all such organisations and implementing the changes to the *RO Act* recommended by the TURC;[204]
- consolidating regulatory functions into a stand-alone Registered Organisations Commission, properly resourced;[205]
- expanding the powers of the regulator and the range of matters able to be investigated under the *RO Act*;[206] and
- increasing obligations (including reporting requirements) and associated penalties in relation to registered organisations.[207]

The government has indicated that it supports the adoption of these recommendations[208] – with recommendations 1 and 2 essentially being matters for State jurisdictions.

In relation to Union Officials, the TURC recommendations (subsequently endorsed by the government) included:

- expanding the definition of 'office' in the *RO Act* to include persons: who participate in decisions affecting the whole or a substantial part of a branch; who have the capacity to significantly affect financial standing; and in accordance with whose wishes the committee of management is accustomed to act (other than professional advisers);[209]
- substantially increasing civil penalties for breaches of statutory duties by officers and employees; drawing a distinction in the legislation between a 'serious contravention' and other contraventions; and introducing criminal penalties for dishonest or reckless breaches;[210]
- prohibiting an organisation from indemnifying, paying or reimbursing a fine imposed on one of its officers;[211]

---

204   TURC *Final Report*, Recommendations 1 and 2.
205   Ibid Recommendations 3 and 4; the creation of the Registered Organisations Commission with the passage of legislation in November 2016 is discussed elsewhere in this chapter.
206   Ibid Recommendations 5–7.
207   Ibid Recommendations 8–23; the 2016 amendments to the *RO Act* increased penalties and some obligations on officials but did not address all of the TURC recommendations in this area.
208   J Massola 'Federal Election 2016: Turnbull government to ban corrupt payments from business to unions', *SMH*, 17 June 2016, http://www.smh.com.au/federal-politics/federal-election-2016/federal-election-2016-turnbull-government-to-ban-corrupt-payments-from-business-to-unions-20160617-gplld.html.
209   TURC *Final Report*, Recommendation 25 (persons of the kind defined as 'officer' in the *Corporations Act 200* (Cth)).
210   Ibid Recommendations 28 and 29.
211   Ibid Recommendation 30.

- stronger disclosure requirements where personal interests are concerned;[212] and
- expanding the provisions in relation to persons disqualified from holding office and the consequences for a person breaching those provisions.[213]

The payment of corrupting benefits was a recurring theme during the TURC's inquiry – and its *Final Report* recognised that for someone to receive a benefit that influenced their conduct, someone else had to have made that payment. The Commissioner's recommendations were in relation to disclosure of payments made to registered organisations, and that offering, promising or giving payments to an official of a registered organisation (other than specified legitimate payments) ought to be a criminal offence, as should the acceptance of such payments.[214] These recommendations were also supported by the government.

Relevant entities – bodies which are not unions but have close links to either a union or its officers – were the subject of many of the TURC's case studies and a number of questionable practices were revealed. Currently, while there are obligations in the *RO Act* for registered organisations to declare transactions with related parties, the regulation of the related entities themselves is beyond its scope.

The Commissioner recommended the amendment of legislation[215] to require financial reporting for controlled entities,[216] to require the registration of election funds[217] and to increase the regulation of worker entitlement funds and employee insurance products (many of which have close links to registered organisations and/or provide them with financial benefits).[218] These recommendations also attracted government support.

Many of the TURC case studies indicated that enterprise agreements negotiated by unions were the vehicle used to institutionalise payments to union-related income protection funds, redundancy funds, training funds and organisations – ostensibly for the welfare of employees. However, the evidence indicated that in many cases these were simply discretionary trusts, which could be selective about whether or not payments were made.

The Commissioner's recommendations, which also attracted government support, were that:

- an organisation that is a bargaining representative be required to disclose any benefit that it or an officer or related entity could reasonably expect to gain from the inclusion of a particular term in an enterprise agreement;[219] and
- it be unlawful to include in an enterprise agreement a requirement to pay contributions to a fund for the benefit of an employee, unless that fund is a registered worker entitlement fund (as discussed in Recommendation 45), a registered charity or a superannuation fund.[220]

---

212   Ibid Recommendations 31 and 32.
213   Ibid Recommendations 36 to 38.
214   Ibid Recommendations 39 to 41.
215   Including the *RO Act* and the *Corporations Act*.
216   TURC *Final Report*, Recommendation 43.
217   Ibid Recommendation 44.
218   Ibid Recommendations 45 and 46.
219   Ibid Recommendation 48.
220   Ibid Recommendation 49.

The Commissioner's recommendation in relation to superannuation – removing the exemption of awards and agreements, which prevents some employees from accessing 'choice of fund' – has already been the subject of legislative drafting by the government.[221]

In relation to competition issues, the Commissioner recommended amendments and increased penalties in relation to the secondary boycott provisions in the *Competition and Consumer Act 2010* (Cth),[222] annual reporting by the ACCC of secondary boycott complaints and the extension of its cartel immunity policy,[223] and giving the building industry regulator concurrent powers with the ACCC in relation to secondary boycotts.[224] These recommendations appear to reflect a view that the ACCC's legislation and regulatory response in relation to unions and secondary boycotts were lacking in these areas.

In relation to the building and construction industry, the Commissioner's recommendations supported: industry-specific legislation for a construction industry regulator;[225] consideration of special legislation in relation to certain CFMEU officials;[226] repealing ss 73 and 73A of the *FW(BI) Act*, which prevented the FWBC from taking enforcement proceedings when other proceedings for the same conduct had been settled;[227] and increasing penalties in the *Fair Work Act* for coercion and prohibited industrial action, as well as recommending confirmation that picketing by employees or unions be regarded as industrial action.[228]

The Commissioner also recommended: the tightening of requirements in relation to union right of entry to workplaces (including the prerequisites for holding a permit), ongoing disclosure requirements while holding a permit, expanding the basis on which a permit can be suspended, and increasing the threshold for exercising entry rights associated with safety matters.[229]

A further issue, canvassed in the TURC's 2015 *Discussion Paper*, was consideration of the US *Racketeer Influenced and Corrupt Organisations Act* (known as RICO)[230] and whether it should be adopted in Australia.[231]

Although one submission[232] urged the adoption of RICO-style legislation, others urged caution and yet others rejected it as unsuitable or undesirable in the Australian IR landscape.[233] The Royal Commission noted the Australian approaches to dealing with organised crime and corruption, including the creation of bodies such as the Australian Crime Commission, which has significant powers, and the adoption of proceeds of crime laws to deal with such issues. The Commissioner also noted the adverse effects that RICO-style laws may have beyond the

---

221   Seeking repeal of parts of s 32C of the *Superannuation Guarantee (Administration) Act 1992* (Cth).
222   TURC *Final Report*, Recommendations 52–5 and 59.
223   Ibid Recommendations 56 and 58.
224   Ibid Recommendation 57.
225   As envisaged in the Coalition's ABCC Bill (ultimately enacted in November 2016); TURC Final Report, Recommendations 61–3.
226   Ibid Recommendation 60.
227   Ibid Recommendation 65.
228   Ibid Recommendation 66.
229   Ibid Recommendations 67–76.
230   18 USC Ch. 96 (1961–1968).
231   TURC *Discussion Paper – Options for Law Reform* (2015) 113–16.
232   Boral Submission to the Discussion Paper: Options for Law Reform.
233   TURC *Final Report*, Vol. 5, 478–84.

construction industry (the sector in which it was asserted to be most needed).[234] Ultimately, the TURC rejected RICO-style laws as a response to the issues that it was dealing with.[235]

5.35.30 Referrals arising from the Royal Commission

Section 6P of the *Royal Commissions Act 1902* (Cth) provides that:

> Where, in the course of inquiring into a matter, a Commission obtains information that relates, or that may relate, to a contravention of a law, or evidence of a contravention of a law, of the Commonwealth, of a State or of a Territory, the Commission may, if in the opinion of the Commission it is appropriate so to do, communicate the information or furnish the evidence, as the case may be, to:
>
> (a) the Attorney-General of the Commonwealth, of a State, of the Australian Capital Territory or of the Northern Territory; or
>
> (aa) the Director of Public Prosecutions; or
>
> (b) [Repealed]
>
> (c) a Special Prosecutor appointed under the Special Prosecutors Act; or
>
> (d) the Commissioner of the Australian Federal Police or of the Police Force of a State or of the Northern Territory; or
>
> (e) the authority or person responsible for the administration or enforcement of that law.

Contravention of a law refers to something that makes a person liable to a criminal penalty or a civil or administrative penalty.[236] A Royal Commission may also communicate information or furnish evidence to the Australian Crime Commission, the Australian Commission on Law Enforcement Integrity (ACLEI) or another Royal Commission, if it relates to the functions of that body.[237]

The provision of information to other bodies in relation to such contraventions is known as a 'referral'. Many referrals arise from findings made in the TURC *Interim* and *Final Reports*. What is the status of these referrals, particularly when they allege breaches of criminal law?

This issue was canvassed in submissions made prior to the TURC *Interim Report* being handed down.[238] The *Interim Report* responded to these matters by noting that even where persons were referred to other agencies in relation to alleged contraventions of particular laws, the Royal Commission (not being a court of law) could not make final determinations in those matters, leaving it up to the relevant agencies, and courts (where appropriate) to consider.[239]

The *Interim Report* and *Final Report* both detailed referrals made to other agencies. These included referrals to: the Australian Federal Police (AFP) and State police forces; the FWC; the FWBC (now the ABCC); ASIC; the Australian Taxation Office (ATO); the Australian Charities and Non-Profits Commission (ACNC); the Office of the Australian Information Commissioner

234   Ibid 484–5.
235   Ibid 484.
236   *Royal Commissions Act 1902* s 6P(1A).
237   Ibid ss 6P(2), 6P(2A), 6P(2B).
238   TURC public hearings, 27 and 29 November 2014.
239   TURC *Interim Report*, Vol. 1, 5–21.

(OAIC); and other State and Territory agencies responsible for administering or enforcing the laws to which the referrals relate.[240]

Most of these matters remain the subject of consideration and/or investigation by these bodies and have not concluded. However, from publicly available information it is apparent that:

- the FWBC successfully prosecuted a CFMEU official in South Australia for intimidation of an FWBC Inspector;[241]
- the Commonwealth DPP successfully prosecuted two former staff of the superannuation fund Cbus for giving false evidence to the Royal Commission;[242]
- the FWC was successful in civil penalty proceedings against two former Branch Secretaries of the TWU's WA Branch, James McGiveron and Rick Burton;[243] and
- substantial criminal charges have been laid against former HSU Secretary, Kathy Jackson, in relation to her use of funds.[244]

Conversely, the ACT Directorate of Chief Minister, Treasury and Economic Development (responsible for the *Work Health and Safety Act 2001* (ACT)) concluded that the limitation period had already expired in relation to a referral made to it by the Royal Commission for the alleged intimidation of a WorkSafe Inspector,[245] and a number of matters referred to the FWBC did not proceed to court.[246]

As a number of the parties referred to other agencies by the TURC were referred to more than one agency (including the police) – with each having to make its own assessment of matters, including admissibility of evidence (not simply relying on the revelations made at Royal Commission hearings) – the process of finalising these referrals may take some considerable time.

5.40 Law reform

5.40.05 Substantive changes to the *RO Act*

Where conduct by a union official does not relate to financial management, the regulator is limited in the recourse that it has. It may seek declarations from the court that the conduct is in

240 Ibid Vol. 1, 30–6 and TURC *Final Report*, Vol. 1, Appendix 2 provide a list of the referrals arising from each of those reports.

241 ABC News 'CFMEU official John Perkovic banned from worksites for bullying government investigator at Adelaide construction site', 23 June 2015, http://www.abc.net.au/news/2015-06-23/cfmeu-john-perkovic-banned-for-bullying-government-investigator/6568224.

242 Australian Financial Review 'Former Cbus employees escape jail', 18 March 2016, http://www.afr.com/news/policy/industrial-relations/former-cbus-employees-escape-jail-20160318-gnm3je.

243 *General Manager of the Fair Work Commission v McGiveron* [2017] FCA 405.

244 B Norington 'Kathy Jackson charged by police over 70 criminal offences', *The Australian*, 31 August 2016, http://www.theaustralian.com.au/national-affairs/industrial-relations/kathy-jackson-charged-by-police-over-70-criminal-offences/news-story/9f1985140bad551c51e485f54463f27e.

245 *Canberra Times* 'Dean Hall slams Royal Commission after intimidation charge dropped', 6 March 2016, http://www.canberratimes.com.au/act-news/dean-hall-slams-royal-commission-after-intimidation-allegation-dropped-20160306-gnc6ci.html.

246 Senate Education and Employment Legislation Committee, Estimates Hearing, 19 October 2016, 74–5.

breach of the organisation's rules.[247] However, declaratory relief alone will generally not provide sufficient response. This can be particularly challenging when the regulator, or union members, are faced with situations where office-bearers are actively involved in contraventions, but those contraventions may not reach the threshold of 'financial management'.

The extension of ss 285 to 288 of the *RO Act* to cover matters other than financial management, such as broader governance and conduct obligations, would seem an appropriate remedy.

While the *Fair Work (Registered Organisations) Amendment Act 2016* established the Registered Organisations Commission and increased penalties for contraventions of the *RO Act*, it largely did not change the substance of the *RO Act*. Consequently, the powers of inquiry and investigation bestowed on the Commissioner (powers formerly held by the General Manager of the FWC)[248] remain confined to matters concerned with the financial management of registered organisations and alleged contraventions of the civil penalty provisions.

This, too, contrasts with the position taken by the Heydon Royal Commission, which recommended the expansion and clarification of these powers.[249]

If those sections are to remain unamended, the introduction of separate provisions to sanction non-financial misconduct should be considered. Examples of such provisions could readily be drawn from the professional conduct and practice rules relating to legal practitioners, medical professionals etc.

5.40.10 State registration for federal unions

As mentioned earlier in this chapter, another aspect of the regulation of unions is the complexity arising from the continuation of State IR jurisdictions.

Constitutional limitations and the reluctance of the States to relinquish IR powers in relation to their own workforces make a single national IR jurisdiction (including both public and private sectors) unlikely.

However, while registration may be a requirement of participation in ongoing State jurisdictions, the system of union registration could be simplified to reduce the number of separate entities occupying the field, which causes confusion for participants and regulators alike.

Under current arrangements, for example, in one union there may be both a State-registered body (referred to as the State union) and a branch of a federally registered organisation (referred to as the State branch) – the former of these bodies being registered with the State IR jurisdiction, and the latter being a reporting unit in the Federal jurisdiction rather than an entity in its own right.[250]

While each jurisdiction is individually dealing with its own registered entity (the State union or the State reporting unit of the Federal union) for purposes *within* that jurisdiction such as adjudicating industrial disputes, registering agreements etc, this situation may be able to be

---

247   *RO Act*, s 163.
248   *RO Act* ss 330 and 331.
249   TURC *Final Report*, Vol. 5, 65–6.
250   This dichotomy is discussed in Creighton and Stewart *Labour Law* (2010), canvassing relevant judgements such as *Williams v Hursey* (1959) 103 CLR 30 and *Moore v Doyle* (1969) 15 FLR 59.

tolerated. However, when fundamental matters such as to whom the funds or assets belong becomes the salient issue – for example, in cases where an official has misappropriated those funds or sought to transfer those assets – establishing just who owns and controls them is a threshold matter for regulators. This has been a live issue for many years, and was particularly apparent following amalgamations of unions, and when established State unions (many with substantial assets) engage with their Federal counterparts.[251]

How can a State or Federal regulator pursue a union official for a breach of their legislation unless and until they can establish that the finances that were mismanaged or misappropriated were within that regulator's jurisdiction?

In some cases, there are arrangements whereby the finances are split 50:50 between the State union and its Federal branch counterpart in that State. In others, they may be vested entirely with the State body and contributions are made from those funds directly to the Federal body (with the State branch as a 'shell', albeit with the same officials) – or indeed the reverse. Further variants may be in place, depending on the circumstances of particular unions, such as their origins (preservation of pre-amalgamation arrangements, for instance), their membership coverage in State and Federal jurisdictions, their geography (Broken Hill being covered by a South Australia-based entity at the Federal level, but its members in State entities still being subject to NSW jurisdiction) and a range of other factors.

So, how to simplify union registration and regulation to provide for legal certainty about which body owns and controls the assets, while preserving the necessary concept of State registration for the purpose of operating in the State systems?

Chapter 5, Division 1 of the *Industrial Relations Act 1996* (NSW) (*IR Act NSW*) seems to hold a possible answer. Sections 218 and 220 of that Act provide that a federally registered organisation may apply for registration under the State legislation, subject to an objections process, if it has the consent of each State-registered organisation whose coverage extends to classes of members covered by the federally registered body. In circumstances where there is another organisation to which members could more conveniently belong or which would more effectively represent them, the Federal entity must give an undertaking to avoid disputes arising from this overlap of eligibility.[252]

How does this provision operate in practice? In August 2015, the NSW Teachers Federation – without doubt an active participant in the State IR jurisdiction – made applications to vary its registration. The applications were to, concurrently, seek the deregistration of the NSW Teachers Federation as a State-registered entity and to seek the registration of the Australian Education Union (New South Wales Teachers Federation Branch), a branch of the Federal entity, as an organisation registered for the purposes of the NSW Act.[253]

On 11 August 2015, the President of the New Soth Wales Industrial Relations Commission, Justice Walton, granted the applications with effect from the following week.[254] This change in registration had the effect that:

251 *Re McJannet; Ex parte Minister for Employment, Training and Industrial Relations (Qld)* (1995) 184 CLR 620, discussed in L Floyd 'The *Fair Work Act*'s forgotten issues' (2010) *Australian Bar Review* 1.
252 *IR Act 1996* (NSW) s 218(1A).
253 NSWIRC *Announcement: Registration of the Australian Education Union New South Wales Teachers Federation Branch*, 13 August 2015, http://www.irc.justice.nsw.gov.au/Pages/IRC_research_information.
254 Ibid.

- the NSW Branch of the federally registered union is now recognised as a registered organisation in the State jurisdiction;
- the old State union has ceased to exist;
- the union is only required to submit one set of financial returns (to the FWC), as the NSWIRC exempted the new organisation from having to lodge with it – being satisfied that the reporting requirements in the *RO Act* met or exceeded those required by the State legislation.[255]

Given that most of the employer and employee organisations registered with State jurisdictions are branches, offshoots or parallel bodies of federally registered organisations, this approach should not be unduly complex.

However, to ensure that all members in the State systems could belong to federally registered organisations, relevant sections of the *RO Act* would need to be amended to facilitate the eligibility rules being able to accommodate such a change, particularly as transitional arrangements in the Act come to an end and a Federal connection is otherwise needed.

By approaching the issue from the perspective of State branches of federally registered unions seeking registration in the State jurisdiction, as in the example of AEU NSW Teachers Federation outlined above, some of the contentious issues associated with State unions moving into the Federal sphere, such as those illustrated in the *AFULE* case regarding conflicts with other unions associated with geographical expansion,[256] might be able to be avoided.

5.45 Union right of entry

5.45.05 The position before the *Workplace Relations Act 1996* (Cth) (*WR Act*)

The role of union officials, in particular full-time elected officials and union employees, and the functions exercised by them are inextricably linked to their ability to represent the industrial interests of those eligible to be members.[257] It is necessary for the union to maintain contact with its members for a range of reasons, including providing members with information in relation to employment-related issues, representing them and assisting them in dealings with their employer, negotiating on their behalf, and responding to related matters such as safety and welfare.

In order to achieve these objectives, a key element is the ability of unions to connect with the workplaces in which their members work, particularly as these members work in varied locations. The ability to enter such workplaces is therefore an important issue. Conversely, employers seek to ensure control of their workplaces and who enters them, and to minimise disruptions to production.

---

255   *IR Act 1996* (NSW) s 281.
256   *Australian Rail, Tram and Bus Industry Union v Australian Federated Union of Locomotive Employees, Queensland Union of Employees* (2008) 172 IR 47.
257   See *Regional Express Holdings Ltd v Australian Federation of Air Pilots* (2016) 244 FCR 344 for a discussion of the extent of this entitlement to represent.

Prior to the *WR Act*, and in a more densely unionised workforce, it appears to have been accepted that union entry to the workplace was part and parcel of doing business, unless that entry was considered to be unlawful trespass or if other breaches occurred. It was more likely that such breaches would arise in circumstances of industrial action or the steps leading to it – an issue discussed in more detail below in relation to industrial action and, more particularly, industrial torts.

This was reflected in provisions such as s 286 of the *Industrial Relations Act 1988* (Cth) (*IR Act 1988*) which enabled officers of a union, authorised by the Secretary of their union, to enter and inspect premises and carry out a range of functions. This was often complemented by a range of other union rights (whether for workplace delegates or union officials) contained in particular awards or agreements.[258] While not all awards or agreements had such provisions, in the environment of provisions such as s 286, it is unsurprising that similar arrangements were widespread, whether explicitly provided for or not. While the *IR Act* made provision for Inspectors of the Department of Industrial Relations to have right of entry and identity cards,[259] there were no similar provisions for permits *per se* in relation to union officials, beyond being authorised by their union.

5.45.10 An overview of the right of entry permit system

The enactment of the *WR Act* in 1996 introduced a scheme whereby a union official was required to be the holder of a right of entry permit to gain access to a workplace.[260] However, it did not require a person who was already an employee, such as the union delegate working within the workplace, to hold a right of entry permit in relation to his/her own workplace. If, however, that person were an office-bearer of the union more broadly – the part-time Vice-President of their union, say – they would require a permit if they wished to exercise the right of entry to workplaces other than their own on union business.

The *WR Act* scheme was administered by the Registry of the Australian Industrial Relations Commission (AIRC) (as it then was). Entitlement to right of entry was linked to whether the permit holder's union was a party bound by an award that applied to that workplace and in which members, or persons eligible to become members, worked.[261] The scheme for entry permits was contained in ss 285A to 285G of the *WR Act*, and s 127AA of the Act made any additional agreement to give additional entry rights unenforceable. These matters are discussed in detail in cases such as *Moranbah*[262] and *Police and Nurses Credit Society*.[263]

---

258   Creighton and Stewart *Labour Law* (2010) 709, noting cases such as *Meneling Station Pty Ltd v Australasian Meat Industry Employees Union* (1987) 18 FCR 51 and *Australasian Meat Industry Employees Union v Thomas Borthwick & Sons (Pacific) Ltd* (1991) 32 FCR 28.

259   *IR Act* ss 85 and 86 and the work of J Shaw and CG Walton 'A union's right of entry to the workplace' (1994) 36 *Journal of Industrial Relations* 546, discussing the pre-1996 system.

260   Division 11A Entry and inspection of premises etc by organisations, contained in Part IX, *WR Act*, which operated in conjunction with s 127AA of that Act.

261   *WR Act* s 285C.

262   *Moranbah North Coal (Management) Pty Ltd v Construction, Forestry, Mining and Energy Union* (2000) 103 IR 267 at 273.

263   *Finance Sector Union of Australia v Police and Nurses Credit Society Ltd* (Unreported, Australian Industrial Relations Commission, Commissioner O'Connor, 29 November 2003) [51] et seq.

Under s 285G of the *WR Act*, the AIRC had the power to revoke a right of entry permit for the purpose of preventing or settling an industrial dispute.[264] The section also specified that if it did so, the AIRC could also make any other order related to preventing or settling the dispute, and about whether to issue a further permit to that person or to any other person.

5.45.15 Right of entry under the *Fair Work Act*

The right of entry provisions formerly in the *WR Act* are now dealt with in Part 3-4 of the *Fair Work Act*, and they largely replicate the *WR Act* provisions. This reflected the approach of the Rudd Government to combat criticism that it would unduly extend union rights.

One significant change was that right of entry under the *Fair Work Act* is now linked to the right of the union to represent the industrial interests of the relevant employees,[265] rather than to coverage by a particular industrial instrument. The FWC has the power to resolve disputes between unions by making a 'representation order' for a particular workplace group.

Another notable change was the removal of the 'conscientious objector' provision (formerly s 762 of the *WR Act*) in relation to right of entry.

Section 512 of the *Fair Work Act* provides that union officials (including employees of that union) have the right to enter premises if they hold a valid entry permit issued under the Act. The process for obtaining a right of entry permit and the requirements that have to be met in order to be granted and retain a permit are outlined in the next section.

A permit-holder may enter a workplace to investigate a suspected contravention of the Act, or of the terms of a fair work instrument provided that it relates to or affects a member of the permit holder's union whose interests it is entitled to represent and who performs work at the premises.[266] The permit-holder may also seek access to non-member records if it can satisfy the FWC that the records are relevant and necessary to the investigation of the suspected contravention.[267] However, s 504 makes it clear that any personal information obtained by a union official must be treated in accordance with the requirements of the *Privacy Act 1988* (Cth).

Permit-holders also have the right to enter premises for the purpose of holding discussions with members or persons eligible to be members, provided that they give the requisite notice of entry (a minimum of 24 hours' notice) and that the right of entry is exercised during a permitted time – during the hours of operation of the workplace, but restricted to work breaks in relation to conferring with members or potential members.[268]

The FWC is empowered to deal with disputes in relation to right of entry, and may issue orders in relation to such disputes. It also has the power to vary or revoke such orders, particularly where the circumstances which led to the making of an order have materially changed.[269]

---

264   Ibid.
265   *Re Maritime Union of Australia* (2016) 68 AILR 102-689.
266   *Fair Work Act* s 481.
267   Ibid s 483AA; *United Voice* [2016] FWC 4454.
268   *Fair Work Act 2009* (Cth) s 487. Failure to comply with the entry permit regime can lead to revocation or restriction of an official's permit: see, for example, *Roberts v Office of the Fair Work Building Industry Inspectorate* [2016] FWCFB 6696, affirming the decision in *Fair Work Commission v Roberts* [2016] FWC 4052.
269   For example, *Maritime Union of Australia v JKC Australia LNG Pty Ltd* [2016] FWC 201 and *Maritime Union of Australia v JKC Australia LNG Pty Ltd* [2016] FWC 3056.

It is an offence for an employer to refuse a union official right of entry where he/she is the holder of a permit and has complied with all the requirements of the legislation outlined above.[270]

Conversely, it is an offence for a permit-holder to seek to abuse entry rights to cause disruption to a business or to refuse to leave a site when reasonably requested to do so.[271] And it will be considered an abuse of the right of entry if a permit-holder repeatedly enters premises with either the intention or the effect of obstructing or harassing an employer or occupier.[272]

Upon entry to a workplace, the *Fair Work Act* (as did the *WR Act* before it) requires that the permit-holder comply with any reasonable directions in relation to safety,[273] the route to be taken within the workplace (unless that would undermine the investigation of contraventions)[274] and where discussions with workers take place.[275] However, this latter issue has been the subject of some dispute, given the potentially conflicting objectives of the employer (seeking to minimise disruption and perhaps also union involvement/exposure) and the union (seeking to meet in advantageous locations such as lunch areas and adjacent to work areas). In such cases, the FWC has been called upon to adjudicate the dispute, with matters such as the reasonableness of the request being relevant considerations.[276]

Significantly, it is still open to some occupiers of premises to invite non-permit-holders onto their sites – however, such persons still cannot exercise any of the statutory rights associated with the right of entry provisions of the *Fair Work Act*, and must leave if/when asked to do so, otherwise their presence will amount to trespass and, in some jurisdictions, also criminal conduct.[277] However, the Federal government's amended *Building Code* (part of the reforms associated with the re-establishment of the ABCC),[278] has the effect of not permitting an employer to invite an officer of a union in the building industry, beyond the requirements of the right of entry provisions in the *Fair Work Act* and the relevant jurisdiction's safety laws onto a work site.[279]

---

270   *Fair Work Act 2009* (Cth) ss 501 and 502. See, for example, *Automotive, Food, Metals, Engineering, Printing and Kindred Industries Union v Byrne Trailers Pty Ltd* [2009] FMCA 1192 in relation to a breach of the equivalent *WR Act* provisions.
271   *Fair Work Act 2009* (Cth) s 500. See also *Darlaston v Parker* (2010) 189 FCR 1.
272   Ibid s 508(4).
273   Ibid s 491; *Darlaston v Parker* (2010) 189 FCR 1.
274   *Fair Work Act 2009* (Cth) s 492A.
275   Ibid s 492. Though note *Central Queensland Services v Construction, Forestry, Mining and Energy Union* [2017] FCAFC 43.
276   *Construction, Forestry, Mining and Energy Union v Central Queensland Services* [2016] FWCFB 288; *Construction, Forestry, Mining and Energy Union v Gittany* [2014] FCA 164; *Transport Workers' Union of Australia NSW Branch v DHL Supply Chain (Australia) Pty Ltd* (2011) 209 IR 242; *Australasian Meat Industry Employees Union v Dardanup Butchering Co. Pty Ltd* (2011) 209 IR 1; *National Union of Workers v Coles Group Supply Chain Pty Ltd* [2014] FWC 1674.
277   See, for example, *Inclosed Lands Protection Act 1901* (NSW) s 4.
278   *Building and Construction Industry (Improving Productivity) Act 2016* (Cth) s 34.
279   Refer *Building Code 2014* s 14.

5.45.20 Applications for permits (and their removal)

Granting of a right of entry permit by the FWC does not occur simply by virtue of a person being a union official. While the holding of a relevant role as a union official (office-bearer or employee) is a necessary prerequisite, it is just the first of several requirements.

The process adopted by the FWC requires the application to be made through the union for whom the proposed permit-holder works. The application must indicate whether the proposed permit-holder is an office-holder or an employee of the union (and specify the position held), and advise whether the permit-holder had previously held a right of entry permit and the status of that permit (returned; lost; not yet expired).[280]

In making an application for a permit, an authorised official (defined to include a member of the union's Committee of Management) is also required to sign the application to verify the matters contained in it: the applicant is an officer or employee of the union; the belief that the applicant is a fit and proper person; the applicant has completed appropriate training; and the applicant has disclosed any relevant matters.[281] The official must also verify the steps taken to confirm the permit qualification matters contained in s 513(1) of the *Fair Work Act*.[282] The proposed permit-holder must make a declaration to the same effect.

It is a criminal offence to knowingly provide false or misleading information in an application for a permit or to make a false or misleading statement in an application for a permit.[283]

Union officials may also hold a WHS Entry Permit for the purposes of exercising functions under the relevant workplace health and safety legislation. In order to do so, the permit-holder must be a union official, have completed prescribed workplace health and safety training and hold an entry permit, as well as complying with the following requirements: 24 hours' notice required to inspect books and records; 24 hours' notice required to consult with and advise workers; but prior notice not required to inquire into a suspected breach.[284]

The ABCC has the right to make submissions in a matter before the FWC that arises under the *Fair Work Act* and involves a building industry participant or building work. This includes any application for a right of entry permit by a building industry participant.

The term of a right of entry permit is 3 years. However, the term of a permit may be extended in circumstances where the permit-holder has lodged a renewal application that has not been finalised by the FWC: that is, where it is still being considered by a tribunal member.[285]

When considering any application (whether by a building industry participant or not), the FWC is required to take into account the permit qualification matters set out in s 513 of the *Fair Work Act*, such as training, convictions, previous revocation or suspension of permits. The FWC may impose conditions on permit-holders or may refuse to issue a right of entry permit

---

280   Non-return or loss of a permit requires the completion of a statutory declaration to explain the failure to comply with *Fair Work Act* s 517.
281   *Fair Work Act 2009* (Cth) s 513 and FWC Form 42.
282   FWC Form 42: Application for Right of Entry Permit (form approved 1 April 2016).
283   *Fair Work Act* s 513 and *Criminal Code Act 1995* (Cth) ss 136 and 137.
284   Model Act ss 116–147, as enacted (for example) in the *Work Health and Safety Act* 2011 (NSW).
285   *Application by Construction, Forestry, Mining and Energy Union and General Division, Queensland and Northern Territory Divisional Branch* [2016] FWC 3389.

where it considers it appropriate, having considered the matters in s 513.[286] These also include circumstances where either the registered organisation or the official has abused permit rights.[287]

5.50 Industrial action

5.50.05 Definition

Industrial Action is defined in s 19 of the *Fair Work Act* as any of the following:

(a)   the performance of work by an employee in a manner different from that in which it is customarily performed, or the adoption of a practice in relation to work by an employee, the result of which is a restriction or limitation on, or a delay in, the performance of the work;

(b)   a ban,[288] limitation or restriction on the performance of work by an employee or on the acceptance of or offering for work by an employee;

(c)   a failure or refusal by employees to attend for work or a failure or refusal to perform any work at all by employees who attend for work;

(d)   the lockout of employees from their employment by the employer of the employees.

However, it does not include action consented to by the employer,[289] or certain safety-related action if particular criteria are met. (The latter is discussed below.)

This definition is not dissimilar from those in earlier iterations of the IR legislation at the Federal level[290] nor the definitions in the States' IR legislation. It is obviously also broader than simply complete withdrawal of labour (strike action).

Industrial action is, *prima facie*, a breach of the employment contract – the employee refusing to work as directed and/or not performing work as part of the 'work–wages bargain'.

However, there are limits to what acts fall within the definition of 'industrial action'. For example, in Australia a distinction has been drawn between the withdrawal of labour (which is industrial action) and those workers taking action in the form of a 'picket line' adjacent to the employer's workplace (which is regarded as not industrial action).[291] This picketing distinction is discussed below.

Action will also not be regarded as being industrial in nature 'if it stands completely outside the area of disputation and bargaining'.[292]

---

286   See, for example, the Full Bench's decision in *Re Maritime Union of Australia* (2014) 241 IR 216 re refusal to issue a permit to the WA Assistant Secretary of that union.

287   *Director, Fair Work Building Industry Inspectorate v Construction, Forestry, Mining and Energy Union* [2016] FWC 811 and, on appeal, *Construction, Forestry, Mining and Energy Union v Director, Fair Work Building Industry Inspectorate* [2016] FWCFB 3241.

288   *Energy Australia Yallourn Pty Ltd v Construction, Forestry, Mining and Energy Union* [2013] FWC 1202 notes that a ban is a prohibition on performing certain work rather than a particular way of working ('work to rule').

289   *Fair Work Act 2009* (Cth) s 19(2).

290   For example, the definition of 'industrial action' inserted in the *Conciliation and Arbitration Act 1904* (Cth) by the *Conciliation and Arbitration Amendment Act (No. 3) 1977* (Cth) and essentially replicated in the *IR Act 1988*, the *WR Act* and now the *Fair Work Act*.

291   *Davids Distribution Pty Ltd v National Union of Workers* (1999) 91 FCR 463.

292   *Automotive, Food, Metals, Engineering, Printing and Kindred Industries Union v The Age Co. Ltd* [2004] AIRC 445.

5.50.10 The right to strike: the international position

Australia is a signatory to many conventions of the International Labour Organization (ILO), including the convention concerning Freedom of Association and Protection of the Right to Organise (ILO Convention 87) and the convention concerning the Application of the Principles of the Right to Organise and to Bargain Collectively (ILO Convention 98).[293]

The ILO's Committee of Experts on the Application of Conventions and Recommendations (CEACR) has observed, as a fundamental aspect of the rights of workers and their unions under Art 3 of ILO Convention 87, that:

> The right to strike is one of the essential means available to workers and their organizations for the promotion and protection of their economic and social interests.[294]

It has also been argued that by being a party to the Universal Declaration of Human Rights, Australia has accepted its fundamental tenets, including respect for the existence of trade unions and all that goes with that (including the right to take industrial action), whether or not we are a signatory to particular conventions.[295] Nevertheless, it is also well established that for international obligations to be imported into Australian law some further step, ordinarily in the form of legislation, is required, in order to give it domestic application.

However, even in the ILO Conventions, despite the 'rights' sentiments expressed, the right to strike is not expressed as being either unfettered or universally applicable. For example, it is expressed as being subject to being exercised in accordance with the laws of the land, as well as having specific 'carve outs' for particular groups of workers.[296] As industrial action is clearly broader than just strikes, these arguments may also be applied to lesser forms of industrial action – those that do not involve the complete withdrawal of labour.

5.50.15 Constraints on the right to strike in Australia

Although a signatory of ILO Convention 87, and despite the right to strike being explicitly recognised in the *IR Act 1988*, in reality there are considerable constraints on the right to strike, or to take other forms of industrial action, in Australia.[297]

Since the advent of the *WR Act* in 1996, industrial laws at the Federal level have drawn a distinction between two types of industrial action: 'protected action' and 'unprotected action'. As the names suggest, one attracts certain legal protections and the other does not (and also brings with it a range of other sanctions). This distinction has continued under the *Fair Work Act*, albeit there has been some tweaking of specific provisions. Protected industrial action, unprotected industrial action and associated issues (including the power of the tribunal to order cessation of industrial action) are discussed in detail below.

---

293   ILO 87 (1948) and ILO 98 (1949), both ratified by Australia on 28 February 1973.
294   ILO 200 (1983) and ILO 147 (1994), cited in S McCrystal *The Right to Strike in Australia* (Federation Press, 2010) 26.
295   Ibid, Chs 2 and 4.
296   ILO Convention 87, Cl 8(1) and ILO Convention 98, Cl 6, by way of examples.
297   See McCrystal *The Right to Strike in Australia* (2010) for a comprehensive analysis.

The *Fair Work Act*, like the *WR Act*, also makes it unlawful for an employer to pay or an employee to demand or request pay for a period of strike action.[298] The application of this requirement to industrial action involving partial non-performance of duties is discussed below, in the section dealing with protected and unprotected action.

Another constraint in relation to industrial action is the existence of 'essential services' legislation. This legislation, found in most States and Territories, provides the relevant government with the power to declare certain industries 'essential services'.[299] This has the effect of allowing the State to intervene to prevent industrial action affecting these industries at particular times, as defined in the relevant legislation. (Interestingly, while mentioning ambulance officers and other 'essential'/emergency service workers, essential services legislation does not mention police – most likely a hangover from the traditional notion that police were not regarded as employees, but rather as direct servants of the Crown.)[300]

5.50.20 Protected industrial action: requirements

Protected industrial action is defined by s 408 of the *Fair Work Act*. As will rapidly become apparent, there are numerous requirements to be met in order for industrial action to qualify as protected industrial action.

First, there is a 'point in time' constraint: employees can take 'protected industrial action' to support or advance claims during collective bargaining, after the nominal expiry date of an existing enterprise agreement and prior to the certification of a new agreement.[301] (Bargaining is discussed in detail in Chapter 4.)

In addition, the action will only be protected if it has been authorised by a ballot: such ballots are mandatory, so the action, to be protected, requires the making of a ballot order as a prerequisite. The ballot is required to specify the types of industrial action for which endorsement is sought from members.[302] For a ballot to occur, an application must be submitted to the FWC, which will consider whether the mandatory requirements of the *Fair Work Act* have been met, namely:

- the applicant union is a bargaining representative for the employees to be balloted;
- the application specifies the group of employees to be balloted;
- a copy was provided to the employer and the AEC within 24 hours of the application;
- the nominal expiry date of the relevant agreement has passed; and
- the union is genuinely trying to reach agreement with the employer.[303]

---

298   *Fair Work Act 2009* (Cth) ss 473–475.
299   For example, the *Essential Services Act 1988* (NSW).
300   Though note the qualifications placed on this distinction by more recent cases such as the High Court's decision in *Jarratt v Commissioner for Police (NSW)* (2005) 224 CLR 44.
301   *Fair Work Act 2009* (Cth) ss 413 and 417.
302   Ibid s 437(3).
303   Ibid ss 437 and 443. See *Australasian Meat Industry Employees Union v Coles Supermarkets Pty Ltd* [2016] FWC 4870 for an example of the tribunal finding that the union had not yet reached this stage, having simply written seeking to open negotiations.

If all of these elements have been satisfied, the FWC is obliged to make a protected action ballot order.[304] The ballot must be a secret ballot conducted by either the AEC (as the default) or another authorised ballot agent.[305] However, the applicant can apply to have a protected action ballot order revoked before voting occurs, in which case the FWC is obliged to revoke the order.[306]

Section 449(2) of the Act requires the AEC to conduct the protected action ballot expeditiously, reflecting the objects in s 436 of the Act: 'a fair, simple and democratic process to allow a bargaining representative to determine whether employees wish to engage in particular protected industrial action'.[307] Section 461 of the Act provides that a technical breach will not necessarily invalidate the conduct of a protected action,[308] with the FWC noting that the intention of the Act is to have 'procedures and outcomes which are not unduly affected by legal technicality or rigid interpretation'.[309]

Even after approval of industrial action by members, in a complying secret ballot, the Act mandates that industrial action will only be protected if bargaining representatives (invariably the union) provide the employer with a minimum period of 3 working days' written notice prior to the action occurring.[310] The FWC has the power to specify a longer period of notice – up to 7 working days – if it is satisfied that there are exceptional circumstances justifying a longer period.[311]

The meaning of 'exceptional circumstances' was considered in the decision in *CEPU v Australia Post*,[312] with the tribunal finding that 'the ordinary and natural meaning of "exceptional circumstances" includes a combination of factors which, when viewed together, may reasonably be seen as producing a situation which is out of the ordinary course, unusual, special or uncommon',[313] and that where these were in relation to an application for an extended notice period 'there must be exceptional circumstances "justifying" the specification of a longer notice period. The notion of justification is critical and calls for a consideration of the purpose of the notice required by s. 441.'[314]

In *Transport Workers' Union v SITA*,[315] a case involving industrial action by the workforce of the Australian Capital Territory's waste management provider, the FWC was not satisfied that the circumstances claimed to justify an extension were of the requisite exceptional nature, and

---

304   *Fair Work Act 2009* (Cth) s 443. See, for example, *United Voice v Ensign Services (Australia) Pty Ltd (t/as Ensign A Spotless Company)* [2016] FWC 3067.

305   *Fair Work Act 2009* (Cth) ss 444 and 449. The AEC Industrial & Commercial Elections Branch conducts protected action ballots as well as elections for registered organisations.

306   Ibid s 448. *National Union of Workers v Toll Transport Pty Ltd* [2016] FWC 7733.

307   *Suez Recycling Recovery Pty Ltd v Transport Workers' Union of Australia* [2016] FWC 3007 at [17] and [18].

308   Ibid [14].

309   *Broadcast Transmission Services Pty Ltd v Automotive, Food, Metals, Engineering, Printing and Kindred Industries Union* [2015] FWC 6340 at [24].

310   *Fair Work Act 2009* (Cth) ss 412 and 441.

311   Ibid s 443(5).

312   *Communications, Electrical, Electronic, Energy, Information, Postal, Plumbing and Allied Services Union v Australian Postal Corporation* (2007) 167 IR 4.

313   Ibid [10].

314   Ibid [11].

315   *Transport Workers' Union of Australia v SITA Australia Pty Ltd (t/as SUEZ Environment and Waste Recovery)* [2016] FWC 2586.

found instead that concerns about notification of the public were 'much overstated' and that asserted health risks could be minimised.[316]

A successful protected action ballot enables protected industrial action (of the kind approved in the ballot) to take place in the next 30 days. However, the FWC has the discretion to extend this for a further period (of no more than 30 days)[317] provided that there is no lengthy delay between the original 30 days and the extension application,[318] and that the parties have participated in conciliation or have refrained from taking industrial action and have bargained constructively during the 30-day period.[319]

Finally, it is important to note that 'employers will also be permitted to take protected industrial action, by locking out employees who have taken industrial action'.[320] In a similar vein, 'employees will also be able to take protected industrial action in response to industrial action taken by their employer (such as a lockout), without a secret ballot'.[321]

It is clear, particularly from the sanctions that flow from it, that the notion of industrial action taken outside the bargaining period,[322] or without notice, or without the other mandatory steps, is not considered by the legislators to be an acceptable means of resolving workplace issues.

5.50.25 Protected industrial action: implications

Where protected industrial action that results in the complete withdrawal of labour (a strike, for example) is taken, s 470 of the *Fair Work Act* stipulates that an employer must withhold payment for the actual period of industrial action. Employees taking industrial action can only lose pay for the actual period of action taken. (Under the *WR Act*, protected action attracted a minimum 4-hour loss of pay for action, regardless of whether or not the action was of less than that duration, and of whether it involved a complete or a partial withdrawal of labour.)[323]

Industrial action sometimes takes the form of partial work bans (only performing part of the role). For partial withdrawal of labour, an employer may withhold payment proportionate to the portion of work refused under the ban.[324] In the case of protected industrial action in the form of overtime bans, if an employee refuses to work overtime and the refusal is a contravention of the employee's obligations under a modern award, enterprise agreement or contract of employment, s 470 provides that payment be withheld for the period when the employee would otherwise have been working overtime.

---

316   Ibid [27], finding that 'the client is the ACT government – not some "tin pot" country council . . . [and it is] unbelievable that three working days notice would be insufficient'.

317   *Fair Work Act 2009* (Cth) s 459(3). *Re Transport Workers' Union of Australia* [2011] FWA 1097.

318   *National Union of Workers v Symbion Pharmacy Services Pty Ltd* [2009] FWA 1284.

319   *Australian Municipal, Administrative, Clerical and Services Union v Flinders Operating Services Pty Ltd (t/as Alinta Energy)* (2011) 209 IR 187; *Maritime Union of Australia v DP World* [2010] FWA 7638.

320   *Fair Work Act 2009* (Cth) s 411.

321   Ibid s 410.

322   *Australian Industry Group v Automotive, Food, Metals, Engineering, Printing and Kindred Industries Union* [2002] FCAFC 386 at [67] per Goldberg and Finkelstein JJ.

323   *WR Act* s 187AA.

324   *Fair Work Act 2009* (Cth) s 471. For an example of FWC determination of such a calculation, see *Independent Education Union (South Australia) v Catholic Schools Endowment Society Incorporated (Catholic Schools Office)* [2016] FWC 1057.

5.50.30 Unprotected industrial action

The *Fair Work Act* regards any action that does not fulfil the requirement for protected industrial action as unprotected industrial action. Consequently, industrial action will not be regarded as protected action where:

- it is taken before the nominal expiry date of an enterprise agreement;[325]
- the parties taking industrial action are not genuinely trying to reach agreement;[326]
- the action is in support of provisions that cannot lawfully be included in an agreement ('unlawful terms');
- bargaining representatives are engaging in 'pattern bargaining'; or
- it contravenes orders already made by the FWC.[327]

As will be seen from the last of these, if the FWC makes orders that protected industrial action cease, then any continuation of that action will be regarded as unprotected action and will bring with it the range of sanctions that apply to that type of action.

Unprotected action, such as a snap strike, is unlawful. Because employers often have no opportunity to prepare for the impact of such action, it can cause significant damage to an employer's business.

The FWC can therefore issue orders to prevent or stop any unprotected industrial action, and if it is unable to determine within 48 hours whether action is unprotected, it can issue interim orders to stop the industrial action.[328] There are, of course, penalties associated with a breach of FWC orders.

In cases of unprotected industrial action, employers are required to withhold 4 hours' pay for *any* incident of unprotected industrial action of up to 4 hours' duration.[329] This includes instances of brief or partial withholding of labour, such as a work ban on a particular task or a stoppage of only a few minutes. Both would be subject to the '4-hour rule' and would require the deduction of 4 hours' pay. The rule is designed to discourage the taking of unprotected action.

The other significant implication of unprotected industrial action, as the name suggests, is to leave those who take it exposed to civil liability associated with the industrial action. The nature of those tort liabilities and the consequences that flow from them are discussed later in this chapter.

5.50.35 Suspending or terminating industrial action

Section 418 of the *Fair Work Act* gives the FWC the power to make an order that industrial action stop, whether that action is current or is threatened or impending. This applies to action

---

325   *Fair Work Act 2009* (Cth) s 417. *Director, Fair Work Building Industry Inspectorate v McCullough* [2016] FCA 1291.
326   *Fair Work Act 2009* (Cth) s 443, although contravention of bargaining orders must relate to the particular industrial action not to a previous non-compliance: *Australian Mines and Metals Association v Maritime Union of Australia* (2016) 242 FCR 210.
327   *Fair Work Act 2009* (Cth) ss 418–421 and ss 423–427.
328   Ibid s 420.
329   Ibid s 474.

by employees or by employers. The power also exists whether the industrial action up until that time (or proposed to be taken) is protected or unprotected action,[330] though there is greater discretion in relation to protected action.[331]

Such an order can extend, for example, to all employees of a company at a particular site or sites, as well as employees of subcontractors engaged on that project,[332] but can exclude protected industrial action, action agreed to or authorised by the company, or action based on a reasonable concern for safety (provided that the employees complied with reasonable directions to perform other safe work).[333] An order may also specify its date of effect and the period for which it operates.[334]

As indicated elsewhere, failure to comply with such orders brings sanctions of its own. The tribunal has also been reluctant, from its earliest days, to assist those who do not abide by the system's dispute resolution processes.[335]

Where protected action is causing or is threatening to cause significant harm to the Australian economy or part of it, or endangers the safety, health or welfare of the population or part of it, the FWC is empowered to order the parties to stop taking industrial action.[336] If further conciliation does not lead to an agreement and the FWC has terminated the industrial action, the FWC may also determine a settlement:

> It may similarly act to end the industrial action and determine a settlement for the bargaining participants where protected industrial action is protracted, is causing or threatening to cause imminent significant economic harm and the dispute will not be resolved in the foreseeable future.[337]

The criteria that the FWC will use to determine a settlement will include:

> matters such as the merits of the case; the interests of the negotiating parties and the public interest; how productivity might be improved in the business or part of the business concerned; the conduct of the bargaining representatives during bargaining and the extent to which they have complied with good faith bargaining requirements; and any incentives to continue to bargain.[338]

---

330   Ibid ss 418–420 and ss 423–427.
331   Ibid s 418 requires that the FWC *must* make an order to stop unprotected industrial action if such an application is made and the FWC is satisfied that it is in fact unprotected action.
332   *Lend Lease Building Pty Ltd v Construction, Forestry, Mining and Energy Union* (Unreported, Fair Work Commission, Commissioner Hunt, 6 May 2016).
333   *Fair Work Act 2009* (Cth) s 19(2).
334   See, for example, *Lend Lease Building Pty Ltd v Construction, Forestry, Mining and Energy Union* (Unreported, Fair Work Commission, Commissioner Hunt, 6 May 2016) at Order 6.
335   A striking example being Higgins J's refusal to hear applications if a union was on strike, even though there were limited prohibitions on strikes at the time. See FWA *Waltzing Matilda and the Sunshine Harvester Factory* 102.
336   *Fair Work Act 2009* (Cth) s 424. See, for example, *Commonwealth of Australia (represented by the Department of Immigration and Border Protection) v Community and Public Sector Union* [2016] FWC 2526.
337   *Fair Work Act 2009* (Cth) Part 2-5. *Commonwealth of Australia (represented by the Department of Immigration and Border Protection) v Community and Public Sector Union* [2016] FWC 7184.
338   *Fair Work Act 2009* (Cth) Part 2-5.

5.50.40 Picketing

Picketing is where persons congregate to express their views publicly and in many cases to restrict access to a site with the intention or consequence of interfering with access to the site.

While it often occurs in the context of IR disputes (for example, as part of a package of actions taken by employees),[339] picketing may just as readily be used in support of a consumer campaign against particular companies or products and/or as part of protest action by particular interest groups.[340] However, action will not be regarded as industrial in character if it is entirely separate from the subject of disputation and bargaining.[341]

Where picketing is peaceful and in effect involves communicating information by way of a public stance or protest, it will not necessarily be regarded as industrial action and would ordinarily not be unlawful. However, if the picketing (particularly in the building industry) involves restricting access to premises, threats or intimidation, or coercion contrary to the *Fair Work Act*, it will be unlawful.[342]

As a consequence of decisions such as *Davids*,[343] picketing that involves infringing free passage in public places and on roads and footpaths may not be regarded as industrial action. Action being not regarded as industrial action is significant, because orders that extend beyond industrial action cannot be made by the FWC. For example, the FWC has the power to order striking workers back to work, but if the picketing is not (in and of itself) industrial action, it does not have the power to make such an order.

In *Transfield Construction Pty Ltd v Automotive, Food, Metal, Engineering, Printing and Kindred Industries Union* [2002] FCA 1413, however, the court drew a distinction: picketing could be industrial action if it had been established 'for the purpose of preventing and deterring or discouraging employees from attending at their employer's premises and from carrying out work'.[344]

While the FWC may be unable to make orders or impose sanctions about non-industrial action, conversely, picketing cannot attract the protections from tort action that protected industrial action has. Therefore, it would still be open to the employer, for example, to commence action seeking the imposition of orders – such as injunctions and damages against picketers – through mainstream courts. Examples of such tort actions are discussed later in this chapter.

The TURC indicated in its Final Report that rather than confining the question of picketing to special building industry legislation, it was 'highly anomalous if the Fair Work Commission cannot stop that kind of tortious industrial conduct when it can make stop orders under s418 in

---

339   *Director, Fair Work Building Industry Inspectorate v Construction, Forestry, Mining and Energy Union* [2015] FCAFC 170; *Construction, Forestry, Mining and Energy Union v Full Bench of the Australian Industrial Relations Commission* [1998] FCA 1404.

340   K Hale 'Peaceful picketing in Australia: the failure to guarantee a basic human right', in *Human Rights Occasional Paper No. 14*, Human Rights & Equal Opportunity Commission (1986).

341   Note to *Building and Construction Industry (Improving Productivity) Act 2016* (Cth) s 47, citing the AIRC decision in *Automotive, Food, Metals, Engineering, Printing and Kindred Industries Union v The Age Co. Ltd* [2004] AIRC 445.

342   See, for example, *Director, Fair Work Building Industry Inspectorate v Joseph McDonald* [2013] FCA 1431.

343   *Davids Distribution Pty Ltd v National Union of Workers* (1999) 91 FCR 463 at [72].

344   [2002] FCA 1413 at 46.

relation to other types of industrial action'. It recommended that 'the FW Act should deal specifically with industrially motivated picketing'.[345]

5.50.45 Industrial action in relation to workplace health and safety issues

Industrial action is often taken in respect of safety issues.[346] Workplace health and safety is discussed in detail in Chapter 8.

For present purposes it is sufficient to note that the *Fair Work Act* makes allowances: if the action taken by the employee 'was based on a reasonable concern of the employee about an imminent risk to his or her health or safety' and the employee complied with a reasonable direction 'to perform other available work . . . that was safe and appropriate for the employee to perform', the action will not be regarded as industrial action that attracts the sanctions of the *Fair Work Act*.[347]

5.55 Industrial action: associated issues and consequences

As indicated earlier in this chapter, legislation in relation to trade unions and their registration often provides that illegality on the grounds of restraint of trade is excluded.[348] The legislation also envisages the operations of unions as 'imposing restrictive conditions on the conduct of any trade or business'.[349] However, while this may preserve unions themselves from being regarded as unlawful associations, it does not necessarily protect their actions.[350] This is particularly so in circumstances where their actions are taken in breach of requirements such as the 'protected action' provisions outlined above, or in contravention of court or tribunal orders.

These actions and their consequences are discussed in two specific contexts below: industrial torts and secondary boycotts.

5.55.05 Industrial torts

Once legislation 'decriminalised' unions, it became a matter for the civil law, in particular torts, to determine what, if any, liability unions and their members had arising from industrial action. These became known as 'industrial torts' and their development can be seen in English cases such as *Taff Vale Railway Co. v Amalgamated Society of Railway Servants* [1901] AC 426.

---

345   TURC *Final Report*, Vol. 5, 475–6.
346   Employees ceasing work when asbestos has been identified, for example.
347   *Fair Work Act 2009* (Cth) s 19(2)(c)(i) and 19(2)(c)(ii) respectively.
348   *IR Act 1996* (NSW) s 304.
349   Ibid s 303.
350   *Australian Industry Group v Automotive, Food, Metals, Engineering, Printing and Kindred Industries Union* [2002] FCAFC 386 at [66] per Goldberg and Finkelstein JJ.

The Dollar Sweets case, discussed below, gives some indication of the sorts of behaviour that will fall foul of the industrial torts. This section of the chapter then goes on to outline the most significant of these torts.

DOLLAR SWEETS PTY LTD v FEDERATED CONFECTIONERS ASSOCIATION OF AUSTRALIA [1986] VR 383[351]

One result of the 1983 National Economic Summit was agreement to return to a centralised system of wage fixing. For 2 years, from September 1983, the Arbitration Commission awarded wage increases in line with the Consumer Price Index (CPI). This was conditional on a union committing to abide by the Commission's wage-fixing principles and processes.

Dollar Sweets was a Melbourne-based food manufacturing company, maker of the well-known 'Hundreds & Thousands' biscuits. Its employees were union members, belonging to the Federated Confectioners Association.

However, as the union had not agreed to abide by the Arbitration Commission's wage-fixing principles, its members were not automatically entitled to the wage rises associated with it. Consequently Dollar Sweets did not have to pay those increases to its employees. In the meantime, the company reached an agreement with its employees to pay them the increases if they (the employees) agreed to abide by the Arbitration Commission's principles.

While the company was paying its employees weekly wages for working a 38-hour week, the union demanded a reduction to 36 hours a week (with maintenance of the weekly amount paid).

Industrial action commenced in support of a 36-hour week. Dollar Sweets advised its employees that it could not agree to the 36-hour week and that they could either continue to work a 38-hour week or find work elsewhere. Some of the employees took up the offer; others did not.

Those who did not accept employment based on a 38-hour week took strike action. The company replaced those workers.

From July 1985 union officials and striking workers maintained a continuous picket of the Dollar Sweets factory. After initially seeking to impede the employees entering and leaving the premises, picketers then sought to prevent deliveries to and from the premises. Union representatives told employees that they would be sacked once the union had broken the company. There were also reports of bomb threats, and parts of the premises were damaged – the locks on the factory doors were destroyed and there was attempted arson. Also, during the picketing, a delivery driver was assaulted and his truck damaged. Telephone wires to the factory were also cut at one stage during the industrial action.

The company stationed security guards at the premises 24 hours a day, apparently at the behest of its insurer. Many transport companies refused to make deliveries because it would involve crossing the picket line, and some suppliers also declined to supply the company.

---

351   This case summary draws on a number of sources, including the judgement in [1986] VR 383 and P Costello 'Dollar Sweets – confronting union power', https://ipa.org.au/library/publication/ 1213763306_document_review39-3_costello-dollarsweets.pdf.

When the company applied to the Arbitration Commission to intervene in the dispute, the Commission recommended that the picket be disbanded. The union ignored this recommendation.

The company took the matter to the Victorian Supreme Court on the basis of intimidation, nuisance and conspiracy to injure its business. Its claim was successful and in December 1985 the Court made orders restraining the picketing, which ended the next day (having lasted for 143 days).

In determining the case, the trial judge observed that the defendants appeared intent on forcing the company out of business – the court found it 'extremely difficult to rationalise such apparently stupid and nihilistic acts'.[352] The union ultimately paid $175,000 as compensation to Dollar Sweets for the losses it suffered.

Contractual interference

As indicated earlier in this chapter, industrial action is *prima facie* a breach of the employment contract. However, this tort may apply to any contract provided the requisite elements are met: namely, the defendant persuades a person to breach their contract with the plaintiff or physically prevents them from performing their contract. (This is often referred to as direct interference).

However, it appears from the case law that this does not extend to persuading a person to do something that would otherwise be lawful, such as seeking to bring their contract to an end.[353]

Another form of this tort is 'indirect interference', where the defendant commits or threatens to commit an act which is unlawful in itself, the effect of which is to interfere with the performance of a contract to which the plaintiff is a party. For example, a union exerting pressure on its members who are employed by a third-party supplier or client of the plaintiff to refuse to deal with goods or services to/from the plaintiff – such conduct would constitute a secondary boycott and would be both indirect interference and a breach of the relevant secondary boycott legislation.[354] Secondary boycotts are discussed separately below.

Conspiracy

The tort of conspiracy may take two forms – 'simple conspiracy' or 'conspiracy by unlawful means'.

Simple conspiracy, also referred to as 'conspiracy to injure', involves two or more persons acting in concert to deliberately inflict loss on the plaintiff. While this appears to be a particularly broad tort, it is in fact limited by the need to establish that the persons were not acting in furtherance of their legitimate self-interest.[355]

---

352   *Dollar Sweets Pty Ltd v Federated Confectioners Association of Australia* [1986] VR 383 at 390 per Murphy J.
353   *Sanders v Snell* (1998) 196 CLR 329; and in *Ansett Transport Industries (Operations) Pty Ltd v Australian Federation of Air Pilots* (1989) 95 ALR 211 the collective action of pilots resigning *en masse* was not itself tortious.
354   Creighton and Stewart *Labour Law* (2010) 798.
355   *McKellar v Container Terminal Management Services Ltd* (1999) 165 ALR 409. This issue is discussed in further detail in Creighton and Stewart *Labour Law* (2010) 799.

By contrast, in conspiracy by unlawful means, motives are irrelevant, as a consequence of either the defendants' purpose being inherently unlawful or the fact that they have used unlawful means. In relation to this tort, unlawful means can be a breach of statute, conduct unlawful as a crime or a tort, or a breach of contract.[356]

However, it should also be noted that proceedings for conspiracy arising from industrial action are not taken only against unions, as evidenced in the 1998 waterfront dispute, involving the lockout of union members by stevedoring employers. In that dispute, the Maritime Union of Australia launched conspiracy proceedings against Patrick Stevedores and the Federal government.[357]

Intimidation

The tort of intimidation arises when the defendant, intending to cause loss to the plaintiff, threatens a third party with harm (including violence or property damage) unless the third party takes action contrary to the plaintiff's interests and resulting in harm.[358]

Unlawful interference?

While a separate tort of unlawful interference has not been specifically adopted in Australia (unlike British decisions such as *OBG Ltd v Allan*),[359] features of the tort, an unlawful act by a defendant inflicting loss upon a plaintiff, have been considered in Australian cases.

For example, in *Northern Territory v Mengel*, it was observed that unlawful interference does not necessarily extend to every unlawful act and that it would require that 'the unlawful act be *directed at* the person injured'.[360] The High Court has since declined to determine expressly whether the tort should be recognised in Australian law.[361]

5.55.10 Remedies in relation to industrial torts

The two chief remedies sought in relation to industrial torts are injunction and damages. However, while some cases may proceed to finality and result in the award of damages, for many the 'interim' result – deciding to grant or refuse interim relief in the form of an injunction – becomes the final relief:[362] the industrial action ceasing as a consequence of the injunction may be (for practical purposes) the end of the matter, with any additional remedy simply 'icing on the cake'.

The granting of an injunction requires more than a court simply determining that there is a serious question to be tried and the balance of convenience favouring an injunction (although these are relevant factors). As indicated in *Patrick Stevedores Operations No. 2 Pty Ltd v Maritime Union of Australia* (1998) 195 CLR 1, the question of whether damages will provide

---

356   *Williams v Hursey* (1959) 103 CLR 30.
357   *Maritime Union of Australia v Patrick Stevedores No. 1 Pty Ltd (in administration)* [1998] FCA 378.
358   *Sid Ross Agency Pty Ltd v Actors Equity* [1971] NSWLR 760.
359   [2008] 1 AC 1.
360   *Northern Territory v Mengel* (1995) 185 CLR 307 at 343 (emphasis added).
361   *Sanders v Snell* (1998) 196 CLR 329 at 341.
362   *Amcor Packaging (Australia) Pty Ltd v Automotive, Food, Metals, Engineering, Printing and Kindred Industries Union* (2006) 157 IR 32.

adequate relief in the absence of an injunction must also be considered. For the grant of an injunction, the court must also consider the consequences that flow from the order sought.[363]

And in relation to industrial disputes particularly, their recurring features (including the fact that interim relief is often final relief) make it appropriate to exercise caution in granting interlocutory relief such as injunctions.[364]

Another question that arises is whether courts should, in fact, intervene in matters that are already before the relevant industrial tribunal. A traditional approach has been to allow the tribunal to carry out its functions in seeking to resolve the dispute.[365] However, in more recent times some courts have rejected that approach.[366] This is disappointing, in that it may serve to undermine the independent dispute resolution function of the tribunal.[367]

In those matters that actually proceed to final resolution (beyond the injunction stage), damages are assessed in accordance with the ordinary tort principles of seeking to put the plaintiff in the position that it would have been in if the wrong had not occurred.[368] The relevant criteria are those related to the loss suffered by the claimant, not the degree of illegitimacy of the action.[369] In many cases, even where the matter proceeds to the damages phase in an acrimonious dispute, agreement on the quantum of those damages may still be reached.[370]

5.55.15 Secondary boycotts

The Fraser Government's enactment of s 45D of the *Trade Practices Act 1974* (Cth) was apparently intended to combat the practice of 'retail price maintenance' whereby unions took industrial action to stop the cutting of prices, with the flow-on effect of protecting union members' jobs. However, the effect of the legislation was much broader: it made unlawful all boycotts which had the purpose or effect of hindering interstate trade and commence or overseas trade and commerce (in keeping with the Commonwealth's legislative powers in this regard).[371]

Section 45D was supplemented in 1980 by the enactment of s 45E, concerning agreements in relation to supplying or acquiring goods and services.

For liability to arise under the secondary boycotts legislation, one party must act in conjunction with another to hinder or prevent a third person supplying goods or services to

---

363   *Australian Broadcasting Corporation v O'Neill* (2006) 227 CLR 57.
364   *Australian Paper Ltd v Communications, Electrical, Electronic, Energy, Information, Postal, Plumbing and Allied Services Union* (1998) 81 IR 15 at 24 to 27 per North J.
365   *Harry M Miller Attractions Pty Ltd v Actors and Announcers Equity Association of Australia* [1970] 1 NSWR 614.
366   See, for example, *National Workforce Pty Ltd v Australian Manufacturing Workers' Union* [1998] 3 VR 265.
367   A view also expressed in Creighton and Stewart *Labour Law* (2010) 806.
368   *Ansett Transport Industries (Operations) Pty Ltd v Australian Federation of Air Pilots (No. 2)* [1991] 2 VR 636.
369   As discussed in McCrystal *The Right to Strike in Australia* (2010) 266–7.
370   See, for example, *Dollar Sweets Pty Ltd v Federated Confectioners Association of Australia* [1986] VR 383, as well as various matters settled by the CFMEU, including *Abigroup v Construction, Forestry, Mining and Energy Union* in relation to the Brisbane Children's Hospital dispute – a settlement which also had the effect of excluding proceedings by the FWBC by virtue of the *FW(BI) Act* ss 73 and 73A.
371   Affirmed in *Actors and Announcers Equity v Fontana Films* (1982) 150 CLR 169.

(or acquiring them from) a fourth person.[372] The conduct must be for a purpose (though not necessarily the sole purpose) of causing substantial loss or damage to the fourth person's business interests and have the likely effect of doing so.[373]

The fourth person cannot be the employer of either of the first two parties (thus the 'secondary' nature of the boycott). And either the third party or the fourth party must be a constitutional corporation, as the legislation relies upon the corporations power in s 51(xx) of the Constitution.

Section 45DB prevented unions and their members taking industrial action in support of the interests of workers in other industries or for other political purposes. Many notable instances of industrial action in earlier decades, such as union refusals in the 1930s to load 'pig iron' bound for Japan, fell foul of the secondary boycott legislation. Section 45DC sought to make unions vicariously liable for the actions of their members and officials by providing that if two or more members or officials engaged in conduct then the union was taken to have acted in concert with them and for the same purpose 'unless the organisation proves otherwise' – in effect, a reverse onus of proof.

The secondary boycott provisions have been criticised over several years by ILO Committees of Experts, as the provisions outlaw 'sympathy action' by other unions and are therefore inconsistent with ILO conventions which permit all forms of peaceful industrial activities, not limited only to employment conditions at a particular enterprise.[374]

Perhaps the best-known case in relation to secondary boycott provisions being used against a union was the *Mudginberri* matter.[375]

MUDGINBERRI STATION PTY LTD v AUSTRALASIAN MEAT INDUSTRY EMPLOYEES UNION (1986) 15 IR 272

Workers at the Mudginberri abattoir in the Northern Territory were employed in an arrangement under which they were not directly employed by the abattoir owner but rather by three contractors. The union, the AMIEU, served a log of claims on Mudginberri, seeking to introduce pay and conditions that were in place at another NT abattoir and demanding union involvement in contract negotiations.

Part of the campaign in support of union demands was the setting up of a picket line at Mudginberri. As the abattoir owner was not legally the employer of the workers, it meant that he was a third party affected by the dispute. Meat Inspectors refused to cross the picket line, thereby stopping production. During the dispute, the NT government facilitated loans to the abattoir.[376]

The Industrial Relations Commission was unable to bring the dispute to an end. The owner of the abattoir sought, and obtained, an injunction under s 45D of the *Trade Practices*

---

372   *Concrete Constructions Pty Ltd v Plumbers and Gasfitters Union* (1987) 15 FCR 31.
373   Now *Competition & Consumer Act 2010* (Cth) s 45D(2).
374   S McCrystal 'The *Fair Work Act 2009* (Cth) and the right to strike', Sydney Law School Legal Studies Research Paper No. 10, F2010, 13–14.
375   *Mudginberri Station Pty Ltd v Australasian Meat Industry Employees Union & ors* (1986) 15 IR 272.
376   *Business Review Weekly* 'Westpac's big role in NT union battle', 2 May 1986.

Act preventing the union picketing at the abattoir. The union refused to remove the picket line, thereby breaching the injunction and being subject to a $44,000 fine. Union assets were subsequently seized for non-payment of the fine, resulting in 3 separate days of national strikes by members of the AMIEU.

Mudginberri was awarded $1.75 million in damages[377] (reduced to $1.48 million on appeal),[378] calculated on the basis of the income that would have been earned and costs that would have been incurred but for the picket.

SUMMARY

Unions remain an integral part of the Australian IR system. Even with the decline in the overall percentage of workers who are union members, an appreciation of trade unions and their role and entitlements remains fundamental to an understanding of IR.

A key reason for this is that there are still many sectors with a substantial union presence (such as nursing and education). Consequently, unions still play a significant role in activities such as the negotiation of enterprise agreements and representing members in proceedings relating to their employment. The right of entry provisions are, in effect, an offshoot of these activities.

With the creation of the ROC, as with the Heydon Royal Commission before it, the government has signalled an increased focus on the regulating of union governance and the conduct of union officials.

Hand in hand with unions is the topic of industrial action. Again, while the incidence of industrial action has declined considerably in recent decades (particularly in relation to full-scale strike action), the existence of protected industrial action as a legitimate form of action in the workplace and its link to workplace bargaining make it an essential area of knowledge in industrial law.

REVIEW QUESTIONS

1. What records must a federally registered union keep?

2. What remedies are available to union members concerned that the leadership of their union is acting improperly?

3. Chapter 7 Part 4 of the *Fair Work (Registered Organisations) Act* 2009 (Cth) is titled 'Disqualification from office'. In what circumstances can disqualification occur and for what offences? What offences did the Royal Commission recommend adding?

4. If a union and its officials encourage their members to take industrial action that is not protected action, what can be the consequences for that union and those officials? Would your answer differ if the action occurred in the construction industry?

5. If you were to become a member of your union's Committee of Management, what are the key responsibilities and obligations that you would have under the *Fair Work (Registered Organisations) Act* 2009 (Cth)?

---

377   *Mudginberri v Australasian Meat Industry Employees Union* (1986) 15 IR 272.
378   *Re Australasian Meat Industry Employees' Union v Mudginberri Station Pty Ltd* (1987) 18 IR 355.

FURTHER READING

Fair Work Australia *Waltzing Matilda and the Sunshine Harvester Factory* (2011).

L Floyd and E Gold 'Jimmy Hoffa: alive and well and living in Australia? The Kennedy legacy and Australian labour law reform' (2016) 49(1) *The International Lawyer.*

A Forsyth and A Stewart 'Swimming against the tide: new challenges for unions under Australian labour law' (2016) 38(1) *Comparative Labor Law and Policy Journal.*

International Labour Organization (ILO) Reports on Freedom of Association in member countries, http://www.ilo.org/global/topics/freedom-of-association-and-the-right-to-collective-bargaining/lang--en/index.htm.

S McCrystal *The Right to Strike in Australia* (Federation Press, 2010).

Royal Commission into Trade Union Governance and Corruption (TURC) *Final Report* (2015). (Volumes 1 and 5: law reform recommendations; Volumes 2, 3 and 4: case studies).

6 THE END OF THE EMPLOYMENT RELATIONSHIP

6.05 Introduction

For many of us, none of these statements is unfamiliar:

'I love *my* job.'

'I loathe *my* job'

'You can't do that, it's *my* job!'

Yet, as Professor Hugh Collins notes, in *Justice in Dismissal*,[1] the legal reality is that there is no proprietary interest in a job.[2] We cannot necessarily hold onto a job until a time of our choosing; nor can we pass a job on to whomever we please when we decide it is time to leave. One of the harsh realities of life is that people can and do lose their jobs for all manner of reasons – and sometimes against their wishes.

That said, Collins also underscores the importance of employment – jobs so often define people's identity – and strong rates of employment add to the economic and social prosperity of the community.[3] It is neither a good thing nor a legally allowable thing for employers to simply terminate an employee's employment on a whim. Indeed, under International Labour Organization (ILO) conventions such as the Convention on Termination of Employment, the notion of preventing unfair dismissal is enshrined. And it must be remembered that employment is governed by a contract of employment (discussed in Chapters 1 and 2 of this book), so the idea of suing for breach of contract may be entertained.

Australian law governs the circumstances in which employment terminates. It endeavours to provide checks and balances between fairness to employees and economic flexibility for business, and to govern the numerous issues that can arise.

The *Fair Work Act 2009* (Cth) provides remedies for unfair dismissal and is available to many Australian employees whose dismissal was 'harsh, unjust or unreasonable'. The remedy is not available for job loss caused by genuine redundancy, nor to those whose employment terminates at the end of a genuine fixed-term contract or who are on qualifying periods. (It does, however, apply to some demotions and constructive dismissals – and there is a Small Business Fair Dismissal Code for those working in small business.) Reasons for dismissals governed by this legislation are many and varied, ranging from alleged poor workplace performance through to after-hours misconduct for misuse of social media. This jurisdiction embeds roles for unions as advocates and promotes conciliation, but lawyers may appear by leave and full trials can occur. The legislation prefers reinstatement as a remedy, but in reality damages are more likely to be awarded if there is irretrievable damage to the employment relationship. The manner in which workplace investigations were conducted prior to dismissal is relevant in unfair dismissal cases.

Contract law also has a role in wrongful dismissal claims. As discussed in Chapters 1 and 2, all employees are employed under a contract of employment. If they are terminated at the behest of the employer and they do not have a remedy under the unfair dismissal laws, there may be a common law avenue if the dismissal is wrongful under contract law. A crucial question in this context is whether the employee was afforded reasonable notice by the

---

1   H Collins *Justice in Dismissal* (Clarendon Press, 1992).

2   Ibid.

3   Ibid 15 et seq.

employer. But in truth, contract law dismissal is fiendishly more difficult than simply addressing that question alone. Difficulties include: what is the situation where the employment contract is part oral and part written? Are there alternative suits for misleading conduct where untrue statements induced the employee to sign on?

Although restraint of trade clauses are typically drafted into an employment contract from its inception, the effects of those clauses can become particularly contentious at the end of the employment relationship, when the former employee seeks to work for another employer. It is at that point that questions involving issues of law and equity have become the subject of litigation and case law. Because job loss can bring into play questions of discrimination and adverse action, there are further laws governing choice of remedy where a dismissal may be both unfair and a case of discrimination (to preclude double dipping).

Particularly where termination of employment was caused by the insolvency of the employer, there are further statutory provisions governing the treatment of accrued employee entitlements (such as long service leave). There are also laws pertaining to transfer of business. And finally, other issues may arise, ranging from reference writing through to whether or not an employer might be able to claw back monies they paid to relocate an employee who is now ending their employment.

This panoply of issues forms the pieces of the termination of employment jigsaw – and that is precisely the puzzle this chapter pieces together.

6.10 Unfair dismissal under the *Fair Work Act*

6.10.05 The statutory provision

Under s 381, the *Fair Work Act* aims to provide a framework for dealing with unfair dismissal that balances the needs of employers and employees; or as *Re Loty and Holloway*[4] put it: to give 'a fair go all round'.

Part 3-2 applies to employees, not contractors. Unfair dismissal is defined in s 385 as requiring the following:

(a) dismissal
(b) that dismissal is 'harsh, unjust or unreasonable'
(c) the dismissal does not comply with the small business code (if it involves a small business) and
(d) it was not a genuine redundancy.

This chapter first discusses what is dismissal, and in that connection considers constructive dismissal, short-terms contracts and demotion. It also raises jurisdictional questions in relation to the Small Business Fair Dismissal Code.

We then consider what constitutes a 'harsh, unjust or unreasonable' dismissal, paying particular attention to job performance, workplace behaviour and after-hours conduct,

---

4   *Re Loty and Holloway* [1971] AR(NSW) 95.

including the use of social media. (Further reasons for dismissal, such as dishonesty and safety breaches, are considered in the review exercises at the end of the chapter.)

The chapter then deals with genuine redundancy, which is a complete defence to an unfair dismissal claim; workplace investigations (which, in turn, have a bearing on the fairness of the dismissal); tribunal procedure (including salary caps, extensions of time limits etc); and the remedies (such as reinstatement).

6.15 Dismissal

A dismissal is said to have occurred if the employee's employment has been terminated at the initiative of the employer (s 386(1)(a)) or if the employee resigned but 'was forced to do so because of the conduct ... engaged in by (the) employer' (s 386(1)(b)).

6.15.05 Constructive dismissal

Interpreting s 386(1)(b) can be problematic. Pauline Thai points out, in 'Constructive dismissal: a re-examination',[5] that there appears to be a split in the authorities as to what this means.[6] There are also questions as to whether some of the legislation's supporting documents, such as the Explanatory Memorandum, refer to concepts (such as the 'common law concept of constructive dismissal')[7] which themselves remain subject to interpretation and debate.[8] Action as blunt as 'resign or be fired' falls within the concept, but there are also questions of degree.[9] Cases (decided before and under the predecessor WorkChoices legislation) such as *O'Meara v Stanley Works Pty Ltd* (2006) 58 AILR 100-528 and *Mohazab v Dick Smith Electronics Pty Ltd (No. 2)* (1995) 62 IR 200 appear to be influential still:[10] objectively, was the employer's conduct such that the employee had no real choice but to resign or that resignation was a probable consequence of the employer's actions?

6.15.10 Fixed-term contracts

There is no unfair dismissal remedy if 'the person was employed under a contract of employment for a specified period of time, for a specified task, or for the duration of a specified season, and the employment has terminated at the end of the period, on completion of the task, or at the end of the season' (s 386(2)). That seemingly straightforward provision can be quite difficult to apply in practice. In that connection, s 386(3)

---

5   P Thai 'Constructive dismissal: a re-examination' (2014) 27 *Australian Journal of Labour Law* 137.
6   Ibid 149 et seq
7   Ibid 151 et seq.
8   The complexity of constructive dismissal – and, indeed, whether it even exists – was discussed in G McCarry 'Constructive dismissal of employees in Australia' (1994) 68 *The Australian Law Journal* 494; as well as Thai 'Constructive dismissal: a re-examination' (2014) from 137.
9   Thai 'Constructive dismissal: a re-examination' (2014) 161.
10   For a useful summary of the area that makes this claim see CCH *Australian Labour Law Reporter* ¶54–345 'How is constructive dismissal relevant to unfair dismissal protection?'; Thai 'Constructive dismissal: a re-examination' (2014) also suggests that these cases are influential (150 et seq).

provides that the above subsection does not apply: 'if a substantial purpose of the employment of the person under a contract of that kind is, or was at the time of the person's employment, to avoid the employer's obligations under this Part'. Two crucial issues arise in practice: determining whether a contract was, in fact, fixed term; and determining what the position is when a succession of fixed-term contracts has been used in respect of a worker.

The issue of whether or not a contract that purports to be fixed term is, in fact, fixed term has been litigated, and the subject of academic commentary, for years.[11] Essentially, if there is an unqualified right to terminate the contract at any time during the so-called fixed term, then the contract may 'lose its element of certainty'.[12] Such an unqualified right to terminate may be different from a right to terminate within the fixed term for reasons of established poor performance.[13]

The use of successive so-called fixed-term contracts may create a difficulty. There could be numerous valid reasons for successive fixed-term appointments, which do not, in fact, detract from the fixed-term nature of the employment. For example, if a worker was engaged during a permanent worker's long service leave and then there was a short-term increase of work which required the substitute worker to remain in the position for a short time.[14] However, if the employer has no business reason for using short-term contracts and the nature of the work is ongoing, there may be an argument as to whether the employment was fixed term or continuing.[15]

Case law, including recent case law, demonstrates the relevance of industrial instruments to the characterisation and use of so-called fixed-term contracts. Unions have been prominent litigators in the area on behalf of their members (especially in the education sector) and some enterprise bargains and awards contain provisions as to the appropriate use of fixed-term contracts.[16]

---

11   See, for example, J Catanzariti 'What to look for in fixed term contracts' (1999) *Law Society Journal* 42–43 discussing *Howarth v Mornington Peninsula Shire Council* (Unreported, Australian Industrial Relations Commission, SDP Williams, 22 January 1999). In that case, the conveying of an unqualified right to dismiss during the life of a so-called fixed-term contract prevents the contract being fixed term – its term becomes uncertain. See also President D Hall, Queensland Industrial Court, in *Department of Justice and Attorney-General v David Carey* [2002] 170 QGIG 306; *Carey v Department of Justice and Attorney-General* [2002] QIC 103; and *Fisher v Edith Cowan University (No. 2)* (1997) 72 IR 464.

12   Catanzariti 'What to look for in fixed term contracts' (1999) 42 and, more recently, *Dale v Hatch Pty Ltd* (2016) 255 IR 132.

13   *P v City of Sterling* [2008] AIRC 1157 as cited in P Munro 'When unfair dismissal possible on a fixed term contract' *Workplaceinfo.com.au*, 23 January 2014.

14   *Department of Justice and Attorney-General v Carey* [2002] QIC 37; *Carey* at 5 per Hall.

15   *D'Lima v Board of Management Princess Margaret Hospital for Children* (1995) 64 IR 19, as cited in both 'The top 3 mistakes you're making with your "fixed term" employment contracts' (2016) *lynchmeyer.com.au/category/legal-updates* (accessed February 2017) and Munro 'When unfair dismissal possible on a fixed term contract' (2014). The latter contrasts *D'Lima* with *Hoschke v Curtain University of Technology* [2012] FWA 3990. For a very early discussion of the emerging issue, see C Oppy and N Ruskin 'The practice of engaging staff on back-to-back fixed term contracts is no "sham" arrangement' (2007) 10(3) *IHC* 24.

16   For example, *Carey* per Hall P and D Marin-Guzman 'NTEU sues Curtin uni for abuse of fixed term contracts' (2015) *Workforce*.

INDEPENDENT EDUCATION UNION OF AUSTRALIA v AUSTRALIAN INTERNATIONAL ACADEMY OF EDUCATION INC (PER JESSUP J) (ORDERS 8 JUNE 2016 FROM MAIN DECISION: [2016] FCA 140)

Clauses of the relevant industrial instrument, the *Educational Services (Teachers) Award 2010*, included the following:

10.2 Terms of engagement

(c) Where the employer engages the employee on a fixed term basis, the letter of appointment will inform the employee of the reason the employment is fixed term, the date of commencement and the period of the employment.

10.6 Fixed term employment

An employee may be employed for a fixed period of time for a period of at least four weeks but no more than 12 months on either a full-time or part-time basis to:

(a) undertake a specified project for which funding has been made available;

(b) undertake a specified task which has a limited period of operation; or

(c) replace an employee who is on leave, performing other duties temporarily or whose employment has terminated after the commencement of the school year. Provided that where the replacement arrangement extends beyond 12 months, the fixed term employment may be extended for up to a further 12 months.

Fourteen school teachers were employed over numerous years under contracts in which they were referred to as replacement teachers. The evidence was not clear as to the nature of the replacement aspect of some of their employment – who they were replacing, and why. Further, not all the paperwork complied with the relevant award. There were found to be multiple breaches of the relevant award and therefore of the *Fair Work Act*.

If a worker is not working under a genuine fixed-term contract, then if they have served their qualifying period (discussed elsewhere in this chapter), they may be able to access unfair dismissal remedies. If the contract was for a fixed term and an employer seeks to terminate before the completion of the fixed term, the employee may try to seek payment for the remainder of the entire period of the contract if there was no provision in the contract for ending the contract early (for reasons of poor performance, for example).

6.15.15 Demotion

Interestingly, there is also no termination if an employee is demoted but there is no significant decrease in their pay (s 386(2)(c)). The CCH *Australian Labour Law Reporter*[17] has a short yet

---

[17]   CCH *Australian Labour Law Reporter* ¶54-335 'Meaning of "Dismissed" in Unfair Dismissal Application' commentary.

useful discussion of demotion where the authors ruminate as to whether a $1 per hour reduction might be significant for a low-paid worker or whether the cessation of supervisory duties for a staff member might also amount to a significant reduction in duties.[18] However, those writers also observe that 'if the contract of employment authorises the employer to change the remuneration and duties of the employee, such a demotion does not constitute a dismissal by the employer under [s] 386(1) since there is no repudiation of the contract'. [19]

6.15.20 An early jurisdictional question: small business Fair Dismissal Code

If one is satisfied there has been a termination, an early jurisdictional question is whether the matter should be dealt with by the Small Business Fair Dismissal Code. Essentially, under s 388 of the *Fair Work Act*, if a business is genuinely a small business (fewer than 15 employees), employees cannot make a claim of unfair dismissal during the first year of employment. If there is a question of dismissal, as long as the employer has followed the checklist provided in the Code, the dismissal is deemed to be fair.[20] The Small Business Fair Dismissal Code is an acknowledgement of the special position of small business – in particular, the fact that small business owners might not have the access to extensive legal advice, and checks and balances that larger corporations do.[21]

If all of the above is satisfied, the question becomes whether or not that termination was unfair or harsh. The further jurisdictional questions are dealt with at 6.30.05.

6.20 Unfair – harsh, unjust or unreasonable

The *Fair Work Act* provision is as follows:

> 387 Criteria for considering harshness etc.
>
> In considering whether it is satisfied that a dismissal was harsh, unjust or unreasonable, the FWC must take into account:
>
> (a) whether there was a valid reason for the dismissal related to the person's capacity or conduct (including its effect on the safety and welfare of other employees); and
>
> (b) whether the person was notified of that reason; and
>
> (c) whether the person was given an opportunity to respond to any reason related to the capacity or conduct of the person; and

---

18   Ibid citing *Moyle v MSS Securities Pty Ltd* (2016) 68 AILR 102-521; [2016] FWCFB 372.
19   Ibid.
20   At the time of writing a copy of the code and checklist were at https://www.fwc.gov.au/about-us/legislation-regulations/small-business-fair-dismissal-code (accessed 12 March 2017).
21   The materials available for small businesses are on the FWC website at https://www.fwc.gov.au/about-us/legislation-regulations/small-business-fair-dismissal-code.

(d)   any unreasonable refusal by the employer to allow the person to have a support person present to assist at any discussions relating to dismissal; and

(e)   if the dismissal related to unsatisfactory performance by the person—whether the person had been warned about that unsatisfactory performance before the dismissal; and

(f)   the degree to which the size of the employer's enterprise would be likely to impact on the procedures followed in effecting the dismissal; and

(g)   the degree to which the absence of dedicated human resource management specialists or expertise in the enterprise would be likely to impact on the procedures followed in effecting the dismissal; and

(h)   any other matters that the FWC considers relevant.

Obviously, as there are myriad circumstances in which jobs can terminate, the notion of a 'harsh, unjust or unreasonable' dismissal has to be broad enough to be able to apply to all those circumstances. Equally, the definition embraces both the *qualitative* decision to dismiss (was there a valid reason? If so, was dismissal still harsh?) as well as *procedural* elements (was the employee notified of the problem? Was there time to improve?).

While no one book or reporting service reports every single dismissal case, two that do an excellent job of covering an extremely large number of cases on this topic are CCH's *Australian Labour Law Reporter* and the Fair Work Commission's (FWC's) *The Unfair Dismissal Benchbook.*[22]

There are obvious themes that can be drawn from the case law as to when a dismissal is likely to be unfair or justified. This chapter will cover the main themes, or the most common and important (or emerging) situations in which fairness is raised: job performance, workplace behaviour or discipline; and after-hours conduct, especially use of social media. The review questions at the end of the chapter deal with further issues, such as dishonesty in the workplace, violence, and breach of workplace health and safety standards. In that context the airline industry and particularly recent cases are raised.

6.20.05 Reasons for dismissal: job performance, workplace behaviour and discipline

The employment relationship is based on contract – an employer contracts with an employee for the performance of a job and that service earns remuneration. It is not an astounding leap, therefore, to acknowledge that if there is a problem with that service – if the worker is incompetent, is no longer necessary for the production of a good or performance of a service, or if the employee behaves poorly so as to damage the workplace (or render production difficult or bring the employer into breach of the other obligations, discussed in this book in Chapter 5, such as workplace health and safety) – the contract of employment and the employment relationship may be terminated. So, generically, if an employee arrives intoxicated for work or if their particular skills are no longer necessary for the running of the business or if they allow personal problems to affect the quality of their work, the employer may need to end the employee's employment. Because Part 3-2 of the *Fair Work Act* aims to provide that

---

22   Both these publications are cited further within this part of the chapter. Other interesting and expansive commentaries include C Sappideen et al. *Macken's Law of Employment* (Law Book Co., 7th ed, 2011).

'fair go all round' and temper the employer's rights with those of the employee, the question is usually where to draw the line – in other words, if, say, an employee arrives for work very slightly 'hungover' (if they were taking Beroccas and complaining of a headache after Australia won the America's Cup, for instance), but does not harm people, might a dismissal of that worker be harsh?[23] If a long-term excellent employee makes a mistake at work whilst grieving the loss of a loved one, might that not be better served with grief counselling than dismissal?[24]

It is not the role of this work to give an exhaustive commentary on the case law on these areas, but it is useful to examine briefly the following situations.[25] What will also become apparent is that there may be interplay or overlap between the question of whether something is fair and the further questions of whether the type of conduct concerned was governed by a workplace policy (discussed in website materials relating to Chapter 2) or there is an alternative or adjoining remedy.

6.20.10 Reasons for dismissal: workplace culture – workplace conduct

What is acceptable behaviour at work is governed by the mores of a society and, to some extent, by the character and culture of that particular workplace. Two interesting and contrasting cases are: *Cahill v Big W* (*Big W*) and *Brown and Fatialofa v Coles Group Supply Chain Pty Ltd* (*Coles*).[26]

CAHILL v BIG W [2000] QIRCOMM 25 (BIG W)

In *Big W*, the employee concerned was summarily dismissed after a complaint was made against him by a union representative. That complaint was made after two warnings had been given to the employee in relation to other matters concerning his conduct at work. The Commissioner hearing the case (Commissioner Swan) had difficulty accepting the evidence of the union representative and also expressed concern about the procedure used by the employer in instantly dismissing the employee – it seems the decision to sack was made before the employee had the chance to address the concern. The dismissal was held to be unfair. Damages were ordered rather than reinstatement, as there had been so much conflict between the parties that a return to work by the employee would 'destabilise' the workplace.

---

23   Although if the employee was intoxicated and represented a danger to others, discipline (and depending on conduct, dismissal) may well be appropriate.

24   Although, once again, if that grieving caused deeply disturbing conduct and violence or gross negligence that could harm others or jeopardise the business, that may well justify discipline – it depends on the facts.

25   Numerous cases in this commentary date back to the predecessor legislation. That is because the concept of unfair dismissal is relatively consistent (stemming from international law concepts) and the cases remain relevant. (McCallum's 2008 book, considered below, acknowledges that older established cases are still highly relevant.) The questions and answers and web materials related to this book contain further and more recent case law. The purpose of this chapter is to establish the principles and the main themes, and to distil the issues and trends.

26   *Big W* [2000] QIRC 25 per Swan C; *Coles* [2008] AIRC 1127 per Cargill C.

Commissioner Swan made some interesting remarks about workplace culture and its influence on what may be construed as appropriate workplace conduct:[27]

> I accept that, as a matter of common sense and knowledge, language used on the dock
> would not necessarily be genteel. Whilst offensive language directed personally at another
> has a greater propensity to offend, in a general sense, conversationally, language which was
> once deemed to be inappropriate is now commonplace. Regrettably, in many areas of work,
> words such as 'f***' and 'd*******', by way of example, are quite common, previously used
> swearwords such as 'bugger' and 'bloody' are deemed to be less offensive, so much so
> that they now have currency on television ads, for example. Those words may well continue
> to be offensive to many people and for those people the use of such words under any
> circumstances in their presence is anathema to them. However, one would not be facing
> reality if one thought that language such as that described above was not becoming more
> the norm.
>
> Notwithstanding those comments, however, abusive language personally directed at
> one's work colleagues, or for that matter anyone, is always fraught with danger. I believe
> that general community standards would continue to deem such occurrences as
> inappropriate.
>
> In the case of Mr Cahill, he called Mr Leader a 'f******', with his back to him and whilst walking
> away from him. While this is still inappropriate, it is somewhat different from openly attacking the
> colleague, and not an offence which should lie as a reason supporting dismissal. Certainly, from
> the employer's perspective, it represented behaviour which was inappropriate and upon which
> comment should be made.
>
> The evidence does show that Mr Cahill could, on occasion, be aggressive and use coarse
> language. However, one must look at this in context. I accept that the applicant was under a
> great deal of pressure whilst working on the dock, and this can be seen as easily conducive to
> frayed tempers. Even if his language was ill-advised, this can at least be deemed as excusable.

While the nuances in that passage make it worth quoting at length, the leeway it may provide
should never be overestimated – especially where the poor language or rough conduct
becomes racist, or bullying, or is a breach of a workplace's company policy. So, for instance,
in *Coles* (below), there were held to be credible complaints about dismissed employees from
witnesses whom the tribunal viewed as not embellishing the evidence but rather being
reserved, hesitant and (by implication) truthful [at 122].

BROWN AND FATIALOFA v COLES GROUP SUPPLY CHAIN PTY LTD [2008] AIRC 1127 (COLES)

In *Coles*, the dismissed employees had addressed their colleagues as 'camel f******'. These
colleagues had twice asked for those comments to stop – and even when they retaliated it

was seen to be in desperation, more than as an acceptance that such language was appropriate. The behaviour was said to be in breach of well-known policies of Coles as to discrimination and bullying:

> I do not accept that Mr Fatialofa's comments can be excused on the basis of a culture of 'friendly banter' involving Mr Zuhair. My observations of Mr Zuhair were that he didn't appear to be the type of person to willingly engage in such 'banter'. He impressed me as being a very serious and reserved individual. I accept that the comments which Mr Zuhair made to Mr Fatialofa were by way of retaliation and said in the hope that Mr Fatialofa would stop picking on him.
>
> I accept Mr Zuhair's evidence that he twice told Mr Fatialofa to stop making comments to him. Mr Zuhair does not seem to be a forthright or forceful person and perhaps Mr Fatialofa did not appreciate the seriousness of his feelings. That however is no excuse.
>
> In my view, whether the conduct of Mr Fatialofa took place over a period of six weeks or a shorter or longer period is not particularly relevant in this case. It was more than just a 'one-off' event and involved derogatory and disparaging remarks, not just the use of swear words in a joking manner, which I accept is common practice in the particular workplace, at least on the evening shift.[28]

6.20.15 Reasons for dismissal: job performance

As far as actual job performance is concerned, obviously an employer requires an employee to be able to perform the job. Likewise, the contract of employment requires the employee to perform their work with reasonable care and skill. So what happens if an employee is not performing their work to the standard required by management? Part of the answer may lie in examining what is being required – is management applying unrealistically high standards to their staff? If so, especially if staff have reasonably complained about workload issues, the dismissal may be unfair – in fact, there may even be a question as to whether the employer is in breach of workplace health and safety law (see *Brunt v Continental Spirits Co.* [2005] NSWIRComm 1133). If the employee is showing signs of personal distress that are affecting the quality of their work, one may ask whether that employee has communicated their problem to their employer. Is the problem work-related, and if it is, has the employer made work-based supports available? It is often the case that the longer a staff member has been employed at a workplace, the more an employer has had to work with the staffer to reasonably overcome the difficulty (unless the negligence or incompetence is so great it strikes at the heart of the contract).[29]

6.20.20 Reasons for dismissal: after-hours conduct

The fact that an employee's conduct after hours can be relevant to their job and justify dismissal is long established.

---

28   Ibid [129] et seq.
29   See also the review questions at the end of the chapter.

ROSE v TELSTRA [1998] AIRC 1592

In *Rose v Telstra* the Australian Industrial Relations Commission (AIRC) dealt with an unfair dismissal application by Mr Rose, who had been dismissed due to his being involved in an after-hours brawl with another Telstra employee. Significantly, that other employee was convicted of criminal charges for attacking Mr Rose with a piece of glass, after being provoked by Mr Rose. (That other employee did not face internal Telstra disciplinary charges but did resign.) At the time of the attack, neither employee was in a Telstra uniform, nor were they on-call. In finding that Rose had been unfairly dismissed, the Commission nonetheless acknowledged that after-hours conduct could justify dismissal in some circumstances. That is because (as noted in Chapter 2 of this book) there is a duty that underpins the employment relationship: the duty of fidelity and good faith to one's employer – or, loosely phrased, not to damage the employment relationship and not to act in a way which is inconsistent with the continuation of employment. The question is the extent to which that duty operates to limit or shape an employee's after-hours conduct. Citing the High Court of Australia in *Blyth Chemicals Ltd v Bushnell* (1933) 49 CLR 66, the Commission noted:[30]

> Conduct which in respect of important matters is incompatible with the fulfilment of an employee's duty. Or involves an opposition, or conflict between his interest and his duty to his employer, or impedes the faithful performance of his obligations, or is destructive of the necessary confidence between employer and employee, is a ground of dismissal ... But the conduct of the employee must itself involve the incompatibility, conflict, or impediment, or be destructive of confidence. An actual repugnance between his acts and his relationship must be found. It is not enough that ground for uneasiness as to future conduct arises ...
>
> The mere apprehension that an employee will act in a manner incompatible with the due and faithful performance of his duty affords no ground for dismissing him; he must be guilty of some conduct in itself incompatible with his duty and the confidential relation between himself and his employer.

The Commissioner cited Spender J in *Cementaid (NSW) Pty Ltd v Chambers* (Unreported, New South Wales Supreme Court, Spender J, 29 March 1995) at 6: one must acknowledge the limits of the link between work and privacy – 'an actual repugnance between the employee's acts and his relationship with his employer must be found'.

In *Rose*, the Commission then went on to consider a number of situations in which an employee's after-hours conduct might be relevant to their employment: if a driver were convicted of drink driving, for example. In numerous other occupations, that would not justify dismissal.

While that case of basic principle was decided in 1998, subsequent cases have explored both the further situations in which the principle is involved as well as its limits. Changing times and technology have also meant that the duty has become relevant to a number of social media platforms. This commentary now turns to those examples.

---

30   See text of judgement surrounding footnotes [17] and [18].

In McCallum's *Top Workplace Relations Cases*,[31] Professor McCallum considered the cases of *McManus v Scott-Charlton* and *Telstra Corporation Ltd v Streeter*.[32]

McMANUS v SCOTT-CHARLTON (1996) 140 ALR 625

In *McManus*, a Commonwealth public servant contacted some of his colleagues after hours to propose marriage. He did so on more than one occasion and, importantly, even after he had been cautioned not to do so. Finn J affirmed the validity of the caution etc; as there was a clear need for the employer to prevent sexual harassment – it was prohibited by law and clearly related to the employment, as the sanctioned public servant had no relationship with the women he called outside work. As McCallum notes (at 103–4), the judgement of Finn J clearly delineates the limits of the employer's capacity to shape conduct after hours (for fear of offending an employee's right to privacy, for example).

TELSTRA CORPORATION LTD v STREETER [2008] AIRCFB 15

McCallum also analysed this case (at 105). Telstra had paid $25 per head for the cost of a dinner, which aimed to be both a Christmas and a farewell function for Telstra staff. Some Telstra employees booked a room at a neighbouring hotel and stayed the night. During that night, employee Carlie Streeter had sex while some of the other staff were present (albeit in the dark – she claimed she thought they were asleep). There were also complaints by Telstra staff in that room that when they needed to urinate they were forced to do so in front of other staff who were naked in the bath together. When staff complained to Telstra, Streeter initially lied about her involvement in the incident. She was dismissed. At first instance, Senior Deputy President Hamberger considered Streeter unfairly dismissed – her conduct was private and she did not think others had seen her having sex. On appeal, the Full Bench majority found in favour of Telstra, finding that Streeter's lies during the initial investigation were a breach of trust between employer and employee. Interestingly, McCallum finds that a harsh judgement (at 108–9), and prefers the view of both the trial judge and the dissenter of the Full Bench, Larkin C – although Streeter lied in the initial interview, it is unsurprising given the highly personal nature of the actions.

Although *Streeter* ultimately hinged on Streeter's behaviour in lying to Telstra, it is obviously relevant regarding after-hours conduct (given what Streeter lied about). The case also showcases some of the evidence that can be relevant to after-hours conduct cases: did the employer pay for the event? (They did in this case.) Was it a collection of people who happened to work for a particular employer or did the subsequent events flow from the employment-related function?

---

31   (CCH, 2008) ¶1102–09.
32   (1996) 140 ALR 625 (*McManus*) and [2008] AIRCFB 15 (*Telstra Corporation Ltd v Streeter*) respectively.

6.20.25 Reasons for dismissal: misusing social media

With the advent of social media – Facebook, Twitter, Instagram, YouTube – one situation that has been litigated is whether the online conduct of the employee can justify dismissal. Quite obviously the answer to that question is in the affirmative, but due to the developing nature of social media, the case law is worth considering in some detail.

LINFOX AUSTRALIA PTY LTD v STUTSEL [2012] FWAFB 7097

In *Linfox*, the leading case, the employee Stutsel posted comments (after hours) on his Facebook page which might be considered discriminatory and offensive – referring to a manager of a particular religion as a 'bacon hater', for example. Importantly, Stutsel's page had been constructed by his wife and daughter and he believed the maximum privacy settings operated (so that his Facebook friends rather than Linfox management would see the posts). Stutsel had a very good employment record spanning 22 years. He had approximately 170 Facebook friends, some of whom were fellow employees of Linfox. Significantly, they had contributed to the conversation in which management was pilloried – but those other staff were not formally disciplined. Stutsel was apparently unaware that he could remove offensive comments. The company had no specific social media policy but rather dealt with this matter relying on pre-existing policy as to discrimination.

At both first instance and on appeal, Stutsel's complaint of unfair dismissal was upheld and reinstatement was ordered. Importantly, there was no direct breach of a specific social media policy and the context in which the comments were made was taken into account, enabling them to be viewed as 'letting off steam' rather than genuine menacing threats. The fact that other staff were not disciplined was significant, as was Stutsel's long and good record of employment and his unfamiliarity with Facebook. But, importantly, the Full Bench rejected the views of the trial judge that this Facebook page was just like 'pub talk'. Instead, the page was more serious as the comments were in writing and could become viral due to the nature of social media (at [25]–[26]). Further, and importantly, the Full Bench considered the new and evolving nature of social media applications (at [34]):

> It is apparent from the recital of these matters that the findings of the Commissioner as to the Applicant's understanding about the use of Facebook were an important part of the circumstances taken into account in concluding that the dismissal was unfair. It is also apparent that, with increased use and understanding about the Facebook in the community and the adoption by more employers of social networking policies, some of these factors may be given less weight in future cases. The claim of ignorance on the part of an older worker, who has enthusiastically embraced the new social networking media but without fully understanding the implications of its use, might be viewed differently in future. However in the present case the Commissioner accepted the Applicant's evidence as to his limited understanding about Facebook communications. We have not been persuaded, having regard to the evidence and submissions presented, that such a finding was not reasonably open.

That passage from *Linfox* is worth quoting at length as it shows:

- the need for social media policies in the workplace.[33] The law pertaining to policy is discussed in the website materials for this book.
- that the nuances involved in applying the law are still unfolding as social media is still a relatively new phenomenon. For many, especially older workers, Facebook is new – so they may not fully comprehend its dangers. That said, if that older worker 'enthusiastically embraces' the technology, then they need to exercise responsibility in that use. The interesting question is what happens when an employee who does not embrace technology snubs it. Where an employer has made it clear that staff are required to understand technology and has provided training to upskill staff, then the snubbing of that technology may become a work performance discipline issue. However, where the person concerned actually runs a workplace and deems technology not necessary (they may write longhand and be highly proficient in a job that does not require them to type), it is hard to see exactly where that (older) worker would be in breach of workplace standards. In fact, they may be amongst the country's most efficient workers.[34]
- anecdotally, some employers are now asking prospective and current staff whether they can become their 'Facebook friends' – presumably so that the employer can monitor the employee's online conduct. For a pre-existing employee, the employer probably cannot require that link in most cases (on grounds of privacy): if the employee maintains appropriate internet content, it is the employee's private concern. Likewise, for a prospective employee at an interview, an employer should not be able to require it. There is an obvious practical question, however – in a crowded job market, could a refusal of this request become one of a number of unstated reasons for the employer refusing to offer the job to that applicant?[35] Some students are now maintaining two Facebook pages, one in their name and one in an alias. In the view of the author, even if there is a second Facebook page with a bogus or code name, if that page includes inappropriate material the employer will still have a strong argument that the conduct justifies dismissal. (In fact, the employee's 'hiding' of the material with an alias may even provide evidence of a guilty conscience, in some cases.)

O'KEEFE v WILLIAMS MUIR'S PTY LTD (T/AS THE GOOD GUYS) [2011] FWA 5311

This is another case involving dismissal and the misuse of social media. In this case one staff member used his Facebook page to call the management obscene names. Many of those reading the page were members of the employer's staff. Clearly, there was a breach and the dismissal was not unfair.

33   L Floyd and M Spry 'Four burgeoning IR issues for 2013 and beyond: adverse action; social media & workplace policy; trade union regulation (after the HSU affair); and the Qantas aftermath' (2013) 37 *Australian Bar Review* 153–74.

34   See L Floyd 'Much ado about nothing: why accepting an invitation did not make Dyson Heydon AC QC appear biased' (2016) 90 *Australian Law Journal* 42–3.

35   Floyd and Spry 'Four burgeoning IR issues for 2013 and beyond' (2013).

Finally, it is important to note that in addition to the above, some contracts of employment may have express clauses dealing with after-hours conduct: for example, a newsreader (or someone in a similar prominent position) may be under an obligation not to behave in a manner that will bring the station into disrepute.

6.25 Genuine redundancy

A dismissal will not be unfair if it is a genuine redundancy. The notion of a genuine redundancy is defined in s 389 of the *Fair Work Act*, which has both inclusionary and exclusionary aspects.[36] Under s 389(1)(a) and 389(1)(b), the dismissal is a genuine redundancy if:

- the person's job is no longer to be performed by anyone because of changes in operational requirements of the enterprise; and
- the employer complied with obligations in relevant modern awards and enterprise bargains to consult about the redundancy.

Even if that is satisfied, there will not be a genuine redundancy if 'it would have been reasonable … for the (employee) to be redeployed within … the employer's enterprise; or … the enterprise of an associated entity of the employer' (s 389(2)(a) and s 389(2)(b)).

In essence, therefore, the question of genuine redundancy turns on three things:

- whether the job is still performed;
- whether there was appropriate consultation; and
- whether redeployment obligations have been complied with.

All three of those elements have been considered in the *Ulan Coal* series of cases considered below.

6.25.05 Ulan Coal series of cases

In *Ulan Coal Mines Ltd v Howarth* (2010) 196 IR 32; [2010] FWAFB 3488 (*Ulan Coal v Howarth*) Boulton J (SDP), Drake SDP and McKenna C considered the meaning of the elements in s 389(1), namely 'job' and 'consultation'.

The relevant facts were, essentially, that in 2009 the company reviewed its NSW mining operations with a view to increasing efficiency. The review resulted in changes, including the introduction of outsourced workers (to deal with ebbs and flows in production), the reduction in non-trade-qualified workers and, importantly, an increase in trade-qualified workers.[37] After voluntary redundancies, the company still dismissed 14 permanent non-trade mineworkers. At first instance, Commissioner Raffaelli found that these workers were not genuinely redundant – because their functions were still being performed and the

36   See *Ulan Coal Mines Ltd v Honeysett* (2010) 199 IR 363; [2010] FWAFB 7578 at [5].
37   *Ulan Coal Mines Ltd v Howarth* (2010) 196 IR 32 (*Ulan Coal v Howarth*) at [9] et seq.

additional qualifications held by the new workers now performing those tasks was something that did 'not meaningfully diminish the fact that the work performed by all mineworkers ... remains essentially the same'.[38] That finding was overruled on appeal, as the Full Bench of FWA formed the view (at [15]–[20]) that the Commissioner at first instance had not taken into account the full nature and circumstances of the changes in Ulan Coal's operational requirements and had misconstrued s 389.[39] In particular, the Full Bench:

- noted the distinction between an individual employee's 'job' and the 'tasks' that employee performs. The statute speaks of a job which is no longer required to be performed. Ryan J, in *Jones v Department of Energy and Minerals* (1995) 60 IR 304, described a job as a '*collection of functions*, duties and responsibilities entrusted, as part of the scheme of the employees' organization, *to a particular employee*' (emphasis added). In a restructure, the tasks of one employee may be redistributed to other new positions, such that although the tasks are still performed, the actual job (of one person doing those tasks) no longer exists (see the Full Bench judgement at [17]–[19]).[40]
- found that the significance of the raising of qualifications by the company was underestimated by the Commissioner at first instance, as those qualifications provided a skills mix which may enable these new qualified tradespersons to work more efficiently (at [14]); as a consequence, there needed to be a reduction in the numbers of employees without trade qualifications;
- cited the Explanatory Memorandum of the Fair Work Bill 2008, which gave examples of possible changes in operational requirements of an enterprise: machines can do work formerly performed by people; a downturn means the business only requires three, not five, people for a particular task; or the employer is restructuring to improve efficiency and the tasks done by a particular employee are distributed between several other employees such that one person's job no longer exists.

In *Ulan Coal v Howarth*, the Full Bench also discussed the requirement to consult about redundancy (at [21] et seq, especially [27]–[29]). The Full Bench noted that many of the consultation requirements that appear in relevant awards and agreements are derived from the original decision of principle, the *Termination Change and Redundancy Case* (1984) 8 IR 34. The basic concept is that once there has been a decision to downsize, there is benefit in bringing employees into discussions – to reduce the adverse consequences of terminations, for instance.

---

38   *Howarth v Ulan Coal Mines Ltd* (2010) 62 AILR 101-087; [2010] FWA 167 at [28] and [29] per Commissioner Raffaelli, as cited in *Ulan Coal v Howarth* (2010) 196 IR 32 at [11]. Commissioner Raffaelli acknowledged that contracting out the work may be able to form a genuine redundancy (at [12]).

39   *Ulan Coal v Howarth* at [13] et seq.

40   In *Rosenfeld v United Petroleum Pty Ltd* [2012] FWA 2445 it was confirmed that the test is whether the job previously performed stills exists – the duties of the previous job may still exist and be redistributed. In that case, a new senior recruit was appointed and took 90 per cent of the work of Mr Anastasiou, who was in turn given Mr Rosenfeld's work – and Mr Rosenfeld was made redundant. It was held this was not a genuine redundancy, as Mr Rosenfeld's job was still being performed. If anyone was redundant, it was Mr Anastasiou.

ULAN COAL MINES LTD v HONEYSETT (2010) 199 IR 363; [2010] FWAFB 7578 (ULAN v HONEYSETT)

The third issue – redeployment – was considered in *Ulan v Honeysett*. In that case, the Full Bench of FWA observed that genuine redundancy is a complete defence to a claim of unfair dismissal, but the employer's capacity to raise that defence is limited/unavailable if the employee could be reasonably redeployed. In defining redeployment the Full Bench stated:

- 'The exclusion poses a hypothetical question which must be answered by reference to all of the relevant circumstances' (at [26]).
- 'The question remains whether redeployment within the employer's enterprise or the enterprise of an associated entity would have been reasonable at the time of dismissal. In answering that question, a number of matters are capable of being relevant. They include the nature of any available position, the qualifications required to perform the job, the employee's skills, qualifications and experience, the location of the job in relation to the employee's residence and the remuneration which is offered' (at [28]).
- In determining whether redeployment with a related entity could have been possible, 'the degree of managerial integration between the different entities is likely to be a relevant consideration' (at [27]).
- Circumstances may have changed materially since the dismissal – there may be new jobs. Although subsequent employment gained by a former employee with an associated entity will be taken into consideration, it is not determinative as to whether redeployment at the time of the dismissal was possible and reasonable (at [28]).

The Full Bench went on to confirm the decision of Commissioner Raffaelli on the matter of redeployment. In essence, the Commissioner had found that the retrenched workers could have been redeployed with the group of companies to which Ulan belonged – namely the Xstrata group – but that Ulan had not redeployed them. The Commissioner observed that simply helping workers find jobs is not redeployment. Further, he noted that Xstrata had overall control of the mining operations of the related entities and that 'there was no evidence that any operational impact would arise if the Xstrata group were to adopt an "activist redeployment process" involving directions for one enterprise in the group to employ surplus employees of another in the group' (at [12]).

In terms of clarifying the law on genuine redundancy, the above material covers the main principles. But there are some important refinements:

- Requiring formal qualifications may mean there is a genuine redundancy even though the new recruit with the formal qualifications continues to do the tasks of the retrenched employee. However, if the formal qualifications are not required, but rather are just for the sake of having an extra qualification, or do not go to the main aspect of the job, there could be an argument that there is not a genuine redundancy.[41]

- Redeployment has been further litigated, and analysed in academic writings:[42] it will be only in rare circumstances that 'redeployment to a contract worker's position will be deemed appropriate'.[43] Further, if a group of companies is strongly segmented and companies do not share management and human resources functions it is not likely that the courts will place a significant burden on the employer to re-employ workers to companies within that group.[44]

The above deals with the pure legal position concerning genuine redundancy. It is important not to use the redundancy process as a mask for dealing with an employee who is simply disliked, underperforming or troublesome.[45] If an employer states an employee is redundant, there is a termination. The issue is whether the redundancy is unfair or genuine. Typically, employers claim a change in economic circumstance as why they need to retrench staff. Coupled with that may be a claimed change in strategic direction or new technology that makes a job or task no long necessary. If asked for evidence as to why the position has to be abandoned, it is not unheard of for an employer to claim 'commercial in confidence'. Despite that, there should be some evidence. The sort of evidence that could prove genuine redundancy includes an examination of the job description of the position to be eliminated and that of the new role. If the former position is genuinely redundant, one would expect to see substantial differences between those two job descriptions.

6.25.10 Spill and fill

One final word on redundancy involves the so-called spill and fill, where jobs are declared vacant and employees must reapply for their position. Typically, there will be fewer jobs than applicants, thus reducing staff numbers. It seems to be increasingly the case that employers adopting this approach will make statements to the effect that 'in applying for positions staff volunteer their application and accept the legality of the process'. With respect, if the only way an employee can remain in their position is to reapply for it, they are not volunteering to reapply for their job at all – they are being forced to do so. It may be advisable for employees in this situation to reapply 'without prejudice' to their legal rights (if they are not successful in

---

41   See *Mackay Taxi Holdings Ltd v Wilson* (2014) 240 IR 409.

42   See E Goodwin 'Genuine redundancy and redeployment under Pt 3-2 of the Fair Work Act 2009 (Cth): the Kestrel Coal decisions' (2015) 21 *Employment Law Bulletin* 110.

43   Ibid 113.

44   Ibid. One of the most notorious cases raising the issue of redeployment was decided under the WorkChoices legislation: *Village Cinemas Pty Ltd v Carter* (2007) AIRCFB 35; (2007) 158 IR 137. At first instance, the employee was successful in an unfair dismissal claim where the employer-cinema had refused to let him take long service leave in the hope the company could find a new position to redeploy him to at the end of the leave. On appeal, the cinema won, the court construing narrowly any redeployment rights/duties and instead holding the view that this was an economic dismissal. In contrast, the subsequent changes to the *FW Act* underscore the importance of redeployment.

45   *The Australian Master Human Resources Guide* specifically raises that danger (paras 6-090, 69-070).

regaining their positions). Further, it may be worth seeking individual legal advice as to whether employees should actually include words to that effect in their application, such as: 'I do not accept the legality of this process.'

6.30 Procedural fairness and dismissal – workplace investigations; standing down

The notion of procedural fairness is important to unfair dismissal claims – a dismissal may be held to be unfair if the employee was unaware of the issue at the heart of the dispute or was denied an opportunity to respond. Those basic elements of procedural fairness are reflected in both the definition of 'harsh, unjust and unreasonable' (when it speaks of allowing a person to respond) and in the case law: in *Big W* the lack of warning to the sacked worker was said to be important, as it was also in *Coles*, and the fact the relevant policies had not been clearly brought to the attention of the dismissed staff was also key.

The need for procedural fairness is why many (especially larger) employers have policies as to performance appraisal, conduct, discipline and workplace investigations. Such policies may help in preventing and defending unfair dismissal claims. However, in some cases, it has been held that a failure to comply (with an exceptionally strict policy, for instance) does not make a dismissal unfair. Equally, following guidelines which are inadequate will not necessarily make something fair.[46]

What goes hand in glove with overarching procedural fairness is the fairness of any workplace investigation. If there has been a complaint about an employee that proceeded the dismissal, was that investigation procedurally fair?

A significant recent decision in which workplace investigations was one issue was *Bartlett v Australia and New Zealand Banking Group Ltd* (2016) 255 IR 309; [2016] NSWCA 30.

BARTLETT v AUSTRALIA AND NEW ZEALAND BANKING GROUP LTD (2016) 255 IR 309; [2016] NSWCA 30 (BARTLETT)

Mr Bartlett was dismissed for allegedly doctoring an internal email about future lending policy and then forwarding the doctored email to a journalist for the *Australia Financial Review*.[47] Crucial procedural issues surrounding the bank's investigation included the fact that there was scant evidence as to how the documents could have been printed and the bank's failure to provide Mr Bartlett with a copy of their handwriting expert's report (which

---

46   CCH *Australian Labour Law Reporter* provides very good lists of the points that should be checked in workplace health and safety (WHS) investigations: see ¶61-405 'Ensuring Procedural Fairness' (accessed 25 April 2017). See also discussion of Full Bench of AIRC in *Appeal by Department of Social Security against Decision and Order of Dight C* (24 December 1997) in ¶3-707 'Procedural Fairness Remains Important'.

47   *Bartlett v Australia and New Zealand Banking Group Ltd* (2016) 255 IR 309; [2016] NSWCA 30 (*Bartlett*) at 311 et seq.

was itself qualified, as the expert had not seen the original of the handwritten envelope containing the doctored email).[48] Further, the bank had not allowed Bartlett to obtain expert opinion on handwriting in response.[49] The investigation also seemed to target a group of employees in Sydney, apparently on the assumption that the email had been posted from Sydney.[50]

The case hinged on the construction of the employment contract.[51] Clause 13 of the contract of employment stated: 'if you fail to comply with the provisions of your employment agreement or any other ANZ performance requirements, ANZ may take disciplinary action which may include suspension with or without pay and in certain circumstances, termination of your employment' with ANZ (see clause 14). Clause 14(b) continued: 'ANZ may terminate your employment at any time, without notice, if, in the opinion of ANZ, you engage in serious misconduct'. There were also extensive policies governing workplace investigations which seemed to provide for an employee right of reply.[52]

Flowing from those provisions, Mr Bartlett argued that clause 13 influenced clause 14.3(b) so the bank had to establish that he had breached before they could dismiss him. In contrast, the bank's argument was that clause 14.3(b) dominated, so they only need to hold the opinion, *bona fide*, that Mr Bartlett had misconducted himself.[53] The Court of Appeal held in favour of Mr Bartlett's approach:[54]

> To construe cl 14.3(b) as permitting termination where there had in fact been no misconduct . . . but only the opinion of the Bank that that had occurred, would be to render the two provisions in conflict. Such a conflict can be avoided by treating the 'opinion of ANZ' referred to in cl 14.3(b) as applicable to the seriousness of the misconduct . . . not its existence. This construction would conform to the contemplation of cl 13 that where there was a breach, termination could only occur 'in certain circumstances'.

What is interesting from the point of view of workplace investigations is the court's consideration of what it viewed as the 'fallback argument'[55] of Mr Bartlett: that the bank had to exercise its powers under cl 14.3(b) reasonably.[56]

In this connection the Court of Appeal, in particular Macfarlane JA, considered a number of cases in which the need for reasonableness had been considered.[57] Significantly, although there were two cases[58] where courts had rejected the existence of implied duties to show procedural fairness before dismissing, those cases could be distinguished as, for

48   Ibid 314, 315.
49   Ibid 314–15.
50   Ibid 313–14 and 322–3.
51   Ibid 315–16 et seq.
52   Ibid 313, 316.
53   Ibid 317 per Macfarlane JA.
54   Ibid 318.
55   Ibid 319
56   Ibid 319.
57   Ibid 320–321.
58   *Intico (Vic) Pty Ltd v Walmsley* [2004] VSCA 90; and *Gramotnev v Queensland University of Technology* (2015) 251 IR 448, cited in *Bartlett* at 320–21.

example, they did not deal with the construction of a specific contractual term with a power to terminate.[59] In contrast, in some cases where one party has the power to affect another, the courts have found that it should do so reasonably.[60] Although the High Court rejected the need to imply a term of trust and confidence in *Commonwealth Bank of Australia v Barker* (2014) 253 CLR 169 (*Barker*),[61] it left open the question of whether contractual powers required a rational exercise. Finally, in the 2015 British decision *Braganza v BP Shipping Ltd* [2015] IRLR 487, Lady Hale suggested that decisions should not be so unreasonable that no reasonable decision-maker should ever have come to them – in essence, she suggested that Wednesbury unreasonableness, a concept of administrative law, may have relevance to employment law.[62]

The NSW Court of Appeal found there to be unreasonableness in this case.[63] Bartlett was awarded damages for unfair dismissal and the court also underscored that at common law the right to summarily dismiss is exercised in narrow circumstances.[64]

In commenting on this decision, Naughton[65] essentially concluded that its future impact remains to be seen, and that it might have been more in line with recent cases if it had focused on considering whether or not the bank's policies on investigation had contractual force and whether or not they were breached.[66] He concludes that workplace investigation 'remains a highly unregulated and uncertain area'.[67]

Some authors have warned that poor workplace investigations may actually be construed as a stressor that may found a WorkCover claim.[68] On the other hand, a competent investigation can protect an employer from a claim of adverse action.[69] It is also important to ensure that investigators avoid conflicts of interest, especially where there is a lot at stake and where the employer is a well-resourced operator such as a government department.[70]

In *The Law of Termination of Employment*,[71] Upex discusses the central elements of fair workplace treatment for cases of misconduct (or underperformance). Relying on the UK

---

59   *Bartlett* at 321.
60   *Service Stations Association Ltd v Berg Bennett & Associates Pty Ltd* (1993) 45 FCR 84 per Gummow J. See also *Burger King Corporation v Hungry Jacks Pty Ltd* (2001) 69 NSWLR 558.
61   Considered in *Bartlett* at 320.
62   *Bartlett* at 321.
63   Ibid 321–23.
64   Ibid 319.
65   R Naughton 'Termination of employment and workplace investigations' (2016) *Employment Law Bulletin* 186.
66   Ibid 188.
67   Ibid.
68   G Beard and R Bryant-Smith 'Delay workplace investigations at your peril' (2008) *Law Institute Journal* 40.
69   J Catanzariti 'Adverse action claim refuted by employer's workplace investigation' (2012) *Law Society Journal* 52.
70   C Molnar 'Apprehended conflicts of interest in employment investigations and decision-making' (2015) *Employment Law Bulletin* 91. For a discussion of investigations in the government context, see also Chapter 7.
71   R Upex *The Law of Termination of Employment* (Sweet & Maxwell, 4th ed, 1994) at 154 et seq.

decision *British Home Stores Ltd v Burchell* [1980] ICR 303, Upex notes that an appropriate investigation requires:[72]

- a belief by the employer that there is a situation to investigate;
- reasonable grounds to sustain that belief; and
- the employer carried out as much investigation as was reasonable in the circumstances.

Upex then considers situations where (investigations and dismissals) have been found unfair, such as when:[73]

- reliance has been placed on the uncorroborated evidence of an anonymous informant (there must be reasonable grounds for relying on statements); or
- there has been a failure to keep or provide notes of investigations; or
- written statements were withheld from employees for no reason.

What that translates to in practice in an Australian context means, for instance:

- The starting point for investigation and discipline should be the relevant policy; if there is one, it should be followed.
- Investigations should not proceed with undue haste (see *Spence v Port of Brisbane Corporation* [2002] QIRComm 59, where the employer sacked the employee within hours of a complaint when the evidence was that the complainant did not want the employee sacked but only wanted the conduct to stop and the employee who was dismissed had been prepared to apologise).
- There should not be undue delay – consider *Smith*, discussed below.
- The employer does not have to follow quite as rigorous a process as a criminal court or police investigation: the standard is *Briginshaw v Briginshaw* (1938) 60 CLR 336. It is still the civil standard of the balance of probabilities, but the weight of the evidence needs to increase to match the seriousness of the allegation. The ultimate question is whether the employer can draw a reasonable inference from the evidence before them (and whether that evidence is reasonable).
- Where there is a disciplinary warning, employers will diarise this and usually have employees sign a written record that this is a meeting for discipline and that if there are further breaches, dismissal may result. (This type of approach was also noted in *Big W*.) Clearly, keeping written records of an investigation is important.
- Particularly difficult situations arise especially when: there is a group of possible wrongdoing employees and there is a question as to whether each one of that group was culpable; or there is possible retribution against a whistleblower; or if too great an amount of the complaint is communicated to the employee.[74]
- As noted in Chapter 7, the public service has sophisticated investigation procedures, although there is case law on when those investigations have miscarried. Ideally, a complainant should be kept separate from the employee about whom the complaint is

---

72   Ibid.
73   Ibid 157–8 considers *Linfood Cash and Carry Ltd v Thomson* [1989] ICR 518 through to *Vauxhaull Motors Ltd v Ghafoor* [1993] ICR 376 as well as *Louies v Coventry Hood and Seating Co. Ltd* [1990] ICR 54.
74   See, for example, J Beck 'Importance of fair workplace investigations' (2012) *Law Society Journal* 46.

made and the substance of the complaint should not become the subject of widespread or idle gossip: see the Defence Department case of *Lee v Smith* [2007] FMCA 59.

- In some industrial instruments and employment contracts, the employer may stipulate that there is a power to suspend an employee while an investigation into their conduct is underway (this is especially common in some forms of public sector employment). In the private sector, without such a contractual stipulation, the option would be to suspend an employee on full pay.[75]

The final case on investigations to be considered in this context is below.

BYRNE v AUSTRALIAN AIRLINES LTD (1995) 185 CLR 410 (BYRNE)

A number of baggage handlers at Sydney Airport were videoed by the Australian Federal Police performing their baggage-handling jobs in a way which reasonably raised questions as to whether they had been involved in long-time theft. Four or five months after the secret video was made, some of the employees were interviewed and sacked. The employees claimed they had been dismissed in contravention of a clause of the relevant award which (similar to today's unfair dismissal laws) included words to the effect that termination of employment could not be harsh, unjust or unreasonable. The employees claimed both breach of the relevant award clause and breach of contract, as they claimed the award clause was imputed into the contract of employment. The latter claim (if successful) would have resulted in substantial damages.

The case is important for two principles of law. First, the High Court found that the award term was not implied into the contract of employment. For a term to be implied, it must be necessary to give the contract efficacy. If the award term were not implied into the contract, the award would still operate; further, the usual implied terms of employment contract law would still apply (namely, that the contract could be terminated on reasonable notice or immediately for a substantial breach) – consequently, there was held to be no contractual void to be filled.[76] To this end the High Court overruled *Gregory v Philip Morris* (1988) 80 ALR 455, which had previously held that award terms (on harsh unjust and unreasonable dismissal) were imputed into a contract regardless of the intention of the parties to that contract.

Second, the High Court found that although there were issues as to procedure (the delay in the investigation), the underlying substantive breach (theft) was so strong that the deficiencies in the procedure did not detract from the validity of the dismissal.

Subsequent to this decision it has also been noted that if facts (justifying a dismissal) are brought to the employer's attention after a dismissal which was technically not fair, those facts (as long as they were subsequently ascertained) can justify the dismissal (see *Byrne*).[77]

---

75   CCH *Australian Labour Law Reporter* ¶71–110 'Types of Disciplinary Action Against Employees'.
76   See also McCallum *Top Workplace Relations Cases* 38–40.
77   *David Russell v Trustees of the Roman Catholic Church for the Archdiocese of Sydney* (2007) 69 NSWLR 198 per Rothman J; on appeal (2008) 72 NSWLR 559.

6.30.05 Futher jurisdictional and procedural questions

The procedure governing the hearing and determination of an unfair dismissal claim is found in Division 5 of Part 3-2 of the *Fair Work Act*. *The Unfair Dismissal Benchbook* provided by the FWC is an excellent practical tool or resource, and summarises some key cases on the meaning of dismissal as well as dealing with significant practical and procedural issues.[78] In order to avoid vexatious claims and ensure that problems can be dealt with in a timely manner, there is both a lodgement fee for an application and a 21-day limit within which applications must be made (ss 394 and 395).[79] It is only in exceptional circumstances that the time limit is extended.[80]

After checking that the applicant has completed any relevant qualifying period and is not in excess of any relevant salary cap, for example,[81] the matter may proceed.[82] There may be a response from the employer, and the parties may agree to an informal hearing with a public servant for conciliation. If that does not occur or does not successfully resolve the claim – or if there are contested facts – there may be a hearing before a member of the FWC (ss 397–399). Such hearings can be struck out if the claim is vexatious (ss 587 and 588) or if the parties have not followed instructions (s 399A).

An appeal will only lie where there is a matter of public interest (s 400).

Although the system is set up to place primary emphasis on representation by unions (s 596), lawyers are often allowed to represent their clients.

6.30.10 Remedies – reinstatement and damages

The remedies for unfair dismissal are governed by Part 3-2 Division 4 (ss 390–393) of the *Fair Work Act*. Importantly, reinstatement to one's job is the preferred remedy and should only be denied where it is 'inappropriate' to do so. If it is inappropriate, an award of compensation is to be made. Where reinstatement is ordered, then one should be restored to one's former position (or as close as possible thereto at either the original employer or a related entity) with continuity of service and an order for lost pay (taking into account any remuneration the employee earned while the unfair dismissal case was being heard). Where reinstatement is deemed inappropriate, compensation – typically capped at 26 weeks – may be awarded, taking into account the remuneration the sacked staffer would have received, their length of

---

78   FWC *The Unfair Dismissal Benchbook*, https://www.fwc.gov.au/documents/documents/benchbookresources/unfairdismissals/unfair-dismissals-benchbook.pdf.

79   *Fair Work Act* ss 394 and 395. For FWC material, go to https://www.fwc.gov.au/termination-of-employment/unfair-dismissal/eligibility. That link refers to *The Unfair Dismissal Benchbook* – which deals with a large range of substantive and procedural issues relevant to dismissal claims. See also forms at https://www.fwc.gov.au/termination-of-employment.

80   An excellent table of cases exists in CCH *Australian Labour Law Reporter* 47–265.

81   The salary cap (defined as one's being above the high-income threshold in s 333) is a matter for regulation and is amended from time to time. At the time of writing the cap was $138,900 and how that is calculated is traversed in the material provided by the Fair Work authorities (in *Unfair Dismissal Benchbook*, for example). Importantly, numerous Australian employees are able to access the remedy because of the wording of the governing provision and the effect it has on the salary cap (ss 333–382).

82   The *Unfair Dismissal Benchbook* also underscores the importance of the issues dealt with in the opening chapters of this book.

service, attempts to mitigate their loss and the employer's capacity to pay. Damages may be payable in instalments. There is no component for hurt feelings etc.

Reinstatement

Although reinstatement is the preferred remedy for unfair dismissal, at the time of writing, the material produced by the FWC demonstrates that it is definitely only in the minority of cases that reinstatement is, in fact, ordered.[83] In the cases discussed here and in the FWC'S *Unfair Dismissal Benchbook*, some themes may be distilled as to when the scales might be more inclined to tilt in favour of reinstatement. They include:

- when there is no fundamental loss of confidence in the relationship: if there was a valid reason for discipline but termination was harsh, and the employee has shown contrition/lack of hostility (such that the employment relationship is not irretrievably damaged).
- where others kept their jobs for similar breaches.
- where the employer is of a size such that they can re-absorb the former employee.
- the gravity of the employee's misconduct and how that balances against resuming employment: have they a strong and long employment record and was this a small lapse?[84]

If an employee is reinstated, the High Court decision of *Blackadder v Ramsey Butchering Services Pty Ltd* (2005) 221 CLR 539 underscores the importance of providing the reinstated worker with a constructive role, and not leaving them idle so that they are a target in a redundancy.

There is an interesting public sector example (under the predecessor *Workplace Relations Act 1996* (Cth) (*WR Act*)) of what is often the difficulty of determining when reinstatement will and will not be granted. In 2005, the Australian Government Solicitor reflected on government dismissal cases which apparently underscored the difficulty of reinstating a public servant.[85] In contrast, one important and interesting decision involving reinstatement is *Trent Smith v Department of Foreign Affairs and Trade (DFAT)* (*Trent Smith*).[86]

---

83   See FWC *Remedies, Results and Outcomes*, https://www.fwc.gov.au/termination-of-employment/unfair-dismissal/remedies.

84   A number of newsletters produced by commercial law firms also underscore the difficulties in distilling themes for reinstatement: Holding Redlich 'Revisiting the appropriateness of reinstatement in unfair dismissal cases' 11 November 2014, https://www.holdingredlich.com/workplace-relations-safety/revisiting-the-appropriateness-of-reinstatement-in-unfair-dismissal-cases; and Clayton Utz (A Casellas and M Clohessy) 'Reinstatement a real risk if you treat employees' safety breaches differently' 17 March 2017, https://www.claytonutz.com/knowledge/2016/march/reinstatement-a-real-risk-if-you-treat-employees-safety-breaches-differently.

85   Australian Government Solicitor (AGS) (2005) 'Reinstatement where the employment relationship has irrevocably broken down' *Litigation Notes* No. 12, which considered *Walsh v Australian Taxation Office* 4 March 2005 [PR 956205]. For an article which discusses that former *Workplace Relations Act* provision and the difference between its test on appropriateness and alternative tests such as impracticality, see H Meggiorin 'Reinstatement under the *Workplace Relations Act* (Cth): is it practicable, appropriate or just plain speculative?' (1999) 27 *ABLR* 438.

86   [2007] AIRC 765 per Deegan C 28 September 2007 (*Smith*). The author thanks Dr Max Spry, Brisbane Bar, for bringing this case to her attention.

SMITH *v* DEPARTMENT OF FOREIGN AFFAIRS AND TRADE [2007] AIRC 765 (SMITH)

In this case, a career public servant with an exemplary employment history, Trent Smith, first was accused of leaking details of the Foreign Minister's conversation to the press. He was later cleared of that but then found guilty (in a departmental investigation) of failing to uphold the values and the integrity of the service (subsection 13(11) Australian Public Service (APS) Code of Conduct) by sending an email to an Opposition staffer advising them that they could obtain information through a Senate Estimates questioning process; and by allegedly seeking the help of a colleague (Matthew Hyndes) to assist in drafting questions or dot points the Opposition could use to embarrass the government. Smith was dismissed as a consequence of the finding. In unfair dismissal hearings before the Commission, Smith was successful and gained reinstatement.

Commissioner Deegan found that many of the findings of the internal DFAT investigation were 'untenable'.[87] The investigators seemed to place more weight on certain witnesses despite the gist of the majority of other credible witnesses.[88] The email that Smith had sent simply directed the Opposition staffer towards information that was on the public record;[89] and the other allegations were made by a witness who lacked credibility.[90] That latter witness, Mr Hyndes, was found to have made the complaint against Mr Smith largely to redeem his own position within the department – which had suffered after a number of significant complaints about his work and conduct.[91] The investigation itself took years and there was a delay with its start – there were also questions as to whether all the evidence had been considered at all times.[92]

In ordering reinstatement, although there had obviously been a full hearing of the matter, Commissioner Deegan acknowledged that the APS is a career service and that Smith had an excellent record and skills which might not be easily transferable to other positions in the private sector – however, these facts were not said to be significant factors in granting the remedy.[93] The significant facts were that the defendant had not breached the trust and confidence of the relationship with the department – he had simply defended himself. Many of the managers responsible for the decisions against him had moved on. The Commissioner stated:[94]

> There is no reason for the applicant not to be placed in the position he would have been in had it not been for Mr Hyndes' allegations. It is not good enough for the Department to argue that, even if the applicant should not have [been] terminated, he should not be reinstated because his contesting (the termination) has affected his relationship with his employer. DFAT is a large department with many overseas posts and offices throughout this country. I am satisfied that

---

87   *Smith* at [291]; see also [262] et seq and [296] et seq.
88   Ibid [291] and [262] et seq.
89   Ibid [260] et seq.
90   Ibid [272] et seq; see also [284] et seq and [288].
91   Ibid [278] et seq and [273] et seq.
92   Ibid [263]. The investigation is further criticised at [308] et seq.
93   Ibid [322].
94   Ibid [323]–[324].

the reinstatement of the applicant is unlikely to adversely affect its operations in any way. I am also certain that the applicant is sufficiently mature and intelligent to know that his attitude upon his return ... will determine his future.[95]

6.30.15 Closing remarks on statutory unfair dismissal

While there is clear utility in the unfair dismissal remedy, there are also clear limits. The cap on damages, the fact that reinstatement does not frequently occur, and the costs and stresses of litigation are all considerations to be taken into account. If parties were at the consultation stage of a restructure, one might ask whether it is strategically wise to argue against the restructure as not being genuine at that stage, rather than letting the matter progress to a possible unfair dismissal dispute. Are there other remedies in the event of unfair dismissal? (See the section below on avoiding double dipping.)

6.35 The role of contract law – wrongful dismissal claims

6.35.05 General rules – what is reasonable notice and when is the remedy to be used?

While the above discussion of the statutory protections against unfair dismissal justifies an entire Part of this chapter – and while that remedy has been labelled a remedy for 'almost all'[96] – there are, nonetheless, those who are not protected by unfair dismissal laws. Importantly, these Australian employees are still not quite in the position of a US worker who (under the US employment-at-will system) can be terminated at any time for any reason.[97] For those Australians not covered by our unfair dismissal system, the termination should be governed by the notice clauses in the contract; where the contract is silent, notice should be reasonable, unless the conduct causing the termination is so serious as to justify instant dismissal (also known as summary dismissal).[98]

There is a useful summary of the factors that influence what is reasonable notice (along with a list of cases where the concept has been explored) in Sappideen et al. *Macken's Law of Employment*.[99] Those factors include: seniority, salary and significance of the job; the nature of the work performed; the length of employment; industry custom and practice; and, sometimes, the employee's age, qualifications and experience, their mobility and how long it may take them to find alternative employment, along with their pension

---

95   Ibid [325].
96   CCH *Australian Labour Law Reporter* Commentary. This is because of the application of those laws to workers employed under industrial instruments, as discussed earlier in this chapter.
97   RA Epstein 'In defense of the contract at will' (1984) 51 *University of Chicago Law Review* 947.
98   For more information on instant dismissal see *Byrne* discussion below.
99   Sappideen et al. *Macken's Law of Employment* (2011) at 286 et seq, especially 289–90 et seq.

entitlements.[100] Sappideen et al. conclude: 'A non-legal, if, for some, unpalatable, rationalization of the cases on reasonable notice is to say that the higher the job on the socio-economic scale, the longer will be the necessary period of notice. The lower the job, the shorter the notice.'[101]

It is on that basis that some scholars (and judges) question the utility of wrongful dismissal as a remedy. In one of the most famous wrongful dismissal cases, *Addis v Gramophone Co. Ltd* [1909] AC 488 (*Addis*) (considered below), Lord Loreburn begins his judgement with this: 'My Lords, this is a most unfortunate litigation, in which the costs must far exceed any sum there may be at stake. A little common sense would have settled all these differences in a few minutes.'[102]

Professor Collins feels that 'rarely is the remedy worth the trouble'.[103] He notes that damages will often be limited to the unpaid amount of a notice period (and for workers who are unskilled, for instance, that could be limited to 1 week's pay). He also notes that the courts will require the complainant employee to mitigate their losses – so that any pay they earn from employment they find promptly will be deducted from any award of damages.[104] When one considers the cost of and stress involved in litigation, and the spoiling of relationships that it can cause, his view is not entirely surprising. But equally obviously there are situations where the action will be worth pursuing. Reasonable damages awarded in a wrongful dismissal suit may include money to cover time during which disciplinary hearings that should have been held could have been held, for instance.[105] There could also be a claim for contractual debt for unpaid redundancy or severance pay.[106]

The circumstances in which instant or summary dismissal may be justified (and hence no notice is required) are discussed in Neil and Chin.[107] Those authors, relying on cases such as *Blyth Chemicals Ltd v Bushnell*,[108] observe that it is 'conduct which in respect of important matters is incompatible with the fulfilment of the employee's duty'[109] that will justify summary dismissal. Such conduct may broadly be described as misconduct, significant negligence or neglect.[110] Examples range from misappropriation of the employer's property through to academics sleeping with their students.[111] Sensibly, Neil and Chin note the pointlessness of relying on any one exemplar decision to govern every similar case – cases will almost always have subtle evidentiary variations of their own, so each one really does turn on its own facts.[112]

The contractual side of termination of employment is far more complex than simply a consideration of what is reasonable notice, however. As Naughton correctly points out,

---

100   Ibid 291 et seq.
101   Ibid 292.
102   *Addis* [1909] AC 488, 489.
103   Collins *Justice in Dismissal* (1992) 30.
104   Ibid 30 and 31.
105   There is an excellent discussion of termination in I Neil and D Chin *The Modern Contract of Employment* (Thomson Reuters, 2012), Ch. 14, especially at 291 et seq.
106   Ibid 302 and 304 et seq. Severance pay is like a golden handshake – an additional payment to compensate the former employee for loss of their position.
107   Ibid.
108   (1933) 49 CLR 66 at 80–81.
109   Neil and Chin *The Modern Contract of Employment* (2012) 247.
110   Ibid 244 et seq.
111   Ibid 248–9 et seq.
112   Ibid 250–8.

'extremely complex common law issues concerning the contract of employment can arise in an unlawful termination claim'.[113]

That complexity stems in part from the fact that there can be legal requirements regulating the contract of employment outside the contract (such as minimum terms in an award or agreement). Consequently, the contract must operate in conjunction with those terms.

Further complexity can also flow from the nature of employment contracts and contract law. First, there is an employment relationship as well as a contract of employment. So, for instance, what happens if one party gives defective notice of termination which the other accepts – will that 'acceptance' overcome the defective notice to terminate? Or what happens if an employee resigns in the 'heat of the moment'?

Even more difficulties may flow from the drafting of contracts. As noted earlier, if a contract purports to be for a fixed term, but also states that it may be ended by either party on the giving of one month's notice (prior to the expiry date), is it really a fixed-term contract at all? What effect will flow if it is not? Similarly, what if one party assumes they will be renewed in their fixed-term contract employment? Does such an expectation carry any weight?

Yet another source of consternation for lawyers might be the position after *Commonwealth Bank of Australia v Barker* (2014) 253 CLR 169, discussed in Chapter 2, as there are questions about the nature of the duty of good faith.

6.35.10 Leading cases and issues on wrongful dismissal

CONCUT PTY LTD v WORRELL (2000) 176 ALR 693

The question for determination in this case was whether Concut (a concrete company, so obviously in the building industry) could rely on a prior wrong of its employee, Mr Wells, to justify its instant dismissal of him. Importantly, the question arose in an unusual context – Mr Wells' employment had been governed by an oral agreement for the first 6 or so years, then was changed to a written contract. The prior wrong came to light during the life of the written agreement, but the wrong (misuse by the employee of employer equipment and materials for the employee's personal use) had occurred during the period of the oral agreement.

The Queensland Court of Appeal majority had found that Mr Wells' employment was governed by two separate and distinct contracts – the oral and then the written contracts. Since a contract of employment is not a contract of the utmost good faith (see *Bell v Lever*

Brothers [1932] AC 161),[114] Mr Wells was under no obligation to declare his own wrong prior to taking up the new written contract of employment and Concut could not rely on the wrong that had occurred under the earlier oral contract.

The High Court unanimously disagreed with the Queensland Court of Appeal majority. It said that the terms of the two contracts and the nature of the work performed were largely similar – the written agreement slightly varied but also consolidated the oral contract. True, Mr Wells was invited to buy shares in Concut at the time the contract was reduced to writing, but that did not alter the flow of the two agreements. There was no intention to dislodge previous substantive rights and obligations and the relationship continued.

Having found Mr Wells' employment to be governed by one contract of employment, the High Court then found that the employer could rely on the earlier misconduct – it had learnt of it only recently (the employer had not known of it for some time and then condoned it, which may have meant the employer was waiving the repudiation). The conduct (secretly misusing the employer's materials for personal uses) was a fundamental breach of the contract of employment – how could an employer be expected to continue to trust Mr Wells (who was in a management and leadership role)?[115]

6.35.15 Wrongful dismissal, repudiation, giving and waiving notice

AUTOMATIC FIRE SPRINKLERS PTY LTD v WATSON (1946) 72 CLR 435

Mr Watson began his employment (as General Manager) in the late 1930s under a contract which was to run for 6 years and then could be terminated by either party on 3 months' notice (in the normal course) or by 1 month's notice if the employer formed the view that Mr Watson was no longer able to fulfil the role. Importantly, the employment contract contained an arbitration clause.

114　Noting that the position is different if an employee is actually asked whether or not they have done something wrong. If there is a direct question, then the employee or would-be employee is under a duty to be frank.

115　For a thoughtful and clear discussion of why the High Court reasoning in *Concut* is correct, see R McCallum *McCallum's Top Workplace Relations Cases: Labour Law and the Employment Relationship as Defined by Case Law* (CCH, 2008) from 128. In contrast, A Stewart and J Carter are critical of the court for (as *they* see it) missing an opportunity to revise the law after *Bell v Lever Brothers* [1932] AC 161: see 'The effect of formalising an employment contract: the High Court misses an opportunity' (2001) 17 *Journal of Contract Law* 181. They also take issue with the High Court characterisation of the written contract as one which merely formalised an earlier agreement.

Mr Watson was wrongfully dismissed by the company on multiple occasions. First, the company gave him notice which was defective, as it was one day short of the requisite 3 months. Later, the employer tried dismissal on 1 month's notice, but the arbitrator found that the company had never really believed he was unfit for the job. Crucially, the employer had also failed to comply with a relevant regulation which required the company to seek formal approval before they terminated an employee's employment. The employer instead had seemed to try to 'get around' the regulation by telling Mr Watson he was terminated as General Manager but would receive less pay for fulfilling a lesser function. After this latter purported dismissal (on 29 September 1944) Mr Watson still continued to come to work and act *as if* he were still the General Manager. On 19 May 1945, when the regulations no longer applied, the company terminated his services and he was blocked from working in the company.

Finding that the original termination was wrongful, the arbitrator then referred the following case stated to the High Court. Essentially: was the 29 May 1944 dismissal ineffectual due to either the national security regulations or Watson's refusal to accept his termination? If the answer to both those questions is 'no', was the measure of damages limited to one day (the day that was not given originally)?

The Supreme Court of New South Wales had answered the first question with a 'yes', so it was not necessary to decide the second. In a High Court decision which was six separate judgements, the appeal was dismissed 4:2, largely because of the operation of the regulation.

The case is said to stand for the proposition that service earns remuneration, rather than simple readiness and willingness to work (in most cases). However, the case is interesting for a number of other reasons. It begs the question of remedies for wrongful dismissal. There might be a quantum meruit (reasonable payment for work performed) if service is performed and accepted. Further, in most cases there is great concern not to insist on specific performance (that is, actual performance) of a contract for personal services. There is also the idea that one party needs to accept a repudiation of a contract before it is said to end. In other words, as noted, there is an employment relationship as well as an employment contract.

The most recent High Court authority where these latter issues were considered is *Visscher v Hon President Justice Giudice* (2009) 239 CLR 361.

VISSCHER v GIUDICE (2009) 239 CLR 361

Essentially, Mr Visscher was a casual, then a full-time, maritime worker. He was appointed Third Hand or Mate, then was promoted to First Mate or chief officer. The relevant union challenged such a speedy promotion. That, combined with instructions from an industrial commissioner, led to the employer, Teekay, rescinding the promotion. The Teekay company claimed Visscher was a Third Mate who would simply be performing higher duties as First Mate. Mr Visscher's pay slips and an attachment to the relevant industrial instrument reflected the company's position. Importantly, however, Visscher refused to accept that he had been demoted – he went on performing the duties of First Mate, basically asserting that that was his substantive role. When Mr Visscher was promoted to Second Mate, still performing higher duties as First Mate, once again he was of the view that he was substantively in the First Mate role. It was only when the company sought to have Visscher actually serve as a Second Mate on ship that Mr Visscher claimed he had been constructively dismissed – that is, forced into resigning due to a demotion, which was akin to being sacked. The company countered that they had neither sacked nor demoted Mr Visscher and that he had resigned of his own accord.

After effectively losing his challenge to the dismissal before a variety of industrial commissioners and Federal Court Judges, the matter went to the High Court on a question of law – and Mr Visscher finally had some success.

The majority of the High Court (Heydon, Crennan, Kiefel and Bell JJ) found that the contract of employment (through which Mr Visscher had been made First Mate) may well still have been on foot. Although the company had repudiated the contract through rescinding Visscher's initial promotion, Mr Visscher had clearly not accepted that repudiation, so possibly the contract remained. It was unlikely that the pay slips or the attachment to the industrial instrument amounted to an acquiescence on his part, and nor did those documents override his objection. The lower courts had erred in law – they had not abided by the rule that there must be acceptance of a repudiation before the contract ends. (The fact that it is unlikely that a court will order specific performance of an employment contract does not change that.) In so finding, the High Court underscored that there is a difference between the employment relationship and the employment contract. The matter was therefore remitted to the industrial commission.

There is an excellent discussion of this decision in Keats, 'What shall we do with a demoted sailor? The High Court decides in *Visscher*'.[116] Keats acknowledges that the case decides the '(two) thorny contractual issues'[117] of whether acceptance of repudiation is necessary to end the contract and the difference between the employment relationship and the employment contract. Usefully, Keats also speaks to the practical relevance of those issues.

As Keats points out, the lower courts in *Visscher* had, incorrectly, applied the automatic theory of termination (that is, the contract ends with the breach), not the correct elective theory (there must be acceptance of repudiation before the contract ends). They had assumed that since a court would not order specific performance of a contract of employment (being a contract for personal services), there was no remedy available, which meant that refusing to accept the repudiation was almost futile. However, as she points out, 'although perhaps uncommon . . . there are situations where an unaccepted repudiation will assume importance'.[118] Visscher's refusal to accept repudiation may well have meant he was still a First Mate, which lays the foundation for his claim of constructive dismissal. Another case Keats points to is *Rigby v Ferodo Ltd* [1988] ICR 29. In that case, an employer reduced an employee's wages; the employee protested but continued in employment and,

116   L Keats 'What shall we do with a demoted sailor? The High Court decides *Visscher*' (2010) 23 *Australian Journal of Labour Law* 121–36.
117   Ibid 131.
118   Ibid 132.

at a future stage, successfully sued for breach of contract for underpaid wages. In deciding the case, Lord Oliver of Aylmerton said: 'I entirely fail to see how the continuance of the primary contractual obligation can be made to depend upon the subjective desire of the contract-breaker.'[119]

The second issue the case decides is to confirm that wrongful dismissal ends the employment relationship even though the contract of employment may continue. The employment relationship continued for years after the repudiation. Keats also considers the situation in the context of another case (which relies on *Visscher*).[120]

The notion that repudiation must be accepted to end a contract is also discussed by Neil and Chin.[121] It is important that notice of termination be clear (and with clear conditions, if the notice is conditional) and in accordance with the terms of the contract – if relevant terms exist.[122] If a resignation is not defective, the employer has little choice but to accept the resignation. If an employee, on the other hand, validly resigns, but does so in the heat of the moment, there can be real issues if that employee seeks to recant. Where the employee has successfully done so is usually when they recant very shortly after the resignation (and in circumstances where their conduct has not permanently undermined the employment relationship), or where the employer is keen to retain the employee's services and has not already set in train irrevocable moves to install a replacement worker. Where an employee resigns (or where they are terminated) it will often be the case that an employer wants to remove the staffer from the work environment – employees at the end of their service may be unproductive, or even disruptive. Where that situation arises, employers can place employees on leave (as discussed in Chapter 2); if the contract of employment or some industrial instrument allows, they can give payment in lieu of notice. In practice, if there is a good employer–employee relationship and the parties are parting company amicably, the employee might benefit from continuing in the workforce and the employer might benefit from an easy handover of the role.

6.35.20 Terminating and not renewing short-term contracts and damages for lost opportunity

A further problem might arise if a short-term contract is terminated before its end date or if there was a presumption that the contract was going to be renewed.

As previously observed, a contract is genuinely fixed term (for a specified period) when it is for a settled or finite period. If this is the case, if the contract simply runs its course there is usually no claim in damages. Likewise, if one party seeks to terminate prior to that contractual completion date, the damages should usually be payment for the remaining period of the fixed-term contract.

---

119   See Keats 'What shall we do with a demoted sailor' 132.
120   Ibid 131 et seq, especially 134. The case referred to is *Tullet Prebon (Australia) Pty Ltd v Purcell* (2008) 175 IR 414.
121   Neil and Chin *The Modern Contract of Employment* (2012) 240.
122   Ibid 234 et seq.

If, on the other hand, the contract stated that it was for a fixed term but either party could terminate on giving 1 month's notice, say, then unless that notice is defective in some way, no damages are available.

The residual question is whether a party could seek damages for lost opportunity to renew the fixed-term contract.

WALKER v CITIGROUP GLOBAL MARKETS AUSTRALIA PTY LTD (2006) 233 ALR 687; [2006] FCAFC 101

Walker was a stockbroker for ABN Amro. He was headhunted by NatWest, at the same time it was being taken over by Citigroup, as it happened. Throughout several months of negotiations with NatWest representatives, Walker made it clear: that he wanted total confidentiality of the negotiations; that he would not leave ABN until his bonus was paid; that he wanted a better job title after a year of service with NatWest; and that he wanted approximately $250,000 in annual salary and the same amount as an annual bonus. When the takeover (by Citi) was first rumoured, Walker sought reassurances from NatWest that his position with them (if he took one) would be secure. A NatWest representative said the position would be secure. ABN then started its own restructuring process. With the knowledge of NatWest, Walker decided not to continue with ABN – as he said, in reliance on NatWest's and Citi's assurances. At that time, things changed with NatWest/Citi. Contradicting their earlier claims that Walker's references were good, representatives began to say that his name was 'mud'. Ultimately, the job offer was withdrawn. Importantly, the contract was both written and oral. There was agreement that Walker's title would upgrade after 1 year, but there were also pro forma written conditions that the contract could be terminated on 1 month's notice by either side. Walker obviously suffered significant career and financial loss and his marriage suffered. He sued for both contract (repudiation) and misleading and deceptive conduct under the former *Trade Practices Act 1974* (Cth) (now the *Competition and Consumer Act 2010* (Cth)).

Before a single Federal Court Judge, *Walker v Salomon Smith Barney Securities Pty Ltd & Anor* [2003] FCA 1099 (*Walker No. 1*) determined liability (and in that judgement the primary judge found some of the evidence of the NatWest staff – about Walker's reputation being mud, for instance – to have been fabricated); *Walker v Citigroup Global Markets Pty Ltd* [2005] FCA 1678 (*Walker No. 2*) and *Walker v Citigroup Global Markets Pty Ltd* [2005] FCA 1866 (*Walker No. 3*) determined the questions of damages and costs. Significantly, the flaw in the judgement, which led all parties to appeal to the Full Court, related to the fact that the primary judge seemed to have found (in *Walker No. 1*) that the contract was oral and written and did include a term that he would continue employment for at least a year; the subsequent decisions homed in on the right of the parties to terminate with 1 month's notice. Clearly there was a repugnance between the two.

The Full Court found that there was definitely a term that Walker would continue in employment for at least a year – the evidence for that was found in the lengthy negotiations during which Walker expressed concern as to his future. Since there was a specifically negotiated term of that nature, it (rather than the pro forma clause that allowed termination on 1 month's notice) was to be the focus in calculating damages. In calculating damages, the court also had regard to the fact that Walker was likely to have had a long career with

Citi. In so doing they cited the decision in *Commonwealth v Amann Aviation Pty Ltd* (1991) 174 CLR 64. The court awarded losses for damage to reputation etc, but that was subsequent to the trade practices claim, not the claim in contract.

On the question of awarding damages for the chance of future continued employment, Neil and Chin[123] point to a spilt in the authorities. The NSW Court of Appeal, in *Murray Irrigation Ltd v Balsden* (2006) 67 NSWLR 73, says they are not available. In the event that such damages may be recoverable, questions go to whether the parties, when negotiating, contemplated such a possibility and whether the performance of the contract was such that renewal was likely.[124]

6.35.25 Damages

Neil and Chin (writing in 2012) note that damages will seldom be awarded for disappointment and distress if an employment contract is terminated.[125] Likewise, diminution of an employee's employment prospects may not lead to an award of damages.[126] With the High Court in *Commonwealth Bank of Australia v Barker* in 2014 finding against an implied term of mutual trust and confidence, it may well be that the chance of damages for reputational injury and lost opportunity for further employment has decreased. There is controversy over whether damages might be awarded if there was psychiatric injury caused by the manner in which the employment was terminated. The judgement of McHugh J in *Baltic Shipping Co. v Dillon* (1993) 176 CLR 344 suggests that it may be (on the basis that such would be a personal injury),[127] but the decision in *Aldersea v Public Transport Corporation* (2001) 3 VR 499 suggested the opposite.[128]

ADDIS v GRAMOPHONE CO. LTD [1909] AC 488

Mr Addis had worked in Calcutta for Gramophone Co. on the basis of a set salary plus commission. His contract of employment was terminable on 6 months' notice. Gramophone terminated his employment with 6 months' pay and immediately installed a new manager – hence depriving Mr Addis of his capacity to earn commission.

The judgements in the House of Lords point to inadequacies in the manner in which the initial trial was run. Those professed inadequacies may well have contributed to what most of their Lordships regarded as the real problem in the case, namely that wrongful dismissal or breach of contract would normally have entitled Mr Addis to 6 months' salary plus the reasonably expected commission, whereas the jury in the case appeared to have also

123   Ibid from 294.
124   See Neil and Chin *The Modern Contract of Employment* (2012) 291 et seq, especially at 299 et seq.
125   Ibid 309–10.
126   Ibid 300–01.
127   Ibid 310 et seq.
128   Ibid 312 et seq.

awarded exemplary or punitive damages – for the manner in which the contract was discharged and the likely damage to Addis' reputation for losing his job and being sent back to the UK before the actual expiry of the 6 months notice period.

The majority of their Lordships noted that exemplary damages were not part of British contract law. Remedy for defamation was a different law suit.

As Neil and Chin note,[129] and as stated above, this case has caused many problems (as to the computation of damages for wrongful dismissal).

Though Neil and Chin are correct, the style of the judgements is endearing in some ways. Lord James of Hereford, for example, refers to Lord Loreburn LC as 'my learned friend on the Woolsack'[130] and laments his days as a junior barrister when he would attempt to find some tortious action because of the limits on contractual damages. Although over 100 years old, the case is well worth reading.

ADAMI v MAISON DE LUXE LTD (1924) 35 CLR 143

Adami was employed as the manager of a hall. The company that controlled the hall ordered Adami to work on Saturdays as they wanted dances to take place at that time. Adami was a bookie and wrote to the company stating that he did not think that was part of his employment, and it was not something he could do. The trial judge sent to the jury the question of whether working on a Saturday was part of Adami's contract of employment. They held that it was not and awarded him substantial damages. On appeal to the High Court, the matter was said to be about a term of the contract and thus not something the jury should have decided. That being the case, the High Court confirmed that the employee should have followed a lawful and reasonable direction. In a separate judgement, Isaacs ACJ found that there should be disobedience of a substantive contractual term before the contract is terminated.

6.40 Further issues
6.40.05 Restraint of trade clauses

These clauses may lead to common law and equitable issues that arise *after* employment ends. One issue that not infrequently arises at the end of the employment relationship is the manner in which the post-employment conduct of an ex-employee can be curtailed by a former employer (so as to protect the legitimate interests of that former employer). The issue can arise in a number of ways.

In the first place, the implied duty of good faith establishes that an employee cannot copy customer lists etc. Although it is a common law duty, and this restraint actually ends with the

---

129   Ibid 293 et seq, where the authors refer to the headnote of *Addis* as limiting damages for the manner in which employment was ended.

130   *Addis* at 488 and 492 per Lord James of Hereford.

termination of the contract, it stands to reason that its operation during the life of the employment contract does confer a limit on a party's post-employment behaviour.

Second, the equitable duty of confidence endures after the employment relationship has formally ceased so that, for instance, any information communicated to an employee (whilst they are employed) in such a way as to command confidentiality, cannot be divulged subsequently, or used in such a manner as to harm the former employer who communicated the information.

The obvious question arises as to how one can practically limit the misuse of such information. That question has caused some to opine that the most effective way to deal with this issue is to prevent the ex-employee from working for a competitor. As Lord Denning MR found in the oft-quoted passage from *Littlewoods Organisation Ltd v Harris* [1978] 1 All ER 1026 at 1479:

> But experience has shown that it is not satisfactory to have simply a covenant against disclosing confidential information. The reason is because it is so difficult to draw the line between information which is confidential and information which is not: and it is very difficult to prove a breach when the information is of such a character that a servant can carry it away in his head. The difficulties are such that the only practical solution is to take a covenant from the servant by which he is not to go to work for a rival in trade.

That idea of having an express contractual term which prevents an employee from working for another (and hence avoiding the risk of an illegal transfer of confidential information) is one of the reasons for express restraint of trade clauses – clauses that prevent an employee working for a competitor for a period after they leave employment – in employment contracts.[131]

6.40.10 Legitimate interest and restraint of trade clauses

Significantly, then, express restraint clauses are designed to protect the legitimate interests of an employer. It follows from the discussion above that such a legitimate interest includes *confidential information*. But there are more legitimate interests that a restraint can also protect. A second legitimate interest that can be protected by such a restraint is the employer's *customer connections* (see *Lindner v Murdoch's Garage* (1950) 83 CLR 628). An employer may have spent considerable money training an employee, and may have business goodwill to consider and protect. Because goodwill is a valuable part of a business, it stands to reason that an employer would seek to give their new employee (who is replacing the former employee) sufficient time to work their way into the new role (proving themselves and establishing relationships with clients) without facing competition from the former employee (who was established in the role).

That last sentence hints at one of the difficulties with the law in this area. The law does not protect an employer from competition; it only seeks to protect a legitimate interest, such as the goodwill of a business (see *Herbert Morris Ltd v Saxelby* [1916] 1 AC 688). There is a difficult balance to be struck between the right of the former employer to protect their business and the right of the employee to use their skills and work. That has prompted authors such as Dean (in

---

131   The clauses are usually in contracts from their inception, but the litigation arises after the end of the employment relationship; hence the inclusion of the topic in this chapter.

Law of Trade Secrets and Personal Secrets) to ask: 'Why is this area of law so confusing?'[132] The answer surely lies in the fact that the cases are about balancing competing interests and they do so against a background of complex legal principles which show the overlap between law and equity.[133]

The law in this area is dynamic. As Dyson Heydon wrote in *The Restraint of Trade Doctrine*,[134] the categories of protected (or legitimate) interest are not closed. So today there is an emerging further type of interest an employer can protect: there are now anti-poaching or non-solicitation clauses, which prevent a former employee approaching those who are still employed by the former employer (see *Hartleys Ltd v Martin* (2002) 52 AILR 7-094). This category acknowledges an employer's legitimate interest in *maintaining a reasonably stable workforce*.

Having established that a legitimate interest potentially justifies a restraint, the balance of the discussion here concerns: what makes for a valid restraint clause? What form might the clause take? What are the more testing issues, academically and practically? And what has been the effect of technology (such as Facebook) on non-solicitation clauses?[135]

6.40.15 A valid restraint: the basic principles

The most basic principle of a valid restraint of trade (in any field, not simply employment) was established well over 100 years ago in *Nordenfeld v Maxim Nordenfeld Co.* [1894] AC 535. For a restraint to be valid, it must be reasonable as to time, place and function – no one has a *carte blanche* right to be protected from competition, and the legitimate interests of an employer in allowing restraint must be balanced against the public interest of facilitating competition. In an employment law context, this is yet another porous test that must be applied itself to an apparently limitless array of circumstances and workplaces. So, for instance, at first blush, a 6-month restraint may seem unduly long in a field such as IT, where programs can change with rapidity, yet it was held to be a valid restraint in a case where the party in breach of the restraint had done so whilst also in breach of their good faith and confidentiality duties (*Portal Software International Pty Ltd v Bodsworth* (2005) 58 AILR 200-211).[136]

There is an excellent and relatively recent discussion of the principles and operation of the law on restraint clauses in an employment law context in the judgement of Brereton J in *Cactus Imaging Pty Ltd v Peters* (2006).

---

132   R Dean and T Thomas *Law of Trade Secrets and Personal Secrets* (Law Book Co., 2002).
133   A further difficulty is the overlap between employment law and copyright: if there is something which is a trade mark, that has a separate governing body of law.
134   JD Heydon *The Restraint of Trade Doctrine* (Butterworths, 2nd ed, 1998).
135   There are other incisive works on restraint of trade, including RP Meagher, JD Heydon and MJ Leeming *Meagher, Gummow and Lehane's Equity: Doctrines and Remedies* (LexisNexis, 4th ed, 2002) as well as CF Spry *The Principles of Equitable Remedies: Specific Performance, Injunctions, Rectification and Equitable Damages* (Law Book Co., 4th ed, 1990).
136   For a very good, relatively recent discussion on what makes for a valid employment restraint and the remedies that might be sought, see G McEwan 'Employment restraint of trade clauses and protection of confidential information from trade rivals' (Parts 1 and 2) (2014) 20 (7 and 8) *Employment Law Bulletin*.

CACTUS IMAGING PTY LTD v PETERS (2006) 71 NSWLR 9

In this case, in addition to a protection of confidential information clause (Clause 7), the relevant restraint was couched in these terms:

9.1 The employee will not directly or indirectly and whether solely or jointly or as director, manager, agent or servant of any person or corporation, do any of the following acts at any time during the course of employment and for 12 months thereafter:

9.1.1 Carry on or be engaged or interested in any business of a nature of the company's business, within New South Wales;

9.1.2 Canvass, solicit or endeavour to entice away from the employer any person who or which at any time during the preceding 12 months were or are clients or customers of the employer or in the habit of dealing with the employer;

9.1.3 Solicit, interfere with or endeavour to entice away any employee, consultant or contractor of the employer; or

9.1.4 Counsel, procure or otherwise assist any person to do any of the acts referred to in clauses 9.1.2 or 9.1.3.

After noting that the central issues went to whether or not the restraint protected legitimate interests of the employer and whether or not they were excessive in scope and duration, Brereton J summarised the key principles of restraint law, from paragraph [10] onwards, and in particular the approach to be adopted to interpreting restraint clauses in New South Wales (which is governed by the *Restraint of Trade Act 1976* (NSW), which allows the court to read down restraint clauses).[137]

His Honour found the clause to be a valid restraint of trade justified by three legitimate interests: confidentiality of the information;[138] customer connection (and hence goodwill); and (as discussed in detail below) the right to maintain a stable workforce. Having found legitimate interests, the question then became whether the restraint was reasonable in scope and duration. In finding that it was, His Honour relied on the fact that although the relevant industry (advertising) was price-sensitive (and not as dependent on clients having faith in a service provider as might be the case in some other fields), it was accepted that there was sufficient contact between employees of Cactus and the outside world that clients had to like the person they were dealing with, otherwise they would take their business elsewhere.[139] Once Mr Peters left employment, it was reasonable to expect that his replacement would take up to 1 year to work for and earn the professional respect of clients, especially those who did not frequently use Cactus. One of the particularly interesting aspects of the case is that the restraint

---

137 Other states do not have the *Restraint of Trade Act 1976* (NSW) and therefore the issue might well be the validity or striking out of the whole clause.

138 For example, information and software that were 'tailor made' for Cactus: *Cactus Imaging Pty Ltd v Peters* (2006) 71 NSWLR 9 (*Cactus*) at [12] et seq.

139 Ibid [25] et seq.

was held to be valid even though it related to people who were not necessarily clients of Mr Peters whilst he was at Cactus (omitting references):[140]

> Were the restraint in cl 9.1.2 supported solely by customer connection, it would be *prima facie* excessive insofar as it prohibited solicitation of customers other than those with whom Mr Peters dealt, and in particular those who had become customers only since he had left . . .
>
> . . . However, such a restraint may be reasonable, notwithstanding that it extends beyond customers with whom the employee has personal contact, in particular where, despite the absence of personal contact, the employee may have acquired influence over or special knowledge of the clientele as a result of the seniority of his or her position, or where the employee's role includes obtaining and extending custom for the employer's business [Mr Peters' position as State Sales Manager places him in that category in respect of the New South Wales clientele, even those with whom he did not personally deal].
>
> . . . Moreover, cl 9.1.2 is supported, not only by protection of customer connection, but also by protection of confidential information. Protection of confidential information could have supported a restraint on employment by a competitor at all, such as is imposed by clause 9.1.1, although Cactus does not seek to enforce it. Clause 9.1.2 can therefore legitimately, in aid of protection of Cactus' confidential information, prohibit solicitation of the existing clientele of Cactus, whether Mr Peters dealt with them or not. That is because his knowledge of pricing parameters and market strategies would advantage him, in the employ of a competitor of Cactus, in soliciting any customer of Cactus, whether or not he had previously personally serviced that customer . . .

His Honour went on to find that the restraint encompassed those who had become clients after Mr Peters had left, for the same reasons.[141] That passage of the judgement also notes that the time for assessing a restraint is traditionally when the contract is made.

6.40.20 Restraint and technology

PLANET FITNESS PTY LTD v BROOKE DUNLOP [2012] NSWSC 1425

This case involved an application for interlocutory relief against a breach of the following Clause 3.5 restraint:

> Restraint of Trade: During the term of this agreement and during the Restraint Period, the Contractor must not directly or indirectly or through any interposed entity (including a corporate vehicle, trust or partnership) without the prior written agreement of the Company, solicit, canvass or secure the custom of any person who is the Company's client. In this clause:
>
> (a) 'Client' means a person who has been a member of the Company (or any other 'Planet Fitness' branded gym) or otherwise attended any 'Planet Fitness' branded

---

140   Ibid [32]–[34].
141   Ibid [35] et seq.

(b) 'Restraint Period' means a period of three months after this agreement is terminated. This clause survives termination of this agreement.

gym at any time whilst the Contractor is providing the Services under this agreement; and

Brooke Dunlop was an independent contractor who supplied personal trainer services to members of the gym. There was no requirement that she work exclusively for the plaintiff. The above restraint focused on not soliciting clients away from Planet Fitness. White J noted:[142]

> There is a strong *prima facie* case that the first defendant has solicited or canvassed persons for whom she provided personal training services when she was contracted to the plaintiff. She did so by posting messages on her Facebook page in which, amongst other things, she advised her Facebook friends that, first, she was in negotiation, and later that she had negotiated arrangements, with Genesis (that is, the second and third defendants), whereby those persons would be able to train at Genesis clubs at a reduced rate for the remaining periods of their contracts with the plaintiff. One of those messages stated:
>
>   '*I have negotiated an amazing deal exclusively for any of my PT* [personal training] *clients, PC members and Class participants.*
>
>   *Please call Sean and the guys at GENESIS Warnersbay* [sic] *NOW ... All you need to do is mention my name and show your current membership tag ...*'

Although there was a *prima facie* breach of the restraint in this case, the problem presenting itself was how to frame the injunction given that the restraint had already been breached: the restraint was to stop breaches, but numerous clients of Planet Fitness had already cancelled their membership and were Facebook friends (and presumably clients of) Ms Dunlop. In the event, the judge did not grant the injunction but noted that if the breach was proved at trial, an award of damages or account of profits would be possible. The offending Facebook posts had already been removed.

ICETV PTY LTD v ROSS [2007] NSWSC 635

This case involved three further interesting questions: whether there could be solicitation if the customer first approached the ex-employee and was then encouraged by that employee; whether the restraint would protect something the employer intended to do but had not yet started; and whether the restraint operated when the employment relationship was terminated by the company.

Vogel and Ross had been employed by a start-up company (ultimately called IceTV), developing TV-related technology. When the company encountered financial problems, Vogel and Ross were terminated by the company. They set up a consulting business and consulted to another company (Mobilesoft), which IceTV regarded as a competitor. Consequently, IceTV alleged breach of paragraph (a) of the non-solicitation clause and (c) of the restraint.

As regards paragraph (a), numerous documents (market announcements, memorandums of understanding with allied service providers, marketing and investment papers) all spoke of the technologies that were being developed and the expectation that there would be a capacity for the company (and its technology) to be able to perform tasks within a short period of time. Although the company (and its technology) was not able to actually complete the task at the moment, the fact that it was working on it and expected to be able to complete the task in the near future meant that those sorts of activities and technologies were part of the business of the company and therefore fell within paragraph (a) of the restraint.[143]

As regards solicitation, although it may be normally the case that this occurs when an ex-employee approaches a client, solicitation can also occur when a client makes the first move in circumstances where the ex-employee 'does not merely indicate a willingness to be engaged, but positively encourages the customer to engage him or her':[144] 'solicitation' means to entice or encourage.[145] In this case, Ross and Vogel had introduced Mobilesoft to the notion that they could produce a business opportunity. It was after that that Mobilesoft made approaches to them.

Although the restraint was being imposed after the company had terminated the services of Ross and Vogel, that was considered not unreasonable. There were many other IT and TV-related jobs the pair could undertake which would not have breached the restraint. Further, IceTV had taken over an earlier company run by Ross and Vogel, the intellectual property of which would in part depend on restraining Ross and Vogel for a period.[146]

6.45 The form of restraint: cascading or especially tailored?
6.45.05 Cascading restraints

One form of restraint which is not infrequently used is the cascading restraint or step clause. An example of such a clause was litigated relatively recently in *OAMPS Insurance Brokers Ltd v Hanna* (2010) 62 AILR 200-400 (*OAMPS*). The clause stated:

2. Restraint period means, from the date of termination of your employment:

  (a) 15 months;
  (b) 13 months;
  (c) 12 months.

143   *Ice TV Pty Ltd v Ross* [2007] NSWSC 635 at [14] et seq, especially [37].
144   Ibid [47] and [48].
145   Ibid [41] et seq, especially [48]–[50].
146   Ibid [60] and [61].

Restraint area means:

(a)   Australia;

(b)   The State or territory in which you are employed at the date of termination of your employment;

(c)   The Metropolitan area of the capital city in which you were employed at the date of termination of your employment.[147]

This clause was found to be valid because it was held to be 'a clear and unambiguous statement that each restraint constitutes a separate and independent provision, severable from the others'.[148] In so deciding, the trial judge relied on previous case law: *JQAT Pty Limited v Storm* [1987] 2 Qd R 162; *Lloyd's Ships Holdings Pty Ltd v Davros Pty Ltd* (1987) 17 FCR 505; and *Hydron Pty Ltd v Harris* [2005] SASC 176. His Honour distinguished *Tyser Reinsurance Brokers Pty Ltd v Cooper* [1998] NSWSC 689 as well as *Northern Tablelands Insurance Brokers Pty Ltd v Howell* [2009] NSWSC 426.[149] The restraint in *Tyser*, for example, was drafted thus:[150]

the periods commencing on the Disassociation Date and expiring one (1) year, two (2) years or three (3) years immediately following such date, to the intent that:

(a)   if any such period shall be held to be invalid, illegal or unenforceable for any such reason by any Court of competent jurisdiction, such invalidity, illegality or unenforceability shall not prejudice or in any way affect the validity of any lesser period specified; and

(b)   all such periods shall bind the employee to the extent that no such finding is made.

Clearly, the fact that cascading restraints may be valid means that some employees are bound by clauses that may have many interpretations – it is really only litigation that will finally determine the meaning of the clause. That fact has led to much academic criticism of these step clauses and suggestions for reform.[151] However, these clauses still do exist and are litigated.

It is, one might suggest, useful to consider tailoring a special restraint clause, rather than relying on cascading restraints. In that context, too, there has been much litigation, especially in New South Wales, as noted earlier.

6.45.10 Anti-poaching clauses: non-solicitation of employees (not simply customers)

As observed earlier, some restraints seek to stop an ex-employee soliciting other staff of the employer to follow them into the new venture. This recognises that an employer has a legal and legitimate interest in a stable workforce, as noted above. These anti-poaching clauses, as

---

147   *OAMPS* [2010] NSWSC 781 para 8.

148   Ibid para 63 per Hammerschlag J.

149   Ibid paras 62 and 66.

150   Ibid citing *Tyser* at para 52.

151   See, for example, A Stewart 'Drafting and enforcing post-employment restraints' (1997) 10 *Australian Journal of Labour Law* 19; and L Floyd and D Cabrelli 'New light through old windows: restraint of trade in English, Scottish and Australian employment laws – emerging and enduring issues' (2010) 26 *International Journal of Comparative Labour Law and Industrial Relations* 167.

they are sometimes known, have been affirmed as a part of Australian law in cases such as *Hartleys Ltd v Martin* [2002] VSC 301 (per Gillard J in the Victorian Supreme Court). While not specifically referring to *Hartleys*, the NSW Supreme Court decision of White J in *Aussie Home Loans v X Inc Services* (2005) ATPR 42-060 also upheld an anti-poaching clause, with the limitation that an employee cannot be prevented from having dealings with *all* staff – rather the limitation should relate to staff the ex-employee knows have special knowledge. Brereton J, too, in *Cactus Imaging Pty Ltd v Peters* (2006) 71 NSWLR 9, reconfirmed that anti-poaching clauses are legal (even where they go beyond the need for protecting confidentiality of information), as there is indeed a legitimate interest for an employer in maintaining a stable workforce. These cases are discussed below – the relevant academic commentary is also considered, as there has been a debate in academic circles, which is relevant given that the judgements are mostly single judge decisions, at this stage.

HARTLEYS LTD v MARTIN [2002] VSC 301 (HARTLEYS)

The relevant employment contracts contained the following clauses:[152]

> HPL has invested a substantial amount of time and effort to develop business relationships with its Clients. To protect HPL's goodwill, you agree that you will not (directly or indirectly) for a period of three months after the termination (including resignation) of your employment, on your own account or for any other person, firm, company or business:
>
> (1)   perform the service of a banking or investment advisory nature for any Client without the prior written consent of HPL; or
>
> (2)   solicit, entice away, interfere with or endeavour to solicit, entice away or interfere with any Client; or
>
> (3)   employ, engage, solicit or entice away or endeavour to employ, engage, solicit or entice away from HPL any Key Employee of HPL.

The Martin brothers had worked for Hartleys (a broking firm which provided investment advice to 100,000 clients, with assets of over $3 billion), starting their employment as trainees. Hartleys paid for the two brothers to attend training conferences, and over time the brothers progressed through the ranks and worked in tandem to obtain large client bases and substantial earnings.[153] In providing their investment advice, the brothers developed close relationships with clients.

The court was satisfied that Hartleys had a proprietary interest in its client base and that ex-employees who had closely advised those clients and had personal knowledge of and influence over those clients might take those clients with them when they left, and that that customer connection was able to be protected.[154] Likewise, the court found that the reasonableness of the clause was to be gauged largely at the time the contract was entered

---

152   *Hartleys* at [71] per Gillard J.
153   Ibid [114].
154   Ibid [116].

into and that it was reasonable for the brothers to be restrained from approaching present as well as former clients, as those clients might have only recently left the firm.

As to the section of the clauses on the poaching of employees, the court was of the view that the secretary of the Martin brothers, Ms Briggs, might be categorised as a 'key employee' under the restrictive covenant – so that part of the clause was valid.

Although the court did not expressly discuss why a personal assistant might be key personnel, it stands to reason that such might be the case – secretaries know the documents of a firm, the personalities of clients and the key aspects of the relationship between different employees and different clients.

Hartleys was roundly criticised by some academics as taking the law on restraint too far.[155] However, that criticism was largely rebutted.[156]

AUSSIE HOME LOANS v X INC SERVICES [2005] NSWSC 285

This case also found anti-poaching clauses to be valid. Clause 14(a)(ii) of this contract required that '[the employee] would not, for a period of twelve months after the termination of his employment, for any reason, solicit, interfere with or endeavour to entice away any employee or contractor of the first plaintiff'.

Although this particular clause was ultimately found to be too broad (and was in fact a restraint against competition *per se*), as it required the ex-employee not to entice away 'any' employee, the prospect that anti-poaching clauses could be legal was maintained. After going carefully through the case law from *Herbert Morris Ltd v Saxelby* [1916] 1 AC 688 and *Littlewoods Organisation Ltd v Harris* [1977] 1 WLR 1472 (especially at 1479) through to *Lindner v Murdoch's Garage* (1950) 83 CLR 628, as well as two differing lines of English authority (*Hanover Insurance Brokers Ltd v Shapiro* [1993] EWCA Civ 2 and *Dawnay, Day & Co. Ltd v de Braconier d'Alphen* [1997] EWCA Civ 1753), the court found:[157]

> This indicates that, just as a general covenant restraining competition may be justified because of the need to protect trade secrets or a trade connection, rather than a more limited covenant against disclosing trade secrets or canvassing customers, so may a restraint against enticing employees be justified by reference to confidential information which the ex-employee has about the relations between his former employer and its employees. It is well established in this area that a legitimate interest may be protected by a wider covenant than one directed specifically to the interest which may legitimately be protected, because of the difficulties of enforcement.

---

155   J Riley 'Who owns human capital? A critical appraisal of legal techniques for capturing the value of work' (2005) 18 *Australian Journal of Labour Law* 1.

156   Floyd and Cabrelli 'New light through old windows' (2010).

157   *Aussie Home* Loans at [26].

It is now accepted that anti-poaching restraints are legal in Australia.[158] In essence, they are legal as long as they are not so broad that they go beyond protecting a legitimate interest.[159] Restraining employment of every employee may be too broad, but a restraint on key personnel (who have knowledge of how the business works, and of the likes and dislikes of clients, and who may possess other confidential information) is legal.

CACTUS IMAGING PTY LTD v PETERS (2006) 71 NSWLR 9 (CACTUS)

It is submitted that this NSW Supreme Court decision puts the matter beyond doubt – there is a legitimate interest in preserving customer connection (even beyond protecting confidential information). Brereton J held:

[53] The controversy has been whether the employer has an interest in staff connection recognised by law as legitimate for the purpose of supporting a covenant. The weight of authority favours the view that there is such an interest. Traditionally, it has been said that the only reason for supporting a restraint is some *proprietary right* of the employer, either trade connection or trade secrets [*Herbert Morris Ltd v Saxelby*, 710 (Lord Parker of Waddington)].

[54] The more recent cases have tended to support restraints on recruitment on the basis of protection of confidential information; thus it has been said that an employer may be able to demonstrate a legitimate interest in maintaining a stable trained workforce, at least if the former employee may seek to exploit knowledge gained of the particular qualifications, rates of remuneration and so on pertaining to other employees which is confidential to the employer [*Dawnay Day & Co. Limited v De Braconier D'Alphen*, [45]–[46]; *Aussie Home Loans*, [24]–[26]; *Kearney v Crepaldi*, [58]] . . .[160]

In that case, a 12-month restraint was found to be reasonable.

In summing up the position on restraints, the following may be said. There must be a legitimate interest and the employer's right to a stable workforce is such an interest. The restraint clause itself must be reasonable as to time, place and function. The clauses are drafted into contracts of employment from their inception and it is recommended that employees (where they are practically able to) discuss those restraints as they are negotiating contracts. Having said that, cascading restraints are legal in many Australian jurisdictions. Litigation on restraints (and whether they are valid) takes place at the end of the employment relationship, yet, in another irony, there may be consideration by the court of the position of the parties at the start of the relationship.

---

158   J Riley 'Sterilising talent: a critical assessment of injunctions enforcing negative covenants' (2012) 34 *Sydney Law Review* 617.

159   Floyd and Cabrelli 'New light through old windows' (2010).

160   *Cactus* at [53]–[54].

6.50 Further issues

6.50.05 Which law suit to bring? Avoiding 'double dipping'

It is clear that termination of employment can form the basis of numerous law suits. This chapter has already raised the distinction between wrongful dismissal (a common law action) and unfair dismissal (where a dismissal is considered harsh, unjust or unreasonable under the *Fair Work Act*).

As stated above, it is often the case that wrongful dismissal is (practically speaking) a remedy most useful for those not covered by the statutory protections and in high-paying positions – where the amount that would cover reasonable notice is a substantial sum. Wrongful dismissal, being contractual, is clearly a suit taken through the civil courts. It is unlikely that damages for the manner of dismissal will be awarded (unless there was physical injury caused by the employer, for instance). Further, there is, as discussed, debate and doubt as to whether further contractual damages can be claimed – for opportunity loss, say.

In contrast, unfair dismissal is more widely available, goes to the merits of the decision to terminate and has a cap on damages. Unfair dismissal claims are taken through the FWC and begin with mediation.

To that broad distinction, cases such as *Walker* add questions as to whether there are alternative causes of action, such as for misleading and deceptive conduct if representations are made during negotiations and those representations are misleading (and the applicant can prove they were made). Once again, that is a matter for the civil courts.

Obviously, a situation can arise where a dismissal is unfair and also discriminatory – or perhaps unfair and a breach of an individual's right to be a union member (in accordance with the adverse action provisions) [unlawful dismissal].

If that situation occurs, then under ss 725–732 of the *Fair Work Act* the commencement of one statutory proceeding for a dismissal precludes a statutory proceeding being brought under the alternative (unless the first is discontinued).[161] Difficulties can arise if the discrimination claim relates to conduct prior to dismissal.[162]

The High Court decision in *Commonwealth Bank of Australia v Barker* militates against a duty of trust and confidence, but there are lingering questions about the nature of good faith.[163]

The special position of public servants is considered in Chapter 7, and in that context remedies such as judicial review have also been canvassed. (See also Figure 6.1.)

6.50.10 Termination through insolvency of the employer or transfer of business

At the time of writing, Yabula – near Townsville, Queensland – was the focus of national attention with the collapse of Queensland Nickel, a company associated with the larger-than-life

---

161   See Figure 6.1

162   *Hazledine v Wakerley & Anor* (2017) FWCFB 500; [2016] FWC 4989. See also *Birch v Wesco Electrics (1996) Pty Ltd* [2012] FMCA 5.

163   J Riley 'The boundaries of mutual trust and good faith' (2009) 22 *Australian Journal of Labour Law* 11.

Figure 6.1   Choice of remedy: multiple action prohibitions in ss 725–732 of the *Fair Work Act*[164]

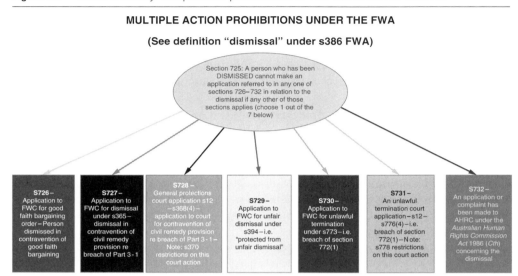

figure Mr Clive Palmer. The insolvency of the company gave rise to the largest claim for unpaid accrued worker entitlements (leave, superannuation, etc) in Australia's history.[165] The position of workers when a business collapses is indeed a very significant legal problem – and Queensland Nickel provides a window to the practical operation of the law and the limits of that law.

6.50.15 Fair entitlements guarantee

If an employee's employment terminates through the insolvency of the employer, then quite obviously that employer (being insolvent) will not have enough money to pay all its debts – and one of the key debts will be what it owes its employees. These (now former) employees will be unsecured creditors of their employer and, as such, will rank behind secured creditors such as banks when a liquidator or trustee in bankruptcy realises assets and distributes those assets amongst creditors. Because employees are seldom able to sustain such a loss – because they have lost their livelihood through no fault of their own – and because of the detrimental effect to the economy when employees are penniless (the businesses they frequent will no longer receive their custom, the banks will not receive their mortgage payments, etc), successive governments have long accepted that employees are in a unique position and it is in society's interest for the government to treat them accordingly. So the government has a scheme through which employees are paid their entitlements out of taxpayer funds and then

---

164   Supplied with permission by Igor Mescher.
165   K Binnie 'Clive Palmer: government to chase refinery owner for $74m owed to Queensland nickel workers', 15 April 2016 (ABC News online), http://www.abc.net.au/news/2016-04-15/queensland-nickel-federal-government-to-pursue-clive-palmer-$74m/7327036 (accessed 12 March 2017).

the government takes the employees' position in the list of ranked creditors and recoups as much money as it can from the company assets.[166]

This scheme was originally called GEERS – General Employee Entitlements on Redundancy Scheme – and it was a creature of policy.[167]

In 2012, it was replaced by the legislation-based *Fair Entitlements Guarantee Act 2012* (Cth) (*FEG Act*). Essentially, under Part 3, employees are entitled to:[168]

- a maximum of 4 weeks' redundancy pay for every year of service;
- payment of unpaid wages for up to 13 weeks;
- payment of lieu of notice of up to 5 weeks' salary;
- annual leave; and
- long service leave.

There are eligibility requirements: normally, payments will not be made to most contractors, directors or family members of directors, and claimants must have met residency requirements. Claims must be made within 12 months and there is capacity to make appeals to the relevant department or the Administrative Appeals Tribunal.[169]

Crucially, the scheme is triggered by redundancy or job loss through the insolvency of the employer – that is, the employer goes into liquidation or is bankrupt (s 4(2)). That point is extremely important: with Queensland Nickel, retrenchments began at the end of 2015 and the start of 2016 and there was no immediate access to this scheme because at that stage the company was only under administration – a restructure of the company was still the legislative objective. It was only after the Voluntary Administrators (FTI Consulting) released their report, recommending liquidation (on 12 April 2016), that the government stepped in and said it would fast-track payments under this legislation. The fact that the payments were confirmed by the relevant Minister on the handing down of the report (and before the final formal vote on the report) does show that there is some flexibility in the scheme. (See Part 7 of the Act – there is some flexibility for contractors to be paid in some cases, also.)

One other feature of the Queensland Nickel case is that the government has announced that it will appoint a Special Purpose Liquidator to attempt to get as much of the unpaid entitlements money back from the company (and therefore into taxpayers or government coffers) as possible.

While the *FEG Act* is clearly a good support for workers, Queensland Nickel has demonstrated that for long-term employees in particular, the scheme will not ensure the repayment of all their entitlements and there was still a delay, during which time some former employees (reportedly) were evicted for non-payment of rent or lost their homes through non-payment of mortgages.[170]

---

166   See also *Corporations Act 2001* (Cth) s 555 et seq.
167   See L Floyd 'Enron and One.tel: Australian renegades championing the American dream' (2002) *Southern Methodist University Law Review*.
168   See CCH *Australian Labour Law Reporter* ¶80-300 'FEG/GEERS Scheme'.
169   Ibid.
170   These stories were recounted in *The Townsville Bulletin* on 17 April 2016, on page 1 and following.

6.50.20 Transfer of business

As noted above, the *FEG Act* does not apply where a business transfers (even if that involves restructuring due to financial issues). Instead, a transfer scenario has its own set of laws in the *Fair Work Act* Part 2-8. The necessity for such legislation stems from the nature of the contract of employment – privity of contract means an employment contract is between the employee and a particular employing entity. When employment passes from one entity to another entity through sale, insourcing or outsourcing, the old contract obviously ends, as it was an agreement between two specific parties who are no longer in an employment relationship. The issues covered by these laws pertain to the conditions of employment (will the former conditions continue with the transferred worker?) and what happens to accrued entitlements (for example, is there continuity of service for the purpose of long service leave?).

The key provision is s 311. Under s 311(1) there is a transfer of employment from the old employer to the new employer if the employee's employment with the old employer has terminated; within 3 months of that termination, the employee becomes employed by the new employer; the work performed by the employee is substantially the same for both the new and old employer; and there is a connection between the old and new employer. Under subsections 311(3)–311(5), such a connection arises where:

- the new employer (or an associated entity) 'owns or has the beneficial use of some or all of the assets (whether tangible or intangible)' of the old employer – and those assets 'relate to, or are used in connection with, the transferring work' OR
- the work transferring from the old to the new employer is performed by one or more transferring employees because the old employer outsourced it OR
- the work being performed is no longer outsourced – in other words it is insourced.

If there is a transfer of work, then the relevant enterprise agreement, determination or award will also transfer to cover employees (ss 312–315).

The provisions of the *Fair Work Act* effectively limit the effect of the High Court decision in *PP Consultants Pty Ltd v Finance Sector Union* (2000) 201 CLR 648. In that case, the St George Bank closed a regional branch and instead allowed some banking work to be performed on a fee-per-transaction basis at a local pharmacy. The question arose as to whether a former St George staffer who worked at the pharmacy should be governed by the conditions of employment they had enjoyed at the former St George Bank branch. In finding that they did not, the High Court examined the transmission of business provisions of the old *WR Act* (which were then in operation) and found that the law would only transmit conditions of work if the character of the new business was substantially the same as the predecessor. Applying that test to the facts of the case, the High Court found that the pharmacy only carried out banking work as a small part of its business: its characterisation was quite different, so the former banking terms of employment did not transmit to the new employment. *PP Consultants* had obviously limited the circumstances in which former conditions of employment could be preserved. By focusing on the nature of the work, rather than the business, the transfer of business provisions aim to have wider application. The addition of Part 6-3A to the Act aims to further broaden the protection of old working conditions in the event that State governments outsource work.

6.50.25 References

At the end of one's employment, an employee might seek a letter of recommendation or reference (to either assist in seeking future employment or simply as evidence of the work that was performed). Depending on the success of the employee's time at the workplace, the seniority and authority (to act on behalf of the employer) of the reference writer, and the nature of the organisation (a branch of government might have a policy not to give official references), a reference might range from something as simple as a statement of service through to something that speaks to the employee's actual ability to perform the work. Some lawyers might seek a reference in settlement at the end of a job, to help their client find another position. Depending on the personal relationships the employee has with colleagues, an employee who leaves work on questionable terms may find that some former colleagues are happy to write a personal reference about their personal experience working with the former employee. That kind of reference will usually not be on letterhead. Today, at a practical level, the emphasis is increasingly on verbal references – or perhaps confidential written references sent directly to the selection committee and which the job applicant/former employee does not see.

One interesting Australian case on reference writing is *Wade v Victoria* [1999] I VR 121 (*Wade*). In that case, Harper J found that the writer of the reference has a duty of care and must not publish inaccurate or misleading information – they must not be negligent.[171] That decision is consistent with the House of Lords' decision in *Spring v Guardian Assurance Plc* [1995] 2 AC 296: where employers choose to write a character reference, they should do so carefully.[172]

It is not clear that the Australian position has reached the levels of the UK in *Spring*, but the Victorian decision in *Wade* does at least indicate that Australian recipients of poor and incorrect references might not be limited to suits for defamation/malice (which is hard to prove, and subject to qualified privilege).

So reference writers might be well advised to take care in their provision of references, as Coventry and Keel suggested in discussing *Wade*.[173]

The residual question relates to confidential references. If a confidential reference is written about an applicant, how does that applicant actually know that malicious words have been said? If the applicant conducts a Right to Information Application/Freedom of Information Application, the next hurdle might be whether the organisation holding the documents releases the documents or whether the Privacy Commissioner is consulted.

SUMMARY

There is no proprietary interest in one's job. Consequently, a worker can lose their job against their wishes. In that event, there may be an issue as to whether the job loss is unfair dismissal under the *Fair Work Act*, or wrongful dismissal under contract law, or there may be some further issue, such as restraint of trade, or transfer of business or the fair entitlements guarantee. It is apparent from other chapters of

---

171   A short but useful case note on this decision is D Coventry and P Keel 'Take care with employee references' (1999) 4 *Employment Law Bulletin* 10.

172   For an excellent discussion of that case and judgement, see T Thawley 'Duty to be careful when giving employees references' (1996) 70 *The Australian Law Journal* 403. The analysis of *Spring* raises the issue of economic loss flowing from poor references.

173   Coventry and Keel 'Take care with employee references' (1999).

this book that dismissal can also bring with it issues of adverse action or discrimination, creating further choices as to cause of action [unlawful dismissal].

Australian law follows ILO conventions in providing some safeguards or remedies in the event of unfair dismissal. This is because one's job is understood to be important to both the worker and the stability of society. Statutory unfair dismissal requires that there be an employer-instigated dismissal (which could include constructive dismissal) and that it is harsh, unjust and unreasonable. A genuine redundancy cannot fall into that category and small businesses employing fewer than 15 are only bound by a code which can deem certain dismissals fair. Matters that can ground dismissal range from poor performance through to after-hours conduct, conduct at the workplace, dishonesty, and safety breaches. Even if there is a valid reason to dismiss, one must consider fairness: was the employee given a chance to improve? How have similar breaches been treated? What is the employee's track record? A developing issue (but it has always been important) is workplace investigations – this acknowledges that the manner in which a matter is investigated might influence the fairness of the dismissal. A question arises as to whether the employer owes a duty of good faith such that matters must be investigated properly – an employer cannot simply outsource their investigatory responsibilities. In a claim for unfair dismissal, there are tribunal procedures to be considered, including appearances by lawyers as well as salary caps and time limits. The statute's favoured remedy is reinstatement, but that is not often ordered. One important consideration when considering granting reinstatement is the employment relationship.

Employees work under a contract of employment. If it ends at the behest of the employer, there might be an issue as to whether notice was reasonable. That issue is not of enormous significance to most workers. But there can be some difficult and technical points that are important, such as the difference between the employment contract and the employment relationship; the acceptance or otherwise of changes in terms of the employment contract; and the continuation (or otherwise) of the employment relationship if the contract is reduced to writing. Particular issues relate to misrepresentations at the start of the contract; whether there can be damages for the manner in which the contract ends; and termination of short-term contracts (this issue also arises in the context of statutory unfair dismissal).

Unfair and unlawful dismissals involve remedies connected to the actual decision to dismiss. Further issues might arise when employment ends. A restraint of trade clause may be in the contract and may become an issue when an employee leaves. To be legal, these clauses should protect a legitimate interest and be reasonable as to time, place and function (what it restrains). The availability of cascading restraints in some Australian jurisdictions puts an emphasis on employees defending the enforcement of restraint clauses. It now seems settled that a legitimate interest an employer can protect with restraints is a stable workforce.

There are further issues at the end of the employment relationship. If there is a transfer of employment, conditions of work should transfer with the workforce if the relevant provisions are complied with. Likewise, there is some protection of accrued entitlements under the *FEG Act* if the job loss is caused by the insolvency of the employer. A significant issue is choice of remedy if a number may be available. Finally, employers are not compelled to write references for former employees, but should not defame an employee if they do.

REVIEW QUESTIONS

1. Problem questions:
    (a) Burt worked as a flight attendant for a leading international airline. The aviation industry is competitive and Burt felt a good deal of stress in his role. Burt alternated between serving

hundreds of economy passengers on long-haul flights and, on other flights, handfuls of first-class customers. During one stop-over in Holland, where the use of recreational marijuana is legal, Burt found that his next flight had been delayed due to a ferocious storm, which had grounded all aircraft. Burt was stressed by this, as his arthritic neck was playing havoc with him. When the pain became unbearable, Burt went to the local coffee shop and, reluctantly, after talking to one of the locals, decided to buy some marijuana and smoke it in the shop. Burt felt better, but when he got up from the table he saw that his supervisor had been observing his actions. The supervisor said: 'You are behaving in a manner which will disgrace the airline. I am reporting you and I hope you are sacked when we return to Australia.' Burt seeks your advice on whether his airline can actually do that. Would your answer differ if Burt was a new employee and there was a workplace policy that prohibited all conduct that might embarrass the airline? Is there further information you would seek in providing your advice?

(b) This time, assume Burt has NOT been discovered smoking the marijuana by his supervisor. Burt, on the return flight to Australia, is serving first-class passengers. Part of the service includes distributing chocolates after dinner. Burt (having recovered from his arthritic attack) remembers his niece's birthday is the same day he returns to Australia. He takes 24 chocolates and places them in his knapsack to give to his niece as a present. His supervisor sees this and sacks him when they land. What is Burt's position in these circumstances? Would your answer differ if a passenger said to Burt, 'Oh for God's sake man, your employer is rich – take the chocolates and give your niece a present'?

2. Problem questions:

(a) Burt's nephew, Ernie, worked as an engineer for the same airline and one evening (after 20 years of faultless service) drove an airline van to the local McDonald's for a Big Mac, even though the airline's policies were adamant that airline vehicles should not be used in that way. Ernie was fired. He seeks your advice on unfair dismissal and reinstatement. Would your answer differ if other colleagues had done the same thing, but had not been sacked?

(b) Instead of the above scenario, this time assume that the position is this: Burt's nephew Ernie fell asleep at work and was fired. Would you need further information to advise on unfair dismissal? If so, what might it be? Would it be significant if Burt was on his first night on the job or if he was taking medication? (In the course of your answer, discuss the general principles governing instant dismissal.)

3. Problem questions:

(a) This time Burt's sister, Penny, was the centre of attention as an employee of the airline. She started a Facebook page on which she and other flight attendants expressed: 'What a terrible day! One of our customers is a misogynist and keeps pinching bottoms. He is too rich to report to anyone, but it really makes me hate men.' When the post comes to the attention of the supervisor, that supervisor seeks advice on the issues arising.

(b) This time, Penny has no Facebook page, but she struggles with the job and the employer finds out she lied on her CV. Advise Penny on the actions the airline can take against her. Is there further evidence you might need? If so, what is it?

4. Research questions:

(a) If an employer pays the relocation costs of an employee, how does the law deal with the situation if the employee does not work out in the job and seeks to return to their place of origin? Can the employee seek a contribution towards the return? Can the employer ever seek reimbursement? Is there a difference between a move within Australia and a move to Australia by an overseas national?

(b) In what circumstances, if any, can an employer ever seek money from an employee for resigning, after either giving too little notice or staying less than an agreed period of time? Are there practical considerations the employer might take into account?

(c) Are there any significant differences between the Federal law and some of the State legislation on dismissal?

5. Group watching brief:

This chapter has discussed workplace investigations and the fact that this is an area that is still developing. Watch the legal developments in this area. In particular, consider:

(a) the notion that there could be a duty of good faith owed between employer and employee;

(b) the notion that employers are being increasingly tempted to 'contract out' – and what should be their obligations if they do so;

(c) case law;

(d) some typical approaches companies, major employers and small businesses use in workplace investigations.

FURTHER READING

M Irving 'Australian and Canadian approaches to the assessment of the length of reasonable notice' (2015) 28 *Australian Journal of Labour Law* 159.

A O'Donnell 'Non-standard workers in Australia: curts and controversies' (2004) 17 *Australian Journal of Labour Law* 89.

C Sutherland 'Streamlining enterprise agreements to reduce complexity: an empirical assessment' (2016) 29 *Australian Journal of Labour Law* 25.

7 PUBLIC WORK

7.05 Introduction

The legal treatment of work in the public sector is as significant as it is complex. Smith's 1987 work, *Public Sector Employment Law*,[1] Professor McCarry's 1988 book, *Aspects of Public Sector Employment Law*,[2] and the more recent *Public Sector Employment in the Twenty-First Century*, by Professor Pittard and the late Professor Weeks,[3] are all testament to the difficulties and uncertainties lawyers face when studying and practising in this field.

Smith observes that a major determinant of public sector work is that key terms of work are drawn from statute rather than contract or industrial instrument of the types studied in the previous chapters of this book.[4] To that may be added the fact that public work often entails meeting some public goal – to give frank and fearless advice, if one is a public service employee; to show fierce independence in the meting out of justice, if one is a judge; or to nurture academic freedom, if one is an academic.

This chapter analyses three key areas of public work:

- *Public sector employment* – The chapter outlines key provisions of the *Public Service Act 1999* (Cth) and the separation of powers doctrine; it discusses recent developments in whistleblower laws and public sector investigations and public sector employment theory.[5]

- *Judicial 'work'* – The chapter discusses something seldom dealt with – the *work* of judicial officers. It is extremely important for lawyers, business people and students of law and business to fully appreciate the work of judges, especially given the recent tendency of some populist commentators to align judges with efficiency principles.[6]

- *Academic employment* – The chapter discusses academic freedom in particular, and the fact that funding for universities stems from government.[7]

This introduction deliberately uses the term 'work' in relation to its treatment of judges and their working conditions. Judges are not employees; they are statutory office-holders. They are appointed under statute and form an independent arm of government – they are not a servant of the elected government of the day. At the outset, then, it is important to note that the term 'officer' is sometimes bandied about, possibly without a great deal of thought for its actual

---

1   G Smith *Public Sector Employment Law* (Butterworths, 1987).
2   G McCarry *Aspects of Public Sector Employment Law* (Law Book Co., 1988)
3   M Pittard and P Weeks *Public Sector Employment in the Twenty First Century* (ANU Press, 2007).
4   G Smith *Public Sector Employment Law* (Butterworths, 1987) 3.
5   This section of the chapter on public sector employment is written by Louise Floyd and much is drawn and developed from her earlier publications: L Floyd 'Reforming Hong Kong public sector employment law after *Lam Siu Po* and *Rowse* – some useful comparisons from Australian Law' (2009) 39 *Hong Kong Law Journal* 457–83; L Floyd 'Whistle blowing and compulsory medical examinations: recent developments in Australian public sector employment law and their relevance to Hong Kong' (2011) 41 *Hong Kong Law Journal* 155–77.
6   The section of the chapter on judicial work is also written by Louise Floyd and is drawn and developed from her earlier publications, cited within.
7   The section on academic employment is written by Professor Jim Jackson and updated by his daughter, Annaliese Jackson. Their work originally appeared in J Jackson and S Varnham *Law for Educators: School and University Law in Australia* (LexisNexis Butterworths, 2007), Jim Jackson having written the relevant chapter on academics.

meaning.[8] McCarry observes that the term was actually used to describe the difference between permanent and temporary employees under the *Public Service Act 1922* (Cth).[9] As will be discussed below, the current *Public Service Act 1999* (Cth) no longer makes that distinction, and instead refers to 'ongoing employees'. Likewise, in academia, the idea that an academic is an officer has been specifically rejected by the High Court.[10] So the best modern example of a statutory office-holder is a judge, whose duties stem from a truly independent source.[11]

This chapter ultimately concludes that the recent changes to the employment law regulating public servants and academics (aimed at introducing further efficiencies into their world) produce both tensions and opportunities. Further, so far as the working environment of judges is concerned, there are administrative measures that some governments might take that could impinge upon the freedoms of the Bench. These need to be guarded against. On the other hand, there are some matters of health and safety that might lend themselves to further consideration.

7.10 Public sector employment[12]

To really appreciate the nature of public service employment, it is necessary to appreciate a fundamental proposition of constitutional law – the separation of powers doctrine. As Black-shield and Williams observe,[13] there is a separation of powers between the three arms of government – legislative, executive and judicial. Put bluntly, the legislative arm makes and changes laws; the executive or administrative arm carries on the business of government (for example, developing policy, administering social services such as public education, housing, transport and health, as well as supervising and financing defence and justice); and the judiciary interprets and applies the law (ascertaining the facts of a case if they are in dispute). The separation creates checks and balances on government power. So, for instance, where the judiciary is required to interpret the distribution of power between the Commonwealth and the States, [14] or where judges are called upon to determine the limits of government power, that judiciary needs to be independent of the government whose power is in question.[15]

---

8   G McCarry *Aspects of Public Sector Employment Law* (Law Book Co., 1988) 11–22. As a practical example, it is worth considering the number of times we hear people speak of safety officers, community liaison officers etc. The term can seem ubiquitous even though perhaps not all who use it are aware of its background and precise legal meaning.

9   Ibid 11–12. Officers were appointed to the career service: they had jobs for life and the role they filled would always need to be filled by a successor when the original appointee moved on; employees, on the other hand, filled roles which were temporary.

10   *Orr v University of Tasmania* [1956] Tas SR 155.

11   McCarry *Aspects of Public Sector Employment Law* (1988) 16.

12   This section of the chapter and the following section on judicial work are written by Louise Floyd. This discussion, in part, is based on and develops her earlier writings in: L Floyd 'Fitness for trial: trial in absence of (unrepresented) litigant; contempt of court and evidentiary issues' (2010) 33 *Australian Bar Review* 56–66; L Floyd 'Reforming Hong Kong public sector employment law after *Lam Siu Po* and *Rowse*' (2009) 457–83; L Floyd 'Whistle blowing and compulsory medical examinations' (2011) 155–77.

13   T Blackshield and G Williams *Australian Constitutional Law and Theory Commentary and Materials* (Federation Press, 5th ed, 2010) 9–10 et seq.

14   Ibid 8.

15   See also G Carney *The Constitutional Systems of the Australian States and Territories* (Cambridge University Press, 2006) 114–15.

The notion of placing limits on monarchical power dates back to the Magna Carta in 1215,[16] and the idea that 'different functions should be vested in different institutions' dates back to Baron de Montesquieu in the 1600s (and Aristotle before that).[17] Professor Carney observes[18] that the concept was particularly inspiring to the framers of the US Constitution in 1787, after that new nation gained independence from Great Britain.[19] Britain, in something of a contrast, has a partial separation of powers in its Westminster system – its doctrine of responsible government sees a link between the legislature and the executive, as the Minister for a particular portfolio (and therefore the person to whom a government department reports) is an elected Member of the Parliament.[20] Judicial independence, however, remains crucial.[21] Influenced by the US, the Australian Constitution has chapters on 'The Parliament', 'The Executive Government' and 'The Judicature'.[22] Influenced by Britain, we have responsible government – the Minister (parliamentarian) must answer to the Parliament for what the public servants in his or her department have done.[23]

7.10.05 Powerful ministerial offices – a new twist on an old problem?

That blurring of the boundaries between the legislature and the executive (and what it means for the employment of public servants) has been considered by Professor Ewing in his essay 'The privatisation of the Civil Service'.[24] Although writing about the British context, Professor Ewing makes a point which is surely valid in an Australian context also, namely: if the public service is restructured (or is even privatised), must that not affect ministerial responsibility? How are public servants really acting under a minister's authority if they are on a contract working for a devolved agency?[25]

Added to that long-asked thorny question is a newer concern. Ewing observes that in Britain[26] – as in Australia[27] – governments increasingly appoint specialist advisers; place emphasis on delivery and outputs rather than constitutional principle and procedure or

---

16   Cf Blackshield and Williams *Australian Constitutional Law and Theory Commentary and Materials* (2010) 54, 55 et seq.

17   Ibid 8 et seq.

18   G Carney 'Separation of powers in the Westminster System' (1994) 8(2) *Legislative Studies* 59 as cited in Blackshield and Williams *Australian Constitutional Law and Theory Commentary and Materials* (2010) 10–11.

19   See, for example, OH Phillips and P Jackson *Constitutional and Administrative Law* (Sweet & Maxwell, 7th ed, 1987) discussing the influence of Blackstone on the US Founding Fathers as cited in Blackshield and Williams *Australian Constitutional Law and Theory Commentary and Materials* (2010) 9 et seq.

20   Blackshield and Williams *Australian Constitutional Law and Theory Commentary and Materials* (2010) 1.

21   Ibid 8.

22   Ibid 11.

23   Ibid 8. See also Carney *The Constitutional Systems of the Australian States and Territories* (2006) 114–15 – the parliament can empower public servants to make delegated legislation. Further note K Ewing 'The privatisation of the Civil Service' in M Pittard and P Weeks (eds) *Public Sector Employment in the Twenty-First Century* (ANU E-Press, 2007) 288.

24   Ewing 'The privatisation of the Civil Service' (2007) 281.

25   Ibid 288.

26   Ibid 285–6.

27   This is discussed below and is part of popular culture in TV programs such as *The Hollow Men*.

reasoned deliberation; and seem to develop policy centrally, in the Prime Minister's office, and then expect the public service to implement that policy.[28] Such an approach may well change the context in which public servants work and present some challenges to some of their core and traditional values.[29]

7.10.10 Management of public service employment: the *Public Service Act 1999* (Cth)

The principal legislation governing the Australian Public Service (APS) is the *Public Service Act 1999* (Cth), which was amended in 2013. That Act sits alongside specialist legislation, such as the *Public Interest Disclosure Act 2013* (Cth), and an assortment of enterprise agreements and directives to form the matrix of codes, values, standards, terms and conditions that govern the manner in which public servants are employed and government departments are managed.

Of crucial importance is the fact that the *Public Service Act* is not heavily prescriptive of terms, conditions and categories of employment – as its predecessor, the *Public Service Act 1922* (Cth), and the associated Public Service Board were seen to be.[30] Rather, it devolves management power (such as much of its recruitment) to agency (department) heads,[31] while establishing core standards (as to conduct and values) that provide the underpinnings of a unified service, with the government as the ultimate employer.[32] The Hon David Kemp MP, in the Second Reading of the Public Service Bill 1999, said this shift in emphasis between the two pieces of legislation was aimed at facilitating a high-performance public service, where departments or agencies had the flexibility to deal with modern stresses as they arise and could fulfil the specific needs of their agency and its clients.[33] In contrast, the Minister viewed the former legislation as a prescriptive straitjacket on performance and creativity.[34]

While the need for flexibility was central to the reform of labour and employment law in the private sector, too – and while it was in keeping with much of the ideological discourse of the day[35] – the public service clearly has an extra dimension to its work.

28 Ewing 'The privatisation of the Civil Service' (2007) 286.
29 This is elaborated upon in Country Profile Chs 2 and Ch. 1, Country Profile Service (Commonwealth Secretariat, London), available on the website of the Public Service Commission, and P Weeks 'The reshaping of Australian public service employment law' in Pittard and Weeks (eds) *Public Sector Employment in the Twenty-First Century* (2007).
30 In addition to McCarry's excellent book, see also P Weeks 'The reshaping of Australian public service employment law' (2007) 13. The *Public Service Act 1922* (Cth) contained detailed rules as to job classification and appointment etc, while the former Public Service Board exercised the majority of human resource functions – and had the capacity to make binding determinations.
31 Pay and conditions are also largely contained in enterprise agreements which are settled at the agency level. See M Molloy 'A revised legislative framework for Australian Public Service employment: the successive impacts of the *Workplace Relations Act 1996* (Cth) and the *Public Service Act 1999* (Cth)' in Pittard and Weeks (eds) *Public Sector Employment in the Twenty-First Century* (2007).
32 Public Service Bill 1999, Second Reading, 30 March 1999, Hon David Kemp MP, House of Representatives, 4683.
33 Ibid 4684.
34 Ibid 4683–4684.
35 These points are made by Molloy 'A revised legislative framework for Australian public service employment' (2007). See also Pittard and Weeks (eds) *Public Sector Employment in the Twenty-First Century* (2007) Ch. 1.

Our public service stemmed originally from the old Whitehall tradition of a career service, driven by merit (not patronage), so that the service – with personnel secure in their jobs – would provide frank and fearless advice (in the name of good governance).[36] To preserve those traditions in a competitive environment, the *Public Service Act* embeds values such as impartiality and merit and ethics – values 'reflecting public expectations of the relationship between the public service and the government, the Parliament and the Australian community'.[37]

Clearly, the lingering question for scholars is how that balance between flexibility and accountability is working. Professor Ewing's work emphasises the need for balance.[38] That question will continue to be relevant – and it in fact was relevant even before the *Public Service Act*, given that some moves towards high performance, flexibility and competition had been made from about 1983.[39]

7.10.15 Key provisions and guides

The objects of the *Public Service Act* are to:[40]

(a) establish an apolitical public service that is efficient and effective in serving the government, the Parliament and the Australian public;

(b) provide a legal framework for the effective and fair employment, management and leadership of APS employees;

(c) define the powers, functions and responsibilities of agency heads, the Australian Public Service Commissioner and the Merit Protection Commissioner; and

(d) establish the rights and obligations of APS employees.

The Act has extra-territorial operation (ss 5 and 13(12)) and uses the term 'ongoing employee' as opposed to 'officer' to describe those who are employed indefinitely or on a continuing rather than short-term basis. The 'ongoing' appointment is the preferred option for employment with the APS (ss 22 and 10A(b)).

The APS Values are listed in s 10. They include:

- *Committed to service* – working professionally, objectively, with innovation and efficiency to achieve the best results;

---

36   See Country Profile Service (Commonwealth Secretariat, London), Ch. 2. (See also Ch. 1: Australian Experience of Public Sector reform). See also Ewing 'The privatisation of the Civil Service' (2007), Molloy 'A revised legislative framework for Australian public service employment' (2007) and Weeks 'The reshaping of Australian public service employment law' (2007).

37   Country Profile Chs 1 and 2.

38   Ewing 'The privatisation of the Civil Service' (2007) and Weeks 'The reshaping of Australian public service employment law' (2007) 40 et seq. See http://www.apsc.gov.au/publications-and-media/archive/circulars-archive/arhive-circular-20087 on new developments in standards of behaviour for ministerial staff (accessed 23 January 2017).

39   See Country Profile Chs 1 and 2; Molloy 'A revised legislative framework for Australian public service employment' (2007) 84 et seq; and Weeks 'The reshaping of Australian public service employment law' (2007) 24.

40   *Public Service Act 1999* (Cth) s 3.

- *Ethical* – the APS is to act with leadership and integrity in all it does;
- *Respectful* – which includes showing respect to the rights and heritage of all people;
- *Accountable* – the APS is open and accountable to the Australian community through the law and ministerial responsibility;
- *Impartial* – the APS is apolitical and provides advice which is frank, honest, timely and based on the best available evidence.

S 10A then lists the APS Employment Principles, which pertain to the overarching functions of the APS but have a particular focus on employment law issues. Those principles state that the APS is a career-based service that:

- makes fair employment decisions based on merit – s 10A(2) states that merit requires 'all eligible members of the community [to be] given a reasonable opportunity to apply to perform the relevant duties'. That is opening the door of the APS, somewhat, from earlier times, when it was considered unusual for an 'outsider' to enter the ranks above entry level;
- will typically engage employees on an ongoing basis;
- expects employees to be effective in their role; and
- provides a safe and flexible workplace.

The enforcement of the APS Values is supported by an APS Code of Conduct (s 13). Essentially, an APS employee must behave and act 'in connection with APS employment':

- honestly and with integrity;
- with care and diligence;
- with respect and courtesy; and
- without harassment.

Likewise, the Code requires APS employees, 'in connection with APS employment', to:

- observe Australian law;
- comply with any lawful and reasonable directions given by someone in the employee's agency who has the authority to give the direction;
- maintain confidentiality in ministerial dealings;
- take reasonable steps to avoid conflicts of duty and interest and also make appropriate disclosure of any material personal interest;
- use Commonwealth resources properly;
- avoid providing false or misleading information; and
- not improperly use inside information or their own authority to seek or gain personal advantage or to detriment the employee's agency.

'At all times' public servants must uphold the APS Values along with the integrity and good reputation of the employing agency.

The Code of Conduct applies to all public servants, including agency heads and statutory office holders (s 14). Significantly, *The APS Values and Code of Conduct in Practice* (the Guide), underscores that s 13 requires that the values must be followed 'in connection with'

APS employment and the integrity of the service must be maintained 'at all times'.[41] It explains: 'The conduct of public servants, both inside and outside the workplace, can have implications for the confidence the community has in the administration of an Agency or the APS as a whole.'[42] Public servants, the Guide insists, 'are entrusted by the Government and the community to undertake important work on their behalf. With this trust comes a high level of responsibility.'[43] The Guide provides useful guidelines as to how public servants might observe the Code of Conduct in the following circumstances:

- Dealing with ministerial advisers (who are employed under the *Members of Parliament (Staff) Act 1984* (Cth)): this is administered by the Minister for Finance and Special Minister of State. Given that Ministers have authority over public servants and their advisers, public servants must ensure that advisers have ministerial authority for any instructions they are giving, and that APS advice is conveyed to the Minister.[44] (Importantly, given the earlier criticisms of Professor Ewing and the later writings of Professor Weeks,[45] there are now also standards of behaviour for ministerial staffers.)[46]

- During election campaigns: the APS is in caretaker mode at these times, so as to avoid political patronage – hence the Guidance on Caretaker Conventions from the Department of Prime Minster and Cabinet must be adhered to.[47]

- Vexatious complaints by the public about public servants: these are dealt with in *Better Practice Guide to Managing Unreasonable Complainant Conduct* (2009) – the significance of the issue was particularly evident after the murder of environment officer Glen Turner.[48]

- After-hours conduct – 'behaviours that, on their face, appear to be largely private [but where] there is a connection between the behaviour and the agency's confidence in the capacity of the employee to perform their duties professionally . . . [or that] . . . impact on the reputation of the Agency or the APS':[49] there are guidelines as to what public servants may post on social media[50] and on the political or other influential activity in which they might engage, and on the gifts they may receive.[51]

41   Australian Public Service Commission *APS Values and Code of Conduct in Practice* (February 2016), 4, http://www.apsc.gov.au/publications-and-media/current-publications/aps-values-and-code-of-conduct-in-practice.

42   Ibid. The breadth of the provision was also acknowledged by C Roles 'Are APS disciplinary processes ahead of the game? Amendments to the APS Code of Conduct' (2014) 21 *Australian Journal of Administrative Law* 57.

43   *APS Values and Code of Conduct in Practice* 4.

44   Ibid. See also *APS Values and Code of Conduct in Practice* Statement of Standards for Ministerial Staff 8.

45   Weeks 'The reshaping of Australian public service employment law' (2007).

46   See http://www.apsc.gov.au/publications-and-media/archive/circulars-archive/archive-circular-20087 (accessed 23 January 2017). This stems from Country Profile Chs 1 and 2.

47   *APS Values and Code of Conduct in Practice* 7.

48   Ibid 13. See also K Hoerr and N Dole 'NSW Farmer Ian Turnbull found guilty of shooting murder of environment officer Glen Turner', ABC News Online, 27 May 2016 (accessed 23 January 2017, http://www.abc.net.au/news/2016-05-27/nsw-farmer-found-guilty-of-murdering-environment-officer/7452728.

49   *APS Values and Code of Conduct in Practice* 18.

50   Ibid 37.

51   Ibid S 5.

7.10.20 Handling misconduct and investigations: the framework

It is one thing to steer public servants in how not to breach the Values and Code of Conduct, but as evident from Chapter 6 (The end of the employment relationship) of this book, the manner in which misconduct is handled (investigated, proven, managed, etc) is extremely important if an employer is to meet its legal requirements to manage staff fairly, and to maintain a healthy and productive working environment, both during and after the alleged misconduct matter. To steer that course the Australian Public Service Commission and Commissioner issues Directions and Guidebooks, in particular *Handling Misconduct: A Human Resources Manager's Guide*.[52] Such guides are issued pursuant to the *Public Service Act* ss 15(3) and 15(4), which require agency heads to establish 'procedures . . . for determining . . . whether an APS employee *or former employee* has breached the Code of Conduct . . . and . . . the sanction (if any) that is to be imposed' (emphasis added) – and those agency procedures 'must comply with basic procedural requirements set out in the Commissioner's Directions; and . . . must have due regard to procedural fairness'. The Public Service Commissioner's Guidelines are still significant and substantial and seem to take into account issues that have arisen in case law and academic commentary. Some of the key issues covered in the Guide include:

- public servants are required to report suspected misconduct;[53]
- once suspected misconduct is reported, there are a number of ways in which the matter can be treated[54] – using the Code of Conduct, or alternative dispute resolution, and/or performance appraisal;[55]
- if the Code of Conduct is invoked, there are considerations relevant to appointing investigators as well as decision-makers, and noting the importance of separating some functions in order for the disciplinary decision to appear fair and unbiased.[56] Obviously, an investigator must be qualified/trained sufficiently to undertake the task and the investigator/decision-maker must have the necessary authority to perform the given role;[57]
- procedural fairness – notifying the subject of the investigation as to its scope etc; fair procedure and due process (what matters will be followed? right of reply?);[58]
- determining the identity of the manager who will determine the sanction, the nature of the sanction, the evidence (including standard of proof) and the record keeping on which it is based.[59]

---

52   Australian Public Service Commission *Handling Misconduct: A Human Resources Manager's Guide 2014.*
53   Ibid 16, referring also to Commissioner's Directions.
54   Ibid diagram on 15 and 21 – the six stages of dealing with misconduct; see also 28–36 et seq.
55   Ibid 28–36 et seq.
56   Ibid 45 et seq.
57   Ibid.
58   Ibid 8 and Ch. 6, 56 et seq.
59   Ibid Ch. 7, 61 et seq. Generally the standard is *Briginshaw v Briginshaw* (1938) 60 CLR 336.

As noted above, the Guide and Commissioner's Directions are the umbrella documents for the agency procedures. As I wrote in the *Hong Kong Law Journal* in 2009,[60] those agency procedures have (in some departments from time to time) included:[61]

- an *informal investigation* (where the manager satisfies themselves whether there is sufficient evidence to warrant a formal investigation); and
- a *formal investigation* (where the public servant who is the subject of the complaint is notified as to the nature of the investigation and its scope and the nature of the complaint). There is not necessarily extensive cross-examination or a formal legal hearing. (Where there is a clear case of abusing time sheets, for example, security logs – showing when a person entered and left a building – may form the basis of the case.) These formal investigations may be briefed out to law firms or other professional workplace investigators (who may give a recommendation at the end of the investigation). The employee being investigated must be given a fair chance to respond – noting that the investigator may test evidence as it is given. One important aspect of the Australian system is that the employee being investigated *may* have a right to legal representation: they may be able to have a lawyer vet documents, probe the case against them for strengths and weaknesses and advise the employee concerned of the ramifications of their statements.[62] This has been alluded to in other jurisdictions, such as Hong Kong, as one of the strengths of the system.

The law outlined above indicates that employees can be investigated even when they have left the APS, to avoid people thinking they can do what they like but avoid the consequences through switching jobs.[63] If there is an adverse finding against the employee, they will have a right of appeal. Termination matters may go to the Fair Work Commission (FWC), while matters falling short of termination, for example Code of Conduct, may go to the Merit Protection Commission (supported by the Australian Public Service Commission). The case law discussed at the end of this section demonstrates the relevance of judicial review.

As regards the strengths and weaknesses of the above system, in my 2009 article I wrote:

In my view, the area of concern is the initial or informal stage of the disciplinary procedure, that is, when the supervisor is determining whether there is sufficient evidence – not to find someone guilty – but rather to warrant a formal investigation. To be fair, it must be said that there is often a legitimate purpose behind this stage. There may be obvious cases where it would be ridiculous to go straight to a formal investigation. For example, a new public servant, fresh from, say, the private sector, may be having difficulty adjusting to public sector culture and may be a bit bumptious in their dealings with others. In such a situation, they may simply need counselling in order to become a constructive public servant, rather than having an entire work group and the metaphoric 'glue' that binds it together placed under the pressure of formal review processes.[64]

---

60   L Floyd 'Reforming Hong Kong public sector law after *Lam Siu Po* and *Rowse* – some useful comparisons from Australian law' (2009) *Hong Kong Law Journal* 471 et seq.
61   Ibid 472–3.
62   Ibid 473.
63   See *Public Service Act* s 15(2A): 'A person who is, or was, an APS employee is taken to have breached the Code of Conduct . . .' See also, generally, Roles 'Are APS disciplinary processes ahead of the game?' (2014).
64   Another example could be where one public servant is complaining about a rival during a promotion round.

However, in my view, there is also an inherent danger in this informal stage. The informal stage may be so informal that a supervisor may simply request a meeting with an employee, stating that they want to discuss a problem in the workplace. When the meeting commences, it may be that the supervisor has their own witness present (typically one of their own subordinates), but the public servant whose behaviour is being considered does not. What follows could be a 'fishing expedition', where the employee in question may feel 'ambushed' or may speak openly, without realising that their statements may be used against them. As there is a duty for public servants to obey reasonable orders, some may feel they would breach that duty if they did not proceed with the meeting once it was called. Where such a meeting begins with a warning that the matter could lead to disciplinary investigations, the employee may instinctively ask for legal representation. There may even be discretion for the supervisor to allow it; the point is that it may be left to the employee whose future is under consideration to know their rights; if they do not know their rights, they may damage their position in such a meeting.

The consequences of such a situation are worth considering further. If a public servant were not guilty, there would be no problem in speaking with a superior. In cases such as time sheet fraud or computer abuse, the strength of the written evidence would be the most important aspect of the investigation. This leaves one other category of investigation, namely investigations into personality matters.

True bullies are a problem in the workplace and breach the Code of Conduct (with its requirement to respect others) as well as workplace health and safety requirements. But what if the supervisor is the bully? What if the public servant they choose to investigate is not a bully but rather someone who is smart, good at their work and better qualified than anyone else in the work group? In other words, what if the public servant being investigated is simply seen as a threat by the supervisor?

Before dismissing this as fanciful, it is worth considering some evidence from Queensland. Under s 85 of the *Public Service Act 1996* (Qld) there was provision for supervisors to commit staff for psychiatric examination 'where the employing authority reasonably *suspects* that the person's ... unsatisfactory performance is caused by mental ... illness' (emphasis added).

Psychiatrists such as Dr Bill Wilkie openly condemned this discretion as something that could be abused by supervisors who were themselves bullies and wanted to terminate employees who were 'inconvenient': 'They're dragging our profession into disrepute. It's an absolute scandal and we should do something to stop it.' [65] Queensland now has the *Public Service Act 2008* (Qld). It is significant that psychiatric testing seems available under s 174 and associated provisions.

There are weaknesses in the public sector disciplinary procedures. Having said that, there are very clear strengths and safeguards and it appears that the second edition of the Guide has taken into account some of the litigation that was decided after the first edition was released. Below, we consider *Jarratt v Commissioner for Police (NSW)* (2005) 224 CLR 44, which underscores the importance of according natural justice to public servants, and *Barratt v Howard* (2000) 96 FCR 428, which shows a very limited practical application or span of natural justice in relation to a top-ranking public servant, namely a department head. We will also

---

65   B Wilkie, as quoted in 'Mental health services abused by managers' (reporter Simon Royal), *The 7:30 Report* (ABC Television) 17 July 2001, http://www.abc.net.au/7.30/content/2001/s331042.htm (transcripts accessed 9 June 2009).

consider the Queensland public service cases[66] of *Queensland v Attrill* (2012) 227 IR 435 (*Attrill*), which underscores the dangers of s 174 mental health orders, and *Wirth v Mackay Hospital and Health Service* [2016] QSC 39 (*Wirth*), which speaks to the nature of natural justice (the availability of documents) as well as the use of legal counsel by public servants at the earlier stages of employment.

These very well-known and important cases have been considered by numerous scholars, including Floyd,[67] the late Professor Weeks,[68] Dr Max Spry[69] and Michael Will.[70] These cases traverse the issue of the relevance of due process in public service dismissal and, in particular, the procedural fairness requirements for dismissal of public servants in higher ranks.

JARRATT v COMMISSIONER FOR POLICE (NSW) (2005) 224 CLR 44 (JARRATT)

Jeff Jarratt, the long-serving and highly respected Deputy Commissioner for Police for New South Wales, was dismissed quite ruthlessly. A press release announcing his dismissal on performance grounds was delivered to his home after hours. Jarratt had no prior warning of the problems alleged and no chance to respond. The *Police Service Act* 1990 (NSW) provided, in s 53, that the appointment could be terminated 'at any time' by the Governor (advised by the Commissioner, acting with ministerial approval).[71]

Before the High Court, the notion that public sector workers of Jarratt's ilk were to serve at the pleasure of the Crown was easily disposed of. The High Court noted not only the relevant legislation but also the advent of administrative law. A disciplined service and fair treatment of staff could co-exist – and where (as was the case here) employment was governed by statute (and not some ancient prerogative), unless natural justice is necessarily excluded, there should be a fair hearing before the employee suffers such a detriment.[72]

BARRATT v HOWARD (2000) 96 FCR 428 (BARRATT)

Paul Barratt was another long-serving highly respected public servant, serving as Secretary of the Department of Defence. However, he had a strained relationship with the Minister of

---

66   I thank Dr Max Spry of the Queensland Bar for raising the cases of *Attrill* and *Wirth* with me in discussions of 4 October and 2 December 2017 (emails and records on file with author).

67   See Floyd 'Reforming Hong Kong public sector law after *Lam Siu Po* and *Rowse*' (2009).

68   See Pittard and Weeks (eds) *Public Sector Employment in the Twenty-First Century* (2007).

69   M Spry 'A review of natural justice principles after *Jarratt*', AIAL Forum No. 48 (2007) 47–51.

70   M Will 'From *Barratt* to *Jarratt*: public sector employment, natural justice, and breach of contract', AIAL Forum No. 48 (2007) 9–16.

71   Ibid 11, a useful table of the provisions relevant to these decisions.

72   For a clear and interesting discussion see Spry 'A review of natural justice principles after *Jarratt*' (2007) 47–8 et seq.

the day and had presided over the department during a difficult time: the introduction of the Collins class submarine. The Secretary of the Department of Prime Minister and Cabinet offered Barratt a position as New Zealand High Commissioner, warning that he faced serious problems in his present role and that 'things in general' were problematic.[73]

As a pre-emptive strike Barratt made an application to the Federal Court for procedural fairness. He scored a pyrrhic victory. The government informed Barratt that the Minister had lost confidence in him and gave only few details. Barratt applied once again to the court. Although the court agreed that Barratt was not working at the pleasure of the Crown and was entitled to procedural fairness, the court also held that the (scant, some would say) reasons given were sufficient grounds for dismissal.

7.10.25 Reconciling the two cases: *Jarratt* and *Barratt*

So two high-ranking, long-serving, well-regarded public servants were both fired; both sued on grounds of procedural fairness and one was successful in a damages claim but the other was not. The content of procedural fairness – what constituted natural justice – differed in the two cases. Reconciling the different outcomes, one author has suggested that it was because Jarratt waited to bring legal action until after management had made the mistake of not giving him natural justice, whereas Barratt applied while still employed, so the employer could then *appear* to give natural justice.[74]

Whether or not that approach should be followed will be left for another day. What can be said, however, in the view of this author, is that natural justice is now a significant part of the employment of most public servants (and indeed this is underscored in the 2014 Guide, as observed above). But the higher up one's employment is – the closer to the Minister one is – it may well be that that actual relationship is increasingly important. In other words, natural justice will be a more demanding requirement for an employer to meet if the public servant is *not* in an extremely high-ranking position where their relationship with the Minister is a determinant of job success.

7.10.30 Public service examinations and investigations – further case law

LEE v SMITH [2007] FMCA 59; (2007) EOC 93–456

The case is important for two reasons: the connection between after-hours sexual conduct and the workplace, and workplace investigations. The case resulted in one of the most significant awards of damages against the Department of Defence and various employees thereof.

73   Floyd 'Reforming Hong Kong public sector law after *Lam Siu Po* and *Rowse*' (2009) 478.
74   Will 'From *Barratt* to *Jarratt*: public sector employment, natural justice, and breach of contract' (2007) 15.

Cassandra Lee worked in an administrative position in the Patrol Boat Landing Class Logistics Office in Cairns, with colleagues from the Navy and the Department of Defence.[75] Ms Lee succeeded in proving a case of sexual harassment and/or sex discrimination[76] (under the *Sex Discrimination Act 1984* (Cth)) in relation to: pornographic images in the workplace (such as calendars in the workplace depicting nude women);[77] menacing conduct (constant innuendo and suggestive conduct despite the rejections of such by Ms Lee);[78] and rape at an after-hours drinks function held at a colleague's home amongst colleagues, and at which Ms Lee was intoxicated.[79] She also succeeded in proving the distress caused by the subsequent handling of her complaint by the relevant department, and by the conduct of her work colleagues (there seemed to be no confidentiality in relation to the matter and the first respondent was able to intimidate her).[80]

Of particular importance in the present context is what the court said in relation to after-hours conduct and the vicarious liability of the employer, the Department of Defence.[81] After citing two separate judgements of Kiefel J, in *Smith v Christchurch Press Co. Ltd* [2001] 1 NZLR 407 and *South Pacific Resort Hotels Pty Ltd v Trainor* (2005) 144 FCR 402 – which spoke of 'necessary connection' – Magistrate Connolly stated in the *Cassandra Lee* decision:

> In the present case, the rape occurred between two current employees and in my view it arose out of a work situation. The Applicant was invited to attend after-work drinks by a fellow employee and indeed the invitation was issued at the behest of the First Respondent to attend dinner at their residence. The Applicant's attendance was clearly because of the original after-work drinks invitation and it was likely that the invitation was provided in that form to ensure the Applicant's attendance. There is no doubt that it not only had the potential to adversely affect the working environment but it did so …[82]

A further interesting part of the judgement pertained to the nature of the evidence given at the hearing, especially the fact that Ms Lee, the complainant, had sent what appeared to be friendly emails to the First Respondent after the alleged incidents.[83] The Magistrate even stated: 'I must admit that the email exchange is not what I would have expected following the events.'[84] Nonetheless, the court accepted the complainant's version of events on the basis that sexual assault can be so distressing that there is no set way a complainant behaves – instead, the weight of the sum total of the evidence and the credibility of all the witnesses must be considered.[85] Scattered throughout the judgement are comments about the need for

75   *Lee v Smith* [2007] FMCA 59 at [2].
76   Ibid [198] et seq and [62] et seq.
77   Ibid [198] and [64].
78   Ibid [94] et seq and [199].
79   Ibid [201] et seq and [117].
80   Ibid [122] et seq.
81   Ibid [201] et seq.
82   Ibid [203]. See generally [206] et seq.
83   Ibid [135] et seq.
84   Ibid [137].
85   Ibid [135]–[143] as well as [121]–[129].

training in workplaces and the need for confidentiality in complaint handling and protecting complainants from intimidation.[86] This case was decided before the recent changes to the *Public Service Act* (where 'at all times' was added), but it underscores the need for public servants to observe that their conduct away from work is relevant to their work.

QUEENSLAND v ATTRILL (2012) 227 IR 435

In this case, the Queensland Court of Appeal found that s 175[87] of that State's *Public Service Act* was inconsistent with the *Anti-Discrimination Act 1991* (Qld) (s 15, for example), and hence repealed the anti-discrimination legislation by implication. Consequently, Queensland public servants cannot rely on the *Anti-Discrimination Act*, with its recourse to the Queensland Civil and Administrative Tribunal (QCAT), if they have a complaint about the ordering of a medical exam under s 175 of the *Public Service Act*. (Note that s 178 governs management options after such a report.)

Ms Attrill was ordered to take a mental health examination so that her superiors could make an assessment as to whether or not she should continue in her role. These orders were made under ss 174–178 of the *Public Service Act* and were brought about because of Ms Attrill's absences from work and consequent questions about her suitability for employment. (She had a known history of mental illness.)

Before QCAT, Ms Attrill complained that the ordering of the examination (which could lead to her termination) was discriminatory. The issue was whether that tribunal had jurisdiction or whether there was a conflict between Chapter 5 Part 7 of the *Public Service Act* and the State's anti-discrimination legislation, such that the more recent *Public Service Act* (2008) impliedly repealed the operation of the earlier anti-discrimination law (1991). The first instance decision maker found that it did.[88] On appeal,[89] Wilson J (still in QCAT) found that it did not – that the two statutes could be reconciled. As long as the order for the exam was based on reasonable grounds related to the employee's capacity to perform the job (and what to do about it), the action would be reasonable.[90] Wilson J also made the comments:

> Indeed, if Chief Executives were not obliged to act in accordance with their obligations under the AD Act, given the lack of prescribed legislative criteria to guide decision-making under s 178 of the PS Act, arbitrary decisions could otherwise be made that disregard the EEO

86   Ibid [21] et seq.
87   Section 175 Chief executive may require medical examination: The chief executive may (a) appoint a doctor to examine the employee and give the chief executive a written report on the examination; and (b) require the employee to submit to the medical examination.
88   *Attrill v Queensland* [2011] QCAT 361.
89   *Attrill v Department of Corrective Services* [2012] QCATA 31.
90   Ibid [48] onwards.

obligations imposed under the PS Act, which recognise, and endorse, the aspects of the AD Act discussed above.[91]

Notwithstanding that, the Court of Appeal (in particular Holmes JA, now Chief Justice Holmes) disagreed with Wilson J's reasoning.[92] In Holmes JA's view, ordering a medical examination would always be a detriment to the person in relation to whom the order was made – it would always be discriminatory – so since s 15 of the *Anti-Discrimination Act* would render s 175 of the *Public Service* Act unusable, the two were inconsistent and s 175 of the *Public Service Act* was to be viewed as repealing s 15 of the *Anti-Discrimination Act*.[93] Justice Holmes did, however, find that s 178 of the *Public Service Act* was not naturally inconsistent with the anti-discrimination legislation.[94]

As a result of Justice Holmes' decision, Queensland public servants have no recourse to QCAT (for discrimination claims) in relation to s 175. It is interesting to note that the Queensland Anti-Discrimination Commissioner intervened in the litigation and argued against that interpretation of that Act. Thinking back to Dr Wilkie's criticisms of the predecessor to s 175, (cited above) it will be interesting to see whether public servants are ever able to use anti-bullying provisions or similar against such an order for a medical examination.

WIRTH v MACKAY HOSPITAL AND HEALTH SERVICE [2016] QSC 39

This decision of Justice Bond of the Queensland Supreme Court underscores the relevance of natural justice to public service Code of Conduct disciplinary proceedings; and addresses two tricky issues about the use of law firms as disciplinary investigations unfold.

The Mackay Health Hospital Service launched an investigation into their emergency room due to decaying relations between staff, which it was feared were affecting operating performance.[95] Significantly, the government department referred the matter to law firm Clayton Utz for investigation, with terms of reference that included:[96]

> As previously discussed, Clayton Utz is instructed by the Mackay Health Hospital Service (Service) to provide legal advice, as required by the Service, in respect of the following matters:
>
> (a) Review and gather all necessary evidence to help identify the cause of the communication and working relationship breakdown between staff at the Emergency Department (Department) **in light of the incidents and complaints involving Dr Peter Wirth and other members of staff of the Department**;

---

91   Ibid [57].
92   *Queensland v Attrill* (2012) 227 IR 435 at [32] per Holmes JA.
93   Ibid [29]–[36] per Holmes JA.
94   Ibid [37] and [38] per Holmes JA.
95   *Wirth v Mackay Hospital and Health Service* [2016] QSC 39 at [1] and [2] et seq.
96   Ibid para 44.

   (b) Consider whether **any staff** of the Department **have acted inappropriately** or in breach of the Code of Conduct or any of the legal requirements; and

   (c) Consider **whether there is sufficient evidence to establish that any staff** of the Department **should be subject to disciplinary or any other action** and the nature of any such disciplinary action.

Crucially, Dr Wirth was never made aware of the fact the investigation was largely focused on his conduct – not even when Clayton Utz interviewed him as part of their investigation: the law firm simply called it a fact-finding mission.[97] Further, when a decision was made to take disciplinary action against Dr Wirth, the government department claimed that the Clayton Utz Investigation Report was privileged.[98] Despite numerous requests,[99] Dr Wirth's lawyers were denied full access to the report (which particularised complaints),[100] even though the relevant department's policies acknowledged the need for natural justice. As Bond J noted:[101]

> The respondents contend that does not matter. They contend that an opportunity to be heard may be satisfied where the gravamen, substance or essential features of any adverse information is disclosed without the entire text or document in which that information is contained necessarily being disclosed. As a general proposition that may be accepted. But the fundamental principle is that the right to be heard '. . . would ordinarily require the party affected to be . . . informed of the nature and content of adverse material'. Moreover, the content of natural justice is fact specific and an examination of the fairness of the process in a practical sense must be essayed.
>
> In the circumstances of this case, it seems to me that natural justice did require what Policy E10 identified as the <u>minimum</u> standard, namely that before a decision was made on the question whether or not an allegation was actually established Dr Wirth would be:
>
>   (a) provided with all the information Ms Douglas intended to rely upon when determining whether an allegation could be substantiated; and
>
>   (b) advised what evidence was being relied upon to support the allegation.
>
> Because he was not given even the summaries of evidence annexed to the Clayton Utz report, Dr Wirth was denied the opportunity of making any countervailing submissions as to credibility of the witnesses whose evidence was adverse to him. He was denied the opportunity of considering whether there were any weaknesses in the versions of events which they had provided to Clayton Utz and of either adducing evidence in response or making submissions thereon. And because he was not given the report itself, he was denied the opportunity of being able to develop any critique of the findings made by Clayton Utz . . .

Justice Bond found in favour of Dr Wirth, stating that the report was not commissioned as legal advice but rather as an investigative report – privilege did not attach thereto.[102]

---

97   Ibid [45], [49] and [50] per Bond J.
98   Ibid [51], [60], [73] et seq.
99   Ibid [97].
100   Ibid [93]–[96] per Bond J.
101   Ibid [71] et seq.
102   Ibid [114]–[118]. In obiter, His Honour pondered as to whether a report which was commissioned for the giving of privileged advice but then used for a different purpose could ever be obtained by a complainant ([119]–[121]).

7.15 Public sector theory

It is clear from the discussion so far that public service employment is no normal job – there are very detailed statutory provisions which underscore the position of trust that public servants occupy, and that trust stems from the view of the public service as one arm of government. While the giddying heights of the Constitution and separation of powers may colour the jurisdiction, there is clearly also a political and ideological or theoretical aspect. Whether the government of the day thinks there should be big or small government and what tasks the government should perform clearly influence how many people are employed by the public sector and how it behaves. Three of the more prominent public service theorists are Max Weber, Julian Le Grande and Phillip Blond. Their work is discussed below.

7.15.05 Outsourcing

Numerous scholars have argued and analysed issues as to the optimal size of government – whether it should enumerate core functions and, if so, what they are – or whether the government should be a big government, shaping many aspects of society.[103] In recent times, two of the more influential, for Australian purposes, have actually been British scholars – Julian Le Grande and Phillip Blond.

Le Grande's *The Other Invisible Hand: Delivering Public Services through Choice and Competition*[104] famously made the case for decentralisation of government services, as something that would lead to efficiency and greater consumer satisfaction.

Continuing down the path of decentralisation is Philip Blond, whose *Red Tory: How Left and Right have Broken Britain and How We Can Fix It*[105] was highly influential on former British Prime Minister David Cameron. Blond came to Australia to address the Liberal Party in the run-up to the victory of former Australian Prime Minster Tony Abbott.[106] In Blond's view, big corporations, big government and big unions should be replaced by Big Society – which would see a dramatic increase in the contracting out of former government work to community groups, co-ops and social enterprises. The inclusion of community-based services would, he claims, enrich the lives of the citizenry and improve the accountability of government.[107]

Blond's views and theories about the public sector beg numerous legal questions, such as how a government might use procurement to include the otherwise disenfranchised in society (might bidders for a government contract be encouraged to employ the long-term unemployed, for instance?). The theory may be viewed as having spawned legislation such

---

103   J Le Grande *The Other Invisible Hand: Delivering Public Services through Choice and Competition* (Princeton University Press, 2007). M Powell (ed) *New Labour, New Welfare State? The 'Third Way' in British Social Policy* (Policy Press, 1999). P Blond *Red Tory: How Left and Right have Broken Britain and How We Can Fix It* (Faber & Faber, 2010).

104   Le Grande *The Other Invisible Hand* (2007). Using procurement and social enterprises has been canvassed in other works such as Powell (ed) *New Labour, New Welfare State?* (1999).

105   Blond *Red Tory* (2010).

106   This was discussed in L Floyd 'Procurement; social enterprises; co-operatives & public service: The UK Government's 'Big Society' and Australian business law' (2012) 40 *Australian Business Law Review* 280.

107   Ibid.

as the *Public Services (Social Value) Act 2012* in the UK, which deals with how small community groups can tender for government contracts and also prove the social value they add to society.[108]

The shrinking of public or government sector employment obviously raises questions clearly relevant to employment law, particularly regarding the accountability of these contractors: how do they uphold the old public sector values? How are they held to account if contracting occurs on a mass scale?[109] It also focuses attention on the working conditions of those who are involved with co-ops and other community-based organisations. Australia's move towards Blond's big society has not gone far, due to the Australian distrust of mass contracting-out.[110]

For those who work in the traditional public service, the work of Max Weber is prescient.[111] The public service, as employer, is a complex beast. It is selfless, yet at the same time employs those with ambition – it serves, yet at the same time sees so many wield power. It is unusual employment, indeed.

7.15.10 Whistleblowing: public interest disclosure

No discussion of public sector employment would be complete without a discussion of whistleblowing or public interest disclosure. The *Public Interest Disclosure Act 2013* (Cth) (*PID Act*) aims to promote public sector accountability and integrity by encouraging public servants to make public interest disclosures. The Act also aims to ensure that those public servants are protected from reprisals and that their concerns are appropriately investigated (s 6).

This Commonwealth statute aims to be an example of how whistleblowing in the private or corporate sector should also be governed.[112] It was passed subsequent to excellent work by Professor AJ Brown in the *Whistling While They Work* report,[113] and further developments in Queensland, for example, and the introduction of protection for journalists at the Federal level.[114]

The *PID Act* applies to public servants in respect of public sector activities.[115] PIDs, or whistleblower complaints, may be made, with protection of the identity of the person making the public interest disclosure,[116] and internally or, after satisfying some

---

108   For a discussion of all issues and legislation, see L Floyd 'The elephant in the room: The *Public Services (Social Value) Act 2012*' (2013) *Law Quarterly Review* 179–83 and Floyd 'Procurement; social enterprises; co-operatives & public service' (2012) 280–302.

109   Ewing 'The privatisation of the Civil Service' (2007); see also Floyd 'Procurement; social enterprises; co-operatives & public service' (2012).

110   The demise of the Abbott, Newman and Bligh governments is a testament to this!

111   See M Weber on bureaucracy: *Max Weber on Capitalism, Bureaucracy and Religion* (Allen & Unwin, 1983).

112   S Lombard and V Brand 'Corporate whistleblowing: public lessons for private disclosure' (2014) 42 *Australian Business Law Review* 5.

113   AJ Brown et al. 'Whistling While They Work: towards best practice whistleblowing programs in public sector organisations', Draft report, July 2009.

114   These measures are discussed in L Floyd 'Whistle blowing and compulsory medical examinations: recent developments in Australian public sector employment law and their relevance to Hong Kong' (2011) 41 *Hong Kong Law Journal* 155–77.

115   *PID Act* ss 6 and 7.

116   Ibid s 10, s 20.

requirements,[117] externally.[118] The statute protects whistleblowers from reprisals[119] but does not necessarily absolve them from blame for their contribution to any wrong.[120] There is also some scope for protecting government contractors under the legislation.[121]

7.15.15 Three key issues under the *Public Interest Disclosure Act 2013* (Cth) (*PID Act*)

1. How does the legislation characterise frivolous, vexatious or revenge complaints?

2. When is it appropriate to go outside the public sector with complaints?

3. How does the legislation intersect with the national security regime?

These issues are considered below. At the time of writing there is no key case law on the operation and interpretation of the Act. However, the Act is under a scheduled legislative review.[122]

Under s 26, the discloser/public official can disclose to people listed in column two of a table set out in connection with that section if the requirements of column three of the same table are also complied with. Without setting that table out in full, the gist seems to be that:

- A whistleblower can go internally to a supervisor or authorised internal recipient if 'the information tends to show, or the discloser believes on reasonable grounds that the information tends to show, one or more instances of disclosable conduct'.

- There can be external disclosure to any person except a foreign public official if the whistleblower disclosed the above-style information internally and 'the discloser believes on reasonable grounds that the investigation was inadequate' or the investigation was not completed within time – and:

  - such external public disclosure is not contrary to the public interest

  - no more information than necessary is made publicly available

  - there is no intelligence information given/an intelligence agency is not involved.

- There is also allowance for disclosure on an emergency basis and to a legal practitioner in some circumstances.

As to whether or not the disclosure (external to the service) is contrary to the public interest, s 26(3) lists a wide variety of factors, including::

- Would the disclosure promote the integrity of the Commonwealth public sector?

- How serious is the conduct?

- What would be the impact of the disclosure on national security?

---

117   Ibid s 26 Table Item 1; see also s 25, s 29.
118   Ibid s 26 Table Item 2.
119   Ibid s 13 et seq.
120   Ibid s 12.
121   Ibid s 29.
122   Ombudsman website: http://www.ombudsman.gov.au. In particular, http://www.ombudsman.gov.au/
      _data/assets/pdf_file/0023/43295/PID-Newsletter-4-November-2016.pdf. See 'Public Interest Disclosure
      E-News', which provides a link to the recent report. At the time of writing, the government was
      considering its response. See also http://www.dpmc.gov.au.

- Is it Cabinet information?
- Is there jeopardy to the administration of justice or legal professional privilege?

Disclosable conduct is defined in s 29 as including public sector conduct that contravenes a law or perverts the course of justice.

It would be interesting to consider the effect, if any, this legislation might have on the outcomes of previously decided cases. In that connection, one may consider *Kessing's case*.

KESSING v THE QUEEN (2008) 73 NSWLR 22[123]

Alan Kessing was employed by the Customs Department at Sydney Airport after the September 11 attacks. He used a public phone near his home to contact journalists from *The Australian* newspaper in relation to weaknesses he perceived in security at the airport. When the leaks were discovered, Kessing – one of only a small number of people who had that information – was investigated and the phone calls were discovered through phone records. Significantly, Kessing had also sent work emails noting his resentment of management.

Kessing was found to have breached the *Crimes Act 1914* (Cth) – he was given a suspended sentence.

7.20 Judicial 'work'[124]

At the 2012 Judicial Conference of Australia (JCA) Colloquium, Justice Wallis presented the paper 'Judges as employees'[125] to deliberately raise the question of the standing of judges when they perform their roles. In commenting on that paper, Hon President Margaret McMurdo AC, of the Queensland Court of Appeal, saw the deliberate irony in the title Justice Wallis had given his speech:[126]

> Discussions like this are important. They enable us to develop best practice ... as Justice Wallis highlighted, that requires vigilance to detect any creeping notion that judges are employees! ... We judges must perform our roles competently, independently and accountably as we apply the rule of law. I am optimistic. I believe this way we can have

---

123   This case is also discussed in Floyd 'Whistle blowing and compulsory medical examinations' (2011). Both this case and the whistleblowing of respected parliamentarian Andrew Wilkie were discussed in the SBS documentary, *Law and Disorder: Andrew Wilkie – The Perfect Whistleblower*.

124   This section of the chapter develops the author's earlier work: L Floyd 'Punch and Jarrod: The pitfalls of Attorney-General (rather than judicial) activism – and the need for an Attorney-General Code of Conduct' (2014) 34 *The Queensland Lawyer* 66; L Floyd 'Fitness for trial: trial in absence of (unrepresented) litigant; contempt of court and evidentiary issues' (2010) 33 *Australian Bar Review* 56–66; L Floyd 'Much Ado About Nothing: why accepting an invitation did not make Dyson Heydon AC QC appear biased' (2016) 90 *The Australian Law Journal* 38.

125   Justice M Wallis 'Judges as employees', JCA Colloquium, Fremantle, 6 October 2012.

126   Hon President Margaret McMurdo 'A comment on Justice Malcolm Wallis' Paper', JCA Colloquium, Fremantle, 6 October 2012.

a respectful, courteous discourse between the three branches of government. Individually and collectively, the judiciary, executive and the legislature can, with public legitimacy, deliver good government to our people. And then the answer to Justice Wallis' question will be that judges, like Cabinet Ministers and members of parliament, collectively govern, not as employees of the executive, but as public officers of their distinct branches of government. Thank you, Justice Wallis, for making us address the challenging question you pose.

It is crucial to note at the beginning of this section that it is being written with respect and mindfulness of the importance of judges being officers, not employees.[127] That notion goes to the heart of our system of government. That independence is something so cherished and essential that it has been the subject of consideration from as far back as Magna Carta, through to Sir Edward Coke, then Lord Mansfield, with his declaration: 'Let justice be done, though the heavens fall',[128] and latterly Lords Devlin and Denning.[129] In Australia, judges have been nothing short of courageous in their defence of judicial independence (as will be expanded upon below).[130] Elegant pieces have been written about the subject by judges ranging from Chief Justice French[131] to Justice Rares[132] and Justice Sackville,[133] and to judges from Justice McPherson[134] through to Justice Thomas.[135] The work of HP Lee is also well known.[136]

So this is written with respect to that tradition, not in spite of it. For judges to perform their work – best viewed as a calling, perhaps – they must be appointed. And they can be removed. This most venerable and ancient institution must today confront modern questions such as:

- the effect of social media on the work of judges (can they be cyber stalked?);
- workplace stress and bullying – and mental health issues;[137] and
- the effect of government administrative measures, such as when the courts do not control their own budgets but rather rely on administrative arrangements made by, for instance, State governments.

---

127   That point has been made again and again. See *Re Australian Education Union; Ex parte Victoria* (1995) 184 CLR 188 at 233 as cited in McMurdo 'A comment on Justice Malcolm Wallis' Paper' (2012).

128   Lord Mansfield in *R v Wilkes* (1770) 4 Burr 2527 at 2562. This is cited in an outstanding and very digestible discussion of the role of judges and the history of judicial independence by Justice S Rares 'What is a quality judiciary?' (2011) 20 *Journal of Judicial Administration* 137–139, especially 138.

129   Once again the work of their Lordships, such as Lord Devlin in *The Judge*, is part of the excellent and brief history found in Rares 'What is a quality judiciary?' (2011) 137.

130   It was originally outlined in Floyd 'Punch and Jarrod' (2014) 66.

131   Chief Justice French 'The State of the Australian judicature' (2016) 90 *ALJ* 400.

132   Rares 'What is a quality judiciary?' (2011) 133.

133   R Sackville AO QC 'Judicial ethics and judicial misbehaviour: two sides of the one coin?' (2015) 89 *Australian Law Journal* 244. Clearly the list is just scratching the surface of the luminous and illuminating pieces written by Australian judges – only some of which are included in this work.

134   B McPherson *The Supreme Court of Queensland 1859–1960: History, Jurisdiction and Procedure* (Butterworths, 1989).

135   JB Thomas *Judicial Ethics in Australia* (LexisNexis Butterworths, 3rd ed, 2009).

136   HP Lee *Judiciaries in Comparative Perspective* (Cambridge University Press, 2011); E Campbell and HP Lee *The Australian Judiciary* (Cambridge University Press, 2001).

137   Raised in insightful articles by Hon Justice Kirby considered further below: Hon M Kirby AC CMG 'Judicial stress and judicial bullying' (2013) 87 *Australian Law Journal* 516 and M Kirby *Judicial stress* (1995) 1 *Australian Bar Review* 101.

All these issues affect the manner in which judges operate professionally. How is their sick leave viewed – can a judge ever be viewed as having taken too much? If they are removed from office, what becomes of their pension? Can a government try literally rearranging a court without the consent of the presiding judge? If they try, is it a justifiable action or an attempt to bully the tribunal head from office? What if the judge is given less than adequate working quarters?

It is in furtherance of the independence of the Bench that I place a discussion such as this in a workplace law text. It is the view of the present writer that it is valuable to underscore to practitioners and law students and community members where the employment of public servants stops and where the work or calling of judges begins, and that the circumstances in which judges perform their work are vital to the workings of our democracy.

7.25 Appointment and removal
7.25.05 Appointments

For the most part, each jurisdiction has its own methodology. Handily, however, the Queensland government is in the process of reviewing its appointment procedures and as part of that exercise has produced the discussion paper *Review of the Judicial Appointments Process in Queensland*, which outlines how the process works for each jurisdiction.[138] The paper references the comparative study by the JCA, *Judicial Appointments Comparative Study*.[139]

The main contribution of this section, therefore, is to highlight that some of the differences between the jurisdictions go to the extent of transparency and consultation for appointment. For example:[140]

- To what extent might there be advertising for vacancies?
- Are there published selection criteria?
- Who appoints, and how?

These questions have been raised in Queensland in the wake of the notorious issues this State has had in recent years.[141] One of the crucial concerns is whether the present Queensland system should be made more formal by means of, for instance, an appointments protocol.[142] At present, there is no advertising for Supreme Court judges and it is largely the State Attorney-General who makes recommendations to the Governor after private consultation with heads of tribunals and the Bar Association.[143]

---

138   Queensland Department of Justice and Attorney-General 'Review of the judicial appointments process in Queensland', Discussion Paper (2015).
139   Judicial Conference of Australia (JCA) 'Judicial appointments comparative study', Research paper (2015).
140   'Review of the judicial appointments process in Queensland' (2015) 25.
141   See R Ananian-Welsh, G Appleby and A Lynch *The Tim Carmody Affair: Australia's Greatest Judicial Crisis* (NewSouth Publishing, 2016).
142   'Review of the judicial appointments process in Queensland' (2015) Minister's foreword, 5.
143   Ibid 7.

7.25.10 Removal of a judge from office

In the JCA's 2009 *Report of the Complaints against Judicial Officers Committee*, Sir Anthony Mason's words were recalled:[144] 'The argument [that some form of judicial accountability mechanism is unconstitutional] is consistent with a tendency of judges to treat judicial independence as a shield for themselves rather than as a protection for the people.' Indeed, that report continued by citing the observations of Justice McClellan in commenting on the paper of Professor Sallmann: 'If the process of investigation and the resolution of complaints [against judges] are not generally accepted, public confidence in the judiciary will be diminished. If that happens the currently accepted conventions which provide for an independent judiciary will come under challenge.'[145]

As with judicial appointment processes, the issue is tricky, because the processes differ from jurisdiction to jurisdiction. Yet again, there is a helpful summary of the various processes in the 2016 paper by Justice Ros Atkinson, 'Judicial accountability: an Australian perspective'.[146]

Her Honour points out that in numerous jurisdictions there is a significant role for politicians in determining whether or not a judge should be investigated and/or should relinquish their office (hence blurring the lines between executive/legislative and judicial arms of government).[147] For example, in some jurisdictions the Attorney-General may determine that there should be an ad hoc committee of (retired) judges which investigates a complaint, and if that committee forms the view (on the balance of probabilities) that there is significant misconduct or incapacity, then the Parliament may vote on their findings. This position is a contrast to that of New South Wales, with its much-vaunted Judicial Commission.[148] That Commission is independent (and comprised of heads of courts as well as members of the community), so it is separate from Parliament. In addition to its educative function and role in monitoring sentencing practices, it receives complaints (and vets for vexatious or frivolous ones). Where complaints have substance but are minor, they are referred to the head of the tribunal (so that private counselling of the judge concerned can occur). Where the Judicial Commission, as opposed to a politician, such as the Attorney-General, determines that a complaint is serious, that complaint goes to the Conduct Division, which investigates to determine whether the matter warrants the judge's removal from office. The report may be made to the Governor and to Parliament for final decision, and the judicial officer is granted an opportunity to show cause why they should not be removed.[149] As Justice Atkinson observes (reflecting on the two approaches), if the Attorney-General decides whether or not there should be an investigation, as opposed to having that decision made by a separate (non-political) body, there is a risk of

---

144   JCA 'Report of the complaints against Judicial Officers Committee' (2009) 4 para 8.
145   Ibid 6 para 12 – the initial paper by Sallmann was presented at the 2005 JCA Colloquium.
146   Justice R Atkinson 'Judicial accountability: an Australian perspective', paper for ANAO Meeting, Mexico (2016). Her Honour outlines the processes for removing judges federally and in the Australian States at 7–13.
147   Ibid 15–16.
148   Those who praise it are legion – see also JCA 'Second report of the complaints against Judicial Officers Committee' (2010). For scholarly acceptance see D Karamicov 'Judicial complaints and the complaints procedure: is it time for an independent commission in Victoria?' (2010) 19 *Journal of Judicial Administration* 232.
149   Atkinson 'Judicial accountability: an Australian perspective' (2016) 8. See also Karamicov 'Judicial complaints and the complaints procedure' (2010) 240–1 – that author also notes the circumspection with which the Commission was originally met in some quarters.

politically motivated investigations – or that an otherwise unimpeachable judge will resign in order to avoid putting themselves and the institution of the courts through a hearing.[150] In making these observations in 2016, Justice Atkinson echoes the thoughts of the JCA in 2010.[151]

There are few instances of Australian judges either being removed from office or being placed under review such that removal is the likely outcome. Justice Atkinson reflects on the two key instances – former Queensland Supreme Court Justice Angelo Vasta and former High Court Justice Lionel Murphy (who, sadly, died of cancer before all the questions raised against him were disposed of).[152] Karamicov outlines situations where magistrates have been called to defend themselves for either falling asleep during trials or seriously delaying the writing of many, many judgements over a considerable time.[153] In the latter situation, the judge was ill and the NSW Parliament did not vote for removal from office.[154]

FINGLETON v THE QUEEN (2005) 227 CLR 166

One of the saddest cases of 'judicial rebuke' was that involving former Queensland Chief Magistrate Diane Fingleton, who was sent to prison for interfering with a witness. On successful appeal, the High Court found that what the Chief Magistrate had done was all covered by s 21 of the *Magistrates Courts Act 1921* (Qld) – she was covered by judicial immunity and, in effect, should never have been charged.

The facts of the case are essentially that Ms Fingleton (whilst defending her decision to transfer Magistrate Cheryl Cornack to Townsville) asked her deputy (Basil Gribbin) to 'show cause' why he should continue in that role. The deputy – hugely respected within the Queensland profession – was openly supporting Magistrate Cornack's appeal, and so he was a party to a proceeding. Characterising the 'show cause' as a payback, the authorities charged Ms Fingleton with threatening a witness. Her evidence in response was that the show cause was not an actual disadvantage (the deputy could still state his case before anything happened) and she was simply trying to run her court in circumstances where she and the deputy had had a number of disagreements.

Convicted on a retrial, Ms Fingleton served a custodial sentence. After release, the High Court handed down its verdict. It was the High Court that raised the s 21 issue. Under s 21A of the *Magistrates Act 1991* (Qld):[155]

---

150   Atkinson 'Judicial accountability: an Australian perspective' (2016) 15–16, citing JCA 'Second report of the complaints against Judicial Officers Committee' (2010) (see JCA para 4) and 12–13.

151   JCA 'Second report of the complaints against Judicial Officers Committee' (2010).

152   Atkinson 'Judicial accountability: an Australian perspective' (2016) 13 and 14 – these two incidents are also discussed in R Sackville AO QC 'Judicial ethics and judicial misbehaviour: two sides of the one coin?' (2015) 89 *Australian Law Journal* 256–8.

153   Karamicov 'Judicial complaints and the complaints procedure' (2010) 237, alluding to a discussion of such cases in Campbell and Lee *The Australian Judiciary* (2001) 107–08.

154   Ibid. On such alleged incapacity as opposed to misconduct see Sackville 'Judicial ethics and judicial misbehaviour: two sides of the one coin?' (2015).

155   See *Fingleton v The Queen* (2005) 227 CLR 166 at [1]–[2] per Gleeson CJ.

A magistrate has, in the performance or exercise of an administrative function or power conferred on the magistrate under an Act, the same protection and immunity as a magistrate has in a judicial proceeding in a Magistrates Court.

As to those further proceedings, s 30 of the *Criminal Code Act 1995* (Cth) provides that:

A judicial officer is not criminally responsible for anything done or omitted to be done by the judicial officer in the exercise of the officer's judicial functions, although the act done is in excess of the officer's judicial authority, or although the officer is bound to do the act omitted to be done.

The High Court began by observing that judicial immunity existed for the benefit of maintaining an independent judiciary. After all, quoting Sandra Day O'Connor, 'if judges were personally liable for erroneous decisions, the resulting avalanche of suits ... would provide powerful incentives for judges to avoid rendering decisions likely to provoke such suits'.[156] And again: 'the public interest in maintaining the independence of the judiciary requires security, not only against the possibility of interference and influence by governments, but also against retaliation by persons or interests disappointed or displeased by judicial decisions'.[157]

The requirement of Chief Magistrate Fingleton to organise the court was part of the administration of justice and a complete defence to the charges laid against her.

Chief Magistrate Fingleton was reinstated as a Magistrate (though not Chief Magistrate) and is now retired. The fact that s 21 was raised only by the High Court (and not at some earlier stage) demonstrates the need for all lawyers to be aware of the law pertaining to the work of judges.

EINFELD v THE QUEEN (NO. 2) [2008] NSWCCA 243

As a retired Federal Court Judge Marcus Einfeld lied (under oath) to avoid a $77 speeding ticket and was subsequently imprisoned for perjury and perverting the course of justice. His lie was bizarre – he stated that a Professor Teresa Brennan had been driving. She had actually died some time earlier, and as those in the know will say: *dead professor don't drive car* ...
Subsequently Einfeld was struck off as a QC.[158]

---

156   Ibid [38] per Gleeson CJ.
157   Ibid [39] per Gleeson CJ.
158   There was an issue as to whether his judicial pension could be taken from him: 'Loophole under review', *Sydney Morning Herald (SMH)*, 21 March 2009 http://www.smh.com.au/national/loophole-under-review-20090320–94kk.html (accessed 22 January 2017).

7.25.15 Conduct guides and misconduct

The above discussion involves judicial appointment and removal from office. But clearly so much falls between those two events and extremes. Sackville observes that there are many ethical choices that guide a judge's conduct inside and outside court.[159] Both he and the former Chief Justice of the High Court, Justice French, have outlined some of the guidelines that govern, shape and assist judges in their lives and roles within and outside the court.[160] The work of retired Queensland Supreme Court Justice Thomas, *Judicial Ethics in Australia*, is, of course, legend.[161]

The *Guide to Judicial Conduct* encourages judges to be part of the community in which they live and also show integrity, diligence, honesty and, centrally, independence.[162] Sackville observes that there is a clear link between judicial ethics and legally enforceable conduct standards, but ethics is broader than that.[163] One very simple example Sackville explores is the idea that judges are expected to be courteous – but to what extent? And surely there could seldom be anything but private admonishment if they were not. In that vein, the Guide must not be prescriptive nor interfere with the independence of the judge.[164]

It is in relation to that middle ground that criticism of some judicial conduct and the manner in which it is treated has arisen. Karamicov finds the current use by some jurisdictions of informal (almost secretive) reprimands of some judges as lacking transparency.[165] She has argued, with some success, for the adoption of a Judicial Commission in Victoria through which an independent tribunal would determine whether conduct was minor and should then be referred to the tribunal head for private counselling.

Media reports in Queensland – which, on all the evidence, has an incredibly efficient judiciary (in 2015–16 its Court of Appeal had a clearance rate of over 100 per cent)[166] – note that people still complain about delays in judgements.[167] The JCA notes that multiple egregious delays over a long period of time may be cause for reprimand.[168] Yet as Justice Rares correctly

---

159   Sackville 'Judicial ethics and judicial misbehaviour: two sides of the one coin?' (2015) 244.

160   French 'The State of the Australian judicature' (2016).

161   Thomas *Judicial Ethics in Australia* (2009) – as a testament to its enduring worth, Hon President MA McMurdo AC cited the book in her speech for the Australian Academy of Law celebrating the 25th anniversary of the establishment of the Queensland Court of Appeal, in 2016.

162   Australian Institute of Judicial Administration *Guide to Judicial Conduct in Australia* (2nd ed, 2007) – discussed in Sackville 'Judicial ethics and judicial misbehaviour: two sides of the one coin?' (2015) 249 et seq.

163   Sackville 'Judicial ethics and judicial misbehaviour: two sides of the one coin?' (2015) 251.

164   Ibid 254. Throughout the article, Sackville considers the adoption of something like the more detailed American *ABA Model Code* for judges. There are also the non-binding *Guidelines for Communications and Relationships between the Judicial Branch of Government and the Legislative and Executive Branches* discussed in French 'The State of the Australian judicature' (2016) 400. See also Floyd 'Attorney General Code of Conduct' (2014) *Queensland Lawyer*.

165   See Karamicov 'Judicial complaints and the complaints procedure' (2010) 238.

166   McMurdo, speech celebrating the 25th anniversary of the establishment of the Queensland Court of Appeal.

167   J Gans 'Baden-Clay's resentencing delayed until High Court hearing', 13 January 2016, https://blogs.unimelb.edu.au/opinionsonhigh/2016/01/13/news-baden-clays-resentencing-delayed-until-high-court-hearing/ (accessed 22 January 2017).

168   JCA 'Second report of the complaints against Judicial Officers Committee' (2010) 37.

reminds us: 'Courts are not sausage factories. Cases are not mere statistics. The real work of the courts in society cannot be totalled up, and measured by, arbitrary business tools, such as key performance indicators, as some commentators, accountants, economists and politicians may believe.'[169] Acknowledging the earlier speech of Chief Justice Spigelman AC, Justice Rares continues:[170]

> Each case presents its own unique set of facts and issues. The role of the judicial branch is to do justice according to law in each case – not in a selected number of cases or by some statistically verifiable methodology. Justice cannot be made to fit the statistician's or bureaucrat's facts or figures. A case that takes a short time to hear may involve legal issues of great significance or difficulty that will take a judge or judges considerable time to consider and resolve, before he, she or they can deliver reasons for judgement.

Justice Rares helpfully outlines some management systems that aid judges in hearing and determining enormously complex litigation (the docket system and the Bench Book, for example).[171] He also observes that so many forget, or simply do not realise, that the court budget also has a role to play in the operation of the courts and therefore the manner in which judges perform their work and roles:

> ... the courts must be adequately funded to ensure they can discharge their functions ... In Australia, two main (funding) models are used: in the federal sphere, the Parliament appropriates a single figure for each of the High Court of Australia, the Federal Court of Australia and the Family Court of Australia. Each of those courts [is] self-administering and the Chief Justice, together with the registrar of each court, is responsible for allocating and spending the amount of the parliamentary appropriation. The Australian States and territories still treat their courts as dependent on an executive department, usually the Attorney-General's Department or the Department of Justice, to provide administrative and functional resources to the courts. Those courts can request, but cannot independently control, the provision or expenditure of any funds or resources.[172]

The courts cannot limit the number of cases that come before them; nor can they control the tendencies of an increasingly litigious society. All of that influences the conditions in which judges work. So neither the public nor the profession should be too quick to condemn the handing down of a decision that takes some time – a gap between hearing and decision may not evidence any blemish on the ability or capacity of the judge. Given the calls to more openly hold judges to account (partly due to community standards), the present writer sounds a note of caution: most Australian workplaces these days have extraordinarily detailed rules and procedures governing workplace health and safety – and worker support (see Chapter 8). If some want to hold judges to account, do we not also have a responsibility to judges to ensure that their working lives are equally well supported?

---

169   Rares 'What is a quality judiciary?' (2011) 133 – the judge considers statements of core values that all judges hold, including *The Beijing Statement of Principles of the Independence of the Judiciary in the LAWASIA Region* and the *International Framework for Court Excellence*.
170   Ibid 144.
171   Ibid 142 and 144 respectively.
172   Ibid 136.

7.30 Judicial working conditions – stress, safety, cyber-stalking and beyond

7.30.05 Basic conditions/allowances/pension

A bland (and ultimately incomplete) answer to questions about the terms and conditions of the work of a judge is that they are often set out in Judicial Entitlements Books on court websites. So, for instance, the Queensland Courts website has an outline of the 'Conditions: President of the Court of Appeal' – it has the same for Chief Justice, Supreme Court and District Court judges.[173] Such documents faithfully inform readers that the President (but only if accompanied by the Associate) can determine that they both travel in business class.

The salary is generous – to ensure impartiality. The pension is also considerable (so that the judge is never tempted through shortage of funds in retirement), and is subject to divorce settlements.[174]

7.30.10 WHS: physical safety

Other judiciary conditions, such as workplace health and safety, seem to be less readily available to the public (no doubt in part to actually safeguard the Bench). Although each court has a security system,[175] in the regions (where judges are infinitely more accessible to the public – and more recognisable), attention needs to be paid to ensuring that such a lack of anonymity never becomes a problem for a judge. Sometimes the health and safety of judges is upheld by the most circuitous of routes. The *R v Ogawa* [2011] 2 Qd R 350 decision is an example of that.[176]

R v OGAWA [2009] QCA 307

Megumi Ogawa was a Japanese law professor undertaking a PhD in Australia. After becoming involved in disputes with the Melbourne Law School, her visa lapsed, so the disputes then escalated to involve the Federal government. Ogawa then started menacing court staff, emailing and ringing literally hundreds of times. Matters came to a head when she rang a Judge's Associate and threatened to kill someone. Rightly, the Associate reported the matter and Ogawa was charged with misusing a carriage service.

Before the District Court, Ogawa (who at that stage had sacked her counsel) behaved remarkably – screaming whilst in court (so proceedings could not continue) then alleging

---

173   http://www.courts.qld.gov.au/.
174   See *Judges (Pensions and Long Leave) Act 1957* (Qld); *Judges Remuneration Act 2007* (Qld).
175   This is particularly a question for the Family Court: 'Leonard John Warwick to stand trial over Family Court bombing, targeted attacks in 1980s', L Carter, ABC, 14 December 2016 (accessed 22 January 2017) http://www.abc.net.au/news/2016-12-14/leonard-john-warwick-to-stand-trial-over-family-court-bombings/8120736.
176   L Floyd 'Fitness for trial: trial in absence of (unrepresented) litigant; contempt of court and evidentiary issues' (2010) 33 *Australian Bar Review* 56–66.

bias against her if proceedings continued in her absence. Disputed reports still circulate today as to whether she poked her naked bottom out at the judge – *The Courier Mail* newspaper described her as 'a Japanese bottom barer'.[177] In the end, she was imprisoned, with the Federal Court pondering whether or not 'much learning doth make thee mad'.[178]

The need for all parties (including self-represented litigants) to have a fair hearing may intersect with the right of the judge and court staff to have a safe workplace. Such a safe workplace involves both physical and mental safety.

7.30.15 WHS: mental safety

Hon Justice Kirby AC was one of the first judicial officers in this country to note the importance of safety in working conditions for a judge, including support mentally and emotionally and freedom from bullying.[179] Judges to further that quest include President McMurdo in her speech before the Judicial College of Victoria Learning Centre[180] and Justice Shane Marshall in a moving interview with Radio National's *Background Briefing*.[181]

An excellent point about the treatment of mental illness in the legal profession and the judiciary was made by academic Frances Gibson.[182] While it is crucial for litigants to receive a fair trial and not have the disability of a judge (or lawyer) interfere with the appropriate treatment of a case, in most occupations mental illness will not be considered something that permanently disables one from performing the work. In fact, one might make the obvious point that some of the most brilliant people in history have suffered mental illness. Reflecting on the position of the terribly tardy and sleepy magistrates (referred to above in relation to discipline/removal from office), Gibson asks whether Judicial Commissions and tribunal leaders are granted sufficient flexibility to deal with illness in such a way that prevents a truly brilliant, decent magistrate or judge being prematurely pensioned off.

7.30.20 Sick leave

Judges have very generous sick leave – it may be considerably longer than most citizens, as long as it is justified to the head of the relevant tribunal.[183] The non-legislative origin of that leave (that is, being a judge is a tenured office) begs a question as to whether there could be some conventions in place which do not unnecessarily interfere with the independence of a judge and their right to hold office, but might deal with the need for a court to continue

177 T Keim 'Japanese bottom-barer faces court', *Courier Mail*, 18 June 2009, cited in Floyd 'Fitness for trial' (2010). For the list of conduct amounting to contempt, see *R v Ogawa* [2009] QCA 307 at [71] and surrounding paragraphs.
178 *R v Ogawa* [2009] QCA 307 at [113] per Keane JA.
179 Kirby 'Judicial stress and judicial bullying' (2013) 516; and Kirby 'Judicial stress' (1995) 101.
180 M McMurdo 'Sources of stress in judicial life', keynote presentation at Balancing the Demands of Judicial Life Workshop, 31 August 2015, Judicial College of Victoria.
181 Ibid citing Marshall J.
182 F Gibson 'Psychiatric disability and the practising lawyer in Australia' (2012) 20 *Journal of Law and Medicine* 391.
183 See Supreme Court of Queensland, *Annual Report 2007–2008.*

functioning in the event of an extremely long illness.[184] A case which is worth noting in this regard is the recent dispute involving FWC Vice-President Michael Lawler.

THE INTRIGUING CASE OF MICHAEL LAWLER

Mr Lawler is reported to have taken 9 months' sick leave on full salary – $430,000 per year.[185] During that time he is said to have assisted his partner, Kathy Jackson, in her attempt to defend herself against charges of misusing union money for personal benefit.[186] To the amazement of most, he also gave a *Four Corners* interview[187] in which he demonstrated how he (possibly illegally) tape-recorded phone calls he had with other tribunal members. Due to his reported activities whilst on sick leave, Mr Lawler's conduct was the subject of a report by former Federal Court Justice Peter Heeley. Mr Lawler resigned before responding to Federal Parliament on that report. At this stage, the report is not publicly available.

7.30.25 Government administrative arrangements and budgets

In 2014, I wrote about Attorney-General activism.[188] Although many have questioned the appropriateness of judicial activism and media comment, in my view more should be done to explore the boundaries that should be placed around what Attorneys-General can do. My article was written in the context of:

- an Attorney-General announcing in the newspaper that he was planning to split the Queensland Court of Appeal before he actually broached the topic with the Appeals Court President;
- then Solicitor-General Walter Sofronoff QC having resigned;[189] and
- then President of the Industrial Court of Queensland, the late Honourable David Hall, also leaving office.

The Queensland government of which that Attorney-General was a part remained in office for only one term, despite having come to power with one of the largest electoral majorities in the State's history.

---

184   In this connection it is worth noting that the Australian Constitution does not actually observe an Opposition Leader, but conventions do so – without being unconstitutional.

185   See, for example, J Norman 'Michael Lawler: Kathy Jackson's partner quits as Vice President of Fair Work Commission', ABC News, 3 March 2016. Also in this context note that the FWC is not a court directly derived from the Constitution. The Constitution's s 51(xxxv) provides the basic head of power from which the FWC can be established, but the actual legislation that sets it up is separate: the *Kable* principle underscores judicial independence for Federal judges and judges in courts exercising Federal jurisdiction.

186   Ms Jackson lost. See L Floyd 'Jimmy Hoffa: alive well and living in Australia?' (2015) 49(1) *The International Lawyer* 21–48.

187   C Meldrum-Hanna, Kl Toft and E Worthington, 'Jackson and Lawler: inside the eye of the storm', *Four Corners*, ABC TV, 20 October 2015, http://www.abc.net.au/4corners/stories/2015/10/19/4332251.htm.

188   L Floyd 'Punch and Jarrod: the pitfalls of Attorney-General (rather than judicial) activism' (2014).

189   The former Solicitor–General is now Hon Justice Sofronoff, President, Court of Appeal, Supreme Court of Queensland.

In my view, it is worth considering the budgetary arrangements and administrative structures of our courts – not only because that will enhance the administration of justice, but also because any issue (even if only perceived) with such budgets and arrangements can affect the working conditions of judges.[190]

In connection with external forces exerted on the courts, in 2016 I wrote an article on the manner in which the Hon Dyson Heydon AC QC was treated while he was conducting the Trade Union Royal Commission.[191] In brief, some unions alleged apparent bias on the Commissioner's part because he accepted an invitation to give a speech on Sir Garfield Barwick to a dinner that was nominally organised by the Liberal Party but was able to be attended by people of all political persuasions – the entire Bar was invited. It is reasonable to ask whether such allegations were an attempt to smear the Commissioner and discredit the Commission's findings.[192]

A point that might be extrapolated from the above relates to health and bullying. There is such a thing as upstream bullying (bullying by underlings of higher-ups). It is encouraging that some of the luminaries of Australian law, such as Justice Kirby, are speaking about judicial mental health and bullying. As the number of lawyers grows, some may envy those who have done better or entered the profession at an earlier time (most judges, for a start), so care must be taken to avoid vexatious complaints and ensure that complaints about judges are not a form of upstream bullying.

7.30.30 Social media and the Bench

As readers would be aware, social media – Facebook, Instagram, Twitter etc – is becoming more frequently used. Its effects in and on the workplace are being litigated – see Chapter 6. The courts have not been immune to the take-up of such technology.[193] The impact of that technology on the working lives of judges is considered in part in the 2016 study 'Challenges of social media for courts and tribunals'.[194] Questions about that latter issue include:

- How can judges be protected from the misuse of social media by outside parties such as litigants – smear campaigns, attempts to influence the judge etc. Should there be a special offence of misusing social media in this way? How could such misuse be detected before the damage is done?[195]

---

190   See The Honourable Justice Margaret A McMurdo AC, 'The Queensland Court of Appeal: the first 25 years', Australian Academy of Law 2016 Queensland Lecture, 24 October 2016, http:// archive.sclqld.org.au/judgepub/2016/MMcmurdo241016.pdf. In the speech President McMurdo reflected on the departure of the first President, Tony Fitzgerald. The local paper, *The Courier Mail*, questioned whether he had effectively been bullied from office.

191   L Floyd 'Much Ado About Nothing: why accepting an invitation did not make Dyson Heydon AC QC appear biased' (2016) 38.

192   Ibid.

193   A Henderson 'The High Court and the cocktail party from hell: can social media improve community engagement with the courts?' (2016) 25 *Journal of Judicial Administration* 175.

194   Dr M Bromberg-Krawitz 'Challenges of social media for courts and tribunals', Issues paper for Symposium of JCA and Australian Institute of Judicial Administration, May 2016.

195   While it is important to protect the judge from smear campaigns and unnecessary interference, the public should never be unnecessarily silenced.

- In addition to the usual protocols and guidelines curbing judges from speaking out, what restrictions should be placed on the use of social media by judges? What if their personal accounts are hacked?

7.35 Academic employment

University staff are not public servants or servants of the Crown or State, and there is no basis for, or tradition of, regarding universities as an extension of government or part of a government department.[196] *Orr v University of Tasmania* [1956] Tas SR 155 (*Orr*) makes it very clear that Australian academics are mere employees of their universities. They are not tenured officers holding a life appointment, allowing removal only upon the most serious cause. Prior to *Orr*, many academics did not see themselves as employees of their universities.[197]

The fact that university staff are employees permitted the registration of industrial unions and ultimately control by Federal industrial machinery.[198] This allowed the handing down of industrial awards and, more recently, enterprise agreements, and agreement-based transitional instruments[199] that are still in effect.

7.35.05 The nature of employment in universities

There are three awards of direct relevance to Australian universities. The main two are:

- *Higher Education Industry—Academic Staff—Award 2010* (MA 000006)
- *Higher Education Industry—General Staff—Award 2010* (MA 000007).

Another award, the *Educational Services (Post-Secondary Education) Award 2010* (MA 0000075) applies, *inter alia*, to staff employed in foundation and language colleges.

A recent example of an approved enterprise agreement is *The University of Canberra Enterprise Agreement 2015–2017.*[200] This agreement contains clauses covering matters such as organisational change, grievance and dispute resolution, types of employment, flexible working arrangements, severance pay, Aboriginal and Torres Strait Islander employment, probation, performance and development, salaries, superannuation, leave, early retirement, suspension, termination, serious misconduct, senior manager agreements, professional staff, and clauses relating specifically to academic staff, such as those relating to intellectual freedom.

---

196   *Clarke v University of Melbourne* [1979] VR 66 at 73; see also *Re National Tertiary Education Industry Union* [1998] AIRC 589.

197   For example, the Orr supporters, Professors Stout and Wright: see C Pybus *Gross Moral Turpitude: The Orr Case Reconsidered* (William Heinemann, 1993) 74, 75. These academics had difficulty reconciling the notion of academic community with the concept of university as master and academic as servant. Academic employees may also be members of their university, a matter not addressed in *Orr*, which may raise natural justice issues: see CW Bartholomew and PG Nash 'Tenure of academic staff' (1959) 1(5) *Vestes* 11; and Professor JL Montrose 'The legal relation of university and its professors' (1958) 29 *Universities Review* 46. See also *University of Western Australia v Gray* [2008] FCA 498 (First instance decision – French J) at [22].

198   *R v Coldham; Ex parte Australian Social Welfare Union* (1983) 153 CLR 297.

199   Agreement-based transitional instruments include various individual and collective agreements that could be made before 1 July 2009 under the former *Workplace Relations Act 1996* (Cth). They also include Individual Transitional Employment Agreements (ITEAs) that were made during the 'bridging period' (1 July 2009–31 December 2009). These agreements will continue to operate as transitional instruments until terminated or replaced by, for example, Australian Workplace Agreements (AWAs).

200   *University of Canberra Enterprise Agreement 2015–2017* [2016] FWCA 909.

The normal academic contract will include obligations to teach and research, but some academics may be engaged to perform one of these tasks exclusively.

Australian academic contracts usually consist of brief written offer letters which may attempt to incorporate into that contract, or otherwise reference, other university documents including an enterprise agreement, code of conduct or other policies of the university.

An example of an unsuccessful attempt to incorporate certain documents by reference is *Gramotnev v Queensland University of Technology* (2015) 251 IR 448, where the Supreme Court of Queensland Court of Appeal held that, with one exception, *none* of the enterprise agreement, university statutes or employment policies under consideration had achieved contractual status. A subsequent amendment to the orders made in that case clarified that the staff misconduct policy had contractually promised that an allegation of misconduct would be dealt with by the relevant enterprise agreement: *Gramotnev v Queensland University of Technology (No. 2)* [2015] QCA 178. Furthermore, the simple promulgation of 'policy' by a university does not give that policy contractual status; nor does it necessarily bind its employees. This area is now considered in detail. Given the case law and significance of intellectual property to academic employment, particular attention is paid to university policies on intellectual property.

7.35.10 The status of university policy in employment contracts

Policy may gain its enforceability because it becomes part of the delegated legislation of the university, is incorporated into an enterprise agreement, or is included in employment contracts. In other instances, some or all of the content of a policy may be characterised as being within the content of the employer's lawful command because it describes the means by which the command may be achieved.

VICTORIA UNIVERSITY OF TECHNOLOGY *v* WILSON (2004) 60 IPR 392

Enforceability of policy was discussed in detail in this case,[201] in the context of employment law and intellectual property law. In simple terms, two staff members used resources of the university to develop and patent electronic technology relating to international exchange. Much of the work was done outside the university. Two actions were brought against the staff members – breach of contract and breach of fiduciary duty. The former failed because the university's intellectual property policy had not become contractual. The latter action was successful.

The intellectual property policy was not approved by council, nor included in the human resources staff manual, nor within the delegated power of the vice-chancellor or deputy vice-chancellor to approve, and was not a subset of other delegations: 'power to approve a policy which could carry the consequence of substantially altering the rights and obligations of the 3,000 academic staff employed by the university' was seen as a matter requiring a specific delegation.[202]

---

201   For a more recent analysis see *Gramotnev v Queensland University of Technology* (2015) 251 IR 448.
202   *Victoria University of Technology v Wilson* (2004) 60 IPR 382 at [87]–[88].

It was found to be insufficient to send the intellectual property policy to the office of research for publication or to the vice-chancellor's office for entry onto a registry database. Council had approved a research management plan but this did not make reference to the policy and it contained some inconsistencies.

On the facts, it was important that it became policy or was incorporated into contracts of employment because this would have established the link to the contract of employment of the staff members involved, which had made reference to 'policy' in one case and the 'staff manual' in the other.

Nettle J stated the law on ownership of inventions:

> ... unless the contract of employment expressly so provides, or an invention is the product of work which the employee was paid to perform, it is unlikely that any invention made by the employee will be held to belong to the employer.[203]

The fact that the staff were engaged to conduct research was not sufficient *per se* to bring the invention within the fields of economics and international trade so as to be treated as research which they were retained to perform.

Nevertheless, Nettle J held that the opportunity to design the system came to them in their capacities as middle-level employees of the university and they began their work in that capacity, only later resolving to work upon the system in their private capacities and to own the intellectual property rights in the invention. This amounted to a breach of their fiduciary obligations because it is clear 'that a fiduciary is not allowed to put himself in a position where his interest and duty conflict and a fiduciary who profits outside the scope of his undertaking can be accountable if the information about the opportunity to make the profit came to him through his fiduciary position'.[204] There was insufficient disclosure to avoid this obligation.

There are a number of lessons from this case:

- First, universities have to be certain that policy, however described, is enforceable.
- Second, universities should not put themselves in a position where policy is enforceable only by staff, and not by the university itself. A university having established and promulgated a policy may find that it is not able to deny the existence of the policy when it turns out it was invalidly created. Staff who have relied on the policy may nevertheless find they can seek any benefits it purported to confer on them.
- Third, policy can become enforceable via effective delegated legislation, its inclusion in enterprise agreements, and via employment contracts.
- Fourth, policy does not necessarily become enforceable simply by promulgation at council level.
- Finally, *Victoria University of Technology v Wilson* makes another strong point: even if the technicalities of intellectual property law do not apply in a particular case, there remains the strong possibility that staff exploiting a university opportunity will be caught under the law relating to fiduciaries.

---

203   Ibid [104].
204   Ibid [141].

The extent to which a university can claim intellectual property in its inventions was also considered in the case of *University of Western Australia v Gray (No. 20)* (2008) 76 IPR 222; *University of Western Australia v Gray* (2009) 179 FCR 346.[205]

UNIVERSITY OF WESTERN AUSTRALIA v GRAY (NO. 20) (2008) 76 IPR 222; UNIVERSITY OF WESTERN AUSTRALIA v GRAY (2009) 179 FCR 346

Dr Gray was a full-time professor of surgery at the University of Western Australia (UWA) and had signed an employment contract setting out his duties and responsibilities, which included the standard obligations to teach and research.

In addition to the terms of the employment contract, UWA imposed obligations on academics through its Patents and Intellectual Property Regulations.

While at UWA, Dr Gray undertook extensive research into liver and bowel cancers. He developed technologies regarding microspheres for the targeted treatment of tumours,[206] and filed several patents relating to those technologies.

UWA argued that:

(a) Dr Gray had breached an implied term in his employment contract that intellectual property developed in the course of his employment belonged to the university;[207]

(b) Dr Gray had breached his fiduciary obligations to UWA, on the grounds that he should have dealt with his inventions in a way that preserved the benefit of the rights in the inventions for UWA and not obtained any secret profit;[208] and

(c) Dr Gray was bound by UWA's Patent and Intellectual Property Regulations.[209]

The Full Federal Court upheld the decision of the primary judge and held that there was no implied duty on Dr Gray to invent.[210] The primary judge found the following factors critical in declining to imply a term in Dr Gray's employment contract[211] (this was upheld by the Full Court of the Federal Court[212]):

First, Dr Gray had no duty to invent anything.[213] His duty was to undertake research and to encourage research amongst staff and students at UWA.

Second, Dr Gray was free to publish the results of his research and any invention developed during that research 'notwithstanding that such publication might destroy

---

205   *University of Western Australia v Gray (No. 20)* (2008) 76 IPR 222 (First instance decision – French J); and *University of Western Australia v Gray* (2009) 179 FCR 346.

206   Ibid [4].

207   (2008) 76 IPR 222 (First instance decision – French J) at [9] and [12].

208   (2009) 179 FCR 346 at [77].

209   Ibid [75].

210   Ibid [165], citing the first instance decision, (2008) 76 IPR 346 at [1360].

211   (2008) 76 IPR 222 at [1366] (First instance decision – French J).

212   (2009) 179 FCR 346 at [206]–[212].

213   (2008) 76 IPR 222 at [1360] (First instance decision – French J).

the patentability of the invention'.[214] Commenting on this aspect of the case, Cabrelli and Floyd note that the nature of academic employment (teaching, researching, disseminating information, etc) is the antithesis of a commercial entity developing a pure 'profit making' invention.[215]

Third, Dr Gray had collaborated with researchers at other institutions; and

Fourth, Dr Gray had to act in an entrepreneurial manner in securing funding for his research from outside sources.

In the 'absence of implication of terms in law, there was no independent fiduciary obligation of a kind and scope that made [Dr Gray] accountable to university for the inventions, applications for patents or patents'.[216] These claims were based upon the success of the claim – via implied contract – entitling UWA to the inventions. The breach of fiduciary duty claims were not pleaded as misappropriated 'opportunities' claims as was the case in the Victoria University of Technology case[217] referred to above.

UWA also alleged that Dr Gray breached his employment contract by failing to disclose his inventions in accordance with UWA's Patent and Intellectual Property Regulations. The primary judge found that Dr Gray's disclosure obligation was contingent on UWA maintaining the patents committee as required by the regulations. The patents committee had ceased to exist in 1988 and so Dr Gray did not have a corresponding obligation to disclose.[218] The additional barrier for UWA was that the IP regulations were found to be invalid. The primary judge found that that 'UWA was authorised by the UWA Act to make regulations relating to the control and management of its own property. It was not authorised by the Act to make regulations acquiring property from others or interfering with their rights.'[219] The primary judge also noted that 'the only secure way for UWA to acquire rights from its academic staff in respect of intellectual property developed in the course of employment would be by express provision in their contracts of employment'.[220]

UWA's application for special leave to appeal to the High Court was refused on 12 February 2010.

The introduction of intellectual property policies in Australian universities raises other interesting legal issues, some of which have been canvassed by Monotti.[221] But the most recent developments concern how universities have reacted to *UWA v Gray* in terms of their commercialisation of research. (This topic is the subject of one of the review questions at the end of this chapter.)

---

214   Ibid [1360].
215   D Cabrelli and L Floyd 'New light through old windows: restraint of trade in English, Scottish and Australian employment laws – emerging and enduring issues' (2010) 26(2) *The International Journal of Comparative Labour Law and Industrial Relations* 167 at 185.
216   (2009) 179 FCR 346 at [213]–[216].
217   Ibid [214].
218   Ibid [116] and [118], citing the first instance decision, (2008) 76 IPR 222 at [257].
219   (2009) 179 FCR 346 at [119], citing the first instance decision, (2008) 76 IPR 222 at [13].
220   (2008) 76 IPR 222 at [14] (First instance decision – French J).
221   A Monotti, 'Who owns my research and teaching materials: my university or me?' (1997) 19 *Sydney Law Review* 24.

7.35.15 Enterprise agreements

The main legal regime controlling industrial conditions in Australian universities remains the enterprise agreement. This agreement contains a collectively agreed set of conditions governing employment conditions at a specific university. The agreements are negotiated at the individual university level, but because of the presence of the National Tertiary Education Union (NTEU) and other unions, and (to a lesser extent) a national employer body, the Australian Higher Education Industrial Association (AHEIA), there is similarity in these agreements across universities. Nevertheless, they are not uniform as to salary or other content and they are likely to become less uniform at each bargaining round. Some of the content in these agreements can be traced to the *Australian Universities Academic Staff (Conditions of Employment) Award 1988* and a further award made in 1995. These awards were argued and made centrally through the Australian Industrial Relations Commission, and applied to *all* universities. Enterprise agreements are made and applied individually at *each* university. As noted above, the university modern awards are now relevant as the comparator for the better off overall test (BOOT).

In some universities there is an agreement covering academic and general staff; others will have two or more agreements covering different staff categories.

The key terms of academic employment are considered below.

7.35.20 Salary

In earlier times, salary levels and classifications were the same across all Australian public universities because these were set and determined by an independent academic salaries tribunal or under an award. Now salaries for the various academic classifications which have remained in most, but not all, universities, Levels A (associate lecturer), B (lecturer), C (senior lecturer), D (associate professor) and E (professor) are agreed in the enterprise agreement process. The enterprise agreements are not decided at the same time at each university, and accordingly, the amounts awarded at the first universities to reach an enterprise agreement with their staff will be influential upon universities that follow.

A university could choose to offer a staff member a higher salary in an individual contract of employment. This does happen, particularly at Level E, though the extent is unclear. Salaries and other conditions for executive levels higher than Level E – for example, Pro Vice Chancellor, Deputy Vice Chancellor and Vice Chancellor – are not usually governed by the enterprise agreement and are a matter for individual negotiation.

7.35.25 Tenure, workplace security and types of employment

Enterprise agreements do not use concepts such as life tenure or tenure to a certain age. The latter is prohibited, typically, by age discrimination legislation. Enterprise agreements will more likely describe and define conditions relating to continuing, fixed-term and casual appointments.

Typically, enterprise agreements confer no special job or life tenure on a university academic beyond that found in other industries. Older notions of 'tenure' have been replaced by 'continuing appointments'. This is in itself not a dramatic change; the more important principle in universities has always been protection against arbitrary dismissal, because this is quite fundamental to the related notion of academic freedom. Of more concern to academic freedom has been the trend towards fixed-term and casual employment.

As will be seen in detail in the section 'Dismissal in Australian universities', protection against arbitrary dismissal does exist in Australian universities, and these procedures operate to best protect, *inter alia*, academic freedom rights; indeed, they have their origins in this critical aspect of university employment.[222]

7.35.30 Organisational change

Organisational change is such an important issue that it is covered in enterprise agreements in clauses which define workplace change, and require the Vice Chancellor or his or her delegate to notify and consult with employees and relevant unions accordingly.

7.35.35 Disciplinary procedures

These procedures relate to two matters: unsatisfactory performance and misconduct/serious misconduct. The latter is considered below in the context of dismissal. The former typically involves a series of procedures, including the giving of notice to the employee of the unsatisfactory performance, counselling and reasonable opportunities to improve. If there is no improvement the academic may face:

   (i) counselling;

  (ii) formal censure;

 (iii) withholding of a salary step;

 (iv) demotion by one or more salary steps. (Demotion has been held by the Fair Work Commission (FWC) not to amount to a termination of employment provided the enterprise agreement has been complied with.[223]);

  (v) demotion by one or more classification levels;

 (vi) termination of employment.

7.35.40 Misconduct and serious misconduct

A typical definition of serious misconduct is found in the University of Melbourne Enterprise Agreement:

> Serious misconduct means: (a) serious misbehaviour of a kind (or conviction by a Court) which constitutes a serious impediment to the carrying out of a staff member's duties or to

---

222   The historical links between academic freedom and protections against arbitrary dismissal are drawn in JG Jackson '*Orr* to *Steele*: crafting dismissal processes in Australian universities' (2003) 7 *Southern Cross University Law Review* 220

223   See *Lollback v University of Southern Queensland* [2014] FWC 2011.

a staff member's colleagues carrying out their duties; or (b) serious dereliction of the duties required of the position.[224]

That enterprise agreement defines misconduct as:

(a) negligence in the performance of the duties of the position held; or (b) misbehaviour (which will include favouritism); or (c) conduct in breach of the staff member's contract or the University's policies, regulations or procedures that does not constitute serious misconduct.[225]

SOLIMAN v UNIVERSITY OF TECHNOLOGY, SYDNEY (2012) 207 FCR 277

The Full Federal Court decision in this case concerned an anonymous complaint from a student that an academic had given students the contents of the exam questions before the exam, during a class. The academic was subsequently demoted. This decision was challenged on various grounds, including whether the exam questions had in fact been given, whether if they had this would constitute misconduct, and whether the disciplinary action taken was proportionate to the misconduct. The court held that the failure by Fair Work Australia to address submissions on mitigating circumstances and the reasonableness of the Acting Vice Chancellor's decision constituted jurisdictional error and remitted the application to Fair Work Australia. In reaching that decision the Full Court commented that even though what the academic did was not formally defined by the university as misconduct, 'the content of the term "misconduct" is to be informed by those with knowledge of the standards to be maintained by university lecturers and is not confined to only that conduct which has been the subject of specific rules, directions or guidelines'.[226]

7.35.45 Redundancy and retrenchment

Enterprise agreements allow for redundancy and retrenchment of staff. This area would normally address matters such as a decrease in student demand or enrolments, a decision to cease offering a course on a particular campus, financial exigency or technological change. Where redundancy and retrenchment are proposed, the Vice Chancellor normally has to enter into discussions with employees and the union to discuss measures which could avert the need for retrenchment or mitigate its effects, such as redeployment, secondment or voluntary separation.

From time to time, issues will arise as to whether a termination of employment is a genuine redundancy. Thus in *Alizadeh v Central Queensland University* [2015] FWC 4595 the FWC made it clear that the decision to make a person redundant and replace that person with a position requiring higher qualifications (a doctorate) was a redundancy under s 389 of

224   *University of Melbourne Enterprise Agreement 2013* [2014] FWCA 1133 clause 61.7.
225   Ibid clause 61.6.
226   *Soliman v University of Technology Sydney* (2012) 207 FCR 277 at [33].

the *Fair Work Act 2009* (Cth), and did not attract the unfair dismissal provisions of that legislation. And in *Kitanovski v University of Newcastle* [2016] FWC 531 the FWC found that it would not have been reasonable to redeploy an employee within the university, and accordingly it was a genuine redundancy. In *Smith v James Cook University* [2016] FWC 6010 the FWC held that the university made decisions about Professor Smith's position in the context of genuine operational considerations about the future direction of its business: that is, his research expertise did not match those directions. This was also held to be a genuine redundancy.

7.35.50 Workloads

Another matter which has achieved prominence in Australian universities is the establishment of consistent, transparent and fair workload policies. Enterprise agreements typically require union and employee consultation through working parties.

7.40 Dismissal in Australian universities

The topic of dismissal commences with the *Orr* case because this is the highest profile dismissal to occur in Australian universities. The controversy surrounding his dismissal and its 10-year duration ultimately strengthened the growth of unions in Australian universities and caused the universities to look to their dismissal processes to avoid further controversies of the same nature as *Orr*.

ORR v UNIVERSITY OF TASMANIA [1956] TAS SR 155

In 1956, the University of Tasmania summarily dismissed Professor Orr following complaints to the Vice Chancellor regarding a number of matters, including an allegation that Professor Orr had seduced an 18-year-old female student. Summary dismissal caused an outrage, though it was not the first time an academic had been dismissed or forced to resign.[227]

Orr sued the university for wrongful dismissal. Green J found that Orr's contract was one of employment and that the relationship of master and servant applied between the university and him. Green J further found that Orr had used his position to seduce his student. An appeal to the High Court was unsuccessful. Orr maintained his innocence until his death in 1966. The combined Australian staff associations placed a black ban on the filling of Orr's Chair which lasted until 1966, when a settlement resulting in compensation to Orr was reached.

---

227   Examples include Professor Read, University of Adelaide (1878); Professors Irvine (1922) and Brennan (1924) at Sydney University; and Professor Marshall-Hall at Melbourne University (1900). A detailed examination of these and other matters is contained in J Jackson, 'Legal Rights to Academic Freedom in Australian Universities', unpublished PhD thesis, University of Sydney, 2002.

7.40.05 Dismissal processes

The decision in *R v Coldham; Ex parte Australian Social Welfare Union* (1983) 153 CLR 297 allowed the Federal registration of an academic union, further strengthening the industrialisation of Australian universities and the handing down of the *Australian Universities Academic Staff (Conditions of Employment) Award 1988*, a Federal award (the 1988 Award). This provided, *inter alia*, extensive discipline procedures. Dismissal was allowed if recommended by a misconduct investigation committee (MIC), and serious misconduct was defined thus:

> **(a)** In the context of these procedures serious misconduct shall mean:
>
> > (i) serious misbehaviour of a kind which constitutes a serious impediment to the carrying out of the member's duties or to other members carrying out their duties; or
> >
> > (ii) serious dereliction of the duties required of the member's office; or
> >
> > (iii) conviction by a court of competent jurisdiction of an offence of a kind which constitutes a serious impediment to the carrying out of the member's duties or to other members carrying out their duties.

This definition is very similar to that found in many current enterprise agreements.

Serious misconduct was initially to be investigated by the chief executive officer (usually the Vice Chancellor). Where an allegation of serious misconduct warranted further investigation, the Vice Chancellor was required to notify the staff member in writing of the nature of the acts or omissions in sufficient detail to enable the staff member to know the precise nature of the allegations and to respond. The Vice Chancellor could suspend in the interim.

If there was a *prima facie* serious misconduct case, the Vice Chancellor was required to refer the matter to an investigation committee which was to investigate, hear evidence and take submissions, and report, with reasons, on the allegations and whether serious misconduct was found. The Vice Chancellor then had to proceed forthwith to exercise one or more of the following powers:

> (i) dismiss the case and remove any suspension previously placed upon the staff member; or
>
> (ii) censure the staff member, withhold an increment of salary for a period not exceeding 12 months, demote the staff member, or dismiss the staff member from the employment of the university.

The award was interpreted as giving the fact-finding and discretionary judgement as to the seriousness of the infractions to the committee and not to the Vice Chancellor.[228] The respective powers of an investigator or misconduct committee and a Vice Chancellor remain a matter for interpretation in certified agreements.

Rice v University of Queensland [1998] IRCA 9 stated the academic freedom rationale for proper procedures relating to dismissal in a university:

---

228   See *Rice v University of Queensland* [1998] IRCA 9.

> When framing the Award, the parties to it evidently had in mind such matters as the intrinsic social importance of the work of academic staff of universities, and the historical phenomenon that some with much to contribute to such work may not necessarily behave in particularly orthodox ways. It is evident that the parties were intent on doing a number of things aimed, on the one hand, at respect for academic freedom while, on the other, at distinguishing between the legitimate scope of such freedom and behaviour which would make it practically intolerable for the continuation of an academic's employment.[229]

In *Chambers v James Cook University* [1995] IRCA 47, Boulton JR made it clear that the principles of natural justice applied to the operations of a misconduct investigation committee. Boulton JR determined that the academic should be reinstated because the committee's decision was vitiated by errors of law. Specifically, he found that there is a requirement that the matters constituting the alleged serious misconduct must be specifically defined[230] and the employee must be informed of precisely what he/she is charged with.[231] Failure to do so denied natural justice to the employee. There was a further procedural concern in *Chambers*. The committee had allowed evidence of separate allegations of sexual harassment to be given at a common hearing in circumstances where there was the possibility of joint concoction of evidence, which may have destroyed the probative value of that evidence.

The *Universities and Post Compulsory Academic Conditions Award 1995* (the Bryant Award) replaced the 1988 Award. Both the 1988 and 1995 awards have been influential on the content of certified agreements in relation to dismissal clauses, and many universities use a process easily identifiable with those awards, though one which may give further discretion to the Vice Chancellor than that demonstrated in the Award in cases such as *Rice*.

Ideally, the legal protection offered by certified agreements includes rights to:

- written allegations;
- answer and be present before an investigator or committee;
- examine witnesses;
- natural justice;
- a misconduct investigation committee or independent investigator to investigate the matters leading to dismissal or other penalty; and
- an in camera process where the academic may be represented, though not usually by a lawyer.

Some university enterprise agreements have significantly modified the above procedures: *inter alia*, the University of Sydney, Charles Sturt University, the University of Canberra, James Cook University and Murdoch University Certified Agreements, and there appears to be a strong

---

229   *Rice v University of Queensland* [1998] IRCA 9 at [13].
230   *Chambers v James Cook University* [1995] IRCA 48 at [24].
231   Ibid [18].

sectorial trend to replace the misconduct investigation committee with an impartial investigator followed by an appeal process. Thus, the University of Melbourne Enterprise Agreement commences the procedure with an impartial investigator who reports his/her findings to a senior staff member, who in turn may make a recommendation to the Vice Chancellor re disciplinary action.[232] A right of review of the recommendation is given, and a Review and Appeals Committee will consider whether there is sufficient evidence to support the finding of misconduct or serious misconduct, whether procedures have been followed and whether the proposed disciplinary action is in proportion to the level of unsatisfactory performance, misconduct or serious misconduct.[233]

It is imperative that procedural fairness is properly accorded to a person subject to misconduct procedures and that the processes in the enterprise agreement are properly followed. This has been recently illustrated in *Frijters v University of Queensland* [2016] FWC 2746, a case where Professor Frijters was accused by the university of not having obtained ethics clearance for a research paper, 'Still not allowed on the bus: it matters if you're black or white!', which had been published jointly by the professor and his doctoral student and had gained some notoriety in Brisbane.

Commissioner Bissett, in a very detailed analysis, made a number of findings against the university in relation to both not following the enterprise agreement, and denying procedural fairness. These included not having properly appointed a supervisor for Professor Frijters.

A matter that has to be examined under every certified agreement is the extent to which a Vice Chancellor is bound to follow the findings of fact of an investigator or misconduct investigation committee.[234]

An equally important matter is whether the university may ignore dismissal procedures contained in an enterprise agreement. *National Tertiary Education Industry Union v University of Wollongong* (2001) 122 IR 110 held that it cannot.

7.45 Dismissal cases
7.45.05 Avoiding dismissal processes

NATIONAL TERTIARY EDUCATION INDUSTRY UNION v UNIVERSITY OF WOLLONGONG (2001) 122 IR 110

In 2001 the University of Wollongong dismissed Associate Professor Steele without notice. The Vice Chancellor's dismissal letter stated:

---

232   *University of Melbourne Enterprise Agreement 2013* [2014] FWCA 1133 clause 61.
233   Ibid clause 62.
234   *National Tertiary Education Industry Union v Southern Cross University Enterprise Bargaining Agreement 2000* [2003] AIRC 944.

a) that you have engaged in serious misconduct by wilful or deliberate behaviour that is inconsistent with the continuation of your employment and

b) that your conduct has caused serious risk to the reputation of the University of Wollongong, your employer.

Accordingly, pursuant to clause 59 of the Enterprise Bargaining Agreement and S 170CM(1) [c] of the *Workplace Relations Act 1996*, I advise you that your employment with the University of Wollongong is terminated, effective immediately.[235]

Steele's alleged conduct was outlined in the dismissal letter, which alleged that he had claimed in the press that he had been instructed to increase the grades of honours students and that he did not substantiate the claims. Upon being instructed to withdraw the claims, the letter asserts that he refused a request from his head of department to correct the public record and repair the damage done to the University.

The university did not use the misconduct investigation procedures in the *University of Wollongong (Academic Staff) Enterprise Agreement 2000–2003*, and the lawfulness of a Vice Chancellor's unilateral decision that an academic had engaged in serious misconduct became the issue in the subsequent litigation.

Branson J rejected the university's interpretation of the enterprise agreement. In light of immense public interest in the case, Branson J made this comment in an explanatory statement attached to the judgement:

Nor was the Court required to address any issue touching on academic freedom or freedom of speech generally. The only issue on which the Court has ruled is an issue concerning the proper interpretation of the Agreement.[236]

Her decision was appealed by the university but the appeal was rejected by the Full Court of the Federal Court.[237] The court stated:

It is unlikely any trade union, today, would accept a proposed enterprise agreement that permitted the employer to dismiss an employee for misconduct without prior warning and an opportunity to make a defence. Common fairness requires the provision of these rights. It is disappointing to find a university, of all employers, claiming not to be under an obligation of common fairness.[238]

There have been other cases involving dismissal in Australian universities.

---

235   The dismissal letter is reproduced in the April 2001 *NTEU National Industry Bulletin* at 2.
236   *National Tertiary Education Industry Union v University of Wollongong* (2001) 122 IR 110 Explanatory Statement, para 6.
237   *University of Wollongong v National Tertiary Education Industry Union* [2002] FCAFC 85.
238   Ibid [35].

7.45.10 Refusal to obey directions in the academic workplace

MILLER *v* UNIVERSITY OF NEW SOUTH WALES [1999] AIRC 1233

This is a case involving the refusal to obey a direction in the workplace.[239] Dr Miller, an associate professor in the School of Physics at UNSW argued before Senior President Harrison of the Australian Industrial Relations Commission (AIRC) that his dismissal was harsh, unjust or unreasonable under s 170CE of the *Workplace Relations Act 1996* (Cth). Miller had been directed by his superior on a number of occasions to take on the position of first-year laboratory director (FYLD) within the School of Physics. He refused to do so, alleging, *inter alia*, that the job would significantly lessen his time for research. Eventually, the Vice Chancellor referred his continued refusal to take on the FYLD task to a Misconduct Investigation Committee.

Dr Miller had argued that it was not lawful to require him to undertake that particular task. Position classification standards at UNSW were examined. These were part of the general conditions of appointment and were also included in a schedule in the enterprise agreement. The FYLD task was within those standards, and accordingly it was lawful to require him to undertake the task.

Significant further litigation ensued on various technical matters, with some measure of victory to Dr Miller, but the original finding of a failure to obey a reasonable and lawful direction and that the dismissal was not harsh, unjust or unreasonable was not overturned.[240]

SAIRA *v* NORTHERN TERRITORY UNIVERSITY (1992) 109 FLR 46

In this case, Saira was found to be validly dismissed for serious misconduct under the serious dereliction of duty limb for failing to deliver four classes after being formally directed to do so. The relevant award was the *Australian Universities Academic Staff (Conditions of Employment) Award 1988*. Kearney J, of the Supreme Court of the Northern Territory, found that the definition of serious misconduct contained an intent element, but 'it is sufficient if the staff member intentionally engaged in conduct which, in all the circumstances in which he engaged in that conduct, it is fairly assessed as a serious dereliction of the duties of his office'.[241] Holding that the academic had intentionally failed to teach, the judge also noted that the academic had failed to avail himself of a complaints procedure after being advised to do so by his supervisor.

---

239   http://www.austlii.edu.au/cgi-bin/disp.pl/au/cases/cth/IRCommA/1999/1233.html.
240   *Miller v University of New South Wales* [2001] FCA 182 at [486], and *Miller v University of New South Wales* (2003) 132 FCR 147.
241   *Saira v Northern Territory University* (1992) 109 FLR 46 at [31].

WILKS v UNIVERSITY OF NEWCASTLE [2016] FWC 6005

In *Wilks* an employee was found to have engaged in serious misconduct by a Committee of Inquiry and was subsequently terminated by the university. He subsequently argued before the FWC that he had been unfairly dismissed. The Commission found no evidence of unfair dismissal and found that the university had defensible reasons for dismissing Dr Wilks. These included the finding that he persistently denigrated his colleagues in written communications which breached the university's code of conduct, and despite directions from his supervisor not to do so. Commissioner Saunders noted: 'Employers are entitled to issue reasonable and lawful directions in the form of policies, procedures and directives and employees are required to conform to such standards in the workplace.'[242] Dr Wilks did not raise any argument related to academic freedom in relation to his speech.

7.45.15 Plagiarism

PETRINA MARIA QUINN v CHARLES STURT UNIVERSITY [2006] AIRC 96

In this case the AIRC found that a member of the general staff who was a senior member of the university's Centre for Enhancing Learning and Teaching had been validly dismissed for plagiarism, and her application for reinstatement was refused. The university argued that 'plagiarism is of a serious nature within a university and constitutes serious misconduct and a form of academic fraud'.[243] Commissioner Roberts continued:

> ... Dr Quinn was guilty of plagiarism in that she used substantial sections of the work of others in papers to which she attached her name. The attachment of her name to the three papers clearly claims ownership of them and her assertion of copyright over two of the papers reinforces my view ...
>
> Dr Quinn was a long term member of the University staff, holding a senior position which partly dealt with the development of strategies to minimise student plagiarism. The concept of plagiarism and its importance within a university must have been apparent to her.

He found that the termination was not harsh, unjust or unreasonable.

---

242   *Wilks v University of Newcastle* [2016] FWC 6005 at [149]. An appeal to the Full Bench of the FWC against this decision was dismissed: *Wilks v University of Newcastle* [2016] FWCFB 7187.

243   *Petrina Maria Quinn v Charles Sturt University* [2006] AIRC 96.

7.45.20 Inappropriate behaviour with a student

The *Orr* case discussed above demonstrates just how seriously courts and universities take allegations of sexual misconduct.

M v AUSTRALIAN NATIONAL UNIVERSITY [1996] IRCA 411

In this serious case, Moore J, of the Australian Industrial Court, made this finding:

> On the evening of 27 December 1991 the applicant abused his position as an employee of the University by pressing himself sexually on a student in the way she described in her evidence. The University had a valid reason to terminate his employment.[244]

Moore J commented that M's behaviour involved a gross abuse of his position within the university and his position as the de facto sponsor of the international student.[245]

SHANAHAN AND UNIVERSITY OF WESTERN SYDNEY [2005] AIRC 473

In *Shanahan*, a number of female students had complained about a lecturer's inappropriate behaviour. A misconduct investigation committee recommended his dismissal, which the Vice Chancellor implemented. In rejecting an appeal from the lecturer against dismissal the AIRC described his behaviour as 'particularly bizarre' and 'totally unacceptable', and found that his termination was not harsh, unjust or unreasonable. The Commission noted that a university has a duty of care to protect its students from the behaviour of a staff member which showed a continued failure to have regard to the proper boundaries between staff and students. This was so regardless of the cause of the behaviour. The lecturer had been diagnosed as bi-polar, but evidence suggested that he had poor insight into his condition with only an intermittent approach to seeking treatment. The Commission concluded:

> The University should certainly not be put in the position where it would have to monitor closely both Mr. Shanahan's conduct and his psychiatric care. It is simply not reasonable to expect the University to continue to employ him as a lecturer in regular contact with young students under those circumstances.[246]

The Commission further noted that it was not possible to be confident that the lecturer would not commit similar conduct in the future.

---

244   *M v Australian National University* [1996] IRCA 411.
245   Ibid.
246   *Shanahan and University of Western Sydney* [2005] AIRC 473.

Medical assessment of staff

In *Shaw v University of Queensland* (1999) 46 AILR 4-120 the university was held to have acted appropriately in requiring a staff member to attend a doctor for medical assessment.

Misappropriation

In *Dadour v University of Western Australia* [2016] FWC 2969 Professor Dadour was found to have no legitimate basis for invoices totalling $38,000 he sent to the university, and accordingly was not able to resist his dismissal, nor able to show that the dismissal was harsh, unjust or unreasonable. Commissioner Williams found that his actions amounted to misappropriation.

Outside work

Universities will normally have policies or provisions in enterprise agreements dealing with whether employees are able to engage in outside work and to what extent. In *Will v Deakin University* [2015] FWC 3130 Dr Will was found to have engaged in serious misconduct because he used university resources to promote his own interests. He was found to have breached a term of his contract and university policy by engaging in outside work in circumstances where he was well aware of the outside work policy. Accordingly, he could not establish that he had been unfairly dismissed.

The holding of political opinions

In *Heathcote v University of Sydney* [2014] FCCA 613 Dr Heathcote unsuccessfully argued, before Driver J in the Federal Court, that his termination was unlawful and was due to his holding certain political opinions. The court found, however, that the redundancy process which preceded the termination had not been undertaken for a prohibited purpose. Had Dr Heathcote been terminated for holding and expressing a political opinion this would have been an academic freedom issue.

7.50 Speech and dismissal: academic freedom

The issue of academic freedom and dismissal raises questions about the basic nature of a university as well as about the need for employees to comply with common law duties (obeying reasonable directions, protecting confidentiality, etc). As discussed in Chapter 2, under common law an employer may give lawful and reasonable directions[247] to an employee, which must be obeyed. This could include a direction not to speak publicly on a certain matter or to curb the manner of disruptive speech, as in *Wilks v University of Newcastle*, above.

---

247   *R v Darling Island Stevedoring & Lighterage Co. Ltd; Ex parte Halliday; Ex parte Sullivan* (1938) 60 CLR 601, per Dixon J. On whether an employee must obey a lawful but unreasonable order, see GJ McCarry 'The employee's duty to obey unreasonable orders' (1984) 58 *ALJR* 327. See also *Miller v University of New South Wales* (2001) 110 IR 1.

LANE *v* FASCIALE (1993) 35 AILR 399

Another example is *Lane v Fasciale*.[248] Lane continued to speak about the closure of the high school where he was principal after having being directed by his employer to stop. Beach J found this to be a reasonable instruction and that the speech was not within the scope of his contract. The absence of an express or implied term in his contract forbidding him to make public statements did not assist Lane. His *bona fide* belief that he had good grounds to comment on matters he thought against the interest of his students was no defence.

In the opinion of the judge, Lane 'was completely free to express his dissent to anyone within the (relevant) hierarchy'.[249] But what he was 'instructed not to do was to express his views publicly because it was perceived by Fr Fasciale that if he continued to do so that could have a disrupting effect upon the College'.[250]

An employee also has duties of confidentiality and good faith. These fundamental obligations could be breached if confidential information were disclosed. A slightly more controversial situation is where there is a public interest in the disclosure of the confidence. It has been held there is 'no confidence as to the disclosure of iniquity',[251] though in *A v Hayden* (1984) 156 CLR 532, Gibbs CJ limited a statement made in *Allied Mills Industries Pty Ltd v Trade Practices Commission* (1981) 34 ALR 105 that 'the public interest in the disclosure . . . of iniquity will always outweigh the public interest in the preservation of private and confidential information' to 'serious crime'.[252] Whistleblower protection legislation may also be of assistance to the employer here. Given this common law context, are there any special privileges that protect academics from dismissal for speech in universities?

7.50.05 Is there a concept of academic freedom in Australia?

The meaning, history and law relating to academic freedom in Australia has been considered in far more detail elsewhere.[253] There have been few occasions when the Australian judiciary has discussed the meaning of academic freedom.

---

248   Supreme Court of Victoria No. BC9304146 (Butterworths Online unreported judgements).
249   Ibid.
250   Ibid.
251   *Gartside v Outram* (1856) 26 LJ Ch. 113.
252   *A v Hayden* (1984) 156 CLR 532 at 545. Dawson and Wilson JJ also noted, at 572: 'It follows that while there may be cases where the triviality of the alleged breaches of the criminal law will not lead a court to withhold relief by way of injunction to restrain a threatened breach of a duty of confidentiality such a submission cannot succeed in this case.'
253   J Jackson 'When can speech lead to dismissal in a university?' (2005) 10 *Australia and New Zealand Journal of Law and Education* 23; 'Express rights to academic freedom in Australian public university employment' (2005) 9 *Southern Cross University Law Review* 107; 'Implied contractual rights to academic freedom' (2006) 10 *Southern Cross University Law Review* 139.

BURNS v AUSTRALIAN NATIONAL UNIVERSITY (1982) 40 ALR 707

In *Burns v Australian National University* Ellicot J described academic freedom as going to the very heart of the university:

> It is vital to the fulfilment of the University's functions as an independent educational institution committed to the search for truth that the tenure of its professorial staff be free from arbitrary attack. I can think of no principle more basic to the existence of a university in a free society. The notion that in the involuntary termination of a professor's appointment it is merely acting under the terms of appointment and not under its basic statute as well, in my view, debases the very principle upon which the university is founded – academic freedom.[254]

In the Linke inquiry into academic freedom in Australia, the following knowledge discovery rationale was provided for academic freedom:

> Academic freedom is basic to the effective operation of higher education institutions in democratic countries. Freedom to inquire, to speak and to publish is the essential ingredient of academic life that secures the advancement and transmission of knowledge and understanding.[255]

It is accordingly a fundamental concept, well worthy of protection at the individual academic level. While this is certainly true, it is instructive to note from US jurisprudence certain matters which do *not* fall under First Amendment protection and are unlikely to come within the ambit of academic freedom in this country either:[256] teaching style;[257] variation by a teacher of curriculum content;[258] a university's demands to lower standards;[259] evaluation of performance, including the use of student evaluations;[260] grievances relating to departmental administration and curriculum;[261] criticising a colleague's tenure denial;[262] and opposing an appointment.[263]

---

254   *Burns v Australian National University* (1982) 40 ALR 707 at 717–18, quoted in Senate Standing Committee on Education and the Arts 'Tenure of academics' (Commonwealth of Australia, 1981) 4.

255   RD Linke 'Report on academic freedom, institutional autonomy and related responsibilities' University of Wollongong, November 1990, 13.

256   WA Kaplin and BA Lee *The Law of Higher Education* (Jossey Bass, 3rd ed, 1995) 306–12.

257   *Hetrick v Martin*, 480 F 2d 705 (1973).

258   *Clark v Holmes*, 474 F 2d 928 (1972).

259   *Lovelace v Southeastern Massachusetts University*, 793 F 2d 419 (1989), but compare *Parate v Isibor*, 868 F 2d 821 (1989).

260   *Carley v Arizona Bd of Regents*, 737 P 2d 1099 (1987), but compare *Cooper v Ross*, 472 F Supp 802 (1979).

261   MW Finkin 'Intramural speech, academic freedom and the First Amendment' (1988) 66 *Texas LR* 1326.

262   Ibid.

263   Ibid.

Protection against arbitrary dismissal of academics for what they have had to say could arise in various ways:

(a)   via adequate and proper dismissal processes (covered earlier);

(b)   under a general or university statute which expressly or impliedly requires the university to protect academic freedom as an essential part of its knowledge discovery object;[264]

(c)   under an academic's contract of employment which confers directly, or indirectly, express or implied rights to academic freedom;[265]

(d)   under an enterprise agreement which confers express academic freedom rights;[266] or

(e)   under university policy which may prevent (estop) the university from denying the existence of an academic freedom right at that university.[267]

7.50.10 Under statute

Australia does not have a direct legal guarantee of academic freedom. This can be contrasted to South Africa, the UK, New Zealand and Ireland,[268] countries which gained academic freedom protection at law during a time when the Australian Vice Chancellors Committee did not support the introduction of such measures.[269]

Australian universities and other higher education providers (HEPs) are now regulated under the *Tertiary Education Quality and Standards Agency Act 2011* (Cth), which mandates a Higher Education Standards Framework (HESF). The Framework does make reference to academic freedom, imposing on governing bodies of HEPs an obligation to take 'steps to develop and maintain an institutional environment in which freedom of intellectual inquiry is upheld and protected'.[270] Later the Framework lists, as part of the criteria for HEP status, that the HEP has 'a clearly articulated higher education purpose that includes a commitment to and support for free intellectual inquiry in its academic endeavours'.[271]

In addition, some university statutes make a passing reference to academic freedom. For example, the legislation establishing each public university in NSW was amended in 2001 to include the following object and function, which also stresses the free inquiry role:

---

264   J Jackson 'Implied contractual rights to academic freedom' (2006) 10 *Southern Cross University Law Review* 160.

265   Ibid 139.

266   J Jackson 'Express rights to academic freedom in Australian public university employment' (2005) 9 *Southern Cross University Law Review* 107.

267   Ibid 132.

268   Legislation passed at that time included *Constitution of the Republic of South Africa 1996* s 16; *Education Reform Act 1988* (UK) s 202; *Education Act 1989* (New Zealand) s 161; and *Universities Act 1997* (Ireland) s 14.

269   Letter sent by the Chairman of the AVCC, Professor Brian Wilson, to the Minister for Education at that time. Copy of letter to the Hon Peter Baldwin, Minister for Higher Education and Employment Services, undated, University of Queensland Archives S435.

270   Higher Education Standards Framework para 6.1.4. This was established under s 58 of the *Tertiary Education Quality and Standards Agency Act 2011* (Cth).

271   Higher Education Standards Framework Part B1.1.

(1) The object of the University is the promotion, within the limits of the University's resources, of scholarship, research, free inquiry, the interaction of research and teaching, and academic excellence.

(2) The University has the following principal functions for the promotion of its object: ...

(b) the encouragement of the dissemination, advancement, development and application of knowledge informed by free inquiry.[272]

Under statute, in the courts, and internationally, academic freedom is a defining and universal feature of a university. But is it merely hope lost in aspiration, or does it have legal meaning which may impact on the rights and obligations of the university and its members?

7.50.15 Express academic freedom protection

If in fact the contract imposes a research and teaching duty, the employing university should put in place conditions necessary for the achievement of the employee obligation. If universities do not place limitations on the precise nature of that research or teaching, academics may have quite a wide ambit in the nature of their research, with a commensurate level of academic freedom as a necessary incident to their work. If academics are employed to carry out a very specific research task, they may well find that on the conclusion of that task they may be made redundant.[273]

In codes of conduct

Many universities now have codes of conduct which address such matters as outside employment, conflict of interests, corruption, computer and other university equipment usage policy, staff and student relationships and rights to make public comment, or more direct clauses on academic freedom.

If universities have carefully drafted appointment letters they can ensure that a code of conduct has contractual force. But where it is not seen as contractual there remains the possibility that a code which purports to create employee rights may prevent the university denying the existence of those rights, under the doctrine of promissory estoppel.[274] If a code of conduct promised a particular level of academic freedom, the university could not deny statements in the code where an academic had relied on the code to their detriment, whether or not the code was contractual. As a matter of administrative law, the university must follow its own statutes and by-laws.[275]

In enterprise agreements

Universities may seek to impose restrictions on speech; for example, by requiring approval before commentary on internal affairs is made. If such a policy is contractual or contained in an

---

272 *Universities Legislation Amendment (Financial and Other Powers) Act 2001* (NSW).
273 See *Smith v James Cook University* [2016] FWC 6010.
274 See *Waltons Stores (Interstate) Ltd v Maher* (1988) 164 CLR 387.
275 Nevertheless, access to administrative law remedies may be difficult: see *Griffith University v Tang* (2005) 221 CLR 99; *Australian National University v Lewins* (Unreported, Federal Court of Australia Full Court, Davies J, Kiefel J, Lehane J, 18 July 1996).

enterprise agreement, and not ultra vires the university, it will the enforceable. Some universities have adopted quite detailed academic freedom clauses.

For example, the University of Adelaide Enterprise Agreement provides:

2.6.1 Academic Freedom

The University is committed to the preservation and protection of the scholarly values of Academic Freedom. Academic Freedom means the freedom of academic staff members to engage in critical enquiry, intellectual discourse and public controversy without fear or favour but does not include the right to harass, intimidate or vilify or to maliciously damage the reputation of the University.

2.6.2 Staff Rights

The University acknowledges that all staff members, without fear of discrimination, are entitled to express freely their opinion about the institution or system in which they work, provided that such free expression does not include the right to harass, intimidate or vilify or to maliciously damage the reputation of the University. This includes freedom from institutional censorship and freedom to participate in professional or representative bodies or associations.[276]

The University of Adelaide clauses reflect well on that university. Academic freedom is not limited to the narrow confines of a particular discipline area, and the rights of academics are clearly described. The placement of the clause in the enterprise agreement removes any uncertainty as to its legal enforceability, at least for staff bound by the enterprise agreement. Other clauses, such as clause 44.3 of the University of Canberra Enterprise Agreement,[277] are narrower, and limit the speech right to 'disseminate their views in areas of their expertise', thereby creating inherent definitional issues at to what these areas may be. The HESF references to intellectual inquiry are not so limited.

7.50.20 Implied academic freedom protection

There are also those university academics who do not have certified agreements, or academic freedom protection in their particular agreement, or in a code of conduct, or expressly in their contract. For this group we have to determine whether it is possible that academic freedom could arise as an implied contractual term.[278]

Breen v Williams (1996) 186 CLR 71 and earlier cases establish that in Australia a term can be implied into a contract by a court. Courts will not imply a term where the contract expressly provides to the contrary, if the term is not clearly definable or just to make a contract reasonable.[279] Nor can the implied term device be used to make an industrial award or an enterprise agreement enforceable as a contract.[280]

A business efficacy term may be included if the parties have not spelt out their contract in full and the implication of the particular term is necessary for the reasonable or effective

276   *University of Adelaide Enterprise Agreement 2014–2017* [2014] FWCA 8614.
277   *University of Canberra Enterprise Agreement 2015–2017* [2016] FWCA 909.
278   Jackson 'Express rights to academic freedom in Australian public university employment' (2005) 107.
279   In *Scally v Southern Health and Social Services Board* [1941] 4 All ER 563 the House of Lords expressly denied that they were doing this (at 572).
280   *Byrne v Australian Airlines Ltd* (1995) 185 CLR 410.

operation of a contract of that nature: see *BP Refinery (Westernport) Pty Ltd v Shire of Hastings* (1977) 180 CLR 266. It has been argued elsewhere in some detail that a business efficacy academic freedom term is necessary to enable an academic to carry out their teaching and research duties and functions at the individual level and the university to discharge its statutory functions at the societal level.[281]

A custom and usage term exists where there is a well-known and acquiesced-in term which has been established by mercantile usage, professional practice or a past course of dealings. Persons making a contract in that situation must reasonably be able to be presumed to have imported it into their contract. As described elsewhere,[282] there is now strong evidence of Australian university traditions of academic freedom which have been built on British inheritance. Admittedly, it is difficult to establish a custom and usage implied term, but there remains a possibility that a form of academic freedom might be implied under this test.

So what can be said with more certainty in relation to implied terms? We can at least say that there is an obligation to be professional. In a school context this has been interpreted in the UK in *Sim v Rotherham Metropolitan Borough Council* [1986] 3 WLR 851 to mean: 'School teachers are members of a profession, are entitled to be so regarded, and ought to be so regarded. They are employed in a professional capacity ... School teachers have professional obligations towards the pupils in their schools. Their contractual duties must include at the least the duty to discharge these obligations.'[283]

In *Victoria University of Technology v Wilson* (2004) 60 IPR 392, Nettle J noted that the activities of the School where the academic was located would inform the content of the academic's research duties.[284] Academics have also been described as professionals with fiduciary obligations, who must avoid conflicts of interest and duty and may not gain at the university's expense.[285] In *Rigg v University of Waikato* [1984] 1 NZLR 149, a lecturer, Rigg, and a student, Buchanan, falsely claimed in a student newspaper that a university laboratory had probably contributed to the deaths of at least four students, and that there was a university cover-up. Rigg petitioned the Visitor against his dismissal from the university. Acting for the Visitor, the Commissaries rejected his claims that his academic freedom had been impinged, noting that universities:

> ought not to use their legal powers to discipline a member of academic staff for conduct which truly falls within the scope of the concept of academic freedom of thought and expression ... The only justification which we can see for a special right to freedom of expression in a university environment is the need for academics, whether teachers or students, to feel free to pursue the search for knowledge and learning and truth without fear of institutional disciplinary action being used to divert them from those purposes in order to force conformity with views held by the university authority.[286]

---

281   Jackson 'Implied contractual rights to academic freedom' (2006) 196.
282   Ibid 139.
283   *Sim v Rotherham Metropolitan Borough Council* [1986] 3 WLR 851 at 870.
284   *Victoria University of Technology v Wilson* (2004) 60 IPR 392 at [109].
285   Ibid [149] per Nettle J.
286   *Rigg v University of Waikato* [1984] 1 NZLR 149 at 207. This is a report of the university's Visitor.

This freedom, which was not an 'uninhibited licence', did not exist without linked responsibilities.[287] Nor was it to be seen as an extramural utterance.

The academic must act professionally in his or her teaching and research, and the university must act in accordance with its statutory obligations. In summary, where a university has not introduced an express term covering academic freedom, there is a possibility that a term as below could be implied, adding an overtone of professionalism to an academic's teaching and writing:

> Where an Australian university academic has legal obligations to teach and to research there are attendant duties to speak and to write in a responsible and professional manner. That professionalism carries with it further obligations to not restrict the speech or writing of colleagues or the learning of students, to work within the law, disclose limitations in the research, and not represent speech as that of the university or colleagues. If the academic choses to criticise the university he/she may do so but that speech or writing carries the same attendant professional obligations as any other speech.[288]

Apart from noting the overarching requirement of professionalism, it is instructive to note what is *not* part of that professionalism. For example, in the US there are no rights to:

(a)   break the law;

(b)   engage in hate speech or incite violence;[289]

(c)   engage in vulgar language that has no academic function;[290]

(d)   defame;[291]

(e)   prevent others exercising their academic freedom or speech rights; for example, by requiring students to pray before a class.[292]

Obviously, these matters are not binding in Australia, though very extensive US jurisprudence in the area of academic freedom could inform our courts.

7.50.25 Reinstatement

Under the *Fair Work Act* ss 190 and 191 there is a reinstatement jurisdiction, as demonstrated by the reinstatement of an expert in literacy, learning and numeracy, Dr Ann Lawless, following her unfair dismissal.[293] Such reinstatements are not common.

Reinstatement was not ordered in the case of *Jin v University of Newcastle* [2013] FWC 1049, even though Deputy President Smith of the FWC had found that Professor Jin was

---

287   Ibid.
288   Jackson 'Implied contractual rights to academic freedom' (2006) 198.
289   *Adamian v* Jacobsen, 523 F 2d 929 (1975). See also RH Miller 'The role of academic freedom in defining the faculty employment contract' (1981) 31 *Case Western Reserve Law Review* 628.
290   *Martin v Parish*, 805 F 2d 583 (1986). See also *Di Bona v Matthews*, 269 Cal Rep 882 (1990) and *Wilks v University of Newcastle* [2016] FWC 6005.
291   *Rigg v University of Waikato* [1984] 1 NZLR 149.
292   *Lynch v Indiana State University Board*, 378 NE 2d 900 (1978) at 905.
293   See *Lawless v Charles Sturt University* [2015] FWC 8859.

guilty of misconduct – not serious misconduct – and dismissal was not an available remedy for mere misconduct. Professor Jin had been dismissed for serious misconduct in relation to the administration of research grants, but the Deputy President doubted whether there was any wilful and deliberate behaviour. He held that compensation was the appropriate remedy.

7.50.30 Final remarks

The decision in *Orr* was a watershed in the development of modern industrial relations in Australian universities. It occurred when academics did not regard themselves as employees of their university, but rather saw themselves *as* the university. In this they had badly miscalculated at the political level, but a positive outcome, from their point of view, was that eventually they were able to organise and register as an industrial union.

The industrialisation of the university has given rise to a university workplace that has much in common with other workplaces and industries, and that is governed by the FWC. In this workplace university employers and unions/employees fight over the terms of enterprise agreements both initially, at the enterprise level, and in commissions and courts later at the individual level, where retrenchment and dismissal are quite common and older notions of collegiality and community battle with modern concerns around casualisation, workloads, bullying, harassment and discrimination.

SUMMARY

There is a separation of powers between the legislature, executive and judiciary, although the fact that Ministers are responsible for their government departments slightly blurs the line between the first two of these.

The *Public Service Act* governs the employment of public servants and seeks to provide flexibility (by devolving management functions to departments, for example) as well as unification of the service as a whole (by providing core values which all public servants should abide by, for example). Those values extend to after-hours conduct. There are questions as to whether there can be abuse of that flexibility in investigations. There are also continuing questions as to how changes in the ways in which government works (such as increased use of contractors and an increasing influence of ministerial staff who may be highly political) can be managed. There are also continuing developments on whistle-blowers. There is a growing body of public service theory.

Judges are not employees: they are statutory office-holders. The hallmark of their role or calling is independence – and our good governance rests upon that. There are many provisions and developments concerning judicial appointment and removal from office. There are also new issues such as judicial stress, safety, bullying and use of social media. There have been calls for making judges more accountable, but those calls are sometimes based on a misunderstanding of the nature and quality of the Australian judiciary.

Academics are not officers. Their employment is governed by a mix of contract and other kinds of bargains. A traditional hallmark of academic life is said to be academic freedom, but at times that concept appears fragile. There is a link between funding and employment. One key area of development is intellectual property and the degree to which the academic and employing university deals with money gained from inventions and research (the commercialisation of research).

REVIEW QUESTIONS

1.   (a)   At the time of writing, the Commonwealth whistleblower laws were under review and there was no significant case law on their operation. What is the outcome of that review? Is there any recent case law? What might the effect of the recent laws be on previously decided cases?

(b)   *Citizen Four* is a docudrama on the whistleblowing activities of former CIA operative Edward Snowden in the US and the role of Wikileaks in his avoiding prosecution. Analyse the relationship between whistleblower legislation and national security protection in Australian law – are there significant differences between the Australian and the US positions?

2.   The complexity of public service employment should now be clear. Draw a diagram of the departments and offices that govern public service employment and employment policy. Include in the diagram the pathways for dealing with dismissal and discipline etc, including any potential avenue for judicial review.

3.   The Queensland government led by Campbell Newman only lasted one term, although it had started its period in office with one of the largest majorities in Queensland's history. That government was roundly criticised by the Law Society, Bar Association and some academics as fundamentally misunderstanding the separation of powers and the work of judges. Analyse the actions of the former government and why those societies, associations and academics reacted as they did.

4.   Sally was a Law Professor at X University. Her specialty was employment law. In the course of a restructure that coincided with an enterprise bargaining round, Sally observed what she regarded as unfair, damaging or illegal conduct on the part of her employing university. The restructure seemed to target highly trained and skilled staff who had been somewhat trouble-some (they had complained about management), while leaving in place academics who did not publish and who had no PhD. The enterprise bargaining round sought to remove all references to academic freedom and also sought to benefit those who favoured non-union bargaining. Sally decided to speak out against this and wrote a stinging article in the local newspaper about her employer. X University then wrote to her stating that she was in breach of her employment contract. Sally now seeks your advice on her legal position. If new facts are added, and Sally is chastised because she has written about the proven ethical breaches of one of the major donors to the university (who is now threatening to withdraw financial support), what would her position be?

5.   Group exercise: research the responses of Australian universities to *University of Western Australia v Gray (No. 20)* (2008) 76 IPR 222; *University of Western Australia v Gray* (2009) 176 FCR 346. How is the issue of research commercialisation being approached? Have universities heeded the obiter of French J's first instance judgement?

FURTHER READING

Public sector employment

J Allsop 'Values in public law' (2016) 13 *Judicial Review* 53–77.

S Argument 'The Strathclyde Review on Secondary Legislation and the Primacy of the House of Commons: possible lessons for Australia' (2016) 27 *Public Law Review* 167–72.

H Dickinson, M Katsonis, A Kay, J O'Flynn and A Tiernan (eds) *Australian Journal of Public Administration* (2015).

S Drake and S Mason 'Frank, fearless and apolitical' (2016) *Ethos* 240 14–15.

M O'Donnell and C Roles 'The *Fair Work Act* and worker voices in the Australian Public Service' (2013) 34 *Adelaide Law Review* 93–117.

C Roles 'Redundancy in the Australian Public Service: some critical reflections' (2013) 41 *Federal Law Review* 41.

Judicial 'work'

S Bogaerts and T Hajan 'Work pressure and sickness absenteeism among judges' (2014) 21 *Psychiatry, Psychology and Law* 92–111.

J Johnston, P Keyzer, M Pearson, S Roderick and A Wallace 'The courts and social media: what do judges and court workers think?' (2013) 25 *Judicial Officers Bulletin.*

W Martin 'Judicial Council on cultural diversity' (2015) 24 *Journal of Judicial Administration* 214–22.

C Strever 'Judging stress' (2015) 89 *Law Institute Journal* 29–32.

F Wheeler 'Constitutional limits on extra-judicial activity by state judges: Wainchu and the conundrum of incompatibility' (2015) 37 *Sydney Law Review* 301–27.

Academic employment

K Blake and A Watkins 'Participation of casual and sessional employees in enterprise agreement ballots: the Full Federal Court says only those "employed at the time" can vote' (2015) 26 *Employment Law Bulletin* 119–21.

P Butler and R Mulgan 'Can academic freedom survive performance-based research funding?' (2013) 44 *Victoria University of Wellington Law Review* 487–519.

M Cochrane 'Protecting intellectual property in employment' (2016) 29 *Australian Intellectual Property Law Bulletin* 66–8.

JJ Furedy 'Free speech and the issue of academic freedom: is the Canadian velvet totalitarian disease coming to Australian campuses?' (2011) 30 *University of Queensland Law Journal* 279–86.

J Macken 'Interim re-instatement in unfair dismissal cases' (2016) 7 *Workplace Review* 5–8.

J Pila 'Academic freedom and the courts' (2010) 126 *Law Quarterly Review* 347–51.

Deep background

G Appleby, N Aroney and T John *The Future of Australian Federalism: Comparative and Interdisciplinary Perspectives* (Cambridge University Press, 2012).

R Hirschl *Towards Juristocracy: The Origins and Consequences of the New Constitutionalism* (Harvard University Press, 2004).

RA Katzmann (ed.) *Judges and Legislators: Towards Institutional Comity* (The Brookings Institute, 1988).

I McLeod *Judicial Review* (Barry Rose, 1998).

S Ratnapala 'The discipline of the separation of powers', PhD thesis, University of Queensland (1994).

8 SPECIALIST LEGISLATION

8.05 Workplace health and safety

8.05.05 Introduction

In addition to the *Fair Work Act 2009* (Cth) and common law, important allied legislation guides and shapes the employment relationship. Broadly speaking, workplace health and safety laws facilitate a safe working environment; anti-discrimination laws aim to ensure that unfair barriers (based on gender, age etc) do not impede the progress of talented people; and taxation law and policy provide obligations to pay money to government, so it has the revenue base to provide services. The links between those objectives and employment is obvious, (even though many of those provisions apply to circumstances beyond the employment relationship, as well). This chapter outlines those laws.[1]

While the workplace relations system for the private sector has become a national scheme regulated by the Federal government – particularly for corporations and private sector employers and employees – the opposite remains largely true in relation to workplace health and safety (WHS).[2]

While most Australian jurisdictions have adopted 'model' WHS provisions by way of enacting complementary legislation from a single template Act and Regulations (referred to as the 'model Act' and discussed in further detail below), the system adopted is one of substantially similar legislation rather than national regulation. Contrast this with the approach adopted by the States (except Western Australia) with the referral to the Commonwealth of power to legislate in respect of private sector industrial relations, which has facilitated a federally legislated scheme.[3]

This s considers the origins and evolution of workplace safety laws; legislative concepts essential to an understanding of the field; safety duties imposed upon parties in the workplace; the compliance and enforcement regime; and the interaction of workplace safety laws with industrial relations and workers' compensation systems respectively.

8.05.10 Origins of modern WHS legislation

Workplace safety legislation in Australia has its origins in the factories legislation of 19th-century Britain. The industrial revolution, the changes that it brought to the world of work, and particularly the conditions in which the work was performed, were the catalyst for early attempts to regulate safety.[4]

Amongst the features of these early British attempts were its industry-specific nature,[5] its reliance upon magistrates and other appointed visitors to attend and make reports (and their

---

1   Throughout this text are acknowledgements that further provisions, including some provisions of the *Fair Work Act*, also relate to safety or anti-discrimination. There may also be issues regarding choice of remedy.

2   The stand-out exception to this being the 2007 amendments bringing corporations which were self-insurers into the Commonwealth's 'Comcare' scheme under the *Occupational Health and Safety Act 1991* (Cth), thereby removing those corporations from State workplace safety and workers' compensation systems.

3   See, for example, the referral of powers legislation such as the *Fair Work (Commonwealth Powers) and Other Provisions Act 2009* (Qld).

4   The framework for this section on the development of workplace safety laws owes much to R Johnstone *Occupational Health and Safety Law and Policy: Text and Materials* (Law Book Co., 1997) especially Ch. 2.

5   See, for example, the *Health and Morals of Apprentices Act 1802*, which only applied to cotton factories.

diligence or otherwise in doing so)[6] and the often-disparate aspects of 'health' and 'welfare' in the workplace that they sought to regulate.[7]

Gradually safety legislation was applied to a broader range of workplaces, particularly the then substantial British textile industry, although these laws remained largely concerned with child welfare in the workplace (or at least the limitation of their working hours). The *Factory Regulation Act 1833*, for example, made the provision of education to children under 14 mandatory, prohibited the employment of children younger than 9 years old, limited the hours worked by children on a daily and weekly basis, and provided for the ubiquitous lime-washing of walls and white-washing of ceilings.[8] However, as Johnstone observes, this particular Act was also notable for another (more durable) reason – the introduction of the notion of enforcement by:

> an independent salaried state inspectorate with broad powers including the right of entry into any factory or mill; the right to make rules, regulations and orders . . . and the right to initiate court proceedings for breaches of the Act.[9]

The notions of industry-specific regulation and an inspectorate funded by the State were adopted in the workplace safety laws enacted by the Australian States. They remained prevalent until the advent of risk-based and 'general duties' legislation in the late 1970s and early 1980s. Indeed, some of the provisions in these laws were similar, if not almost identical, to provisions in 19th-century British laws.[10]

The key feature of safety regulation in both Britain and Australia, prior to the adoption of 'Robens-style' legislation, was that it was both specific and prescriptive. For example, regulations could specify the height of protective guarding and the material from which it was to be made, and could mandate limits for certain categories of employees (notably women and young workers) in relation to the weight of items that they were permitted to lift.[11]

8.05.15 The notion of general duties (the Robens reforms)

The shortcomings of prescriptive workplace safety laws, which were rigid, increasingly complex and only applied to certain workplaces (and even then lacked uniformity), led the British government to appoint a Commission of Inquiry in 1970, headed by Lord Robens, to examine the interaction of the law, workplace safety and its regulation.

This was also an issue in Australia, where research indicated that while there had been a focus by unions on supporting and obtaining compensation for injured workers, for many unions this did not necessarily translate into safeguarding their members' health by way of

6   P Bartrip and P Fenn 'The evolution of regulatory style in the nineteenth century British Factory Inspectorate' (1983) 10 *British Journal of Law and Society* 201.
7   For example, the abovementioned *Health and Morals of Apprentices Act 1802* sought to regulate working hours of children (to no more than 12 hours per day); to ensure separate accommodation for males and females; and to have factory walls lime-washed twice yearly and windows for ventilation.
8   *Factory Regulation Act 1833*.
9   Johnstone *Occupational Health and Safety Law and Policy* (1997) 39.
10 See, for example, the observation in relation to *Factories Shops and Industries Act 1962* (NSW) s 27(1) and its similarity to *Factories Act Amendment Act 1844* s 21, cited in B Creighton and A Stewart *Labour Law* (Federation Press, 5th ed, 2010). See also N Gunningham *Safeguarding the Worker: Job Hazards and the Role of Law* (LBC, 1984).
11 See *Factories Shops and Industries Act 1962* (NSW) s 36. No. such limits applied to adult male workers.

preventive strategies.[12] Rather, it seemed that in many industries, such as demolition, the focus was on addressing the lack of safety in workplaces through the payment of 'danger money'.[13]

The Report of the Committee on Safety and Health at Work – the Robens Report – recommended the enactment of safety laws based on a single legislative umbrella, the imposition of general safety responsibilities on 'duty holders' and the use of regulations and codes of practice where further details were required.[14]

Britain adopted the Robens recommendations via the *Health and Safety at Work Act 1974* (UK). Australia responded to Robens gradually and, as time elapsed, comprehensively. The first attempt, in South Australia, actually pre-dated the legislative response in the UK.[15]

Using NSW as an example, the adoption of 'general duties'-based safety legislation followed the conduct of an inquiry[16] that included an assessment of the existing range of safety-related legislation[17] and the regulations associated with them. It also considered the experience of other jurisdictions and contrasted prescriptive safety regimes with those that were 'performance based' – where the focus was on the safety outcome rather than on the specific requirements to be met. The inquiry recommended the adoption of Robens-style legislation based on general duties, risk control and a cooperative approach. The legislative response was the *Occupational Health and Safety Act 1983* (NSW).

A key feature of legislation adopted progressively in the Australian States – particularly in measures such as the 1983 Act in NSW and its Victorian counterpart, the *Occupational Health and Safety Act 1985* (Vic) – was the extension of workplace safety laws to all industries and occupations, including some which had not specifically been covered previously. This represented something of a conceptual watershed in certain industries (including agriculture).

The legislation in each State, Territory and the Commonwealth prior to harmonisation was based on the same broad principles: hazard identification, risk assessment, risk control and a mix of performance standards, general safety duties and specific provisions for certain high-risk activities (such as those involving electricity and/or chemicals). However, each Australian jurisdiction maintained its individual variations and, in some cases, its additional legislation for particular industries, such as mining.

There were also variations in the compliance philosophies adopted by regulators and in the enforcement responses in each State.[18] In addition, there were controversial differences as to where the onus of proof lay in relation to whether or not a safety measure was reasonably practicable: did the regulator have to prove that it was, or was lack of practicability a defence available to the duty holder (usually the employer)? These matters are discussed below.

12   M Quinlan and P Bohle *Managing Occupational Health and Safety in Australia: A Multidisciplinary Approach* (Macmillan, 1991) 360.
13   An extra payment to persons because the work they are performing is unsafe. See Quinlan and Bohle *Managing Occupational Health and Safety in Australia, A Multidisciplinary Approach* (2000) 446.
14   *Report of the Committee on Safety and Health at Work 1970–72* (HMSO, 1972), cited in Creighton and Stewart *Labour Law* (2010) 442.
15   The *Industrial Safety and Welfare Act 1972* (SA) enacted by the Dunstan Government.
16   TG Williams *Report of the Commission of Inquiry into Occupational Health and Safety*, 3 June 1981.
17   Such as the *Factories Shops and Industries Act 1962* (NSW) and the *Construction Safety Act 1912* (NSW).
18   Canvassed in Creighton and Stewart *Labour Law* (2010) Ch. 15.15 and in greater depth (in relation to Victoria) in R Johnstone *Occupational Health and Safety, Courts and Crime* (Federation Press, 2003).

8.05.20 Harmonised national scheme (and exceptions)

From this system of similarity in principles but disparity in both detail and enforcement, the Workplace Relations Ministers' Council in 2009 committed to adopting uniform standards and enforcement polices and to move towards 'model' legislation.[19] This approach was adopted in preference to the enactment of national legislation.

Australia adopted the International Labour Organization (ILO)'s Occupational Health and Safety Convention 1981 No. 155,[20] so the use of the external affairs power in s 51(xxix) of the Constitution to enact Commonwealth legislation to give domestic effect to this Convention was available. (However, the ratifying country putting in place other suitable measures to implement the convention can also satisfy the requirements of the Convention.)

Consistent with the principles of the model Act, the jurisdictions which have adopted it have done so with minor local alterations, such that the key concepts and definitions – worker; person conducting a business or undertaking (PCBU); risk; and reasonably practicable – are essentially the same in each of the adopting jurisdictions. Currently the only States not to have adopted the model Act are Victoria and Western Australia.

Figure 8.1:   Map showing adoption of the model WHS legislation.
Adapted from Minter Ellison HR & IR Update: *Quarterly Update on WHS Harmonisation and Bullying,* 3 April 2013

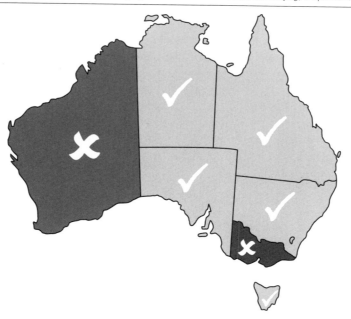

19   Communiqué issued by the Workplace Relations Ministers' Council (WRMC), May 2009.
20   Ratified by Australia on 26 March 2004.

8.05.25 Concepts of 'risk' and 'risk control'

In both the model Act and its Robens-style predecessors, 'risk' is a fundamental concept. It is a relatively straightforward concept:

> Hazard means a situation or thing that has the potential to harm a person. Hazards at work may include noisy machinery, a moving forklift, chemicals, electricity, working at heights, a repetitive job, bullying and violence at the workplace.
>
> Risk is the possibility that harm (death, injury or illness) might occur when exposed to a hazard.[21]

Section 19(3) of the *Work Health and Safety Act 2011* (Cth) (referred to in this chapter as the *WHS Act* though it is, in fact, a separate Act in each of the jurisdictions) deals with risk management, providing examples of what may be considered means of obviating risks:

- the provision and maintenance of a work environment without risks to health and safety, of safe plant and structures; and of safe systems of work;
- safe use, handling, and storage of plant, structures and substances;
- adequate facilities for the welfare of workers, including ensuring access to those facilities;
- information, training, instruction or supervision to protect persons from risks to their health and safety arising from work carried out;
- health monitoring in appropriate circumstances (for exposure levels, for example).[22]

Risk is a significant concept because the legislation is framed in terms of risks and controlling them. Therefore, prosecutions for breaches by duty holders, unless otherwise specified, deal with the failure to address safety risks rather than the consequences that are evidence of the risk (the injury).

An illustration of this is the matter of *Thiess Pty Ltd v Industrial Court of New South Wales* (2010) 78 NSWLR 94,[23] in which a worker was found deceased in a large sediment pond (28m long, 6m wide, 3m deep at one end) – the duty holders had fenced it on three sides but had removed the physical barrier on the fourth side. The prosecution was based entirely upon risk (necessarily so, as the post-mortem indicated that the worker had died of a heart attack).[24] The defendants' attempts to focus on the incident itself were unsuccessful, as was the argument that the risk was remote – the risk of injury posed by an unfenced large body of water being clear.

While the specifics of managing risk are left in the hands of the PCBU, the method of controlling risks can be summed up in a framework referred to in the 'hierarchy of controls'.

---

21   Safe Work Australia *Code of Practice – How to Manage Work Health & Safety Risks*, December 2011, 4 (republished by the various State regulators), http://www.workcover.nsw.gov.au/__data/assets/pdf_file/0009/15201/how-manage-work-health-safety-risks-code-of-practice-3565.pdf.

22   *Work Health and Safety Act 2011*(Cth) s 19(3)(a) and s 19(3)(g) and largely identical provisions in other States which have adopted the model Act.

23   *Thiess Pty Ltd v Industrial Court of New South Wales* (2010) 78 NSWLR 94 (appeal); *Theiss Pty Ltd v Inspector Stephen Jones (WorkCover Authority of New South Wales)* (Unreported, Chief Industrial Magistrate's Court of New South Wales, Chief Industrial Magistrate Miller, 19 August 2008) (first instance).

24   Ibid [8].

Previously enshrined in some States' regulations,[25] the hierarchy is an established methodology for controlling risks whereby the 'higher order' control measures are to be deployed first. These are, first, to eliminate the risk if possible, and second, should elimination fail, to use the following types of measures (in the order listed below):

(a)   substitute an item/substance/process of lesser risk;

(b)   implement an engineering control (such as machine guarding);

(c)   establish administrative control measures (such as the use of personal protective equipment); and

(d)   provide training and instruction.

8.05.30 Concept of 'worker'

A central concept in model Act jurisdictions is that of 'worker' – it is defined in the *WHS Act* and is broader than the common law definition of an 'employee'.

Section 7(1) of the *WHS Act* defines a 'worker' as someone who 'carries out work in any capacity for a person conducting business or undertaking', and includes:

- an employee;
- a contractor or subcontractor;
- an employee of a contractor or subcontractor;
- an employee of a labour hire company, assigned to work in the business or undertaking;
- an outworker;
- an apprentice or trainee;
- a student gaining work experience;
- a volunteer (as defined by the *WHS Act*).[26]

This definition captures a large cross-section of persons involved in the workplace, recognising that those engaged in work are not all employees. Nevertheless, the definition does not capture everyone affected by the activities of a person conducting a business or undertaking (PCBU). The legislation deals with this by making provision for others to whom a safety duty is owed. These are discussed in more detail in the next s.

8.05.35 Concept of 'person conducting a business or undertaking' (PCBU)

Recognising the realities of modern workplaces and the limitations on a safety duty framed in employer–employee terms, the *WHS Act* uses the broader terms of 'worker' and 'person conducting a business or undertaking'. As will be seen in the s on bullying, these concepts (and their definitions) have now been exported to other fields.[27]

---

25   For example, *Occupational Health and Safety Regulation 2001* (NSW) Reg 5.
26   *WHS Act* s 7(1)(a) to 7(1)(i), including 'a person of a prescribed class' who may be declared by the legislation to be a worker.
27   See, for example, the Bullying section of this chapter.

The primary duty owed under the legislation is of a PCBU towards workers and others.[28] This is not dissimilar from the primary duty under the various States' predecessor legislation, which imposed a duty on employers in respect of the safety of their employees and others affected by the conduct of their undertaking.[29] Other persons to whom PCBUs owe a duty are discussed later in this s.

PCBU is defined in s 5 of the *WHS Act*. It provides that the business or undertaking can be conducted alone or with others and whether or not the business or undertaking is conducted for profit or gain (s 5(1)); and includes a business or undertaking by a partnership or an unincorporated association (s 5(2)).

It is apparent from this that a PCBU may be an individual (either individually or with others), a corporation (on the same basis), or a government agency.[30] However, a person is not himself/herself regarded as a PCBU if he/she is engaged solely as a worker in, or as an officer of, a business or undertaking (s 5(4)); or he/she is acting in his/her capacity as an elected member of a local authority (s 5(5)). Obviously, if a person is involved in a business or an undertaking other than in those capacities, he/she may be a PCBU for those other purposes.

With volunteer organisations there is an additional criterion. A volunteer association will not be a PCBU if, while working together for a community purpose or purposes, none of the volunteers (either alone or jointly) employs any person to carry out work for the association. In short, associations with people paid to perform work for them will be regarded as PCBUs (ss 5(7) and 5(8)).

Section 5(6) also provides that the Regulations may specify circumstances in which a person may be taken not to be a PCBU.

As Marks indicates, the legislation seems to intend to make a distinction between organised and ongoing activity, which may be regarded as a business or undertaking, and a one-off purchase or sale of an item, which may not (usually). An exception would be that in the example considered by Marks; the purchase of an old vehicle for the purpose of stripping it and selling the components as spare parts 'would arguably constitute an undertaking, if not a business'.[31]

Even with the broad notion of 'worker', the range of persons affected by the activities of a PCBU, and therefore to whom a safety duty is owed, does not end there. The duties of PCBUs, set out in ss 19 and 20, stretch well beyond a PCBU's own workers. They encompass:

- workers engaged, or caused to be engaged, by the PCBU (s 19(1)(a));
- workers whose activities in carrying out the work are influenced or directed by the PCBU (s 19(1)(b));
- other persons exposed to risk from work carried out as part of the conduct of the PCBU (s 19(2));

---

28   *WHS Act* s 19.

29   For example, *Occupational Health and Safety Act 2000* (NSW) ss 8(1) and 8(2); *Workplace Health and Safety Act 1995* (Qld) ss 28(1) and 28(2).

30   Affirmed in *Balthazaar v Department of Human Services (Cth)* (2014) 241 IR 390 (discussed in the Bullying section below); see also *WorkCover Authority of New South Wales (Inspector Keelty) v Crown in Right of the State of New South Wales (Police Service of New South Wales)* [2000] NSWIRC 234 regarding the status of the Crown and its agencies.

31   F Marks, D Dinnen and L Fieldus *The New Work Health & Safety Legislation: A Practical Guide* (Federation Press, 2013) 24.

- where a PCBU has management or control (including partial control) of workplaces – any risks arising from those places, including access and egress (s 20);
- where a PCBU manages or controls fixtures, fittings or plant – any risks arising from those items (s 21).

The legislation also defines 'workplace' broadly – encompassing vehicles, vessels and other mobile structures, associated waters and installations.[32]

8.05.40 Other duty holders

In addition to the duties imposed on a PCBU, the legislation also imposes safety duties upon designers (s 22); manufacturers (s 23); importers (s 24); suppliers (s 25); those who install, construct or commission equipment (s 26); officers of an entity that has a safety duty (s 27); workers (s 28); and persons other than workers present at a workplace (s 29).

Summarised briefly, the obligations upon duty holders under ss 22 to 26 aim to ensure, as far as reasonably practicable, that their item of plant, substance or structure (as the case may be) does not give rise to risks to the health and safety of those who come into contact with it, via handling, storing or otherwise working with it. This includes using it not just in a particular work process, but also in ancillary activities such as cleaning.

The duty imposed upon officers is to exercise 'due diligence' to ensure that the entity of which they are an officer complies with its safety duties. Section 27(5)(a)–27(5)(f) specifies that due diligence includes the officer taking reasonable steps to:

- acquire and keep up-to-date knowledge of safety matters;
- gain an understanding of the operations of the PCBU and of the hazards and risks associated with those operations;
- ensure that the PCBU has available and uses appropriate resources and processes to eliminate or minimise risks to health and safety from work carried out by the PCBU;
- ensure that the PCBU has appropriate processes for dealing with information about incidents, hazards and risks and responding in a timely manner;
- ensure that the PCBU has, and implements, processes for complying with its duties under the Act – including, for example, obligations in relation to consultation, training and instruction, and incident notification; and
- verify the provision and use of resources outlined above.

In the case of a corporation, the definition of 'officer' is the same as that contained in s 9 of the *Corporations Act 2001* (Cth) and includes company director, company secretary, a person who makes or participates in making decisions that affect the whole or a substantial part of the business or have the capacity to impact its financial standing, and a person on whose instructions the directors are accustomed to act. It can also include a receiver, manager, liquidator or administrator in circumstances where they are involved in the running of the business.[33]

The duties imposed upon workers (s 28) are to:

---

32   *WHS Act* s 8.
33   Marks et al. (2013) 87. *Corporations Act 2001* (Cth) s 9.

- take reasonable care for his/her own health and safety;
- take reasonable care that their acts or omissions do not adversely affect the health and safety of others;
- comply, as far as reasonably able, with reasonable instructions given by the PCBU to enable them to comply with the legislation; and
- cooperate with any reasonable safety-related policy or procedure of the PCBU in relation to safety that has been notified to workers.[34]

While the duties to take reasonable care and to comply and cooperate with reasonable instructions and policies have carried over from previous safety legislation, in some jurisdictions the duty of the worker to take care for his/her own health and safety has been added as a new requirement.[35]

However, the duty imposed upon workers is subservient to the primary duty imposed on the PCBU in s 19 of the *WHS Act*: 'take reasonable care' as distinct from 'ensure, as far as reasonably practicable'.

The duties imposed upon others, including visitors to the workplace, are similar to those imposed upon workers:

- take reasonable care for his/her own health and safety;
- take reasonable care that their acts or omissions do not adversely affect the health and safety of others; and
- comply, as far as reasonably able, with any reasonable instruction given by the PCBU to enable them to comply with the legislation.[36]

Safety duties extend to not engaging in 'prohibited conduct' (such as victimising or otherwise disadvantaging) in relation to a person who raises a safety issue.[37] However, this does not extend to the safety issue being used as a shield to every action that the complainant takes. For example, in *Dowling v CardCall Pty Ltd*, the dismissal of an employee who sent an email to a large number of the employer's customers to inform them of safety complaints was held to have been fair as the effect of the email amounted to gross misconduct which could not be justified by any legitimate safety complaint, being:

> ... unequivocally harmful to the employer's business interests. Although the applicant had some reasonable basis for compliant about an occupational health and safety issue, this complaint did not entitle the applicant to deliberately damage the employer's business by circulation of the offending email.[38]

34   *WHS Act* s 28(a)–28(d).
35   *Occupational Health and Safety Act 2000* (NSW) s 20, for example, did not contain this duty. By contrast, the equivalent Tasmanian legislation at the time saw prosecutions of workers who failed to ensure their safety.
36   *WHS Act* s 29(a)–29(c); for examples, see *Patrick Stevedoring Pty Ltd v Chasser (Victorian WorkCover Authority)* (2011) 215 IR 411 and *Director of Public Prosecutions (Vic) v Acme Storage Pty Ltd* [2017] VSCA 90.
37   *WHS Act* ss 104–106. For a prosecution under the equivalent provision, see *Occupational Health and Safety Act 2000* (NSW) s 23: *WorkCover Authority of New South Wales (Inspector O'Neil) v Galdgin Pty Ltd t/as Strictly Aquariums* (Unreported, Chief Industrial Magistrates Court of New South Wales, Magistrate Hart, 27 July 2006).
38   *Dowling v CardCall Pty Ltd* [2006] NSWIRComm 1013 at [5].

In order to sustain a complaint of prohibited conduct or disadvantage arising from a safety compliant, the applicant must establish a link between the safety complaint and the action taken against them.[39]

8.05.45 Health and safety representatives (HSRs) and consultation

Since the introduction of Robens-style legislation, there have been (to a greater or lesser extent) duties to consult with those who work in the workplace. In some cases, these duties were prescriptive and an end in themselves – for example, the requirement to have a safety committee in workplaces of more than 20 employees.[40] In other cases, they were focused on consultation as part of the safety management process.[41]

This latter approach was gradually adopted in other jurisdictions, providing for a range of arrangements – safety committees, health and safety representatives (HSRs), a combination of these, or other agreed arrangements – the purpose of which was to make consultation an element of safety management.

The *WHS Act*, which was based largely upon the Victorian and Commonwealth legislative experience, adopted the approach of HSRs in designated work groups as the basis for workplace consultative arrangements, with committees generally playing a broader policy and oversight role.[42] Failure to consult with other duty holders is also regarded as a breach of a PCBU's duties and has, in one case, resulted in prosecution.[43]

Also consistent with the Victorian and Commonwealth approaches up to that time, the *WHS Act* empowered HSRs to attempt to resolve safety issues through a mix of consultation and the issuing of Provisional Improvement Notices (PINs)[44] identifying apparent safety breaches, which the PCBU must either comply with or seek a review of from the regulator. The regulator may revoke the PIN or confirm it and issue an Improvement Notice (non-compliance with which is an offence under the Act).[45]

8.05.50 Incident notification and associated requirements

The *WHS Act*, like its predecessors and non-model counterparts, contains obligations on PCBUs to notify serious incidents[46] and to preserve and not disturb the site of the incident until instructed by the regulator, except to the extent that is necessary to render emergency aid and make the location safe.[47]

---

39   *Hogan v Police and Community Youth Clubs* [2010] NSWIRComm 23.
40   See *Occupational Health and Safety Act 1983* (NSW) s 23.
41   Se *Occupational Health and Safety (Commonwealth Employment) Act 1991* (Cth).
42   *WHS Act* Part 5 and Safe Work Australia *Code of Practice – Workplace Consultation*.
43   *Boland v Trainee and Apprentice Placement Service Inc* [2016] SAIRC 14.
44   *WHS Act* s 90.
45   Ibid s 102.
46   Ibid ss 35–38.
47   Ibid s 39.

The purpose of such provisions is apparent when one considers the regulator's function in enforcing the legislation and investigating alleged breaches. The preservation of an incident site and the reporting of injuries are a fundamental part of that process.

The first prosecution under the NSW enactment of the *WHS Act* was for failure to notify a reportable incident and disturbing/failing to preserve the incident scene, which had undermined the regulator's investigation of the incident.[48]

8.05.55 Reasonable practicability

Another central concept in WHS, and one which qualifies the duty of care imposed on a PCBU, is the notion of 'reasonable practicability'.

'Reasonable practicability' is not so broad a concept as to encompass anything and everything that it was possible to do. Nor does it reflect an expectation that incidents never happen.[49] It is an objective test referable to the standard expected of a reasonable person placed in the duty holder's position.[50]

The High Court considered 'reasonable practicability' in its judgement in *Silvak v Lurgi (Australia) Pty Ltd* (2001) 205 CLR 304,[51] from which the following findings may be drawn:

1. 'reasonably practicable' is something narrower than 'physically possible';

2. reasonable practicability is to be judged based on what was known at the relevant time; and

3. to determine what is reasonably practicable, one must balance the likelihood [and seriousness] of the risk against the cost and difficulty of averting that risk.[52]

As these are objective tests, the element of reasonable practicability may still be found in circumstances where the duty holder says they did not know at the relevant time or they believed that the cost and difficulty outweighed the taking of particular safety measures. For example, the regulator and the courts will consider matters such as the availability of safety codes of practice and guidance material in the relevant field,[53] along with information developed by or in conjunction with the relevant industry, such as Australian Standards. Given the broad range of topics covered by such material (from machine guarding and electrical installations through to confined spaces and risk management itself),[54] while 'reasonable practicability' is an element of the duty, it does not represent an excuse to be used by a PCBU to simply dismiss safety measures that it chooses not to take.

---

48   *WorkCover Authority of New South Wales v Ali Mohammed El Ibrahim* (Unreported, Local Court of New South Wales, 9 October 2013).

49   *Holmes v R E Spence & Co.* [1992] VSC 227.

50   CBP Lawyers *Work Health and Safety: The PCBU's Duty to Do what is Reasonably Practicable*, 11 December 2012, citing *Director of Public Prosecutions (Vic) v Esso* [2001] VSC 263.

51   (2001) 205 CLR 304, cited in Master Builders Australia *Losing Control? – The Impact of the Primary Duty of Care* 2011.

52   *Silvak v Lurgi (Australia) Pty Ltd* (2001) 205 CLR 304 at 53 per Gaudron J.

53   Indeed, under *Occupational Health and Safety Act 1995* (Qld) s 26, adherence to a relevant Code of Practice was regarded as a defence available to the duty-holder.

54   Australian Standards AS 4024, AS3000 (also known as the 'Wiring Rules'), AS2865 and AS4801 respectively.

These principles are reflected in s 18 of the *WHS Act*, which defines 'reasonably practicable' as that which:

> ... is, or was at a particular time, reasonably able to be done ... taking into account and weighing up all relevant matters including:
>
> (a) the likelihood of the hazard or risk concerned occurring; and
> (b) the degree of harm that may result from the hazard or the risk; and
> (c) what the person concerned knows, or ought reasonably to know, about:
>   i. the hazard or the risk; and
>   ii. ways of eliminating or minimising the risk; and
> (d) the availability and suitability of ways to eliminate or minimise the risk; and
> (e) *after* assessing the extent of the risk and the available ways of eliminating or minimising the risk, the cost associated with available ways of eliminating or minimising the risk, including whether the cost is grossly disproportionate to the risk (emphasis added).[55]

It is also important to consider the question of reliance upon expertise. Can a PCBU fulfil its duty and/or be excused from liability if it has relied upon the expertise of another party?

This issue was particularly considered in two cases: *Kirk v Industrial Court (NSW)* (2010) 239 CLR 531 (*Kirk*) and *Laing O'Rourke (BMC) Pty Ltd v Kirwin* [2011] WASCA 117.

In *Kirk*, an experienced farm manager was killed when the four-wheeled 'quad bike' vehicle that he was riding overturned. The vehicle was unfortunately (and perhaps incorrectly) referred to as an all terrain vehicle (ATV) in the proceedings. Mr Kirk and his company were prosecuted for breaches of the *OHS Act 2000* (NSW).

The breaches that comprised the charge were poorly particularised, in some instances no more than a recital of words from the statute with the addition of the words to the effect of 'in particular the ATV'.[56] When coupled with procedural defects – such as the defendant being called as a prosecution witness – this was fatal to the case. The High Court found that the Industrial Court of NSW[57] had erred in acting beyond its jurisdiction.

Importantly for the issue of reasonable practicability, the High Court also considered the question of whether the principal (Mr Kirk) was entitled to rely upon the expertise of another person to fulfil its duty of care. In this matter, the deceased was an experienced farm manager – far more experienced than Mr Kirk, who had no experience in farming. The Court, in very plain terms, endorsed the position that a principal may rely upon expertise in fields where the person engaged clearly has greater expertise. It concluded that:

> it is absurd to have prosecuted the owner of a farm and its principal on the ground that the principal failed to ensure the health, safety and welfare of his manager, who was a man of optimum skill and experience – skill and experience much greater than his own – a man whose conduct in driving straight down the side of a hill instead of on a formed and safe road was inexplicably reckless.[58]

---

55   *Model Act* s 18.
56   *Kirk* at [22].
57   That is, the Industrial Relations Commission of NSW, in court session.
58   *Kirk* at [125].

The *Laing O'Rourke*[59] matter arose from serious injuries incurred by workers sheltering in company huts known as 'dongas'. During a cyclone, the huts overturned. The company was convicted on the basis that it had failed to ensure that the dongas were safe in an area that was cyclone-prone. The judge found that the company should have engaged an engineer to inspect the buildings to ensure that they were safe. However, on appeal, the Supreme Court of WA found that the company had no reason to believe that the buildings were not constructed to the appropriate standard (the welded tie-downs were inadequate), as they had been approved by the local council authority, and that there was no evidence that an engineer would necessarily have found the deficiency.[60]

This notion, that a step *could* have been taken was considered by the High Court in *Baiada Poultry Pty Ltd v The Queen*, in which the Court affirmed that the duty holder did not have to take every possible step, but only those that were reasonably practicable. The Court also observed: 'Bare demonstration that a step could have been taken and that, if taken, it might have had some effect on the safety of the working environment does not, without more, demonstrate that the employer has broken the duty.'[61]

Having considered the question of reliance upon the expertise of others, it is important to point out that this is not a blanket protection. In *Inspector Duncan v Kell & Rigby (ACT) Pty Ltd*, the principal on a supermarket construction site had engaged scaffolders in relation to the erection and certification of scaffolding. However, the scaffolding was inadequate and did not have guardrails to prevent falls. In that case, the court found that the principal's failure to act on an obvious risk (and apparently a contractual requirement) and not seeking to have it remedied but instead accepting the certification when key features were missing, was a failure on the part of the principal.[62]

The degree of influence and control that a principal can exercise is an important consideration. While contractual arrangements may be an indicator of this, elements of control and influence may still exist. This was considered in the matter of *Inspector Nicholson v Pymble No. 1 Pty Ltd & Molinara (No. 2)*,[63] in which the developer successfully argued that it did not have control of the site while the principal contractor engaged for the construction had control of the site. However, the court noted that if the developer had established a regime to inspect the works and give directions, the right to influence and control would have been retained.

Before the adoption of the *WHS Act* in NSW and Queensland, the legislation in those jurisdictions dealt with the topic of reasonable practicability by making it a defence for the duty holder, rather than an element of the primary duty.[64] So in proceedings for offences against the Act, the onus was on the prosecutor to prove all elements of the breach of duty beyond reasonable doubt (but without 'reasonable practicability' being one of them). It was left to the duty holder to raise reasonable practicability as a defence – which then had to be proved on the balance of probabilities.

59   *Laing O'Rourke (BMC) Pty Ltd v Kirwin* [2011] WASCA 117.
60   MBA *Losing Control? – The Impact of the Primary Duty of Care* 5.
61   *Baiada Poultry Pty Ltd v The Queen* (2012) 246 CLR 92 at [15].
62   *Inspector Duncan v Kell & Rigby (ACT) Pty Ltd* [2011] NSWIRComm 25.
63   *Inspector Nicholson v Pymble No. 1 Pty Ltd & Molinara (No. 2)* [2010] NSWIRComm 151.
64   *OHS Act 2000* (NSW) s 28; *Workplace Health and Safety Act 1995* (Qld) s 37(1)(c).

This was variously (and inaccurately) referred to by critics of the legislation as either 'the reverse onus of proof' or 'guilty until they could prove their innocence'.[65] It was also said to be the cause of higher rates of prosecutions and convictions in those jurisdictions and was particularly compared to the Victorian experience, where reasonable practicability had long been an element of the duty that the prosecutor was required to prove.[66] What that critique failed to give sufficient weight to was that: (a) for many years Victoria appeared more reluctant to use prosecutions as a compliance tool;[67] and (b) that conviction rates in excess of 90 per cent are common in criminal proceedings.[68]

With the adoption of the *WHS Act* in NSW and Queensland, reasonable practicability is now an element of the primary duty, with the prosecutor required to prove it as an element of the offence.[69]

8.05.60 Compliance and enforcement

The *WHS Act* and many of its State predecessors provide a range of measures for achieving compliance with the legislation, including enforcement and sanctions for non-compliance.

Notionally, these measures are regarded in the shape of a pyramid – the less serious and more frequently used at the base (provision of advice), and the more serious and less frequently used (prosecution) at the top. The use of these measures may be assessed by referring to the regulator's compliance and enforcement policies, which are now largely consistent across jurisdictions.[70]

As the following illustration indicates, the compliance tools available to regulators under the *WHS Act* include:

- Improvement Notices (identifying an apparent breach of the legislation and providing advice and directions in relation to remedying it within a specified timeframe);[71]
- Prohibition Notices (with immediate effect, prohibiting the performance of particular work or the use of particular equipment or substance until the safety breach has been remedied);[72]
- Penalty Notices/Infringement Notices (also known as on-the-spot fines, issued for breaches of the legislation considered serious enough to receive a sanction but which would not be prosecuted in the ordinary course of events);[73]
- Enforceable Undertakings (steps agreed between the party in breach and the regulator, which are an alternative to prosecution and are intended to promote safety improvements);[74] and
- Prosecution.[75]

---

65   CBP Lawyers *Work Health and Safety* 2012.
66   For example, *Occupational Health and Safety Act 1985* (Vic) (now *Occupational Health and Safety Act 2004* (Vic)) s 21.
67   Johnstone *Occupational Health and Safety, Courts and Crime* (2003).
68   G Fisher *Sentencing Severity for 'Serious' and 'Significant' Offences: A Statistical Report* (Sentencing Council of Victoria, 2011) 10.
69   *WHS Act* s 19, adopted in NSW and Queensland as the *Work Health and Safety Act 2011*.
70   See, for example, the *National Compliance and Enforcement Policy* adopted by the jurisdictions as the principles underpinning their approach to compliance (accessed 4 July 2016), http://www.safeworkaustralia.gov.au/sites/SWA/about/Publications/Documents/618/National%20Compliance%20aand%20Enforcement%20Policy.doc.
71   *WHS Act 2011* (NSW) ss 191–194.
72   Ibid ss 195–197.
73   Ibid s 243.
74   Ibid Part 11 (ss 216–222).
75   Ibid s 230.

Figure 8.2:   Pyramid showing compliance and enforcement tools.

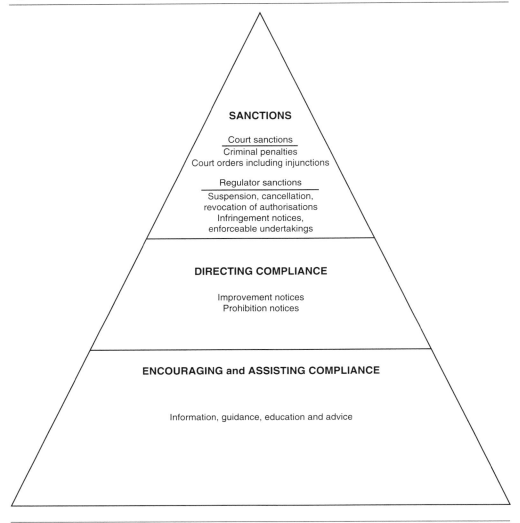

The regulator will generally also publicise the outcomes of its prosecution proceedings.[76] However, it has been held that this is not appropriate in circumstances where no conviction has been recorded.[77]

---

76   See, for example, WorkCover QLD court summaries (http://www.worksafe.qld.gov.au/laws-and-compliance/prosecutions/court-summaries) and SafeWork NSW prosecution summaries (http://www.safework.nsw.gov.au/law-policy/enforcement/prosecutions).

77   *HG v Queensland (represented by the Department of Justice and Attorney-General)* [2013] QSC 89, in which no conviction was recorded in respect of the individual defendant, on which basis the Supreme Court found that the individual should not be identified in the prosecution summary on the regulator's website.

The *WHS Act* provides three categories of penalties for a failure to comply with a safety duty:

Category 1: Reckless conduct (s 31) – conduct that exposes an individual (or individuals) to risk of death or serious injury or illness, for which the maximum penalty ranges from $300,000 for a person to $3 million for a corporation, and may also include up to 5 years' imprisonment for person who recklessly breaches their safety duty;[78]

Category 2: Failure to comply coupled with exposing an individual to risk of death or serious injury or illness, but without the element of recklessness (s 32), for which the maximum penalty ranges from $150,000 for a person to $1.5 million for a corporation;[79] and

Category 3: Failure to comply, but without the element of a risk of death or serious injury (s 33), for which the maximum penalty ranges from $50,000 for a person to $500,000 for a corporation.

8.05.65 WHS and workers' compensation

It is easy to confuse or conflate workplace health and safety with workers' compensation. Certainly, there may be the common features, but the purposes of the two are different: one is to ensure safety in the workplace; the other is to compensate for injury and to deal with associated matters after an injury has occurred.

To maintain the distinction and to highlight important differences, the topics are addressed separately.

8.05.70 WHS and industrial relations

There is a strong link between workplace safety and industrial relations – whether in terms of the perennial 'safety disputes' in some industries or the more recent phenomenon of WHS Entry Permits being required for union officials.

Part 7 of the *WHS Act* details the requirements for obtaining such a permit (such as completion of prescribed training and being the holder of a permit under the *Fair Work Act 2009* (Cth)) as well as the powers of union officials for WHS purposes and the circumstances in which notice of entry is required.

Even in those jurisdictions where the model WHS legislation has not been adopted, it is clear from the case law that the right of entry provisions in the *Fair Work Act* and State/Territory safety laws 'are intended to operate interactively'.[80]

In relation to workplace safety disputes, while each case turns on its own facts, the reality is that the right of a worker or groups of workers to refuse to perform unsafe work (on certain

---

78   The first Category 1 prosecution is reported to be that of *Boland v Safe is Safe Pty Ltd and Munro*, SA Industrial Court.

79   The courts have shown a preparedness to impose fines commensurate with these new maximums, with a fine of $1 million being imposed by the District Court of NSW in a prosecution under the *Work Health and Safety Act 2011* (NSW) s 32: *SafeWork NSW v WGA Pty Ltd* [2017] NSWDC 92.

80   *Communications, Electrical, Electronic, Information, Postal, Plumbing and Allied Services Union of Australia (Western Australian Division) v Fortescue Metals Group Ltd* (2016) 310 FLR 1, citing *Ramsay v Sunbuild Pty Ltd* (2014) 221 FCR 315.

conditions if they are not to lose pay)[81] and the genuine risks to safety that still arise in many workplaces, will see safety and industrial relations continue to be linked (see Chapter 5) in relation to industrial action and right of entry permits.

However, a promising development in this field is the inclusion in the *WHS Act* (now adopted by most jurisdictions) of the power of Inspectors appointed by the relevant work safety regulator to take an active role in resolving workplace safety disputes.[82] It is hoped that this will bring safety matters that are ostensibly the cause of a dispute to the forefront for resolution, rather than using safety as a pretext in a broader industrial dispute.[83]

8.10 Workers' compensation

Workers' compensation refers to statutory insurance schemes, usually 'no fault' schemes, implemented to deal with work-related illness and injury.[84] Such schemes are intended to ameliorate difficulties associated with injured workers having to seek remedies through the courts, and to provide insurance coverage to employers to deal with the financial impost of such claims, which may be particularly burdensome in the case of substantial or multiple claims.

Modern workers' compensation schemes also go beyond a simple model of payments, from a pool of premiums, to workers for particular injuries. Schemes now incorporate rehabilitation and return to work programs (often collectively referred to as 'injury management'). As will be seen below, this approach is not only an altruistic desire to see workers return to pre-injury duties if possible, but also a way to address the financial burdens of the schemes.

8.10.05 Precursor to statutory schemes

Prior to the adoption of statutory workers' compensation, compensation for injuries sustained by workers had to be pursued through the courts in the same way as compensation for other injuries or wrongs. As well as being a potentially expensive exercise, the claimant also invariably had to prove 'fault'.

Historically, this took two forms. The first was the notion of the 'deodand', whereby the family of a person killed could sue in relation to the thing that had caused the death. This was, however, something of a lottery, with the quantum of compensation linked to the value of the object that had caused the death.[85] The provision was abolished in 1846.

---

81   *WHS Act* ss 83–89 (and compare Clause 13 of ILO Occupational Health and Safety Convention 1981).
82   Ibid ss 141–143.
83   See, for example, *Director, Fair Work Building Industry Inspectorate v Construction, Forestry, Mining and Energy Union* [2016] FCA 772 (another instalment in the protracted disputes between the CFMEU and Grocon).
84   Applicants may still need to prove fault/negligence if they seek to pursue *additional* compensation in those schemes where it is available.
85   In English law in medieval times, a 'deodand' was an animal or article that, having been the immediate cause of the death of a human being, was forfeited to the Crown to be applied to pious uses. The provision was abolished in 1846 (9 & 10 Victoria Ch 62 *Deodands Act 1846*). For further detail see D Pietz 'Death of the deodand: Accursed objects and the money value of human life' (1997) 31 *Res* 97–108.

The other, quite substantial, impediments to injury compensation for workers derived from what came to be known as the 'unholy trinity' of defences to actions by injured workers:

1. contributory negligence;

2. common employment; and

3. voluntary assumption of risk.[86]

Contributory negligence presented difficulties for injured workers in circumstances where, prior to apportionment legislation, any contributory negligence on the part of the worker was a complete defence to a claim.[87] 'Common employment' presented another hurdle, being the principle that an injured employee could not sue their employer in respect of an injury caused by a fellow employee.[88] The third of the trinity, voluntary assumption of risk, carried with it the inference that by virtue of undertaking work, the worker was taken to have assumed all risks associated with it.

In the face of these impediments to pursuing compensation through the courts it is unsurprising that there was a push for the implementation of statutory schemes of compensation.

8.10.10 Statutory workers' compensation schemes

Statutory compensation for work-based injuries was first introduced in the various Australian jurisdictions between 1900 and 1914[89] – each statute compensated injury arising in the course of employment. Over time, schemes were extended to cover most occupations.[90] These statutory schemes arose from the inadequacy of the common law (court-based claims) as a means of compensating injured workers.[91]

As a consequence of each jurisdiction establishing its own scheme, there are now 11 separate schemes operating in Australia: one for each State and Territory and three Commonwealth schemes.[92] Australia is also one of few countries where State governments have primary responsibility for workers' compensation.[93] The extent to which the Commonwealth can or should expand its coverage in the field of workers' compensation remains the subject of debate – as with workplace health and safety, one of the key issues is whether to move to a

---

86   Discussed in greater detail in Johnstone *Occupational Health and Safety Law and Policy* (1997) 52–55.

87   Under apportionment legislation it is now only a partial defence, generally resulting a reduction in damages rather than exclusion from compensation.

88   *Priestly v Fowler* (1837) 150 ER 1030.

89   The original statutes were: *Workmen's Compensation Act 1900* (SA); *Workers Compensation Act 1902* (WA); *Workers' Compensation Act 1905* (Qld); *Workmen's Compensation Act 1910* (NSW); *Workers Compensation Act 1910* (Tas); *Workmen's Compensation Act 1912* (Cth); and *Workers' Compensation Act 1914* (Vic).

90   For example, *Workers Compensation Act 1926* (NSW).

91   B Creighton and A Stewart *Labour Law*, (Federation Press, 3rd ed, 2000) 443.

92   Safe Work Australia *Comparison of Workers' Compensation Arrangements in Australia and New Zealand* (2010) 7.

93   R Guthrie, K Purse and F Meredith 'Workers compensation and self-insurance in Australia – national priority or Trojan Horse' (2006) 17(3) *Insurance Law Journal* 256.

nationally consistent framework administered by separate jurisdictions (harmonisation) or to implement/expand a national scheme.[94]

A century of development of separate State schemes has, unsurprisingly, resulted in many inconsistencies, including differences in premiums paid across States by employers in the same industry; the level of benefits; and whether certain workers are even covered for workers' compensation. Such disparity presents challenges, particularly with an increasingly mobile workforce, changes in work arrangements and employers operating across several jurisdictions.[95]

There are, however, many common features among the schemes, including:

- compulsory insurance for employers[96] (with very limited exceptions);
- 'no-fault' schemes – statutory benefits for injured workers do not require the employer to be *at fault* in relation to the injury (there simply has to be the necessary *connection* between work and injury);
- a core definition of 'worker', based on the employment law principle of a 'contract of service';[97]
- provisions for deeming others (outside the core definition) to be 'workers';[98]
- commitment to rehabilitation of injured workers and their return to work; and
- opportunities for large employers to 'self-insure'.

In broad terms, workers' compensation schemes are funded by employers paying premiums[99] (just like any other form of insurance policy), the premiums for which are calculated using a formula which takes into account claims history; the amount of the employer's payroll; and the industry that the employer is operating in. The formula is designed to reflect the claims experience performance of a business compared to other employers in the same industry.[100]

The claims history or 'experience' element of the premium is intended to provide an incentive to employers to improve their claims experience through strategies such as improving workplace safety and encouraging good injury management and return to work processes.

Claims on the scheme are based on incident notifications and the insurer determining whether the injured person, their injury and the circumstances in which it occurred fall within the parameters of the scheme. These factors, including the definitions of 'worker' and 'injury' and the element of connection to work are discussed below. Fraudulent claims may be the

94   J Howe 'Possibilities and pitfalls involved in expanding Australia's National Workers Compensation Scheme' (2015) 39(2) *Melbourne University Law Review* 472.

95   Personal Injury Education Foundation *2007–2011 Strategic Plan* 5; and Australian Business Limited *National Workers Compensation and Occupational Health & Safety Frameworks – Submission to the Productivity Commission Public Inquiry* (2003).

96   J Macken et al. *The Law of Employment* (Law Book Co., 5th ed, 2002) 126; Safe Work Australia *Comparison of Workers' Compensation Arrangements in Australia and New Zealand* (2010) 8.

97   WorkSafe Victoria 'Defining workers, employees, and contractors', in *Multi-State Workers' Compensation Guidance Material* (2009).

98   Macken et al. *The Law of Employment* (2002) 42.

99   And for failure to take out any or an adequate level of workers' compensation, sanctions such as prosecution and payment of double the amount of the avoided premium by way of penalty.

100   ICARE workers insurance: premiums, https://workersinsurance.icare.nsw.gov.au/premiums-and-policies/calculate-your-premium#gref.

subject of criminal prosecutions by the regulator.[101] Service providers may also be the subject of either prosecution or civil proceedings if they have received payments that the scheme considers they are not entitled to.[102]

Depending on the individual claim and the type, nature and severity of the injury, an injured worker may be eligible for one or more of the following benefits:

- weekly payments based on pre-injury earnings (with the rate of these payments generally reducing after defined periods);
- permanent impairment benefits;
- medical, hospital and rehabilitation expenses;
- death benefits and funeral expenses;
- compensation for property damage;
- work injury damages/common law damages (although access to these is limited in most schemes).

8.10.15 Definition of 'worker' for workers' compensation

Each State and Territory uses the 'common law' definition of employment – the existence of a contract of service between employer and employee – as the *core* definition for eligibility for workers' compensation.[103] The core definition does not include contractors or others falling outside of it (such as self-employed persons). However, most jurisdictions have 'deeming' provisions to enable additional groups to come within an extended definition of 'worker' – and workers' compensation policies are required to cover such deemed workers.[104]

As a consequence, the 'common law' distinction between employees and contractors lies at the heart of the current system of eligibility in each State. It is also the distinction used in the workers' compensation schemes of many other countries.[105]

The traditional position, that employees are eligible for workers compensation and contractors (generally) are not, remains the starting position in each Australia jurisdiction. But it is apparent from the categories of deemed worker in each scheme that the intention is to cover

101 For example, *WorkCover Authority of New South Wales v Veronica McGrath* (Unreported, Local Court of New South Wales, Magistrate Morahan,13 March 2013) (first instance) and *WorkCover Authority of New South Wales v McGrath* (Unreported, District Court of New South Wales, Blanch CJ, 11 June 2013) (appeal), in which the defendant was initially sentenced to 6 months' imprisonment, varied on appeal to an Intensive Corrections Order of 12 months, as well as being ordered to pay restitution to the scheme in the amount of $71,221.

102 For an example of such civil proceedings, see *Workers Compensation Nominal Insurer v Khaled Zoud* [2015] NSWSC 476.

103 For example, *Workers Compensation Act 1987* (NSW) s 4 defines a worker as 'a person who had entered into or works under a contract of service or apprenticeship with an employer' (and see Chapter 5).

104 *Workers Compensation Act 1951* (ACT) s 8; *Workers Rehabilitation and Compensation Act* (NT) s 3; *Workplace Injury Management and Workers Compensation Act 1998* (NSW) s 5 and Schedule 1; *Workers Compensation and Rehabilitation Act 2003* (Qld) s 11; *Return to Work Act 2014* (SA) s 4; *Workers Rehabilitation and Compensation Act 1988* (Tas) ss 4–4E and 5–6B; *Workplace Injury Rehabilitation and Compensation Act 2013* (Vic) s 3; *Workers Compensation and Injury Management Act 1981* (WA) ss 3, 6–17, 175 and 175AA.

105 Associated Workers Compensation Boards of Canada *Scope of Coverage – Industries and Occupations* (2010).

groups regarded as potentially vulnerable and thus requiring the protections of workers' compensation regardless of the contractual arrangements applying to them, and who would not otherwise be eligible. For example, volunteer fire-fighters in each State and Territory are covered for workers' compensation, as are State Emergency Service (SES) volunteers while they are performing those emergency roles.[106]

The views of employers and unions have often differed in relation to deeming provisions, with unions seeking broad use of deeming provisions; employer groups seeking definitions as close as possible to the 'common law' employee/contractor test.[107]

While in each jurisdiction it is mandatory for employers to hold a workers' compensation insurance policy covering their workforce, the coverage of that policy usually does not extend to individual 'employers' (sole traders, partners of partnerships and company directors) themselves if they are injured. They may seek cover for themselves by taking out income protection insurance, but such insurance is not mandatory (and would be in addition to the cost of workers' compensation for their other workers).

Ultimately, when contractors and other self-employed people suffer catastrophic injury or are killed at work, usually the only recourse that they have is the (often lengthy) option of a civil claim for compensation through the courts – if they can show that some other party has contributed to their loss. With over one million people Australia-wide reported to be independent contractors in their 'main job', with a further 975,000 classified as 'other business operators',[108] this means a substantial proportion of the workforce is without coverage.

8.10.20 Injury

As with the definition of 'worker', the definition of 'injury' for workers' compensation purposes is quite similar across jurisdictions.[109]

By way of illustration, 'injury' includes: a personal injury arising out of or in the course of employment, diseases of gradual onset[110] and psychological injury,[111] as well as the aggravation, acceleration or exacerbation of any disease, illness or condition.[112]

For an injury to be considered work-related and therefore compensable under workers' compensation, employment must be a substantial contributing factor,[113] with the injury

---

106   See, for example, WorkCover SA *Guide to Definition of Worker: Workers Rehabilitation and Compensation Act 1986* (March 2008).

107   Hon J Macken *Report of Inquiry into the Definition of a Worker* (2005).

108   ABS *Forms of Employment: Australia*, Cat. No. 6359.0, 29 April 2010, 17, which defines 'Other business operators' as 'people who operate their own business, with or without employees, but are not operating as independent contractors. They generally generate their income from managing their staff or from selling goods or services to the public, rather than providing a labour service to a client.'

109   *Workers Compensation Act 1951* (ACT) s 4; *Return to Work Act* (NT) s 3A; *Workers Compensation Act 1987* (NSW) s 4; *Workers Compensation and Rehabilitation Act 2003* (Qld) s 32; *Return to Work Act 2014* (SA) s 4; *Workers Rehabilitation and Compensation Act 1988* (Tas) s 3; *Workplace Injury Rehabilitation and Compensation Act 2013* (Vic) s 3; *Workers Compensation and Injury Management Act 1981* (WA) s 5.

110   See *Workers Compensation Act 1987* (NSW) ss 15 and 16; however, dust diseases such as asbestosis and silicosis are sometimes covered by their own specific legislation/scheme, such as the *Workers Compensation (Dust Diseases) Act 1942* (NSW).

111   *Workers Compensation Act 1987* (NSW) s 11A.

112   Ibid s 4(b)(i).

113   *Workers Compensation & Rehabilitation Act 2003* (Qld) s 32(1)(a).

occurring in the course of or arising out of the worker's employment. For aggravation of a pre-existing injury, it must be shown that employment was a substantial contributing factor in the worsening of the condition. Likewise, in relation to a disease, the connection with employment must have been a substantial contributing factor to the disease.

8.10.25 Journey claims and recess claims

Injuries received on a regular periodic journey (from home to work and back, say) may be compensable under some schemes, provided there is no interruption or deviation that materially increases the risk of injury.

However, in more recent years journey claims have either been excluded by some schemes[114] or access to them has been significantly reduced through the introduction of additional requirements, such as having to demonstrate a link between work and the injury (above and beyond it just being a journey to or from work).[115]

Injuries sustained during a break from work, known as a 'recess claim', may also be compensable,[116] provided that workers do not subject themselves to any abnormal risk of injury during that break. For example, an injury incurred during strenuous lunchtime sporting activities may not be compensable unless a sufficiently strong connection to work can be established. Factors such as the provision of uniforms by the employer, encouragement to participate via the employer's email facilities, use of work time to travel to the event etc are matters that would be taken into account when assessing work-relatedness.

INJURY ON A DAY OUT: HATZIMANOLIS v ANI CORPORATION LTD (1992) 173 CLR 473

Rent-free accommodation at a campsite was provided by ANI for its workers. The campsite was located 15 or 20 minutes' walk from the town of Newman (WA). An air-conditioned cabin was given to each worker. Workers other than those employed by ANI also lived in the camp, which included a mess building (for meals), a swimming pool, a TV room, plus bathroom/toilet facilities.

The company had also hired two vehicles that were used, amongst other things, to transport employees to and from their workplace.[117] The hired vehicles were made available to the employees to use on days off work – for driving them around the town, collecting them from the local Show etc.

One day, the supervisor told employees, 'I'm organising a trip to Wittenoom this weekend for anybody who cares to come along', and all but one of the employees decided to go. Food for the trip was provided by the mess staff at the request of the supervisor.[118]

---

114   Such as the Comcare scheme.
115   See, for example, the amendments enacted in 2012 to the *Workers Compensation Act 1987* (NSW), now embodied in s 10 of that Act.
116   *Workers Compensation Act 1987* (NSW) s 11.
117   *Hatzimanolis v ANI Corporation Ltd* (1992) 173 CLR 473 at [3].
118   Ibid [4] and [5].

On the return journey, the appellant was seriously injured when one of the vehicles over-turned. The injury occurred during an interval within an overall period of work – a sightseeing tour organised by the employer on workers' day off.

A critical issue in this case was that the phrase 'in the course of employment' covers 'not only actual work which a person is employed to do but also the natural incidents connected with the class of work'.[119] The company argued that the supervisor had organised the trip in his private capacity as a fellow worker and not as an ANI supervisor.

However, the court concluded that his position in relation to the other employees, his role as spokesman for the company in explaining the nature, terms and conditions of their employment, and his part in organising and providing the vehicles and food for the 800-kilometre trip, meant that:

> the most cogent conclusion to be drawn from the evidence is that he acted on behalf of ANI when he organised the trip and invited the appellant and the other employees 'to come along'. In the absence of any denial from [the supervisor] or other officers of ANI, the inevitable conclusion is that [he] was authorised to make the company's vehicles available for the use of the employees on their day off and that his authority extended to organising and making the vehicles available for sightseeing journeys of the kind embarked on this particular Sunday.[120]

This therefore amounted to the employer inducing or encouraging employees to spend intervals or interludes in the course of their employment in a particular way or at a particular place.

As can be seen from *Hatzimanolis* above, something that is an ostensibly personal activity (having lunch, participating in an activity during a break etc) is not precluded from being a compensable injury for workers' compensation purposes – provided that the relevant criteria have been met.

This is particularly illustrated in cases where workers have sustained injuries while required to be somewhere other than their usual place of work. Having to shower while on an overnight stay required by the employer has been regarded as arising out of or in the course of employment,[121] even where the employer did not direct the worker as to how to spend their leisure hours.[122]

These issues have been revisited by the High Court in recent years, most notably in the case of *Comcare v PVYW* (2013) 250 CLR 246, a matter involving a Commonwealth employee who was injured during an overnight stay required of her work. However, the injuries sustained (head injuries and psychological injuries) occurred in the course of engaging in sexual intercourse. The injured worker claimed workers' compensation and the matter went through various appeals[123] before finally being determined by the High Court. During that appeals

---

119   Ibid [7].
120   Ibid [20].
121   *Comcare v McCallum* (1994) 49 FCR 199.
122   *Baudoeuf v Department of Main Roads* (1968) 2 NSWR 93, Jacobs JA holding that it went too far to hold that an injury might not be compensable simply because, at the time of its occurrence, the worker was using the hotel premises in the same way that he would use his own home (cited in *Comcare v PVYW* (2013) 250 CLR 246 at [98]).
123   The Administrative Appeals Tribunal, Federal Court (single judge) and Full Bench of the Federal Court.

process (prior to the High Court), arguments were put forward as to whether the conduct engaged in was an ordinary incident of an overnight stay, an activity not countenanced by the employer,[124] or a lawful activity engaged in during a work-related trip.

The High Court ultimately concluded that the test in *Hatzimanolis* was the correct one to be applied – that the circumstances in which the employee was injured must be connected to an inducement or encouragement by the employer.[125]

8.10.30 Psychological claims

As indicated in the s on definition of 'injury' above, psychological injury comes within the definition of injury for workers' compensation – provided that the psychological disorders (like all other types of injury) are diagnosable medical conditions. Therefore, medical certificates (known in some jurisdictions as 'certificates of capacity') need to specify the particular medical diagnosis (anxiety, post-traumatic stress disorder etc) rather than the more generic 'stress'.

In more recent years, jurisdictions have tended to move towards imposing thresholds before certain types of claims can be made. For example, since 2002, workers in NSW who suffer a psychological injury must have suffered a degree of permanent impairment of at least 15 per cent before they may claim compensation for that permanent impairment and pain and suffering.[126]

In addition, for a psychological injury to be compensable as a work-related injury, employment must be *the* major significant contributing factor,[127] not simply a significant contributing factor, as with other types of injury.

8.10.35 Excluded claims

Even though statutory workers' compensation schemes are regarded as 'no-fault' schemes, this is in the context of the injured worker not having to prove fault on the part of the employer or another party in order to access compensation – in contrast with fault-based matters such as common law negligence claims.

However, there are particular circumstances where a worker's claim for compensation will be excluded by virtue of conduct. These include where there is insufficient connection between the injury and the employment – as in matters such as *Comcare v PVYW*.[128]

Another example, particularly relevant to psychological injury claims, is where the injury arises from reasonable management action, conducted in a reasonable manner, in which case the injury is not compensable.[129]

The other significant basis on which workers' compensation claims are excluded is that of serious and wilful misconduct. Mere misconduct, or failure to follow a particular procedure, will not of itself reach this threshold. The 'serious and wilful misconduct' element is required,

---

124   Though it was agreed by the parties that the claimant's actions were not misconduct.
125   (2013) 250 CLR 246.
126   However, those under the threshold are still eligible for other entitlements, such as medical expenses and (capped) weekly benefits for income, if relevant.
127   *Workers Compensation and Rehabilitation Act 2003* (Qld) s 21(1)(b).
128   (2013) 250 CLR 246.
129   *Workers Compensation and Rehabilitation Act 2003* (Qld) s 32(5).

as it excludes claims other than for the most serious of injuries.[130] A parallel can be drawn with the position adopted by workers' compensation schemes to exclude deliberately self-inflicted injuries from compensation.[131]

8.10.40 Injury management, rehabilitation and return to work

Workers' compensation has evolved from merely a system of payments for injuries sustained to schemes with a broader focus on their own financial sustainability and the goal of returning injured workers to work, where possible. A necessary accompaniment to this is an increased emphasis on injury management, rehabilitation and the provision of suitable duties to injured workers to facilitate that return to work. This brings with it obligations on the parties involved.

There are obligations on employers to participate in the injury management process for injured workers[132] and to provide suitable duties for injured workers to assist them in their return to work.[133] The legislation will often also require employers to designate a person as their 'return-to-work coordinator'.[134]

As the premiums paid by larger employers are 'experience adjusted' for the cost of workers' compensation claims, not assisting an employee to return to work after injury is likely to increase the cost of the claim and therefore the subsequent burden on the employer of higher premiums.

There are complementary obligations on workers to participate in the injury management and rehabilitation process, comply with return-to-work programs, undertake suitable duties where offered, and attend medical examinations when required to do so.[135] Failure to meet any of these requirements may result in reduction or cessation of workers' compensation payments.

8.10.45 Employment issues following injury (including dismissal)

Most workers' compensation statutes in Australia provide protections for injured workers in relation to dismissal – in particular seeking to protect them in the months immediately following their becoming unfit for work due to work-related injury.[136] This is consistent with s 352 of the *Fair Work Act*, which provides that an employee not be dismissed for a temporary

130   *Workers Compensation Act 1987* (NSW) s 14(2); *Workers Compensation and Rehabilitation Act 2003* (Qld) s 130.
131   *Workers Compensation Act 1987* (NSW) s 14(3), albeit that this was not contained in the original legislation – anecdotally, because the notion of self-infliction of injury to gain compensation for the lost body part (as set out in the grimly named 'Table of Maims') was thought somewhat incredible.
132   *Workplace Injury Management and Workers Compensation Act 1998* (NSW) s 46.
133   Ibid s 49; *Workers Compensation and Rehabilitation Act 2003* (Qld) s 228.
134   *Workers Compensation and Rehabilitation Act 2003* (Qld) s 226.
135   *Workplace Injury Management and Workers Compensation Act 1998* (NSW) ss 47 and 48.
136   In NSW, for a period of 6 months following injury: *Workers Compensation Act 1987* (NSW) s 248; in Queensland, 12 months: *Workers Compensation and Rehabilitation Act 2003* (Qld) s 232B.

absence due to illness or injury. Under workers' compensation laws, dismissal during the 'relevant period' post-injury is also an offence which the regulator may prosecute.

In some cases these were contained within the State's industrial relations laws.[137] However, the enactment of the 2005 amendments to the *Workplace Relations Act 1996* (Cth) (*WR Act*), which had the effect of expanding Federal industrial laws, prompted State governments to transfer the relevant provisions from the industrial relations legislation to the workers' compensation legislation. The rationale for this was that while the *WR Act* (and the *Fair Work Act* subsequently) applied in relation to national system employers and employees 'to the exclusion of all State and Territory industrial laws so far as they would otherwise apply',[138] the legislation explicitly preserved the operation of State laws in respect of matters such as workers' compensation and workplace safety.[139]

After the prescribed period of protection has elapsed, if the employee's injury or continued incapacity means that they are unable to perform the inherent requirements of their role (subject to reasonable adjustments being made), an employer may be able to validly terminate the worker's employment. An employer should be cautious about coming to this conclusion too quickly, particularly where the employee is still on suitable duties or amended working hours as part of an approved return-to-work program.

Conversely, if an employee is able to demonstrate that they can perform the duties of the role, the dismissal is likely to be considered unfair.[140]

8.10.50 Interaction between State and Commonwealth schemes

Separate from the State workers' compensation schemes are the three Commonwealth schemes. The most relevant of these is the Comcare scheme, which covers the Commonwealth public sector, businesses that were formerly Commonwealth agencies (such as the Commonwealth Bank and Telstra) and in more recent times 'non-Commonwealth licensees': corporations that had in the past been in competition with government business enterprises.

This latter category arose from a 2004 report into workers' compensation,[141] particularly regarding employers operating in multiple jurisdictions. This led the Howard Government to expand the Comcare scheme to enable those corporations to join the scheme and thereby exit the State schemes.[142]

As a consequence of these changes, the Comcare scheme has come to be seen by the States as something of a drain on their schemes – removing corporations that were in many cases large contributors to revenue for their workers' compensation funding.

---

137   See, for example, *Industrial Relations Act 1996* (NSW) ss 91–100.
138   *Fair Work Act 2009* (Cth) s 26(1), with s 26(2) defining 'State or territory industrial' law to include, amongst others, the *Industrial Relations Act 1996* (NSW) and the *Industrial Relations Act 1999* (Qld).
139   *Fair Work Act 2009* (Cth) s 27(2).
140   *Cooper v Balfours Bakery Pty Ltd* (2011) 63 AILR 101-405.
141   Productivity Commission *Report into National Workers' Compensation and Occupational Health and Safety Frameworks* (AGPS, 2004).
142   Guthrie, Purse and Meredith 'Workers compensation and self-insurance in Australia – national priority or Trojan Horse' (2006).

Notwithstanding this competition, there has been a significant degree of cooperation and a degree of consistency has already been achieved amongst the jurisdictions,[143] much of it through the Heads of Workers Compensation Authorities (HWCA) group. While differences between schemes remain (particularly in relation to issues such as the levels of premiums and benefits payable), the prospect of consistent approaches is encouraged by successful initiatives such as multi-State guidance material;[144] a National Audit Tool for self-insurers; consistent criteria for accrediting rehabilitation providers;[145] and a simplifying of arrangements for businesses operating across State borders.[146]

8.15 Bullying

This section deals with the law as it relates to bullying in a workplace context. Except where it touches on that context, it does not deal with the issue of bullying in a broader community or non-work situations.

Bullying is a substantial workplace issue in both the public and private sectors,[147] across a range of industries, and responding to it is a challenge. Indeed, regulators and law enforcement agencies themselves have not been immune to it, as evidenced by the number of accepted compensation claims[148] and parliamentary inquiries involving such agencies.[149]

The law has responded in a variety of ways – from seeking to regulate or sanction the specific bullying behaviour (assaults, threats, etc) through to placing the onus on the employer to deal with the matter and, if that does not succeed, using a compliance and enforcement response (the workplace health and safety approach), through to the setting up of a specific jurisdiction to deal with bullying matters.

The following pages deal with the threshold issues of the definition of bullying and examples of how it manifests itself; the relationship between bullying and common law duties owed by employers and employees; the notion of bullying as a workplace health and safety issue and a workers' compensation issue respectively; and the operation of the Fair Work Commission's anti-bullying jurisdiction.

---

143   M Skulley 'States find common ground on Workplace Cover', *Australian Financial Review*, 28 August 2006; and Guthrie, Purse and Meredith 'Workers compensation and self-insurance in Australia – national priority or Trojan Horse' (2006).

144   WorkSafe Victoria *Defining Workers, Employees, and Contractors* (2009).

145   Heads of Workers Compensation Authorities (HWCA) *Communiqué of Meeting Outcomes* (2 October 2009).

146   WorkCover NSW *Cross Border Guide – Cross-Border Arrangements for Workers Compensation*, publication no. WC04814 (December 2009).

147   Safe Work Australia *Psychological Health and Safety and Bullying in Australian Workplaces: Indicators from Accepted Workers Compensation Claims, Annual Statement* (2015) (SWA 2015) indicates that 2070 out of 9610 accepted workers' compensation claims for mental health matters (some 21.5 per cent) were explicitly identified in the sub-category 'work-related harassment and/or workplace bullying'.

148   With 'Public Order and Safety Services' ranking third highest amongst the industries in terms of accepted workers' compensations claims arising from bullying and harassment (SWA 2015, 3).

149   See, for example, NSW Legislative Council General Purpose Standing Committee No. 1 *Report on Allegations of Bullying in WorkCover NSW*, 19 June 2014, https://www.parliament.nsw.gov.au/committees/DBAssets/InquiryReport/ReportAcrobat/5110/GPSC%20No%201%20-%20Report%2040%20-%20Allegations%20of%20bullying%20in.pdf.

8.15.05 Definition

The most broadly accepted definitions of bullying in a workplace context, and certainly those adopted in both the *Fair Work Act* and in the workplace health and safety guidance material, have the following common features. Bullying is:

- the repeated less favourable treatment of a person;
- by another or others in the workplace;
- behaviour which may be considered unreasonable and inappropriate workplace practice;
- behaviour that intimidates, offends, degrades or humiliates a worker.

'Unreasonable behaviour' is conduct that a reasonable person would see as victimising, humiliating, undermining or threatening in the circumstances.

Bullying may manifest as 'direct' (abusive language, 'initiations') or as 'indirect' or 'covert' (withholding information, increasing workload unreasonably). It can be directed sideways (most commonly, worker against worker); upwards (workers against a manager); or downwards (supervisor against a subordinate). And it can be intentional or unintended.

A single act – for example 'unfriending' on Facebook – will not, on its own, satisfy the definition.[150] However, in *Roberts*, the Facebook conduct was one of 18 incidents. The case is also authority for the proposition that repeated unreasonable behaviour does not necessarily mean repeating the *same* behaviour.

8.15.10 Reasonable management action

Not all conduct that is considered unfavourable to a worker is considered bullying. As is the case with workers' compensation, there is an exclusion in circumstances where the conduct directed to the worker was in fact reasonable management action, reasonably conducted.

As will be seen below, this notion has also been imported into the FWC's anti-bullying jurisdiction in s 789FD(2) of the *Fair Work Act*.[151]

8.15.15 Case law

Prior to the advent of the FWC's anti-bullying jurisdiction, and indeed still, mainstream courts have been a forum for bullying matters – whether arguing a breach of common law duties by an employer and/or fellow employees, breach of contract,[152] or on some other basis, such as negligence. Many matters also touch on other areas of the law, such as discrimination. One example of a matter in this latter category is the horrific behaviour – racial vilification, sexual assault and harassment both within and outside the workplace – to which the applicant had been subjected in the matter of *Nationwide News Pty Ltd v Naidu* (2007) 71 NSWLR 471.

---

150   *Roberts v VIEW Launceston Pty Ltd* (2015) 252 IR 357; see also *Harpreet Singh* [2015] FWC 5850, in which a single incident was found not to enliven the FWC's bullying jurisdiction.

151   *Applicant v Respondent* (2014) 66 AILR 102-283.

152   As in *Goldman Sachs JB Were Services Pty Ltd v Nikolich* (2007) 163 FCR 62.

'PUT SOME LIPPY ON': KEEGAN v SUSSAN CORPORATION (AUSTRALIA) PTY LTD [2014] QSC 64

Gabrielle Keegan was Assistant Manager at a North Queensland outlet of a fashion store. She had just returned from maternity leave, in September 2010, when her manager, who had been appointed while she was on leave, began harassing her.

Ms Keegan was subject to unwarranted criticism, often delivered in an aggressive manner (including holding a mop about 10cm from her face during a confrontation about cleaning). The bullying also involved 'excluding Ms Keegan from knowledge of and participation in matters of business management, ignoring Ms Keegan's offers of assistance and warning her of the consequences of a drop in standards'.[153]

Ms Keegan reported her concerns to the company's Queensland Business Manager. Despite Ms Keegan contacting them in tears complaining about her manager's bullying, the company's representative did not respond appropriately. Instead, Ms Keegan was allegedly told to 'put some lippy on and go home to your bub' while the matter was dealt with.

The company told the bullying manager about the complaint. The manager then confronted Ms Keegan. When Ms Keegan complained again to the Queensland Business Manager, she was told that she had to work it out for herself.

(It was revealed during the case that the Queensland Business Manager had hired the bullying manager in spite of a negative reference about her lack of management skills and people skills.)

The court found that the company's approach in dealing with the matter was inconsistent with its own bullying and harassment policy, that the complaint was not treated sufficiently seriously and that 'confidentiality was not respected ... [and] no attempt was made to investigate the complaint'.[154] The court also noted that the company's failure to act heightened the prospect of Ms Keegan's distress worsening and that the risk to her mental state and consequent injury was reasonably foreseeable.

The company was found liable and was ordered to pay Ms Keegan $237,770 in damages.

Amongst the many other examples of such matters is *Bailey v Peakhurst Bowling Club* [2009] NSWDC 284, which involved the applicant being subjected to threatening behaviour (including as to her continued employment), being prevailed upon to breach liquor laws, and being required to resign from her union.

8.15.20 Bullying as a workplace health and safety issue

As indicated above, persons conducting a business or an undertaking (PCBUs) have obligations in relation to the health and safety of workers and others in the workplace, and this extends to the risk of psychological injury and workplace violence.[155]

---

153   *Keegan v Sussan Corporation (Australia) Pty Ltd* [2014] QSC 64 at [7].
154   Ibid [124].
155   See also *Occupational Health and Safety Regulation 2001* (NSW) (repealed) at Clause 9(2)(j) for an example of this obligation in workplace safety law.

This means that it is open to workplace health and safety regulators to take enforcement action in relation to workplaces where the risk of bullying is present. This action can range from an Improvement Notice issued to implement bullying polices and training of staff through to prosecution for bullying-related safety offences.

While such prosecutions could hardly be described as common occurrences, a handful of cases (particularly in NSW and Victoria) have served to highlight the issue and its consequences.

In the *Coleman Joinery* matter,[156] a company, its directors and several employees were all prosecuted in relation to an 'initiation' incident in which a worker was wrapped in plastic by his co-workers, covered in sawdust and glue, including inside his clothes and mouth, and then had a fire hose sprayed on him to wash out his mouth, during which time he was coughing and choking.

Each of the defendants was found guilty. Fines were imposed on the company, the directors (whose fines were increased on appeal) and one of the employees; the other employees were placed on bonds.

In the more recent case of *Inspector Estreich v Zaccardelli* [2012] NSWIRComm 47, Work-Cover NSW prosecuted four workers (one of whom was the supervisor) for their conduct on a construction site towards a fellow worker. The conduct included grabbing the worker, tying him to steel reinforcing mesh, tearing his clothes, breaking eggs on his head, pouring petrol in a circle around him and igniting it. Two of the workers were fined and the other two were put on bonds with no conviction recorded. Significantly, the supervisor had also separately been convicted of assault in relation to the incident.

The first of the Victorian cases involved a radio announcer who bullied staff. The radio station at which the announcer worked did not take adequate steps to deal with his conduct. Both the employer and the bully were prosecuted by WorkSafe Victoria under that State's *Occupational Health and Safety Act* and were convicted and fined.[157]

In a more recent case, the regulator prosecuted a Mildura laundry owner who tormented his workers in various ways, including threatening employees with acid and telling them they should have been drowned.[158] He was convicted in the Magistrates Court and fined $50,000. He appealed, apparently unrepentant, but the Country Court upheld the conviction and fine.[159]

But by far the most prominent workplace health and safety prosecution in Victoria was that arising from the death of a young worker, Brodie Panlock.[160] Ms Panlock had committed suicide following sustained bullying from her co-workers in and out of the workplace.[161]

---

156   *Inspector Gregory Maddaford v M A Coleman Joinery (NSW) Pty Ltd* [2004] NSWCIMC 42 (first instance) and *Inspector Gregory Maddaford v Graham Gerard Coleman* [2004] NSWIRComm 317, (appeal by WorkCover against the leniency of the sentence).

157   *WorkSafe Victoria v Ballarat Radio* (Unreported, Ballarat Magistrates Court, 12 August 2004) and *WorkSafe Victoria v Reginald Mowat* (Unreported, Ballarat Magistrates Court, 22 July 2004).

158   *Victorian WorkCover Authority v Kevin James Andrews* (Unreported, Melbourne Magistrates Court, 5 December 2012) (first instance); and *Andrews v VWA* (2013) VCC 1615 (appeal); http://www.austlii.edu.au/au/cases/vic/VCC/2013/1615.html.

159   Ibid.

160   *Victorian WorkCover Authority v MAP Foundation (trading as Café Vamp)* (Unreported, Magistrates Court of Victoria, Magistrate Lauritsen, 8 February 2010). Prosecution summary at http://www1.worksafe.vic.gov.au/vwa/vwa097-002.nsf/content/LSID164635-1.

161   http://www.coronerscourt.vic.gov.au/home/coroners+written+findings/finding+-+inquest+into+the+death+of+brodie+panlock.

In addition to the Inquest and prosecution, Ms Panlock's death resulted in the enactment of 'Brodie's law': amendments to s 21A of the *Crimes Act 1958* (Vic) extended the definition of 'stalking' to include serious bullying.[162]

The 'Brodie's Law' provision in the *Crimes Act* was recently utilised in a prosecution which resulted in the perpetrator of long-term bullying at a Woolworths supermarket being sentenced to a term of imprisonment.[163]

8.15.25 Bullying as a workers' compensation issue

It should be reasonably apparent that as psychological injury may be a compensable injury for the purposes of workers' compensation, victims of workplace bullying may be able to access the workers' compensation scheme. As with other work-related injuries, there must be a diagnosed injury or medical condition, with work as a substantial contributing factor.

By way of example, in another fatality preceded by bullying, Alec Meikle was subjected to several incidents of workplace bullying, including being sprayed with flammable liquid, having his work apparently sabotaged, and threats being made that he would be assaulted with an object if his errors reached a certain cumulative point.[164]

While the Inquest into the death of Alex Meikle was unable to conclude that *the* cause of death was in the jurisdiction where the bullying had occurred[165] – due to his death occurring overseas some months after the bullying incidents – there was a sufficiently clear link between the conduct in the workplace and his diagnosed psychological injuries for his medical treatment to be the subject of a successful workers' compensation claim.[166]

As with other workers' compensation cases, reasonable management action is also an exclusion in bullying-related claims.

A recent Tasmanian case considered a claim for workers' compensation arising from alleged workplace bullying, in which the employer sought to rely on the defence of reasonable administrative action (the relevant equivalent in that State's workers' compensation legislation).[167] In that matter, the tribunal confirmed that the threshold to be met is that 'the action be reasonable and that it be taken in a reasonable manner. It is not necessary for the action to be worker friendly, or that it be taken with the utmost sensitivity and delicacy.'[168]

---

162   Similar provisions exist in some other States, such as *Criminal Code* (Qld) s 359B in relation to unlawful stalking.

163   *R v Sean Clare* (Unreported, La Trobe Magistrates Court, 25 November 2015). See also 'Woolworths employee jailed over workplace bullying at Moe store', 5 July 2016, http://www.abc.net.au/news/2015-11-25/woolworths-employee-jailed-over-workplace-bullying-at-moe-store/6973828

164   *Inquest into the Death of Alec Samuel Meikle*, Coroner's Court of NSW, December 2013. See report of Deputy State Coroner McMahon, http://www.coroners.justice.nsw.gov.au/Documents/meikle,%20alec%20samuel%20-%20findings.pdf.

165   The relevant requirement under *Coroner's Act 2009* (NSW) s 18 to give jurisdiction where the death has occurred outside the State.

166   *Inquest into the Death of Alec Samuel Meikle*, 5.

167   *C v Community and Public Sector Union* [2015] TASWRCT 16, dealing with s 25(1A), *Workers Rehabilitation and Compensation Act 1988* (Tas).

168   *Headway Support Services v Wickham* [2009] TASSC 99, Blow CJ at [13], cited in [2015] TASWRCT 16 at [7].

8.20 Fair Work Commission and bullying – the statutory scheme

The statutory anti-bullying jurisdiction introduced by Part 6-4B of the *Fair Work Act*[169] was enacted via amendments that took effect on 1 January 2014, vesting the Fair Work Commission (FWC) with the power to deal with these matters.[170] The amendments followed a parliamentary inquiry into bullying which reported in November 2012. Its recommendations included seeking a clear definition of bullying and promoting and strengthening legislative and regulatory frameworks.[171]

The establishment of the anti-bullying jurisdiction was predicted to lead to many thousands of applications being received by the FWC. In fact, in the first 6 months in which the jurisdiction operated, 343 applications were lodged.[172] Reasons for those statistics will be discussed below. They include the eligibility requirements themselves.

As with other matters dealt with by the FWC, legal representation is not an automatic right, but may be granted on the basis that it would be unfair to refuse it in the particular circumstances or that legal representation will facilitate the matter being dealt with more efficiently.[173]

In many cases, in accordance with s 593 of the *Fair Work Act*, the FWC has made a determination to supress the identity of one or more of the parties, but again, it does not do so automatically and must be satisfied that there are substantive reasons for doing so.[174]

8.20.05 Eligibility: worker constitutionally covered

Like the current statutory schemes for workers' compensation and workplace health and safety, a central concept in the FWC anti-bullying jurisdiction is the concept of 'worker'.

Like the workplace health and safety sphere, the definition of 'work' for the purposes of an application to stop bullying are quite broad (but not universal). Section 789FC of the *Fair Work Act* specifies that (with the exception of the Defence Force) 'worker' has the same meaning as in the *WHS Act*.[175]

The worker must also be engaged or employed by a person conducting a business or undertaking[176] that is a 'constitutionally covered business' as defined in s 789FD(3) of the *Fair Work Act*: a constitutional corporation; or the Commonwealth; or a Commonwealth authority; or a body corporate incorporated in a Territory; or a business or undertaking conducted principally in a Territory or Commonwealth place.[177] Consequently, reference must be made

---

169   *Fair Work Act 2009* (Cth) ss 789FA–789FL.
170   A Queensland anti-bullying jurisdiction, taking effect from 1 March 2017, was introduced by the *Industrial Relations Act 2016* (Qld) ss 272–277.
171   House of Representatives Standing Committee on Education and Employment *Workplace Bullying: We Just Want it to Stop*, tabled on 26 November 2012.
172   Fair Work Commission *Annual Report 2013–14*.
173   *H v Centre* [2014] FWC 6128; *Re Applicant* [2014] FWC 7378.
174   *Justin Corfield* [2014] FWC 4887, applied in *Bowker v DP World Melbourne Ltd* (2014) 246 IR 138.
175   *Work Health and Safety Act 2011* (Cth) s 7(1).
176   Again consistent with the meaning in the *WHS Act*.
177   *K.L. v Trade & Investment Queensland* [2016] FWC 4174; *Re Amzalak* (2016) 262 IR 284 (the latter dealing with the question of the extent to which Victoria had referred powers in relation to bullying).

to s 5 of the *WHS Act* for the scope of 'person conducting a business or undertaking' (PCBU). Section 5 is a broad definition. However, s 5(8) excludes volunteer associations where the volunteers are working (unpaid) for one or more community purposes and where none of the volunteers (either alone or jointly) employs any person to carry out work for the association.

In *Re McDonald* (2016) 258 IR 99 it was confirmed that volunteers can apply for an order to stop bullying, but for them to be regarded as workers requires consideration of whether the organisation was a PCBU for the purposes of the *WHS Act*. In that matter, all of those involved were volunteers and they were not eligible to access the FWC's bullying jurisdiction as, without the employment of anyone, the organisation was not a PCBU that was constitutionally covered.

Contrast this with *Marie Pasalskyj* (2015) 67 AILR 102-483, in which a community services organisation providing services for offenders, ex-prisoners and their families was held to be a trading corporation (and therefore a constitutionally covered business) as 11 per cent of its income came from trading activities and this was held to be significant and sufficient to impact the character of the organisation.

As indicated in the part of this chapter dealing with workplace health and safety, a PCBU may be an individual or individual members of a partnership or of a joint venture.[178] However, for the purpose of enlivening the anti-bullying jurisdiction, the PCBU must also be an entity that falls within s 789FD of the *Fair Work Act*.

Thus a sole trader or partnership conducted principally in a State is unlikely to fall within the jurisdiction, nor would State government departments or local councils, despite the fact that each of these would meet the definition of a PCBU under the model *WHS Act* adopted in each State other than Victoria and WA.

Importantly, the criteria of 'worker' and 'business or undertaking' is a two-step test and also requires a link between the work performed and the business or undertaking being conducted. In *Balthazaar v Department of Human Services (Cth)* (2014) 241 IR 390, the FWC concluded that the work of a carer could be work for the purposes of the Act but that the receipt of social security benefits in the form of a carer's allowance was not work performed *for* the Department of Human Services.

Section 789FD of the *Fair Work Act* refers to 'bullied at work', so what constitutes 'at work' arises. A Full Bench of the FWC considered this question in *Bowker v DP World Melbourne Ltd* (2014) 246 IR 138. In that matter, the Full Bench found that the phrase 'at work' means performing work or engaged in employer-authorised activities and when engaged in some other activity authorised or permitted by the employer. It also held that the alleged bullies need not be at work at the time of their conduct, and rejected the argument that social media posts had to have occurred at work, noting that the behaviour continues as long as the posts are online. Being subjected to bullying behaviour when seeking to enter the workplace has also been held to have sufficient connection.[179] It is also possible that behaviour upon leaving the workplace may also be so regarded.[180]

---

178   Marks et al. *The New Work Health & Safety Legislation* (2013) 26.
179   *Worker A, Worker B, Worker C, Worker D and Worker E v Automotive, Food, Metals, Engineering, Printing and Kindred Industries Union* [2016] FWC 5848.
180   See, for example, *Kedwell v Coal & Allied Mining Services Pty Ltd (t/as Mount Thorley Operations/ Warkworth Mining)* [2016] FWC 6018 (an unfair dismissal case involving harassment of a co-worker on the way home from work).

8.20.10 Eligibility: bullying has occurred

Section 789FD(1) of the *Fair Work Act* states that a worker is bullied at work if:

    (a) while the worker is at work in a constitutionally covered business:
        (i) an individual; or
        (ii) a group of individuals;
        repeatedly behaves unreasonably towards the worker, or a group of workers of which the worker is a member; and
    (b) that behaviour creates a risk to safety.

Consistent with the notion that bullying does not extend to reasonable management action, in *Mac v Bank of Queensland Ltd* (2015) 247 IR 67 the FWC found that while the applicant had a genuinely held belief that they had been bullied, placing the applicant on a Performance Improvement Plan was not an unreasonable action, and that while the employer's conduct was neither best practice nor beyond criticism, it did not reach anywhere near the required level of unreasonableness for the manner in which it was done to constitute bullying.

Likewise, it is apparent that there needs to be some genuine connection between the person engaged in the alleged bullying and the purported victims of that conduct. For example, in the matter of *Millman v Essential Energy* [2016] FWC 2653,[181] two employees contended that they had been the subject of unreasonable management action, allegedly at the behest of the Chief Executive Officer, in being denied redundancy and being left without meaningful roles and meaningful or sufficient work. The FWC ultimately found that it was unreasonable for the employer to have denied these two workers voluntary redundancy in circumstances where they were then left with no meaningful work and, in the specific circumstances, considered it appropriate to order that the employer accept the redundancy applications of these two workers.[182] However, it also found that the company's adoption of a particular approach (not accepting redundancy applications from employees who would be entitled to a payment in excess of 52 weeks), while having implications for the two employees, could not imply that the policy was directed at either of them personally and not so directed by the CEO.[183]

Bullying applications, by their nature, deal with matters of behaviour, the appropriateness of that behaviour and whether or not it falls within the definition of bullying – in relation to either its having occurred or its being an ongoing risk. However, as indicated in *Re Gore* [2016] FWC 2559, while alleged bullying is 'highly contextual', Parliament clearly distinguished between an applicant's self-belief and feelings of discomfort on the one hand and reasonable workplace conduct on the other, noting that 'the legislation does not provide for an applicant's self-belief or self-conviction to trump all other factors'.[184]

8.20.15 Eligibility: ongoing risk

As well as having to be satisfied that a worker has been bullied at work by an individual or group of individuals, another prerequisite for the FWC to be able to make orders to stop

181   The matter number also incorporates a related dispute resolution matter, *CFMEU v Essential Energy*.
182   *Millman v Essential Energy* [2016] FWC 2653 at [112].
183   Ibid [86] to [88].
184   *Re Gore* (2016) 257 IR 257 at [73].

bullying is that 'there is a risk that the worker will continue to be bullied at work by the individual or group'.[185]

Consequently, if it can be shown that the worker is no longer at ongoing risk of bullying, the FWC is precluded from making orders under that section. Aside from the (perhaps optimistic) instance of the bullying behaviour actually having stopped, the clearest circumstance in which 'no ongoing risk' could occur is where one or more of the participants are no longer part of the equation: for example, where the applicant is no longer working for the organisation.[186] In these circumstances, the FWC has usually been prepared to dismiss an application as having no reasonable prospect of success. In *Re Bayly* (2017) 263 IR 200, however, appearing to recognise the prospect that dismissal or other disciplinary action may frustrate the bullying claim, the FWC made orders effectively preventing disciplinary action or dismissal while the matter remained before the FWC.

Notably, the Commission has also drawn the distinction that if a person is no longer performing work for an organisation but could reasonably expect to do so in the future, and if the working relationship itself has not been concluded, an application will not necessarily be dismissed. This is particularly so where neither party concedes that there has been either a resignation or a termination.[187]

Where the person(s) alleged to have engaged in the bullying behaviour are no longer employed there may again be no evidence of ongoing risk and an application may be dismissed as having no reasonable prospects of success without needing to make findings as to the nature of the behaviour itself.[188]

However, action by the employer to remove the alleged perpetrator from the particular workplace but putting them to work in a different (but related) business with ongoing contact with the original workplace may not meet this threshold.[189]

8.20.20 Defences

The provisions of *Fair Work Act* s 789FD(2), excluding reasonable management action from the scope of bullying and allowing it as a complete defence if made out, makes it, not surprisingly, a widely utilised defence.

Taking the notion of 'defences' in the broadest sense and including jurisdictional objections to bullying applications, other responses to bullying actions regularly include challenges on the basis that:

- The applicant is no longer working for the organisation and therefore there is no risk of continued bullying;[190]

---

185   *Fair Work Act 2009* (Cth) s 789FF(1).

186   *Mitchell Shaw v Australia and New Zealand Banking Group Ltd* [2014] FWC 3408; *Willis v Capital Radiology Pty Ltd* [2016] FWC 716; *Atkinson v Killarney Properties Pty Ltd* [2015] FWCFB 6503; *Obatoki v Mallee Track Health & Community Services* (2015) 249 IR 135; *Ravi v Baker IDI Heart and Diabetes Institute Holdings Ltd* [2014] FWC 7507.

187   *Justin Simounds* [2016] FWC 2040.

188   *Lisa Fsadni* [2016] FWC 1286.

189   *Lokteeva v Woolworths Ltd* [2016] FWC 3603; *CF v Company A* (2015) 252 IR 377. Though contrast with *Darren Lacey and Chris Kandelaars v Murrays Australia and Andrew Cullen* [2017] FWC 3136, where transfer was sufficient to avoid the need for orders.

190   See, for example, *Shaw v Australia and New Zealand Banking Group Ltd* [2014] FWC 3408; *Willis v Capital Radiology Pty Ltd* [2016] FWC 716; *Atkinson v Killarney Properties Pty Ltd* [2015] FWCFB 6503; and *Obatoki v Mallee Track Health & Community Services* (2015) 249 IR 135.

- The person(s) alleged to have engaged in the bullying behaviour are no longer employed and therefore there is no ongoing risk;[191] and/or
- The organisation falls outside the jurisdiction because it not constitutionally covered.[192]

The FWC has also made findings that where an applicant has elected to treat earlier conduct by the employer as a dismissal for other purposes (such as recovery of entitlements or an unfair dismissal claim), they may be held to such an election when it comes to assessing factors such as whether the applicant is employed by the respondent employer and whether or not there is any reasonable prospect of the applicant returning to the workplace as a worker.[193]

A Full Bench of the FWC has also held that a tribunal member may find that some incidents occurred at work and were not reasonable management action and yet still conclude that the threshold of repeated unreasonable behaviour at work warranting the making of orders to stop bullying has not been met.[194]

8.20.25 Remedies

The nature of the orders available to the FWC in the anti-bullying jurisdiction is expressed in *Fair Work Act* s 789FF(1) in terms of 'any order it considers appropriate' to prevent the worker from being bullied by the relevant individual or group. However, the same section expressly excludes the FWC from making any order requiring payment of a pecuniary amount: the awarding of compensation or other damages falls outside of the scope of the FWC's anti-bullying jurisdiction.

Similarly, the anti-bullying jurisdiction is not a 'catch all' jurisdiction in which to agitate a raft of workplace-related grievances such as unpaid or underpaid entitlements. Such grievances can be lodged with the relevant regulator, such as the Fair Work Ombudsman, and it is up to the applicant to do so and not expect the FWC to refer matters elsewhere where they go beyond the scope of anti-bullying.[195]

Likewise, the eligibility requirements for an anti-bullying order – such as remaining engaged in work or likely to be engaged in work and as such at ongoing risk of bullying – preclude remedies such as reinstatement. Put simply, if you can't succeed in a bullying application because you're no longer employed, termination-related remedies can't be given to you by the FWC's anti-bullying jurisdiction. Whether a person is able to separately succeed in an unfair dismissal or general protections claim against that former employer is another matter entirely.

8.20.30 Outcomes from the FWC's bullying jurisdiction

For a jurisdiction dealing with such a disputed and emotionally charged area, it may be somewhat surprising that the majority of the 'stop bullying' orders issued by the FWC have been by consent.

---

191   *Lisa Fsadni* [2016] FWC 1286.
192   *A.B.* [2014] FWC 672 (where the applicant was employed by a State government department); and *Gaylene May McDonald* [2016] FWC 300 (the applicant was a volunteer in an organisation comprised only of volunteers).
193   *KM* [2016] FWC 2088 and noting the decision of the Full Bench in *Atkinson v Killarney Properties Pty Ltd* [2015] FWCFB 6503 that reinstatement is one factor.
194   *Hammon v Metricon Homes Pty Ltd* [2016] FWCFB 1914.
195   *KM* [2016] FWC 2088.

Indeed, in many matters, even where there are different versions of events, the incidents themselves are either not disputed or the areas in dispute are minor or a question of the inferences that may be drawn.

The first orders made by a Commissioner in the anti-bullying jurisdiction appear as a model of both the issuing of orders by consent (and indeed their variation by consent) and of orders ultimately no longer being required.

That matter, referred to by the anonymous pseudonym *Applicant*, was the subject of consent orders in March 2014, a variation of these orders by consent in September 2014, and a December 2014 decision of the Commissioner revoking the earlier orders following receipt of information regarding an improved working relationship and a desire to make 'a new start in the new year'.[196] Subsequent orders in other matters have also tended to be by consent.[197]

Even where there have been findings of unreasonable conduct, it may be that the circumstances of a particular bullying case at the time the FWC is called on is such that the Commission member elects not to make orders.[198] Alternatively, where the matter involves broader issues, such as those in *Millman v Essential Energy* [2016] FWC 2653, it may be that other applications and other orders (beyond orders to stop bullying) provide an appropriate response.

8.20.35 Relationship of bullying to other matters dealt with by the FWC

In reality, the FWC's role in bullying matters is not confined to the anti-bullying jurisdiction. There are a number of reasons for this, not least of which being that some employers choose to take action against the perpetrator of the bullying (rather than the arguably more traditional approach of blaming the victim). However, as the examples below indicate, there are also cases in which the employee has alleged bullying-related issues as part of a termination complaint.

There are several examples of unfair dismissal cases in which employees have contested their dismissal and the employer has argued, successfully, that there was a valid reason for the dismissal – that being the employee's bullying conduct.[199] For example, in *Carroll v Karingal Inc* [2016] FWC 3709, the FWC upheld the dismissal of an employee arising from bullying complaints that included inappropriate behaviour and micromanagement. The extent to which workplace policies are in place and instruction and training on appropriate conduct are provided is also important. In *Salloum v Jayco Unit Trust (t/as Jayco Caravan Manufacturing)* [2016] FWC 3746, an employee who was sacked for inappropriate workplace behaviour that occurred even after bullying and harassment training had been provided was found to have been fairly dismissed.

---

196   PR548852 (21 March 2014), PR555329 (10 September 2014) and [2014] FWC 9184 (16 December 2014) respectively.

197   See, for example, *Blenkinsop* (PR555521, 15 September 2014) and *CF and NW v Company A and ED* [2015] FWC 5272.

198   See, for example, *Re LP (No. 2)* (2016) 256 IR 39; *Ari Kypuros* [2017] FWC 3082.

199   For example, *R and Y v Toll Holdings Ltd* [2016] FWC 4140; *Hansen v Calvary Health Care Adelaide Ltd* [2016] FWCFB 5223.

Adverse action matters have also canvassed bullying issues. In *Jones v Queensland Tertiary Admissions Centre Ltd (No. 2)* (2010) 186 FCR 22, the Federal Court considered the question of whether commencing an investigation into bullying complaints against a person who was a bargaining representative amounted to adverse action. The court held that commencing an investigation into bullying complaints, when there were reasonable grounds for doing so, was not adverse action, though it recognised that in other circumstances such a response might be unreasonable.

In *Lisha v St Vincent de Paul Society NSW* [2016] FWC 2080, the applicant argued that termination of his employment was as a consequence of his raising a bullying complaint. While the FWC did not find that his employment was terminated for that prohibited reason, the Commissioner observed that the decision to terminate employment with immediate effect 'lacked decency [and was] hard to reconcile with the Christian mission' of the organisation.[200]

8.25 Anti-discrimination

In her pioneering works – *Anti-Discrimination Legislation in Australia*[201] and *Affirmative Action and Sex Discrimination: A Handbook on Legal Rights for Women*[202] – Ronalds discusses the range of international treaties and conventions that seek to guard against discrimination. All ratified by Australia, the International Labour Organization (ILO) Convention concerning Discrimination in Respect of Employment and Occupation, United Nations International Covenant on Civil and Political Rights, United Nations Convention on the Elimination of All Forms of Racial Discrimination and the United Nations Convention on the Elimination of All Forms of Discrimination against Women largely form the basis on which successive Federal governments, using the international affairs power of the Constitution, have enacted legislation aiming to prevent discrimination.[203]

Helpfully, as well as Ronalds, services such as CCH's *Australian and New Zealand Equal Opportunity Commentary* provide a complete and up-to-date list of all the discrimination law at both Commonwealth and State level.[204] That includes the key Federal statutes:

- *Racial Discrimination Act 1975*;
- *Sex Discrimination Act 1984*;
- *Disability Discrimination Act 1992*; and
- *Age Discrimination Act 2004*.

There are also adverse action provisions of the *Fair Work Act* (see Chapter 3). Further, the *Workplace Gender Equality Act 2012* (Cth) places an obligation on institutions of higher learning and entities employing 100 or more to establish workplace equal opportunity programs. Finally, there is a *Human Rights Commission Act 1986* (Cth), which provides a

---

200   *Lisha v St Vincent de Paul Society NSW* [2016] FWC 2080 at [37].
201   C Ronalds *Anti-Discrimination Legislation in Australia* (Butterworths, 1979) 2 et seq.
202   C Ronalds *Affirmative Action and Sex Discrimination: A Handbook on Legal Rights for Women* (Pluto Press, 1987) 16–17 et seq.
203   CCH *Australian and New Zealand Equal Opportunity Commentary* 2-440, 2-970 (accessed on CCH Intelliconnect November 2016).
204   Ibid 2-780.

mechanism through which parties may seek alternative dispute resolution of discrimination complaints and through which research and inquiries can be undertaken into human rights issues.

Given the international law background, there are many similar concepts that arise in many of the various anti-discrimination and human rights Acts.[205] However, there are also significant differences.[206] While clearly human rights is an important motivation and reason for this legislation, it is interesting that the virtues of reasonable protections against discrimination have been traversed by scholars of law and economics[207] who have canvassed the arguments around whether it is more efficient for business and the economy to utilise talent than to discriminate against talent because of gender etc.

Statistically, a significant number of the employment-related complaints involve gender discrimination.[208] Against that background, this commentary analyses the key concepts of the Commonwealth *Sex Discrimination Act 1984* (*SD Act*), namely direct and indirect discrimination – respectively, 'less favourable treatment' which is 'on the ground of' gender, and rules which seem fair in form but are disadvantageous in their effects on women. These concepts provide a useful base for consideration of all discrimination laws. The discussion then moves to a consideration of equal opportunity (and how that relates to the older concept of affirmative action). The commentary concludes by discussing specific current legal issues in the broader discrimination field: *Racial Discrimination Act 1975* s 18C, the recent series of cases relating to that provision, and the relationship s 18C bears to employment law.

8.25.05 Discrimination: types and prohibitions

There are two types of discrimination – direct and indirect. Direct discrimination is basically 'facial' discrimination – where, *on the face of the evidence*, one person has been treated less favourably than another on the basis of their gender. In contrast, indirect discrimination involves *rules which, on their face, seem non-discriminatory* – the problem instead lies in their inequitable effect. The primary anti-discrimination legislation pertaining to gender in Australia is the *SD Act*. It prohibits discrimination based on gender and other related attributes, such as marital status,[209] in employment – be that engagement, promotion, termination, conditions offered etc.[210]

---

205   Some of those were alluded to by Hon Judge Jarrett in QUT at para 39 – for example, the concept of humiliation in sexual harassment (*Sex Discrimination Act 1984* s 28A) and s 18C claims under the *Racial Discrimination Act 1975*.

206   See CCH *Australian and New Zealand Equal Opportunity Commentary* 4-420 'Concept of reasonableness', which discusses the differences between the various State and Federal statutes on reasonableness in indirect discrimination as well as the onus of proof. See also 4-480 'Reasonableness'.

207   S Schwab, 'Employment discrimination' (2000) 3 *Encyclopedia of Law and Economics* 31 (also at http://cornell.edu/facpub/530).

208   Australian Human Rights Commission *Annual Report 2014–15*, Appendix 1: Complaint statistics 136, https://www.humanrights.gov.au/sites/default/files/document/publication/AHRC_Annual%20Report%202014%E2%80%9315_Web%20version.pdf (accessed 19 January 2017).

209   *SD Act* s 6 – see also s 7 et seq.

210   Ibid s 14.

8.25.10 Direct discrimination

Under s 5(1) of the *SD Act*, one person discriminates against another 'on the ground of the sex of the aggrieved person if, by reason of' that aggrieved person's gender or a characteristic of that gender 'the discriminator treats the aggrieved person less favourably' than they would treat someone of a different gender in similar circumstances.[211] So there are two elements: treating someone less favourably; and doing so on the ground of their gender (causation).

WARDLEY v ANSETT (1984) EOC 92-002

The earliest major direct discrimination case and still one of the most notable cases on how these elements are met is *Wardley v Ansett* (1984) EOC 92-002.[212] Mrs Wardley had qualifications from the University of Melbourne, a commercial pilot's licence and 500 hours of flying experience, and performed well in the interview for a position as pilot with the old Ansett Airlines. Despite that, her application was unsuccessful. She was beaten for the position by males who had not performed as well as she in the application process. The evidence demonstrated that she failed to gain the position due to her child-bearing potential. Some members of the selection panel were concerned about the effect that might have on scheduling (for example).

As one can imagine, there are, sadly, numerous cases on direct discrimination. As with dismissal, it is not often that one would come across cases with identical facts, so arguing a point generally rests on extrapolating from one case to another.

Two significant cases to consider are *Waterhouse v Bell* (1991) 25 NSWLR 99 and *Boehringer Ingleheim v Reddrop* [1984] 2 NSWLR 13.

WATERHOUSE v BELL (1991) 25 NSWLR 99

Waterhouse v Bell involved the now famous and well-respected racehorse trainer Gai Waterhouse. Mrs Waterhouse was the daughter of respected trainer Tommy Smith, had attended the respected Catholic girls' school Kincoppal in Sydney; and had even performed an acting stint on the respected old television show *The Young Doctors*.[213] Not that those facts were the centre of the litigation, but the point is that there was nothing that stood out as a blemish on Mrs Waterhouse's character – in fact, the evidence was quite to the contrary. However, Mrs Waterhouse was married to Robbie Waterhouse – a man who had been

---

211   Ibid 5(1).
212   See also R McCallum *McCallum's Top Workplace Relations Cases: Labour and the Employment Relationship Defined by Case Law* (CCH, 2008).
213   These facts are well known, especially to the author, who in her heyday was something of a fan of the show!

warned off Australian racecourses by the Australian Jockey Club due to his association with the Fine Cotton ring-in scandal – where, unbelievably – a horse was actually dyed a different colour to fool punters and therefore influence betting!

Mrs Waterhouse was rejected for a trainer's licence by the Australian Jockey Club (AJC). After seeking reasons for the denial but initially being declined her request, Mrs Waterhouse's inference (that despite all that respectability in *her* background, she was regarded as tainted because of who she was married to)[214] seemed to be confirmed in a letter from the AJC of 9 March 1990, which stated:[215] 'Mrs Waterhouse was not refused a trainer's licence because she is a married person but because she is married to a person who has been warned off every racecourse in Australia and elsewhere.' The letter also referred to the need for the AJC to protect racing standards. It claimed its rejection of Mrs Waterhouse was a necessary decision due to the finding of the court in the earlier case, *Boehringer Ingleheim v Reddrop* [1984] 2 NSWLR 13.

Mrs Waterhouse appealed on the basis that the decision must rest on an assumption that women (generally, including herself) can be corrupted by their husbands. Remember, there was nothing in *her* background to suggest a doubtful character, so where would any doubts come from? Surely it must stem from concerns about *his* background and suspicions that the fact that *he* had done something shady would *influence her*.

The court agreed – this was discrimination based on a characteristic that was imputed to women: they would be influenced by their roguish husbands and not stand strong as individuals. In particular, the court pointed out that:[216]

- there was no evidence to slight Mrs Waterhouse's character;
- the evidence was that Mrs Waterhouse had an excellent character;
- most of the decision to reject Mrs Waterhouse spoke of problems with Mr Waterhouse; and
- the internal decision of the initial AJC investigators was to accept Mrs Waterhouse – that was reversed by the final internal committee of the AJC without any apparent investigation.

In short, the belief was that 'the plaintiff was liable to be corrupted by Robbie Waterhouse simply because she was married to him'.[217] To put it another way, 'the plaintiff was liable to be corrupted because, and only because, she was married to a man both deceitful and manipulative'.[218] There was no evidence that she had 'personal character deficiencies which rendered her vulnerable to the corrupting influence of her husband',[219] so there must have been an assumption that she *like women generally* would be corrupted by their husbands. That point is borne out most vividly when one considers the further evidence that Mr Waterhouse knew Mrs Waterhouse's father, Tommy Smith – but at no stage did anyone think Mr Smith would be corrupted – no, there must have been an assumption that *wives* were corruptible.[220]

The NSW Court of Appeal in *Waterhouse* distinguished *Reddrop*, which is considered below.

214   *Waterhouse v Bell* (1991) 25 NSWLR 99 especially from 100.
215   Ibid 101 per Clarke JA.
216   Ibid 110–112 et seq.
217   Ibid 111.
218   Ibid 110.
219   Ibid.
220   Ibid 115.

BOEHRINGER INGELHEIM v REDDROP [1984] 2 NSWLR 13

Boehringer Ingelheim had refused a job to a woman applicant whose husband was employed by a rival company. However, significantly, the evidence showed: 'if (the decision maker) had known that any applicant had a close relationship with an employee of a competitor they would have eliminated him or her as a candidate'.[221] This caution of Boehringer was due to security reasons – the idea that *any two people living closely* (not just husbands and wives) might accidentally 'let something slip' or be overheard in a conversation or leave sensitive documents lying around.[222] Security might be breached despite the best efforts and integrity of the staffer concerned: 'The decision in ... *Reddrop* [was] ... grounded upon a characteristic which was particular to Mrs Reddrop (and was not generally imputed to married women), that is, that she had a close relationship with an employee of a competitor.'[223]

The court in Waterhouse distinguished *Reddrop*. Indeed, in a quite tongue in cheek section of the *Waterhouse* judgement, Clarke JA, in reflecting upon *Reddrop*, pondered whether there is no breach of the discrimination provisions when what is in question are the proclivities of the particular spouse rather than something more general: 'I do not think the [provision] would prevent an employer refusing to engage as a live-in cook a man who was cohabiting with Typhoid Mary.'[224] The job loss would be because of the risk of typhoid (he was at high risk of getting it) rather than marital status or a characteristic of married people.[225]

8.25.15 Indirect discrimination

Under s 5(2) of the *SD Act* indirect discrimination occurs if a party imposes a condition or practice likely to have a disadvantaging effect on people of the same gender as the aggrieved person. Unlike direct discrimination, there is a defence of reasonableness in s 7B. So, if the condition is reasonable there is no discrimination – such an inquiry typically involves a consideration of the nature and extent of the disadvantage suffered, the result sought to be achieved by imposing the condition, and the feasibility of changing it.[226] The burden of proving reasonableness lies with the alleged discriminator under s 7C.[227]

The High Court of Australia considered indirect discrimination in the case below.

AUSTRALIAN IRON AND STEEL v BANOVIC (1989) 168 CLR 165

Most Australians would be familiar with the 'last on, first off" concept in redundancy: confronted by a situation where they have to lose staff for economic or structural reasons,

---

221   Ibid 102, citing *Boehringer*.
222   *Waterhouse v Bell* (1991) 25 NSWLR 99 at 115.
223   Ibid 115. See also, generally, *Boehringer*.
224   *Waterhouse v Bell* (1991) 25 NSWLR 99 at 104.
225   Ibid 115.
226   For an excellent discussion of the concept as it applies to each of the discrimination statutes see CCH *Australian and New Zealand Equal Opportunity Commentary* 4-480 'Reasonableness' and 4-420 'Concept of reasonableness'.
227   But the position is complex – in relation to the approaches taken in the various legislation, see ibid.

rather than misconduct by any staff, an employer might chose to make the most recent people employed the first people to leave – it is one approach to a situation where there must be job losses but there is no blame to be attributed to individual staff. That policy was applied in *Banovic*'s case. Although it is actually a well-known approach in this country, it was held to be discriminatory in this instance.

Significantly, Australian Iron and Steel employed 7698 men and only 510 women – of a total 553 iron workers retrenched, 32 were women.[228] Those statistics led to quite a complex series of judgements in the High Court as to how one applies the indirect discrimination sections, and what groups should be used as comparisons. There were four separate judgements handed down with the decision. But by a 3:2 majority, the 'last on, first off' approach was said to be discriminatory in this instance (even though there were roughly equal proportions of men and women laid off) due to the particular circumstances: this employer had a poor track record on engaging women staff (at the relevant time it had only recently sought to turn that poor track record around through recruiting new staff who were women). In those circumstances, the 'last on, first off rule' would disadvantage those women and therefore have a discriminatory effect or repeat the discrimination of the past (with no arguable justification for so doing).[229]

8.25.20 Genuine occupational requirement

If an employee of a particular gender is sought because that is a 'genuine occupational requirement', that will not offend the legislation.[230] Such a requirement might include reasons of decency (working in change rooms) or authenticity (dramatic arts). It does not typically include strength.[231]

8.25.25 Exemptions to prohibition against discrimination

There are exemptions to the prohibition on discrimination listed in s 30 and following of the *SD Act*. Those exemptions include religious schools (s 38). The reason for such an exemption is because people send their children to school not only for the standard syllabus education but also to be inculcated into their religious faith, or as Pope John Paul II put it:

> Through you, as through a clear window on a sunny day, students must come to see and know the richness and the joy of life lived in accordance with Christ's teaching, in response to his challenging demands. To teach means not only to impart what we know, but also to reveal who we are by living what we believe. It is this latter lesson which tends to last the longest.[232]

---

228   *Australian Iron and Steel v Banovic* (1989) 168 CLR 165 at [3] per McHugh J.
229   Ibid [27] per Dawson J; at [23] per Deane and Gaudron JJ.
230   *SD Act* s 30.
231   See, for example, CCH *Australian and New Zealand Equal Opportunity Commentary* 52-740.
232   Marist College Canberra *Teaching in Catholic Schools – A Statement of Principles* (copy on file with author).

Despite there being exceptions in the prohibition, there are limits to those concessions. So, for instance, in the Queensland case of *Walsh v St Vincent De Paul Society Queensland (No. 2)* (2009) EOC 93-522, a volunteer of St Vincent de Paul (a Roman Catholic charity), who was Christian but not a Catholic, was held to have been discriminated against when told to become Catholic or lose the position to which they had been promoted. The ultimatum was given after the individual had served successfully for years in the organisation. The Queensland Tribunal distinguished between positions aimed at inculcating faith (that would be exempt) and positions and functions that were mainly practical (such as this) that were not exempt.

8.25.30 Sexual harassment

In addition to prohibiting acts or rules that have a limiting effect on women, s 28A of the *SD Act* prohibits sexual harassment, which is defined as conduct of a sexual nature (element one) which is unwelcome (element two). So the act or rule need not create an obvious career disadvantage, such as a refusal to employ a woman, but the act in question must be something that causes humiliation due to its unwanted and sexual nature. In that latter regard, the section introduces a reasonable person test: the section bans unwelcome sexual conduct where a 'reasonable person, having regard to all the circumstances, would have anticipated the possibility that the person harassed would be offended, humiliated or intimidated' (s 28A(1)(b)). In making that latter determination, regard should be had to the sex and age of the person harassed and the relationship between the person harassed and the individual in relation to whom the complaint has been made (s 28A(1A) and 28A(2)). So it is an *objective reasonable person test* – which has subjective elements to it (having regard to the circumstances of the case).

HALL v A & A SHEIBAN PTY LTD (1989) 20 FCR 217

In this case (decided under an earlier and different version of the section, which spoke of disadvantage),[233] a doctor asked applicants for a receptionist position questions that one may regard as quite creepy and intrusive – whether or not they were on the pill etc.[234] Those applicants were successful in obtaining the job and that type of treatment of them (along with evidence of physical contact) continued after employment.

Clearly, the conduct was of a sexual nature, but an issue arose as to whether it was unwelcome and whether the applicants had suffered the requisite intimidation, as the applicants actually were offered and accepted the job. The Federal Court found that in the circumstances (some of the applicants had been unemployed for some time and desperately needed the job) an individual may be more likely to tolerate conduct which is in fact unwelcome.[235]

---

233   In addition to the standard commentaries such as CCH, there is an interesting commentary of the history of sexual harassment law in the University of Queensland *Australian Feminist Judgement Project*: see Professor H Douglas et al. 'Sexual harassment case studies', https//law.uq.edu.au/files/5957/sexual harassment.pdf (accessed 14 May 2017).

234   That is just the tip of the iceberg – the three applicants all gave evidence of what was asked as well as the actions of the doctor. Much of that evidence was accepted by the court (at 223–8).

235   *Hall v A & A Sheiban Pty Ltd* (1989) 20 FCR 217 at 235–6 per Lockhart J; at 249–51 per Wilcox J; at 265 et seq; and at 278 et seq per French J – once again acknowledging that the case was decided under a differently worded section.

As to whether or not conduct must be repeated before the person engaging in that conduct must be said to know it is unwelcome, the Federal Court was of the view that some conduct is so innately offensive as to offend in only one instance.[236]

Below are two other examples of conduct which amounts to sexual harassment.

ASHTON v WALL (1992) EOC 92-447

CCH categorised this case as raising the issue of love gone wrong.[237] In other words, sometimes couples meet in the workplace and have a consensual relationship. If that relationship sours, will one party then retrospectively re-characterise the relationship as harassment? In *Ashton*, a relationship had persisted for months and there were, for example, cards of endearment. When the relationship ended, the female argued sexual harassment and tendered evidence that she had tolerated the relationship due to something akin to Stockholm Syndrome (where someone taken captive by a hostage-taker 'believes' they are in love with that person to make the degradation they are facing more tolerable in their own mind). The court did not accept that argument, especially in light of the length of the relationship and the notes which passed from one to the other over time.

HORNE v PRESS CLOUGH JOINT VENTURE (1994) EOC 92-556

The environment in which one works might itself constitute harassment. In this case, the complainants – the few women employed – complained about pornographic material on the walls of the workplace. Their complaints were met with derision and further material was displayed. The complainant women employees were successful in their court action, the judge finding that sexual material permeated the workplace to a degree that meant that the few women working there could not quietly enjoy their workplace.

8.25.35 Remedies

Comprehensive guides to the quantum of damages/nature of remedies awarded in cases are detailed in services such as CCH's.[238] Many practitioners find analogous cases and make submissions as to remedies by way of similarity.

---

236   Ibid 279–80 per French J.
237   CCH *Australian and New Zealand Equal Opportunity Commentary* 79-162.
238   Ibid 89-960 'Damages awarded in reported equal opportunity cases'.

8.25.40 Equal opportunity

Direct and indirect discrimination deal with complaints about actual events of discrimination and rules that have a discriminatory effect, respectively. But discrimination runs deeper than that. There is a wealth of literature on systemic discrimination in our society.[239] Tradition (the idea that there are some things women 'just don't do'); family responsibility (the fact that women are typically primary care-givers); stereotyping (the caricature of the 'dumb blonde'); and network opportunities, or the fact that some networks for men are so strong they may automatically think of one of their associates for an opportunity, rather than opening the doors to a new, female candidate – all place barriers in women's career paths that are difficult to pinpoint, but which do at least as much damage as particular discriminatory events.[240] Statistically, therefore, there is, sadly, much literature on the segregation of women in employment and the concentration of women in low-level positions – for instance, only 23 per cent of Australian corporate directors are women whereas around 40 per cent of clerical positions are held by women.[241] Equal Employment Opportunity programs are aimed at that type of (almost faceless, often historical) discrimination – they aim to give women (and sometimes other disadvantaged groups as well) an equal opportunity through allowing special measures to achieve equality.[242]

Equal opportunity laws in this country stem from Australia's international commitments under the ILO Convention concerning Discrimination in Respect of Employment and Occupation and the United Nations Convention on the Elimination of All Forms of Discrimination against Women. In its typically excellent and up-to-date commentary, CCH observes that most anti-discrimination legislation will allow the taking of special measures in order to facilitate equal employment opportunity (EEO).[243] The main specialist piece of legislation on EEO in Australia is the *Workplace Gender Equality Act 2012* (Cth).[244]

Under that legislation, which applies to all employers and employees, the Workplace Gender Equality Agency educates all employers on the importance of workplace equality and advises on the means by which their organisation can pursue equality at work.[245] Employers with over 100 employees report to the Agency on the progress they have made – such as meeting benchmarks for equality – and such reported information can form part of the Agency's research into further enhancing equality measures.[246] The Agency helps develop the

239   See generally Ronalds *Anti-Discrimination Legislation in Australia* (1979) and *Affirmative Action and Sex Discrimination* (1987).
240   See speech by Hon President Margaret McMurdo AC to Women Judicial Officers Conference 2014. In fact, there can be even further networking issues: for example, what if the opportunities presented to women are predominantly presented to relatives of influential males?
241   Australian Institute of Company Directors statistics, http://www.companydirectors.com.au/director-resource-centre/governance-and-director-issues/board-diversity/statistics (accessed 19 January 2017); compared to Workplace Gender equality agency 'Gender composition' (2016), https://www.wgea.gov.au/sites/default/files/Gender%20composition-of-the-workforce-by-industry.pdf; and https://www.wgea.gov.au/sites/default/files/Gender_composition_of_the_workforce_occupation.pdf.
242   See CCH *Austalian and New Zealand Equal Opportunity Commentary* 15-120 'International Convention' and 15-140 'Special measures to achieve equality'.
243   For the complete list, see ibid 15-140 'Special measures to achieve equality'.
244   Ibid 15-190 'Why is the *Workplace Gender Equality Act* 2012 needed?', which also provides the background to the Act.
245   *Workplace Gender Equality Act 2012* (Cth) ss 10 and 2B.
246   Ibid.

benchmarks against which equality at workplaces can be considered and reports to the relevant Minister – even naming employers who have failed to comply.[247] Significantly, the statute also covers men.[248] That may well prove significant in professions such as teaching, where there is now an under-representation of males.[249]

The statute's benchmarks stop short of mandating quotas of women in key positions. Some political parties, for instance, have introduced these types of measures.[250] However, that is not the approach Australia has traditionally taken. In one of the earlier commentaries on the dangers of having mandated quotas (as opposed to goals) if such detracts from the merit principle, *Affirmative Action: The New Discrimination*,[251] Professor Gabriel Moens observes that appointing women to positions on bases other than merit may damage opportunities for later generations of women workers. Where is the benefit of deliberately discriminating against better qualified males if that damages the institution for those who come next?[252] Clearly, there is logic in that argument, but the statistics quoted earlier equally remind readers of the need to keep a sharp eye on the issues.

Some of the softer equality programs that are adopted in this country are canvassed on the Agency's website.[253] They include scholarships directed at women applicants so they can acquire the skills necessary for particular roles.[254]

We will now consider some legal issues – of particular prominence at the moment – that may lead to law reform.

Racial Discrimination Act 1975 (Cth) s 18C[255]

Section 18C of the *Racial Discrimination Act* (*RD Act*) states:

> (1)   It is unlawful for a person to do an act, otherwise than in private, if:
>
>   (a)   the act is reasonably likely, in all the circumstances, to offend, insult, humiliate or intimidate another person or group of persons; and

---

247   Ibid.

248   See 'Women's Work/Men's Work', https://www.wgea.gov.au/learn/womens-work-mens-work (accessed 12 March 2017) which underscores the limits stereotypes can place on people.

249   'The Great Man shortage hits Australian classrooms', *Sydney Morning Herald Online*, 8 November 2015 (accessed 19 January 2017), http://www.smh.com.au/national/education/male-teachers-rare-breed-but-still-sought-after-20151030-gkmpp0.html. The issue has been debated in KF McGrath 'We need to rethink recruitment for men in primary schools', *The Conversation*, 17 October 2016, https://theconversation.com/we-need-to-rethink-recruitment-for-men-in-primary-schools-66670 (accessed 19 January 2017).

250   Emily's List Australia *Status of Women Report 2015*, http://www.emilyslist.net.au/wp-content/uploads/file/Status%20of%20Women%202015.pdf (accessed 19 January 2017).

251   G Moens *Affirmative Action: The New Discrimination*, CIS Policy Monographs 8 (1985).

252   Ibid 27 et seq.

253   Workplace Gender Equality Agency 'Employer of choice', https://www.wgea.gov.au/lead/employer-choice-gender-equality-0 (accessed 19 January 2017).

254   Such as the Promoting Women Fellowship, https://www.uq.edu.au/equity/content/promoting-women-fellowships.

255   Based on content from the Federal Register of Legislation at 08 February 2017. For the latest information on Australian government law go to https://www.legislation.gov.au. At the time of writing (May 2017), the government's attempt to modify s 18C had been blocked in the Senate. M Kozial et al. 'Senate kills off Turnbull Government's changes to 18C race discrimination law' *SMH* online, 30 March 2017 (accessed 14 May 2017).

   (b)   the act is done because of the race, colour or national or ethnic origin of
         the person or of some or all of the people in the group.
(2)   For the purposes of subsection (1), an act is taken not to be done in private if it:
   (a)   causes words, sounds, images or writing to be communicated to the public; or
   (b)   is done in a public place; or
   (c)   is done in the sight or hearing of people who are in a public place.

Section 18D defines some exemptions:

   Section 18C does not render unlawful anything said or done reasonably and in good faith:

   (a)   in the performance, exhibition or distribution of an artistic work; or
   (b)   in the course of any statement, publication, discussion or debate made or held
         for any genuine academic, artistic or scientific purpose or any other genuine
         purpose in the public interest; or
   (c)   in making or publishing:
      (i)   a fair and accurate report of any event or matter of public interest; or
      (ii) a fair comment on any event or matter of public interest if the comment is
            an expression of a genuine belief held by the person making the comment.

The provision has proven to be controversial because its operation has raised issues as to the
balance between protecting free speech and guarding against humiliation of others on the
basis of race – as demonstrated in the case law, discussed below.

PRIOR v QUEENSLAND UNIVERSITY OF TECHNOLOGY (QUT) (NO. 2) [2016] FCCA 2853

This was an application (under rule 13.10 Federal Circuit Court Rules 2001) by three
students, who were respondents in this matter, to have the complaint against them stayed
or dismissed, on the basis that, *inter alia*, it had no reasonable prospect of success. Their
claim succeeded, and in so doing has become noteworthy in Australian jurisprudence.[256]
      Essentially the facts were that the three QUT students (Wood, Powell and Thwaites) entered
the University's Oodgeroo Unit computer lab. The complainant, Ms Prior, who was an administration officer, approached the three and asked them if they were Indigenous. When they stated
that they were not, Ms Prior stated that the unit was 'an indigenous space' and the three should
use computers elsewhere on campus.[257]
      The three left, but they then started a Facebook conversation on 'QUT Stalker
Space'.[258] Wood posted: 'Just got kicked out of the unsigned Indigenous computer room.
QUT stopping segregation with segregation ...?'

---

256   *Cynthia Prior v Queensland University of Technology (QUT); Mary Kelly; Anita Lee Hong; Alex Wood;
      Jackson Powell; Callum Thwaites; and Chris Lee (No. 2)* [2016] FCCA 2853 at paras 14 and 15.
257   Ibid para 1.
258   Ibid paras 2 et seq.

Powell then posted, and responded to other posts with:[259]

- 'I wonder where the white supremacist computer lab is.'
- 'it's white supremacist, get it right. We don't like to be affiliated with those hillbillies.'
- 'Chris Lee today's your lucky day, join the white supremacist group and we'll take care of your every need!'

Under the name of Thwaites was apparently posted: 'ITT niggers.'[260] (As noted below, Thwaites has always stated he did not, in fact, write this.)

Ms Prior claimed the posts breached s 18C and sought an apology and damages – noting (to underscore why this case is being discussed here) that she included her employer, QUT, in the claim.

In dismissing the claim against the three students,[261] Judge Jarrett provided an overview of the law on s 18C,[262] including an outline of some of the leading cases: in particular, *Eatock v Bolt* (2011) 197 FCR 261 (considered below) and *Bropho v Human Rights & Equal Opportunity Commission* (2004) 135 FCR 105. Although s 18C is found in the part of the Act pertaining to racial hatred, it should not be read down to apply only to actual hatred or violence.[263] Having said that, 'an objective test must be applied in determining whether the act complained of has the necessary offensive, insulting, humiliating or intimidatory quality'.[264] The question is not how the act affected the particular complainant, but rather 'would the act, in all the circumstances in which it was done, be likely to offend ... a person or a group of people of a particular racial, national or ethnic group'?[265] Proof of actual offence is not the key; instead one looks for evidence of reasonable likelihood of offence.[266] Consideration is to be given to the values and circumstances of people in the group concerned and their likely reaction.[267] The section is not about general community standards.[268] However, it does not provide a cause of action where 'the intolerance of the receiver of the message rather than the intolerance of the speaker ... is responsible for causing the offence'.[269] The offence taken must not be a mere slight.[270] Crucially, particularly for this QUT case, the reasons for the act are important – the relevant act must be done because of race etc.[271]

The main reasons why the students, Wood and Powell, succeeded in their application was because of the lack of a causal nexus between what they wrote and race; and because what was

259   Ibid para 3.
260   Ibid para 4.
261   Dismissal took place under *Federal Circuit Court Act 1999* (Cth) s 17A(2) and relied on discussion of *Spencer v Commonwealth* (2010) 241 CLR 118 – which considers the similar provision of the *Federal Court of Australia Act 1976* (Cth) s 31 (cf paras 18 et seq of the QUT judgement).
262   *Cynthia Prior v Queensland University of Technology (QUT) ... and Chris Lee (No. 2)* [2016] FCCA 2853 from paras 29–31.
263   Ibid [30].
264   Ibid [30] point e.
265   Ibid.
266   Ibid [30] points c and d.
267   Ibid [30] point j.
268   Ibid [30] point k.
269   *Eatock v Bolt* (2011) 197 FCR 261, cited in [30] point l.
270   *Prior v Queensland University of Technology (No. 2)* [2016] FCCA 2853 at [30] point o.
271   Ibid [30] points r–u.

written was more in the nature of a slight.[272] Thwaites succeeded because he denied writing the Facebook post and there was no proof offered by the complainant of the provenance of the post.[273]

The judge accepted that the students did not know Ms Prior was Indigenous.[274] Wood's comments were not directed at a race or person but rather at a policy of QUT – and if anything he was rallying against racism by providing evidence that he decried segregation based on race.[275] The remarks of Powell, although tasteless, were meant to be a joke – and the student attested that he would have reacted the same way if QUT had had a James Joyce Unit set up only for students of Celtic extraction.[276]

So the complainant's case was not proven – she had no evidence that denied the students' arguments.[277] In the Judge's view, it was not:

> reasonably likely that a hypothetical person in the position of the applicant, or a hypothetical member of the groups identified by Ms Prior who is a reasonable and ordinary member of either of the groups who exhibits characteristics consistent with what might be expected of a member of a free and tolerant society and who is not at the margins of those groups would feel offended, insulted, humiliated or intimidated . . .[278]

At the time of writing, an appeal of Ms Prior had just been dismissed by Dowsett J in the Federal Court. Previously, significant costs had been awarded against her.[279] Shortly after the QUT decision, a s 18C complaint against the late Bill Leak was dropped.[280]

In *Prior v Queensland University of Technology (No. 2)*, Judge Jarrett was not required to deal with s 18D or the tensions and nuances in the authorities on the interpretation of that provision.[281] His Honour did note that Justice French (as he then was), in *Bropho v Human Rights and Equal Opportunity Commission* (2004) 135 FCR 105, made the following comments in relation to s 18C:[282]

> freedom of expression is not limited to speech or expression which is polite or inoffensive … but also [includes] … 'those [expressions] that offend, shock or disturb the State or any sector of the population. Such are the demands of that pluralism, tolerance and broad mindedness without which there is no democratic society'.

---

272   Ibid [32].
273   Ibid [74] and [75].
274   Ibid [53] and [68].
275   Ibid [49] and [51]: the student had said he was concerned that 'racial segregation was policy administered on the campus of my university'. He said that mixing with people of many cultures was an invaluable part of a university education.
276   Ibid [68].
277   Ibid [75], [68] and [55].
278   Ibid [49].
279   *Prior v Wood* [2017] FCA 193 per Dowsett J. See http://www.couriermail.com.au/news/queensland/crime-and-justice/cindy-prior-ordered-to-pay-costs-over-qut-racial-discrimination-case/news-story/466f3168375a6afec461b78e25c98154.
280   A Gartrell 'Racial discrimination complaint against cartoonist Leak dropped', *Sydney Morning Herald* (accessed 13 November 2016).
281   *Prior v Queensland University of Technology (No. 2)* [2016] FCCA 2853 at [80].
282   Ibid [31], citing French J at 69 in *Bropho v Human Rights and Equal Opportunity Commission* (2004) 135 FCR 105, citing *Handyside v United Kingdom* (1976) 1 EHRR 737.

EATOCK v BOLT (2011) 197 FCR 261

This is one of the most well-known cases where s 18C and D – and hence the relationship between freedom of speech and freedom from racial hatred – were discussed.

The case concerned two articles written by Andrew Bolt: 'It's so hip to be black' and 'White fellas in the black' published by the Herald & Weekly Times (in the *Herald Sun* newspaper). The gist of both articles (which were appended to the judgement) was that there is a 'trend' in Australia for people of mixed racial descent to elect to define themselves through the Aboriginal part of their lineage.[283] For some, the article continued, there is a question as to whether such election has been made on the basis of the entitlements made available to Aboriginal people.[284] Mr Bolt then discussed a dozen or so prominent Australians who identify as Indigenous (and have mixed heritage) in sarcastic tones, such as 'but chose Aboriginal, insisting on a racial identity . . . She also chose, incidentally, the one identity open to her that has political and career clout'.[285] There were factual inaccuracies in the article[286] – some of the Indigenous Australians discussed had been *brought up* Indigenous rather than choosing to associate themselves with Aboriginality in later life.[287] In a small section of the article, Mr Bolt praised one Australian of mixed race who had praised both their Indigenous and white background.[288] Mr Bolt also wrote: 'I'm not saying any of those I've named chose to be Aboriginal for anything but the most heartfelt and honest reasons. I certainly don't accuse them of opportunism, even if full-blood Aborigines may wonder how such fair people can claim to be one of them and in some cases take black jobs.'[289] One of the articles concluded: '[people should] be proud only of being human beings set on this land together, determined to find what unites us and not to invent such racist and trivial excuses to divide'.[290]

In finding that the articles had breached s 18C and that the s 18D defence was not available, Justice Bromberg held that despite the apparent rider about heartfelt reasons (noted above), the overwhelming weight of the article was derisive towards the people discussed[291] – there was example after example of sarcastic commentary (like the one also noted above).[292] Readers would be of the view that the article was about the 'trend' of people having chosen to identify as Aboriginal for career gain.[293] The link between the article and race was clear.[294] The article also considered Aboriginality as something biological, without reference to being raised in accordance with ancestral culture.[295]

---

283   *Eatock v Bolt* (2011) 197 FCR 261 at [57] per Bromberg J.
284   Ibid [27], [28], [33], [50] and [442].
285   Ibid [29], cited by Bromberg J. Many other examples of that type of sarcasm were given: see [49]–[50].
286   Ibid [289] and [402].
287   Ibid [89]. See also [398] et seq.
288   Ibid [34].
289   Ibid [29]
290   Ibid [34], cited in Bromberg J.
291   Ibid [414].
292   Ibid [36], [35] and [54] et seq.
293   Ibid [33] and [55].
294   Ibid [314]–[316].
295   Ibid [31].

Importantly, in the present context, Bromberg J made a number of comments about freedom of speech. After considering the judgement of French J in *Bropho*,[296] he considered whether the argument could be made that Mr Bolt had really been writing about whether or not there is a just allocation of opportunities for Aboriginal people – whether advantaged Aboriginal people had been taking opportunities meant for disadvantaged Aboriginal people:[297]

> An approach rationally related to the making of a public interest point about injustice in the distribution of opportunities to Aboriginal people would have directed attention to demonstrating that all the people in the 'trend' (not merely some) are advantaged, rather than that they are all of mixed biological heritage and of pale skin. A rationally related approach would have directed primary attention to the policies which served to create the alleged unjust distribution and the people responsible for them, rather than on the choice made by the recipients of the opportunities to identify as Aboriginal people. The extent to which the public interest matter relied upon and the imputations bear a rational relationship does not significantly contribute to the reasonableness of the conduct in question.[298]

And again:[299]

> It is important that nothing in the orders I make should suggest that it is unlawful for a publication to deal with racial identification including challenging the genuineness of the identification of a group of people. I have not found Mr Bolt and HWT to have contravened s 18C simply because the Newspaper Articles dealt with subject matter of that kind. I have found a contravention because of the manner in which that subject matter was dealt with.

Such high-profile cases as *Bolt* and *QUT* – along with the discontinuation of the Leak complaint – have led to s 18C becoming a much debated part of the *RD Act*.[300] In practical terms, for those employed, it is clearly relevant to a person's working life, especially as artists, cartoonists, journalists and commentators. What is still unfolding is discussion of the precise nature of the protections afforded artistic work under s 18D. The *QUT* case demonstrates how a complainant may join an employer as a respondent, even when people not employed by the employer (but rather students of the employer) are key respondents.[301] In the aftermath of *QUT*, there have been questions regarding the procedures of the Human Rights Commission and whether it should be more vigorous in exercising its

---

296   Ibid [411] and [426].

297   Ibid [445].

298   Ibid [446].

299   Ibid [461].

300   R Lewis et al. 'Peter Dutton ups the pressure on Gillian Triggs to fall on her sword', *The Australian*, 11 November 2016.

301   In the days that followed the QUT case, J Forrester, A Zimmermann and L Finlay 'QUT discrimination case exposes Human Rights Commission failings', *The Conversation*, 7 November 2016 observed that Ms Prior was still suing QUT – the authors of that article cite her original damages claim as for nearly $250,000.

capacity to strike out claims[302] (see below). There is an ongoing debate as to whether the section should be amended to address conduct which vilifies rather than offends.[303]

8.25.45 The tribunals – Human Rights Commission

At a Federal level, under the *Human Rights Commission Act 1986* (Cth), complaints are brought before the Human Rights Commission (HRC). Highly importantly, the Commission will investigate matters in the first instance and it has a power to terminate a matter if it is lacking substance. If the matter does not lack substance, in the view of the HRC, and the complainant seeks to continue, the HRC will conciliate, but it has no power to legally find discrimination has occurred. If conciliation is not possible, the matter may be taken by the complainant to a court hearing.[304] A similar process applies to resolution of matters under the various State acts.[305] In addition to attempting to conciliate matters, the HRC also develops policy on discrimination and inquires into matters of national importance.[306]

8.30 Taxation

Taxation law and employment law go hand in glove. As a general rule and as a starting point, an employee who earns over the tax threshold must pay tax; and an employer must pay that employee's superannuation. Less obvious, perhaps, but equally important, as Smith and Koken observe in *Tax and Remuneration Planning*,[307] are remuneration packages (blending monetary benefits with other benefits, such as a car or school fees), which can nurture valuable staff while minimising employer on-costs.[308]

The above examples arise at the level of the employment relationship, and enable employers and employees to comply with the rudiments of relevant Australian law. But there are broader policy implications of the tax–work equation. In *Labour Law and Labour Market Regulation*,[309] Howe notes that tax breaks can influence behaviour of investor corporations by encouraging them to employ local workers.[310] At an even broader policy level, recent

---

302   Ibid. The authors ask whether 'the punishment is the process' – the original complaint was made 3 years before the matter was struck out by the Federal Circuit Court Judge – and the delay was not the judge's fault.

303   Lewis et al. 'Peter Dutton ups the pressure on Gillian Triggs', 11 November 2016. See also footnote 255 and *Prior v Queensland University of Technology (No. 2)* [2016] FCCA 2853 at [14] and [15].

304   See Human Rights Commission website. See also CCH *Ausrtalian and New Zealand Equal Opportunity Commentary* 89-350 'Dispute resolution in the Human Rights Commission'.

305   For the relationship between the Anti-discrimination Commission Queensland and the Queensland Civil and Administrative tribunal see http://www.qcat.qld.gov.au/matter-types/anti-discrimination-matters.

306   Human Rights Commission *Annual Report 2015–2016*.

307   B Smith and E Koken *Tax and Remuneration Planning* (Australian Tax Practice, 3rd ed, 2000).

308   Ibid 2 [1 010]. See, generally, Chapter 1.

309   J Howe 'Money and favours': government deployment of public wealth as an instrument of labour regulation' in C Arup et al. *Labour Law and Labour Market Regulation* (Federation Press, 2006).

310   Indeed, that essay observes, correctly, that government can use a range of financial investment incentives and subsidies to attract new investment and therefore employment opportunities. A famous recent example of this has occurred in Queensland with the State government highlighting potential employment opportunities flowing to depressed regional Queensland from the Carmichael mine: 'Adani Coal: Queensland-first workforce promised for Carmichael Mine', ABC News, 6 December 2016, http://www.abc.net.au/news/2016-12-06/adani-carmichael-mine-queensland-first-workforce/8096402.

parliamentary debate has centred on the ' backpacker tax' – the tax level applied to those who holiday in Australia and pick up work as they go (they are not actually moving here for their careers).[311] Farmers urged the government not to place too burdensome a tax rate on such workers, as the farmers relied on them to perform work for which they cannot find Australian workers. And at an international level, the G20 made a point of noting that some large corporations make millions of dollars of profits in some countries yet pay minimal tax in those countries by establishing their headquarters in tax shelter countries.[312] The question is, why should workers be expected to pay their full load of tax and make efficiency increases at work if some rich corporations hardly pay any tax?[313] Or as the Henry Review asked years ago: what is the correct balance of tax between labour, capital, consumption and resources, and how can we ensure that there is a stable revenue base for the Australian government given the ageing of the population and the changing working patterns of the country's citizens and residents?[314]

The above are some of the questions around tax and employment law. The following provides a brief outline of the main taxes relevant to employment law.[315]

8.30.05 Income tax

The *Income Tax Assessment Act 1997* (Cth) governs the taxation obligations of most Australians. The country has a 'progressive' taxation system: the greater one's earnings, the more tax is paid.[316] It is typically the obligation of an employer to withhold tax from an employee's earnings.[317] At the end of the financial year, the employer then provides the employee with an earnings statement, which the employee tenders to the Australian Taxation Office (ATO) along with a list of deductions (which might include some moneys spent in the course of earning, charitable contributions etc). If the employee earns money from other sources, such as investment, that income may also be taxable. The difference between earnings (income) and deductions is a person's taxable income.

There has long been a debate about tax rates:[318] whether tax levels are so high as to act as a disincentive to work; bracket creep (whether the tax rates have adequately taken into account

311 'Changed rules for working holiday makers', Australian Parliament House website, http://www.aph.gov.au/About_Parliament/Parliamentary_Departments/Parliamentary_Library/pubs/rp/BudgetReview201516/Holiday (accessed 9 December 2016).

312 *G20 Leaders Summit: Financial Regulation Session*, http://www.oecd.org/ctp/g20leaderssummitfinancialregulationsession.htm (accessed 9 December 2016). See E Mercurio 'Arguments for an international tax base revenue' (2012) 22(1) *Revenue Law Journal*; JG Gravelle 'Tax havens: international tax avoidance and evasion', 15 January 2015, https://fas.org/sgp/crs/misc/R40623.pdf (accessed 12 March 2017).

313 Obviously some corporations have a tremendous culture of benefaction. The debate is about ensuring that both working people and corporations have an equal share of tax burden and responsibility.

314 K Henry et al. *Australia's Future Tax System Review* (*Henry Review*), https://taxreview.treasury.gov.au/Content/Content.aspx?doc=html/home.htm (accessed 16 January 2017). See also N Warren 'Tax: facts, fiction and reform', Australian Tax Research Foundation (ATRF) Research Study No. 41 (2004).

315 This commentary aims to be a useful starting point for a debate some mistakenly view as divorced from employment.

316 JP Smith 'Taxing popularity: the story of tax in Australia' ATFR Research Study No. 43, 103.

317 See Woellner, *Australian Taxation Law* (CCH, 2014) especially Chs 3 and 4 on income tax, https://www.ato.gov.au.

318 See Henry Review and the series of papers produced by the ATRF referred to above.

inflation); and whether trickle-down economics (the idea that reducing tax rates will automatically mean more spending, which will stimulate economic growth) actually works.[319]

Obviously, as a matter of legal practice, the tax area is a complex specialty. Each year, the ATO advises of crackdowns – for example, on barristers, academics, the self-employed – during which individuals in those areas will be particularly carefully vetted.[320] Travel entitlements, for instance, might be vetted to ensure that travel was work-related. If employees earn income in a foreign location, the ATO will determine whether or not that work leads to Australian tax obligations.[321]

8.30.10 Superannuation

Superannuation is an important obligation on employers and investment for employees. As a basic rule, under the Superannuation Guarantee legislation,[322] employers in Australia should pay 9.5 per cent of an employee's earnings into a superannuation fund. That money is not to be accessed by the employee until they reach their preservation age.[323] The idea is that employees will be able to rely on that money in their retirement rather than relying on the public purse (pension). As Woellner reflects,[324] that makes superannuation 'the cornerstone of the federal government's retirement incomes policy', especially given the ageing of the Australian population and the shrinking tax revenue from the traditional workforce.[325] So important is superannuation that the obligation extends to include contractors.[326]

The law governing superannuation is fiendish in its complexity. Superannuation funds hold trillions of dollars.[327] There are a variety of types of funds, from industry funds – often originally established for a particular industry and with strong links to unions (often with unionists on their boards)[328] – through to retirement savings accounts for those with intermittent employment.[329] The superannuation industry is governed by the Australian Prudential

---

319   See https://www.whitehouse.gov for President Trump's taxation plan for the US, which is based on so-called trickle-down economics (accessed 14 May 2017).

320   For example, F Chung 'ATO reveals dodgiest deductions', http://www.news.com.au/finance/money/tax/ato-reveals-dodgiest-deductions/news-story/3f76c532512e8e4ddc8d0399ecd05edf (accessed 16 January 2017).

321   For a very early discussion of this important topic see RL Deutsch *Taxation of Foreign Source Income* (Legal Books, 1993). More recently, see the Taxation Institute of Australia's concerns about taxing Australians who earn income overseas (*Income Tax Assessment Act 1997* (Cth) s 23AG), https://www.taxinstitute.com.au/seminar-papers/expatriates-section-23ag-exemption-paper (accessed 16 January 2017)).

322   *Superannuation Guarantee (Administration) Act 1992* (Cth) and *Superannuation Guarantee Charge Act 1992* (Cth).

323   See https://www.ato.gov.au/Individuals/Super/Accessing-your-super/ (accessed 16 January 2017).

324   Woellner, *Australian Taxation Law* (2014) Ch. 23.

325   Ibid.

326   See https://www.ato.gov.au/Business/Super-for-employers/Working-out-if-you-have-to-pay-super/Contractors/ (accessed 16 January 2017).

327   Woellner, *Australian Taxation Law* (2014) at [28-000].

328   This is apparent from the annual reports of numerous industry funds (such as Q Super), as unionists are representatives of their employee members – and those employee union members are also members of the fund.

329   Woellner, *Australian Taxation Law* (2014) at [23-000].

Regulatory Authority (APRA) as well as the *Superannuation Industry Supervision Act 1993* (Cth) and is widely regarded as a strong investment that is well regulated.[330]

Despite that, there are some questions. At the time of writing, research carried out for Industry Super Australia found that $2.8 billion in superannuation contributions had not been made, as sham contractors and employers have failed to meet (or possibly understand) their legal obligations.[331] In a similar vein, Tria Investment Partners (researching for Cbus, the Building Industry Superannuation Fund) found that $800,000 in contributions for employees had gone missing due to the cash economy, where worker are being paid cash 'off the books'.[332] This late 2016 research adds to earlier research, as does the proposal by the Federal government in its 2017 budget to adopt a superannuation home deposit saving scheme.[333]

Further, in the TURC *Final Report*,[334] Commissioner Heydon AC QC paid particular attention to the relationship between industry superannuation funds and trade unions. Under some enterprise agreements negotiated by unions, certain of these funds are the default fund into which the superannuation of the employee members is paid. The Royal Commission questioned whether there should be greater choice of superannuation funds for workers, and whether some of these funds are too closely related to trade union leaders. In other words, are they really the best superannuation investment vehicle for employee-members? In that connection, the Royal Commission was concerned to review the governance of those funds.[335]

One further word of caution relates to knowing the terms of the relevant superannuation trust deed. Funds such as Unisuper (for academics) are strongly performing funds and yet in the early 2000s there were instances of the fund switching members from a defined benefit (which provides a *certain* benefit amount on retirement) to an accumulation benefit (which may be variable) should certain events take place. Similarly, one term of the Unisuper deed enabled the fund to consider *redefining* what the defined benefit actually was if certain triggering events occurred (an economic downturn, for example). Another public sector fund issue arose when the Queensland government recently flagged that profits of QSuper (the superannuation fund of the public service) might be used to commence infrastructure projects, rather than leaving the money for the direct benefit of employees.[336]

Having said all that, superannuation remains one of the most significant investments in the lives of most Australians. It gets favourable tax treatment, and some scholars point out[337] both

---

330   Ibid from [23-000].
331   P Gallagher, 'Overdue: time for action on unpaid super' (Industry Super Australia, 2016).
332   Tria Investment Partners Cbus – see generally S Maher 'Two million Aussies shortchanged by $3.8bn on superannuation', *The Australian* online, http://www.theaustralian.com.au/national-affairs/treasury/two-million-aussies-shortchanged-by-36bn-on-superannuation/news-story/149af04f145cc9cf0573f9a40d749b3f (accessed 9 December 2016).
333   See A Freiberg 'Bang Bang Maxwell's Silver Hammer? Superannuation rime in the 1990s' (1996) 24 *Australian Business Law Review (ABLR)* 217 and A O'Connell 'Superannuation – protection for investors' (1994) 23 *ABLR* 436. See also Hon Scott Morrison, Treasurer, *Federal Budget Speech*, 9 May 2017.
334   JD Heydon Royal Commission into Trade Union Governance and Corruption (TURC), *Final Report*.
335   Ibid Vol. 6 Ch. 6, https://www.tradeunionroyalcommission.gov.au/reports/Pages/Volume-5.aspx (accessed 14 May 2017).
336   'Queensland Government poised to raid public servants' super to fund infrastructure', ABD News online, 24 May 2016, http://www.abc.net.au/news/2016-05-24/qld-government-could-raid-superannuation-fund/7440278 (accessed 10 December 2016).
337   WH Simon 'The prospect of pension fund socialism' (1993) 14 *Berkeley Journal of Employment and Labor Law* 251.

the relative security such funds often give retired workers, and the good the funds can do for society if fund managers use their powers to invest conscientiously.

8.30.15 Remuneration planning, salary packaging and fringe benefits tax

As Smith and Koken point out, remuneration planning and salary packaging – taking some of one's remuneration in entitlements, such as a car, rather than receiving it all in money/income – is popular and can make a great deal of sense for an employee who seeks to reduce tax.[338] In lieu of the employee paying income tax, the employer instead pays fringe benefits tax (FBT) (tax on the value of the benefit).[339] That 'set off' (if it can be called that) stops the government missing out on tax revenue.[340] The employer is still under a duty to pay the legal entitlements and salary of the employee,[341] and the employer can still gain a financial advantage if the effect of the package reduces their liability.

However, as with almost everything in taxation law, this is a complex area, and the nature of the tax benefit – and, importantly, whether there actually is a benefit – depends on, for example:[342]

- the length of the arrangement – there may be changes to tax law that reduce or negative a benefit;
- the type of entity or business organisation the employer is.

In addition to being an issue in the context of salary sacrifice and remuneration planning, FBT may arise if, for instance, an employee travels a lot with work and tags lengthy personal holidays onto the end of a work trip.[343]

8.30.20 Employee share schemes

One of the more interesting examples of employees receiving a benefit rather than money is an employee share ownership scheme.[344] These have been considered in government reports.[345] They have also been the subject of other research.[346]

Such plans aim to align the interests of employees with those of shareholders, and to give employees a sense of ownership of or inclusion in the company. But as always, there are

---

338 Smith and Koken *Tax & Remuneration Planning* (2000) Ch. 1, 'Remuneration Planning'.
339 Ibid. See also Woellner, *Australian Taxation Law* (2014) Ch. 26, especially [26-000], discussing the *Fringe Benefits Tax Act 1986* (Cth).
340 Ibid.
341 Smith and Koken *Tax & Remuneration Planning* (2000) Ch. 1.
342 Ibid.
343 Woellner, *Australian Taxation Law* Ch. 26.
344 *Income Tax Assessment Act 1997* (Cth) s 83A et seq.
345 See House of Representatives Standing Committee on Employment, Education and Workplace Relations, *Shared Endeavours – An Inquiry into Employee Share Ownership in Australia* (2000).
346 See A Barnes et al. 'Employee share ownership plans: evaluating the role of tax and other factors using two case studies' (2007) *Australian Business Law Review* 73l; A O'Connell 'Employee share ownership in unlisted entities: objectives, current practices and regulatory reform' (2009) 37 *Australian Business Law Review* 211; and I Landau et al. 'Broad based employee share scheme ownership in Australian listed companies. An empirical analysis' (2009) 37 *Australian Business Law Review* 412.

complexities in the regulation of these schemes (and any tax treatment thereof), and benefits and drawbacks to their adoption. Given that some regulations changed in 2015, useful starting points for considering these are the websites of the Australian Tax Office and the Australian Securities and Investment Commission.[347] The CCH *Australian Federal Tax Reporter* also underscores the complexities of the area and the legal issues that might arise.

8.30.25 Payroll tax

Payroll tax is typically administered by State government offices such as the Office of State Revenue and governed by State legislation such as the *Payroll Tax Acts*. However, the system is harmonised throughout the country so there are similar dates for lodgement of returns etc.[348] Basically, it is a tax levied on employers who have a wages bill exceeding a specified amount. Consideration can include amounts paid to some contractors and non-monetary benefits might be considered. Employers are required to register for the purposes of this tax regime.

8.30.30 Termination payments

There are also special tax provisions that apply to termination payments; they depend on the nature of the termination payment.[349]

8.30.35 Corporate tax evasion? The G20, the 'Panama Papers' and their relevance to employment

A significant issue in taxation – which may not at first glance seem to connect with employment law – is 'multinational profit shifting and tax base erosion'.[350] Essentially, most of our tax laws were developed in the industrial age. The emergence of the new economy, globalisation and the digital age have enabled corporations to – quite legally – move their wealth into tax havens, thus reducing their tax burden. The result is that a company may make considerable profit in one country through business activity in that country, but not pay much, if any, tax in that country. This topic was earmarked for global action at the G20 in Brisbane in 2014.[351] Reports, discussion papers and legal developments have included the OECD's *Addressing Base Erosion and Profit Shifting (Action Plan)* and Australia's *Tax Laws Amendment (Countering Tax Avoidance and Multinational Profit Shifting) Act 2013*.

---

347   See https://www.ato.gov.au/general/employee-share-schemes/ess-basics/latest-changes/ (accessed 10 December 2016) and https://www.moneysmart.gov.au/investing/shares/employee-share-schemes (accessed 10 December 2016).

348   http://www.payrolltax.gov.au/harmonisation (accessed 10 December 2016).

349   CCH *Australian Federal Tax Reporter* 799-155 'Treatment of Superannuation Lump Sums and Employment Termination Payments (formerly eligible termination payments)'.

350   CCH *Australian Taxation Law* (24th ed, 2014) 24-910.

351   CCH *Australian Taxation Law* (24th ed, 2014).

But much work remains to be done, and that was demonstrated early in 2016 with the emergence of the 'Panama Papers'. Essentially, leaked documentation from tax havens such as Brazil underscored the millions of dollars that wealthy companies and individuals were relocating into those tax havens. Some of the money was linked to organised crime, but significantly, a lot of the money was *legally* deposited (through use of separate corporate entities). The question therefore was whether corporate and tax law should be (indeed could be) changed so as to tax this money.[352]

The link to employment is basically that if employees are taxed, if they can 'lose' super-annuation, if employers pay FBT etc, why should corporations be able to avoid tax simply because they can utilise artificial legal entities to take advantage of global tax havens? How is that fair? How is it in the national economic interest when corporations earn so much more than people who are employees and in an era when there may be reduced employment and therefore reduced tax revenue anyway?

The thorny issues of tax base erosion have been canvassed numerous times before. They link to employment not simply because employees and employers need to be taxed fairly, but because the ageing of the population and the changing work patterns influence the tax base government relies on to run services.[353]

SUMMARY

Though having its origin in common law duties to workers, protection from workplace harm is now firmly an area of legislative intervention. The model *WHS Act* makes it clear that persons conducting a business or undertaking (PCBUs) have duties to ensure the safety of workers and others as far as reasonably practicable. This is regarded as the 'primary duty of care' in the legislation, and other workplace participants (including suppliers and manufacturers) also have safety obligations.

Rather than a seismic shift in safety laws, the *WHS Act* reflects an evolution which had occurred in its predecessor Acts in each jurisdiction – the recognition that dealing with workplace safety issues effectively goes well beyond a simple employer–employee relationship.

Statutory compensation schemes for workplace injury are a feature of every Australian jurisdiction. While the core definitions of 'worker' and 'injury' are quite similar across jurisdictions – and encompass disease and psychological injury using the substantial contributing factor test – the prospect of a single workers' compensation scheme (or even 'model' legislation) still appears to be distant.

However, the shift in focus to greater emphasis on 'injury management', return to work and the cost effectiveness of the schemes, and away from (or limiting) lump sum payments, does seem to represent a common approach in each workers' compensation jurisdiction.

The increased focus on bullying, including workplace bullying, in recent years has flowed on to the work of courts, tribunals and (more recently) Parliament. A significant question in this field is whether the remedies available – via the FWC anti-bullying jurisdiction, safety and compensation laws, and common law actions – provide sufficient recourse for victims.

352   See CCH *Australian Tax Week* 'Tax administrations develop actions on Panama Papers' *Australian Tax Week*, 15 July 2016, 533.
353   The international nature of the issue is further highlighted by the UK government's study into pensions.

As with injuries arising from workplace safety incidents, specific bullying complaints can be just the most obvious manifestation of workplace behavioural and cultural issues. Contrary to the practice of relocating the victim in the hope that the issue will go away, the most effective response to workplace bullying complaints (for both the victim and the employer) is to take timely, proportionate and well-documented action against the perpetrator(s).

Anti-discrimination

International human rights law underpins anti-discrimination law, so there are similarities between statutes governing different forms of discrimination law, but there are also differences. Sex discrimination is a good example, as numerous cases are raised in an employment context.

Direct discrimination is facial – someone is treated less favourably than someone of a different gender, on the ground of gender. Indirect discrimination is not facial – the rule appears fair in form but is unfair in application. Sexual harassment might not involve blatantly holding a person back from an opportunity – the harm is done through the degradation of that person by unwanted conduct of a sexual nature. Equal opportunity (related to the old idea of affirmative action) addresses societal discrimination such as the effects of years of previous discrimination. In Australia, generally we have targets as opposed to quotas for engagement of minorities. There are limited exceptions to some anti-discrimination prohibitions, such as genuine occupational requirement.

Tribunals such as the Human Rights Commission aim to conciliate. Matters can go to court if no agreement is reached. Recent issues concerning the *RD Act*'s s 18C raise questions about the balance between free speech and racial vilification – this is especially relevant to journalists in the course of their employment. There are also questions regarding when the Human Rights Commission may discontinue a matter.

Taxation

Tax has clear links to employment due to the requirement to pay income tax and superannuation, and the desirability and complexity of remuneration planning. In addition, there is a broad policy connection: income tax forms an important part of the government's revenue base, and changing patterns of work might lessen that revenue base. Corporate tax evasion, as revealed in the 'Panama Papers', for instance, is equally significant and begs the question of fairness in taxation – why not pursue corporations, as the government would pursue individual employees who do not pay tax? That issue has been considered by the G20.

REVIEW QUESTIONS

1. (a) In what circumstances can a worker refuse to perform work because of safety concerns and still be permitted to receive pay?

    (b) What are the essential elements for a claim for workers' compensation to succeed?

2. Consider the facts in *Inspector Estreich v Zaccardelli* [2012] NSWIRComm 47, (http://www.austlii .edu.au/au/cases/nsw/NSWIRComm/2012/47.html). On the basis that all involved remained employees of the same employer afterwards, if the conduct occurred after 1 January 2014, could these events form the basis for a successful bullying complaint to the FWC?

3. Gerald was the supervisor of a beachware shop called Venice Beach Hotties, located at Bondi Beach, Sydney. His new recruit, Betty, was young and very insecure, as this was her first job. The basic culture of the workplace was that staff wore little clothing, to show off their fantastic bodies, and they mixed regularly after-hours to promote a relaxed 'vibe' in the workplace. In the lead-up to Christmas, a number of staff (during working hours and using the workplace computer) sent emails to each other planning a Christmas drinks night on the beach. Nothing was being paid for by the employer company, but only staff were invited. Before the start of the beach party, there were a number of small groups of staff who went off to various bars for drinks to fill in time before the party started. The weather was hot, most people were dehydrated and the alcohol being consumed seemed to have a devastating effect on those who attended these events. The morning after the Christmas drinks, Betty woke up stunned to find Gerald in her bed at her home. Gerald said to her, 'Darling Betty, I always thought you loved me ...' Horrified, Betty alleged sexual harassment. Advise Gerald of his legal position and the likely remedy, if any. Is there further information you would need to refine your answer? Could the employing company be joined in the action? Why?

4. At the time of writing, the Queensland Police Service announced that it was appealing a Federal Court judgement which found officers had breached the *Racial Discrimination Act* in the course of their work on Palm Island in Queensland. What are the key points in that case that are relevant to discrimination and employment law? Also discuss complaint and court procedures in the anti-discrimination jurisdiction and the onus of proof.

5. Class exercises:

    (a) Discuss the legal difficulties involved with remuneration planning and employee share schemes.

    (b) Study the superannuation deed of a leading super fund. What are some of the clauses that might cause employee-members consternation?

FURTHER READING

WHS

Fair Work Commission *Anti-Bullying Benchbook* (2015) http://benchbooks.fwc.gov.au/antibullying/.

F Marks, D Dinnen and L Fieldus *The New Work Health & Safety Legislation: A Practical Guide* (Federation Press, 2013).

Anti-discrimination

D Allen 'Supporting working parents: findings from the AHRC's national inquiry into the prevalence of pregnancy and return to work discrimination in the workplace' (2014) 27 *Australian Journal of Labour Law* 281.

A Chapman 'Is the right to request flexibility under the *Fair Work Act* enforceable?' (2013) 26 *Australian Journal of Labour Law* 118.

S Edwards '*Purvis* in the High Court: behaviour, disability and the meaning of direct discrimination' (2004) 26 *Sydney Law Review* 639.

A Heron and S Charlesworth 'Effective protection of pregnant women at work: still waiting for delivery?' (2016) 29 *Australian Journal of Labour Law* 1.

T MacDermott 'Affirming age: making federal anti-discrimination regulation work for older Australians' (2013) 26 *Australian Journal of Labour Law* 141.

N Rees, S Rice and D Allen *Australian Anti-Discrimination Law* (Federation Press, 2nd ed, 2014).

B Smith and M Hayes 'Using data to drive gender equality in employment: more power to the people?' (2015) 28 *Australian Journal of Labour Law* 191.

B Smith and T Orchiston 'Domestic violence victims at work: a role for anti-discrimination law?' (2012) 25 *Australian Journal of Labour Law* 209.

M Thornton 'Proactive or reactive? The Senate Report on the *Equal Opportunity for Women in the Workplace Amendment Bill 2012* (Cth)' (2012) 25 *Australian Journal of Labour Law* 284.

Taxation

Australian Master Tax Guide (Wolters Kluwer, 60th ed, 2017).

Australian Tax Forum (The Tax Institute).

KE Emmerton, RK Fisher and HM Hodgson *Tax Questions and Answers* (Thomson Reuters, 2004).

D Pinto and K Sadiq *Australian Tax Review* (Thomson Reuters, 2012).

K Sadiq et al. *Principles of Taxation Law* (Thomson Reuters, 2014).

9 EMERGING ISSUES AND NEW FRONTIERS

9.05 Introduction

Most of this book has dealt with labour and employment law insofar as it applies to Australians in Australia. There is every justification for that. Most people still work in one country or for an employer based in one country – and live their lives centred on a community.[1]

However, times are changing. Not infrequently, corporations operate transnationally; there are global supply chains; and an employee based in one country may transfer to an overseas office of their employer. Such developments raise numerous questions, ranging from how the law balances the power of the global corporation with that of the local worker, through to how a conflict of laws may be resolved in a particular instance. As Professor Ewing recently observed, to neglect transnational labour law is an 'extraordinary omission, given the impact of globalisation on workers' rights and the power of global capital. Extraordinary too, in light of the developing body of principles, rules and practices regulating transnational corporations.'[2]

Parallel to those changes in the basic nature of work and the law, there are further developments around the manner in which work is performed. Not infrequently, volunteers will perform important work (in sometimes dangerous places), and issues may arise as to whether there is an employment relationship there at all. Beyond that, some people are watching a world in which their very job seems to be disappearing with the advent of new technology and automation.[3]

Indeed, labour and employment law face many emerging issues and new frontiers – and this chapter discusses those:

- *Issue 1: Transnational and international labour and employment law issues.* As observed in Chapter 3, there has always been a tension between international trade and labour. Likewise, there has long been a study of the influence one country's laws might have on the employment laws of another. The advent of large transnational corporations and global supply chains beg questions as to how best to develop such transnational and international labour laws. Solutions may rest in corporate codes of conduct and regional trading agreements, as well as International Labour Organization (ILO) treaties and international law suits. Transnational labour law seeks to extend beyond the nation state, yet relies on nation states contributing to its development and enforcement. In international labour law there may be conflicts of law when an employee from one country works for the overseas office of their employing company: which law will apply in any given situation? There are specific issues that arise in these contexts. The growing influence of China on the world stage has created specific issues in employment law, such as how to raise Chinese labour standards when the culture of the Chinese people is not to make complaints against authority figures. Some industries, such as aviation, are truly global in nature; what implications does that raise for employment law? The UK's decision to leave the European Union (EU) heralds change for UK employment law, but does it also signal a rejection of EU law? That question is important, as the EU is a truly supranational organisation. Does

---

1   See R McCallum 'Conflicts of laws and labour law in the new economy' (2003) 16 *Australian Journal of Labour Law* 3.

2   K Ewing '*Transnational Labour Law*, by Antonio Ojeda-Aviles, Alphen aan den Rijn, Wolters Kluwer, 2015' (2016) 27(1) *King's Law Journal* 132–5.

3   The scholarly sources discussing volunteers and automation are outlined and discussed infra.

Britain's decision to leave provide a lesson for how supranational law and transnational law should develop? And, if so, what does that mean for Australia?

- *Issue 2: Immigration and employment.* In an Australian context, most obviously this pertains to 457 visas – which are under review at the time of writing and pose interesting questions regarding the impacts of immigration on employment. (That issue was also at the heart of Brexit.)

- *Issue 3: Volunteers and work experience.* Volunteering is worth millions to the Australian economy each year, but there remain questions as to the status of volunteers, especially in the event of injury in particularly dangerous situations. Equally, there are questions as to whether the growing trend towards unpaid work threatens the conditions of paid employees or facilitates exploitation of those doing work experience. Recent case law and reports are considered.

- *Issue 4: Robots and automation.* Robots might ultimately replace far more manual labour jobs than was first thought, given the development of artificial intelligence and the dexterity of today's robots. What might their impact be and what might the law do to 'protect' workers?

9.10 Transnational and international employment law

9.10.05 Origins of transnational labour law

Comparative labour law has been written about for over a century. In a British Commonwealth context, and as discussed in Chapter 3, Beatrice and Sydney Webb wrote about 'the exciting development in the Britains beyond the seas' when they studied the development of the arbitration system in Australia (which was so different from that in England).[4] US scholars have spread their ideas on collective bargaining to Canada and post-war Japan.[5]

As discussed in Chapter 3, for example, the regulatory links between trade and labour may be seen in the early work of the ILO[6] (as members raised questions about whether cheap labour not only violated human rights but also negatively affected trade). The failed International Trade Organisation (which preceded the General Agreement on Tariffs and Trades (GATT) and the World Trade Organization (WTO)) also considered the relevance of fair labour standards.[7]

---

4   S and B Webb *Industrial Democracy* (Longmans, Green and Co., 1902) 1-927 and *The History of Trade Unionism* (Longmans, Green and Co., 1920) 1-784. See K Walker 'Compulsory arbitration in Australia' in J Lowenberg (ed.) *Compulsory Arbitration: An International Comparison* (Lexington Books, 1976).

5   H Arthurs 'Reinventing labor law for the global economy: The Benjamin Aaron Lecture' (2001) 22 *Berkeley Journal of Employment and Labor Law* 278–9. In fact, early US greats, such as Benjamin Aaron and Clyde Summers, appreciated the links between trade and labour – the stronger US exports were, the more confident US trade unions became in seeking better conditions for workers. Those trade unions themselves had found voice since The New Deal, which owed its mores in part to John R Commons' knowledge of overseas ideas.

6   L Floyd 'Castles in the sand: a study of Australian strike law and its effects on trade union power' (1998), unpublished LLM thesis.

7   Arthurs 'Reinventing labor law for the global economy' (2001) 279.

Consequently, in addition to the labour law of nation states (national law), standards that extended beyond nations were being raised. The seeds were being sown for transnational and international labour law – standards that apply beyond borders, cooperation between states and the monitoring of conditions by international bodies.

9.10.10 Key issues

Two of the issues central to international and transnational law are the link between trade and labour and the reliance on nation states to embrace and enforce international standards.

Any discussion of the links between trade and labour always starts with the obvious point – whether cheap labour costs in one country will drive down production costs in that country and therefore cause a 'race to the bottom' on working conditions throughout the world.[8] A good discussion of the intricacies of that debate may be found in the work of the late Professor Hepple[9] and Professor Compa.[10] Regulatory competition (that is, deliberately reducing labour costs to attract investment and production) is clearly at work; however, both authors, independently, argue that high labour standards can also strengthen productivity – by providing safe conditions of labour and rewards that encourage workers to do their jobs more proficiently, for instance. Some level of redistribution of wealth in society (through fair wages) also adds to peace and stability, which in turn aids investment.[11] Rather than 'sweating' workers, Compa argues that there should be concentration on 'introducing new technology, better production flows, superior materials, responsive marketing and customer service, and other innovations'.[12] Similarly, Hepple wrote of the production achievements of nations such as Japan over the years: it is an advanced nation that, despite its economic woes, has traditionally treated workers with respect.[13]

Sharpening the point at issue in a labour and trade law context, Lester, Mercurio and Davies[14] examine the trade/labour nexus by extracting a passage from the WTO's own website:

> On the one hand, some countries argue … [that] WTO rules and discipline … would provide a powerful incentive for member nations to improve workplace conditions and 'international coherence' …
>
> On the other hand, many developing countries believe the issue has no place in the WTO framework. They argue that the campaign to bring labour issues into the WTO is actually a bid by industrialised nations to undermine the comparative advantage of lower wage trading partners, and could undermine their ability to raise standards through economic development, particularly if it hampers the ability to trade. They also argue

---

8   The 'race to the bottom' is discussed in ibid; R Hepple *Labour Laws and Global Trade* (Hart Publishing, 2005); and L Compa 'Labor rights and labor standards in international trade' (1993–94) 25 *Law and Policy International Business* 165–91. For a review of a number of books on the topic, see DM Trubek 'Recent books on international law' (2006) *American Journal of International Law* 733.

9   Hepple *Labour Laws and Global Trade* (2005) 253.

10 Compa 'Labor rights and labor standards in international trade' (1993–94) 168–9.

11 Ibid 168.

12 Ibid.

13 Hepple *Labour Laws and Global Trade* (2005) 252, discussed in Trubek 'Recent books on international law' (2006) 729.

14 S Lester, B Mercurio and A Davies *World Trade Law: Text, Materials and Commentary* (Hart Publishing, 2nd ed, 2012) 872.

that proposed standards can be too high for them to meet at their level of development. These nations argue that efforts to bring labor standards into the arena of multilateral trade negotiations are little more than a smokescreen for protectionism.

At a more complex legal level is the question of the relationship between the International Labor Organization's standards and the WTO agreements – for example whether or how the ILO's standards can be applied in a way that is consistent with WTO rules.[15]

While that passage shows the two extremes of the debate, there is, of course, the further argument of industrialised nations – namely that the low-wage conditions of some countries are actually an unfair trade mechanism being used by developing nations.[16] Lester, Mercurio and Davies continue:

Thus, not only did trade negotiators in the 1940s identify the link between labor and international trade, they also recognised that unfair labor conditions create difficulties or distortions in the market by lowering the price of goods below what would normally exist in a competitive market and should be eliminated. It is clear that the drafters explicitly recognised labor as being related to trade.[17]

Scholars, including the present writer,[18] note the unequal distribution of wealth within many developing countries, such as China. There is thus an argument that it is the *governments* of those countries that are a problem for the poorest people in those developing nations – and international labour standards will help those most in need. Without Western intervention, many working-class and rural Chinese people, for example, would scarcely benefit from China's new industrial expansion.[19] The particular position of China is considered in more detail later in the chapter.

So given the complexity of the trade–labour debate, the best answer probably lies in incremental improvement and change, in developing a flexible transnational system of (hard and soft) labour law and linking it to trade in such a way as to allow for growth in developing nations (so long as such growth is shared by all citizens in those countries).[20] Emerging transnational labour law is considered immediately below.

9.10.15 Transnational labour law

The emerging transnational labour law has a panoply of provisions[21] – these range from ILO Conventions and UN Human Rights Treaties through to corporate codes of conduct, and the

---

15   See https://www.wto.org. See also Compa 'Labor rights and labor standards in international trade' (1993–94) 168.

16   M Cabin 'Labor rights in the Peru Agreement: can vague principles yield concrete change? (2009) 109 *Columbia Law Review* 1047, cited in L Floyd 'When old meets new: some perspectives on recent Chinese legal developments and their relevance to the United States' (2011) 64 *Southern Methodist University Law Review* 1226–7.

17   Lester, Mercurio and Davies *World Trade Law: Text, Materials and Commentary* (2012) 874, citing R Chartes and B Mercurio 'A call for an agreement on trade-related aspects of labor: why and how the WTO should play a role in upholding core labor standards' (2012) *North Carolina Journal of International Law and Commercial Regulation* 672–706.

18   Floyd 'When old meets new' (2011).

19   Ibid.

20   See Compa 'Labor rights and labor standards in international trade' (1993–94) 168.

21   Most scholars agree there will be a type of tapestry of instruments: see Hepple *Labour Laws and Global Trade* (2005) 248 et seq; Arthurs 'Reinventing labor law for the global economy' (2001) 291–4; Compa 'Labor rights and labor standards in international trade' (1993–94) 176 et seq.

use of litigation against transnational corporations (where that litigation attempts to apply the domestic laws of the company's home country to their workers located throughout the world). The latter approach obviously involves complex questions of conflicts of law. A lingering debate relates to whether there should be internationally binding laws and sanctions on labour – and to the relevance of regional agreements. While this might seem to draw together a disparate group of sources of law, Arthurs points out that this is nothing new for a law which is still developing. In presenting the Benjamin Aaron Lecture at the University of California Los Angeles, Arthurs concluded:[22]

> It is difficult to imagine that governments, unions, corporations, and social movements might create and administer a system of global labor law by pasting together a collage of treaties and conventions, best practices, corporate codes, ad hoc settlements, and vestigial remnants of national legislation. But this, after all, is pretty much how we originally constructed our 'old' system of labor law. Lest we forget, there was collective bargaining before the Wagner Act, employer- and union-sponsored welfare funds before Social Security, and grievance arbitration before the War Labor Board. Thus, I want to conclude by arguing that it is just possible that in these scattered, episodic episodes of rule making and dispute resolution, we may spy the shape of the future.

The patchy nature of transnational labour law is also said to give the law flexibility – so that it can apply and be relevant to the many different cultures of the world and meet the circumstances of many different cultures and stages of national development. But as Reich reminds us in *Supercapitalism*,[23] some of today's corporations have greater wealth than some small nations, and transcend national barriers. There is a politically neoliberal element to globalisation, as so much is about the pushing of ideas and finances beyond the boundaries of one nation's laws.[24] It is no easy thing to regulate transnational workers' rights.

The various types of transnational laws are discussed below.

9.10.20 Methods of achieving the regulation of transnational/international labour law

Methods of regulating transnational labour law have been discussed by a range of scholars.[25] Below is a distillation of the common threads and issues.

9.10.25 ILO (and UN) treaties and conventions

Instruments such as the UN's Universal Declaration of Human Rights speak to the need for fair wages and reasonable working conditions.[26] As discussed in Chapter 3, the ILO works in close association with the UN on labour law issues and regulation. Its conventions and recommendations provide international labour standards. The ILO examines the compliance

---

22   Arthurs 'Reinventing labor law for the global economy' (2001) 291 and 293–4.
23   R Reich *Supercapitalism: The Transformation of Business, Democracy and Everyday Life* (Knopf, 2007).
24   See also Arthurs 'Reinventing labor law for the global economy' (2001) opening pages.
25   Compa 'Labor rights and labor standards in international trade' (1993–94); Arthurs 'Reinventing labor law for the global economy' (2001); Hepple *Labour Laws and Global Trade* (2005); Trubek 'Recent books on international law' (2006).
26   Compa 'Labor rights and labor standards in international trade' (1993–94) 176–7.

with and promotion of those standards in member states.[27] However, as with many international law and human rights bodies, there are questions about the effective enforcement of its standards. One significant problem is that some of its member states do not actually ratify ILO standards and enact them into domestic law. There is little by way of sanctions that the ILO can rely on to enforce its conventions and some of its labour standards may simply be too high for some developing countries to meet immediately upon joining (if they were to do so).[28] For these reasons, debate has turned to the manner in which the work of the ILO can be improved and 'buttressed'.[29] The methods of doing so are considered below.

There are two significant parallel developments: the emergence of Core Labour Standards (CLSs) and moves to incorporate further labour conditions within WTO agreements. The CLSs are the ILO standards on which there is an international consensus:[30] a safe workplace with adequate wages, reasonable working hours and freedom from discrimination; the right to organise into unions and collectively bargain; and prohibitions on forced labour and child labour. The discussion about protectionism (above) underscores the controversy that surrounds placing labour standards within the purview of the WTO, although the links between trade and labour are clear and long established. The case in support is that the CLSs are broadly accepted internationally and are so significant that they are human rights – and hence should be enforced by the WTO, rather than left to the ILO, which does not have a perfect record on enforcement.[31]

9.10.30 Transnational law – regional agreements and sanctions

Given the issues with ILO enforcement and questions as to whether some ILO standards are simply too high for developing nations to meet, attention has been paid to the EU, and to other forms of regional standards and enforcement where, for instance, there has been free movement of workers between unified states and sanctions for breach.[32]

At the time of writing, the EU was undergoing significant change after the Brexit vote – whereby 51.9 per cent of Britons (in a non-compulsory referendum vote) voted to leave the EU. That vote has inspired other member states, such as France, to consider a Frexit referendum (although at the time of writing, Emanuel Macron, a supporter of the EU, had just been elected French President).[33] It is unclear, therefore, what the future holds for the EU. That

---

27   Ibid 177–9.
28   On all these points see, for example, discussion in Hepple *Labour Laws and Global Trade* (2005) in Trubek 'Recent books on international law' (2006) 726 et seq and Lester, Mercurio and Davies *World Trade Law: Text, Materials and Commentary* (2012) 871 et seq.
29   Trubek 'Recent books on international law' (2006) discussing Hepple *Labour Laws and Global Trade* (2005) at 726 et seq.
30   Compa 'Labor rights and labor standards in international trade' (1993–94) 169 et seq. The concept is also considered in Lester, Mercurio and Davies *World Trade Law: Text, Materials and Commentary* (2012) from 873.
31   Lester, Mercurio and Davies *World Trade Law: Text, Materials and Commentary* (2012) 878.
32   See Trubek 'Recent books on international law' (2006) 729–30.
33   A Evans-Pritchard 'Madame Frexit looms large as the French political centre disintegrates', *The Telegraph*, 8 February 2017, http://www.telegraph.co.uk/business/2017/02/08/madame-frexit-looms-large-french -political-centre-disintegrates/ (accessed 11 February 2017). As to French Presidential elections, see ABC News 24 in week beginning 7 May 2017.

situation and its impact on labour law is considered later in this chapter. Still, regional solutions may be seen to be worthwhile, in that such an approach gives flexibility and avoids having only global standards that apply to all nations, irrespective of their level of development and their specific cultural considerations.[34]

9.10.35 Trade regulation

The US now clearly includes labour standards in its free trade deals,[35] and there is a side arrangement on labour in NAFTA (the North American Free Trade Agreement).[36] Further, international funding for development has been linked to the meeting of basic workers' rights.[37]

9.10.40 Codes of conduct

In the opening to this section, attention was drawn to the fact that the new transnational labour law will involve a mix of hard and soft law measures to improve labour conditions in the many different cultures in the world, bearing in mind their different stages of development. In this context a consideration of codes of conduct is apposite.

Scholars observe that transnational corporations increasingly adopt global codes of conduct in relation to labour conditions, in a quest to both improve labour conditions in the countries where their suppliers are based, and avoid negative criticisms and litigation if the working conditions are found to be poor.[38] Such codes take many forms, and vary as to the force of the language used, the topics covered and the monitoring provided.[39] There may be internal codes (written statements of policy about standards of labour) produced by the companies themselves (for example, Wal-Mart's voluntary internal code of conduct),[40] and there are external codes, which are either agreed between countries or put in place by non-government organisations (often through the imprimatur of the ILO).

The earlier codes of conduct were put in place either after multinational companies had experienced public relations difficulties when the sweatshop conditions of their suppliers were discovered, or they were a response to government pressure or incentive.[41] One government agreement, the Apparel Industry Partnership, is a coalition of apparel producers, church groups, unions and non-government organisations in the clothing industry established by former President Clinton.[42] Its creation is interesting.[43] After veteran US television presenter Cathie Lee Gifford found that sweatshop labour was being used to produce her line of clothing

---

34   See Trubek 'Recent books on international law' (2006) 730.
35   Compa 'Labor rights and labor standards in international trade' (1993–94) 179.
36   Ibid 180.
37   Ibid 181–2.
38   R Blanpain et al. *Global Workplace International and Comparative Employment Law: Cases and Materials* (Cambridge University Press, 2007) from 590.
39   Ibid 591 et seq.
40   KE Kenny 'Code or contract: whether Wal-Mart's code of conduct creates a contractual obligation between Wal-Mart and the employees of its foreign suppliers' (2007) 27 *Northwestern Journal of International Law and Business* 456–59.
41   Ibid 456 et seq.
42   Ibid.
43   See H Revak 'Corporate codes of conduct: binding contract or ideal publicity?' (2011–12) 63 *Hastings Law Journal* 1651–2.

for Wal-Mart, she teamed with the Clinton Administration to form these independent standards. While that development is obviously positive, the social group Sweatshop Watch has asked questions about how well enforced and policed the standards are.[44]

But the actual case which underscores the difficulties in enforcing codes of conduct is a different law suit involving Wal-Mart. The subject of scholarly consideration by many,[45] *Doe v Wal-Mart* is considered below.

DOE v WAL-MART STORES INC (US COURT OF APPEALS, 9TH CIRCUIT, NO. 08-55706, 2009)[46]

The Doe in the title of the case stands for Jane Doe and John Doe – the faceless workers who suffered the alleged sweatshop exploitation in countries ranging from China to Swaziland (where suppliers for Wal-Mart were based). This case involved class action litigation against Wal-Mart. It was argued that Wal-Mart's Code of Conduct is part of its supply contract (that is, suppliers are to meet that standard in order to remain suppliers for Wal-Mart); and that Wal-Mart is therefore obliged to monitor compliance and ensure commitment to those standards – if it does not, it is breaching its representation to its customers and its supply agreements. In essence, it was argued that Wal-Mart failed to leverage its economic and actual control to force suppliers to comply with labour standards, and so it was a party to the breach of standards relating to workers' rights.[47]

In dismissing the case, some of the key issues considered by the courts were:

- *The effect of the code* – One of the factors the courts will consider in determining whether a code creates a binding contractual obligation is whether the language is sufficiently promissory, contractual and well publicised that an employee (or subcontractor) would consider it part of a contractual offer.[48] (In other words, there is a similarity between the US law on policies governing the Wal-Mart case and some of the law governing policies in Australia.)[49] While the Wal-Mart code was well publicised, it was not so much promissory to *workers*, but rather set out some guidelines as to when Wal-Mart might take action against *suppliers* (for example, Wal-Mart 'reserved the right to make periodic inspections', it would 'favor suppliers who meet industry practices' and 'failure to supply complete and accurate

---

44   Ibid and Kenny 'Code or contract' (2007) 456.
45   Blanpain et al. *Global Workplace International and Comparative Employment Law* (2007); Kenny 'Code or contract' (2007) 456–59; Revak 'Corporate codes of conduct' (2011–12) 1645; J Van de Walle 'Doe v Wal-Mart: revisiting the scope of joint employment' (2011) 30 *Berkeley Journal of Employment and Labor Law* 546.
46   Extracts of the court documents are set out in Blanpain et al. *Global Workplace International and Comparative Employment Law* (2007) from 592. The case was dismissed in 2007 *Doe v Wal-Mart Stores Inc*, US Dist LEXIS 98702 (CD Cal March 30, 2007), and the appeal was dismissed in 2009 (*Doe v Wal-Mart Stores Inc*, 572 F 3d 677 (2009)): 'Appeal Dismissed' Washington Legal Foundation: Litigation Update, wlf.org/upload/litigation/litigationupdate/072109walmart.pdf (accessed 11 May 2017).
47   Ibid 592 et seq; and see generally Revak 'Corporate codes of conduct' (2011–12), Van de Walle and Kenny 'Code or contract' (2007).
48   Kenny 'Code or contract' (2007) 459 et seq.
49   *Goldman Sach JB Were Services Pty Ltd v Nikolich* (2007) 163 FCR 62 – such cases are considered in connection with the Chapter 2 internet materials.

commercial invoices may result in cancellation of orders').[50] Even when there was an absolute prohibition on accepting goods from forced labour, there were no provisions regarding how the use of such would be uncovered – there was always something vague or in need of interpretation such that the agreement was likely to hinge on when Wal-Mart might eliminate a supplier rather than on guarantees of worker rights.[51]

- *The corporate structure/independent contractor laws* – Further problems arose in trying to construe Wal-Mart as a joint employer of the labour in China and of the other suppliers. This is because the litigants were not able to prove that Wal-Mart had day-to-day control over the employment of labour at these factories or that somehow Wal-Mart had positively contributed to the problem.[52] Sadly, the law does not seem to take into account economic realities: the fact that Wal-Mart exercises such economic influence over its suppliers that if it insisted on higher labour standards and further audits of conditions, things almost certainly would improve. The law does not seem to sufficiently factor in capacity to indirectly control supplier conduct.[53]

- *Unlimited liability disincentive to improve* – Some scholars make the point that a good Samaritan who throws a rope, pulls a drowning man halfway to shore and then (for no good reason) abandons him to drown may be held liable.[54] By the same token, if those good Samaritan notions were carried too far (in an international trade context) so that any attempt by a corporation to improve the conditions of overseas workers could make them liable (even though the corporation has no day-to-day control over the endless breaches that could arise) then perhaps the law would be going too far.[55] So the question for most of the authors in this field is whether corporate codes are enforceable (or do they at least have some real worth) or are they just good publicity for the companies? As Blanpain said, there is promise and peril in international self-regulation and associated US litigation.[56]

Perhaps the last word should be left with Kenny,[57] who reminded us of the benefit of international law suits: they shine a spotlight on injustice and can shock a multinational into doing something (whether the actual law suit is settled or lost). She also noted the relevance of procurement law in fostering better labour conditions.[58] In places like San Francisco, ordinances require those seeking work with the government to meet certain labour standards. It seems a blend of legal strategies is the most appropriate approach.

9.10.45 Application of domestic laws abroad

Doe v Wal-Mart Stores Inc demonstrates that codes of conduct can be used to apply the labour or other laws/standards of an advanced country such as the US (generally the home

---

50   Kenny 'Code or contract' (2007) 463 et seq.
51   Ibid 465 et seq.
52   Van de Walle '*Doe v Wal-Mart*' (2011) 571–3.
53   Ibid 597 et seq.
54   Revak 'Corporate codes of conduct' (2011–12) 1664.
55   Ibid 1667.
56   Blanpain et al. *Global Workplace International and Comparative Employment Law* (2007) 591.
57   Kenny 'Code or contract' (2007) 470 et seq.
58   Ibid.

of a transnational corporation) to workers in developing countries (typically the home of suppliers of transnational companies).[59]

Over and above these kinds of approaches is the deeper issue of conflicts of laws. One of the most obvious conflicts involves situations where there are completely different types of legal system and culture in play. For example, what occurs when Western Christians work in Islamic nations? It is unlikely that an Islamic court would hold in favour of many standards Westerners take for granted.[60] (See also the section on anti-discrimination law in Chapter 8.)

The opening of this section highlighted how US labour law scholars have noted the changing nature of labour law – how international elements are affecting the lives of many workers, whereas in the past, labour law was considered a more local type of practice.[61] The same point has been well made in an Australian context by Professor Ron McCallum,[62] who observes that previously workers would build lives for themselves in local communities and local workplaces, but increasingly workers travel abroad for promotion, or at least make overseas visits with work, or are employees of a multinational, some of whose work may be performed oversees. To use a current example, there are now Indian call centres that work with Australian customers. While the issues discussed above are especially relevant to lifting the standards of overseas workers who are part of global supply chains – or stopping such workers' conditions forcing down the labour conditions of employees in developed nations – there remain these very important questions: what law applies to work done by an Australian while they are working overseas? What of a foreign national working in Australia for a multinational? What is the place of conflicts of laws in a labour law context?

The starting point and essence of conflicts of laws is threefold, according to Tilbury, Davis and Opeskin:[63]

• *Establish jurisdiction (lex fori)* This arises typically where one party (usually the defendant) is not present in the jurisdiction or where the court the plaintiff claims has jurisdiction seems inappropriate;

• *Establish the correct choice of law (lex loci)* What is the proper law? Here one considers whether there is a connection with a foreign system of law that is so strong that it is illogical to apply the law of Australia.

• *Ask whether a foreign judgement is enforceable in Australia.*

---

59 Another interesting example involving Wal-Mart relates to that company's code of conduct, which prohibited intimate relationships between staff and provided a type of dobber line for those who had suspicions the policy was being breached. That provision was in breach of German laws on workplace privacy – see Hastings at 1567 and Kenny 'Code or contract' (2007) 462–3. Seldom does domestic legislation operate on an extra-territorial basis.

60 Excellent books on Islamic law include Y Haddad and B Stowasser *Islamic Law and the Challenges of Modernity* (Altamira Press, 2004). Books are available on the laws of most countries as primers: see R Chandran *Employment Law in Singapore* (Pearson Prentice Hall, 2005) and M Vranken *Death of Labour Law? Comparative Perspectives* (Melbourne University Press, 2009).

61 Arthurs 'Reinventing labor law for the global economy' (2001) 274–8: Arthurs makes the point that localisation of labour law is an especially significant point in the US, a globaliser of others – it influences the world more than most countries.

62 R McCallum 'Conflicts of laws and labour law in the new economy' (2003) 16 *Australian Journal of Labour Law* 3.

63 M Tilbury, G Davis and B Opeskin *Conflicts of Laws in Australia* (Oxford University Press, 2002) 3–5.

McCallum provides a very useful survey of the types of employment issues that have arisen and might arise, and some of the broad principles that apply from the decided cases.[64]

Parties may choose the proper law of their contract, which will frequently apply – unless it is overruled by statute. If parties have not chosen (either expressly or by implication), then the courts usually apply the law with the 'closest and most real connection to the contract'.[65] So, in *Sheldrick v WT Partnership (Australia) Pty Ltd* (1998) 89 IR 206, Einfeld J was confronted by a situation in which an Australian national left an Australian company to work in Kuala Lumpur for a related company doing work on a Malaysian airport. When summarily terminated from his employment, the employee sought recourse to the Australian courts. Einfeld J held that the real decision to terminate was taken in Melbourne and adopted by the overseas related company, hence Australian law applied.[66] In contrast, in *Amery v Coopers & Lybrand Actuarial Services Pty Ltd* [1999] VSC 29, Australia was not the correct forum as the contract was made in Singapore, the employer was a Singapore corporation and the termination occurred in Singapore – where most of the witnesses also resided.[67]

While those are examples of termination cases, there are special issues arising in a tortious context. The High Court of Australia in *John Pfeiffer Pty Ltd v Rogerson* (2000) 203 CLR 503 found that the locality of the tort will usually determine the applicable law.[68] That approach can have harsh consequences, such as for an Australian who is injured while on a short overseas trip with work (say to Indonesia) and ends up unable to access Australian workers' compensation systems.[69] McCallum suggests that employees consider suing in contract for failure of the implied term to take reasonable care of the employee's safety.[70]

9.15 Special cases in international law
9.15.05 China

One of the world's most respected scholars of Chinese law is Professor Jerome Cohen. As he observed, culture and history play an important role in the interpretation and operation of Chinese law.[71] Throughout many periods in Chinese history (such as Tiananmen Square and the Cultural Revolution), the state has had a crushing influence on dissenters. That may well have bred both disrespect for laws espousing individual rights and a fear of trying to exercise individual rights. Culturally, building relationships has long been important in China, as has the concept of 'saving face'. Consequently, while a written contract may say one thing, its operation may show deference to the relationship between the parties.[72]

---

64   McCallum 'Conflicts of laws and labour law in the new economy' (2003) 16.
65   Ibid 27.
66   Ibid 30–31.
67   Ibid 32–33.
68   Ibid 37.
69   Ibid 40.
70   Ibid 40–41 et seq.
71   J Cohen, Y Chan and HY Ming *Contract Laws of the People's Republic of China* (Longman, 1988).
72   Similar points have been made by numerous subsequent scholars, such as P Blazey 'Culture and its relationship to undertaking business in China' in P Blazey and Kay-Wah Chan, *The Chinese Commercial Legal System* (Law Book Co., 2008).

What this means in a labour law context is that while the Chinese government has introduced many laws relating to workers' rights,[73] there is a gap between the words on the statute books and the operation of those laws in practice.[74] Trade unions and church groups operate to help workers, but only so long as they have the imprimatur of the state.[75] Vast rural populations (who do not speak English, who perform manual labour, and/or who may not be able to take on executive work in large Chinese cities) may either not know their rights or be too afraid to try to enforce them.[76] While the ILO reports that things have improved, there is a very long way to go before Chinese working conditions catch up with those in the West. As noted above, there is concern in the meantime as to whether Chinese standards may actually drag down Western standards or have a negative impact on trade.[77]

Other crucial issues confronting Australians dealing with China relate to ethics and the lack of transparency of the Chinese legal system. Chinese 'relationship building' must not amount to a transgression of Australian business ethics – there have been documented cases where taking relationships too far has led to disciplinary action being taken against the Australian.[78] Further, when some Australians have acted in ways that might be seen to embarrass the Chinese government, there have been questions as to whether those individuals have suffered reprisals.[79]

The crux of the difficulty is that in China the law is inextricably linked to the culture and the government. Even if there is a written agreement or labour law, the actual words on the page may not take effect as a Westerner expects because of those cultural and political realities.

9.15.10 The international transport industry – HR issues and international organising

The chapter has, so far, discussed the application of international/transnational law and standards on matters that have often previously been local. But some industries are innately global – such as international air transport, maritime businesses and IT. Particularly in the transport field – where there are numerous unskilled or lower-skilled jobs – there are significant questions about workplace governance in our international age.

International cargo ships are frequently registered under 'flags of convenience' – not the flags of the nations with which they have the strongest connection (ownership or ultimate benefit), but rather the flag of a country that has made an industry out of providing registration for businesses (such as Panama).[80] There is much debate and concern about the use of such flags of convenience. Where the ultimate beneficiary or owner places shell companies

---

73   For instance, the Chinese Labor Contract Law, discussed in HK Josephs 'Measuring progress under China's labor law: goals, processes, outcomes' (2008) 30 *Comparative Labor Law and Policy Journal* 337.

74   See, for example, Floyd 'When old meets new' (2011).

75   Ibid 1221.

76   Ibid 1224 et seq.

77   See Floyd 'When old meets new' (2011).

78   Ibid 1233 et seq.

79   Ibid.

80   M Gianni and W Simpson *The Challenging Nature of High Seas Fishing: How Flags of Convenience Provide Cover for Illegal, Unreported and Unregulated Fishing* (Australian Department of Agriculture Fisheries and Forestry, WWF and International Transport Workers Federation, 2005).

between themselves and the vessel, it may be hard to determine who actually controls the vessel's operation. Obviously, that begs questions as to whether such arrangements mask illegal activity or make investigation of environmental and human rights offences difficult. For those reasons, there are international instruments, such as the UN Convention on the Law of the Sea, which seek to solidify links between ownership and operation and registration of vessels. But as the International Transport Workers Federation notes, there are major issues of labour law for seamen.[81] The Federation correctly observes that workers on the high seas are largely hidden from view. If their ship is registered to a low-wage country, those low wages will be the standard for their work (regardless of where the workers are from and regardless of whether the ultimate beneficiary of the ship's work is a business in a developed country).[82] The ILO's Maritime Labour Convention of 2006 opposes the use of flags of convenience and the International Transport Workers' Federation (ITWF) uses its influence to force inspections of ships when they come ashore, to examine working conditions.[83]

The international airline industry may not be quite as bad as the maritime field, but there is a growing trend for airlines to form alliances and share arrangements where they (at the very least) sell tickets for each other and use each other's aircraft.[84] Against that background, crew swapping clearly becomes an issue. In the US there have been culture shocks and confusion through the use by one airline of another airline's staff. There is also a need to avoid a race to the bottom on terms and conditions of employment and a need to avoid sexism where crews are being shared between carriers whose nation of origin has extremely conservative views about the place of women (even though clearly they allow them to work).[85]

Even within carriers there can be workplace issues on crew swaps. A reading of the Flight Attendants Union website shows that within the Qantas group there have been questions about what rules will apply when crews swap between the airline's various arms.[86] At the very least, there needs to be careful checking that no terms of enterprise bargains are breached (in situations where there is a different agreement for a different arm of the carrier).

More broadly, there are international trade union-style bodies – not only the ITWF mentioned above, but also, for instance, the International Federation of Airline Pilots[87] – which take up generic issues. So, for instance, when there was a question about whether some of the Middle Eastern airlines were being subsidised by rich oil interests and hence had a competitive advantage over the US airlines, that issue was ventilated by the unions.[88]

---

81   http://www.itfglobal.org.

82   Ibid.

83   Ibid and http://www.ilo.org/global/stanolards/maritime-labour-convention/lang/en/index.htm.

84   D Whitelegg *Working the Skies: The Fast-paced Disorienting World of the Flight Attendant* (New York University Press, 2007) 60 et seq.

85   Ibid.

86   See https://faaa.org.au (for example, Tripswapping – Across Category/Contracts) (accessed 11 May 2017).

87   See http://www.itfglobal.org, which is an international federation of transport workers'. See also https://www.ifalpa.org (airline pilots). At an Australian level, see the Australian Federation of Air Pilots website, http://www.afap.org.au.

88   See Partnership for Fair and Open Skies 'US airlines, unions reveal evidence of $42 billion in subsidies by QATAR and the UAE to their state carriers', http://www.openandfairskies.com.

9.15.15 Brexit

On 23 June 2016, a British referendum decided, 51.9 per cent to 48.1 per cent, to exit the European Union (EU) or to 'Brexit', as it is known.[89] Given that EU labour and employment standards and institutions affect British employment law (by laying down minimum standards or by maintaining the jurisdiction of the European Court of Justice in some areas), there is an obvious question about what happens to UK labour and employment law in the coming years.[90] A parliamentary briefing paper records the UK government's pledge that nothing will change:[91]

> Commentators differ in their opinions on what the Government will do with EU employment law, but the Brexit Minister, David Davis, said in mid-July: 'All the empirical studies show that it is not employment regulation that stultifies economic growth, but all the other market-related regulations, many of them wholly unnecessary.'

But some of the most insightful considerations of the topic doubt that can be the case.[92] Careful consideration suggests those commentators should not be ignored. There are two broad categories of issue:

- what happens to the physical human beings who work throughout the EU essentially as EU citizens;[93] and
- what happens to the detail of the British law and law enforcement mechanisms, some of which clearly rest upon EU principles.[94]

Extremely importantly, any consideration of those issues takes place in the most uncertain of environments. At the time of writing, the House of Commons had only just voted to trigger Art 50 of the Treaty of European Union, the provision by which a member of the EU can start exit negotiations.[95] Prime Minister May had only just delivered her keynote address on the 12 points on which Britain's Brexit negotiations would rest.[96] Significantly, the Prime Minister indicated that Britain would seek what has been called a 'hard Brexit', rather than what some commentators had suggested was the more likely and desirable 'soft Brexit', which would have placed Britain in a situation similar to that of Norway: Britain would have remained in the single European market,

---

89   V Bogdanor 'Brexit, the Constitution and the alternatives' (2016) 27(3) *King's Law Journal* 314–22. See also Electoral Commission figures, http://www.electoralcommission.org.uk/find-information-by-subject/elections-and-referendums/past-elections-and-referendums/eu-referendum/electorate-and-count-information (accessed 11 February 2017).

90   Even in the short time that has elapsed since the referendum, this question has been considered by numerous British lawyers. See footnotes below.

91   House of Commons Library, *Brexit; impact across policy areas*, Briefing Paper 26, August 2016, http://www.parliament.uk.

92   P Thompson 'Roll up that mat' (2016) *New Law Journal*, newlawjournal.co.uk and M Ford 'The effect of Brexit on workers' rights' (2016) 27(3) *King's Law Journal* 398–415.

93   Treaty on the Functioning of the European Union, Art 21.

94   EV Miller 'Brexit: impact across policy areas' (House of Commons Briefing Paper No. 07213 26, 2016).

95   The vote took place in the House of Commons on 9 February 2017, after a court challenge mandated a parliamentary vote: see discussion of *R (Miller) v Secretary of State for Exiting the EU* [2016] EWHC 2768 (Admin) in KD Ewing Editor's Introduction (2016) 27(3) *King's Law Journal* 289–96.

96   Speech delivered by T May, 17 January 2017, https://www.gov.uk/government/speeches/the-governments-negotiating-objectives-for-exiting-the-eu-pm-speech. Website materials will include updates.

but not be an actual member of the EU.[97] The EU is truly supranational – it is a body with its own pillars and freedoms, such as freedom of movement of persons within the EU (akin to EU citizenship) and a single market (a form a trading bloc amongst the European nations which does not necessarily commit members to all EU actions and obligations). The EU's freedoms and pillars exist separately from the institutions and laws of the nations who are EU members – and indeed can influence those national laws. If Britain remained in the single market but was not a member of the EU (a soft Brexit), the UK would still have to adhere to freedom of movement of persons (and therefore workers). The UK government has decided against this, claiming that it is exactly those migration-related issues that led to the referendum result.[98]

Even taking those uncertainties into account, it is useful to consider the key employment law issues confronting the UK after Brexit, as they underscore the key issues at the heart of this chapter.

9.15.20 Freedom of movement of persons/workers

Under one of the freedoms fundamental to the EU – freedom of movement (of persons) – many workers came to the UK from other EU nations and many Britons worked in other parts of the EU.[99] Any restrictions on their capacity to work were less tightly controlled than those placed on citizens of non-EU nations.[100] It has been suggested that those who have already secured permanent residency or citizenship will be untouched, but what will happen to others? Will they be subject to visas? If so, will there be a special category of visa for those in the so-called Shengen area (which takes into account much of the EU)?[101] What happens to Britons who are used to working abroad? This question underscores the links between labour and migration laws.

9.15.25 UK employment laws and law enforcement

The leading commentary on this issue at the time of writing is Michael Ford QC's 'The effect of Brexit on workers' rights' (which also alludes to his advice to the Trade Union Council [TUC]).[102] In that article, Ford neatly summarises the position of British employment law vis-à-vis the EU:[103]

> What we do know, as I explained in detail in an advice written for the TUC prior to the referendum, is that most employment rights in the UK are at present guaranteed by EU law. The rights include protection against discrimination in the work sphere; the principal health and safety regulations; rights to collective information and consultation on

---

97 Ibid point 8. 'Brexit Bill: Theresa May gets her way over hard Brexit as Corbyn hit by key resignations', *The Independent* online, 9 February 2017, http://www.independent.co.uk/news/uk/politics/brexit-bill-vote-commons-parliament-article-50-a7570411.html (accessed 11 Feb 2017). It goes against what some commentators had suggested. For the soft Brexit concept, see S Dhingra 'Salvaging Brexit: the right way to leave the EU' (2016) 95 *Foreign Affairs* 90. For an excellent outline of the options available for Brexiting as well as the pillars and organisations that make up the EU, see Bogdanor 'Brexit, the Constitution and the alternatives' (2016) 318.

98 T May speech, 17 January 2017, point 8.

99 T McGuinness, *Brexit: What impact on those currently exercising free movement rights*, House of Commons Briefing Paper No. 7871, 19 January 2017.

100 Ibid 7.

101 Thompson 'Roll up that mat' (2016).

102 Ford 'The effect of Brexit on workers' rights' (2016). For a further discussion see E Slattery and J Broadbent 'A long and winding road' (2016) *New Law Journal*.

103 Ford 'The effect of Brexit on workers' rights' (2016) 399 (internal footnotes omitted).

redundancies, transfers and beyond; working time rights; protections of workers on transfers of undertakings and in insolvency; rules on the treatment of fixed-term, agency and part-time workers; and other, more peripheral, rights such as data protection. The principal purely domestic exceptions are the individual rights not to be unfairly dismissed, to the national minimum wage and to redundancy payments, and the labyrinthine procedure for compulsory trade union recognition.

Ford is sceptical of the government's reassurance that workers' rights will be entrenched after Brexit. Essentially, the UK government is planning a Great Repeal Bill: 'While the jurisdiction of the European Court of Justice (ECJ) will end, according to Mrs May the existing *aquis* of EU law will be converted into UK law, to be repealed, revoked or amended at leisure in later years.'[104]

According to Ford, the end of the jurisdiction of the ECJ will probably reduce workers' rights.[105] Britain will miss any worker protections that were gained by virtue of being a member state of the EU.[106] Even if laws remain on the statute books, the enforcement mechanisms may change, making it harder for workers to assert their rights (could enforcement be privatised, for instance, or could costs be attached for applications to assert rights?).[107]

A further significant issue is the impact of Brexit on Scottish employment law. Scotland voted 1,661,191 to 1,018,322 to remain in the EU.[108] However, Scotland is still a stateless nation: although it is a nation, it is part of the UK, which is the state, and there are numerous matters that have not been devolved to its own parliament.[109] It must follow Westminster's lead on those and, therefore, it too must Brexit. This state of affairs has prompted debate as to whether there should be another independence referendum in Scotland. If there were and it succeeded, an independent Scotland (if one emerges) would then reapply for EU membership.[110]

Beyond that, there are questions about the future of the EU itself. Matthias Matthijs observes:[111]

> As the British historian Alan Milward argued in his 1992 book *The European Rescue of the Nation-State,* Europe's ruling elites established the European Economic Community (EEC) in the 1950s not to build a new supranational power but to rehabilitate the system of

104   Ibid 398.
105   Ibid 414–15.
106   Ibid 404 et seq and 414–15.
107   Ibid 401 et seq and 414–15. See also KD Ewing and J Hendy 'Editors' preface' (2016) 27(1) *King's Law Journal* 22–3, which contains a useful overview of all articles on these issues. See also H Jewitt 'Now the dust has settled' (2015) *New Law Journal*, considering the employment implications of a David Cameron (now Theresa May) victory in the 2015 UK election.
108   See Electoral Commission figures, http://www.electoralcommission.org.uk/find-information-by-subject/elections-and-referendums/past-elections-and-referendums/eu-referendum/electorate-and-count-information (accessed 11 February 2017).
109   http://www.parliament.scot/visitandlearn/education/18642.aspx (accessed 11 February 2017).
110   J Elgot 'Sturgeon: second Scottish referendum is likely to be held in event of hard Brexit', *The Guardian* online (16 October 2016), https://www.theguardian.com/politics/2016/oct/16/nicola-sturgeon-second-scottish-referendum-likely-in-event-of-hard-brexit (accessed 11 February 2017). The issue has also been raised in *Brexit Unknowns*, Cabinet Briefing Paper 7761, 9 November 2016.
111   M Matthijs 'Europe after Brexit: a less perfect union' (2017) 96 *Foreign Affairs* 87 and 94.

European nation-states after the horrors of World War II. They realized that if their countries were to survive, they would need some degree of continental coordination to help provide economic prosperity and political stability. Europe's leaders need to return to Milward's basic idea that Europe was meant not to cage its nation-states but to rescue them. Democratic legitimacy, for better or worse, remains with Europe's national governments.

And that is an appropriate place to leave the discussion of transnational labour law. As nations trade, as corporations operate transnationally, questions naturally arise as to the balance between trade promotion and the protection of labour law and human rights. The law and the issues are still emerging. The sources of transnational labour law are disparate and take varying forms – from transnational treaties through to regional (yet still transnational) agreements (such as the EU), corporate and industry codes of conduct and law suits. Conflict of laws is another difficulty. One of the ironies is that those transnational standards must be embraced and enforced by nation states. In the current political climate, those national governments are dealing with an apparent fear of migration and surge in nationalism. In the context of Brexit, Ewing ends his review of a leading transnational law text on a rather dark note:[112]

> The question now is whether [transnational labour law] will be a labour law of empowerment or a labour law of containment. My sense is that we have reached the summit of what is likely to be achieved, in the former sense, at least for the time being, and that the new focus will be one of adapting to the reality of a new diminished global standard . . . There are no governments queuing up to unleash latent transnational labour power. The paradox of transnational labour law is that like national labour law, it needs state support if it is to be a force for good. Although addressed to transnational actors and activities, at least on the labour side the effectiveness of transnational action depends on its legality, and its legality still depends on the decisions of legally 'sovereign' states . . . [The] transnational actors are bigger than the states on whose laws unions rely . . . the immediate prospects for a progressive transnational labour law look bleak, in a world in which political power has failed effectively to enfranchise those with the greatest economic need.

9.20 Migration and employment – subclass 457 visas

Possibly reflecting Ewing's concern (above) and clearly demonstrating the fear, in some quarters, of the free flow of workers, the Australian Prime Minister announced a review of the 457 visa system and a renewed commitment to promoting Australian workers in April 2017.[113] It is apposite to examine the key elements of the 457 system and the issues underlying the debate and law reform in this part of the chapter. Under the *Migration Act 1958* (Cth) and the associated *Migration Regulations 1994* (Cth), subclass 457 visas

---

112   Ewing '*Transnational Labour Law*, by Antonio Ojeda-Aviles, Alphen aan den Rijn, Wolters Kluwer, 2015' (2016) 135.

113   M Turnbull, as quoted in *The Courier Mail*, April 2017. See D Atkins (opinion) 'Party games: reason behind Malcolm Turnbull's 457 visa ban' *The Courier Mail*, 18 April 2017.

exist in order to facilitate the entry into Australia of skilled workers to fill temporary shortages in the workforce. Essentially, the program involves an employer sponsoring a worker to work in Australia for a period that can vary from months to years. The visa can be renewed, secondary visas can be granted to family members and the holders of such visas can apply for permanent residency.[114] The scheme is one of temporary rather than permanent migration – although permanent migration can follow – which makes it something of a contrast to the historical Australian position, which emphasised permanent migration for jobs.

While the idea might seem simple enough, it can be difficult to implement these types of schemes well. In other words, while there is a need to fill genuine labour shortages, there is also a need to protect local jobs and a duty to prevent the exploitation of migrant workers. Tham and Campbell observe:

> The relationship between these purposes and, in particular, the extent to which they can be reconciled depends on the design of the temporary migrant schemes and, importantly, broader labour regulation. The goals of addressing shortages and protecting the employment opportunities and working conditions of local workers can come into conflict: the supply of temporary migrant workers will inevitably impact upon the employment opportunities and working conditions of Australian workers engaged in similar industries. Whether these two purposes can be reconciled depends on the definition of labour shortages and how such shortages are demonstrated. Is employer say-so sufficient or are there strict evidential requirements? At what level of wages and conditions are the shortages to exist? If the requisite level is placed at the lower end, there is then the risk of migrant workers underpricing local workers, thereby displacing them.
>
> There is also a close relationship between protecting local workers and protecting the working conditions of migrant workers.[115]

In terms of mechanisms that could be used to deal with these issues, a number of options can be considered: placing limits on the number of workers an employer can sponsor; requiring minimum levels of skills (for workers) and minimum conditions of work (from employers); and requiring employer-sponsors to train local workers (not simply import workers from abroad).[116]

The difficulties in maintaining that balance, as well as the significance of the scheme, is reflected in the fact that temporary skilled migration has been embraced in some form by both major political parties since the 1990s – and there have been numerous reports and reviews into how the system should work.[117]

---

114   J-C Tham and I Campbell *Temporary Migrant Labour in Australia: The 457 Visa Scheme and Challenges for Labour Regulation* (2011) Centre for Employment and Labour Relations Law, Melbourne Law School, Working Paper No. 59 2, 7 et seq.

115   Ibid 7–8.

116   Ibid 8 – those authors raise Singapore (which has had foreign worker levy rates) as an example of how foreign workers are treated.

117   This point is made in J Azarias et al. *Robust New Foundations: A Streamlined, Transparent and Responsive System for the 457 Program – An Independent Review into Integrity in the Subclass 457 Programme* (2014) 7 et seq, 20–23, 105 et seq, as well as Tham and Campbell *Temporary migrant labour in Australia* (2011) 9–18 which sets out a detailed history (including regulation numbers and legislative changes) starting with the original scheme in 1996.

At various points in time, the scheme has rested upon:[118]

- labour market testing (the employer-sponsors test the local market to determine whether there are Australians they can employ);
- connection between sponsorship of workers and a specified list of occupations (possibly an extensive list generated by the Australian Bureau of Statistics);
- stringent English language testing with only a few countries exempted from that requirement;
- a requirement that the migrant worker be paid no less favourably than a ministerially determined minimum (that is, a temporary skilled migration income threshold) – except where the amount earned reaches a prescribed level (such as $180,000). Once the threshold is met, payment is also made with reference to what other Australians in the relevant business are being paid (a form of market rate);
- consideration of the record of the employer-sponsor for maintaining conditions of employment of migrant workers; and contributions by employers to training schemes.

One of the most recent reports (the Azarias Report) was released in September 2014. Whilst advocating tighter enforcement of the relevant laws and harsh penalties for breach,[119] the report is generally deregulatory, and seems to transfer some responsibility from the employer to the government. For example, the report recommends:

- the removal of labour market testing and its replacement with a tripartite committee to advise government on labour shortages – such committee may also assist in determining the list of occupations to which 457 visas apply (Recommendation 1);[120]
- relaxation of the English-language requirements (Recommendation 7);
- relaxation of the income threshold underpinning the system (Recommendation 5);
- replacing the current system for training Australians with an annual training contribution to be paid to government ($400 per worker) (Recommendation 6).

Interestingly, the report also leaves open the possibility of further situations in which 457 workers could be recruited and different methods through which they could come to Australia. There may be greater scope for recruiting 457 workers in some regions through a lower income threshold, for instance.[121]

On 18 March 2015, the government responded to the Azarias Report, supporting most of the recommendations and commencing a review of thresholds for wages.[122] Parallel to that, Immigration Instrument IMMI 15/149 (December 2015) exempted certain Chinese executives from labour market testing.

---

118   Tham and Campbell *Temporary Migrant Labour in Australia* (2011) 15–17 and Azarias et al. *Robust New Foundations* (2014) 8, 22.

119   Azarias et al. *Robust New Foundations* (2014) Recommendations 12, 17, 18, 21 and 22.

120   Ibid Recommendations 8 and 9.

121   Ibid Recommendation 14.

122   For regulations governing 457 visas see, for example, *Migration Regulations 1994* Reg 2.75 et seq; *Migration Act 1958* (Cth) s 140GBA and associated provisions. But the situation is fluid, and further change (probably along the lines of Australia First) has been clearly foreshadowed by the government, as noted above.

But that already complex situation has become even more complicated, as a result of two subsequent developments. A subsequent Senate Report was released.[123] That report recommends, *inter alia*: strengthening labour market testing, altering the constitution of the advisory committee; increasing the rigour behind the calculation of wages; and, highly significantly, publishing labour agreements and prohibiting the replacement of local workers with 457 visa holders. The report also highlights the links between different forms of migration and work.

The decision on Brexit, plus the election of President Trump in the US (with his constant message of 'America First' and promoting US jobs), has influenced the Australian discourse on the links between labour and immigration and the need to promote Australian jobs.[124] Although the various economic debates, theories and statistics on whether that nationalistic mantra is warranted are beyond the scope of this text, it is interesting to observe that there is great debate as to whether Brexit and Trump will in fact increase the numbers of jobs available for working people in the UK and the US respectively. As just one example, on 6 February 2017 British press outlets were reporting concerns about whether the Vauxhall car plants in the UK would close as French (read EU) interests gained a greater influence in that company.[125] The question is whether the UK plants, which relied on importing European parts, are less viable as an investment now that Britain is leaving the EU. Of course the impact of President Trump's policies on jobs remains to be seen, but the early phase of the administration, with all its turmoil, has led some respected economic commentators to ask whether the market (and therefore jobs) will ultimately be destabilised, rather than supported.[126]

At the time of writing, the area of 457 visas is fluid – as it has been for years. This commentary seeks only to place readers in a position where they know the theory behind the system, the basic elements of the system, and the key developments and debates so far.[127]

9.25 Unpaid or especially dangerous work

While the bulk of this book deals with paid employment (and to some extent independent contractors), unpaid work is of increasing importance to labour and employment law. Volunteers for charities or in times of national emergency; interns (perhaps eager law

---

123   Senate Education and Employment References Committee *National Disgrace: The Exploitation of Temporary Work Visa Holders* (March 2016).

124   For example, in the wake of the US election Opposition Leader Bill Shorten criticised 457 visas on a tour of high-unemployment North Queensland, even though he had previously supported them: R Baxendale 'Bill Shorten's stance on foreign workers breathtaking hypocrisy: PM', *The Weekend Australian* online, 15 November 2016. President Trump's catch-cry was notorious throughout the election campaign, was reiterated in his inauguration speech and has been reiterated on a daily basis since: R Revesz 'President Trump tells inauguration crowd "From this day on, it's America First"', *The Independent* online, 20 January 2017, http://www.independent.co.uk/news/world/americas/donald-trump-us-president-inauguration-speech-america-first-winning-rulers-nation-borders-jobs-roads-a7538091.html (accessed 18 February 2017).

125   BBC TV News, 16 February 2017.

126   'QUEST MEANS business' CNN TV, 16 February 2017.

127   An interesting body of research on 457 visas is being developed: see J Howe 'Does Australia need an expert commission to assist with managing its labour migration program?' (2014) 27 *Australian Journal of Labour Law* 233; 'Enterprise migration agreements under the subclass 457 visa: much ado about nothing?' (2014) 27 *Australian Journal of Labour Law* 86; and 'Regulation of Australia's migration program: is there a case for including fairness?' (2016) 26 *Australian Journal of Labour Law* 58.

students who cannot wait to experience a piece of courtroom action); and those undertaking either unpaid test period work or in vocational training (who need practical experience in order to graduate) together represent a significant portion of society, and their work arrangements and conditions have implications for employment law and governance. Some of the more significant questions in connection with unpaid work are considered below. They are:

- What are the definitions of these types of work? Is there any chance the work being performed is actually employment (in a legal sense) and not volunteer or intern work? In other words, should it be paid work? What are the implications for labour law and regulation flowing from the growth of the unpaid work sector?

- Even if work is being performed by volunteers or interns (who, therefore, should not be paid), what is the relevance of other legislation such as workplace health and safety or workers' compensation? And what of insurance?

9.25.05 What is a volunteer?

The value of volunteer work to the Australian economy is enormous: the number of volunteer hours worked have been calculated as representing around $9 billion in a year (if those doing it were *paid*, rather than *unpaid*).[128]

Most scholars – and for that matter lay people – would agree that the basic character of volunteer work is that the individual is working without remuneration (other than perhaps the reimbursement of reasonable expenses) for a purpose other than themselves: for example, to further the charitable endeavours of a non-profit organisation or something similarly altruistic.[129] But there are nuances to that definition.[130] Court-ordered community service is not really treated as volunteering (as it is not voluntary).[131] Volunteers may be formal (for an organisation such as the Red Cross); episodic (individuals who assist with big events such as the RSPCA's Million Paws Walk); or 'impulse'.[132] One sad example of the latter occurred in Japan after the 2011 earthquake, tsunami and nuclear power plant explosion at Fukushima. Such was the scale of the disaster that Japanese from all walks of life – students, the unemployed, business people, the elderly and home-based carers – simple 'dropped everything' to help.[133]

Obviously, such nuances mean that, from time to time, litigation and/or debate arises as to the status of an individual as a volunteer.

---

128 M McGregor-Lowndes 'Volunteer protection in Queensland' (2003) 24 *Queensland Lawyer* 81.
129 Ibid 86; see also A Stewart and R Owens *The Nature, Prevalence and Regulation of Unpaid Work, Internships and Trial Periods in Australia: Experience or Exploitation?* (2013) Report for Fair Work Ombudsman, 5; and J Tarr 'Volunteers piggy backing off their private insurance: an uncertain protection against liability' (2013) 41 *Australian Business Law Review* 30.
130 Tarr 'Volunteers piggy backing off their private insurance: an uncertain protection against liability' (2013) 30 et seq.
131 Ibid.
132 Ibid 31.
133 See M Willacy *Fukushima* (Macmillan Australia, 2013) and L Floyd 'Long road to recovery' *The Courier Mail*, 13 December 2013.

BERGMAN v BROKEN HILL MUSICIANS CLUB LTD (T/AS BROKEN HILL MUSICIANS CLUB) [2011] FWA 1143 (BERGMAN)

In this case, the question was whether someone who had been paid $50 per week for about 5 years for calling numbers for bingo matches was an employee who could sue for unfair dismissal or a volunteer (and therefore could not). In finding against an employment relationship,[134] Commissioner Steel acknowledged that there were some conflicts in the evidence; some gaps in the memories of witnesses; and some instances in which the club had referred to the applicant as an employee. However, there was no intention to create binding legal relations:

- The applicant had not been formally offered a 'job' but rather the arrangement developed out of her relationship with her predecessor;
- Although the club had the applicant's tax file number, they did not withdraw tax. The amount paid was not linked to hours of work, nor did it index to inflation over time – it was more in the nature of an honorarium or simple acknowledgment of some services rendered;
- There were no sanctions for breach of contract within the contemplation of the parties; and
- The applicant had undertaken other activities at other clubs due to an interest in bingo – not simply for profit.

CUDGEGONG SOARING PTY LTD v HARRIS (1996) 13 NSWCCR 92

This case, raised by Commissioner Steel in *Bergman* (above),[135] found a live-in carer to be an employee although they were not paid cash but rather were given board. The notion that there might be consideration for an employment contract without the actual payment of money has also been raised by others, who have alluded to a blurring of the line between volunteer and employee where a law student might work for a Community Legal Centre, partially for altruistic reasons but also to develop their legal skills and experience.[136]

TEEN RANCH PTY LTD v BROWN (1995) 87 IR 308

The court held there was a volunteering relationship where an applicant worked sporadically at times of their choosing over a period of years, not for money but for board.[137]

---

134 *Bergman* at [38]–[48] per Commissioner Steel.

135 Ibid [34].

136 Stewart and Owens *The Nature, Prevalence and Regulation of Unpaid Work, Internships and Trial Periods in Australia* (2013) 5, considered later in the chapter.

137 The case is also considered in *Bergman* at [41] and Stewart and Owens *The Nature, Prevalence and Regulation of Unpaid Work, Internships and Trial Periods in Australia* (2013) at 224–25. It is interesting to note that the *Teen Ranch* decision is questioned in J Murray 'The legal regulation of volunteer work' in C Arup et al. *Labour Law and Labour Market Regulation* (Federation Press, 2006) 708.

9.25.10 Employment law and volunteers: liability; workplace health and safety

It follows from the above cases[138] that volunteers are not covered by dismissal law; nor are they covered by the general protections of the *Fair Work Act*. That seems a logical consequence of the basic nature of the relationship: they are driven by altruism more than an intention to personally or financially gain; and there is no intention to create binding legal obligations.

But there is one vital matter that arises despite all that – and that is the issue of workplace health and safety, which connects to workers' compensation and liability for injury to others caused by volunteers. Indeed, Professor McGregor-Lowndes and Professor Tarr observe that volunteers operate often in dangerous emergency conditions, and they may have differing levels of experience (WHS and insurance are genuine concerns).[139] It is understandable – even to be expected – that volunteers might suffer injury, or injure someone else.

Typically, volunteers are protected by the 'employer's' obligation[140] to provide a safe workplace (so long as the charity has at least some paid employees in addition to the volunteers and is not simply a voluntary unincorporated association with no employees at all). Sometimes volunteers are deemed employees for the purposes of workers' compensation schemes (even though they are obviously outside the traditional definition of employee) – examples include certain volunteer fire-fighters and emergency volunteers.[141] However, many times they are not covered for that same reason.[142] In such circumstances insurance becomes a critical legal issue.[143] These duties and laws were considered in detail in Chapter 8.

Throughout most Australian States,[144] there is legislation (such as Queensland's *Civil Liability Act 2003*) which limits the liability of volunteers for damage caused by their acts or omissions, so long as their actions have been part of an organised activity and have not been due to drunkenness, and they were not outside the scope of the charity's activities and they are not criminal in nature.[145] The vexed question is whether the volunteer organisation can be made vicariously liable for the damage caused by the volunteer (as an employer often is for the acts of an employee).[146] On top of that, there are different contexts in which people volunteer (as noted above) along with differences in legislation covering volunteer liability. The difficulties those differences can cause can be seen in this example, raised by Professor Tarr:

---

138   See, for example, F Parry, J Phillips and A Herbert *National Workplace Relations* (Thomson Reuters, 2012) 'Who is covered?'.

139   See generally Tarr 'Volunteers piggy backing off their private insurance' (2013) and McGregor-Lowndes 'Volunteer protection in Queensland' (2003).

140   McGregor-Lowndes 'Volunteer protection in Queensland' (2003) 90. See also a useful summary in Stewart and Owens *The Nature, Prevalence and Regulation of Unpaid Work, Internships and Trial Periods in Australia* (2013) 104 et seq.

141   Australian Employment Law Guide (CCH Intelliconnnect online service) 'Workers Compensation Obligations' [6 905].

142   R Parsons, J Wynyard and J Loyola *Workers Compensation Manual NSW* (Thomson Reuters) 2.205 Volunteers.

143   See generally Tarr 'Volunteers piggy backing off their private insurance' (2013).

144   Ibid 31 and 32.

145   McGregor-Lowndes 'Volunteer protection in Queensland' (2003) 86 considering the *Civil Liability Act 2003* (Qld) ss 39 et seq.

146   Ibid 90 et seq.

In Queensland, an employee might be instructed by their employer to volunteer for a charity due to the corporate social responsibility commitments of the employer. So, they will be on the payroll of the employer, yet performing work for the charity. That worker may have to rely on the *Workers Compensation and Rehabilitation Act* rather than the *Civil Liability Act* as the law might regard them as performing work for the employer.[147]

Amidst all the questions of classification, there is a clear message here. Impulse volunteers are likely to be hard-pressed to claim legal protections – and all volunteers (and, if relevant, those facilitating volunteer opportunities) need to consider their insurance coverage. Due to the complexity of the law and the nature of liability that can arise, peak bodies such as Volunteers Australia produce useful guides to the rights of volunteers and obligations of those who use their services.[148] These are useful starting points for consideration, at a practical level, before possibly seeking specific legal advice.

In the absence of protection under statutory schemes or other forms of insurance, it may well be that questions arise as to who might bear responsibility for injury to someone who undertakes unpaid work for an unincorporated association. Whilst that question goes beyond the scope of this book and moves into the area of associations law, it would be naive for an employment law student or practitioner not to be aware of the links between the performance of work and insurance, as well as tortious and other liability.[149]

9.25.15 Emergency services: paid and unpaid work

The above commentary on volunteers canvassed some issues about volunteers and the emergency services (especially in terms of dealing with injury, health and safety). But it is not only volunteers who work in emergency services. Employees also work in emergency services, and there are issues beyond health and safety, such as what to do with employees when a workplace shuts down because of the effect a natural disaster has had on it. Given the inherent link between volunteers and employees in the wake of natural disasters, that issue is considered here.

Mark observed that the best approach for an employer is to plan ahead: for example, have a disaster management plan to relocate employees or have employees work from home, so that the business can continue even if the place of work is physically affected by natural disaster.[150] Whether or not such a plan exists, the provisions of the *Fair Work Act* are relevant. In particular, s 524 allows employers to stand down employees (without pay – but with continuity of service) when they cannot be redeployed. If the business can continue to operate after a disaster (and even if it cannot), there may be some staff who seek leave to participate in the emergency services relief effort. The *Fair Work Act* also

---

147   Tarr 'Volunteers piggy backing off their private insurance' (2013) 32.

148   Such as *The Volunteers' Guide: The Essential Guide for Work Health and Safety for Volunteers* and *National Standards for Involving Volunteers in Not for Profit Organisations*. There are useful fact sheets and checklists on the Volunteering Australia website, https://www.volunteeringaustralia.org.

149   See McGregor-Lowndes 'Volunteer protection in Queensland' (2003). K Fletcher, *The Law Relating to Non-Profit Associations in Australia and New Zealand* (Law Book Co., 1986) 34.

150   See K Mark 'Employer response to natural disasters' (2011) 2(3) *Workplace Review* 101.

deals with this situation. Under ss 108–112, staff can take reasonable time off for this purpose – such a term is, of course, subject to any enterprise bargaining term that may be more beneficial (and perhaps may allow for payment). An employee in this position can also avail themselves – if necessary – of adverse action relief and dismissal protection under ss 341 and 772.[151]

Eburn considers the question of special terms and conditions of employment for those involved in emergency services.[152] This chapter only gives a sample of the issues. Key issues to be considered include:

- What powers do emergency services workers have that can protect them from being accused of assault? What is the effect on those powers of a government declaration of a state of emergency?

- What is the law governing the driving of emergency vehicles at speed?

- When does a commander declare that a situation is too dangerous for workers? Can workers volunteer for especially hazardous work? (Thinking of the Japanese nuclear power catastrophe at Fukushima, some of the workers in the power station knew they were undertaking a suicide mission. Can staff ever be compelled to undertake such work, or must they be volunteers?)

- What equipment and safety training should be given to staff? If staff work in areas of disease overseas, should they be isolated on returning home so as not to affect their Australian colleagues? (This issue arose during the 2014 Ebola scare.)[153]

Many emergency services personnel and aid workers work in countries other than Australia. It is interesting to note that most large volunteer and emergency groups, such as Peace Boat and Medecins Sans Frontieres, are highly organised and have well-established plans for dealing with employment issues in the world's trouble spots.[154] International bodies such as the UN or the ILO also have specific provisions dealing with these topics.[155]

9.25.20 Unpaid work: ongoing concerns

In 2013, Professors Stewart and Owens released their report, *Nature Prevalence and Regulation of Unpaid Work Experience, Internships and Trial Periods in Australia: Experience or*

---

151   Ibid, making the point that the *Fair Work Act* provisions, when applicable, lessen the need for employers to rely on *force majeure* or frustration of contract principles to stand down staff.

152   See M Eburn *Emergency Law* (Federation Press, 2013).

153   'Cairns Ebola scare: two doctors stood aside amid review at hospital in Far North Queensland' ABC News website, 14 October 2014, http://www.abc.net.au/news/2014-10-13/two-doctors-stood-aside-amid-ebola-scare-review-at-cairns-hospit/5810412 (accessed 18 February 2017).

154   See, for instance, the Disaster Relief Volunteer Centre Guides by Peace Boat, https://mail.google.com/mail/u/0/#search/japan+relief+workers/14157ef6a16b4f18?projector=1. Alternatively, see Peace Boat, *Annual Report 2011–12*, http://peaceboat.org/english/content/documents/2011_PBV_web.pdf (accessed 18 February 2017).

155   See ILO *Employment and Decent Work in Situations of Fragility, Conflict and Disaster: Guide and Tool Kit* (5 October 2016) and UN International Civil Service Commission *Danger Pay*, http://icsc.un.org/secretariat/hrpd.asp?include=dp (accessed 18 February 2017).

Exploitation?[156] The report had been commissioned by the FWO after reports surfaced of exploitation of unpaid workers – supposedly in workplaces to gain experience but in effect performing a substantive role within the organisation.[157] The obvious practical effect of misclassifying workers is clear: if someone (supposedly on unpaid work experience) is actually an employee, they should be paid the minimum wage, and be covered for workers' compensation. The report highlights the prevalence of the problem and the difficulty of applying the relevant legislation (and in some cases the paucity of that law). In a fairly clogged job market – such as the legal profession, where the number of graduates far exceeds the number of places available for lawyers – numerous graduates will seek work experience to 'get a foot in the door' or give them a practical, job-ready edge.[158] Similarly, migrant workers, unaware of their rights, might drift into precarious work arrangements.[159] These sorts of workers might be used to fill roles that are productive and essential to the operation of the workplace – is that truly work experience performed for the benefit and training of the worker, or is it a method of an employer procuring cheap labour (and therefore undercutting both that worker and others who might look to that position as a full-time employment option)?

At a basic level, the Fair Work Ombudsman provides a series of sheets that seek to direct employers and workers on their position if they perform work through an unpaid trial, work placement or unpaid work experience.[160]

From a legal standpoint, the main relevant provisions are ss 12 and 13 of the *Fair Work Act*, which exempt (from employment and therefore employment obligations such as wages) a 'vocational training' scheme. Essentially, if a period of work experience is essential for completion of an approved course, then it is exempt from payment. While the Stewart and Owens report, in analysing the provision, argue that the section is not particularly well drafted,[161] effectively it means that unpaid legal placements necessary for the completion of a law elective or for admission into legal practice (when they are approved) are covered by this exemption.[162]

Perhaps more troubling is unpaid work experience – or internships.[163] In his article, Moore compares the Australian position to the UK position – in the latter, the purpose of the engagement plays a significant role in determining whether the relationship is unpaid (work experience or intern) or paid (an employee).[164] In Australia, however, the position is not the same. The decision in *Pacesetter Homes Pty Ltd v Australian Builders Labourers Federated Union of Workers (WA Branch)* (1994) 57 IR 449 found work experience people not to be employees as there was no intention to create legal relations – the experience was for a limited

---

156   Stewart and R Owens *The Nature, Prevalence and Regulation of Unpaid Work, Internships and Trial Periods in Australia* (2013).

157   Ibid ix and 1.

158   Ibid. See discussion of R Perlin *Intern Nation: How to Earn Nothing and Learn Little in the Brave New Economy* (Verso, 2012) 17 et seq and various outlines of the position of workers: 24, 31, 37 et seq.

159   Ibid.

160   See http://www.fairwork.gov.au.

161   Stewart and Owens *The Nature, Prevalence and Regulation of Unpaid Work, Internships and Trial Periods in Australia* (2013) from 75.

162   Ibid.

163   See S Moore 'Interns or employees?' (2016) 7 *Workplace Review* 56.

164   Moore relies on *Wiltshire Police Authority v Wynn* [1981] 1 QB 95 per Lord Denning: in finding that a police cadet was not an employee, His Lordship pondered whether the primary purpose of the arrangement was teaching a trade or serving a master.

time and much of it was observing others in order to develop skills in people who were previously unemployed. In *Rowe v Capital Territory Health Commission* (1982) 2 IR 27 (per Northrop Deane and Fisher JJ), however, a student nurse was found to be an employee – although there, the extent of her work and its significance to the enterprise could not be ignored. Moore concludes that the character, conduct and substance of the relationship – the extent and nature of the work performed – is more important in this country than the description of the relationship or its purported purpose. The longer the length of the engagement and the more substantive the task (as opposed to learning and observation) the more likely it is that the relationship will be characterised as one of employment.

9.25.25 Concluding remarks on volunteers

Whether or not someone performing work without pay is an employee or volunteer is a significant legal issue to be addressed: so that employers do not, in error, underpay workers who in truth are employees; to ensure that workers who are permitted to access workers compensation can in fact do so; and to prevent the routine exploitation of students and migrants.

Key questions are whether the parties intended to create binding legal relations and, if so, whether the relationship is a contract of service. In that connection, an important point is whether non-monetary consideration can actually colour a work experience arrangement so as to show a binding contract.[165]

The application of the vocational training exemption is also important. How the courts will observe unpaid work experience schemes generally and whether or not they will characterise them on their substance is a developing area.

9.30 Robots and automation
9.30.05 The question

The spectre of robots 'taking human jobs' or of mankind potentially becoming redundant is not new. Publications ranging from press reports[166] through to scholarly articles[167] and monographs[168] have been canvassing the issue, to various extents, since the 1980s. What is critical

---

165   Stewart and Owens *The Nature, Prevalence and Regulation of Unpaid Work, Internships and Trial Periods in Australia* (2013) 45 et seq and 75 et seq.

166   MY Vardi 'Are robots going to steal your job? Probably', *The Guardian*, 7 April 2016; 'Technological unemployment – the next big global economic issue', independentaustralia.net (30 August 2012).

167   AJ Mikva 'Hard times for labor' (1985) 7(3) *Industrial Relations Law Journal* 345; R Story Parkes 'Bargaining over the introduction of robots into the workplace' (1983–84) 21 *San Diego Law Review* 1135; B Napier 'Computerization and employment rights' (1992) 21 *Industrial Law Journal* 1; CB Craver 'The labor movement needs a twenty-first century committee for industrial organisation' (2005–6) 23 *Hofstra Labor and Employment Law Journal* 69.

168   HA Hunt and TL Hunt *Human Resource Implications of Robotics* (Kalamazoo Michigan E Upjohn Institute for Employment Research, 1983) – reviewed by Professor Emeritus Robert Aronson in (1984–85) 38 *Industrial and Labor Relations Review* 673; AS Bix *Inventing Ourselves Out of jobs? America's Debate over Technological Unemployment 1929–1981* (Johns Hopkins University Press Baltimore, 2000); J Rifkin *The End of Work: The Decline of the Global Work-force and the Dawn of the Post-Market* (GP Putnam & Sons, 1995); and GR Woirol *The Technological Unemployment and Structural Unemployment Debates* (Greenwood Press, 1996).

today, however, is the nature and extent of technological change – especially the introduction of vastly more efficient robots and possible artificial intelligence. The question, it seems, is not whether technology will replace some humans who will then have to retrain, but rather whether machines will take over so many human work functions and require such a degree of retraining that there will be a fundamental change in the nature of society – and in labour and employment law.

9.30.10 A practical example – the waterfront (in Australia and throughout the world)

Just one case in point is the waterfront. The epic disputes on the waterfront have been well analysed.[169] While those disputes involved stevedoring company Patrick using corporate restructures to allegedly oust union employment, the current dispute on the waterfront involves the introduction of robots – and the effect that has on both employment and enterprise bargaining.[170] The *Australian Financial Review* has reported that: '[a] $350 million investment in the same robot cranes that populated Patrick's Brisbane terminal would result in the loss of 270 Port Botany jobs.'[171] The union's response was to argue for reduced working hours per person but with the maintenance of wages: 'the theory is that with automaton there's reduced requirement for workers ... We think if we have fewer hours we'll save jobs.'[172]

While the position on Australia's waterfront is an unfolding story at the time of writing, it is a microcosm of an issue that has arisen throughout the world's maritime industry – and in fact throughout many global industries. The *New York Times* examined the position of the US longshoreman's union in these terms:[173]

> The list of longshore jobs that technology has rendered obsolete is long and poignant. [The] tower workers are gone. The cube workers, who calculated the cubic volume of loose cargo, are gone. The coopers, who sewed torn sacks and repaired broken pallets, are gone. The water boys, working in the steamy reaches of the hold, are gone, as well.
>
> In the 1960s, when New York was the world's busiest port, there were more than 35,000 longshoremen on the city's docks. Today, there are 3500.
>
> This thinning of the ranks has stiffened the necks of the New York chapters of the longshoremen's union, which have been among the most successful in the country at preserving benefits for their members. The coveted remaining jobs, usually secured through referrals from other union members, pay well ...

169   G Orr 'Conspiracy on the waterfront' (1998) 11 *Australian Journal of Labour Law* 159–85; and L Floyd 'Weipa and the wharves: the right to strike and trade union power' (1999) 18 *University of Tasmania Law Journal* 62.
170   See, for example, M Stevens 'Patrick's national strike is fuelled by the MUA's revenge on robots', *Australian Financial Review*, 19 January 2016; E Hannan 'Patrick hit with new 48-hour strike on waterfront', *Australian Financial Review*, 21 April 2016; P Karp 'Wharf strikes: union fights for job security in the age of automation', *The Guardian (Australia)*, 12 April 2016.
171   Stevens 'Patrick's national strike is fuelled by the MUA's revenge on robots' (2016).
172   MUA Sydney branch secretary Paul McAleer, as cited in Karp 'Wharf strikes: union fights for job security in the age of automation' (2016).
173   A Feuer 'On the waterfront, rise of the machines', *New York Times*, 28 September 2012.

9.30.15 The evidence – government reports

While the waterfront presents an important practical example of an ongoing dispute and negotiation about the introduction of technology in the workplace, studies by the CSIRO and the NSW government, for example, provide useful evidence of the creeping problems of technological unemployment.[174] According to Dudley,[175] people will be less likely to expect to hold jobs with one employer for lengthy periods; there will be significantly greater use of robotics; workers will freelance and possibly share a platform (like an app) for what is dubbed the 'peer-to-peer' economy; there will be far greater need for high-calibre education and training (especially in robotics and IT); and there will be a much greater emphasis on creativity and entrepreneurship (as workers will not simply *do*, but rather *think*).[176] Clearly the manual labour sectors will be hard hit and human resource managers will have to place a premium on talent at the point of engagement. Apart from the obvious emphasis this 'new world' places on independent contracting and the viability of post-work restraints,[177] Dudley laments: 'The question of how workers will be protected in this new paradigm, including how employment and industrial laws will keep pace with these changes and how the role of unions might change, are left unanswered.'[178]

9.30.20 The scholarship

Strangely enough, part of the beginnings of some form of answer to that very 2017 question being considered in Australia may lie in a US article from 1985 and an academic conversation initiated recently by Cornell University, New York (in particular, in its Industrial and Labor Relations School). And although it is US material, it is central to this problem that many nations in fact share. This is a global issue, so international consideration is important.

In 1985, Judge Abner Mikva wrote 'Hard times for labor'.[179] He began by reflecting on the character Dorothy's discovery of the very bad wizard behind the curtain in *The Wizard of Oz*.[180] That story of exaggerated expectations – when the answer may have lain somewhere else (perhaps within) – is the allegory on which the judge bases his consideration of the US's *Wagner Act*, which is essentially the basis of the collective US labour law system.[181] In particular, he observes: 'These changes in the business structure and the economy have produced no concomitant shift in the primary law governing labor.'[182] (In other words, the governing workplace laws of many nations may not be keeping pace with changes in the manner in which people work.)

Surely the same observation can be made about numerous elements of the Australian system – there are old established elements that may not be able to deal with modern

---

174   L Rudd et al. *Tomorrow's Digitally Enabled Workforce*, CSIRO, 2016 and *NSW Intergenerational Report 2016: Future State NSW 2056*, NSW Treasury, 2016.
175   B Dudley 'Future trends in the way we work: what are they and what are the lessons for employers?' (2016) 22 *Employment Law Bulletin* 219.
176   Ibid especially 221.
177   Ibid.
178   Ibid 220.
179   Mikva 'Hard times for labor' (1985).
180   Ibid 345.
181   Ibid 345 et seq.
182   Ibid 347.

problems. So what are the problems and possible solutions? As Mikva and numerous other scholars have observed and questioned:

- Could there be a right for unions to represent workers not only as regards the effects of the introduction of technology (such as redundancy), but also in the actual decision of whether the particular technology will be adopted? Rather than simply considering the position of investor shareholders, might there not also be consideration of the position of the workers who have invested their working lives in the company?[183]

- Can governments better regulate for corporate social responsibility (and against abuses of the corporate veil)? Similarly, might there be tax reform for more equitable redistribution of wealth?[184]

- If businesses become uncompetitive without robots, there will be job losses anyway, so how do unions deal with bargaining in the robotic age?[185] Should they restructure themselves to have technology committees?[186] How do unions actually unionise the new workforce of highly educated and creative individuals?[187]

- If there are going to be large numbers of people either unemployed (former labourers, say) or in highly precarious employment, can there be a law guaranteeing a genuine right to work for a real wage? Can some form of job security become a topic of legislation just as health and safety has?[188]

These are some of the questions now under consideration in an initiative of Cornell University's Industrial and Labor Relations School: *The Technology and Employment Sustainability Initiative* of the Institute for Compensation Studies.[189]

At the time of writing, the Australian Labour Law Association had advertised its forthcoming Biennial Conference, a part of which seems to be geared towards discussing the future of work. One must surely applaud the decision to have that discussion – and the publications that, no doubt, will flow from it. As has been stated earlier, labour law, unions, employers and the very manner in which work is performed will all reshape themselves in the years ahead. It would be only an ostrich with its head in the sand that did not welcome a discussion on labour and change.

SUMMARY

Since the foundation of the ILO, consideration has been given to the setting of international/transnational standards as well as the links between trade and labour. As corporations operate transnationally, as global supply chains emerge and as companies second staff to work in overseas branch offices, transnational labour law and standards are increasingly important. An inherent problem is enforcement –

---

183   Ibid 349. This question was also raised by Napier 'Computerization and employment rights' (1992) 49.
184   Mikva 'Hard times for labor' (1985) 348–54. Similar observations were made by Napier 'Computerization and employment rights' (1992) 46 and 49 et seq.
185   Napier 'Computerization and employment rights' (1992) 49.
186   Craver 'The labor movement needs a twenty-first century committee for industrial organization' (2005-6).
187   Napier 'Computerization and employment rights' (1992) 49.
188   Mikva 'Hard times for labor' (1985) 351–2.
189   https://www.ilr.cornell.edu/institute-for-compensation-studies/.

the law is still emerging, and includes law suits against multinationals, transnational corporate codes of conduct and reliance on nation states to embrace and enforce core labour standards. Debate continues about the balance between trade and labour –are high standards too onerous on developing nations or are low standards providing developing nations with an unfair trade advantage? There are ongoing attempts to link labour standards with trade agreements. Specific issues and challenges include: China (although numerous ILO conventions have been acted upon, the culture of the country makes enforcement and observation difficult); truly international industries such as airlines, maritime operations and IT; plus Brexit in the UK and the election of Trump in the US. The latter suggest a rise in nationalism in employment and employment law, although there is ongoing debate as to whether either will deliver the benefits touted. These developments also underscore the links between labour and immigration.

Australia has a long history of linking (permanent) migration to labour. Recently the 457 visa scheme – short-term migration – has been used to fill labour shortages. Underlying tensions, relating to the balance between protecting Australian jobs and recruiting from abroad, have surfaced. Numerous government reports have canvassed how that balance should be struck (and at the time of writing, the Turnbull Government had foreshadowed further changes in the law).

Volunteer work takes numerous forms. Some is highly organised, some is occasional and some is ad hoc. One of the key issues for determining whether or not someone is a volunteer (not an employee) is whether or not there was an intent to create legal relations. Workplace health and safety is important for both employees and volunteers, especially in dangerous situations.

There are increasing numbers of workers, many of them young, undertaking unpaid work experience etc. There are also work-integrated learning schemes in many universities. Questions include whether a desire to learn can ever ground a contract of employment, and whether non-monetary consideration can exist in an employment contract.

Robots are able to do more things and be more flexible than we had at first thought. Consequently there is an issue as to large-scale redundancy – human workers being replaced by machines, especially in low-skill areas. Governments issue labour force reports about the shape the modern workforce is likely to take. These often include increasing reliance on short-term employment, use by individuals of IT platforms to market themselves, and the 'gig economy'. What is the legal response to that? As corporations are beneficiaries, should corporations law promote corporate social responsibility more forcefully? Should it address the corporate veil?

REVIEW QUESTIONS

1. Research question: US States sometimes have 'right to work' laws, but those laws are conceptually very different from the 'right to work' alluded to by Mikva. Discuss both. What do they mean for Australia? In the course of your discussion, pay particular attention to Caterpillar – the US company at the centre of numerous recent labour disputes.

2. Group monitoring projects: This chapter deals with emerging issues and new developments. As a group or class project, monitor the following new developments:
    (a) What are the Australian government's proposed changes to the 457 visa scheme? What was the legal catalyst for change? Follow the issue.

    (b) In their report (on work experience etc), Stewart and Owens spend a lot of time considering Work Integrated Learning (WIL) in law schools and placements by universities. What are the chief concerns of those authors? Does your university have a WIL scheme or job placements – if so, how do they fit within the law? What are the latest developments on payment and work experience?

3. Individually, monitor the developments in:
    - the UK on labour law as Brexit unfolds
    - the US on labour law during the Trump Administration.

4. On 10 February 2016, the *Financial Times* published an article by JM Brown: 'UK self-employed plumber wins court battle for workers' rights: Ruling against Pimlico Plumbers has bearing for gig economy'. Read *Pimlico Plumbers v Gray* [2017] EWCA Civ 51. How is the law (and the UK government) dealing with changes in the way people work? What implications are there (if any) for Australia?

5. **(a)** Study the response of Australian emergency services to Cyclone Yassi in 2011. To what extent did the crisis involve work by emergency services, volunteers and the armed services? What legal lessons were learnt, from an employment law perspective?

    (b) Research the use of volunteers in police services throughout Australia – are there special employment law issues that arise?

FURTHER READING

B Barrett and D Lewis 'Is the *Employers Liability (Compulsory Insurance) Act 1969* fit for the purpose?' (2016) 45(4) *Industrial Law Journal* 503–24.

H Carty 'The modern functions of the economic torts: reviewing the English, Canadian, Australian and New Zealand positions' (2015) 74 *Cambridge Law Journal* 261–83.

E Dorotheou 'Reap the benefits and avoid the legal uncertainty: who owns the creations of artificial intelligence?' (2015) 21 *Computer and Telecommunications Law Review* 85–93.

B Longstaff 'Changing times, changing relationships at work . . . changing law?' (2016) 45 *Industrial Law Journal* 131–43.

A Ojeda-Aviles, *Alphen aan den Rijn Transnational Labour Law* (Wolters Kluwer, 2015).

INDEX

457 visas, 394, 409–12, 423
   Azarias Report, 411

ability to engage other staff, 15
academic employment, 300
   disciplinary procedures, 306
   dismissal. *See* dismissal in
      Australian universities
   enterprise agreements, 305
   misconduct and serious
      misconduct, 306–7
   nature of employment in
      universities, 300–1
   organisational change, 306
   redundancy and
      retrenchment, 307–8
   salary, 305
   status of university policy in
      employment contract,
      301–4
   tenure, workplace security
      and types of
      employment, 305–6
   workloads, 308
academic freedom
   concept of in Australia, 317–19
   dismissal and, 316–17
   express. *See* express
      academic freedom
   implied protection, 321–3
   under statute, 141–2
adverse action, 93–4
   elements of, 214
anti-bullying statutory scheme,
   361
   bullying has occurred, 363
   defences, 364–5
   ongoing risk, 363–4
   outcomes from, 365–6
   relationship to other Fair
      Work Commission
      matters, 366–7
   remedies, 365
   worker constitutionally
      covered, 348
anti-discrimination, 367–8, 389,
   See also discrimination
Apparel Industry Partnership,
   399
approval process for enterprise
   agreements

approval by Fair Work
      Commission, 139–40
   better off overall test, 141
   effect of approval, 142
   'genuinely agreed', 140
   pre-approval steps, 138–9
   undertakings, 141–2
Australian Accounting Standards,
   163
Australian Building and
   Construction
   Commission, 173–4,
   186, 193
Australian Charities and
   Non-Profits Commission,
   176, 186
Australian Commission on Law
   Enforcement Integrity,
   186
Australian Competition and
   Consumer Commission,
   185
Australian Crime Commission, 186
Australian Electoral Commission,
   124, 172, 197
Australian Federal Police, 186
Australian Human Rights
   Commission, 145
Australian Industrial Relations
   Commission, 10, 80, 86,
   100–1, 191
Australian labour law system
   practical, historical and
      constitutional
      development of. *See*
      development of
      Australian labour law
      system
Australian Prudential Regulatory
   Authority, 385
Australian Public Service Code of
   Conduct, 274
Australian Public Service
   Commission
   Australian Public Service
      Employment Principles,
      274
   Australian Public Service
      Values, 273–4
   Australian Public Service
      Values and Code of

      Conduct in Practice,
      274–5
   Better Practice Guide to
      Managing
      Unreasonable
      Complainant Conduct,
      275
   formal investigation, 277
   Handling Misconduct:
      A Human Resource
      Manager's Guide, 276
   informal investigation, 277
   inherent danger in informal
      investigation, 278
   strengths and weaknesses of
      investigative system, 277
Australian Securities and
   Investments
   Commission, 176
Australian Standards, 340
Australian Taxation Office, 7,
   186, 383
Australian Workplace Agreements,
   80–2, 95, 112
automation. *See* robots and
   automation
awards. *See* modern awards
Azarias Report, 411

bargaining for enterprise
   agreements
   approval process. *See*
      approval process
      for enterprise
      agreements
   commencement of, 124
   good faith bargaining
      requirements. *See* good
      faith bargaining
      requirements
   majority support
      determination, 124–5
   notice of employee
      representational rights,
      125–6
   protected industrial action
      in support of claims, 133
better off overall test, 82, 100, 148
   approval process for
      enterprise agreements
      and, 141

425